The Practitioner's Guide to Psychoactive Drugs

SECOND EDITION

TOPICS IN GENERAL PSYCHIATRY

Series Editor:
John C. Nemiah, M.D.
*Psychiatrist-in-Chief, Beth Israel Hospital
and Professor of Psychiatry, Harvard Medical School*

HYPNOSIS
Fred H. Frankel, M.B.Ch.B., D.P.M.

THE FRONTIER OF BRIEF PSYCHOTHERAPY
David H. Malan, D.M., F.R.C. Psych.

SOCIOCULTURAL ROOTS OF MENTAL ILLNESS
John J. Schwab, M.D., and Mary E. Schwab, M.D.

SHORT-TERM DYNAMIC PSYCHOTHERAPY
Peter E. Sifneos, M.D.

THE PRACTITIONER'S GUIDE TO PSYCHOACTIVE DRUGS
Second Edition
*Ellen L. Bassuk, M.D., Stephen C. Schoonover, M.D., and
Alan J. Gelenberg, M.D.*

The Practitioner's Guide to Psychoactive Drugs

SECOND EDITION

Edited by

Ellen L. Bassuk, M.D.
Stephen C. Schoonover, M.D.

Beth Israel Hospital and Harvard Medical School
Boston, Massachusetts

and

Alan J. Gelenberg, M.D.

Massachusetts General Hospital and Harvard Medical School
Boston, Massachusetts

PLENUM MEDICAL BOOK COMPANY
New York and London

Library of Congress Cataloging in Publication Data

Main entry under title:

The Practitioner's guide to psychoactive drugs.

(Topics in general psychiatry)
Includes bibliographies and index.
1. Psychopharmacology. 2. Psychotropic drugs. I. Bassuk, Ellen L. II.
Schoonover, Stephen C. III. Gelenberg, Alan J. IV. Series. [DNLM: 1. Psychotropic drugs. QV 77 P8952]
RC483.P726 1983   615′.78   82-22468
ISBN 0-306-41093-1

First Printing — March 1983
Second Printing — May 1984

© 1983 Plenum Publishing Corporation
233 Spring Street, New York, N.Y. 10013

Plenum Medical Book Company is an imprint of Plenum Publishing Corporation

Printed in the United States of America

To Sherry, Sara, David, and Rebecca

———

To Mary Nell Schoonover

———

In Memory of Molly Bassuk

Contributors

Alan J. Gelenberg, M.D. Associate Professor of Psychiatry, Harvard Medical School, and Chief, Special Studies Clinic, Department of Psychiatry, Massachusetts General Hospital, Boston, Massachusetts 02114

Steven A. Hoffman, M.D. Clinical Fellow in Psychiatry, Harvard Medical School, and Chief Resident in Psychopharmacology, Massachusetts Mental Health Center, Boston, Massachusetts 02215

Carol R. Koplan, M.D. Assistant Professor of Psychiatry, Emory University School of Medicine, Atlanta, Georgia 30322

Steven M. Mirin, M.D. Associate Professor of Psychiatry, Harvard Medical School, and Director, Drug Dependence Treatment Unit, McLean Hospital, Belmont, Massachusetts 02178

Thomas F. O'Hare, J.D. Staff Attorney, Department of Legal Services, McLean Hospital, Belmont, Massachusetts 02178

Carl Salzman, M.D. Associate Professor of Psychiatry, Harvard Medical School, and Director of Psychopharmacology, Massachusetts Mental Health Center, Boston, Massachusetts 02215

Stephen C. Schoonover, M.D. Instructor in Psychiatry, Harvard Medical School, and Director, Inpatient Psychiatry, Beth Israel Hospital, Boston, Massachusetts 02215

Jeffrey B. Weilburg, M.D. Clinical Fellow in Psychiatry, Harvard Medical School, and Clinical Fellow in Psychiatry, Department of Psychiatry, Beth Israel Hospital, Boston, Massachusetts 02215

Roger D. Weiss, M.D.   Instructor in Psychiatry, Harvard Medical School, and Psychiatrist-in-Charge, Drug Dependence Treatment Unit, McLean Hospital, Belmont, Massachusetts 02178

Foreword

Books, like people, are born, and, if they survive the trauma of birth, mature in response to a changing environment. This volume is no exception. It immediately proved its usefulness to psychiatric clinicians upon its publication six years ago, and it is not surprising to find it now entering a new phase of life in a second edition. The many and significant changes that the reader will find herein reflect not only the rapid growth of knowledge in the field of psychopharmacology but also the editors' wise awareness of the need to incorporate that knowledge into clinical practice. Important new sections have been added on the management of elderly patients, on the pharmacological approach to those with temporal lobe epilepsy, and on the use of psychoactive medications during pregnancy. The existing clinical sections have been expanded, and the format has been altered to make the volume more practically useful for the harried clinician. Most important of all, the discussions of individual drugs have been carefully revised to update information about those medications that have stood the test of time and to include those newer pharmacological agents that have appeared on the clinical scene since the publication of the first edition. This last task has been significantly aided by the addition of Dr. Alan J. Gelenberg to the family of editors; his clinical and scientific knowledge nicely complements that of Drs. Bassuk and Schoonover, and its influence is evident throughout.

Increased in stature, clothed in new finery, broadened by the wisdom of experience, the second edition of *The Practitioner's Guide to Psychoactive Drugs* provides the clinician of the 1980s with an indispensable manual of patient care.

John C. Nemiah, M.D.

Boston

Preface

Although scarcely three decades old, the field of psychopharmacology has had a tremendous impact on the practice of medicine in general and psychiatry in particular. With the help of medication, many chronic schizophrenics have left the back wards of public institutions and rejoined their communities, and patients suffering from mood disorders have had acute symptoms relieved and, in many cases, recurrences prevented. Similarly, various drugs now treat anxiety and insomnia without causing excessive sedation.

The decade of the 1950s spawned a revolution in drug therapies: virtually every major agent now with us was introduced then. During the ensuing period, we have begun to understand the effects of medication on brain chemistry and have developed biological models of psychiatric illness (largely based on drug actions). These advances have enhanced our ability to select agents for specific patients. Psychopharmacology also has nurtured the growth of empirical science and rigorous experimental technique in psychiatry.

The practitioner newly introduced to the field of psychopharmacology is apt to feel bewildered by the plethora of available agents and the complexities governing their use. However, as in all clinical therapeutics, similarities among groups of drugs outweigh dissimilarities, and diligent application of basic principles most often leads to effective results for most patients. Our book attempts to guide the mental health and medical practitioner through this exciting and rapidly expanding field, focusing primarily on clinically applicable information and practical guidelines.

To ensure a broad understanding of pharmacotherapy and to make this book useful for everyday clinical practice, we focus on the following:

1. Specifying the degree to which various psychiatric presentations are drug responsive.
2. Accurately describing the assets and limitations of available drug regimens.

3. Discussing the relationship of drug treatment to nonbiological therapies.
4. Presenting a pragmatic approach for the assessment and management of patients with medication-responsive syndromes.
5. Providing a framework for understanding pharmacotherapy, interpreting "new data," and encouraging a positive attitude toward medicating patients.

We have organized the major sections of the book according to clinical syndromes (i.e., depression, bipolar illness, psychosis, anxiety, insomnia, and substance abuse). In separate sections on pediatrics, geriatrics, pregnancy, and temporal lobe epilepsy, we discuss the special problems of these patients. The format of each chapter follows the steps in clinical decision making. From a discussion of medicable syndromes and general therapeutic measures (with an emphasis on the importance of the doctor–patient relationship), we proceed to a complete presentation of the various psychoactive drugs, including chemistry and kinetics, mechanism of action, clinical effects, adverse reactions, preparations, and clinical applications.

Since its first printing, the *Practitioner's Guide* has been widely read. It is time for another edition; we have thoroughly revised and expanded the original book. Dr. Alan J. Gelenberg has joined Drs. Ellen L. Bassuk and Stephen C. Schoonover in this new volume. Dr. Gelenberg edits the *Massachusetts General Hospital Newsletter, Biological Therapies in Psychiatry* and is actively involved in research, consultation, and teaching in psychopharmacology. Drs. Bassuk and Schoonover return to this edition with their own clinical perspectives and broad experience in practice. Both are psychotherapists and general hospital psychiatrists specializing in emergency and inpatient psychiatry, respectively.

Dr. Gelenberg would like to acknowledge his intellectual indebtedness to mentors like Drs. Gerald L. Klerman and Ross J. Baldessarini, who provided his earliest introduction to the field. He would also like to thank the members of the Department of Psychiatry at the Massachusetts General Hospital and the Erich Lindemann Mental Health Center for providing a rich and fertile environment for study and practice. The staff of the Special Studies Clinic has been available and loyal through his arduous work and frenetic activity, and particular thanks go to his devoted and loving wife and children.

We would like to thank Hilary Evans, Senior Medical Editor at Plenum, for her continued support, enthusiasm, and encouragement in the preparation of this volume. Also, special thanks to Ellen Spencer for her patience and forbearance with our demands and for her meticulous work in the typing and retyping of the lengthy manuscript. Without her persistence, we would never have completed this project.

Note: Initially, the text contained both male and female pronouns in sentences that did not have a specific referent. However, to improve clarity and flow, we made an editorial decision to include only masculine pronouns.

E.L.B.
S.C.S.
A.J.G.

Boston

Contents

2. Depression

Stephen C. Schoonover, M.D.

3. Bipolar Affective Disorder and Recurrent Unipolar Depression

Stephen C. Schoonover, M.D.

4. Psychoses

Alan J. Gelenberg, M.D.

5. Anxiety

Alan J. Gelenberg, M.D.

6. Insomnia

Alan J. Gelenberg, M.D.

7. Substance Abuse

Steven M. Mirin, M.D., and Roger D. Weiss, M.D.

8. Geriatric Psychopharmacology

Carl Salzman, M.D., Steven A. Hoffman, M.D., and
Stephen C. Schoonover, M.D.

9. Pediatric Psychopharmacology

Carol R. Koplan, M.D.

10. The Use of Psychotropic Drugs during Pregnancy and Nursing
Carol R. Koplan, M.D.

11. Temporal Lobe Epilepsy

Jeffrey B. Weilburg, M.D.

12. Legal Issues in Prescribing Psychoactive Medications

Thomas F. O'Hare, J. D.

The Practitioner's Guide to Psychoactive Drugs

SECOND EDITION

1

Introduction: The Practice of Pharmacotherapy

STEPHEN C. SCHOONOVER, M.D.

I. HISTORICAL PERSPECTIVE

Experimentation with drugs that alter mood, thinking, or perception represents a timeless human enterprise. Although largely aimed at the relief of suffering, the utilization of various pharmacological agents also reflects different cultural, religious, and political ideologies. Frequently, the implementation of effective pharmacological treatments depends more on social issues, economic considerations, and serendipity than on clinical factors. A historical account of both the discovery and introduction of psychoactive drugs in the United States highlights these patterns.

The medical community has only recently employed psychoactive drugs to treat mental illness. In the 1840s clinicians prescribed bromides as sedative agents. These chemicals effectively diminished anxiety, but their prolonged use caused significant central nervous system complications. The experience with bromides was portentous; they effectively alleviated psychological symptoms but had hidden long-term dangers. In the latter part of the 19th century, other sedative agents were synthesized, including paraldehyde, urethane, sulfonal, and chloral hydrate. During this same period, Sigmund Freud suggested that cocaine was a useful psychoactive drug, and Emile Kraepelin started the first laboratory for testing drugs in humans.

STEPHEN C. SCHOONOVER, M.D. • Department of Psychiatry, Harvard Medical School and Beth Israel Hospital, Boston, Massachusetts 02215.

At the beginning of the 20th century, researchers introduced the barbiturates. Because they more effectively relieved anxiety than any previously used drug, they largely displaced other agents from general use. Their mood-altering properties, complicated by their addictive potential, promoted widespread use. Since that time, over 2500 barbiturates have been synthesized, but only 50 have been used clinically. No additional clinical advances occurred until the 1950s. However, during the intervening period, researchers unwittingly discovered many of the major drug classes. In 1931, Sen and Bose first reported giving a rauwolfia alkaloid, originally developed for its hypotensive and sedative properties, to psychotic patients.[1] Although the results were unremarkable, they were the first to link the properties of these reserpinelike drugs with their potential effectiveness in psychiatric patients.

Shortly thereafter, Charpentier developed promethazine, a phenothiazine derivative, as an antihistamine and sedative. Clinical trials proved unremarkable, but luck was again close at hand. During this same period, three other important pharmacological groups were synthesized and used clinically—the benzodiazepines, lithium salts, and the tricyclic antidepressant, imipramine (Tofranil® and others). By the 1940s, researchers had discovered each of the major chemical groups currently used in psychopharmacology. All were originally synthesized for purposes other than their subsequent clinical use. It took many more years before researchers and clinicians defined guidelines for their administration.

The revolution in psychopharmacology really began in 1949. Promethazine, although disappointing when used alone, effectively potentiated the sedative properties of barbiturates. Based on this finding, researchers developed other phenothiazines to aid in anesthesia. In 1949, Charpentier synthesized chlorpromazine (Thorazine® and others). By 1952, several individuals had noted the beneficial effects of chlorpromazine on mania, paranoia, and other psychoses.[2] They observed that patients improved primarily because of a decrease in disorganized thoughts, feelings, and behaviors rather than because they were sedated. Once researchers identified the "neuroleptic" properties of these drugs, they began to develop similar antipsychotic agents.

Chlorpromazine, which was introduced for general use in the United States in 1954, created a revolution in patient care.[3] Thereafter, other phenothiazines were rapidly developed. In 1958, while attempting to find a more effective analgesic agent, Janssen synthesized haloperidol (Haldol®), a butyrophenone with strong neuroleptic properties. Since then, other researchers have discoverd additional classes of antipsychotic drugs including the thioxanthenes, the dibenzoxazepines, and the dihydroindolones.

In 1940, lithium chloride was given to cardiac patients as a salt substitute, but many developed severe toxic reactions. This initial experience significantly retarded its acceptance as a psychopharmacological agent in the United States. Despite the apparent toxicity of lithium, Cade continued his experimentation. He gave lithium to animals to determine if it increased the solubility of uric acid. Noting its sedative properties, he gave the salt to several manic and agitated patients. In 1949, based on these results, Cade reported lithium's antimanic effects.[4] However, because of continued concerns about toxic reactions, the drug was not approved for use in the United States until 1970.

In 1950, the search for sedative–hypnotics safer than the barbiturates led to the discovery of propanediol carbamates [e.g., meprobamate (Miltown® and others)]. Unfortunately, these compounds proved as troublesome as the drugs they replaced. Physiological tolerance, dependence, and severe withdrawal reactions made them a poor choice for treating anxiety. In 1957, Sternback synthesized the benzodiazepine chlordiazepoxide (Librium®).[5] The finding that it calmed animals without producing marked sedation spurred clinical trials in humans. Since then, various benzodiazepines have largely replaced other drugs for the treatment of anxiety and insomnia. In part, this stems from both their clinical effectiveness and broad margin of safety. However, it also reflects an age-old social phenomenon—an epidemic urgency to find relief from anxiety, tension, and worry. Recently, the use of these agents has decreased somewhat. However, physicians still write about 100 million prescriptions for sedative–hypnotic agents each year, of which over 60 million are for the benzodiazepines [chlordiazepoxide (Librium®) and diazepam (Valium®) account for about 75%].

As with most other psychotropic agents, the antidepressant properties of various drugs were identified fortuitously. For example, clinicians noticed that tuberculosis patients treated with isoniazid (INH®, Nydrazid®, and others) and iproniazid experienced elevated mood; this led to the further investigation of the monoamine oxidase inhibitors (MAOI). In 1952, these agents were administered to patients with depression, and by the late 1950s, this class of drugs became part of common clinical practice. However, when authors reported severe, life-threatening hypertension in patients who failed to eliminate amine precursors from their diet, these agents fell into disfavor. The introduction of safer monoamine oxidase inhibitors, clearer clinical guidelines, and reports citing effectiveness in selected patients with depression and phobic states have rejuvenated their use.

The tricyclic antidepressant imipramine was initially synthesized in the 1940s as a promazine analogue. In 1958, Kuhn successfully treated a group of severely disturbed patients with imipramine.[6] (The drug did little for psychotic individuals but significantly helped those who were depressed.) Thereafter, researchers and clinicians defined guidelines for the use of imipramine to treat "endogenous" depressions. Soon afterwards, several other heterocyclic antidepressants* with similar properties were synthesized. More

---

*Since many of the currently used thymoleptic drugs are not tricyclic in structure, we have adopted this term to represent the various cyclic antidepressants. From: Baldessarini R. J.: Overview of recent advances in antidepressant pharmacology. Part II. *McLean Hosp J* 7:1–27, 1982.

recently, researchers have developed new antidepressants including amoxapine (Asendin®) and trimipramine (Surmontil®) and several nontricyclic agents [such as maprotiline (Ludiomil®)].

The effectiveness of antianxiety drugs and antidepressants stimulated researchers to pursue many other avenues of investigation. Interest in brain chemistry grew rapidly. Researchers developed and began testing hypotheses about symptom etiology. Moreover, an increase in the reliability and validity of diagnostic categories resulted in better-designed studies. These diverse areas of investigation led to the development of clinically useful treatments, various models as frameworks for further research, and a more complex view of the interaction between biological and nonbiological factors. Researchers now realize that new clinical approaches must account for the interaction of biology, experience, and environment on the expression of illness.

II. CURRENT TRENDS IN PSYCHOPHARMACOLOGY

A. Definition of Clinical Syndromes

Although many diverse diagnostic frameworks exist, they often do not help the practitioner decide whether or not to prescribe drugs. In the past, diagnosis often was based on presumed cause (e.g., endogenous vs. reactive depressions). More recently, DSM-III was developed to define discrete diagnostic groups according to symptom profiles and inclusion and exclusion criteria. This framework provides reliable diagnoses and consistent criteria for research and encourages accurate communication among professionals. However, it does not specify drug-responsive disorders. Some researchers, studying the outcome of specific drug treatments, have delineated **symptom profiles** that respond to pharmacotherapy. Unfortunately, despite these advances, many patients still do not receive effective medication trials. Some individuals with similar presenting symptoms have disorders requiring different drugs, whereas other patients with disparate symptoms may respond to similar treatments. To remedy this problem, investigators are trying to widen their knowledge of drug-responsive presentations and develop **biological methods of diagnosis.**

B. Development of Brain Chemistry Models and New Pharmacological Agents

Perhaps the most significant recent advance in psychopharmacology is the evolution of biological models of disease based on increased knowledge of brain chemistry. Despite their limitations, the **dopamine hypothesis** for schizophrenia and the **catecholamine hypothesis** for depression have provided useful starting points for research. For example, biochemical models of depression have undergone various modifications to account for evidence that norepinephrine (NE), serotonin (5HT), and acetylcholine may each have a role in depression. The brain chemistry models have stimulated the search for drugs that produce hypothetically effective neurohumoral changes and fewer adverse reactions.

On the other hand, new compounds whose effects are not consistent with postulated biochemical alterations (like the antidepressant iprindole which does not block the reuptake of either 5HT or NE) promote the revision of existing hypotheses. In addition, with increasing knowledge of neurotransmitters, investigators are attempting to develop new diagnostic methods (e.g., urinary MHPG levels and the dexamethasone suppression test for depressive disorders). At present, these advances have only limited pragmatic usefulness for the clinician, but the future promises the development of more definitive approaches.

C. Pharmacokinetics

Ideally, the practitioner should know the pharmacokinetics of each agent including its complete metabolic pathway. However, the characteristics of many psychoactive compounds and the limitations of current laboratory technology often make these goals impossible. The kinetics of many drugs are not known or are not readily available to the clinician because of problems developing affordable, accurate assays. Moreover, many agents have active metabolites that also must be measured, since they, too, are clinically effective. With medications that are protein bound, the percentage of "free drug" may represent only a small fraction of the total; sometimes, current methods do not differentiate the bound from unbound portions.

In addition to studying the kinetics of drugs (see Section IV.B.4), pharmacologists are attempting to define clinical correlates of biochemical tests. For example, they have tried to correlate factors such as clinical effectiveness and unwanted effects and toxicity with the blood level of the drug (and any active metabolites). In addition to actual measurements of the serum concentrations of the drugs themselves, radioactive receptor binding assays are helping to evaluate the total effects of certain classes of drugs including dopamine-blocking activity (for antipsychotic drugs) and anticholinergic activity (for antiparkinson drugs). Moreover, in patients taking MAO inhibitors, some researchers have noted a relationship between the extent of platelet monoamine oxidase (MAO) inhibition and clinical response.

D. Design of Drug Studies

The methodology of clinical investigations in pharmacology has improved vastly over the past few decades. The introduction of **double-blind**

techniques, blind raters, "active placebos," and sophisticated analyses has brought the light of science to previously insoluble clinical dilemmas. Nevertheless, many methodological problems still beset clinical pharmacology. Drug studies are expensive: it may take as much as $50 million to bring a drug to market. This means that if a drug does not appear to have potential for profit, it may never be adequately studied. Furthermore, the validity of a clinical study depends on the diligence of an investigator in selecting appropriate patients and adhering rigorously to a study protocol. Moreover, the heterogeneity of many psychiatric disorders, such as unipolar depression, can explain divergent results when different investigators study the same antidepressant drugs. Despite these difficulties, however, a surprising consensus has emerged from research studies in recent years, and if funding is available for future studies, prospects appear bright.

III. PERSPECTIVES ON CLINICAL PRACTICE

In clinical practice, each practitioner must develop various skills such as the ability to identify drug-responsive syndromes and to implement effective medication trials. However, becoming a proficient clinical pharmacologist is often difficult. Our wish to believe that available drugs actually can cure psychiatric disorders sometimes obscures recognition of the limitations of these compounds. Guidelines for prescribing these drugs are still unclear, and many patients continue to experience persistent symptomatology despite their use. Since both acute and chronic psychiatric illnesses vary greatly from patient to patient, discriminating the effects of the drugs from other factors, such as stress or psychotherapy, is sometimes impossible. Despite the confounding features of psychiatric illness, pharmacotherapy cures some patients and alleviates suffering in many others. Therefore, what must the practitioner know and do to provide effective care?

A. Matching Medications with Drug-Responsive Syndromes

Diagnostic distinctions may confuse the clinician. Many syndromes reflect groups of illnesses or clusters of symptoms. More specific delineation of discrete disorders responsive to particular medications requires further understanding of brain chemistry. However, the practitioner currently can rely on careful observation, mental status signs, presenting symptoms, family history, and the course of psychological symptoms to define various clinical syndromes. Once the clinician defines the nature of the disorder, he should determine if it is drug responsive. In addition, he often can identify features that may indicate a decreased response to pharmacotherapy (such as rapid cycling of manic episodes in patients with bipolar affective disorders).

B. Properties of Medication

The clinician should know the various properties of each medication prescribed, including its **clinical action, adverse reactions, kinetics, methods and routes of administration, preparation and dosage, toxicology, and cost.** The characteristics of a psychoactive agent contribute to the practitioner's management of a drug trial. For example, although the mechanisms of action may be largely unknown, clinical experience has helped to define the time required for the onset of clinical effects (e.g., for antidepressants, 2 to 3 weeks in therapeutic doses). Caretakers also must consider the possibility of short- and long-term adverse reactions and toxic responses. The clinician must not only understand these potential risks but know what to do when they occur.

C. Attributes of the Clinician

The practitioner's attitudes and behaviors may have profound effects on the outcome of pharmacotherapy. A positive result may be encouraged or enhanced by optimism and faith in the drug. At a procedural level, the therapist's attitude is reflected by his persistence in completing drug trials and his consistency, emotional availability, and attentiveness to the patient's concerns. Similarly, a clinician who devalues the need for medication, expresses pessimism about the outcome, or develops ambivalent or even hostile feelings toward the patient may negatively affect the treatment course.

D. Attributes of the Patient

The characteristics of each patient always influence compliance and the course of treatment and often affect outcome. In fact, some studies indicate that less than one-half of those taking drugs over a long period reliably follow directions and that lack of compliance accounts for the majority of treatment failures. Therefore, the clinician must consider the psychosocial variables that affect therapy, such as the individual's attitudes toward and understanding of his illness, psychodynamic issues, character style, ability to relate in a therapeutic relationship, coping skills, social supports, attitude toward drug-taking, and motivation. For example, if the patient has a negative self-image or if those close to him disapprove of pharmacotherapy, compliance with treatment recommendations is often poor. Each individual also tends to manifest his own pattern of drug taking that usually becomes evident during the early phases of drug treatment. The most typical clinical manifestations include:

1. Overuse or inappropriate use because of
   a. Impulsiveness.

  b. Misunderstanding of the risks of the drug, its mechanism of
     action, or the regimen prescribed.
  c. Inadvertent polypharmacy (e.g., taking a substance such as alco-
     hol without realizing that it may potentiate the effects of other
     agents).
2. Underuse (which is most common in clinical practice) because of
  a. Fear of adverse reactions.
  b. Concern about dependence and addiction.
  c. Inconvenience of the medication regimen.
  d. Misunderstanding about the prescribed regimen.
3. Inappropriate use because of
  a. Struggles with the clinician for control.
  b. Tendency toward self-regulation of feeling states.

In addition to its effects on drug taking, the patient's attitude toward his
therapy may also influence the biological course of the syndrome. Active support from both the clinician and persons close to the patient may have similar
influences.

E. Pharmacotherapy and Psychotherapy

Often pharmacotherapy and psychotherapy are considered competing
ideologies. The report of The Group for the Advancement of Psychiatry,
Pharmacotherapy and Psychotherapy: Paradoxes, Problems and Progress,
published in 1975, emphasized the synergism between these two forms of
treatment.[7] However, defining the critical psychotherapeutic factors has been
difficult. Nonspecific factors (e.g., the therapist's values, the therapist's
regard for the patient, the patient's feelings about the therapist) often dominate a specific type or style of treatment. In addition, psychotherapeutic techniques are difficult to delineate and to implement consistently enough to
study. Despite significant methodological problems, researchers and clinicians
have developed various beliefs about combining pharmacotherapy and
psychotherapy.

  1. In some severe disorders, particularly acute affective and psychotic
     episodes, psychotherapy may contribute little to short-term outcome.
  2. In many situations, drugs may be necessary but not sufficient for
     optimal outcome. The clinician should combine medication with a
     nonbiological approach (e.g., antipsychotic medication and milieu
     therapy for schizophrenic episodes; MAO inhibitors or heterocyclic
     antidepressants and psychotherapy for panic states and phobias;
     antidepressant medication and milieu therapy or psychotherapy for
     acute depressive episodes).
  3. In depressive episodes, medication and psychotherapy each affect a

different part of the disorder. Psychotherapy improves the patient's interpersonal relationships; pharmacotherapy improves mood and reduces symptoms. Combined effects appear to be greater than those produced by either treatment alone.[8]

4. For patients with less severe symptoms (particularly depression and anxiety), psychotherapy alone may be as effective as pharmacotherapy. For example, several recent studies have shown that Beck's cognitive treatment is as effective as drugs for treating depression.[9] Well-designed studies are needed to define the interaction between psychotherapy and pharmacotherapy and the effects of each modality when used alone. For instance, although some patients' hypomanic symptoms diminish with increased therapeutic contact, most individuals (perhaps 90% or more) develop subsequent affective episodes if their lithium is stopped.

When a specific psychotherapy is combined with drug treatment, the interaction may be easier to see. However, to some extent, the success of each drug trial rests on basic psychotherapeutic skills. The clinician must tolerate the patient's symptoms while maintaining his faith in the therapeutic task. Since drugs often have conflicting meanings for both patient and clinician, each may experience various discomforting feelings, including ambivalence, fear, and anger. For the practitioner, many pitfalls exist. In the most severe cases, therapists sometimes blame or ignore patients because of ineffective results or adverse reactions. In other instances, pills may be used as a substitute for talking. This can take two forms—inappropriate trials of medication or appropriate medication without meaningful human contact. Even the most sincere practitioner sometimes administers halfhearted drug trials that are born out of acquiesence to the patient or that result from a sense of medical obligation (without conviction about success).

Focusing on drug giving also may cause the therapist to ignore the patient's viewpoint. Psychiatric illnesses often are stigmatizing. Patients may stop using available supports. Just as often, persons close to the patient may become distant or turn away. These same tendencies may operate in the therapeutic relationship. Sometimes, both transference and countertransference feelings compound the clinician's difficulties in establishing an empathic, caring human bond with the patient. Therefore, we must always remember that pharmacotherapy entails a psychotherapeutic interaction.

IV. GENERAL CLINICAL GUIDELINES

A. Patient Evaluation

Each clinician should develop a comprehensive approach to medicating patients. This does not require memorizing all the details of psychopharma-

TABLE 1. Common Organic Causes
of Anxiety States

Endocrine disorders
   Cushing's disease
   Hyperthyroidism
Metabolic disorders
   Hypoglycemia
   Hypocalcemia
Drugs and medications
   Caffeine
   Amphetamines
   Withdrawal states from addictive drugs
   Steroids

cology but rather developing a framework for care that includes guidelines for assessment, thoughtful differential diagnosis, methods for implementing a drug trial and monitoring adverse reactions, and access to essential information.

The first step in providing quality care involves taking a thorough psychiatric history and review of systems and administering appropriate parts of the mental status examination. When the patient is too disorganized or withdrawn, the clinician should interview friends or family members. On the basis of these findings, the clinician must differentiate functional from organic causes. Often caretakers feel overwhelmed by the array of possible medical disorders mimicking or contributing to primary psychiatric illnesses. Organic disorders sometimes present with psychological symptoms (see Tables 1, 2, and 3), whereas medicable psychiatric disorders sometimes present as an organic brain syndrome (i.e., disorganized schizophrenic states, bipolar affective disorders, and "pseudodementia" of depression).

TABLE 2. Organic Causes of Psychosis

Space-occupying lesions of the CNS
   Brain abscess (bacterial, fungal, TB, cysticercus)
   Metastatic carcinoma
   Primary cerebral tumors
   Subdural hematoma
Cerebral hypoxia
   Anemia
   Lowered cardiac output
   Pulmonary insufficiency
   Toxic (e.g., carbon monoxide)
Neurological disorders
   Alzheimer's disease
   Distant effects of carcinoma
   Huntington's chorea
   Normal-pressure hydrocephalus

(continued)

TABLE 2. Organic Causes of Psychosis (*Continued*)

Temporal lobe epilepsy
Wilson's disease
Vascular disorders
    Aneurysms
    Collagen vascular diseases
    Hypertensive encephalopathy
    Intracranial hemorrhage
    Lacunar state
Infections
    Brain abscess
    Encephalitis and postencephalitic states
    Malaria
    Meningitis (bacterial, fungal, TB)
    Subacute bacterial endocarditis
    Syphilis
    Toxoplasmosis
    Typhoid
Metabolic and endocrine disorders
    Adrenal disease (Addison's and Cushing's disease)
    Calcium
    Diabetes mellitus
    Electrolyte imbalance
    Hepatic failure
    Homocystinuria
    Hypoglycemia and hyperglycemia
    Pituitary insufficiency
    Porphyria
    Thyroid disease (thyrotoxicosis and myxedema)
    Uremia
Nutritional deficiencies
    B_{12}
    Niacin (pellagra)
    Thiamine (Wernicke–Korsakoff syndrome)
Drugs, medications, and toxic substances
    Alcohol (intoxication and withdrawal)
    Amphetamines
    Anticholinergic agents
    Barbiturates and other sedative–hypnotic agents (intoxication and withdrawal)
    Bromides and heavy metals
    Carbon disulfide
    Cocaine
    Corticosteroids
    Cycloserine (Seromycin®)
    Digitalis (Crystodigin®)
    Disulfuram (Antabuse®)
    Hallucinogens
    Isoniazid (INH ® and others)
    L-DOPA (Larodopa® and others)
    Marijuana
    Reserpine (Serpasil® and others)

TABLE 3. Organic Causes of Depression

Neurological disorders
  Alzheimer's disease
  Cerebral arteriosclerosis
  CNS degenerative disorders
  Huntington's chorea
  Multiple sclerosis
  Normal-pressure hydrocephalus
  Parkinson's disease
  Postconcussion syndrome
  Subdural hematoma
Metabolic and endocrine disorders
  Addison's disease
  Cushing's disease
  Diabetes
  Hepatic disease
  Hyperparathyroidism
  Hyperthyroidism
  Hypokalemia
  Hyponatremia
  Hypopituitarism
  Pellagra
  Pernicious anemia
  Porphyria
  Uremia
  Wernicke–Korsakoff syndrome
  Wilson's disease
Infectious diseases
  Brucellosis
  Encephalitis (viral)
  Hepatitis
  Influenza
  Mononucleosis
  Postencephalitic states
  Subacute bacterial endocarditis
  Syphilis
  Tuberculosis
  Viral pneumonia

Effects of tumors
  Cancer of the bowel
  Cancer of the pancreas
  Carcinomatosis
  Cerebral metastases and tumors
  Oat cell carcinoma

Drugs, medications, and poisons
  Alcohol
  Amphetamine withdrawal
  Antipsychotics
  Barbiturates
  Bromides
  Carbon disulfide
  Carbon monoxide
  Cocaine
  Digitalis
  Heavy metals
  Lead poisoning
  Methyldopa
  Opiates
  Oral contraceptives
  Other sedatives
  Propranolol (Inderal® and others)
  Reserpine
  Steroids

Miscellaneous disorders
  Anemia
  Cardiac compromise
  Chronic pyelonephritis
  Epilepsy
  Lupus erythematosus
  Pancreatitis
  Peptic ulcer
  Postpartum state
  Rheumatoid arthritis

Confusion between organic and functional disorders frequently leads to extensive and unnecessary laboratory testing. Studies show that generally, the clinician can medically screen a patient by taking a careful medical history, reviewing organ systems, completing a physical examination, and obtaining laboratory studies to follow up positive findings. Several factors may complicate the interpretation of the data. Emotional difficulties caused by a stressful event or significant environmental causes tend to obscure biological factors. In addition, rigid or distorted character defenses sometimes alter or hide the usual presenting symptoms of medicable syndromes.

B. Principles of Drug Use

1. Use Nonbiological Treatments When They Are as Effective as Pharmacotherapy

Many psychological conditions respond to support, crisis intervention, and various therapies (e.g., behavioral treatment for simple phobias or perhaps cognitive or insight-oriented therapies for moderately severe depressions). Each clinician must consider that drug therapies may have significant physical and psychological morbidity. In addition, patients often request medications (particularly sedative–hypnotic agents) for inappropriate reasons.

2. Do Not Deny a Patient Appropriate Medication

In many cases, clinicians overlook the signs of a medicable syndrome or withhold medication because symptoms seem to be "reactive." Patients often suffer needlessly and occasionally harm themselves or others.

3. Choose the Drug with the Best Risk/Benefit Ratio

The practitioner should prescribe the medication with the fewest adverse reactions and the greatest clinical effects.

4. Understand the Pharmacokinetics of Psychotropic Agents

A clinician should understand the kinetics of psychotropic agents, since the clinical characteristics of a drug are determined, in part, by biological factors that affect its ability to reach and exit from its site(s) of action. These pharmacokinetic factors—**absorption, distribution, metabolism, and excretion**—have been studied and understood increasingly in recent years and have enhanced our capacity to use drugs rationally.

Knowledge about the kinetics of a drug can help the clinician guide its actions in a patient and also may be useful in the selection of a particular compound. The rate of drug **absorption** from the gastrointestinal tract, for example, largely determines the speed of onset of action after a single oral dose. Drugs that are absorbed rapidly produce a faster and more intense onset of clinical effects, whereas the reverse is true for more slowly absorbed compounds. Termination of a drug's effects after a single oral dose is largely determined by the rate and extent of the drug's **distribution.** For example, highly lipid-soluble compounds tend to be rapidly and extensively distributed throughout the body's tissues, which indicates a relatively brief duration of clinical effects following a single dose. Distribution, rather than the elimination half-life of the drug, determines its duration of action after a single dose, but after repeated dosing, the elimination half-life becomes clinically important. The elimination half-life determines the rate at which a drug accumulates in body tissues: drugs with longer half-lives accumulate more gradually (steady-state concentrations are achieved after approximately four half-lives). In addition, drugs with long half-lives disappear from the body more gradually following discontinuation, whereas those with shorter half-lives are eliminated more rapidly (which for some drugs can result in the rapid appearance of an intense withdrawal syndrome). The half-life also can guide a clinician in choosing the frequency of dosing intervals: drugs whose half-lives exceed 24 hr usually can be administered once each day.

5. Learn the Differences between Preparations

Parenteral preparations generally have a more rapid onset of action, whereas all oral preparations, whether in capsule, tablet, or liquid form, provide equivalent amounts of medication with equal speed. Therefore, clinicians should avoid prescribing concentrates except for patients who have trouble swallowing medication. These preparations usually cost more than others and may cause mucosal irritation and contact dermatitis.

Occasionally alternative preparations may be useful. In drugs with a long half-life, sustained-release preparations offer no advantage over tablets or capsules. However, since lithium has a short half-life, and adverse reactions accompany fluctuations in serum level, a sustained-release preparation might reduce some of these problems in occasional patients. In addition, depot preparations of antipsychotic medication may benefit some patients over the long term.

6. Minimize Drug Use

Every practitioner should administer the lowest dose of medication for the shortest period of time. For antipsychotic drugs, this may reduce the incidence of tardive dyskinesia. Sometimes drugs can be avoided or used in smaller doses when other forms of support or treatment are available. Since individuals on lithium maintenance have developed kidney changes, clinicians have been prompted to review the dosage and occasionally maintain lower plasma levels. For both acute regimens and maintenance treatments, the clinician should also consider criteria for stopping or tapering medication over time.

7. Prescribe the Simplest Drug Regimen to Increase Compliance

Most patients, particularly those who require chronic medication, do not take it reliably. To increase compliance, clinicians often can give a single bedtime dose. In drugs with a long half-life (like heterocyclic antidepressants) that are administered in gradually increasing doses, once-a-day medication can be started at the beginning of treatment. Other drugs with a long half-life, such as antipsychotic agents, also may be given in a single dose, but only after several weeks of administration. Although patients often prefer to take benzodiazepines in divided doses, the long-acting agents within this drug class can be given once a day with the same clinical effect. Lithium, because of its short half-life, is the major exception to once-a-day administration. Wide fluctuations in blood level may lead to various adverse reactions. Three times a day is standard, although some patients tolerate twice daily medication. Delayed-release preparations may provide a means of giving drugs like lithium in twice-a-day doses.

8. Avoid Polypharmacy

Combinations of psychoactive drugs generally are not more effective than a single agent. Because of additive properties or drug interactions, polypharmacy may increase the incidence of adverse reactions. Combinations of medication are often promoted for commercial reasons. Moreover, patients already on drugs may have persistent symptoms and demand immediate relief. Clinicians, feeling frustrated, may respond by dispensing additional medications. Despite the evidence against polypharmacy, the average state hospital patient still takes three different medications. However, in the following situations, combinations of drugs may be indicated:

1. When a potential beneficial synergistic effect outweighs the risk of an adverse reaction. For example, sometimes heterocyclic antidepressants used alone do not alleviate the patient's depression. In rare situations, however, their synergistic effect with other drugs such as the antipsychotics, MAO inhibitors, methylphenidate (Ritalin®), thyroid hormone or thyroid-stimulating hormone may relieve the patient's symptoms.
2. When the diagnosis is in question and the need for immediate treatment outweighs the risk of a serious adverse reaction. For instance, the clinician may administer a combination of a heterocyclic antidepressant and an antipsychotic agent to depressed patients with disorganizing psychotic symptoms.
3. When adverse reactions caused by a psychotropic drug require treatment. For example, antipsychotic-drug-induced extrapyramidal reactions should be treated with antiparkinson drugs; severe anticholinergic symptoms secondary to heterocyclics, antipsychotics, or antiparkinson drugs can be treated acutely with physostigmine.
4. When changing from an acute regimen to maintenance treatment, the use of two preparations may overlap. In schizophrenia, depot

fluphenazine (Prolixin®, Permitil®) is started while the patient still receives an oral antipsychotic agent. Sometimes, in an acute manic patient who is taking haloperidol, lithium may be started for maintenance therapy before the antipsychotic medication is discontinued.

5. When a patient has two significant symptoms that do not respond to one drug. Sleeping medication may be indicated in depressed patients with persistent insomnia even after they have been started on an antidepressant regimen.

9. Provide the Most Cost-Effective Treatment

Theoretically, the clinician should help patients save money by prescribing drugs by their generic names. Unfortunately, the bioavailability (i.e., the amount of drug absorbed into the plasma) of different preparations may vary significantly. In practice, the clinician should try to prescribe the least expensive and most appropriate drug first. If this is done, he should discuss possible problems of bioavailability with the patient. In addition, he should encourage the patient (and/or family) to inquire about possible changes in the brand when prescriptions are refilled and to monitor closely the appearance of adverse reactions or the reemergence or worsening of clinical symptoms.

Because of the possible changing effectiveness of the preparations administered, the practitioner may also have to adjust dosage. At present, only a few medications are available in generic preparations. These include lithium, chlorpromazine, chlordiazepoxide, and the antidepressants imipramine and amitriptyline (Elavil®). However, other drugs will soon follow, since their patents will expire over the next several years.

10. Exercise Special Care with Medically Ill Patients

Prescribing psychoactive drugs to medical patients may require special measures. These patients often are older—the risk of adverse reactions increases, and tolerance to medication decreases. The elderly often are taking medication that may interact with psychoactive agents. The medical condition itself may represent a relative contraindication to drug treatment or may obligate the clinician to alter the dosage or methods of administration significantly. Because of these limitations, the clinician should:

1. Monitor possible drug interactions, adverse and toxic reactions, and special metabolic problems.
2. Assess the role of the medical condition in the etiology of the psychological symptoms.
3. Administer the lowest possible effective dose.

11. Establish an Ongoing Therapeutic Relationship

After evaluating the attributes of the patient and his illness and choosing the appropriate drug, the clinician should encourage an active collaboration. At the most basic level, this involves talking openly with the patient and providing accurate information. However, the practitioner's job entails many subsequent steps. He should help the patient acknowledge and resolve negative feelings and distorted beliefs about medication. In addition, the clinician must clarify roles and responsibilities for both himself and the patients. In practice, this process often requires time and the development of a trusting relationship.

At a pragmatic level, the clinician must negotiate a collaborative treatment plan with the patient that evolves from an open discussion of possible risks (i.e., common and serious adverse reactions) and potential benefits of pharmacotherapy and possible alternative treatments. Sometimes, if a disorganized patient cannot give informed consent, the caretaker must involve relatives, friends, guardian, or lawyer. The clinician should record in the patient's chart discussions about treatment, overall care, and any significant changes (e.g., dosage changes, severe adverse reactions and their treatment, mental status changes such as suicidal ideation or psychotic symptoms). The structure of treatment varies from case to case. However, at the least, the clinician should see the patient intermittently and be available (often by telephone) during periods of acute distress. Even after acute symptoms subside, a structured treatment program helps to increase medication compliance and may improve the patient's attitude. In addition, the practitioner should periodically reevaluate the need for medication and develop criteria for discontinuing medication.

12. Complete Each Drug Trial

A full clinical drug trial consists of administering adequate therapeutic doses of medication for an appropriate length of time. The trial culminates with one or a combination of the following:

1. Acceptable clinical result.
2. Intolerable adverse effects.
3. Poor response after an appropriate blood level is reached or the drug is administered for a time period specific for the illness (e.g., about 3 weeks for heterocyclic antidepressants or 3 to 6 weeks for antipsychotics).

By following these guidelines, caretakers can usually provide effective and safe care. Moreover, just as any clinical talent, skill in pharmacotherapy requires a combination of knowledge, practice, positive attitude, humility, and persistence.

V. CONCLUSION

As drug-responsive syndromes become more clearly defined, practitioners increasingly use pharmacotherapy as the primary treatment for many psychiatric disorders. Based on clinical experience and new research findings, medication options have greatly increased. Many new agents with fewer adverse reactions, lower toxicity, and somewhat different effects on brain chemistry have become available. These advances have improved patient care, and the future holds even greater promise. Increased understanding of brain chemistry and pharmacokinetics will significantly change clinical practice. And, as investigators define the interactions between biological and nonbiological interventions, more comprehensive treatment approaches will evolve.

REFERENCES

1. Sen G., Bose K. C.: Rauwolfia serpentina, a new Indian drug for insanity and high blood pressure. *Indian Med World* 2:194–201, 1931.
2. Laborit H., Huguenard P., Alluaume R.: Un nouveau stabilisateur vegetatif, le 4560 RP. *Presse Med* 60:206–208, 1952.
3. Lehmann H. E., Hunrahan G. E.: Chlorpromazine, a new inhibiting agent for psychomotor excitement and manic states. *Arch Neurol Psychiatry* 71:227–237, 1954.
4. Cade J. F. J.: Lithium salts in the treatment of psychotic excitement. *Med J Aust* 2:349–352, 1949.
5. Sternback L. H., Randall L. O., Gustafson S. R.: 1,4-Benzodiazepines: Chlordiazepoxide and related compounds, in Gordon M. (ed): *Psychopharmacological Agents*. New York, Academic Press, 1964, vol 1, 137–224.
6. Kuhn R.: The treatment of depressive states with G22355 (imipramine hydrochloride). *Am J Psychiatry* 115:459–464, 1958.
7. Group for the Advancement of Psychiatry: *Pharmacotherapy and Psychotherapy: Paradoxes, Problems and Progress,* report 93. New York, Group for the Advancement of Psychiatry, 1975, vol 9.
8. Weissman M. M.: The psychological treatment of depression: Evidence for the efficacy of psychotherapy done in comparison with, and in combination with, pharmacotherapy. *Arch Gen Psychiatry* 36:1261–1269, 1979.
9. Beck A. T., Rush A. J., Shaw B. F., et al: *Cognitive Therapy of Depression.* New York, Guilford Press, 1979.

2

Depression

STEPHEN C. SCHOONOVER, M.D.

I. INTRODUCTION

A. Psychological Models

Melancholia has accounted for severe human suffering throughout history. Numerous individuals have poignantly described the various symptoms and feelings that accompany severe depressions. However, it was not until the beginning of the 20th century that both psychological and constitutional theories were developed. Abraham postulated intense oral fixation in depressed individuals and differentiated grief from morbid depression.[1] Moreover, he viewed depression as aggression turned toward the self. Freud embraced these ideas but elaborated the concept of object loss.[2] He contended that the real or fantasied loss of an ambivalently loved person precipitates an ego regression with introjection and intense anger toward the lost object. This process results in self-deprecating, guilty feelings. Many authorities have argued that depression is not simply the result of aggression turned inward. Overt expressions of hostility do not relieve depressive symptoms. Weissman et al. emphasize that depression and aggression are separate affects that frequently coexist in depressed individuals.[3]

Other investigators have broadened our theoretical understanding of depression. Bibring viewed depression as a discrete ego state resulting from an individual's inability to achieve his ego ideal.[4] He felt that aggression was not the driving force behind depression; depleted self-esteem was the primary issue and secondarily led to hostility.

In addition to models that emphasize loss and self-esteem, some researchers and clinicians have discussed the role of deprivation during criti-

STEPHEN C. SCHOONOVER, M.D. • Department of Psychiatry, Harvard Medical School and Beth Israel Hospital, Boston Massachusetts 02215.

cal developmental stages. The Harlows, Spitz, Ainsworth, Bowlby, the Robertsons, and Mahler have contributed to our understanding of early attachments and the process of separation–individuation.[5–10] Early deprivation resulting from the loss of or separation from a major attachment (i.e., mothering figure) may have permanent ramifications if it occurs during a critical period and is not replaced by a meaningful relationship. Spitz observed that infants separated from their mothers during the first year of life developed various symptoms that progressed from apprehension and crying to withdrawal, motor slowing, despair, and, finally, detachment and even retarded physical and emotional development. This "anaclitic depression" was also described by Robertson and Bowlby in older children and by Harlow in primates. Clinical studies have since corroborated the importance of developmental deficits in the etiology of depression.

More recently, self-psychology has added another framework for understanding mood disorders.[11] Patients who have a poor sense of self and a lack of soothing self-objects frequently feel overburdened, helpless, worthless, and depressed. In clinical practice, those with severe narcissistic disorders and borderline states often develop adult "anaclitic" conditions marked by feelings of emptiness, loneliness, and lowered mood, even in the presence of others.[12]

Changes in psychoanalytic theory and practice have contributed to a broader view of depression: developmental deficits leave the individual exquisitely sensitive to feelings of deprivation and loss, which are stirred up by dynamically important life events and precipitate low self-esteem, loss of self-love, and self-deprecation.

Along with psychodynamic formulations, other authors have developed various psychological models to explain depressions. From foundations in Ellis' rational emotive therapy and ego psychology, Beck et al. envision depression as primarily a disorder of thinking.[13] Like the psychoanalysts, Beck postulates that distorted views of the self, the world, and the future result from early learning. This negative set consists of disordered cognitive "schemata" and cognitive "errors" that are stimulated by events in the patient's life and cause the patient to feel hopeless and helpless in the face of life's difficulties. Beck, in a way, bridges the psychodynamic and behavioral models.

Learning theory and behavioral psychotherapies brought a new focus to the study of depression. Seligman introduced the concept of "learned helplessness."[14] He hypothesized that people get depressed when they feel a loss of control over positively reinforcing experiences. Seligman thinks that some individuals exposed to unavoidable aversive stimuli will respond with passivity and helplessness to similar "stresses" in the future. In addition, this reaction can become a generalized personality trait; the individual believes that all adaptive efforts will eventually fail. Lewinsohn et al., like Seligman, view the lack of reinforcing stimuli as central to the development of depression.[15] However, they state that the important deficit is the low number of positive reinforcements "contingent" on the efforts of the individual. Moreover, according to this model, patients exposed to punishing or nonreinforcing responses from their environment may stop behaving in ways that will yield rewarding responses.

Other behavioral causes for depression have also been postulated. Some investigators feel that passive, self-deprecating, or depressed behaviors may become linked to other more fundamental sets of feelings. For example, depressed behaviors may elicit attention or affection, or they may cause others to gratify need-satisfying impulses (secondary gain).

Some authors have focused on social and existential themes. They emphasize not only the importance of relationships but also the broader social context. Problems with role status, individual purpose and meaning, and cultural myths may contribute to a person's sense of alienation and despair.[16]

B. Biological Models

More recently, investigators and clinicians have turned their attention to the biology of depression. Theoretical formulations followed the fortuitous discovery of agents that alleviated severe depression. Researchers found that the tricyclic antidepressants and monoamine oxidase inhibitors had significant effects on various brain neurotransmitters. In particular, Schildkraut and others hypothesized a relative synaptic **biogenic amine deficit** in depression and an excess in mania.[17]

Since the early reports, investigators have studied many aspects of brain functioning for evidence of the biological nature of depression, including neurotransmitter effects, metabolism and reuptake of monoamines, neuroendocrine feedback mechanisms, cell membrane and cation balance, brain peptides, and receptor phenomena (including the roles of adenylate cyclase and cyclic AMP). Deficits of both catecholamines (norepinephrine) and indoleamines (5-HT) have been suggested in depressed patients. More recently, researchers have proposed that both **serotonin-deficit** and **norepinephrine-deficit** depressions exist.[18] In addition, the interaction between these two neurotransmitter systems (particularly in the switch between mania and depression) has been described.[19] Several authorities postulate a permissive theory in which a serotonin deficit results in a vulnerability to affective illness; a lowered catecholamine level precipitates depression, and a raised level results in mania. **Although the changes in monoamines during depression may be significant, investigators now think that a variety of relationships between the parts of the central nervous system must be considered in the etiology**

of severe depression. This feeling stems not only from research illustrating changes in various brain subsystems but also from the clinical effectiveness of new drugs that might not affect norepinephrine or serotonin levels (e.g., the experimental drugs iprindole and mianserin).

C. Integrative Model

Any cogent theory of depression must integrate information from various levels of observation. Akiskal and McKinney envision **depression as a psychobiological "final common pathway of the various interlocking processes at chemical, experiential, and behavioral levels."**[20] They think that many factors including biological vulnerability, developmental deficits, and physiological and psychosocial stressors can contribute in varying degrees to a functional impairment of diencephalic centers that help to maintain mood, motor activity, appetite, sleep, and libido.

Even with the remarkable progress in our understanding of depression, the roles and relationships of various contributing factors to depressive symptoms await clarification. Therefore, we must treat each patient's problem individually by combining biological and nonbiological interventions.

II. DIAGNOSTIC CONSIDERATIONS

A. Clinical Presentations

To define disorders for which pharmacotherapy is strongly indicated, the clinician must differentiate normal from abnormal mood. Individuals frequently experience sadness and depression as a normal response to stress, disappointment, and crisis. Others exhibit depressive symptoms as part of their character style or in response to unconscious themes. Some individuals even appear to have mood changes related to natural rhythms (like the seasons). Many episodes of lowered mood require little or no intervention. However, some reactive, recurrent, or chronic depressions mentioned above require support, psychotherapy, or even pharmacotherapy.

Some individuals with abnormal mood develop more severe, autonomous depressive symptoms (i.e., "endogenous" or "melancholic") that respond to medication. These patients usually have a persistently lowered mood accompanied by feelings of worthlessness, hopelessness, helplessness, guilt, self-deprecation, blame, and pessimism. They also may have self-destructive impulses and impaired functioning. Somatic preoccupations and vegetative signs, including anorexia and weight loss, constipation, anhedonia, decreased libido, psychomotor retardation and/or agitation, and sleep distur-

TABLE 1. Major Depressive Illness[21]

Dysphoric mood (depression) and
At least four of the following for at least 2 weeks:
    Poor appetite or weight loss or increased appetite or weight gain
    Sleep disorder
    Loss of energy
    Psychomotor agitation or retardation
    Loss of interest or pleasure
    Feelings of self-reproach (may be delusional)
    Complaints or evidence of diminished ability to think or concentrate
    Recurrent thoughts of death or suicide
Melancholic subtype includes:
    Loss of pleasure
    At least three of the following:
        Distinct quality of depressed mood
        Diurnal mood swings (i.e., worse in morning)
        Early awakening
        Marked psychomotor agitation or retardation
        Poor appetite or weight loss
        Excessive or inappropriate guilt

bance (including fitful sleep and early awakening) are frequent in more severe depressions. Many individuals also manifest diurnal mood swings—the most serious symptoms occur in the morning, with improvement as the day progresses. In the most severe cases, patients may experience somatic or paranoid delusions.

The DSM-III specifies criteria for major depressive illness (see Table 1).[21] Some individuals, however, who present atypically also respond to medication. They include chronic complaining patients ("crocks"), individuals with "reactive" depressions, elderly with "pseudodementia," and those with hypochondriasis and chronic pain syndromes, phobic and anxiety states, "hysteroid dysphoria," Briquet's disease (hysteria), some severe psychoses (particularly with paranoia), and catatonic states.

Moreover, although severe depressions occur more commonly in patients with significant character problems, drug-responsive conditions are often missed by clinicians. These patients frequently appear lonely, empty, angry, manipulative, or object hungry and regressed rather than classically depressed. In addition, patients with severe obsessional character traits may mask a major depression with ruminations, compulsions, and intellectual defenses. In these individuals, the clinician must diagnose an underlying depression by a careful assessment over time or from a successful trial of antidepressant medication. Sometimes nonpsychiatric medications or medical conditions (see Table 3 in Chapter 1) may contribute to or cause major depressive episodes that require medication for their resolution.

B. Classifications

Historically, depressions have been subtyped according to dichotomous categories (e.g., endogenous–reactive and neurotic–psychotic). Recently, this view has been refined and broadened to include primary–secondary and unipolar–bipolar. In general, endogenous depressions correspond to the melancholic subtype of major depressive illness. The abandonment of the endogenous–reactive dichotomy has been important, since it implied that some depressions do not have exclusively environmental causes and require pharmacotherapy, whereas others result from life stresses and should be "worked through" psychotherapeutically. This clinical stance would preclude the use of pharmacotherapy for patients with "reactive depressions" and the use of psychotherapy for "endogenous" depressions. In fact, the decision to medicate with antidepressants relies not so much on presumed causality but on the presence of particular symptom clusters. The neurotic–psychotic classification of depressions is equally misleading, since the definitions of these terms are variable and do not correlate well with drug response.

More recently, diagnosticians have reclassified depressions. The primary–secondary dichotomy avoids some of the problems of the older continua. In primary depressions, there is no previous history of psychiatric illness except for episodes of depression or mania; secondary depressions occur in patients with a previously documented psychiatric disorder (other than an affective episode) or a medical illness. Investigators originally thought that primary depressions might preferentially respond to antidepressants. However, secondary depressions generally have similar symptoms and responses to medication. Clinically, patients with secondary depressions have a somewhat greater incidence of somatic and psychotic symptoms, phobias, anger, and suicidal behaviors. Winokur, in particular, believes that secondary depressions represent an acute process superimposed on a chronic set of problems.

The unipolar–bipolar dichotomy represents a further subclassification of primary affective disorders. Bipolar disorders must have a history of both depression and mania. In contrast, a unipolar depressive disorder must include a history of depressions only, although the number and frequency of depressions require further definition. Recently, by studying families, Winokur has further subdivided primary depression into pure depressive disease, depressive spectrum disease, and sporadic depressive illness (nonfamilial). Pure depressive disease occurs most often in older males who have one or more first-degree relatives with depressions. This condition appears equally in men and women. Depressive spectrum disease, in contrast, occurs most frequently in women under 40 years of age. Their female relatives have an increased frequency of depression, and first-degree relatives have a high frequency of alcoholism or antisocial characteristics. Males with depressive spectrum disease usually have alcoholic or antisocial symptoms.

Sporadic depressive disorders comprise the largest group of unipolar depressions (about 40%). Although unipolar illnesses can be divided into relatively homogeneous groups, the clinical ramifications of these findings await clarification. In addition, researchers must further correlate epidemiologic, familial, and clinical data with biochemical findings.

The DSM-III is the currently adopted diagnostic framework for psychiatric disorders. However, because DSM-III must insure a high degree of reliability and validity, some more atypical presentations of depression are excluded. Despite limitations, it defines a group of major depressive disorders (see Table 1) that are generally:

1. Recurrent and severe (70 to 80%).
2. Responsive to antidepressant medications.

C. Biological Diagnosis

As a result of biological research, investigators have identified biochemical markers that often occur in severely depressed patients. **Urinary 3-methoxy-4-hydroxyphenylglycol (MHPG) levels** and **dexamethasone suppression** are the two experimental tests currently used in clinical settings as biological correlates of major depressive illness. However, much uncertainty surrounds both procedures.

1. Amine Metabolites

Two related theories of depression, based initially on the biological effects of antidepressant drugs, postulate that inadequate levels of either norepinephrine or serotonin result in melancholic disorders. To study this hypothesis, researchers began to monitor levels of these neurotransmitters during pharmacotherapy by measuring their breakdown products [particularly urinary and cerebrospinal fluid (CSF) MHPG and CSF 5-HIAA].

Unfortunately, alterations in urinary MHPG (a metabolite of norepinephrine) levels have been highly variable in patients with affective disorders.[22] Patients with bipolar illness sometimes have lowered MHPG (<1000 mg/24 hr).[23] Some authorities have noted that patients with unipolar depressions separate into two groups: one with lowered MHPG and one with elevated MHPG.[24,25] A few studies show that patients with low urine MHPG also tend to have elevated levels of CSF 5-HIAA (an indoleamine breakdown product), whereas those with elevated MHPG often have low CSF 5-HIAA. The various antidepressants have different effects on the reuptake of norepinephrine and serotonin. Therefore, investigators have proposed that patients

with low MHPG (and presumably a norepinephrine deficit) should respond
to drugs such as desipramine (Pertofrane®, Norpramin®) that more selectively block the reuptake of norepinephrine, whereas patients with higher urinary MHPG (implying a serotonin deficit) should respond to drugs such as
amitriptyline (Elavil® and others) that more specifically block the reuptake of
5HT.[26-28]

Although some studies corroborated the diagnostic and treatment implications of these research findings, much of the emerging data have been contradictory. Accurate 24-hr urine collections are difficult to obtain in
depressed patients; laboratory procedures frequently are not adequately stan-
dardized; and many extraneous factors (e.g., caffeine intake, diet, exercise)
can affect the results. In addition to these problems, the amount of urine
MHPG that comes from brain metabolites varies widely (20 to 60%), making interpretation of urinary data difficult. The remainder originates from
peripheral sources and may be significantly affected by motor activity and
anxiety. The accumulating evidence seems to indicate that urinary MHPG
measurements may contain too many artifacts for routine clinical use. Moreover, several newer agents have significant antidepressant properties without
major effects on serotonin or norepinephrine.

Some investigators have also found that a 20- to 30-mg dose of amphetamine (a strong norepinephrine-blocking drug) sometimes quickly improves
symptoms in depressed patients who subsequently respond preferentially to
imipramine (Tofranil® and others) or desipramine. (Both drugs strongly
block the reuptake of norepinephrine.) This procedure, however, is still experimental and remains to be corroborated.

2. Cortisol Metabolism

A majority of melancholic patients secrete increased amounts of cortisol,
perhaps indicating abnormal limbic system activity and disinhibition of the
hypothalamic–pituitary–adrenal axis. In addition, the usual diurnal cortisol
suppression commonly does not occur in these individuals. In depressed people, a central catecholamine deficit may result in suppression of the hypothalamus and an oversecretion of corticotropin-releasing factor (CRF). The synthetic steroid dexamethasone (Decadron® and others) usually suppresses
pituitary ACTH and, therefore, circulating adrenal steroids. However, some
researchers report that up to half of endogenously depressed individuals
escape suppression at some time during the 24 hr following the administration of dexamethasone.[29] Brown has observed that individuals failing to suppress had more depressive episodes and responded better to pharmacotherapy
(particularly imipramine and desipramine).[30,31] Because of these and other
data, researchers have proposed that the dexamethasone suppression test
(DST) may be helpful in choosing antidepressants and monitoring the progress of drug therapy.[32]

In practice, although widely used, the DST only infrequently helps the clinician. Some research suggests that the DST has few false positives (i.e., patients who escape suppression but are not endogenously depressed). However, a rate of 50% false negatives (i.e., patients who do have major depressive illness with melancholia but do suppress with dexamethasone) makes it a very limited diagnostic tool. Patients with melancholic depression usually are medicated regardless of the outcome of the test. Escape from suppression only confirms the clinician's impressions, whereas normal suppression should not overrule the clinician's judgment that a drug-responsive syndrome is present. Occasionally, if a patient's clinical presentation does not conform to the diagnostic criteria for major depressive illness, a positive DST might encourage a practitioner to give an antidepressant drug. In addition, clinicians usually discontinue antidepressant medication on an empirical basis. In depressed patients with a positive DST, some authorities feel that the test can be used to monitor the course of treatment. However, in practice, a return of dexamethasone suppression provides only a rough indicator that the underlying disturbance in brain function has remitted.

Guidelines for the clinical use of the DST include:

1. Reserve the DST for patients in whom the diagnosis is in doubt.
2. After taking 10 cc of blood for a base-line cortisol measurement, give 1 mg of dexamethasone at 11:00 p.m.
3. Take blood for subsequent measurements at 4:00 p.m. on the following day.
4. Assay the blood samples for cortisol (dexamethasone normally suppresses serum cortisol to <5 mg/100 ml of serum over a 24-hr period).

The identification of biological markers that correlate with diagnosis parallels the development of more complex models of brain behavior. Although these tests currently have limited clinical applications, with further research and investigation, biological methods of diagnosis may become practical aids.

D. Symptom Profiles and Drug Responsiveness

Generally, DSM-III criteria for major depressive illness correspond to those disorders responding to antidepressant medications. However, many investigators have searched for more specific characteristics of responders and nonresponders.

Researchers have delineated various factors correlating with drug responsiveness (see Table 2), including anorexia and weight loss, "middle and terminal" (rather than early) insomnia, diurnal mood variation, psychomotor retardation or agitation, autonomous symptoms, decreased functioning, acute

TABLE 2. Predictors of Heterocyclic Responsiveness

Positive predictors
    Vegetative symptoms (anorexia, weight loss, middle and terminal insomnia)
    Diurnal mood variation (with worst mood in the morning)
    Psychomotor retardation or agitation (including decreased functioning)
    Autonomous and pervasive symptoms
    Acute onset
    Family history of depression and drug responsiveness
    Dose of imipramine (or equivalent dose of another heterocyclic) above 125 to 150 mg per
        day
    Blood levels of desmethylimipramine or imipramine and desmethylimipramine above 200
        ng/ml and nortriptyline between 50 and 150 ng/ml
Negative predictors
    Coexistence of other significant psychiatric disturbances (particularly with hysterical or
        externalizing features)
    Chronic symptoms
    Psychotic features (particularly mood incongruence)
    Hypochondriacal concerns or predominant somatic symptoms
    Previous drug trial failure(s)
    History of sensitivity to adverse reactions

onset, family history of depression and/or family history of response to an antidepressant, and previous response of drug therapy. Poor responders more frequently exhibit other psychiatric disturbances (particularly hysterical or externalizing styles), chronic symptoms, mood-incongruent psychotic features (particularly delusions), prominent hypochondriacal concerns and/or somatization, and previous drug trial failures. (Some of these patients, however, respond to other biological therapies, e.g., MAO inhibitors.)

In practice, both the DSM-III definitions of depression and the experimental profiles of drug responders probably represent heterogeneous groups of disorders that may respond differentially to the various drugs. For example, a few studies suggest that depressed patients with psychotic symptoms, anxiety and/or agitation, and middle and late insomnia more often exhibit low MHPG levels. Some authorities believe that these individuals should receive a medication (such as imipramine or desipramine) that blocks the reuptake of norepinephrine. These guidelines, however, have not proven very reliable. Therefore, both symptom clusters and MHPG levels currently provide limited guidance in the choice of antidepressant.

Monoamine oxidase inhibitors have roughly the same therapeutic profile as **heterocyclic antidepressants.*** Some experts feel that these agents

*Since many of the currently used thymoleptic drugs are not tricyclic in structure, we have adopted this term to represent the various cyclic antidepressants. From: Baldessarini R. J.: Overview of recent advances in antidepressant pharmacology. Part II. *McLean Hosp J* 7:1–27, 1982.

may have a selective advantage with hysteroid, hypochondriacal, or extremely obsessive individuals and for patients with nonmelancholic depressions that show "reversal" of sleeping, eating, and diurnal mood disturbances (i.e., hypersomnia and a sleep onset disorder, increased appetite, and worsening mood late in the day).

At present, available data about drug responsiveness can help structure expectations and may imply the effectiveness of a particular class of drug (i.e., heterocyclics for melancholic depressions, MAOIs for selected nonmelancholic depressions, and a combination of a heterocyclic and an antipsychotic for depressions accompanied by psychotic symptoms, particularly delusions). However, these guidelines, developed from an analysis of large groups of patients, may fail to predict outcome in a given individual.

III. GENERAL THERAPEUTIC MEASURES

A broader understanding of the relationships among brain chemistry, behavior, thinking, and feeling has fostered a more open environment for investigation. In fact, as we clarify the multidetermined nature of depressive illness, we also have started to develop a range of therapeutic techniques for depression. Research has demonstrated the effectiveness, if not the necessity, of using somatic treatments in severe mood disorders. However, recent studies also have shown that various psychological techniques may represent an effective alternative for treating depressed patients.[13,33]

A. Milieu and Crisis Techniques

Many depressed patients manifest intense suffering, suicidal impulses, and poor self-care, requiring immediate and intensive care. Others require hospitalization because of uncertain diagnosis or medical problems that may confound somatic treatment. In these cases, inpatient care offers various therapeutic advantages and possibilities. At the most basic level, the ward milieu contains symptoms and provides protection.

Frequently, depressed individuals exhibit self-destructive thoughts and behaviors that develop, in part, as a result of self-punitive thinking and disengagement from social supports. A therapeutic milieu can interrupt the depressive cycle and provide at least some measure of protection. Patients intent on dying, however, usually succeed. Because severe suicidal impulses often last only a few days, close observation and enforced human contact often help the patient live through the acute crisis. An inpatient milieu offers other therapeutic advantages as well, including relief from a self-demeaning or disorganizing interaction with persons close to the patient, emotional support and self-validation, structured interpersonal interactions, correction of cognitive distortions, maladaptive patterns, and self-punishing rituals, and the practicing of new behaviors. These psychological interventions can also be provided in other settings (e.g., day care) and by other personnel (e.g., home visit and crisis teams). In fact, most intensive care settings employ crisis techniques that have a focused, here-and-now, time-limited, reality-based orientation. The therapeutic approaches include mobilizing the patient's natural supports, adopting an active and supportive (and sometimes directive) role for the therapist, reviewing, labeling, and correcting maladaptive behaviors and cognitive distortions, and learning new coping and problem-solving techniques. In many ways, this approach integrates aspects of "cognitive therapy," behavioral techniques, and the short-term psychodynamic therapies.

B. Psychotherapy

Recent investigations have indicated that many depressive syndromes respond well to various types of psychotherapy. Researchers in the Boston–New Haven Collaborative Study found that antidepressant therapy (amitriptyline 100 to 200 mg per day) and psychotherapy both worked better than a mock treatment for patients with a nonpsychotic major depressive illness. Both drug therapy and combined drug and psychotherapy provided equal symptom relief and prevention of relapse. However, psychotherapy alone offers somewhat less symptom relief but more improvement in measures of social adjustment.[34]

Partly as an outgrowth of this work, these investigators developed an "interpersonal" psychotherapy for depression.[35,36] It consists of 12 to 16 once-a-week sessions focusing on recent interpersonal relationships and using both directive and interpretive interventions. For moderately severe mood disorders, this treatment seems quite effective. Other investigators and clinicians using both short-term intensive psychodynamic treatment and various forms of crisis intervention have shown that they are also beneficial to many depressed individuals. Longer-term psychodynamic treatment may be necessary to treat depressive symptoms related to deep-seated intrapsychic conflicts. For the less experienced psychotherapist or medical practitioner, however, consultation from someone accustomed to treating severe depression with both psychotherapy and pharmacotherapy may be appropriate.

Beck and others have approached the psychotherapy of affective disorders from a different perspective. They developed a therapy that focuses on the distorted cognition in depressed patients.[13] This therapy aims to correct underlying negative assumptions and errors in thinking that may generate feelings of hopelessness and helplessness. Beck feels that patients have unrealistically negative views of themselves, the world, and the future ("cognitive triad") and that they perpetuate them by cognitive errors and negative cognitive schemata. Therapy to correct these misattributions consists of about 20 sessions over 12 to 20 weeks. The therapist takes an active and directive stance while helping the client to focus on and confront a "list" of target symptoms. (In this process, the clinician addresses both manifest and unconscious dysfunctional thoughts.)

More behaviorally oriented therapists use similar techniques to treat depression.[37] In addition to identification and confrontation of cognitive structures, behaviorists employ formal cognitive restructuring, skills training (including assertiveness training), and environmental manipulation.

In general, evidence indicates not only that structured psychotherapies help many depressions but also that they frequently may be equal to or better than pharmacotherapy. However, we must be careful in drawing a definitive conclusion. Studies often have employed antidepressants and specific psychotherapeutic methods inadequately. No investigations comparing psychotherapy and pharmacotherapy have addressed the problem of "fit" between a patient and a particular drug or a specific model of therapy. In addition, the accumulating evidence in psychotherapy research indicates that many factors other than the type of therapy significantly promote positive outcome, including a patient's positive attitude toward therapy and the therapist, a therapist's positive feeling about the patient, and the patient's motivation.

Which depressed patients should receive psychotherapy? Every patient should be involved in a therapeutic relationship. Individuals taking drugs should receive emotional support and encouragement and the opportunity to address their feelings about the depressive episode. Moreover, for individuals with significant character pathology (e.g., borderline states, narcissistic personality disorders, masochistic or depressive characters) who develop mild to moderately severe depressions in response to chronic disappointment and low self-esteem, long-term insight-oriented psychotherapy is the treatment of choice. These patients, however, frequently develop more severe and autonomous depressive symptoms accompanied by vegetative signs; such symptoms may improve with medication. In addition, some therapies may be equal to or better than medication for individuals who become depressed in response to severe stress, life crises, real or fantasied losses, or from a severely negative view of the self, world, or others.

C. Electroconvulsive Therapy

1. Introduction

Although its mechanism of action is unknown, **electroconvulsive therapy (ECT) effectively treats most patients with severe depression.** In fact, 60,000 to 100,000 individuals receive this treatment each year, most without significant morbidity. However, questions of efficacy, concerns about the development of an organic brain syndrome, and occasional abuses have stigmatized this procedure.[38] In addition, antidepressant medication offers an effective and often more acceptable alternative to ECT. Thus, some patients do not receive ECT even when it is the treatment of choice. In the last decade, however, investigators have attempted to define more precisely the various clinical effects and indications and contraindications of ECT.

2. Mechanism of Action

Although no consensus exists about the therapeutic mechanism of ECT, researchers have documented profound central nervous system changes resulting from its use. Some experts believe that it alters neurotransmitter availability similarly to the effects of antidepressant medications. However, electroshock not only increases serotonin levels and increases MAO activity, dopamine, and cyclic AMP but also may lower catecholamine levels. Alternatively, ECT may produce its effects by increasing the sensitivity of postsynaptic neurotransmitter receptors.[39]

3. Indications

Numerous controlled studies demonstrate that ECT works better than placebo and at least as well as heterocyclic antidepressants in the treatment of severe depression. In addition, ECT may be more effective than heterocyclics alone for treating psychotic depressions, particularly when accompanied by agitation. Electroconvulsive therapy also alleviates the symptoms of extreme agitation and catatonia in schizophrenics who respond poorly to medication, making these patients more amenable to other treatments.

Electroshock therapy offers significant advantages over medication in certain clinical situations. The strongest indications include:

1. Previous good response to ECT without significant untoward effects.
2. Strong family history of positive response to ECT.
3. Depression characterized by psychotic features, particularly somatic or nihilistic delusions.
4. Relative or absolute contraindication to medication, such as in patients with significant cardiovascular disease or other medical disorders that preclude an adequate trial of drugs.
5. Need for immediate containment of symptoms (e.g., severely suicidal patients, severe mania, extremely agitated or assaultive patients, and individuals with severe retarded depression that impairs self-care and feeding).

6. Poor response to trials of medication.
7. Severe, persistent behavior problems or mildly disorganized thinking in schizophrenic patients.

Electroconvulsive therapy should be strongly considered for psychotically depressed patients and those who have not responded to medication. In this situation, the clinician may start or continue an antidepressant drug, since ECT and heterocyclics may work synergistically. However, the anesthesia procedure occasionally may produce additional risk of cardiotoxicity from the combination of ECT with antidepressants and antipsychotics. Therefore, a clinical decision should be made together with an anesthesiologist. In addition, **patients receiving lithium have a greater risk of developing significant CNS impairment during a course of ECT;** therefore, lithium treatment should be discontinued before ECT and restarted after treatment has ended.[40,41] Many patients require a psychoactive drug after ECT to prevent relapse. Although less than a quarter of patients on a heterocyclic antidepressant or lithium relapse after 6 months, more than half of individuals without maintenance pharmacotherapy subsequently have a recurrence. However, the guidelines for starting long-term drug therapy following ECT require further clarification. In rare cases, maintenance ECT is needed and helpful.

Sometimes ECT does not provide adequate relief from depressive symptoms. Factors that correlate with poor outcome include hypochondriasis, hysterical character stucture, absence of vegetative symptoms (i.e., sleeping, eating, bowel function, motor activity), absence of a family history of depression, absence of delusions, presence of reactive factors, and presence of a marked personality disorder. Clinically, however, this list of negative criteria does not provide much guidance, since individuals with these attributes also respond poorly to other treatment modalities.

4. Contraindications and Adverse Reactions

Several medical conditions may limit the use of ECT. Increased risk generally stems from the anesthesia, the induced seizure, or the transient increase in CNS pressure and blood flow. Relative contraindications include **a recent myocardial infarction, active pulmonary inflammation, central nervous system tumors, increased intracranial pressure, and recent carbon monoxide poisoning.** (ECT occasionally has resulted in brain damage in these cases.)

The risks that attend preparatory anesthesia include significant respiratory depression, allergy to premedications, and cardiac failure. The main adverse effects of ECT are confusion and short-term memory loss (which may last five times as long in elderly patients). Both are significantly less with unilateral treatments.[42]

5. Technique

The clinician should inform the patient about what he will experience during and after the procedure: he will be asked to lie down, a sedative will be administered, and he may wake up with some discomfort (and rarely with a sense of being paralyzed). In addition, each individual should know the possible risks (particularly memory loss) and treatment alternatives. The practitioner should obtain informed consent (from a relative or guardian, if necessary) and should carefully document discussions and procedures.

The procedure begins with the administration of an anticholinergic agent (scopolamine or atropine), a short-acting anesthetic agent (usually a briefly acting barbiturate), and a muscle relaxant [succinylcholine (Anectine®)]. The barbiturate usually takes about 1 min to work. During anesthesia, because of muscle paralysis, assisted ventilation with oxygen is required. A physician then applies a brief, low-energy unilateral electrical stimulation (a new apparatus decreases both the time and intensity of the current) to the nondominant hemisphere. The electrical impulse is titrated to produce a generalized CNS seizure of about 40 to 60 sec duration. The strong muscle relaxant protects the patient from physical injury but paralyzes the respiratory and limb muscles. Therefore, to monitor the seizure, the clinician can tighten a blood pressure cuff on one arm, which will prevent the succinylcholine from affecting that limb, and allow the seizure activity to be observed. Alternatively, the clinician may use an EEG tracing to observe the spike-and-wave pattern. After the seizure, recovery usually takes about 10 to 20 min.

The number and frequency of treatments vary with the clinical needs of the patient. Therapy should be administered until the patient experiences complete recovery. **The typical regimen usually consists of every-other-day or twice-weekly treatments for a total of five to ten sessions.** Sometimes, additional treatments or bilateral stimulation may be needed to produce significant results. Some authorities think that recovery may be proportional to the total seizure time.[43]

IV. PHARMACOTHERAPY

In the 1950s and early 1960s, the discovery of monoamine oxidase inhibitors (MAOIs) and imipramine and related tricyclic antidepressants was among the most significant developments in the pharmacotherapy of depression. Since that time, we have made great theoretical advances. However, most new agents were developed by testing the effects of drugs (i.e., those with minor alterations of the basic tricyclic structure) in animal behavioral paradigms. Therefore, the subsequently developed tricyclic antidepressants have offered no increase in efficacy and only small improvements in the spectrum of adverse reactions. Recently, however, researchers have begun to test compounds with more diverse effects and chemical structures.[52–54] The introduction of amoxapine (Asendin®), maprotiline (Ludiomil®), trimipramine (Surmontil®), and trazodone (Desyrel®) in the United States brings the total of available heterocyclic antidepressants to ten. Most of these new agents have properties similar to the previously developed drugs. However, amoxapine produces extrapyramidal reactions and may have antipsychotic effects, and trazodone seems to cause significantly fewer cardiac and anticholinergic effects than any of the currently used heterocyclic antidepressants.

The United States has been somewhat slower than other countries in adopting new antidepressant drugs. For instance, clorimipramine, a tricyclic antidepressant that may offer advantages in the treatment of phobic anxiety conditions and severe obsessive–compulsive states, is approved for use in Canada (the FDA has concerns about possible toxicity). In addition, clinicians in other countries employ more than a dozen antidepressant agents not available in the United States. Most of these resemble the traditional tricyclic antidepressants, although some (like mianserin and iprindole) differ significantly in both structure and pharmacological effects. In particular, these drugs have fewer cardiac and anticholinergic effects.

Beyond the drugs available for clinical use, many other agents with diverse structures and properties are being tested. Researchers have found possible antidepressant properties in many nontricyclic drug classes including bicyclic and tetracyclic compounds, phenylpiperazine derivatives, oximethers of aralkylketones (fluvoxamine), benzodiazepines (alprazolam), a chloropropriophenone (bupropion), tetrahydroisoquinoline (nomifensine), a β-adrenergic stimulant (salbutamol), a natural metabolite (S-adenosyl methionine), three new MAO inhibitors, and the amino acids tryptophan and tyrosine. In addition, a great deal of current investigation focuses on developing drugs with more selective effects. Many new agents more specifically block the reuptake of norepinephrine or serotonin, and some experimental MAO inhibitors selectively block type A (e.g., clorgyline) or type B (e.g., deprenyl) monoamine oxidase. Researchers hoped that type B MAOIs would have significant antidepressant properties. By sparing type A MAO in the gut, these agents would not lead to hypertension from the "cheese effect" (by allowing metabolism of tyramine-containing foods in the GI tract). Unfortunately, although type A MAOIs appear to be effective antidepressants, type B MAOIs are not.

In addition to their special effects on neurotransmitters, many new antidepressants cause fewer adverse effects of some types. For example, some,

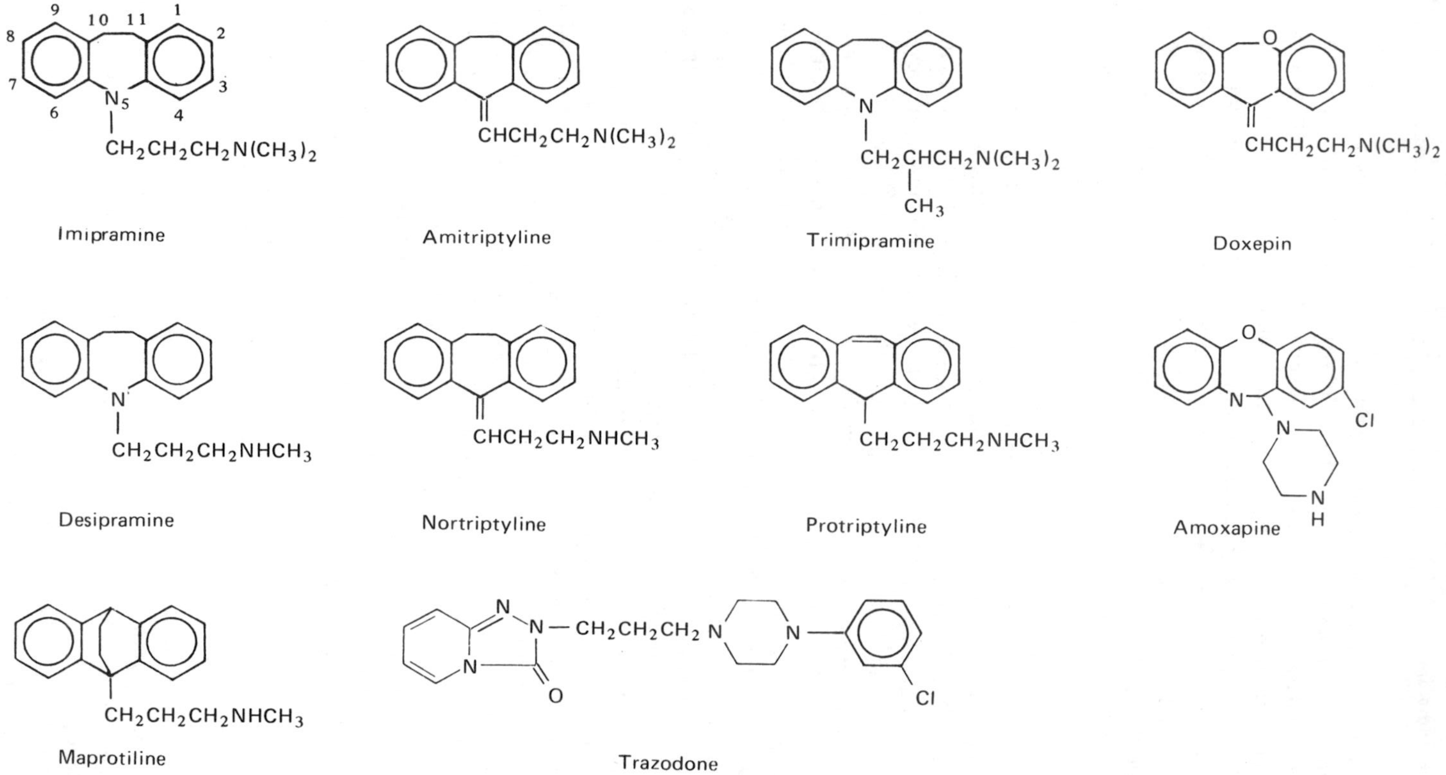

FIGURE 1. Heterocyclic antidepressants.

including trazodone, zimelidine, fluoxetine, and fluvoxamine, produce few anticholinergic reactions. These new developments already offer us greater clinical choices. Moreover, in the near future, these "second generation" antidepressants may provide safer and more specific treatment for patients with various depressive subtypes.

Clinically, we know that various heterocyclic antidepressants and monoamine oxidase inhibitors provide significant relief from many severe depressions and are the treatment of choice. By defining some characteristics of drug responders, investigators have started to specify particular indications for pharmacotherapy. In addition, practitioners have found that the antidepressants provide relief from less severe depressions with unusual symptoms and from various other clinical syndromes (see Fig. 1). Experimentally, the various antidepressant drugs produce a range of brain chemistry effects that may make them effective in some patients but not in others with similar symptoms. However, in practice, the heterocyclic medications are quite similar to one another in their clinical effects and adverse reactions. In addition, work with antipsychotic drugs and benzodiazepines (particularly alprazolam) indicates that depressive syndromes may be significantly affected by diminishing anxiety. Although available drugs already help many depressed individuals, the future should bring more specific, effective, and easily monitored pharmacotherapies.

A. Heterocyclic Antidepressants

1. Chemistry

This group of compounds effectively relieves many severe autonomous depressions. Most heterocyclics have three interlinked carbon rings; one (amoxapine) has a tricyclic nucleus with an additional ring on the side chain, another (maprotiline) has a four-ring nucleus, whereas trazodone has a structure dissimilar from other available antidepressants (see Table 3).

The heterocyclic antidepressants are equally effective clinically and have similar metabolic pathways. However, they are divided into several subgroups according to potency, secondary pharmacological properties, and adverse reactions:

1. The original group (imipramine and amitriptyline).
2. Monomethylated or "secondary amine" compounds [nortriptyline (Aventyl®, Pamelor®), desipramine, and protriptyline (Vivactil®)], which can have an initial activating effect but show no differences in antidepressant activity.
3. Doxepin (Sinequan®, Adapin®), a dimethylated compound structurally similar to amitriptyline.

TABLE 3. Amine Uptake-Blocking Properties
of Heterocyclics

Drug	Norepinephrine	Serotonin
Amitriptyline	Low	Moderate
Imipramine	Moderate	Moderate
Doxepin	Moderate	Moderate
Trimipramine	Moderate	Moderate
Nortriptyline	High	Low
Desipramine	Very high	Very low
Protriptyline	High	Very low
Amoxapine	High	Low
Maprotiline	Very high	Very low
Trazodone	Very low	Very high

4. Amoxapine, a dibenzoxazepine similar in structure to the antipsychotic loxapine.
5. Maprotiline, a tetracyclic compound.
6. Trazodone, a phenylpiperazine derivative of triazolopyridine with very few anticholinergic and cardiac effects.

2. Mechanism of Action

Investigators have developed several interesting hypotheses to explain the therapeutic action of heterocyclic antidepressants. Since no model completely accounts for all of the available facts, many experts think that biologically dissimilar depressions probably exist. Until recently, researchers primarily focused on the way antidepressants affected the availability of amine neurotransmitters.[44] Antidepressants were thought to work by blocking the reuptake of norepinephrine or serotonin (see Table 3). However, recent findings refute or at least complicate this general hypothesis. Some effective antidepressants (such as mianserin, which is unavailable in the United States) do not seem to significantly block the reuptake of norepinephrine or serotonin.[45] Moreover, antidepressants require a few weeks to work, even though their CNS blocking effects are immediate.

Sulser presents a divergent viewpoint.[46] He proposes that depressions result from increased norepinephrine activity and that antidepressants promote a "down-regulation" of activity by decreasing β-adrenergic receptor sensitivity. Other research has described how the heterocyclics may take a few weeks to increase postsynaptic receptor sensitivity or decrease presynaptic inhibition by desensitization of the α receptor (resulting in a larger release of NE per nerve impulse).[48] Even the existence of a CNS antidepressant substance has been proposed. This has been supported by the recent finding that binding sites fairly specific for imipramine exist.[49] Janowsky et al. also suggest that acetylcholine has an important role in affective disorders. They feel that an imbalance between acetylcholine and norepinephrine or serotonin is important in producing depression and mania (e.g., a predominance of ace-tylcholine leads to depression). They therefore propose that antidepressants work, at least in part, because of their anticholinergic properties.[50]

The current evidence emphasizes that we probably cannot expect to find a common mechanism for all antidepressants. In addition to the existence of depressive subtypes, each distinct syndrome may result from a complex inter-action of presynaptic, neurohumoral, and postsynaptic receptor properties of specific neural pathways (see Tables 3 and 4). As Maas postulates, anti-depressants may act in various complicated ways to restabilize an unbalanced system.[51]

3. Adverse Reactions

The clinician should know a drug's adverse reactions and a patient's sus-ceptibilities. Some of these effects cause minor discomfort, but others may interfere with drug trials or produce serious morbidity. Of the common reac-tions, cardiac, anticholinergic, and CNS effects produce the most clinical morbidity. Untoward effects occur more often when heterocyclics are coad-ministered with other drugs or when a patient has a coexisting physical disor-der. The heterocyclic antidepressants generally have similar adverse reac-tions. However, the new drug amoxapine more closely resembles antipsychotic agents in structure and brain chemistry effects; therefore, it occasionally causes amenorrhea, galactorrhea, and extrapyramidal effects. Although no cases of tardive dyskinesia have been reported so far, clinicians should exercise caution when using amoxapine for an extended period of time.

a. Gastric

Although mucosal irritation, resulting in nausea and vomiting, can occur, these symptoms usually result from psychogenic factors. Heterocyclics

TABLE 4. Pharmacodynamic Actions of Heterocyclic Antidepressants[a]

Immediate actions
    Block amine uptake (NE, 5HT)
    Reduce firing rate and turnover (NE, 5HT cells)
    Block ACh receptors (3° > 2° amine agents)
    Inconsistent effects on 5HT, α_1, and H_2 receptors
    No MAO inhibition (or very weak)
Later actions
    Block amine uptake
    Increased firing rates
    Decrease sensitivity of α_2 and β NE receptors
    Increase NE release per impulse
    Increase 5HT sensitivity but decrease $5HT_2$ binding

[a]Adapted from Ross J. Baldassarini, M.D.

can also cause heartburn, which can usually be alleviated by administering the medication after meals or at bedtime.

b. Hematological

i. Leukocytic Effects and Purpura. Heterocyclics only rarely produce alterations in white cell count. Clinicians have reported leukocytosis, leukopenia, Loeffler's syndrome, eosinophilia, thrombocytopenia, and purpura. These conditions should be medically evaluated, although they seldom cause significant morbidity. The patient can usually continue the medication at the same dosage.

ii. Agranulocytosis. Both the heterocyclics and the phenothiazines rarely cause agranulocytosis, but the incidence is much lower with the antidepressants. Death from infection occurs infrequently if the drug is discontinued immediately and the patient placed immediately in reverse isolation. White cell numbers usually return to normal within several weeks of discontinuing the drug. Most reported cases have occurred with imipramine (although this may be an artifact, since it is the drug most often studied).

Agranulocytosis seems to be an allergic response of sudden onset that usually appears 40 to 70 days after initiation of the medication. Patients have a greater risk with advancing age and concomitant physical illnesses. The clinical syndrome is characterized by a low white count (composed almost completely of lymphocytes), normal red count, and infection (usually involving the oropharynx) accompanied by fatigue and malaise.

Routine blood studies do not help with early detection, since the syndrome develops very rapidly. Instead, the clinician should evaluate and treat any sign of infection, especially of the pharynx. He should discontinue the heterocyclic and never administer it to that patient again. The practitioner might try an antidepressant with a different structure and follow the patient closely for adverse hematological effects.

c. Hepatic

Less than 0.5 to 1% of patients treated with heterocyclics develop liver toxicity. This adverse reaction seems to be a hypersensitivity response similar to that caused by the phenothiazines.

Most often, the toxicity produces abnormal liver function tests without clinical jaundice. Mild, transient jaundice preceded by abdominal pain, anorexia, fever, and transitory eosinophilia may occur during the first 2 months of treatment. In these cases, the patient has abnormal liver function tests. Most often, individuals have a high conjugated bilirubin and congested bile canaliculi without hepatocellular damage. After the drug is discontinued, recovery from this syndrome usually takes several weeks. When a toxic reaction occurs, the clinician should lower the dosage or switch to another type of antidepressant.

d. Endocrine

Heterocyclics have fewer endocrine effects than the phenothiazines. Unlike the phenothiazines and amoxapine, the other heterocyclics have produced no clear-cut cases of amenorrhea or galactorrhea. Rare patients, however, may develop menstrual irregularities.

Antidepressants may lower blood glucose in patients with diabetes mellitus but do not seem to provoke or worsen diabetes. In rare cases, idiosyncratic nephrogenic diabetes insipidus has occurred.

Patients with preexisting thyroid disease may show altered tolerance to heterocyclics. Euthyroid patients who are given tricyclics and triiodothyronine (T_3) or thyroid-stimulating hormone (TSH) simultaneously sometimes show quicker resolution of the depression while still remaining euthyroid. The combination of dexamethasone and heterocyclics also reportedly produces more rapid results. These two treatments, however, remain experimental.

e. Ocular

Unlike the phenothiazines, the heterocyclics do not produce ocular pigmentation. They do, however, commonly cause **blurred vision.** This is caused by a failure of accommodation, which usually leaves distant vision intact. This anticholinergic effect results from ciliary muscle relaxation. Tolerance sometimes develops over the first few weeks of drug treatment.

In patients with **narrow-angle glaucoma,** heterocyclics can cause significant damage. Anticholinergic properties cause pupillary dilation, which can precipitate an acute episode. The problem arises with undiscovered, unreported, or untreated cases. If open-angle glaucoma, however, is being treated, the patient **can** take heterocyclics. To detect patients at risk for the narrow-angle variety, the clinician should perform an examination with a penlight and take a good history including questions about blurred vision, halos around lights, and eye pain. To do a flashlight test, the practitioner should shine a light laterally across the iris. If it illuminates the entire iris, the patient probably does not have glaucoma. If angle closure exists, the iris bunches and will block the laterally shining light. Angle-closure glaucoma usually requires surgery, whereas the more common open-angle type is usually well treated with drugs.

f. Cardiovascular

The cardiac effects of heterocyclic antidepressants in particular are among the most frequent and potentially severe adverse reactions. Therefore, investigators have worked to answer several questions:

1. Do heterocyclics cause cardiac morbidity in patients with cardiac disease?
2. How dangerous are the various heterocyclics in individuals with cardiac problems?

3. Which heterocyclics cause the fewest cardiac effects?
4. How do different dosage levels produce or perhaps even help cardiac arrhythmias?

To date, researchers have only partially answered these questions.

Heterocyclic antidepressants in general cause numerous cardiovascular adverse reactions, including postural hypotension, tachycardia, rare heart failure, arrhythmias (often refractory to treatment in overdoses), and occasional sudden death.[55] Postural **hypotension and tachycardia occur frequently.** These effects appear most often after a rapid dose increase or in elderly patients or those with evidence of preexisting cardiovascular disease or pretreatment postural changes. In most patients, tolerance develops in the first weeks of treatment, although in many individuals, postural hypotension persists. This reaction is most common with imipramine and other tertiary amines and less common with nortriptyline and other secondary amines. In the early phases of treatment, patients at risk of hypotension should have their blood pressure monitored about ½ hr after each dose and should be advised to lie down if they become dizzy. Because symptomatic individuals often have a vascular system that responds slowly to postural changes, they should be told to change positions slowly (i.e., lying to sitting, sitting to standing). If emergency vascular support is necessary, the patient should receive norepinephrine (since epinephrine may produce a paradoxical lowering of blood pressure). In severe cases, the clinician should discontinue treatment and start a new medication.

Most of the ECG changes induced by heterocyclics are benign and reversible. These drugs commonly cause tachycardia and Q–T prolongation and T-wave inversion or flattening. Patients receiving a toxic dose most often exhibit broadened P–R and QRS intervals, ST segment depression, A–V block, intraventricular conduction defects, and frequent premature ventricular contractions.[56] These drugs may act at several sites to produce cardiac symptoms. They have a mild negative inotropic effect (decreased myocardial contractility) and inhibit intracardiac conduction and autonomically controlled regulatory reflexes.

Although most patients with cardiac disease do not develop cardiac complications from heterocyclics, these individuals do have a significantly increased risk of complications. Some patients with cardiac disease taking heterocyclics (usually amitriptyline) have died suddenly. In addition, patients who have had a recent myocardial infarction should not receive heterocyclics. Since these drugs may represent a threat to these patients, the clinician should take a careful history and review of systems and ask specific questions about cardiac functioning. Rarely, hypertension occurs with heterocyclics, presumably because of a paradoxical response. In toxic doses, most of these drugs also seriously compromise cardiac function (see Section IV.A.5 for assessment and management).

Beyond the general cardiac effects of this class of drugs, investigators have tried to determine risks from specific agents. **Among tricyclics, doxepin and desipramine may cause fewer direct cardiotoxic effects.** The other desmethylated tricyclics, nortriptyline and protriptyline, and imipramine may cause a moderate number of untoward effects. **Amitriptyline seems to produce the most frequent and severe reactions. Amoxapine and maprotiline may have fewer cardiac effects, whereas trazodone causes very few reactions.** Other experimental drugs such as mianserin and perhaps nomifensine may have significantly fewer cardiac effects than all the currently available antidepressants except perhaps trazodone.

Cardiotoxic effects result from a complex interaction of several factors that include dosage levels (which may vary greatly between patients), individual sensitivities, direct and secondary (e.g., anticholinergic) cardiac effects, and different actions of the various drugs on heart muscle, cardiac conduction, and reflexes. Most studies have not been able to control for every variable. In addition, investigators only recently have monitored cardiac response without intrusive techniques. Glassman, Bigger, and others have begun to use various methods (EKG, echocardiography, Holter monitoring, and radionculeotide ventriculography) to document cardiac responses more precisely.[57] These studies not only may answer some of the remaining questions about cardiotoxicity but also offer clinical guidelines where few now exist.

Guidelines for Clinical Use

1. Take a careful cardiac history and review of systems before starting medication.
2. Educate the patient about possible effects, particularly tachycardia and postural hypotension.
3. In young patients without cardiac problems, the choice of drugs should be based primarily on clinical symptoms (i.e., choice of desired secondary pharmacological properties).
4. In older patients or those with cardiac problems:
   a. Choose a heterocyclic with few adverse reactions
      i. Trazodone for sedation.
      ii. Desipramine or maprotiline for a less sedating response.
   b. Monitor pulse, orthostatic changes in blood pressure, plasma drug levels, and ECG (every day or two) if high doses of antidepressant are required.
   c. Complete a more extensive cardiac workup in symptomatic patients put on medication (which should include consultation with an expert psychopharmacologist and/or cardiologist and might

include specific tests such as 24-hr Holter monitoring, echocardiography, and perhaps ventriculography or even exercise ventriculography).
d. Consider ECT.
e. Take an ECG once or twice a year in elderly patients on maintenance heterocyclics.
5. Divide or reduce the dose of medication in patients who develop hypertension or hypotension.
6. If plasma levels are obtained, lower the dose in all patients whose total level exceeds 500 ng/ml.
7. Perform periodic ECGs in any patient on unusually high doses of drug (i.e., >300 mg) or with high serum levels (i.e., >500 ng/ml).
8. Discontinue medication in those who have persistent alterations of blood pressure, cardiac arrhythmia, fainting, heart failure, or evidence of cardiac compromise on ECG.
9. Avoid coadministration of drugs that affect the cardiovascular system, and closely monitor when synergistic drugs are given (see Tables 5 and 6).
10. Immediately hospitalize and continuously monitor patients who have overdosed or who are toxic (see Section IV.A.5).

g. Neurological

The heterocyclics produce numerous central nervous system effects. In addition to their anticholinergic properties, these agents also cause **sedation** directly. Drowsiness most often occurs with doxepin, amitriptyline, and trazodone; less with imipramine, maprotiline, and amoxapine; and infrequently with demethylated agents (protriptyline, nortriptyline, and desipramine). In therapeutic doses, demethylated tricyclics such as nortriptyline can cause CNS activation during the initial part of treatment. All of the heterocyclics may cause **psychomotor slowing and difficulty concentrating and planning,** which may be greater with the more anticholinergic agents. The patient should be told about these effects, particularly if he must perform active physical or mental tasks. **Muscle weakness and fatigue, nervousness, headaches, agitation, vertigo, neuropathies, tremors, ataxia, paresthesias, dysarthria, nystagmus, and twitching occasionally occur.** Heterocyclics also **lower the seizure threshold** (some more than others) in a manner similar to the phenothiazines. Therefore, the clinician should start patients with seizure disorders on lower doses of the antidepressant and raise doses more gradually **(maprotiline may be somewhat more epileptogenic).**

The relationship between heterocyclics and extrapyramidal reactions remains somewhat confusing. These drugs are better than placebo in the

TABLE 5. Drug Interactions with Heterocyclics

Increased heterocyclic clinical effects and adverse reactions
  A. Direct increase in antidepressant effect
    1. Thyroid hormone (Euthroid® and others)
    2. Methylphenidate (Ritalin®)
    3. Dexamethasone (Decadron® and others)
  B. Increased plasma levels through metabolic alteration
    1. All antipsychotic agents
    2. Monoamine oxidase inhibitors
    3. Acetylsalicylic acid
    4. Chloramphenicol (Cloromycetin®)
    5. Thyroid hormone
    6. Thyroid-stimulating hormone (Thytropar®)
    7. Methylphenidate
  C. Increased plasma levels through increased kidney
     reabsorption
    1. Acetazolamide (Diamox® and others)
    2. Thiazides
    3. Sodium bicarbonate
  D. Increased anticholinergic stimulation
    1. Alcohol
    2. Antihistamines
    3. Benzodiazepines
    4. Antiparkinson agents
    5. Antispasmodics
    6. All antipsychotic agents
    7. Meperidine (Demerol® and others)
    8. Glutethimide (Doriden® and others)
Decreased heterocyclic clinical effects and adverse reactions
  A. Decreased plasma levels through induction of liver microsomal enzymes
    1. Alcohol
    2. Lithium (Eskalith®, Lithonate®, Lithobid®, and others)
    3. Oral contraceptives
    4. Barbiturates
    5. Primidone (Mysoline® and others)
    6. Chloral hydrate (Noctec® and others)
    7. Smoking
  B. Decreased plasma levels by increased kidney excretion from acidification of urine
    1. Ascorbic acid
    2. Ammonium chloride (Dextrotussin® and others)
  C. Decrease in antidepressant effect
    1. Centrally acting antihypertensives
      a. Clonidine (Catapres®, Combipres®)
      b. α-Methyldopa (Aldomet® and others)
      c. Propranolol (Inderal®, Inderide®)
    2. Oral contraceptives

TABLE 6. Heterocyclic Interactions with Other Drugs

Agent	Effects	Mechanism
Meperidine (Demerol® and others)	Respiratory depression	Combined CNS depression
Amphetamine (Benzedrine®) Epinephrine (Adrenalin® and others) Norepinephrine (Levophed®)	Peripheral sympathetic stimulation (including hypertensive responses that can be severe with amphetamines)	Inhibition of catecholamine uptake
Over-the-counter cold medicines	Sedation	Combined CNS depression
Acute barbiturate ingestion	Sedation, stupor, coma	Competition for liver metabolism
Coumarinlike drugs (Dicumarol® and others)	Prolonged and/or increased anticoagulant effect	Competition for liver metabolism
Sedative–hypnotic drugs	Sedation	Combined CNS depression
Antipsychotic drugs	Sedation	Combined CNS depression
Amphetamine	Behavioral excitement, hypertension (occasionally severe)	CNS synergism, inhibition
Guanethidine (Esimil®, Ismelin®)	Decreased antihypertensive effect and occasionally severe hypotension	Inhibition of neuronal uptake of the drug
Clonidine (Catapres®, Combinpres®)	Decreased antihypertensive effect	Inhibition of effects on central α receptors
α-Methyldopa (Aldomet® and others)	Behavioral excitement	?
Propranolol (Inderal®, Inderide®)	Decreased antihypertensive effect	?
Ethchlorvynol (Placidyl®)	Delirium	CNS synergism
Ethyl alcohol	Cardiac arrhythmias	?

treatment of parkinsonism (through their anticholinergic effects) and may offer some protection from extrapyramidal symptoms when used simultaneously with the phenothiazines. The heterocyclics may, however, rarely cause parkinsonism and other extrapyramidal effects. **Amoxapine differs from other heterocyclics; it has specific dopamine-blocking properties like the antipsychotics. In fact, it can cause all of the common extrapyramidal**

reactions. Treatment with antiparkinson agents sometimes work. In addition to extrapyramidal effects, a persistent, rapid, fine action tremor of the upper extremities, head, and occasionally the tongue may occur in as many as 10% of patients (particularly the elderly). All extrapyramidal reactions and tremors abate when patients discontinue medication. Moreover, individuals usually tolerate these adverse reactions long enough to provide an adequate trial of medication. **Since amoxapine resembles antipsychotic drugs chemically and clinically, the practitioner should also watch for tardive dyskinesia with long-term use.**

Some patients have developed a **toxic delirium** (i.e., central anticholinergic syndrome) at high doses of the heterocyclics (although sometimes at therapeutic levels). The symptoms disappear when medication is stopped (see Section IV.A.5.b.ii. for treatment with physostigmine).

Sometimes heterocyclic administration may produce **paradoxical reactions.** These drugs may cause marked increases in anxiety and worsening of some depressions, particularly mild depressions. They may also produce insomnia and nightmares. Heterocyclics can also induce paradoxical mania in predisposed patients and may cause psychotic reactions or confusional states with delusions, hallucinations, and disorientation both in patients with underlying psychotic disorders and in "normal" individuals. When the drug is discontinued, symptoms remit rapidly in this latter group. In addition, these patients show no increased susceptibility to schizophrenia. If mania or another acute psychosis develops, the patient should receive specific therapies for these conditions after antidepressant medication is discontinued.

Heterocyclics do not cause addiction, but rapid discontinuation of these drugs may result in a **mild "withdrawal syndrome,"** marked by variable symptoms. These include malaise, muscle aches, coryza, chills, nausea and vomiting, dizziness, anxiety, or an akathisialike motor restlessness. Therefore, the clinician should generally taper the dose of heterocyclic antidepressants over a few days.

All anticholinergic drugs can produce mild CNS effects such as drowsiness, confusion, or clouded thinking. In its pathological form, a **"central anticholinergic syndrome"** develops (see Section IV.A.5). In clinical practice, selected symptoms from the syndrome may also appear.

h. Cutaneous

Heterocyclics cause few dermatological problems. Occasionally, they produce maculopapular rashes or petechiae that can be treated by giving an antihistamine or stopping the drug. Like the phenothiazines, they can occasionally produce a photosensitivity response, which can be prevented by avoiding exposure or by using a sunscreen [paraaminobenzoic acid (PABA and others)]. Rarely, cases of urticaria occur.

TABLE 7. Pharmacological Properties of Heterocyclic
Antidepressants

Sedation	Antihistaminic	Anticholinergic
High	High	High
Amitriptyline	Doxepin	Amitriptyline
Trimipramine	Trimipramine	Imipramine
Doxepin		Trimipramine
Trazodone		Doxepin
Moderate	Moderate	Moderate
Imipramine	Amitriptyline	Amoxapine
Amoxapine	Maprotiline	Nortriptyline
Nortriptyline		Maprotilene
Maprotiline		
Low	Low	Low
Desipramine	Imipramine	Desipramine
Protriptyline	Trazodone	Protriptyline
	Amoxapine	
	Protriptyline	
	Nortriptyline	
	Very low	Very low
	Desipramine	Trazodone

i. Autonomic

Heterocyclics, like the phenothiazines, produce numerous autonomic effects. These are predominantly anticholinergic (see Table 7). Patients most commonly report **dry mouth** (usually early in treatment). Generally, physiological tolerance develops to this adverse reaction. However, in some, dry mouth persists and may cause discomfort, mouth infections, and dental caries (sometimes rampant). In severe cases of xerostomia, the clinician should intervene by:

1. Encouraging adequate hydration.
2. Lowering the dosage of medication if possible.
3. Discouraging the use of sugar-laden drinks, chewing gum, or candy.
4. Providing alternative means of mouth lubrication
   a. "Sugarless" gums (although these actually have sugars that in high doses can contribute to the formation of caries).
   b. Fluroride lozenges.
   c. Direct lubricants (a saliva substitute).
5. Administer bethanecol chloride (Urecholine® and others), a cholinergic agent, 25 mg up to three times per day, in patients whose symptoms do not respond to conservative measures, who would not be able to

> complete a drug trial because of the severity of symptoms, and who
> are not at increased risk from cholinergic stimulation (e.g., patients
> with asthma, potential cardiac compromise, or ulcer disease).
> 6. If all of the above measures fail, stop medication and switch to a drug
> with fewer anticholinergic properties (such as trazodone or
> desipramine).

The major cardiovascular anticholinergic effect is **tachycardia.** Tolerance to this reaction usually develops quickly. **Blurred vision,** resulting from failure of accommodation, occurs in up to 20% of patients. This symptom appears at the beginning of treatment and rapidly resolves without dosage adjustment. If a patient has severe blurring, and the dosage cannot be lowered, the clinician can give 1% pilocarpine nitrate (Ocusert®) eyedrops for a short time.

Patients on heterocyclics also experience both **increased and decreased sexual desire,** and men occasionally have **retarded ejaculation.** The cause of these symptoms may be difficult to assess, however, since depression so commonly affects libido.

Among the most worrisome autonomic reactions are those that affect gastrointestinal and genitourinary functioning. A significant **decrease in intestinal motility** occurs in up to half of those treated. This occurs much more often in the elderly and may be compounded by the vegetative symptoms of the depression itself. They are particularly susceptible to the development of **paralytic ileus.** Symptomatic treatment with stool softeners and milk of magnesia usually suffices. **Urinary retention** also may cause severe problems. Some patients have died from acute renal failure following the development of an atonic bladder. This condition often results from the coadministration of drugs with anticholinergic properties such as higher doses of the most anticholinergic heterocyclics (e.g., amitriptyline). Fortunately, severe bladder compromise occurs rarely. If it appears, the patient should stop medication immediately and have a medical consultation. Since most patients develop tolerance to the anticholinergic properties of heterocyclics, clinicians can usually prevent serious problems by monitoring symptoms and lowering dosages or allowing more time for accommodation before increasing the amount.

Atropinelike effects resulting in autonomic stimulation also result from antidepressant medication. **Pathological sweating,** which occurs in approximately 25% of patients, is the most common sympathomimetic effect. Interestingly, it occurs along the distribution of the superior cervical ganglion (affecting the head, neck and upper extremities) and usually occurs at night or only episodically during the day. No treatment is required. Other stimulatory effects include **anorexia, insomnia, and psychomotor stimulation.**

j. Drug Interactions

Heterocyclic antidepressants react with many other pharmacological agents. These interactions occur in many ways: induction of microsomal enzymes, competition for binding sites, additive CNS depressant anticholinergic effects, and alterations in metabolic breakdown and absorption (see Table 5).

k. Miscellaneous Adverse Reactions

Rarely, heterocyclics cause tinnitus, weight loss, anorexia, appetite increase and weight gain, black tongue, parotid swelling, alopecia, and an allergic response manifested by generalized edema, edema of the face and tongue, or orbital edema.

4. Precautions for Administration during Pregnancy

No psychiatric drug should be routinely prescribed during the first trimester of pregnancy. Heterocyclic antidepressants, however, have been given during this period without harmful effects on the fetus. Occasionally, the newborn of a mother who took heterocyclics may exhibit irritability, hyperhidrosis, tachycardia, tachypnea, and cyanosis for several days following delivery. These symptoms do not seem to cause long-term morbidity. Therefore, the pregnant patient with a severe depression accompanying a serious suicidal risk or an inability to care for herself might receive a trial of heterocyclic antidepressants. The clinician and patient should carefully weigh the risks and benefits (see Chapter 10).

5. Acute Toxicity

a. Intoxication Syndromes

Individual patients show a variable tolerance to the heterocyclics. Usual clinical doses may occasionally cause toxic responses resulting from special sensitivity or from interaction with coadministered medications. Most often, however, patients develop CNS depression and/or cardiotoxicity from an acute or chronic overdose of heterocyclics. The clinician should treat each overdose aggressively because of the possibility of refractory cardiac arrhythmias and circulatory or respiratory collapse. Prolonged observation is mandatory, since recovery from acute ingestions can be delayed because of rapid and extensive tissue distribution.

Symptoms develop 1 to 4 hr after the overdose and depend on the age of the patient, individual tolerance, and dose. Frequently, **doses equivalent to 1.2 g imipramine are toxic** (although doses of <1.0 g occasionally cause severe reactions and death), and **more than 2.5 g is commonly fatal.** Prior to a marked decrease in consciousness, hallucinations, sensitivity to sounds, delirium, or agitation may occur. A "hyperactive" coma may develop and progress to a deeper nonreactive coma. Hypotension or hypertension, dilated, sluggishly reactive pupils, and hypothermia also occur. Patients sometimes die from the severe hyperpyrexia secondary to central anticholinergic effects. Myoclonic seizures and bilateral plantar responses on neurological examination are common. Arrhythmias, which are difficult to control, include ventricular tachycardia, atrial fibrillation, and atrioventricular and intraventricular block. Manifestations of cardiac effects appear on EKG as bundle branch block, varying degrees of heart block, ventricular extrasystoles, and bizarre QRS complexes.

A large acute overdose may have a somewhat different character. Deep coma often appears rapidly. Reflexes decrease, and bilateral plantar responses occur. Patients frequently exhibit seizures, arrhythmias, and respiratory arrest. The pupils may be of normal size, but they will react sluggishly or not at all. The pulse rate increases, and blood pressure and body temperature decrease.

Management of serious heterocyclic overdoses poses serious difficulties since cardiorespiratory collapse, arrhythmias, and coma present both an immediate and persistent life threat (see Table 8). In fact, every patient who overdoses even with small amounts of medication should have at least 2 days of cardiac monitoring. The first and perhaps most important procedure is induced emesis followed by gastric aspiration and lavage (particularly since the heterocyclics themselves may decrease GI motility and thus inhibit their own absorption). Thereafter, the clinician should administer activated charcoal (20 to 30 g every 4 to 6 hr for 24 to 48 hr).[58] The physican should also start a temporary transvenous pacemaker, institute monitoring, insure adequate ventilation, and obtain basic blood chemistry studies and a heterocyclic blood level. In addition, he should insert a routine pulmonary artery catheter to monitor blood gases, pulmonary artery pressures, left atrial wedge pressure, and cardiac output continuously.[58] If the overdose is mild to moderate, lavage and monitoring may suffice. If confusion, delirium, agitation, or coma ensue, the clinician should consider giving physostigmine (Antilirim®), 1 to 2 mg IV every 30 to 60 min as necessary. This centrally active anticholinesterase combats the anticholinergic symptoms of all psychoactive drugs and is useful in treating the central anticholinergic syndrome.[59,60] Many phenothiazines, thioxanthenes, antiparkinson drugs, and heterocyclic antidepressants commonly cause these effects. Often, in these patients, symptoms abate quickly, although some confusion, tremulousness, and agitation may persist for days. **Physostigmine must be used cautiously, since it may produce hypotension, bradycardia, increased bronchial secretions, bronchoconstriction, and a lowered seizure threshold** (particularly in a setting of cardiorespiratory compromise). Therefore, in such circumstances, physostigmine must be administered only with careful monitoring.

TABLE 8. Management of Overdose

Initial measures
  A. Induce emesis
  B. Implement gastric aspiration and lavage [with activated charcoal (Charcodote® powder), 20 to 30 g, every 4 to 6 hr for 24 to 48 hr]
  C. Complete physical examination and obtain vital signs
  D. Adequately ventilate; monitor by ECG
  E. Insert an intravenous line with cardiac pacing capacity
  F. Insert pulmonary artery catheter
  G. Obtain blood chemistries including heterocyclic serum level
Maintenance procedures
  A. Monitor vital signs, electrolytes, serum heterocyclic levels, and ECG
  B. Maintain fluid and electrolyte balance
  C. Insure adequate ventilation and skin care if the patient is comatose
Hypertension
  A. Implement osmotic diuresis (e.g., mannitol)
  B. Administer phentolamine (Regitine®), 5 mg (if persistent and severe)
Hypotension
  A. Elevate legs
  B. Adequately hydrate
  C. Administer norepinephrine (Levophed®); avoid epinephrine
Seizures
  A. Administer diazepam (Valium®), 5 to 10 mg IM or IV PRN (avoid barbiturates)
Central and peripheral anticholinergic syndrome
  A. Slowly inject physostigmine (Antilirium®), 1 to 2 mg IV every 30 to 60 min PRN
Hyperpyrexia
  A. Use ice mattress, ice packs, or cold sponges
Cardiac interventions
  A. Avoid type 1 antiarrhythmics [procainamide (Pronestyl® and others) and disopyramide (Norpace®)]
  B. Use lidocaine (Xylocaine® and others) for ventricular arrhythmia
  C. Use lidocaine or phenytoin (Dilantin® and others) for heart block arrhythmia
  D. Use physostigmine for supraventricular arrhythmia
  E. Implement volume expansion for decreased left atrial pressure
  F. Use dopamine (Intropin®) for increased left atrial pressure
  G. Give IV $NaHCO_3$ (acid imbalance may predispose to ventricular irritability)
Persistent arrhythmia with heart failure
  A. Use cardiac pacing or cardioversion

With the most serious overdoses, the patient may require other measures. Caretakers can manage seizures with intravenous diazepam 5 to 10 mg PRN. Since barbiturates may synergistically depress respiration, they are contraindicated. Hypertension should be managed with osmotic diuresis (mannitol) and, if it is severe and persistent, phentolamine (Regitine®), 5 mg, should be administered. Hypotension is generally to be treated conservatively. If this fails, hypotension may be counteracted with norepinephrine, not epinephrine. Peritoneal or hemodialysis helps little in removing the drug, since it is mostly protein bound and highly lipid soluble. In rare cases, dialysis has been used to lower body temperature if conservative measures fail (e.g., ice mattress, ice packs, sponging). Ventricular arrhythmias are best managed with lidocaine (Xylocaine® and others); heart block with lidocaine or pheny-toin (Dilantin® and others); and supraventricular arrhythmias from atropine-like effects with an anticholinesterase [physostigmine or pyridostigmine (Mestinon®, Regonol®)]. **Clinicians should avoid using type I antiarrhyth-mics such as procainamide, quinidine (Quinidex®, Quinora®, and others), or disopyramide (Norpace®)** (since they may exacerbate the impaired conduc-tion caused by heterocyclics) and propranolol (since it may add significantly to depression of cardiac contractility). When severe arrhythmias persist, patients may require cardioversion or cardiac pacing. In addition, **external cardiac massage and oxygenation should be continued for extended periods (i.e., 2 to 3 hr)** in unresponsive but previously healthy patients, even with complete asystole (since one patient recovered, possibly as a result of drug redistribution from continued perfusion).[61]

b. Anticholinergic Syndromes

i. Description. Most psychoactive drugs have both peripheral and cen-tral anticholinergic effects. They occur with heterocyclic antidepressants, antipsychotics, some hypnotics, antihistamines, and antiparkinson agents. Combinations of these drugs, such as a psychoactive drug (antidepressant or antipsychotic or both) and an antiparkinson agent, may produce additive anticholinergic effects. Older patients seem particularly sensitive. Acute over-doses of the abovementioned agents also frequently cause anticholinergic crisis.

The anticholinergic syndrome may present with a mixture or a predomi-nance of either peripheral or central symptoms. In its florid state, **the CNS picture consists of confusion, delirium with disorientation, agitation, visual and auditory hallucinations, anxiety, motor restlessness, pseudoseizures (myoclonic jerks and choreoathetoid movements with EEG seizure activity), and a thought disorder (e.g., delusions). The peripheral syndrome may be manifested by decreased bowel sounds and constipation, urinary retention, anhidrosis (decreased sweating), mydriasis (increased pupillary size), dry mouth, cycloplegia (decreased accommodation), increased body tempera-ture, motor incoordination, flushing, and tachycardia.** When these syn-dromes are caused by the heterocyclic antidepressants, there is also a high risk of life-threatenting arrhythmias. Aliphatic and piperidine phenothiazines [especially thioridazine (Mellaril®)] and the tricyclics amitriptyline and imi-pramine are the most anticholinergic. A combination of the above drugs or of these drugs with other anticholinergic agents greatly increases the risk of an anticholinergic syndrome.

ii. Anticholinesterase Therapy. Anticholinesterase therapy has proven very effective for the treatment of anticholinergic syndromes. All anticholinesterases counteract the peripheral manifestations of the syndrome. However, clinicians should use either **physostigmine** or **pyridostigmine** because they cross the blood–brain barrier and therefore counteract the central symptoms. Most clinical studies have focused on physostigmine, but equivalent doses of pyridostigmine also are effective.[58,59] In general, **the clinician should avoid using physostigmine in patients with unstable vital signs.** In these cases, cardiac arrhythmias from cholinergic stimulation are common. Cholinergic effects can also produce seizures (particularly with rapid injection of physostigmine) and respiratory arrest in selected patients. Although practitioners have tried many different regimens, **physostigmine salicylate, 1 to 2 mg IM or IV,** will relieve symptoms dramatically. The clinician should **infuse the drug very slowly (e.g., 1 mg over 2 min), monitor the cardiac status, and have means for respiratory support available. If no improvement occurs within 15 to 20 min, another dose of 1 to 2 mg should be given. Up to 4 mg may be administered over 10 to 15 min.** The body degrades physostigmine almost completely within 1½ to 2 hr. Since the toxic agents may disappear more slowly, additional 1- to 2-mg doses at 30-min intervals may be necessary, even if the initial treatment is successful.

Although physostigmine treatment provides dramatic and sometimes life-saving relief from heterocyclic-induced arrhythmias, it also has risks from cholinergic stimulation. Excessive acetylcholine can result in tearing, salivation, rhinorrhea, sweating, pallor, bronchial constriction, hypotension, muscle weakness and fasciculations, nausea and vomiting, abdominal cramps, urinary frequency, and bradycardia. The antidote is atropine.

6. Pharmacokinetics

Heterocyclic antidepressants are generally well absorbed from the gastrointestinal tract. They typically peak in the plasma within 30 to 60 min and remain unbound for about 30 min. Eighty to 90% of the drug is protein bound, although individual differences in binding can produce a fourfold variance in the amount of free drug. Tissue distribution and the first step in metabolism of tertiary heterocyclics, demethylation, occur rapidly. Heterocyclics have a high volume of distribution because they are quite lipid soluble and actively bind to various tissues. Patients usually achieve a steady state for each dosage after 1 to 3 weeks (depending on the drug used). Liver metabolism, including demethylation, hydroxylation, and glucuronide conjugation, also accounts for large variations in heterocyclic serum levels. Individual differences in patients' microsomal enzyme activity produce steady-state plasma concentrations (bound and unbound) that may vary as much as 40-fold. These characteristics suggest that individual patients may require widely varying doses to produce clinically effective serum levels.

During the initial pass through the liver, about 80% of circulating heterocyclics are degraded ("first past effect"). The first demethylation of tertiary amines results in an active compound (demethylated heterocyclics), whereas a second demethylation and hydroxylation at the 2-position of the central ring produce degradation products (probably therapeutically inactive but which may have cardiotoxic effects). Glucuronidation occurs after hydroxylation and makes the derivative water soluble. Initially, about 50% of the heterocyclics are excreted through the bile, but because of an active enterohepatic circulation, two-thirds of the drugs are eventually eliminated in the urine. Clearance of the heterocyclics is relatively slow, but they have a wide range of half-lives (see Table 9). Because of the dual pathways of excretion, the clinician can safely administer these drugs in lower doses to patients with liver or kidney disease.

The coadministration of heterocyclics and other drugs can cause a change in the drugs' metabolism (see Table 8).

7. Therapeutic Plasma Levels

Research on clinical correlation of plasma levels of antidepressants has resulted in contradictory findings.[62-64] For the monomethylated tricyclic antidepressants, particularly nortriptyline, investigators have proposed a curvilinear dose–response relationship; these agents probably have a specific range of effective plasma levels (**"the therapeutic window"**) for each individual patient. **Therefore, for nortriptyline, clinical results decrease with serum levels below 50 ng/ml or above 150 ng/ml.** Comparable data do not exist for either desipramine or protriptyline. With nortriptyline, some investigators have used a 24- or 48-hr plasma level of nortriptyline drawn after a 50-mg loading dose to predict a steady-state therapeutic dose. Pragmatically, individual patients may have widely varying clinical responses and adverse reactions. Therefore, providing gradually increasing doses of each of the heterocyclics until the usual therapeutic range is reached and then obtaining a

TABLE 9. Mean Half-Life of Heterocyclics[a]

Drug	Time (hr)
Trazodone	5
Imipramine	16
Amitriptyline	16
Desipramine	22
Nortriptyline	24
Amoxapine	30
Maprotiline	47
Protriptyline	126

[a]Half-life varies greatly among patients and tends to increase significantly with age.

plasma level within a week or two (a steady state usually occurs within about 2 weeks) most often suffices.

The dimethylated tricyclic antidepressant imipramine seems to have a positive linear dose–response curve. The dose–response curves for amitriptyline and doxepin are less clear. In addition to the administered compound, each of these dimethylated drugs has a therapeutically active monomethylated derivative that by itself may have a separate relationship to treatment outcome. For example, although it is highly variable, the administration of imipramine usually yields a steady-state ratio of 1.0/1.4. between imipramine and its active desmethyl derivative, desipramine. For imipramine, therapeutic response is most likely at serum levels of the parent compound plus its demethylated derivative over 200 ng/ml. Increasing numbers of patients with melancholia seem to respond at higher serum levels.

Researchers have not yet defined adequate dose–response curves for the new heterocyclics such as trimipramine, amoxapine, maprotiline, and trazodone. Clinical effects, however, may occur at 200 to 300 ng/ml for trimipramine and maprotiline and 160 to 800 ng/ml for amoxapine and its hydroxy metabolites. Current information seems to indicate that certain plasma levels of antidepressants are required for a therapeutic result but that large individual variations exist. Therefore, how should the clinician use heterocyclic plasma monitoring? In practice, the physician must determine each individual patient's response to a particular drug and should provide the patient with a complete drug trial and only obtain plasma levels to help make specific treatment decisions (see Tables 10 and 11). (Some investigators have documented a correlation between saliva heterocyclic levels and serum concentrations. In any one individual, consistent results can be obtained. However, general clinical application is limited, since very large differences in saliva concentrations exist among patients, and since the research data are inconsistent.)

TABLE 10. Reasons for Monitoring Heterocyclic Plasma Concentrations

To determine a "low" therapeutic dose for an elderly patient who develops or may develop serious adverse reactions

To determine if a potentially effective dose of medication has been given to a patient in whom adverse reactions prevent further increases

To document inadequate serum levels of heterocyclics in "nonresponders" on high doses of medication

To determine if a reticent patient is taking medication

To provide guidance in lowering dosage (or switching to a new heterocyclic) in responsive patients who develop intolerable adverse reactions

To monitor plasma levels in overdose cases

To monitor plasma levels in medically ill patients

To document serum levels within the "therapeutic window" for nortriptyline (and perhaps desipramine and protriptyline)

**TABLE 11. Precautions in Obtaining
Heterocyclic Plasma Levels**

Do not use vacutainer tubes
Do not use rubber stoppers
Take blood samples 12 hr after the last drug dosage
Use a laboratory with proven reliability

8. Preparations and Dosage

The wide range of effective clinical doses of heterocyclic antidepressants results in part from individual differences in plasma binding and liver enzyme activity. The dimethylated tricyclic compounds amitriptyline and imipramine and the tetracyclic maprotiline have usual dose ranges of 150 to 300 mg/day. The monomethylated derivatives nortriptyline and desipramine are about twice as potent, whereas protriptyline is about four times as potent. Doxepin is somewhat less potent than the other dimethylated tricyclics. Amoxapine and trazodone are about half as potent as imipramine, with clinically effective doses ranging from 150 to 600 mg/day. Concentrates and parenteral and slow-release preparations offer no clinical advantages over standard preparations (see Table 12).

B. Monoamine Oxidase Inhibitors

1. Chemistry

Monoamine oxidase inhibitors (MAOIs), after a period of diminished use, have reemerged as useful agents for treating severe autonomous depressions, various atypical affective disorders, and certain anxiety states.[65] Based on their structure, we can divide these agents into two categories: **hydrazines** and **nonhydrazines.** The hydrazines include isocarboxazid and phenelzine. They act within 3 to 4 weeks and have a lower incidence of unwanted effects than the nonhydrazines. The only marketed nonhydrazine is tranylcypromine which has stimulant amphetaminelike qualities that often produce clinical improvement within about 10 days. However, it also has a high incidence of adverse reactions, particularly cardiovascular.

2. Mechanism of Action

Monoamine oxidase inhibitors inhibit the various subtypes of MAO throughout the body (gut, liver, brain, platelets, and blood vessels). They elevate body levels of epinephrine, norepinephrine, 5-HT, and dopamine by irreversibly binding to the degradation enzymes of these substances. Investiga-

TABLE 12. Preparations and Dosage of Heterocyclic Antidepressants

Heterocyclic	Brand name	Preparations	Initial dosage	Usual therapeutic dosage
Amitriptyline	Elavil®, Endep®, Amitril®	10-, 25-, 50-, 75-, 100-, 150 mg tablets; 25-, 20-mg capsules; vials of 10 ml with 10 mg/ml	25 to 75 mg	150 to 300 mg
Imipramine	Tofranil®, Presamine®, Imavate®, Janimine®, Sk-Pramine®, Philips-Roxane Imipramine®	10-, 25-, 50-, 100-mg tablets; 75-, 150-mg capsules; ampules of 20 ml with 25 mg/2 ml	25 to 75 mg	150 to 300 mg
Doxepin	Sinequan®, Adapin®	10-, 25-, 50-, 75-, 100-, 150-mg capsules; solution of 10 mg/ml	25 to 75 mg	150 to 300 mg
Nortriptyline	Aventyl®, Pamelor®	10-, 25-mg capsules; solution of 10 mg/5 ml	20 to 40 mg	75 to 150 mg
Desipramine	Norpramin®, Pertofrane®	25-, 50-, 75-, 100-, 150-mg tablets; 25-, 50-mg capsules	25 to 75 mg	75 to 200 mg
Protriptyline	Vivactil®	5-, 10-mg tablets	10 to 20 mg	20 to 60 mg
Trimipramine	Surmontil®	25-, 50-mg capsules	25 to 75 mg	75 to 300 mg
Amoxapine	Asendin®	30-, 100-, 150-mg tablets	50 to 150 mg	150 to 600 mg
Maprotiline	Ludiomil®	25-, 50-mg tablets	25 to 75 mg	75 to 300 mg
Trazodone	Desyrel®	25-, 50-, 100-mg tablets	50 to 100 mg	150 to 600 mg

tors hypothesize that the increased availability of CNS norepinephrine and serotonin may account for the antidepressant activity of MAO inhibitors. Recently, two types of monoamine oxidase have been identified (types A and B). Type B (accounting for about 80% of CNS MAO) degrades mostly dopamine and phenylalanine, whereas type A (accounting for 20% of CNS MAO but most of the gastrointestinal MAO) primarily degrades serotonin and norepinephrine. Although the MAOIs that are currently available affect both enzymes, experimental agents (such as clorgyline) that selectively inhibit type A MAO seem to be more effective in treating depression than selective inhibitors of type B MAO [such as L-deprenyl or some available drugs used for other purposes, including pargyline (Eutonyl®, Eutron®), procarbazine (Matulane®) or furazolidone].

3. Adverse Reactions

The MAOIs can produce many serious adverse reactions. Although some of the untoward effects resemble those produced by heterocyclic antidepressants, notable exceptions include **severe hypertension, hyperthermia, and hypertonic reactions.**

a. Cardiovascular

Monoamine oxidase inhibitors can cause both mild and life-threatening effects. Orthostatic hypotension, tachycardia, and palpitations are common. In cardiac patients, these agents can eliminate or delay the onset of angina pectoris by blocking the response of the cardiovascular system to the stress of exercise and thereby promoting situations that predispose to a myocardial infarction. The most worrisome cardiovascular side effect is hypertension. This can occur at therapeutic doses but usually appears when high doses of MAOI are taken, the drug is combined with a heterocyclic antidepressant or a sympathomimetic agent, or a high-tyramine-content diet is consumed. Patients taking tranylcypromine and phenelzine most frequently have hypertensive reactions resulting from the release of catecholamines in the peripheral nervous system in the face of monoamine oxidase inhibition. This can result in an alarming and dangerous elevation of blood pressure. A severe, atypical headache may herald an impending crisis that can end in a cerebrovascular accident and death. The hypertensive syndrome is usually characterized by headache, palpitations, flushing, nausea and vomiting, photophobia, and occasionally hyperpyrexia, arrhythmias, and pulmonary edema (see Section IV.B.6).

Patients should avoid foods with high tyramine content. Because this product results from fermentation of protein, the patient should be told to avoid any food with aged protein (see Table 13).

Monoamine oxidase inhibitors may synergize with several other phar-

macological agents to produce a hypertensive crisis. These include amphetamine, dextroamphetamine, methylamphetamine, ephedrine, some procaine
preparations (which contain norepinephrine), epinephrine, methyldopa, and
phenylpropanolamine (over-the-counter cold preparations).

b. Autonomic

The most common autonomic effects include dry mouth, hyperhidrosis,
blurred vision and photophobia, decreased gastrointestional motility and
bladder tone, orthostatic hypotension and tachycardia, epigastric distress,
delayed ejaculation, impotence, dry skin, and hypertension.

c. Gastrointestinal

Constipation is the most frequent adverse reaction, but anorexia, abdominal pain, diarrhea, and nausea are frequently reported.

d. Neurological

Central nervous system effects occur often, particularly dizziness, agitation, and insomnia. Other reactions include vertigo, ataxia, drowsiness, dullness, impaired memory, tremulousness, hyperreflexia, euphoria and hypomania, fasciculations, seizures, headache, precipitation of psychotic
symptoms, and confusional states with disorientation and sensory distortions.

e. Hepatic

Monoamine oxidase inhibitors, like the antipsychotics and heterocyclic
antidepressants, cause hepatic reactions. However, they usually cause direct
hepatocellular damage rather than cholestasis. Since severe jaundice and
liver failure can occur, the clinician should stop the medication if symptoms
of hepatic impairment appear.

f. Drug Interactions

Interactions between MAOIs and other drugs are summarized in Table
13.

g. Miscellaneous Adverse Reactions

Hypoglycemia, which occurs rarely, generally does not lead to clinical
symptoms. This reaction usually results from the coadministration of heterocyclics and MAOIs. Many patients develop mild, asymptomatic leukopenia.
Other miscellaneous effects include rare anemia, maculopapular rash, peripheral edema, weight and libido changes, photosensitivity, black tongue, rare
peripheral neuropathies and optic neuropathy, edema of the glottis, myalgias,
and hyperpyrexia.

TABLE 13. Adverse Reactions with MAOIs

Food and drugs that cause hypertension with MAOIs
Cheeses
  1. High tyramine content: boursault, camembert, cheddar, gruyere, stilton
  2. Moderate tyramine content: gouda, parmesan
  3. Low tyramine content: American
Other foods
  1. High tyramine content: lox, pickled herring
  2. Moderate tyramine content: salted herring, chicken liver, figs, raisins, broad beans
     (fava beans), yeast products, pickles, sauerkraut, coffee, chocolate, cocoa, soy sauce,
     sour cream, snails, avocado, banana peels, licorice
Beverages
  1. High tyramine content: chianti
  2. Moderate tyramine content: sherry, beer
  3. Low tyramine content: champagne, Italian red wine, riesling, santeone, "hard" liquor
Additives
  1. Cyclamates, monosodium glutamate
Drugs
  1. Amphetamine (Benzedrine®), dextroamphetamine (Dexedrine®), methylamphetamine
     (Desoxyn®), ephedrine (Tedral® and others), procaine preparations (Novocain® and
     others) (which often contain epinephrine), epinephrine (Adrenalin® and others), meth-
     yldopa (Aldomet® and others), phenylpropanolamine (Dimetane®, Coricidin®, and oth-
     ers) or ephedrine (in over-the-counter cold preparations), pseudoephedrine (Actifed®,
     Sudafed®, and others), dopamine (Intropin®), methylphenidate (Ritalin®), heterocyclic
     antidepressants, or another MAOI
Drugs that can cause severe hypotension with MAOIs (including occasional deaths reported
     from cardiovascular collapse)
  1. Narcotics, alcohol, analgesics, phenothiazines, thiazides, anesthetic agents, antihista-
     mines, insulin (Iletin® and others), reserpine (Serpasil®, Diupres®, and others), antipar-
     kinson agents, barbiturates
Drugs that cause other adverse reactions with MAOIs
  1. Insulin and other hypoglycemics: hypoglycemia
  2. Heterocyclic antidepressants: severe anticholinergic syndrome marked by delirium, sei-
     zures, tremors and hypertonia, hyperpyrexia, and occasionally death
  3. Meperidine (Demerol® and others): enhanced narcotic effect, hyperpyrexia, and rigid-
     ity (may be very severe syndrome)
  4. Alcohol and phenothiazines: decreased monoamine oxidase inhibition
  5. Anesthetics, alcohol, chloral hydrate, cocaine, minor tranquilizers, barbiturates,
     codeine: significant CNS depression
Surgical precautions
  1. If possible, discontinue MAO inhibitor 2 weeks prior to surgery
  2. When a MAO inhibitor is being administered, warn the anesthesiologist about possible
     complications regarding the use of pressor agents

4. Contraindications

The clinician should administer MAOIs only after a careful medical and psychiatric history and review of systems. In various medical situations, however, the clinician should use MAOIs with caution. These include **liver dis-**

ease, advanced renal disease, pheochromocytoma, cardiovascular disease,
hypertension, asthma, or chronic bronchitis (since pressor agents like epinephrine or theophylline may be necessary). In addition, MAOIs should seldom be given to patients who are over 60 years of age or who take drugs
that may produce dangerous synergisms.

5. Use during Pregnancy

The safe use of MAOIs during pregnancy has not yet been documented.
The practitioner should select an alternative treatment first when an antidepressant is required (see Chapter 10).

6. Toxicity

Monoamine oxidase inhibitors can cause severe acute toxic reactions.
The signs of intoxication often do not appear until 11 or more hours after
ingestion. Therefore, a patient who has overdosed on MAOI requires prolonged monitoring. Clinically, the patient experiences gradual onset of headaches, often accompanied by nausea and vomiting, tachycardia, mydriasis,
and photophobia. Trismus and laryngeal stridor may be present. If the overdose is large, two other serious effects may develop: central nervous system
stimulation and hypertension. Individuals often develop central symptoms of
hyperactivity, hyperreflexia, hyperpyrexia, confusion, hallucinations, delusions, convulsions, and, eventually, coma. Hypertension poses the most severe
risk. The elevation of blood pressure can precipitate pulmonary edema, circulatory collapse, or intracranial hemorrhage.

The clinician usually manages a serious overdose with conservative measures including acidification of urine or dialysis to hasten the elimination of
MAOI and maintenance of sugar and temperature balance. Since hypertension may be acutely life threatening, aggressive treatment with phentolamine (Regitine®) (a short-acting α adrenergic blocking agent), 5.0 mg IV, is
indicated. Phentolamine, 0.25 to 0.5 mg IM every 4 to 6 hr, may be used
thereafter to control blood pressure. If this drug is not available, chlorpromazine is an appropriate alternative. The clinician should administer an initial dose of chlorpromazine, 50 mg IM, with 25-mg IM doses every 1 to 2 hr
thereafter to control the hypertension. Caretakers should carefully monitor
blood pressure during the treatment of hypertensive episodes, since marked
hypotension may follow.

7. Pharmacokinetics

Monoamine oxidase inhibitors are rapidly and fully absorbed from the
gastrointestinal tract. They undergo biotransformation in the liver and are

excreted very quickly through the intestinal tract and, to a lesser extent, via the kidneys. Their half-life in the body is very short. However, the MAOIs have long-lasting pharmacological effects, since they permanently inactivate enzymes. Therefore, adequate inhibition continues for a week or more after discontinuation of the drug. The body must resynthesize the enzymes before normal metabolism of body amines resumes, a process taking 1 to 2 weeks.

The hydrazine MAOIs are inactivated in the liver by acetylation. Studies have shown that there are two populations of acetylators: slow (a Mendelian recessive trait) and fast (Mendelian dominant). About 50% of white and black populations but only 10 to 15% of Orientals, are slow acetylators. This genetic polymorphism of a liver enzyme system markedly affects the metabolism of MAOIs. Recent studies, however, cast doubt on the usefulness of acetylator status in predicting response to treatment. In contrast, inhibition of platelet monoamine oxidase by greater than 80% 2 weeks after the initiation of treatment predicts that the patients will have a positive response to phenelzine therapy after 6 weeks. (This has not been documented for other MAOIs, however.)

8. Preparations and Dosage

Each MAOI is produced in a single preparation (see Table 14). Usual doses vary widely among patients but generally are about 1 mg/kg of body weight per day for phenelzine and one-third as much for isocarboxazid and tranylcypromine.

C. Evaluation of the Depressed Patient

The depressed patient can present with many different clinical symptoms and signs. Mood disturbances frequently accompany major losses and other stressful events, particular character styles, and certain psychodynamic constellations. More often, depressed patients come to both medical and psychiatric clinicians with physical complaints. This may take many forms, from

TABLE 14. Preparations and Dosages of Monoamine Oxidase Inhibitors

Generic name	Trade name	Preparation	Usual dosage range (mg/day)
Isocarboxazid	Marplan®	10-mg tablets	10 to 30
Phenelzine	Nardil®	15-mg tablets	45 to 90
Tranylcypromine	Parnate®	10-mg tablets	10 to 30

a request for a physical examination, complaints of fatigue, weight loss, or
insomnia, to specific somatic symptoms (often careful questioning reveals
that several organ systems are involved). Along with or instead of physical
manifestations, the patient frequently has both emotional (e.g., lowered
mood, anhedonia, negativism) and psychological symptoms [e.g., irritability,
loss of interest, ruminations, poor concentration, suicidal preoccupations, and
even pseudodementia (see Chapter 8)]. In addition to defining the specific
nature and history of the mood disorder, the clinician should also evaluate
the other important components of the patient's life that might affect treatment: his environmental supports and important relationships, family history,
coping style, and ego strengths.

In Each Depressed Patient, the Practitioner Should

1. Look for life-threatening symptoms (i.e., poor self-care, suicidal and
   homicidal impulses).
2. Take appropriate measures to address suicidal impulses.
3. Assess the patient's diet.
4. Define medication-responsive symptom clusters (see Tables 1, 2, and
   15).
5. Obtain a history of the present illness, focusing on possible
   situational, constitutional, and biological contributions to the mood
   disturbance.
6. Inquire about a history of previous affective episodes, their course,
   treatment, and response(s) (including adverse reactions).
7. Inquire about a family history of affective episodes, their course,
   treatment, and response(s).
8. Define the patient's strengths, including coping mechanisms and
   environmental supports.
9. Determine the patient's attitude toward help and medication.
10. Take a complete medical history (including a review of organ systems
    and documentation of both prescribed and nonprescribed drugs) (see
    Table 16).
11. Complete or arrange a physical examination (and perhaps other base-
    line studies such as an ECG when clinically indicated.
12. Avoid the nonselective use of extensive medical screening and
    biochemical tests for major depressive illness.
13. Get appropriate consultation if psychological or medical symptoms are
    not clarified by the evaluation.
14. Inform the patient (and perhaps persons close to him) about the
    findings of the evaluation, the recommended treatment(s), benefits,
    risks, and possible alternatives.
15. Document conversations and recommendations.

16. Establish rapport with the patient and enlist him (and often family members) in the treatment.

After completing a careful evaluation, the clinician should decide how to manage acute symptoms, possible precipitants, and sequelae of the affective episode (e.g., stigmatization, lowered self-esteem, alienation from social supports).

D. Drug Therapy for the Depressed Patient

1. Initiating Treatment

After reaching a diagnostic decision and assessing the physical status of the depressed patient, how does the practitioner choose a drug for individuals

TABLE 15. Possible Indications for Heterocyclic Antidepressants and Monoamine Oxidase Inhibitors

Heterocyclics
 Established uses
  Major depressive illness
  Panic anxiety
  Phobic states
  Prevention of recurrent depressions
  School phobia in children
 Other possible uses
  "Secondary" depressions
  Migraine headache
  Chronic pain
  Narcolepsy
  Nightmares
  Hyperactivity in children
  Severe obsessive–compulsive symptoms
  Hysteroid dysphoria
  Enuresis
  Acute, severe dysphoria in borderline states
Monoamine oxidase inhibitors
 Established uses
  Major depressive illness (in patients refractory to heterocyclics)
  Panic anxiety
  Phobic states
 Other possible uses
  "Secondary" depressions
  Hysteroid dysphoria
  Depression with severe obsessive–compulsive symptoms, hypochondriasis, or hostility and agitation
  Atypical depression with increased appetite and sleep, lethargy, early insomnia, labile emotions, and worse mood late in the day.

TABLE 16. Drugs Associated with Depression[a]

Antihypertensives	Antiinfectious agents (*cont.*)
Guanethidine (Ismelin®)	Griseofulvin (Fluvicin® and others)
Methyldopa (Aldomet® and others)	Metronidazole (Flagyl®)
Reserpine (Serpasil® and others)	Antineoplastic agents
Hydralazine (Apresoline® and others)	Mithramycin (Mithracin®)
Propranolol (Inderal®, Inderide®)	Azathioprine (Imuran®)
Sedative–hypnotic agents	Bleomycin (Blenoxane®)
Alcohol	L-Asparaginase (Elspar®)
Chloral hydrate (Noctec®)	Cardiac drugs
Benzodiazepines	Digitalis (Crystodigin® and others)
Steroids	Procainamide (Pronestyl® and others)
Oral contraceptives	Propranolol (Inderal®, Inderide®)
Cortisol (Solu-Cortef® and others)	Clonidine (Catapres®, Combipres®)
ACTH (Acthar®)	Stimulants
Antipsychotic medications	Amphetamines (Benzedrine® and others)
Analgesics	Fenfluramine (Pondimin®)
Opiates	Other drugs
Antiinflammatory agents	L-DOPA (Sinemet® and others)
Phenacetin (A.P.C. tablets, Emprazil® and	Amantadine (Symmetrel®)
others)	Methysergide (Sansert®)
Phenylbutazine (Butazolidin® and others)	Acetazolamide (Diamox® and others)
Pentazocine (Talwin®)	Carbamezapine (Tegretol®)
Estrogen withdrawal (Premarin® and others)	Choline (Trisilate® and others)
Antiinfectious agents	Disulfiram (Antabuse®)
Sulfonamindes	Physostigmine (Antilirum®)
Clotrimazole (Lotrimin®, Mycelex®)	Ethambutol (Myambutol®)
Ethionamide (Trecator-SC®)	Indomethacin (Indocin®)

[a]Association does not mean causality. Some agents (e.g., reserpine and steroids) have a clear relationship with depression, whereas many other drugs do not.

with syndromes generally responsive to heterocyclic antidepressants or mono-amine oxidase inhibitors? (See Table 15.) If the patient or a close relative has previously responded to a particular medication, use that drug (if it can be given safely). Since the currently available drugs have similar properties, and biochemical tests still do not adequately define differences on which to base a choice, **the clinician should choose a medicine according to various rough guidelines such as potential adverse reactions, secondary properties (including anxiolytic or sedative effects), and current understanding of effects on brain chemistry** (see Table 7). If the caretaker is not primarily concerned about cardiovascular or anticholinergic effects, he can start therapy with any of the heterocyclics. If sedative or anxiolytic properties are required, trazodone, amitriptyline, doxepin, or maprotiline work well. Otherwise, imipramine or a secondary amine can be used.

Both imipramine or amitriptyline can usually be started in doses of 50 to 75 mg/day (see Table 12 for equivalent doses of other heterocyclics). The clinician should start elderly individuals, children, and small patients on lower doses. **Most people can take the entire dose of medication at bedtime,** since the half-life for these drugs is about 1 day. If bothersome adverse reactions develop (e.g., oversedation, nightmares, or frightening dreams) or if multiple doses are preferred by the patient for emotional reasons, he can take the drug two or three times a day. Most patients will become partially tolerant to the anticholinergic effects and then, when an optimal therapeutic dose is achieved, can return to a single dose at bedtime. Usually, patients have fewer adverse reactions and less need for coadministered sleeping medication when the drug is given once in the evening. A bedtime regimen also results in less motor and mental slowing and better compliance. If a patient takes a nightly dose, medication may be increased gradually (i.e., 25 mg/day) or by 75 mg every 3 days until a therapeutic range is reached or intolerable adverse reactions develop.

Individuals usually experience an antidepressant effect at 150 to 300 mg/day with imipramine or amitriptyline. However, some patients require much higher doses (even 600 to 700 mg) to achieve a therapeutic plasma level. This may entail a more prolonged drug trial and careful monitoring for adverse reactions. In these cases, the practitioner should obtain psychopharmacological consultation, monitor blood levels (with doses exceeding 300 mg/day), and carefully document risk, benefits, and information imparted to the patients.

If the clinician has concerns about cardiac or anticholinergic effects (e.g., in the elderly or cardiac patient), antidepressants other than imipramine or amitriptyline should be tried first (perhaps trazodone, desipramine, or maprotiline), and medication should be administered more slowly with more careful monitoring of adverse reactions.

In the anxious melancholic, trazodone and maprotiline produce few adverse reactions and significant sedation (and perhaps secondary anxiolysis in some patients). The clinician can administer maprotiline in a manner similar to imipramine; trazodone doses are about twice as much. **In individuals who have significant psychomotor retardation, a monomethylated tricyclic antidepressant (e.g., desipramine or protriptyline) is a good choice.** These secondary amines often have a stimulating or activating effect that plateaus after the first week of administration. They sometimes aggravate preexisting tension and anxiety, particularly in the elderly. These agents do not, however, produce a true antidepressant effect more quickly than the other heterocyclics. The patient may subjectively feel initial mild relief and then a slower resolution over a few weeks, as with the other antidepressants. If the patient experiences the stimulating effect but not a true antidepressant effect, he may suffer a subjective "relapse" after a week or two. On the other hand, some individuals find the initial stimulatory properties disturbing, producing a "nervous" or "jittery" sensation.

In all cases of acute outpatient therapy, the clinician must balance practical reality against suicidal risk. The seriously self-destructive patient should be hospitalized. With less suicidal individuals, the practitioner should closely monitor treatment by frequent contact with the patient (and family members) and by careful assessment of depressive symptoms and suicidal thoughts and plans. **Initially, to prevent lethal overdose, prescriptions should be entrusted to a family member or limited to less than 1.00 to 1.25 g if given to the patient.** Once a patient has improved and has established rapport with the clinician, larger amounts of medication may be dispensed. In addition, the clinician should inform all individuals receiving antidepressants about their high lethality. For example, borderline patients may sometimes take a few pills in a suicide attempt of low intent but, because they do not understand the dangerousness of these drugs, may develop serious medical problems.

2. Completing a Medication Trial

The clinician should initiate therapy mainly by talking with the patient about symptoms, prescribing recommended dosages, and monitoring adverse reactions. Sometimes, assays of heterocyclic plasma levels are indicated (see Table 10). Although some heterocyclic agents allegedly work faster than others, **a clinical response usually requires 2 to 3 weeks at therapeutic doses.** The monomethylated tricyclics sometimes stimulate motor activity in the beginning of treatment. The new antidepressants, maprotiline and amoxapine, originally thought to work within a week probably are not actually faster acting than other heterocyclics. However, with any antidepressant, some symptoms may remit within the first week. Generally, the sleep disorder and anxiety improve first, followed by a decrease in psychomotor retardation or agitation and somatic concerns. The depressed mood and diminished self-esteem usually remit last. The clinician should explain this progression to the patient to prevent him from becoming discouraged and discontinuing his medication. Generally, the clinician and family members notice that the patient has improved before the patient does. In individuals who only partially respond, higher doses of medication, longer treatment, and more active means of support should be provided.

Antidepressants occasionally cause a significant increase in appetite. This usually occurs with the most antihistaminic heterocyclics (e.g., doxepin, amitriptyline, trimipramine) (see Table 7). In cases in which this effect leads to noncompliance or severely impaired self-esteem, the clinician might switch to a secondary amine or trazodone.

If little or no clinical response occurs after 3 weeks of administering adequate amounts of any heterocyclic antidepressant, the practitioner should obtain a serum level (12 hr after the last dose). If the patient has a very low level (perhaps less than 50 ng/ml), the clinician should question the individual about compliance and then increase the dosage for 2 to 3 weeks to provide an appropriate serum concentration. In patients who subsequently fail to respond, a second antidepressant should be chosen on the basis of desired secondary pharmacological properties and the risk of adverse reactions (although some authorities advocate choosing drugs on the basis of their different pharmacological effects on NE or 5HT).

If a patient has a poor response to two successive trials of medication, the practitioner should review his diagnostic assessment. He might search for organic or characterologic factors limiting improvement. In addition, he might administer a dexamethasone suppression test (although only 50% of melancholic depressed patients have a positive result). If he reconfirms the diagnosis, the clinician should consider ECT, a MAOI, or a combined drug treatment for resistant depressions (see Section IV.D.11). Patients receiving ECT may also continue antidepressant medication. Although there may be potential hazards (particularly cardiovascular), some authorities advocate this combination because of possible synergistic effects. One always must weigh the risks of adverse reactions against a possible beneficial synergism.

3. Discontinuing Medication

After a satisfactory clinical effect is achieved, heterocyclics may be continued at the same doses for several months if the patient has few adverse reactions. If untoward effects are prominent, the clinician should slowly lower the dosage to a tolerable level. In some patients, a **rapid lowering of dosage causes a cholinergic rebound syndrome** characterized by mild transient nausea, diaphoresis, diarrhea, headaches, malaise, chills, coryza, muscle aches, and sleep and dream disturbances (vivid dreams, nightmares, etc.).

If a patient has had a good response to medication in a first depression or in a depressive illness with widely spaced episodes, **continue the drug treatment about 6 more months after "complete symptom suppression"** (the usual projected length of a depression is 6 to 12 months). **The practitioner should discontinue medication over a period of weeks,** observing the patient for the reappearance of symptoms. If the patient previously has escaped dexamethasone suppression, the return of appropriate suppression may be a sign that the clinician can stop the drug (it marks the end of underlying hypothalamic–pituitary–adrenal disinhibition). In the rare cases in which these data are available, treatment should continue if the test remains positive.

4. Maintenance Therapy for Chronic or Recurrent Depressions

As many as 15% of patients with depressive illness have chronic symptoms or recurrent episodes that require not only acute treatment but also maintenance therapy. The clinician should collaborate with the patient in any decision about chronic medication. Severity and length of depressions and the frequency of episodes should be considered, along with adverse drug reactions and the patient's attitude.

Both lithium and heterocyclic antidepressant maintenance are effective in preventing relapse of depressive illness characterized by lengthy periods of depression or by multiple, shorter episodes[66] (see Chapter 3). The clinician should search for at least one manic episode, since the depressions related to bipolar illness respond best to lithium maintenance. In unipolar depressive illness, both agents seem equally effective. As with lithium prophylaxis, maintenance heterocyclic treatment does not completely eliminate the risk of subsequent depressions. A regimen of 75 to 150 mg amitriptyline or its equivalent decreases the risk of severe depression. In many individuals, lower doses (i.e., 25 to 50 mg/day) can decrease the recurrence of affective episodes. Some patients do relapse despite ongoing maintenance treatment, and about half of the patients on prophylaxis have intermittent periods of mild to moderately severe depressive symptoms. The choice of lithium or heterocyclic maintenance for chronic depressive syndromes depends on many factors:

1. If depressive episodes are infrequent, the clinician must decide whether the morbidity from possible intermittent episodes is greater than the untoward effects of the drug.
2. The choice of a maintenance regimen should partly depend on the physical status of the patient and the adverse reactions of each of the drugs.
3. If a patient has previously responded to one regimen, it should be continued; if he has an unsatisfactory response (even after dosage adjustment), another maintenance medication should be tried.

In general, **if other factors do not favor the use of lithium, patients usually tolerate maintenace heterocyclics better.**

Although there are no known long-term effects from heterocyclics, the clinician should determine the lowest effective maintenance dose to guard against potential long-term adverse reactions. Since long-term lithium therapy can cause kidney changes, some experts recommend trying lower levels of lithium (i.e., 0.4 to 0.6 mEq/liter) during maintenance.

Many patients have been maintained on lithium or heterocyclic antidepressants for more than a decade without the development of long-term adverse effects. Therefore, although maintenance therapy may not cure affective disorders, it can safely change the course of chronic depressive illnesses.

5. Depressive Episodes in Bipolar Affective Disorders

Depressive episodes in bipolar illness occur much more frequently than manic or hypomanic states. Lithium may provide some relief for acute depressions, but it mainly prevents the recurrence of manic episodes. Therefore, the depressive episodes of manic depressive illness should be treated by giving heterocyclic antidepressants along with lithium maintenance. If this treatment fails, some authorities advocate treating acute episodes with MAOIs added to the lithium (since they feel that MAOIs are more specific for depressive episodes in bipolar patients).

6. Agitated, Anxious, or Hostile Depressions of Moderate Severity

This group of depressions comprises about 80% of those coming to clinical attention. Approximately 75% are characterized by marked anxiety and moderately severe depressive symptoms. The other 25% include anxious depressions with overt hostility. All may be accompanied by agitation.

These depressions probably comprise several different syndromes and represent a more diffuse clinical entity than the more severe depressions. Some experts feel that treatment is basically symptomatic and primarily aimed at alleviating anxiety. In controlled studies, **heterocyclic antidepressants and antipsychotic agents** provide better results than placebo. Although antipsychotic drugs with strong sedative effects seem to relieve anxiety symptoms, many other antipsychotics (e.g., piperazine phenothiazines and thiothixene) also are effective. Therapeutic doses usually range from one-third to one-half of the amount used for acute psychosis.

Clinically, the choice of drug for these depressions can be confusing. When in doubt, use a heterocyclic antidepressant with sedative properties (e.g., trazodone, maprotiline, amitriptyline) that will theoretically diminish anxiety symptoms while correcting neurotransmitter imbalances. **For hostile or agitated depressions that do not respond to heterocyclics or that have obsessive features, hypochondriasis, or other indicators for MAOI use (see Table 15), isocarboxazid or phenelzine may be helpful.** In the future, drugs such as alprazolam (Xanax®), a new benzodiazepine with antidepressant properties, may prove helpful for disorders with both lowered mood and anxiety.

7. Mild Depressions

Many patients with transient, mild, and nonmelancholic depressions do not have the symptom clusters that indicate the need for antidepressant therapy. The short-term use of benzodiazepines may provide significant relief, particularly when anxiety is a prominent component.

8. Psychotic Depressions

Psychotic depressions present a conflict for the clinician. Overt psychotic symptoms such as paranoia and somatic delusions may sometimes accompany a major depressive illness. Sometimes, these psychotic symptoms seem disproportionate to the degree of depression. In these individuals, the clinician may have difficulty determining whether the patient has a depression with psychotic symptoms or a schizoaffective disorder that may follow a course similar to schizophrenia. In either case, **a combination of a heterocyclic antidepressant and an antipsychotic agent should be considered.** This not only contains psychotic symptoms but may more effectively resolve the depressive episode. (The amitriptyline–perphenazine combination has been used most widely.) The clinician can administer about half the usual dose of both the antipsychotic and the antidepressant. In general, precombined preparations should be avoided, since doses of each drug cannot be adjusted individually. In patients who have very severe symptoms or who do not respond adequately to a combined regimen, ECT should be considered.

Although researchers have yet to complete appropriate studies, amoxapine may have both antidepressant and antipsychotic effects. In the steady state, amoxapine and one active hydroxy metabolite (7-OH-amoxapine) block dopamine. This property and clinical evidence of extrapyramidal reactions and hyperprolactinemia may indicate that amoxapine is similar to the antipsychotics.

9. Depression in Schizophrenic Patients

In schizophrenics who develop depressive symptoms, the clinician must consider several possible explanations. The patient may have:

1. A schizoaffective disorder that could respond to antidepressant therapy.
2. A worsening psychotic picture marked by withdrawal.
3. An apathetic state secondary to chronic psychosis.
4. An adverse reaction to antipsychotic therapy (e.g., oversedation or akinesia).
5. Depressive symptoms related to despair about his condition.

In each case, the practitioner should reevaluate the patient's condition. For those individuals with the symptoms of major depressive disorder, antidepressants may help. For others, some adjustment of antipsychotic medication may provide relief. Most often, however, the clinician can do little by pharmacological methods. Instead, he should offer support, consistency, and a forum for addressing the patient's problems functioning and relating to other people.

10. "Atypical" Depressions

Monoamine oxidase inhibitors (MAOIs) are perhaps slightly less effective than heterocyclics in major depressive illness. However, some patients who do not respond to heterocyclics respond to the MAOIs. Moreover, they may be the treatment of choice for some patients with atypical depressions, phobic states, and panic anxiety (see Table 15). In these cases, the practitioner should educate the patient about the dangers of MAOIs (particularly the food and medication prohibitions) and then prescribe one of these agents in divided doses. For example, phenelzine, the most used MAOI, is given in 15-mg doses three times a day for 2 to 4 weeks. Medication may be increased to 75 to 90 mg if the initial dosage fails to provide adequate improvement. After a clinical effect is observed, clinicians should generally reduce the dosage to 15 to 30 mg for a few more months. The dosage range for isocarboxazid and tranylcypromine is about one-half to one-third that for phenelzine.

11. Resistant Depressions

Most depressions improve with time or respond to standard pharmacotherapy. Occasionally, however, a debilitating depression will not respond to successive trials of antidepressant medications or ECT. In these cases, several other approaches can be tried. One of these regimens consists of **combining a MAOI and a heterocyclic antidepressant.** Despite the increased risk from this combination, it usually does not cause problems if **diet is controlled, and the heterocyclic is started first (usually 50 mg amitriptyline, trimipramine, or doxepin), and subsequent dosage increases are alternated in half the usual amounts for each drug.** Remember that a previously administered MAOI must be stopped for at least 1 week prior to beginning heterocyclic treatment (i.e., adding a heterocyclic to a MAOI may be dangerous). In contrast, if a trial of a heterocyclic proves ineffective, the practitioner may add small doses of MAOI. Isocarboxazid and phenelzine may be the MAOIs of choice, since they seem to produce the fewest adverse effects in a combined regimen. **(Experts recommend avoiding MAOI/imipramine or desipramine combinations.)** The patient who is already on a clinically appropriate dose of heterocyclics should take a 5-mg dose to test for sensitivity while blood pressure is being carefully monitored. If this dose is still tolerated after 1 or 2 days, the MAOI should be increased to 10 mg and maintained at that level for about a week. Thereafter, it can be increased by 10 mg each week until a level of 30 mg is reached. An adequate trial of combined medication consists of a clinical response within 3 or 4 weeks or the onset of prohibitive adverse reactions. The most common unwanted effects from combination medication include fatigue, constipation, and dizziness.

Investigators have tried other combined drug regimens. Some studies indicate that the coadministration of **triiodothyronine** (T_3) (Cytomel®, Thyrolar®) and a heterocyclic antidepressant yields a higher percentage of drug responders with faster results (often in 1 to 5 days rather than 10 to 21 days). Researchers have made similar claims for heterocyclics combined with **methylphenidate** (Ritalin®) or dexamethasone. These approaches are still experimental and should be considered only by experienced pharmacotherapists for patients who are unresponsive to all other measures.

12. Use of Stimulants for Depression

Clinicians should generally avoid using stimulants including amphetamine and its derivatives and methylphenidate. Their effectiveness in hyperactive children is well established, and the short-term use of methylphenidate with tricyclic antidepressants in resistant depressions has been justified by some studies. However, their use is usually contraindicated in other clinical situations. These agents produce frequent untoward effects, their stimulant properties may exacerbate or precipitate psychotic symptoms, and they have a severe abuse potential.

V. CONCLUSION

The biological treatment of depressive disorders has advanced remarkably in recent years. We not only have new antidepressants with fewer adverse reactions but also the promise of safer agents that have diverse effects on brain chemistry. In addition, new brain chemistry models of depression, biological methods of diagnosis, and approaches to monitoring treatment are evolving rapidly. Alongside these advances, researchers and clinicians continue to explore and clarify the relationships between biology and human experience. We now have a broad, although at times confusing, range of psychotherapeutic and pharmacological treatment options. For the patient, this will mean a more effective armamentarium for treating and preventing mood disturbances and the suffering that accompanies them.

REFERENCES

1. Abraham K.: *Notes on the Psychoanalytic Investigation and Treatment of Manic–depressive Insanity and Allied Conditions (1911).* New York, Basic Books, 1960, pp 137–156.
2. Freud S.: *Mourning and Melancholia,* Standard Edition (1916). London, Hogarth Press, 1971, vol XIV.
3. Weissman M. M., Fox K., Klerman C.: Hostility and depression associated with suicide attempts. *Am J Psychiatry* 130:450–455, 1973.

4. Bibring E.: The mechanism of depression, in Greenacre P. (ed): *Affective Disorders.* New York, International Universities Press, 1965, pp 13–48.

5. Harlow H., Harlow M.: Learning to love. *Sci Am* 54:244–272, 1966.

6. Spitz R.: Anaclitic depression. An inquiry into the genesis of psychiatric conditions in early childhood. *Psychoanal Study Child* 2:313–342, 1942.

7. Ainsworth M.: Object relations, dependency and attachment. *Child Dev* 40:969–1025, 1969.

8. Bowlby J.: Childhood mourning and its implications for psychiatry. *Am J Psychiatry* 118:481–498, 1961.

9. Robertson J., Robertson J.: Young children in brief separation: A fresh look. *Psychoanal Study Child* 26:264–315, 1971.

10. Mahler M. S.: On sadness and grief in infancy and childhood: Loss and restoration of the symbiotic love object. *Psychoanal Study Child* 16:332–351, 1961.

11. Kohut H.: *The Analysis of the Self.* New York, International Universities Press, 1971.

12. Kernberg O.: *Borderline Conditions and Pathological Narcissism.* New York, Jason Aronson, 1975.

13. Beck A. T., Rush A. J., Shaw B., et al: *Cognitive Therapy of Depression.* New York, Guilford Press, 1979, pp 1–34.

14. Seligman M., Maier S., Geer J.: The alleviation of learned helplessness and the dog. *J Abnorm Soc Psychol* 73:256–262, 1968.

15. Lewinsohn P., Biglar A., Zeiss A.: Behavioral treatment of depression, in Davidson P (ed): *The Behavioral Management of Anxiety, Depression and Pain.* New York, Brunner-Mazel, 1976, pp 91–146.

16. Decker E.: *The Revolution in Psychiatry.* London, Collier–Macmillan, 1964, pp 108–135.

17. Schildkraut J. J.: Catecholamine hypothesis of affective disorder. *Am J Psychiatry* 122:509–522, 1965.

18. Maas J. W.: Biogenic amines and depression: Biochemical and pharmacological separation of two types of depression. *Arch Gen Psychiatry* 32:1357–1367, 1975.

19. Bunney W. E., Murphy D. L., Goodwin F. K., et al: The "switch process" in manic-depressive illness. I. A systematic study of sequential behavioral changes. *Arch Gen Psychiatry* 27:295–317, 1972.

20. Akiskal H. S., McKinney W. I. Jr: Overview of recent research in depression; integration of ten conceptual models into a comprehensive clinical frame. *Arch Gen Psychiatry* 32:285–305, 1975.

21. American Psychiatric Association: *Diagnostic and Statistical Manual of Mental Disorders,* ed 3. Washington, American Psychiatric Association, 1980.

22. Schatzberg A., Rosenbaum A.: Studies on MHPG levels as predictors of antidepressant response. *McLean Hosp J* VI(2):138–147, 1980.

23. DeLeon-Jones T. D., Maas J. W., Dekirmenian H., et al: Diagnostic subgroups of affective disorders and their urinary excretion of catecholamine metabolites. *Am J Psychiatry* 132:1141–1148, 1975.

24. Schlidkraut J. J.: Norepinephrine metabolites as a biochemical criteria for classifying depressive disorders and predicting responses to treatment: Preliminary findings. *Am J Psychiatry* 130:695–699, 1973.

25. Maas J. W.: Biogenic amines and depression: Biochemical and pharmacological separation of two types of depression. *Arch Gen Psychiatry* 32:1357–1361, 1975.

26. Maas J. W., Fawcett J. A., Dekirmenian H.: Catecholamine metabolism, depressive illness and drug response. *Arch Gen Psychiatry* 26:252–262, 1972.

27. Beckman H., Goodwin R. K.: Antidepressant response to tricyclics and urinary MHPG in unipolar patients: Clinical response to imipramine or amitriptyline. *Arch Gen Psychiatry* 32:17–21, 1975.

28. Rosenbaum, A., Schatzberg A. F., Maruta T., et al: MHPG as a predictor of antidepressant response to imipramine and maprotiline. *Am J Psychiatry* 137:1090–1092, 1980.

29. Carroll B. J.: Neuroendocrine function in psychiatric disorders, in Lipton M. A., DiMascio A., Killam K. F. (eds): *Psychopharmacology: A Generation of Progress*. New York, Raven Press, 1978, pp 487–497.

30. Brown W.: The dexamethasone suppression test in the identification of subgroups of depression differentially responsive to antidepressants. Read at the New Clinical Drug Evaluation Unit Meeting, Key Biscayne, Florida, May 27–29, 1980.

31. Brown W. A.: The dexamethasone suppression test: Clinical applications. *Psychosomatics* 22:951–955, 1981.

32. Gold M. S., Pottash A. L. C., Extein I., et al: Dexamethasone suppression tests in depression and response to treatment. *Lancet* 1:1190, 1980.

33. Weissman M. M.: The psychological treatment of depression. *Arch Gen Psychiatry* 36:1261–1268, 1979.

34. Weissman M. M., Prusoff B. A., DiMascio A., et al: The efficacy of drugs and psychotherapy in the treatment of acute depression episodes. *Am J Psychiatry* 136:555–558, 1979.

35. Herceg-Baron R. L., Prusoff B. A., Weissman M. M., et al: Pharmacotherapy and psychotherapy in acute depressed patients. A study of attrition patterns in a clinical trial. *Compr Psychiatry* 20:315–325, 1979.

36. Weissman M. M., Klerman G. L., Prusoff B. A., et al: Depressed outpatients: Results one year after treatment with drugs and/or interpersonal psychotherapy. *Arch Gen Psychiatry* 38:51–55, 1981.

37. Kovacs M.: The efficacy of cognitive and behavior therapies for depression. *Am J Psychiatry* 137:1495–1501, 1980.

38. Frankel F. H.: Current perspectives on ECT: A discussion. *Am J Psychiatry* 134:1014–1019, 1977.

39. Grahme-Smith D. S., Green A. R., Costain D. W.: Mechanism of the antidepressant action of electroconvulsive therapy. *Lancet* 1:254–256, 1978.

40. Small J. G., Kellams J. J., Milstein V., et al: Complications with electroconvulsive treatment combined with lithium. *Biol Psychiatry* 15:103–112, 1980.

41. Mandel M. R., Madsen J., Miller A. L., et al: Intoxication associated with lithium and ECT. *Am J Psychiatry* 137:1107–1109, 1980.

42. Squire L. R., Slater P. C.: Bilateral and unilateral ECT: Effects on verbal and nonverbal memory. *Am J Psychiatry* 135:1316–1320, 1978.

43. Maletsky D. M.: Seizure duration and clinical effect in electroconvulsive therapy. *Compr Psychiatry* 19:541–550, 1978.

44. Baldessarini R. J.: The basis for amine hypothesis in affective disorders. A critical evaluation. *Arch Gen Psychiatry* 32:1087–1093, 1975.

45. Wilson E. G., Petrie W. M., Ban T. A.: Possible lack of anticholinergic effects with mianserin: A pilot study. *J Clin Psychiatry* 41:63–65, 1980.

46. Sulser F.: New perspectives on the mode of action of antidepressant drugs. *Trends Pharmacol Sci.* 1:92–94, 1979.

47. Crews F. T., Smith C. B.: Presynaptic alpha-receptor subsensitivity after long-term antidepressant treatment. *Science* 202:322–324, 1978.

48. deMontigny C., Aghajanian G. K.: Tricyclic antidepressant: Long-term treatment increases responsivity of rat forebrain neurons to serotonin. *Science* 202:1303–1306, 1978.

49. Briley S., Langer S. Z., Raisman R., et al: Tritiated imipramine binding sites are decreased in platelets of untreated depressed patients. *Science* 202:303–305, 1980.

50. Janowsky D., El-Yousef K., Davis M., et al: A cholinergic adrenergic hypothesis of mania and depression. *Lancet* 2:632–635, 1972.

51. Maas J. W.: Neurotransmitters in depression: Too much, too little or too unstable? *Trends Neurosci* 2:306–308, 1979.

52. Feigner J. P.: Pharmacology: New antidepressants. *Psychiatr Ann* 10:388–395, 1980.
53. Shopsin B.: Second generation antidepressants. *J Clin Psychiatry* 41:45–46, 1980.
54. Hollister L. E.: "Second generation" antidepressant drugs. *Psychosomatics* 22:872–879, 1981.
55. Risch S. C., Groom G. P., Janowsky D. S.: Interfaces of psychopharmacology and cardiology. *J Clin Psychiatry* 42:23–34, 1981.
56. Langou R. A., VanDyke C., Tahan S. R., et al: Cardiovascular manifestations of tricyclic antidepressant overdose. *Am Heart J* 100:458–464, 1980.
57. Glassman A. H., Bigger J. B., Cantor S. J., et al: Cardiovascular effects of imipramine. *NCDEU Intercom* 7:8–12, 1978.
58. Crome P., Dawling S., Braithwaite R. A., et al: Effect of activated charcoal on absorption of nortriptyline. *Lancet* 2:1203–1205, 1977.
59. Granacher R. D., Baldessarini R. J.: Physostigmine: Its use in acute anticholinergic syndrome with antidepressant and antiparkinson drugs. *Arch Gen Psychiatry* 32:375–379, 1975.
60. Burks J. S., Walker J. E., Rumack B. H., et al: Tricyclic antidepressant poisoning: Reversal of coma, choreoathetosis and myoclonus by physostigmine. *JAMA* 230:1405–1407, 1974.
61. Orr D. A., Bramble M. G.: Tricyclic antidepressant poisoning and external cardiac massage during asystole. *Br Med J* 283:1107–1108, 1981.
62. Risch S. C., Huey L. Y., Janowsky D. S.: Plasma levels of tricyclic antidepressants and clinical efficacy. Review of the literature, Part II. *J Clin Psychiatry* 40:58–69, 1979.
63. Amsterdam J., Brunswick D., Mendels J.: The clinical application of tricyclic antidepressant pharmacokinetics and plasma levels. *Am J Psychiatry* 137:653–662, 1980.
64. Baldessarini R. J.: The status of psychotropic blood level assays and other biochemical measurements in clinical psychiatry. *Am J Psychiatry* 136:1177–1180, 1979.
65. Quitkin F., Rifkin A., Klein D. F.: Monoamine oxidase inhibitors: A review of antidepressant effectiveness. *Arch Gen Psychiatry* 36:749–760, 1979.
66. Schou M.: Lithium as a prophylactic agent in unipolar affective illness: A comparison with cyclic antidepressants. *Arch Gen Psychiatry* 36:849–851, 1979.

3

Bipolar Affective Disorder and Recurrent Unipolar Depression

STEPHEN C. SCHOONOVER, M.D.

I. INTRODUCTION

Lithium (Lithonate®, Lithane®, Eskalith®, and others), a naturally occurring salt, has been used for various medical purposes since the 1800s. Initially, it was given to patients who suffered from urinary calculi and gout. Later, it was combined with bromides and used as a sedative. In 1949, Cade observed that lithium calmed agitated psychotic patients: ten manic patients responded, six schizophrenic and chronically depressed psychotic patients did not, and one patient's symptoms reappeared after lithium was stopped.[1] During this same period, lithium was introduced in the United States as a salt substitute for cardiac patients, but it caused numerous toxic reactions and several deaths. Thus, even with the emergence of convincing evidence that lithium was safe and effective in manic–depressive illness, it was not accepted in the United States until 1970.

Lithium currently is employed to treat **acute hypomanic** or **manic episodes** and **recurrent affective disorders.** Despite its effectiveness, however, its mechanism of action remains unclear. Some authorities postulate that lithium corrects an ion-exchange abnormality.[2] Other researchers have shown that it increases neuronal release of norepinephrine, serotonin, and dopamine, increases the reuptake and metabolism of norepinephrine, alters serotonin receptor sensitivity, and may decrease the availability of acetylcholine. Forn

---

STEPHEN C. SCHOONOVER, M.D. • Department of Psychiatry, Harvard Medical School and Beth Israel Hospital, Boston, Massachusetts 02215.

TABLE 1. Syndromes That May Respond to Lithium Maintenance[a]

Two episodes in any 2-year period or a total of three or more episodes with the following characteristics:

A. Unipolar depressive disorder
  1. Dysphoric mood (depression)
  2. At least four of the following for at least 2 weeks:
    a. Poor appetite or weight loss or increased appetite or weight gain
    b. Sleep disorder
    c. Loss of energy, fatigue, or tiredness
    d. Psychomotor agitation or retardation
    e. Loss of interest or pleasure
    f. Feelings of self-reproach (may be delusional)
    g. Complaints or evidence of diminished ability to think or concentrate
    h. Recurrent thoughts of death or suicide
B. Unipolar manic disorder
  1. Distinct, persistent period(s) of predominantly elevated, expansive, or irritable mood
  2. At least three of the following (four if mood is only irritable):
    a. Hyperactivity (often inappropriate)
    b. Pressure of speech
    c. Flight of ideas or subjective feeling of racing thoughts
    d. Grandiosity
    e. Decreased sleep
    f. Distractibility
C. Bipolar affective disorder
  Criteria for depressive and manic disorders fulfilled by a combination of history and current symptoms
D. Schizoaffective disorder
  1. Criteria for either a unipolar or bipolar affective disorder or both
  2. Consistence with the criteria for schizophrenia, including at least one of the following:
    a. Delusions of being controlled or influenced
    b. Thought broadcasting
    c. Thought insertion or withdrawal
    d. Preoccupation with a delusion or hallucination to the relative exclusion of other symptoms or concerns
    e. Auditory hallucinations with a running commentary on patient's behavior or thoughts, or two or more voices conversing with one another
    f. Verbal hallucinations of more than one or two words spoken to the patient on several occasions
    g. Hallucinations of any type lasting throughout the day for several days or intermittently for at least 1 month
    h. Formal thought disorder if accompanied by either blunted or inappropriate affect, delusions, or hallucinations of any type, or grossly disorganized behavior
  3. Overlap of affective and psychotic schizophrenic symptoms

[a]Presumptive diagnostic criteria derived from DSM-III classification of psychiatric disorders.[8]

and Valdecasas hypothesize an alteration of the adenylate cyclase system that affects membrane permeability by changing the functioning of postsynaptic receptor sites.[3]

    The major affective illnesses (see Table 1) affect 10 to 20% of people in a lifetime. Manic–depressive illness and recurrent unipolar depressions are among the most common and treatable disorders of this type. In most patients, the illness recurs, with episodes becoming more severe and frequent with age. Clinicians have successfully treated these disorders with pharmacological agents, particularly lithium salts. In fact, **70 to 90% of patients with "typical" bipolar illness respond to lithium.** In addition, other periodic disorders with an affective component that may be related to manic–depressive illness (e.g., schizoaffective disorder) can sometimes be effectively treated with lithium. Less clearly defined periodic disturbances (see Table 2) are also occasionally responsive to lithium and include periodic catatonia,[4] periodic alcoholism (particularly accompanied by depressive affect),[5] emotionally unstable character disorders,[6] cyclothymic personality disorders,[7] and obsessive–compulsive states.[8] A possible role for lithium in the treatment of schizophrenic patients remains to be elucidated.

In practice, how quickly and how well does lithium work? In acute hypomanic or manic episodes, lithium is frequently effective within 1 to 2 weeks but may require several more weeks or even a few months to contain the affective episode fully. Sometimes an antipsychotic agent [like haloperidol (Haldol®)] should be used acutely to manage behavioral excitement and acute psychotic symptoms. After diminishing the acute symptoms, lithium maintenance therapy decreases the number, severity, and frequency of affective episodes. Even with drug treatment, some patients experience various symptoms, intermittent periods of distress, or unwanted effects. To achieve optimal results, the clinician may need to experiment with various dosage levels and continue maintenance therapy for a year or longer. In addition, patients with acute depressive symptoms tend not to respond to lithium alone.

Initially, the clinician should fully evaluate the patient to make an accurate diagnosis and then develop a comprehensive approach to care. Therefore, to establish a framework for safe and effective clinical care, we discuss the following practical guidelines:

1. Defining symptom profiles and diagnosing patients responsive to medication.
2. Delineating clinical effects, pharmacokinetics, and adverse reactions.
3. Specifying acute and maintenance medication regimens for bipolar affective episodes and recurrent unipolar depressions.
4. Developing a medication philosophy that emphasizes risks and

TABLE 2. Other Possible Uses for Lithium

Paranoia	Drug abuse
Periodic psychosis	Obsessive–compulsive disorders
Premenstrual tension	Phobic behavior
Alcoholism	Various childhood disorders
Impulse-ridden character disorder	Cyclothymic personality

benefits and effective collaboration with the patient within a caring therapeutic relationship.

II. MANIC–DEPRESSIVE DISORDER (BIPOLAR AFFECTIVE DISORDER)

Manic–depressive illness is characterized by episodic mood swings. Different patterns include

1. Episodes of mania alternating with depression. These mood "switches" may occur frequently (every few days) or may be widely spaced.
2. Episodes of mania followed by an intervening period of normal mood and then by the onset of depression. In this subgroup, intermittent depressive episodes followed by a period of normal mood may occur without the development of hypomania or mania.
3. Rare cases of unipolar mania with episodes varying in length (up to several decades in some untreated cases).[9]

The clinician can use the severity and pattern of a patient's illness as a base line for monitoring the effectiveness of pharmacotherapy. Because of the range of clinical presentations and the wide variation in the course of bipolar illness, the clinician must carefully follow each individual.

A. Clinical Presentation

Bipolar affective illness, primarily a disorder of mood, occurs in about 0.3 to 0.4% of the general population. Patients usually develop their first affective episode (usually mania or hypomania) between the ages of 20 and 40 (average 32). In mania, elevated mood is common but not universal. Sometimes depressive symptoms break through a facade of emotional lability. Pressure of speech, flight of ideas, increased motor activity, and decreased sleeping time often accompany the sense of elation and well-being. These patients are very self-involved but often can sense the vulnerabilities of others and become inappropriate and intrusive. If mania progresses, the patient's sense of humor may border on anger and irritability. Pressure of speech may deteriorate into fragmented sentences and clang associations, and a sense of well-being may escalate into grandiosity. In the most extreme form, the patient becomes psychotic. Auditory hallucinations, delusions, and paranoia are frequent, and incoherence, sensory distortions, agitation, and combativeness may accompany the most disorganized states.
    Clinicians have described some cases of prolonged mania or intermittent

mania. Most commonly, however, the illness is bipolar. Depressions occur more frequently than mania in most bipolar patients (ratio of about 5 : 1). Usually, the depression is indistinguishable from a major depressive disorder. The DSM-III carefully defines the symptom criteria which include persistently lowered mood, psychomotor retardation, feelings of helplessness, hopelessness, and worthlessness, vegetative symptoms, and various somatic concerns. However, many patients who may have other psychiatric disturbances that also respond to lithium therapy do not exactly conform to classical clinical profiles.

B. Course of the Illness

Both manic and depressive episodes are usually time limited, (generally 3 to 9 months). As patients grow older, however, the episodes generally occur more frequently and last longer. Most often, the manic and depressive episodes of bipolar illness are shorter and more frequent than in pure mania or major depressive illness. Patients with rapid cycling (over four episodes per year) between mania and depression have a more guarded prognosis. Despite these general trends, the course of bipolar disorder varies considerably in different individuals. Many patients have episodes every few years; others have clusters of episodes; some show worsening in both frequency and intensity over a period of years.

In depressive disorders, about half of those patients with a single episode will have a second one. Those with more than one depressive episode are at even greater risk of developing future depressive episodes.

Despite the general usefulness of statistical descriptions, the clinician should look beyond them to define the nature and course of each patient's illness individually. An appropriate treatment plan can be developed only after assessing the impact and meaning of the illness in the patient's life.

III. GENERAL MEASURES FOR TREATING MANIC–DEPRESSIVE ILLNESS AND RECURRENT DEPRESSIONS

Many approaches, including electroconvulsive therapy (ECT), pharmacotherapy (antipsychotic drugs, lithium, and heterocyclic antidepressants*), milieu therapy, and various psychotherapies are used to treat bipolar illness and recurrent depressions.

---

*Since many of the currently used thymoleptic drugs are not tricyclic in structure, we have adopted this term to represent the various cyclic antidepressants. From: Baldessarini R. J.: Overview of recent advances in antidepressant pharmacology. Part II. *McLean Hosp J* 7:1–27, 1982.

A. Electroconvulsive Therapy

Electroconvulsive therapy is an effective treatment for the depressive episodes of manic–depressive disease and major depressive illness (see Chapter 2).

Circumstances That May Warrant the Use of ECT as the Primary Treatment

1. Previous good response to ECT.
2. Medical contraindication for antidepressant drugs.
3. Immediate threat of suicide or homicide or serious withdrawal or regression that interferes with self-care.
4. Failure of successive trials of pharmacotherapy.
5. Acute disorganization or combativeness that requires immediate behavioral containment (in these cases, ECT may prove useful in combination with antipsychotic agents or lithium).

B. Milieu Therapy

To insure a manic patient's safety and to contain his symptoms, inpatient care may be necessary. These patients, however, frequently disrupt the ward milieu. The patient's infectiously elevated mood may stimulate reinforcement from the staff and other patients, and his irritability and hostility can be highly provocative. Structuring daily activities, correcting cognitive distortions, and limiting external stimulation by staff and patients may reduce the patient's excitement. Caretakers should remember that milieu therapy and pharmacotherapy should be synergistic. A safe and stable environment promotes medication compliance, and the salutary effects of drugs increase insight, emotional availability, understanding, and formation of social attachments.

C. Group Therapy

Recently, Fieve organized "lithium groups" to discuss issues related to maintenance therapy.[10] This approach is not only time efficient for clinicians but also advantageous for patients. Sharing similar concerns about medication usage can be both supportive and growth producing while it increases compliance.

D. Psychotherapy and the Therapeutic Relationship

Clinicians have treated manic–depressive patients with a wide range of psychotherapies. Since the advent of lithium therapy, most therapeutic approaches are ego supportive and do not attempt to achieve definitive structural changes in the individual's personality. The predisposition to manic–depressive mood swings may represent a genetic diathesis that may occur in patients with various character structures. Psychotherapy research has done little to clarify whether or not change in character structure alters the course of the mood swings. Unfortunately, a very high percentage of patients who discontinue lithium have subsequent affective episodes. Some experts believe that patients with mood disorders improve more with combined psychotherapy and pharmacotherapy.[11] Therefore, drugs may be a necessary, but not sufficient, component of treatment. Even in supportive approaches, the relationship with the therapist probably promotes a positive outcome.

IV. PHARMACOTHERAPY

A. General Clinical Considerations

Pharmacological agents have markedly decreased the morbidity associated with bipolar illness, recurrent depressions, and several other cyclic psychiatric disturbances. The antipsychotic drugs provide an effective means of controlling the behavioral symptoms and thought disorder that accompany mania and hypomania. Antidepressant medications contain depressive episodes. Lithium can diminish the symptoms of acute mania and, over the long term, suppress both manic and depressive episodes. New research shows that carbamazepine (Tegretol®) may also have mood-stabilizing effects.[12,13]

In general, patients with the DSM-III criteria for bipolar illness constitute the major group of lithium responders. However, investigators have developed additional criteria for predicting lithium's effectiveness for both acute treatment and chronic maintenance. Responders more often have the following characteristics: premorbid cyclothymic features, prior manic symptoms, onset of the affective illness with mania, history of alcohol abuse, family history of mania, and symptoms of euphoria and grandiose delusions. Other attributes include fewer than four episodes of mania and depression, positive response to lithium in relatives, florid psychotic features during both mania and depression, and improved sleep during the initial phases of lithium administration. Patients who respond poorly most often exhibit a withdrawn personality, thought disorder accompanied by paranoia or depression, obsessive traits, anxiety, "rapid cycling" between mania and depression (four or more episodes per year), predominantly depressive symptoms (particularly retardation), or onset of the illness after age 40.[14] As with all statistical predictors, the clinician should apply this profile cautiously to the individual patient.

Antipsychotics and lithium are both useful in the treatment of mania.[15,16] Antipsychotics, particularly haloperidol, can rapidly diminish increased motor activity and also suppress other symptoms of this disorder. These agents have definitive advantages over lithium for the treatment of acute behavioral excitement. However, the antipsychotic drugs only initially suppress the symptoms. Questioning reveals that these patients continue to feel internally disorganized. Lithium, in contrast, has more specific antimanic effects than the antipsychotics and usually diminishes manic symptoms within 5 to 14 days. However, the time required to control the manic syndrome fully with lithium may vary from days to several months. The depressive episodes of bipolar illness have a clinical course similar to other depressions and should be treated with standard antidepressant medication. Sometimes, antipsychotic drugs may be required to contain the symptoms of a psychotic depression. In general, lithium does not help acute depressive episodes.

Eliminating significant mood swings is the optimal clinical response to lithium maintenance therapy. However, mood fluctuations, and even the recurrence of an affective episode, do not indicate that lithium treatment has failed. Some clinicians feel that manic or depressive symptoms that occur within a few months of the initiation of treatment represent a relapse of the initial episode. To find a clinically therapeutic blood level, the clinician may initially have to vary the dosage. Patients on a maintenance lithium regimen also may develop mild manic and depressive symptoms that subside spontaneously or respond to interpersonal support or a transient increase in lithium.

Long-term studies have consistently demonstrated that lithium maintenance suppresses mood swings in most bipolar patients.[17] However, individuals must take appropriate amounts of medication consistently. In fact, failures of lithium therapy are quite frequent. Most occur during the first year of treatment and result from inadequate resolution of the initial episode, inadequate regulation of dosage, or lack of patient compliance. About 20 to 30% of patients discontinue lithium therapy on their own.

The Most Common Reasons for Stopping Medication

1. Denial of the illness.
2. Unawareness of the consequences of stopping medication.
3. Feeling no effects from the drug.

4. Intolerable adverse reactions.
5. Longing to be "high."
6. Fear of diminished competence, productivity, or creativity.[18]

By discussion of these and other concerns with the patient, the number of treatment failures attributed to poor patient compliance (three-fourths of the total) should be diminished.

B. Pharmacokinetics

Lithium is administered clinically as the citrate or carbonate. In the body, lithium circulates as a small ion with a single positive electrical charge. It is rapidly and usually fully absorbed after oral administration. Although the exact sites of absorption are somewhat unclear, blood levels after single oral doses peak in about 3 hr. However, complete absorption often takes 8 hr. In practice, the clinician should obtain serum lithium levels 12 hr after the last dose. Standard levels are based on this reference time (which insures accurate measurement after a steady state is achieved). A single dose of 300 mg usually produces an abrupt rise in serum lithium of about 0.2 mEq/liter.

Lithium is distributed unevenly, with high concentrations in the kidney, moderate concentrations in muscle, bone, and liver, and low concentrations in brain tissue. It equilibrates slowly and at different rates in various tissues. In chronic intoxication, tissue sites (particularly bone) act as reservoirs. The serum:cerebrospinal fluid ratio for lithium is usually 3:1 to 4:1 during chronic administration. Lithium also is actively transported across many cell membranes, and a steady state is established after about 1 week of administration.

Lithium is excreted almost entirely by the kidneys, with insignificant amounts appearing in the sweat and feces. Lithium is fully filtered and about 80% reabsorbed in the proximal tubules. Smaller amounts are reabsorbed in the loop of Henle. Under normal body conditions, the amount of lithium filtered and reabsorbed is constant. Lithium excretion is, therefore, proportionate to plasma concentrations, and lithium clearance is relatively constant for each patient. With a single dose of lithium, 50% is excreted within 5 to 8 hr. In patients on maintenance lithium, the half-life is about 24 hr. However, depending on the age and kidney status of patients, the half-life may vary widely (approximately 18 hr in young, healthy individuals to 36 hr in older patients).

Effective regulation of lithium depends on the sodium and fluid balance of the body. When lithium is initially administered, a cation balance among lithium, sodium, and potassium occurs; sodium and potassium excretion increases. Clinically, the balance between lithium and sodium is important for the following reasons:

1. Sodium depletion can result in marked lithium retention and possible toxicity.
2. High levels of lithium can lead to sodium excretion.

In cases of toxicity, the loss of body sodium obligates more lithium retention by the kidney, prolonging the toxicity. Decreased fluid intake also can diminish lithium excretion.

Since the lithium ion distributes throughout the body, practitioners have monitored its level in various body fluids. Most often clinicians use plasma levels to monitor treatment. Although controversial, some investigators feel that a genetically determined high erythrocyte-to-plasma lithium ratio predicts a positive treatment outcome. Erythrocyte levels are usually about 30% of plasma levels; responders often have levels of 50% or greater.[19]

C. Adverse Reactions

1. Endocrine

The long-term use of lithium carbonate may cause various endocrine abnormalities.

a. Thyroid

Lithium therapy can produce significant changes in thyroid functioning. It inhibits several steps in the process of synthesis and degradation, including iodine uptake by the thyroid gland, iodination of tyrosine, the release of T_3 and T_4, the peripheral degradation of thyroid hormones, and the stimulating effects of TSH (thyroid-stimulating hormone). Patients can usually compensate for the initial decrease in thyroid hormones. Approximately 5% of patients treated with lithium develop signs of hypothyroidism; another 3% develop a diffuse, nontender goiter.[20] This latter effect usually occurs in women between 5 months and 2 years after commencing treatment. In addition, about 30% of patients develop consistently increased levels of TSH indicated by elevated hormones or abnormal clinical signs and symptoms.[21] Each of these thyroid abnormalities remits when lithium is stopped.

Clinically, hypothyroidism can be confused with a depressive disorder. Therefore, the practitioner should always search for the clinical manifestations and laboratory findings indicative of thyroid disease.[22]

Since lithium affects thyroid function so profoundly, what measures should the clinician take during the various stages of maintenance therapy?

Before Starting Treatment

1. Screen for signs and symptoms of preexisting thyroid disease.
2. Obtain laboratory tests, including TSH (thyroid stimulating hormone), T_4 (thyroxine), T_4I (free thyroxine index), and T_3RU (resin uptake).

During Treatment

1. Obtain a TSH measurement every 6 months during the first year and yearly thereafter.
2. Follow up any elevated TSH with a complete battery of thyroid tests.
3. Initiate thyroid replacement therapy if hyperthyroidism occurs (discontinuing lithium is not necessary).

In addition, some clinicians treat elevated TSH with replacement therapy. However, present evidence does not indicate that this procedure has either positive or negative effects. Therefore, we recommend that practitioners treat low thyroid reserve (elevated TSH) only if the patient has a low normal level of thyroid hormone (T_4), a poor clinical response to lithium maintenance therapy over time, or mild symptoms of thyroid deficiency (a subclinical alteration in thyroid function may affect mood).

b. Diabetes Mellitus

Lithium has many effects on carbohydrate metabolism, including altered glucose tolerance. Occasionally, patients develop mild diabetes mellitus.[23] In these cases, the clinician must decide whether or not the risk from diabetes outweighs the morbidity of the individual's affective disorder.

Generally, diabetic patients tolerate lithium well. Sometimes, however, this agent causes increased sensitivity to insulin, requiring a dosage readjustment.

2. Renal

a. Polydipsia and Polyuria

Lithium therapy causes polydipsia and polyuria in about 60% of patients; it persists in 20 to 25%. These symptoms appear early in treatment but may reappear after several months or even several years. This adverse reaction may result from an inhibition of the interaction between antidiuretic hormone (ADH) and adenylate cyclase in the renal tubule and collecting duct system.[24] Clinically, polydipsia and polyuria may prompt many patients to discontinue medication. In spite of the patient's discomfort, these effects are usually benign and reversible; theoretically, the practitioner can safely continue lithium therapy. Lowering the dosage might prove helpful.

b. Diabetes Insipidus

Occasionally, a nephrogenic diabetes-insipidus-like syndrome develops in which the patient cannot concentrate urine. These individuals excrete very large amounts of urine (greater than 3 liters/day by definition and sometimes greater than 9 liters/day) and must drink comparable amounts of water to avoid dehydration. The condition does not seem to be dose related and is almost always reversible if lithium is stopped.[25,26]

If the Clinician Suspects That a Patient Has Diabetes Insipidus

1. Check urine osmolality (avoid performing a 12-hr dehydration test, since it can be dangerous in these patients).
2. If the kidney cannot adequately concentrate urine, either discontinue lithium or administer a thiazide (which may paradoxically reverse the polyuria by an unknown mechanism).[27]
3. If thiazide is given, lower the dose of lithium immediately and follow blood levels closely until a new equilibrium is established (the thiazides markedly decrease lithium clearance).

---

c. Structural Kidney Damage

Perhaps the most worrisome adverse reaction is the occurrence of permanent structural changes in the kidney after long-term lithium treatment. Although in most patients it does not cause significant clinical morbidity, the physician should carefully monitor the patient. This chronic tubulointerstitial nephropathy may be characterized by focal glomerular atrophy, interstitial fibrosis, and significant impairment of tubular functioning.[28] Clinically, impaired renal concentrating capacity appears in most patients after even short-term use, and as many as 10 to 20% of patients may develop structural changes after as little as 1 year of lithium therapy. Generally, the appearance of decreased tubular functioning correlates roughly with the length of exposure to lithium. In addition, the degree of functional impairment seems roughly correlated with the degree of cellular damage.[29] Often, persistent polyuria (over 2 liters/day) may be an early warning of possible kidney damage. Also, other drugs commonly used with lithium (i.e., antipsychotics and perhaps heterocyclic antidepressants) may increase the incidence of polyuria and, perhaps, of subsequent damage.

Since many patients develop polyuria during maintenance treatment, and since our current knowledge suggests that kidney damage occurs but rarely causes significant morbidity, the clinician is faced with a difficult problem. Some researchers believe that kidney changes may be caused by intermittently high levels of lithium from dehydration, intermittent fluctuations, or maintenance levels that are too high. Therefore, to minimize risk, the clinician should always monitor the lithium level carefully. Several factors, however, seem related to renal changes and include individual sensitivity, length and level of exposure to lithium, and synergism with other medications. To explain the nephropathy, one group of investigators even suggested that patients with affective disorders may be predisposed to kidney damage.[30]

To Minimize the Risk of Renal Damage

1. Take a careful medical family history to detect possible kidney disease.
2. Do a careful review of systems to discover other causes of kidney impairment (hypertension or diabetes mellitus, etc.).
3. Fully assess renal functioning prior to initiating therapy. Complete the following studies:
   a. Urinalysis, BUN, and electrolytes.
   b. Estimate of 24-hr creatinine clearance calculated by using the Cockcroft and Gault formula: creatinine clearance = (140 − age) (weight in kg) [0.85 (female only)] (72) (serum creatinine)[31]
   c. 24-hr urine volume.
   d. 12-hr dehydration followed by a measurement of urine osmolality (>600 mOsm/kg or >1.01% specific gravity is acceptable).
4. Reassess kidney functioning every 6 months (more often in patients with previous abnormal findings).
5. Closely follow patients who have a urine volume of greater than 3 liters/day.
6. Avoid coadministration of heterocyclics and antipsychotic agents if possible.
7. Use the minimum effective maintenance dose (may be between 0.4 and 0.6 mEq/liter for many patients).

8. Encourage adequate fluid intake to avoid dehydration.
9. Minimize fluctuations in blood levels of lithium. A sustained-release preparation may be preferable for some patients.
10. Consider the possibility of discontinuing lithium if significant kidney impairment persists or worsens after the above precautions are taken.

d. Other Kidney Effects

In addition to lithium's effects on fluid balance, several other adverse reactions may occur. Some patients develop a reversible nephrotic syndrome. During acute intoxication, some individuals may develop renal failure.

Lithium and sodium are managed similarly by the kidney. When lithium is first administered, sodium may be excreted in unusual amounts. Re-equilibration usually occurs within 1 week. Perspiration, diarrhea, or vomiting may produce a significant increase in the lithium level, necessitating careful monitoring. The physician should discuss this possibility with the patient and encourage clinical contact during these periods.

3. Hematological

Mild to moderate elevations of the white blood cell count (12,000 to 15,000 cells/mm^3) occur with both acute and chronic administration of lithium.[32] Neutrophils and lymphocytes are most affected. The disorder is clinically benign and reversible and can develop at various doses and at any stage of treatment. Investigators have not yet discovered the factors causing this condition or any significant medical problems resulting from it.

4. Cardiovascular

Lithium has significant effects on the heart. However, adverse reactions in clinical practice are rare. Perhaps because of its effects on potassium balance, lithium causes ECG T-wave flattening or inversion in about 20% of individuals.[33] Sometimes with normal doses, U-waves also appear. Since these are common changes, the clinician should obtain a base-line ECG prior to starting therapy.

Adverse cardiac reactions are rare even in patients with known heart disease. **Several types of conduction problems have appeared during lithium therapy,** including first-degree atrioventricular block, irregular or slowed sinus node rhythms (particularly in elderly patients), and increased numbers of ventricular premature contractions.[34,35] Some individuals have also developed severe congestive heart failure, cardiomyopathy, and ventricular tachycardia. However, the degree to which lithium therapy contributed to the development of these disorders was unclear.

During toxic states, some patients have developed persistent ventricular tachycardia, atrial fibrillation, advanced A–V block, and vascular collapse.[36]

> **Because Cardiac Reactions May Produce Serious Morbidity in an Occasional Patient**
>
> 1. Take a careful cardiac history.
> 2. Obtain a base-line ECG.
> 3. Follow the patient's cardiac status at least by monitoring clinical signs and symptoms.
> 4. Fully evaluate any conduction abnormalities that occur during therapy.
> 5. Consider lowering dosage in patients with conduction changes if continued lithium therapy is a high priority. Similarly, in individuals with irregular or slowed sinus rhythm, consider a pacemaker if other measures fail to provide cardiac stability.
> 6. Discontinue lithium in those who develop heart failure, ventricular tachycardia, or cardiomyopathy.

5. Cutaneous

Lithium occasionally causes bothersome skin problems. A pruritic, maculopapular rash may appear during the first month of therapy. This allergic response has a variable course which sometimes can progress to a serious dermatitis. Other observed dermatologic effects include acneiform lesions, hyperkeratotic papules, xerosis cutis, cutaneous ulcers, thinning and drying of scalp hair, exacerbation or appearance of psoriasis, chronic folliculitis, and anesthesia of the skin. Only the more serious responses require the discontinuation of lithium. Many of these reactions respond to conservative treatment, remit over time, or may not reappear if lithium is stopped and then restarted.

6. Gastrointestinal

Gastrointestinal (GI) reactions occur frequently during initial lithium therapy or as a result of dosage changes and include **gastric irritation, anorexia, abdominal cramps, nausea, vomiting, and diarrhea.** Because symptoms most often follow abrupt changes in the blood level, reducing these fluctuations may help. In addition, GI symptoms often indicate impending toxicity. Individuals, however, vary greatly in their sensitivity to changes in dosage or preparation and in the persistence of their symptoms.

To Cope with Gastrointestinal Reactions

1. Check the serum lithium level of any patient who develops gastrointestinal symptoms after the start of treatment.
2. Treat gastric irritation by administering lithium after meals, lowering the dose, further dividing dosages, or using a sustained-release preparation.
3. Treat other GI symptoms by changing or further dividing the dose or switching to another preparation (tablets, capsules, or sustained release).

7. Central Nervous System and Neuromuscular

Lithium commonly produces CNS and neuromuscular effects at therapeutic doses. The most common reactions occur at the beginning of treatment and include **mental dullness, decreased memory and concentration, headache, fatigue and lethargy, muscle weakness, and tremor.** These symptoms most often remit quickly and usually do not require changing the dosage.

A fine hand tremor of irregular rhythm and frequency (usually between 5 and 10 cycles per second) accompanies lithium therapy in about half of all patients. It is an action tremor (made worse by purposeful movements) that may persist from the beginning of treatment, appear at any point, or recur.[37] However, it usually appears when therapy starts and decreases over time (with a 4% incidence after 2 years). Central nervous system stimulants, caffeine, anxiety, muscle tension, and occasionally, antiparkinson drugs worsen the tremor, whereas sedative–hypnotic agents may improve it. Patients with other forms of action tremor (i.e., familial, idiopathic, senile) develop lithium-induced tremors more frequently. Rarely, tremulousness may involve the upper extremities, face, or eyelids. Lowering the dose of lithium may provide relief. However, if the tremor still persists, **propranolol (Inderal®, Inderide®), 20 to 160 mg per day,** may help.[37] Some controversy exists about using this drug, particularly since it can cause depressive reactions. Although the hand tremor does not indicate any known CNS lesion, patients discontinue treatment on their own.

Lithium also causes various other troublesome symptoms, including dysarthria, vertigo, ataxia, tinnitus, nystagmus, autonomic slowing of bladder and bowel function, visual distortion, muscle irritability (e.g., twitching, fasciculations, facial spasm, increased tendon reflexes, clonus, and choreoathetosis), and even a full organic brain syndrome.

Extrapyramidal reactions, although sometimes occurring without any apparent predisposition, are more likely in the elderly, those taking antipsychotic medication, and those who are toxic. Cogwheeling and more generalized muscle rigidity are more common symptoms.[38] Sometimes these reactions appear during the first months of therapy at therapeutic levels of lithium. However, they more often accompany serum lithium levels greater than 1.5 mEq/liter. With levels above 3.0 mEq/liter, patients show profound neurotoxic effects that can progress to seizures and incontinence, stupor, coma, brain damage, and death.

In addition to the adverse reactions already mentioned, rare cases of irreversible brain damage with usual doses of lithium may occur (see Chapter 4). This occurs most often in patients who are elderly, schizophrenic, or impaired neurologically.

To Minimize CNS Effects

1. Take an appropriate history for schizophrenia, possible central nervous system disease, tremors, and antipsychotic medication usage.
2. Note and carefully follow any mild, initial neurological symptoms (i.e., mental dullness, poor concentration, weakness, lethargy, or tremors).
3. Discontinue lithium and obtain a serum level in patients who develop any significant neurological symptoms (particularly an organic brain syndrome).
4. Treat hand tremors by reassurance, adjustment of dosage, or administration of 20 to 160 mg of propranolol per day.

8. Ocular

Lithium therapy rarely causes adverse reactions involving the eyes. Sometimes tearing, itching, burning, or blurring may occur during the first few weeks of treatment. With decongestant eyedrops and time, most of these reactions abate. Occasionally, more significant reactions develop, including exophthalmos, worsening of cataracts, and two reported cases of bilateral papilledema. However, the role of lithium in these disorders remains unclear.

9. Weight Gain

Reports vary widely about weight gain during lithium therapy. Twenty to 60% of patients gain more than 20 lb.[39] Although the etiology of this effect is unclear, many causes have been hypothesized, including altered carbohydrate and lipid metabolism, increased fluid intake and retention, improved appetite with the resolution of affective episodes, diminished thyroid functioning, and increased intake of high-caloric fluids. Since this adverse reaction is frequent, patients should be warned and instructed about possible dietary restrictions. For those who gain weight, limiting calories usually results in appropriate weight loss.

10. Other Adverse Reactions

These include metallic taste and pretibial edema.

11. Pregnancy

Various congenital abnormalities have been reported in babies exposed to lithium in utero, particularly anomalies of the heart and great vessels (Ebstein's anomaly). Therefore, lithium therapy should be avoided during pregnancy, particularly during the first trimester. In addition, infants born to mothers taking lithium occasionally develop temporary adverse reactions antepartum. Also, lithium's concentration in breast milk may significantly affect nursing infants (see Chapter 10).

D. Drug Interactions

Lithium and other drugs, particularly the diuretics, have various synergistic effects (Table 3). Thiazide diuretics commonly cause increased levels of lithium by decreasing clearance. This reaction can occur quickly, resulting in significant increases in blood levels and, finally, in toxicity. The potassium-retaining diuretics, spironolactone, ethacrynic acid, and triamterine, may also cause moderate increases in the lithium level over time. Some other diuretics, notably osmotic drugs and carbonic anhydrase inhibitors, result in decreasing lithium levels as a result of increased excretion. The clinician should be especially cautious if he administers lithium and methyldopa together; they may cause both hypertension and toxic symptoms at normal blood levels.

Antipsychotic agents are commonly prescribed with lithium for acutely disorganized patients. This practice is usually safe. However, some individuals have developed acute neurotoxicity and/or permanent brain damage (par-

TABLE 3. Drug Interactions

Increased levels of lithium
    Thiazide diuretics
    Ethacrynic acid (Edecrin®)
    Triamterene (Dyazide®, Dyrenium®)
    Spironolactone (Aldactazide®, Aldactone®, and others)
    Phenylbutazone (Azolid®, Butazolidin®, and others)
    Indomethacin (Indocin®)
    Ibuprofen (Motrin®)
    Mefenamic acid (Ponstel®)
    Naproxen (Naprosen®)
    Sulindac (Clinoril®)
    Zomepirac (Zomax®)
    Antipsychotic agents
Decreased levels of lithium
    Osmotic diuretics
    Carbonic anhydrase inhibitors
    Caffeine
    Theophylline (Tedral® and others)
    Theobromine diuretic (Athemol®)
Increased adverse reactions
    Cardiovascular toxicity: hydroxyzine (Atarax®, Vistaril®, and others)
    Somnambulism: antipsychotic agents
    Toxic symptoms with normal blood levels: methyldopa (Aldomet® and others)
    Hypertension: methyldopa (Aldomet® and others)

ticularly with haloperidol). These reactions occur rarely and may reflect lithium toxicity only or a neuroleptic malignant syndrome (see Chapter 4). Whether or not a combined toxic effect occurs is still unclear.

Other adverse drug reactions include increased cardiovascular toxicity with hydroxyzine, somnambulism with antipsychotic agents, increased levels of lithium with prostaglandin synthetase inhibitors (phenylbutazone, indomethacin, ibuprofen, mefenamic acid, naproxen, sulindic, and zomepirac), and increased excretion of lithium with xanthines (e.g., caffeine, theophylline, and theobromine).

To Minimize Possible Drug Synergisms

1. Avoid polypharmacy whenever possible, including periods of combined antipsychotic and lithium usage.
2. Lower the dosage of lithium in patients starting on lithium-retaining diuretics (particularly thiazides).

3. Monitor serum lithium levels more often in patients on osmotic diuretics or a carbonic anhydrase inhibitor.
4. Administer furosemide as a diuretic if it fits the patient's medical needs (this drug may not affect blood levels).
5. Discontinue lithium and obtain a blood level in any patient who develops symptoms of an organic brain syndrome while taking antipsychotic medication.
6. Avoid abruptly discontinuing caffeinated beverages (e.g., coffee, tea, colas) and monitor blood levels more closely in patients who markedly change their consumption of caffeine.
7. Avoid the use of methyldopa and hydroxyzine with lithium.

E. Toxicity

Lithium causes two types of toxic response. The first, occurring at low serum levels, is characterized by fine hand tremor, gastric irritability, anorexia, vomiting, diarrhea, and thirst. These effects, coinciding with large fluctuations in serum lithium levels, usually abate over the first few weeks of therapy and do not require special measures.

The second type of toxic response may result either from an acute overdose or from the chronic administration of an inappropriately high dosage. Toxic reactions most often occur at serum levels in excess of 2.0 mEq/liter, although in some sensitive individuals, they can occur at lower levels. In these patients, gastrointestinal symptoms may initially appear, followed or accompanied by central nervous system depression. This may include somnolence, sluggishness, the various hallmarks of an organic brain syndrome, dysarthria, seizures, choreoathetoid movements, increased muscle tone and increased deep tendon reflexes. Most often, more severe symptoms occur at serum lithium levels greater than 3.0 mEq/liter. Cardiovascular collapse marked by lowered blood pressure, irregular cardiac rhythm, decreased urine output, and conduction abnormalities (and ECG changes) may be life threatening.

Acute intoxication causes significant CNS depression. Patients develop pyramidal tract signs and impaired consciousness or coma. Individuals who take too much medication chronically gradually develop CNS impairment. Sluggishness and drowsiness may progress over a period of days. Often, gastrointestinal symptoms, slurred speech, ataxia, and coarse tremor accompany these changes. If the initial signs of chronic intoxication are overlooked, a more florid CNS syndrome may develop, most often manifested by hyperpyrexia and stupor or coma. It may also include neurological asymmetries, nystagmus, stiff neck, and hyperextension of the extremities.

Lithium toxicity is generally managed by supportive measures. If the toxicity occurs as part of an acute medication regimen or minor overdose, and kidney function is intact, careful observation usually suffices. Since lithium is excreted rapidly, the syndrome most often abates within a few days. However, in a large or chronic overdose, very large total body lithium stores may accumulate. In these cases, the patient often suffers persistent (several days or longer) life-threatening CNS depression and cardiovascular impairment.

Management of Serious Toxic States

1. Rapidly assess (including clinical signs and symptoms, serum lithium levels, electrolytes, and ECG), monitor vital signs, and make an accurate diagnosis.
2. Discontinue lithium.
3. Support vital functions and monitor cardiac status.
4. Limit absorption.
   a. If alert, provide an emetic.
   b. If obtunded, intubate and suction nasogastrically (prolonged suction may be helpful, since lithium levels in gastric fluid may remain high for days).
5. Prevent infection in comatose patients by body rotation and pulmonary toilet.
6. In all cases, vigorously hydrate (ideally 5 to 6 liters per day); monitor and balance the electrolytes.
7. In moderately severe cases.
   a. Implement osmotic diuresis with urea, 20 g IV two to five times per day, or mannitol, 50 to 100 g IV per day.
   b. Increase lithium clearance with aminophylline, 0.5 g up to every 6 hr and alkalinize the urine with IV sodium lactate.
   c. Insure adequate intake of NaCl to promote excretion of lithium.
8. Implement peritoneal or hemodialysis in the most severe cases. These are characterized by
   a. Serum levels between 2.0 and 4.0 mEq/liter with severe clinical signs and symptoms (particularly decreasing urinary output and deepening CNS depression).
   b. Serum lithium levels greater than 4.0 mEq/liter. Most patients completely recover from lithium toxicity; several may die; some develop permanent neurological damage.

TABLE 4. Lithium Preparations and Dosages

Lithium carbonate 300-mg capsules
    [Eskalith® (S, K & F), Lithonate® (Rowell), PFI-LITH® (Pfizer), Phillips-Roxane Lithium
    Carbonate]
Lithium carbonate 300-mg tablets
    [Lithane® (Dome), Phillips-Roxane Lithium Carbonate, Lithotabs® (Rowell)]
Lithium carbonate 300-mg slow-release tablets
    [Lithobid® (CIBA)]
Lithium citrate concentrate of 8 mEq/5 ml
    [Cibalith-5® (CIBA), Phillips-Roxane Lithium Citrate Syrup]

F. Preparations and Dosage

In the United States, lithium comes mostly as a carbonate salt in oral preparations of 300 mg (8.12 mEq). This dosage and composition usually meet most clinical needs (see Table 4). However, a few patients exhibit sensitivities to various preparations.

In Individuals Who Develop Adverse Reactions

1. Further divide doses by administering portions of scored tablets.
2. Switch between tablets and capsules (or vice versa).
3. Administer lithium citrate syrup (to try a different salt) or give smaller doses.
4. Give slow-release tablets to minimize serum level fluctuations.

V. CLINICAL APPLICATIONS

A. Diagnostic Evaluation

Prior to instituting lithium treatment, the clinician should carefully assess and diagnose the nature and severity of the disorder. In particular, he should search for the symptoms of bipolar affective disorder, schizoaffective illness, or recurrent unipolar depression (see Table 1). However, many patients do not exhibit typical bipolar symptoms. Instead, their symptoms may be indistinguishable from schizophrenia, or they may have an unusual presentation (e.g., irritability, anger, and distractability). In addition to making a primary diagnosis, the practitioner should familiarize himself with the factors that help predict outcome. He also should assess current stressors and precipitating events; psychodynamic, characterologic, and interpersonal issues; and ego strengths and environmental resources. The development of an initial rapport that contributes to a growing therapeutic relationship occurs simultaneously with this information-gathering process.

Some patients with cyclic affective disorders should be considered for maintenance therapy. The following individuals have the greatest likelihood of developing recurrent episodes:

1. Two affective episodes in any 2-year period.
2. Three or more affective episodes in a patient's history.
3. Onset of illness after the age of 30.

The presence of two of these factors strongly indicates the need for lithium. Patients with one factor might also receive medication. However, in clinical practice, decision making is more complex. Some individuals with severe affective episodes might benefit from medication even if they do not fit the above criteria. Others with milder symptoms, shorter episodes, or a good response to alternative treatments should be followed before submitting them to the potential risks of long-term maintenance. In each case, the clinician must exercise his judgment about the appropriateness of lithium treatment and provide ongoing care and support.

Factors Predicting Lithium Responsiveness

1. Positive response
    a. Cyclothymic personality features
    b. Family history of mania
    c. Response of family member to lithium
    d. Prior manic episode
    e. Onset of illness with mania
    f. Alcohol abuse
    g. Florid psychotic features in both manic and depressive episodes
    h. Euphoria and grandiose delusions
    i. Diagnosis of primary affective disorder
2. Negative response
    a. Rapid cycling (more than four episodes/year)
    b. Thought disorder with depression and paranoia
    c. Anxiety
    d. Obsessive features
    e. Onset after age 40

Eventually, researchers may develop biochemical criteria for prediciting who will respond to lithium. Already, investigators have correlated clinical effectiveness with various factors including lithium retention, the serum calcium/magnesium ratio (i.e., >2.62 in responders), a marked increase in serum magnesium during the initial phase of lithium therapy,[40] and an increased erythrocyte/plasma lithium ratio (>0.5 in responders).[19] These results are experimental and need further clinical validation.

B. Medical Evaluation

The clinician should complete a medical history, including a review of organ systems and a physical examination, before starting lithium therapy. The patient should be screened for pregnancy, thyroid disease, epilepsy, renal disease, cardiovascular disease, and evidence of brain damage. If the patient has any of these conditions, lithium should be administered more cautiously. Significant renal disease, cardiac disease, brain damage, and pregnancy (particularly in the first trimester) represent relative contraindications for lithium therapy.

Appropriate Medical Screening

1. Base-line complete blood count
2. Base-line ECG
3. Urinalysis, BUN, electrolytes
4. Estimate of 24-hr creatinine
5. 12-hr dehydration test
6. Serum TSH, T_4, T_4I, RT_3, and thyroid antibodies
7. Fasting blood sugar

C. Initiating Treatment

The therapeutic relationship provides a foundation for all drug therapies. In acute situations, a caretaker may use his position to establish quick rapport and, when necessary, to confront or limit set. His initial approach should include various crisis intervention techniques such as mobilization of environmental resources. Involvement of persons close to the patient generally increases medication compliance. However, maintenance therapy requires the formation of a trusting collaboration between clinician and patient. With many patients, open discussion about the illness sets the tone for the ongoing dialogue. Most individuals have some trouble accepting their illness and its possible ramifications. Therefore, the clinician should try to understand how the affective episodes impact on the patient's life. He should explore how each episode has interfered with the patient's relationships and major roles.

During the early phase of treatment, patients with bipolar illness most often want to know:

1. Where did I get it?
2. Is my problem permanent?
3. What is the treatment?
4. How effective is therapy?

These queries frequently encompass more fundamental, but less obvious, concerns about control, dependency, personal defectiveness, and "loveableness" in personal relationships. Therefore, the clinician should try to clarify both the explicit and implicit concerns and requests before providing answers that might close off continued discussion. No matter what course is taken, however, discussion of the potentially inherited nature of bipolar illness and its possible chronic course should be coupled closely with explanations about the effectiveness of lithium maintenance and the importance of the therapeutic relationship. Establishing an open relationship may take many months. The clinician should encourage the patient to become an active partner in maintenance therapy. For example, the patient (and sometimes the family) should take responsibility for detecting emerging hypomanic and depressive symptoms. The clinician and patient together should delineate a list of symptoms that are early manifestations of the patient's affective illness and require immediate clinical contact (like sleeplessness, spending extra money, or anorexia). Also, the patient should be informed about medical conditions that might affect the lithium level.

Reasons to Contact the Physician for a Lithium Level

1. Signs of toxicity, including nausea, vomiting, diarrhea, increasing fatigue, or mental dullness.
2. Symptoms of mania, including euphoria, irritability, hyperactivity, inappropriate actions, inability to complete tasks, persistent insomnia.
3. Symptoms of depression, including lowered mood, self-deprecating behavior, guilt, decreased activity, insomnia, weight loss, poor appetite.
4. Changes in dose.
5. The development of medical disease, particularly those that cause fever or diarrhea.
6. Significant increases in sweating (e.g., move or visit to a warmer climate or marked increase in exercise).
7. The institution of steroids, diuretics, antipsychotic drugs, or sodium bicarbonate.

8. Question of pregnancy.
9. Change in salt intake or diet.
10. Signs of thyroid deficiency.

The discussion of these aspects of treatment often stimulates other questions, including:

1. How long will treatment last?
2. How will we know when to stop lithium?
3. What are the risks of treatment?
4. How will I feel on the medicine?
5. Does lithium interact with other drugs?

Again, these questions should be answered only after determining what they mean to the patient and how he will use the information. In addition, the clinician has a human and legal responsibility to discuss adverse reactions and potential toxicity (see Table 5), alternative treatments, limitations of maintenance therapy, and long-term prognosis.

D. Bipolar Affective Disorder

1. Acute Manic Episode

To contain behavioral symptoms and begin lithium treatment, the acutely manic patient probably should be hospitalized. The usual initial treatment regimen consists of both an **antipsychotic drug and lithium.** However, because of reports of increased adverse reactions and occasional neurotoxicity, controversy exists over combining these agents. **Haloperidol** works best for acute behavioral excitement and the disorganized thinking of manic psychosis. Some investigators claim that haloperidol has specific antimanic properties, but most agree that all of the commonly used antipsychotic drugs in large enough doses can contain acute psychotic states. However, haloperidol is a potent neuroleptic with a wide dosage range and can be parenterally administered.

Severely agitated and disorganized patients who require immediate behavioral control may be managed by **rapid neuroleptization;** this involves administering divided doses of haloperidol every few hours until high doses are reached. Rapid, high-dose medication, however, should be reserved for selected patients, since severe adverse reactions (e.g., laryngospasm) and death can occur. Practitioners may use other antipsychotic agents if the patient develops serious adverse reactions to haloperidol. Chlorpromazine is often given, but in high doses it may cause cardiovascular effects such as severe postural hypotension (see Chapter 4).

TABLE 5. Adverse Reactions to Lithium

Initial	Potentially indicative of toxicity (*cont.*)
Nausea and vomiting	Slurred speech
Diarrhea	Confusion
Lethargy	Vertigo
Drowsiness	Coarse tremor and twitching
Muscle weakness	Muscle weakness
Fine tremor	Persistent but benign
Increased thirst (polydipsia)	Increased thirst
Increased urination (polyuria)	Increased urination
Potentially indicative of toxicity	Fine tremor
Nausea, vomiting, diarrhea	Weight gain
Drowsiness and mental dullness	Edema

Lithium may more specifically resolve manic symptoms than antipsychotic drugs. Unfortunately, lithium usually takes 5 to 14 days to work. When a crisis approach and/or a therapeutic relationship helps to contain the patient, lithium alone may suffice. However, individuals who need behavioral control may need an antipsychotic agent coadministered with lithium. Each clinician should remember that antipsychotic drugs suppress mania but leave many patients internally disorganized. Therefore, the clinician may find it necessary to prescribe combined or overlapping drug regimens for a substantial period of time. Usually, the clinician determines if the lithium is having an adequate antimanic effect by gradually decreasing the antipsychotic after achieving both behavioral control and therapeutic serum levels of lithium (i.e., from 0.8 to 1.3 mEq/liter).

In general, if the patient is stable, start withdrawing haloperidol after about 5 days of lithium therapy. Tapering the drug usually requires 1 to 2 weeks. The clinician can assess whether or not manic symptoms are reappearing by carefully evaluating the patient's feelings and thoughts. Many manic patients, in fact, will report racing thoughts even when they appear calm.

Initially, practitioners should prescribe lithium in divided doses, follow the serum levels, and then increase the amount as necessary. Cooper et al. have reported an accurate method for quickly predicting lithium dosage requirements.[41,42] They administer a priming dose of 600 mg lithium with 100 cc water and, after 24 hr, determine the serum lithium level. By using a table, the clinician can then accurately predict the amount of lithium that produces a blood level necessary to manage acute mania. Administering a higher initial dose may save time and diminish suffering. However, in clinical practice, this method often does not work. Most laboratories are not reliable enough; many patients are not cooperative enough; and other factors (such as coadministered drugs) can result in a "false" level.[43]

As a general rule, the clinician should start lithium in three divided 300-

mg doses on the first day of treatment. On day 2, he may increase the dose to 1200 to 1800 mg, depending on the clinical state and physical health of the patient. Doses of lithium should always be divided because of the high frequency of unwanted effects related to large serum fluctuations. Giving medication following meals can also diminish initial adverse reactions. During manic episodes, patients might require three to four times more lithium than nonmanic patients to maintain a specific blood level (although this is controversial). This level of medication should be maintained for the first week, while equilibration occurs. The clinician should follow blood levels and note the clinical response to that dose. This regimen usually results in blood levels of 0.8 to 1.4 mEq/liter.

The clinician should obtain lithium serum levels on day 3 or 4 and on day 7 of acute treatment. Each level should be measured 12 hr after the last lithium dose. In the initial phase of therapy, the dosage requirement may vary significantly with the clinical state of the patient. The practitioner may need to monitor the serum lithium once or twice a week until the patient's symptoms and dosage level stabilize. Each change requires a full week to equilibrate. Because the excretion of lithium is quite rapid, each full day without lithium produces a drop in the blood level of about one-half. Therefore, if a patient has missed a few doses, a low serum level does not give the clinician any relevant information about that particular patient's previous steady-state level. If the patient has taken lithium within 4 hr of the determination, an increase over the steady-state level of about 0.2 mEq/liter will occur. Therefore, if a quick estimate is necessary, a lithium level can be obtained and the dosage corrected.

The patient in poor physical health may still tolerate maintenance lithium. The clinician can administer one tablet a day for the first week, with every-other-day lithium determinations. After about 1 week, a steady state occurs. The clinician can then add another tablet each day and frequently determine serum lithium levels. This procedure should be followed until a low prophylactic level of 0.5 to 0.8 mEq/liter is reached.

After a clinical effect has occurred, the patient's lithium requirement might decrease. In fact, toxic levels may result from keeping compensated patients on the dosage schedule for acute mania.

After the first week, lithium levels should be determined weekly for a few weeks and then once a month. When the manic episode resolves, the clinician must make a decision about maintenance therapy. If a patient has had very infrequent episodes, or if the present episode is the first, lithium should be continued for the projected length of a manic episode (usually about 6 months) and then discontinued.

2. Hypomania

Clinicians often can begin lithium treatment in hypomanic patients without hospitalization. Lithium is relatively easy to start once the patient has been medically cleared. Give 300 mg of lithium carbonate twice or three times a day for 1 week and then draw a serum level. Inform the patient about the blood-drawing procedure and instruct him to allow 10 to 12 hr between the last dose and the serum measurement. For each dosage change, a steady-state level is achieved after 1 week. After drawing the first serum level, the clinician can usually estimate a maintenance dose. In maintenance therapy, 0.5 to 1.0 mEq/liter is the usual effective range, although 0.4 mEq/liter may maintain some patients, whereas others may require 1.2 mEq/liter.

During the first week of therapy, the initial administration of lithium has few risks because of rapid clearance and low total dosage. Therefore, telephone contact or short office visits usually suffice unless the patient requires additional support and reassurance. Gastrointestinal symptoms are common during initial treatment and during dosage shifts. If these symptoms are severe, however, smaller doses or a different preparation may help. If the dose is changed, another serum level should be obtained a week later. Once the desired level is reached, monthly checks are adequate. The clinician should remember that hypomanic and manic persons retain lithium. Therefore, before the number of serum levels is diminished, the patient's mood should be stable. For fully stabilized patients, the clinician can obtain lithium levels every 3 months. In any patient on lithium, and particularly in those stopping medication, the caretaker should educate the patient and relatives about the signs of incipient mania and the ability of lithium to abort a manic episode. Some patients may want to carry a wallet card indicating their condition.

Lithium may provide dramatic relief for both manic and hypomanic symptoms. However, a maintenance regimen for the treatment of acute affective episodes may require the administration of lithium for 12 to 18 months before the clinician can determine its effectiveness.

3. Maintenance Therapy

The practitioner must shift his therapeutic stance when introducing the possibility of a maintenance regimen to a patient. Many clients are, in essence, "well patients" who can and must have a responsible role in treatment. In fact, only the patient can control many of the vital aspects of therapy. Therefore, the clinician should openly discuss with the patient the nature of the affective illness and the clinical effects and pharmacokinetics of lithium. He should also inform the patient about possible adverse reactions, normal precautions, and the importance of monitoring the serum lithium (see Table 5). For example, the patient should be advised to maintain a stable salt intake and contact the physician when there are significant changes in salt balance [e.g., after marked sweating, diarrhea from an illness, institution of a low-sodium diet, when another medication is coadministered (particularly diuretics), or when pregnancy is planned or expected]. The patient also should be told about common adverse effects: hand tremor, gastrointestinal upset, polydipsia and polyuria, and weight gain. In addition, patients should be instructed to stop lithium and contact the physician if any of these symptoms persist or get worse, or if dizziness, drowsiness, slurred speech, or ataxia appear. Sometimes, we give patients a "log" to highlight important information, reinforce their role, and provide a means of following their treatment. The development of a collaborative relationship usually instills feelings of confidence and competence and improves compliance.

At least in some individuals, symptoms are precipitated by stressful events. Therefore, many patients benefit from treatment that helps to alter a negative self-image or a destructive relationship to their environment. In all instances, a trusting, constant, collaborative helping relationship is prerequisite. Moreover, formal psychotherapy may sometimes offer the patient a more self-directed means of preventing, suppressing, understanding, or resolving some of the affective symptoms.

In practice, clinicians may start maintenance lithium (as described in Section V.D.2) or achieve a maintenence regimen by reducing the drug from the high levels used to treat mania. Stabilized patients usually require about ½ mEq/kg of body weight per day (about 900 to 1500 mg) to maintain serum levels between 0.5 and 1.0 mEq/liter. This level, however, varies widely among patients and requires individual titration. Once a patient equilibrates on a maintenance schedule, lithium levels remain remarkably constant. After once-a-week and then once-a-month checks for the first year, the clinician can check serum lithium approximately every 3 months.

In any chronic drug treatment **practitioners should provide the lowest possible effective dose, the least total amount of medication, and the simplest regimen.** Although no specific guidelines exist, physicians have successfully prescribed twice-a-day dosages (particularly with the new slow-release preparation)[44] and lower maintenance doses (yielding serum levels less than 0.5 mEq/liter). Studies and clinical experience, however, have not yet clarified the effects of these altered schedules.

Because of the evidence that lithium can cause hypothyroidism and structural damage to the kidney, **clinicians should intermittently evaluate thyroid and renal functioning.** A consensus about appropriate tests and their timing does not exist. However, we recommend a measure of creatinine clearance (which can be calculated from a serum creatine by the Cockcroft–Gault formula) and a 12-hr dehydration test (to measure tubular concentrating ability) every 6 months and a thyroid-stimulating hormone (TSH) level every 12 months. In addition, patients with polydipsia and polyuria (greater than 3 liters/day) should be checked more frequently for renal impairment. In individuals with renal damage, the clinician must weigh the risks of further kidney damage against the potential morbidity caused by affective episodes.

In addition, the potential for kidney damage with chronic use and the possibility, although rare, of sudden death in patients with significant cardiac disease highlight the importance of administering the lowest possible doses or perhaps even discontinuing treatment under certain circumstances.[1,2] At present, only impressionistic and anecdotal reasons have been given for stopping successful chronic medication regimens. These include character changes, identification and avoidance of specific environmental precipitants, or formation of a patient–therapist alliance capable of identifying premonitory symptoms. However, the criteria must be very strict, and the therapeutic relationship stable, since up to 90% of those with bipolar illness who discontinue lithium may have a recurrence.[45]

E. Acute Depressive Episode

The clinician should treat patients with bipolar illness who develop an acute depression with **antidepressants or ECT.** Although heterocyclics are used most often, some authorities feel that MAOIs may be most effective for the depressions of bipolar illness. Occasionally, antidepressants can cause a mood reversal, resulting in mania. Although studies indicate that lithium can prevent depressive episodes, it does not have powerful antidepressant properties. Some reports indicate that heterocyclics may be more effective when coadministered with lithium. Although clinicians should generally try to avoid polypharmacy, in depressed patients, lithium usually can be continued during antidepressant therapy.

F. Recurrent Depression

Lithium maintenance therapy effectively prevents depression in many patients with recurrent unipolar episodes (although this application is not presently FDA approved). The clinician should follow the usual procedure for maintenance therapy. In addition, maintenance antidepressant drugs may be as effective as lithium in these individuals. Therefore, clinicians have two drug choices for preventive therapy that have very different pharmacological properties.[46,47] For most patients, antidepressants cause fewer adverse effects. However, we must await the completion of studies in progress to learn about selective usage of these two regimens.

G. Schizoaffective Disorder

Differentiating among schizophrenia, schizoaffective disorder, and manic–depressive illness is often difficult. Some patients who are initially diagnosed as manic–depressive ultimately develop schizophrenia. At least some cases of schizoaffective illness may be variants of the affective disorders and not a discrete illness or a subtype of schizophrenia. This is suggested, in part, by the fact that manic–depressive patients with schizoaffective relatives are more likely to respond to lithium than patients without schizoaffective relatives. Differentiating among diagnostic groups is important in clinical practice, since some authorities believe that lithium can produce neurotoxic effects and a worsening of psychotic symptoms in selected schizophrenic patients.[48] However, lithium is effective in many cases of "atypical" mania that may have a clinical picture indistinguishable from a schizoaffective disorder. Therefore, lithium is clearly indicated for manic states with psychotic symptoms and should be used with caution in patients with schizophrenic disorders.

When a patient develops cyclic mood swings in which the psychotic symptoms are disproportionate to the mood disturbance, the nature of the primary problem (i.e., thought disorder vs. mood disorder) becomes clouded. However, the probability of positive clinical outcome usually outweighs the risk of developing an organic brain syndrome, an exacerbation of the psychotic symptoms, or even possible brain damage. "Neurotoxicity" seems to occur only rarely in patients with an underlying schizophrenic disorder. Therefore, patients with schizoaffective illness should receive the same treatment as those with bipolar disease.

In the group of responders, lithium stabilizes the mood swings and contains the aggressive behavior but may not eliminate the thought disorder. These results are less satisfactory than those with more typical cases, but the treatment may be more effective and certainly is more benign than the long-term use of antipsychotic agents. Occasionally, the clinician should add antipsychotic medication to lithium in patients whose affect becomes normal but whose thoughts remain disordered. For these patients, the combined maintenance regimen requires careful monitoring to assess each drug's effect and to detect possible adverse reactions.

H. Other Possible Applications

1. Emotionally Unstable Character Disorders

Studies have not demonstrated conclusively that lithium effectively treats any disorder other than mania, manic–depressive illness, and unipolar depressions. However, clinicians have occasionally reported impressive results in other cyclic disorders, particularly hyperaggressive components of character disorders, brain-damaged children, temporal lobe seizures, and even schizophrenia.[6] These preliminary results may indicate that lithium has antiaggressive as well as antimanic properties. The clinician may administer a clinical trial of lithium if all other treatment modalities have failed and if the probability of morbidity from lithium is very low.

2. Premenstrual Tension

This periodic disorder is characterized by a sense of physical discomfort and irritability. In its extreme form, patients may exhibit periods of agitation alternating with depression. Occasionally, this disorder markedly diminishes the quality of the patient's life. Although double-blind studies indicate that lithium helps no more than placebo, 900 mg in divided oral doses given for 1 week starting 10 days prior to the expected onset of menstruation has proven effective in occasional patients.[49]

VI. CONCLUSION

The clinician faces a challenging task in planning appropriate therapies for patients with bipolar illness and recurrent depressions. Research demonstrates that mania and hypomania respond impressively to lithium therapy, and that the mood swings of both bipolar illness and recurrent depressions are diminished with maintenance treatment. Occasionally, lithium also helps other cyclic psychiatric disturbances. However, in practice, the clinician has a broader mandate than giving drugs. He must combine knowledge about medication and diagnoses within the context of a therapeutic relationship. Each practitioner must also understand the unique characteristics of lithium, such as the proximity of therapeutic and toxic doses and the nature of common adverse reactions (particularly thyroid, renal, and neurological). In addition, caretakers must tailor trials of lithium and other medications (e.g., antipsychotics and antidepressants) to fit the clinical syndrome and the emotional needs and medical characteristics of each patient. By combining these elements, the clinician can provide successful and gratifying therapy for most individuals with bipolar illness and recurrent depressions.

REFERENCES

1. Cade J. F. J.: Lithium salts in the treatment of psychotic excitement. *Med J Aust* 11:349–352, 1949.
2. Davis J. M.: Overview: Maintenance therapy in psychiatry: II. Affective disorders. *Am J Psychiatry* 133:1–13, 1976.
3. Forn J., Valdecasas F. G.: Effects of lithium on brain adenyl cyclate activity. *Biochem Pharmacol* 20:2773–2779, 1971.
4. Gjessing L. R.: Lithium citrate loading of a patient with periodic catatonia. *Acta Psychiatr Scand* 43:372–375, 1967.
5. Kline N. S., Wren J. C., Cooper T. B., et al: Evaluation of lithium therapy in chronic and periodic alcoholism. *Am J Med Sci* 268:15–22, 1974.
6. Rifkin A., Quitkin F., Carrillo R., et al: Lithium carbonate in emotionally unstable character disorder. *Arch Gen Psychiatry* 27:519–522, 1972.

7. Gottfries C. G.: The effect of lithium salts on various kinds of psychiatric disorders. *Acta Psychiatr Scand* [*Suppl*] 203:157–167, 1968.

8. American Psychiatric Association: *Diagnostic and Statistical Manual of Mental Disorders*, ed 3 (*DSM–III*). Washington, American Psychiatric Association, 1980, pp 202, 208–217.

9. Nurnberger J. R., Roose S. P., Dunner D. L., et al: Unipolar mania: A distinct clinical entity? *Am J Psychiatry* 136:1420–1423, 1979.

10. Fieve R. R.: The lithium clinic: A new model for the delivery of psychiatric services. *Am J Psychiatry* 132:1018–1022, 1975.

11. Weissman M. M., Prusoff B. A., DiMascio A., et al: The efficacy of drugs and psychotherapy in the treatment of acute depressive episodes. *Am J Psychiatry* 136:555–558, 1979.

12. Ballenger J. C., Post R. M., Bunney W. E.: Carbamazepine in manic–depressive illness: A new treatment. *Am J Psychiatry* 137:782–790, 1980.

13. Okuma T., Inanaga K., Otsuki S., et al: Comparison of the antimanic efficacy of carbamazepine and chlorpromazine: A double-blind controlled study. *Psychopharmacology* 66:211–217, 1979.

14. Ananth J., Pecknold J. C.: Prediction of lithium response in affective disorders. *J Clin Psychiatry* 39:95–100, 1978.

15. Garfinkel P. E., Stancer H. C., Persad E.: A comparison of haloperidol, lithium carbonate and their combination in the treatment of mania. *J Affect Disord* 2:279–288, 1980.

16. Prien R. F., Caffey E. M. Jr, Klett C. J.: Comparison of lithium carbonate and chlorpromazine in the treatment of mania. *Arch Gen Psychiatry* 26:146–152, 1972.

17. Fieve R. R.: Overview of therapeutic and prophylactic trials with lithium in psychiatric patients, in Gershon S., Shopsin B. (eds): *Lithium. Its Role in Psychiatric Research and Treatment*. New York, Plenum Press, 1973, p 336.

18. VanPutten T.: Why do patients with manic–depressive illness stop their lithium? *Compr Psychiatry* 16:179–183, 1975.

19. Mendels J.: Lithium in the treatment of depression. *Am J Psychiatry* 133:373–378, 1976.

20. Schou M., Anderson A., Eskajaer-Jensen S., et al: Occurrence of goiter during lithium treatment. *Br J Med* 3:710–713, 1968.

21. Emerson C. H., Dyson W. L., Utiger R. D.: Serum thyrotropin and thyroxin concentration in patients receiving lithium carbonate. *J Clin Endocrinol Metab* 36:338–346, 1973.

22. Jefferson J. W.: Lithium carbonate-induced hypothyroidism—its many faces. *JAMA* 242:271–272, 1979.

23. VanderVelde C. D., Gordon M. W.: Manic–depressive illness, diabetes mellitus and lithium carbonate treatment. *Arch Gen Psychiatry* 21:478–485, 1969.

24. Singer T., Rotenberg D.: Mechanism of lithium action. *N Engl J Med* 289:254–260, 1973.

25. Angrist B. M., Gershon S., Levitan S. J., et al: Lithium-induced diabetes insipidus-like syndrome. *Compr Psychiatry* 11:141–146, 1970.

26. Rabin E. Z., Garston R. G., Weir R. V., et al: Persistent nephrogenic diabetes insipidus associated with long-term lithium carbonate therapy. *Can Med Assoc J* 121:194–198, 1979.

27. Levy S. T., Forrest J. W. Jr, Heninger G. R.: Lithium-induced diabetes insipidus: Manic symptoms, brain and electrolyte correlates, and chlorothiazide treatment. *Am J Psychiatry* 130:1014–1018, 1973.

28. New C., Manschreck T. C., Flocks J. M.: Renal damage associated with long-term use of lithium carbonate. *J Clin Psychiatry* 40:460–463, 1979.

29. Hestbech H., Hansen H. E., Amdisen H., et al: Chronic renal lesions following long-term treatment with lithium. *Kidney Int* 12:205–213, 1977.

30. Coppen A., Bishop M. E., Bailey J. E., et al: Renal function in lithium and non-lithium-treated patients with affective disorders. *Acta Psychiatr Scand* 62:343–355, 1980.

31. Cockcroft D. W., Gault M. H.: Predictors of creatinine clearance from serum creatinine. *Nephron* 16:31–41, 1976.
32. Shopsin B., Gershon S.: Pharmacology–toxicology of the lithium ion, in Gershon S., Shopsin B. (eds): *Lithium: Its Role in Psychiatric Research and Treatment*. New York, Plenum Press, 1973, pp 107–146.
33. Schou M.: Electrocardiographic changes during treatment with lithium and with drugs of the imipramine type. *Acta Psychiatr Scand [Suppl]* 169:258–259, 1963.
34. Roose S. P., Nurnberger J. L., Dunner D. L., et al: Cardiac sinus node dysfunction during lithium treatment. *Am J Psychiatry* 136:804–806, 1979.
35. Jaffe C. M.: First-degree atrioventricular block during lithium carbonate treatment. *Am J Psychiatry* 134:88–89, 1977.
36. Worthley L. J. C.: Lithium toxicity and refractory cardiac arrhythmia treated with intravenous magnesium. *Anesth Intens Care* 2:357–360, 1974.
37. Jefferson J. W., Griest J. H.: Adverse reactions—neurological tremor, in Jefferson, J. W., Griest, J. H. (eds): *Primer of Lithium Therapy*. Baltimore, Williams & Wilkins, 1977, pp 139–150.
38. Ghandirian A. M., Lehman H. E.: Neurological side effects of lithium: Organic brain syndrome, seizures, extrapyramidal side effects, and EEG changes. *Compr Psychiatry* 21:327–335, 1980.
39. Vestergaard P., Amdison A., Schou M.: Clinically significant side effects of lithium treatment: A survey of 237 patients in long-term treatment. *Acta Psychiatr Scand* 62:193–200, 1980.
40. Carmen J. S., Post R. M., Teplitz T. A., et al: Divalent cations in predicting antidepressant response to lithium. *Lancet* 2:1454, 1974.
41. Cooper T. B., Bergner P. E. E., Simpson G. M.: The 24-hour serum lithium level as a prognosticator of dosage requirements. *Am J Psychiatry* 130:601–603, 1973.
42. Cooper T. B., Simpson G. M.: The 24-hour serum lithium level as a prognosticator of dosage requirements: A 2-year follow-up study. *Am J Psychiatry* 133:440–442, 1976.
43. Naiman I. F., Muniz C. E., Steward R. B., et al: Practicality of a lithium dosing guide. *Am J Psychiatry* 138:1369–1371, 1981.
44. Cooper T. B., Simpson G. M., Lee H., et al: Evaluation of slow-release lithium carbonate formulation. *Am J Psychiatry* 135:917–922, 1978.
45. Jamison K. R., Gerner R. H., Goodwin T. K.: Patient and physician attitudes toward lithium. *Arch Gen Psychiatry* 138:1369–1371, 1981.
46. Prien R. F., Klett C. J., Caffey E. M.: Lithium carbonate and imipramine in the prevention of affective disorders. *Arch Gen Psychiatry* 29:420–425, 1973.
47. Schou M.: Lithium as a prophylactic agent in unipolar affective illness. *Arch Gen Psychiatry* 36:849–851, 1979.
48. Shopsin B., Gershon S.: Pharmacology–toxicology of the lithium ion, in Gershon S., Shopsin B. (eds): *Lithium. Its Role in Psychiatric Research and Treatment*. New York, Plenum Press, 1973, pp 107–147.
49. Sletten I. N., Gershon S.: The premenstrual syndrome: A discussion of pathophysiology and treatment with lithium. *Compr Psychiatry* 7:197–199, 1966.

4

Psychoses

ALAN J. GELENBERG, M.D.

I. INTRODUCTION

The focus of this chapter is on antipsychotic agents—drugs also known as neuroleptics, antischizophrenic agents, and major tranquilizers (a misnomer). This pharmacological family has become a mainstay in the treatment of schizophrenia and other psychotic disorders as well as many nonpsychotic conditions. We deal primarily with the phenothiazines and related antipsychotic drugs but briefly discuss various experimental agents. The chapter also describes other approaches to treating psychoses and concludes by discussing future directions.

The most firmly grounded indication for using antipsychotic drugs is in the treatment of schizophrenia. These agents can suppress the more florid and acute symptoms of schizophrenic psychosis such as hallucinations, delusions, other aspects of thought disturbance, and excited, aggressive behavior. In addition, they may alleviate similar symptoms in patients with other syndromes, such as paranoid disorders, schizophreniform disorder, brief reactive psychosis, schizoaffective disorder, atypical psychosis, and psychosis associated with affective disorders such as melancholia and mania. Furthermore, antipsychotic drugs may alleviate psychotic symptoms or excited and assaultive behavior in patients with organic mental disorders, retardation, and childhood psychoses. At times, these ubiquitous chemicals have helped in the treatment of patients with severe pain syndromes and difficult personality disturbances.

The almost never-ending list of disorders treated with antipsychotic agents, which practically spans DSM–III, far exceeds the experimental data base that should ideally bolster clinical practice. The most convincing data

ALAN J. GELENBERG, M.D. • Department of Psychiatry, Harvard Medical School and Massachusetts General Hospital, Boston, Massachusetts 02114.

support the use of these drugs to treat schizophrenic patients. Some experimental evidence also exists suggesting their effectiveness for other disorders such as affective psychoses, but for various illnesses the literature is merely anecdotal. However, even when scientific research has not kept pace with clinical practice, patients continue to require medication; therefore, this chapter discusses the most up-to-date information on the use of these compounds, blending evidence from scientific research with data from clinical experience.

II. OTHER TREATMENTS

A. Nonbiological

A mixture of interpersonal approaches has been developed to treat psychotic individuals. These therapies have been based on varied theoretical frameworks, practical considerations, and common sense. Attempts to dissect experimentally what works from what does not work and under what conditions have been hampered by the heterogeneity of disorders (e.g., schizophrenia) and by difficulties in defining and standardizing therapeutic techniques.

In general, clinicians should treat acutely psychotic patients with respect, concern, and empathy, tempered with appropriate distance, a low-stimulation environment, and clearly delineated rules and limits. Recommended approaches range from supportive to insight-oriented therapy as well as individual, family, and group treatment. The type of psychotherapy recommended by a physician will depend on an assessment of the patient's needs and available resources. When a patient is evaluated, especially for a more insight-oriented approach, particular attention must be given to favorable prognostic factors, prediction of transference regression, and the existence of environmental supports. Supportive treatment aims at minimizing dysfunction and maximizing individual strengths by mobilizing ego resources and the environment. Controlled studies of acute schizophrenic inpatients show that psychotherapy alone does not significantly reduce psychopathology and that drug therapy results in greater short-term improvement. Moreover, shortening the period of acute psychosis by the administration of drugs can mean a better long-term prognosis.[1] Psychotherapy is far more effective in discharged patients who are followed in a comprehensive aftercare program. The benefits of psychotherapy become more apparent after 1 to 2 years of ongoing treatment and if they are evaluated in terms of psychosocial functioning rather than symptom suppression.[2] In the long term, various therapeutic modalities (e.g., psychotherapy, rehabilitation measures, social case work, public health nursing) should be combined with drug therapy to diminish the likelihood of a psychotic relapse and assist the patient to maintain his routine living patterns.

Depending on a patient's personality, internal and external resources, and the nature of the illness, different therapies may provide a number of benefits. For example, for chronic schizophrenic patients, family and individual psychotherapy may help alleviate intrafamilial patterns that exacerbate and precipitate episodes of psychosis. At times, concrete advice and counseling can change a harmful living situation. Similarly, occupational and vocational therapy may expand a patient's job opportunities. A recent review concluded that psychotherapy with schizophrenics was most effective when it was combined with somatic treatment and focused on everyday issues rather than nonspecific psychological concerns.[3] Many patients with mood disorders find the insights gained during psychotherapy helpful in improving their sense of well-being, their marital and family relationships, and their social functioning in general, and possibly in diminishing the impact of their mood swings. Behavioral therapy is often valuable in various psychotic conditions, usually as an adjunct to antipsychotic drugs.

B. Nondrug, Biological

1. Electroconvulsive Therapy

Electroconvulsive therapy (ECT) can play a dramatic, even life-saving, role in the treatment of psychotic depression. It also suppresses acute mania. A wealth of clinical anecdotes testifies to similarly impressive results in many cases of catatonic schizophrenia (however, not all catatonia is schizophrenia, which may cloud the issue[4]). It is possible that ECT may have a role in the treatment of selected schizophrenic patients with other subtypes.[5] However, the efficacy of ECT in the treatment of other forms of schizophrenia is less clear, and treatment courses tend to be longer than in patients with affective illness.

2. Psychosurgery

The frontal lobotomy, used to treat many schizophrenic patients earlier in the century, has largely been abandoned because of an unfavorable risk/benefit ratio. More restrictive psychosurgical procedures, such as cingulotomy, may effectively treat patients with chronic, severe depressions and intractable pain syndromes, but no substantial evidence supports the use of psychosurgery in the treatment of psychosis.[6]

3. Megavitamin Therapy

Although the original idea of using a vitamin (niacin) to treat schizophrenia involved a single agent in pharmacological doses and was based on a rational hypothesis (the transmethylation theory), orthomolecular theories and megavitamin therapy have subsequently become more a cult than a scientifically based clinical approach. The dogma is muddled, the therapeutic approaches chaotic (using a plethora of supposedly "organic" substances), and the scientific grounding virtually nil. Although occasional cases of behavioral disturbances might reflect dietary inadequacies or toxicity (which, in an affluent society, is most likely to reflect food faddism), there is no evidence to suggest that localized cerebral vitamin deficiences or allergies produce schizophrenia or any other form of psychiatric illness.[7] Similarly, although it is conceivable that some neuropsychiatric disturbances may be alleviated by selective dietary chemicals (e.g., lecithin, tyrosine, tryptophan), the approaches used by orthomolecularists and megavitamin therapists are unlikely to be helpful and may, in fact, be harmful (e.g., through the use of contaminated substances sold in "health food" establishments).[8]

III. ANTIPSYCHOTIC DRUGS

A. Introduction and Terms

The introduction of the first antipsychotic drugs—reserpine and the phenothiazines—in the early to mid-1950s revolutionized psychiatry. For the first time, chemotherapy offered more than sedation to acutely disturbed and psychotic patients. Ultimately, antipsychotic drugs helped to diminish the previously sharp increase in the number of hospital beds in the United States occupied by schizophrenic patients. Many of these individuals could now function in their communities with periodic admission to psychiatric units, often in general hospitals. Psychiatric wards became quieter and less violent. The subspecialty of psychopharmacology was born, and many other important classes of psychopharmaceuticals have emerged. Unfortunately, the advent of antipsychotic drugs has not eliminated the problem of chronic schizophrenia. With the passage of the Community Mental Health Centers Act in 1963, President John F. Kennedy mandated a "bold new approach" to the treatment of the mentally ill. However, because of political and fiscal pressures, many severely ill patients were too rapidly "deinstitutionalized" to nonexistent community programs. The sad result has been the re-creation of back wards in the community, with many chronic schizophrenic patients poorly medicated, hardly managed, and barely cared for.[9]

The rauwolfia alkaloid reserpine caused a number of problems, but the effects of the phenothiazine chlorpromazine (Thorazine® and others) were impressive. From this prototypical phenothiazine emerged a host of sister compounds with similar actions and effectiveness but differing in potencies (i.e., milligram dosages) and unwanted effects. During the past three decades, various classes of antipsychotic compounds have been synthesized. They sometimes differ structurally from chlorpromazine but are pharmacologically and clinically similar.

Clinicians and researchers have labeled antipsychotic drugs with various synonyms, but the terms often have resulted in both semantic and conceptual confusion. When they were first used, these pharmaceuticals often were called major tranquilizers. This term developed from the observation that chlorpromazine and reserpine produce somnolence and relaxation and the consequent misbelief that their major action was sedative. However, relatively nonsedating antipsychotic compounds just as effectively combat psychotic symptoms. Moreover, patients often become tolerant to the sedating effects of antipsychotic drugs but not to the antipsychotic effects themselves. Finally, because of the implication that "major tranquilizers" are on a spectrum with, but more powerful than, sedative–hypnotic and antianxiety agents (sometimes called "minor tranquilizers"), this term is best avoided.

Because antipsychotic drugs frequently produce signs of neurological dysfunction, most notably Parkinson's syndrome and other extrapyramidal reactions, the term "neuroleptic" was coined. In fact, researchers originally believed that (1) any drug effective in combating psychosis must produce extrapyramidal effects and (2) in any given patient, the induction of extrapyramidal signs indicated an optimal therapeutic dose. However, based on the following evidence, these assumptions are incorrect:

1. The piperidyl phenothiazine thioridazine (Mellaril®) produces a relatively low incidence of short-term extrapyramidal effects, yet is as effective as any other antipsychotic agent.
2. Clozapine, an experimental dibenzoxazepine compound, is an effective antipsychotic agent which produces few, if any, extrapyramidal effects.
3. Many patients show marked clinical improvement in psychotic symptoms without experiencing parkinsonian signs or related reactions.

Therefore, although all antipsychotic agents on the United States market at the time of this writing are, in fact, neuroleptics, an antipsychotic drug need not be neuroleptic—a fact presenting a challenge for future research. Furthermore, **when treating individual patients, clinicians should try to avoid the emergence of neurological effects.**

B. Effects on Behavior and the Nervous System

In animals, antipsychotic drugs inhibit conditioned avoidance behavior, suppress electrical intracranial self-stimulation, block vomiting and aggression produced by the dopamine agonist apomorphine, and produced cataleptic immobility resembling human catatonia. In early testing, researchers observed that antipsychotic drugs potentiated anesthesia and produced a state called "artificial hibernation." Chlorpromazine, the prototype phenothiazine, did not by itself induce anesthesia but rather promoted sleep and diminished interest in the environment; animals required increased stimulation or motivation to perform tasks. Antipsychotic drugs have relatively little tendency to suppress vital centers in the brainstem: coma, respiratory depression, and cardiovascular collapse are rare, even at very high doses.

In the electroencephalogram (EEG), phenothiazines and other antipsychotic chemicals produce slowing and synchronization and a decrease in arousal-induced changes—effects that are reversed by dopamine agonists. The low-potency agents (e.g., chlorpromazine) also tend to lower the seizure threshold. Clinically, this effect is particularly important in patients predisposed to seizures, such as those with epilepsy, and in individuals undergoing withdrawal from sedative–hypnotic drugs (including alcohol) (see Chapter 11).

Most antipsychotic agents (with thioridazine as an interesting exception) have antiemetic effects. They can protect against the nausea and vomiting that usually follow administration of apomorphine, presumably by blocking the latter's dopamine agonistic effects in the chemoreceptor trigger zone of the medulla.

C. Mechanism of Action

The antipsychotic drugs block dopamine receptors in various pathways within the brain, which probably accounts for their therapeutic effectiveness as well as for some of their more prominent unwanted effects. According to widely held theories, antipsychotic activity depends on the blockage of postsynaptic receptors in dopamine-mediated pathways that run from the midbrain to the limbic system (septal nucleus, the olfactory tubercle, and the amygdala) (see Fig. 1) and to the temporal and frontal lobes of the cerebral cortex. In fact, the effectiveness of antipsychotic drugs in blocking dopamine receptors correlates with their clinical potency (i.e., usual daily doses). Presumably, tolerance to the dopamine-blocking action of antipsychotic drugs does not develop in these mesolimbic and mesocortical pathways, explaining the impression that tolerance does not develop to their antipsychotic efficacy.

Antipsychotic drugs also block dopamine receptors in the pathways from the substantia nigra in the midbrain to the head of the caudate nucleus in the basal ganglia (see Fig. 1). Interruption of communication in this nigrostriatal pathway is thought to account for Parkinson's syndrome—bradykinesia, rigidity, and tremor. In this neuronal network, tolerance to the dopamine-blocking action of the drugs does seem to develop. Chemically blocked dopa-

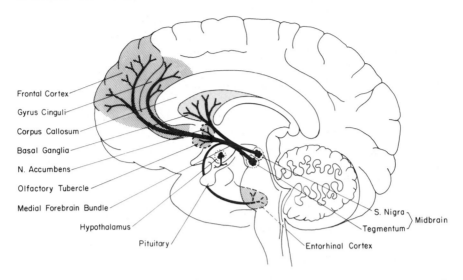

Frontal Cortex
Gyrus Cinguli
Corpus Callosum
Basal Ganglia
N. Accumbens
Olfactory Tubercle
Medial Forebrain Bundle
Hypothalamus
Pituitary
S. Nigra
Midbrain
Tegmentum
Entorhinal Cortex

FIGURE 1. Some dopamine tracts in human brain (longitudinal representation). From Lader.[44]

mine receptors are initially underactive and then become normally active to overactive, developing what is analogous to denervation supersensitivity. Underactivity of the striatal dopamine receptors results in parkinsonian signs; overactivity causes tardive dyskinesia, a syndrome of abnormal involuntary movements. Acetylcholine and γ-aminobutyric acid (GABA) mediate transmission within adjacent connecting neuronal systems. Treatment of both Parkinson's syndrome and tardive dyskinesia may involve drugs purported to act on any or all of these three neurotransmitters (see Section III.G.1.a).

Researchers believe that a third important dopamine pathway, the tuberoinfundibular system, is affected by antipsychotic drugs. It projects from the arcuate nucleus of the hypothalamus to the median eminence, where it acts to inhibit (directly or indirectly) the release of prolactin from the anterior pituitary (see Fig. 1). By blocking dopamine neurotransmission in this system, antipsychotic drugs cause increased prolactin secretion and hyperprolactinemia, producing unwanted effects and possible long-term toxicity (see Section III.G.6). Although researchers have believed that tolerance did not develop to the prolactin-elevating effect of antipsychotic drugs, it now appears that at least partial tolerance may develop over a period of many months and even years. Some have suggested that the elevation of prolactin in plasma could be used as an index of the clinical effectiveness of antipsychotic drugs; however, maximum prolactin elevation occurs at much lower doses than those usually required to treat a psychotic disorder.

Must parkinsonian and hormonal effects accompany antipsychotic activity? The discovery of clozapine, which produced few (or perhaps no) extrapyramidal effects and had only a weak prolactin-elevating action, suggested that the answer is no. Moreover, neurophysiological differences among the dopamine systems can mean that pharmacological agents may act differentially at different dopamine receptors. The goal, then, is to discover new drugs that are more selective dopamine blockers.

The potent effects of antipsychotic agents on the autonomic nervous system explain many of their adverse reactions. They block α-noradrenergic receptors, which probably accounts for their hypotensive action, particularly on a postural basis. At common clinical doses, low-potency antipsychotic drugs tend to be more potent at α-adrenergic receptors and to produce a greater drop in orthostatic blood pressure. The same low-potency agents also cause more sedation, which may reflect α-adrenergic antagonism at brain receptors. Central effects on noradrenergic systems might be involved in antipsychotic activity as well.

Antipsychotic agents block muscarinic acetylcholine receptors, producing other autonomic effects (see Section III.G.2). As a group, antipsychotic drugs tend to be much less potent as anticholinergic agents than the heterocyclic antidepressants* (see Chapter 2). The most potent antimuscarinic drug among antipsychotic agents available in the United States is the phenothiazine thioridazine, which approaches the heterocyclics in anticholinergic activity. High-potency antipsychotic agents act relatively weakly at cholinergic receptors.

Antipsychotic drugs produce other effects on neurotransmission, although their significance is unclear. Similarly to heterocyclic antidepressants, they block the reuptake of norepinephrine, but this effect is probably outweighed by their tendency to antagonize norepinephrine receptors. Antipsychotic drugs also block serotonin and histamine receptors; the latter might account for some of their sedative and appetite-increasing tendencies. Other effects involve β-adrenergic receptors, GABA, and peptide neurotransmitters.

The hypothalamus mediates various antipsychotic drug effects. In addition to effects on prolactin, antipsychotic drugs inhibit the release of growth hormone (which might have implications for their use in children). Some of their effects on autonomic activity may also result from actions within the hypothalamus. Furthermore, they impair the temperature-regulating mechanisms by making the normally homeothermic mammalian system poikilothermic (i.e., the body temperature drifts toward that of the environment), which has resulted in cases of hypo- and hyperthermia. In the extreme, antipsychotic drugs have created what has been termed the neuroleptic malignant

---

*Since many of the currently used thymoleptic drugs are not tricyclic in structure, we have adopted this term to represent the various cyclic antidepressants. From: Baldessarini R. J.: Overview of recent advances in antidepressant pharmacology. Part II. *McLean Hosp J* 7:1–27, 1982.

syndrome (see Section III.G.1.d), also thought to involve the hypothalamus. Increase in appetite, yet another hypothalamic effect, often results in weight gain.

D. Classes and Chemistry

Table 1 presents a list of antipsychotic drugs grouped by chemical classes that are currently available by prescription in the United States. The first group, the phenothiazines (chlorpromazine is the prototype), are three-ring (tricyclic) molecules made up of two benzene rings linked by a sulfur and a nitrogen atom. The nitrogen atom, which is attached to a carbon side chain, determines the phenothiazine subtype. A straight chain of carbon atoms attached to the nitrogen indicates an aliphatic phenothiazine (e.g., chlorpromazine). When the amino nitrogen at the end of the chain is incorporated into a cyclic structure, the molecule is a piperidine (e.g., thioridazine). A somewhat different cyclic structure results in the piperazine phenothiazines [e.g., trifluoperazine (Stelazine®)]. When a piperazine phenothiazine has a terminal hydroxyl (OH) group, esterifying it with a fatty acid results in a highly fat-soluble hybrid that diffuses into the body's adipose tissue, releasing the parent phenothiazine over a period of weeks. Examples are the enanthate and decanoate esters of the piperazine phenothiazine fluphenazine (Prolixin®).

Replacing the nitrogen atom in the central ring with a carbon atom produced a second group of effective antipsychotic substances, the thioxanthenes. They have either aliphatic [e.g., chlorprothixene (Taractan®)] or piperazine [e.g., thiothixene (Navane®)] structures and are chemically and pharmacologically similar to the phenothiazines.

The butyrophenones, developed by Janssen, appear structurally quite different from the phenothiazines but are pharmacologically very similar to the piperazines. The only butyrophenone labeled for antipsychotic use in the United States is haloperidol (Haldol®), although the anesthetic agent droperidol (Inapsine®) also appears to have antipsychotic properties. Closely related to the butyrophenones are the diphenylbutylpiperidines, currently undergoing experimental investigation. This class includes pimozide, an extremely potent blocker of the neurotransmitter dopamine, and penfluridol, which has a prolonged duration of action enabling it to be administered only once weekly by mouth.

The dibenzoxazepine drugs are a fourth antipsychotic group with a three-ring structure. The only member currently labeled as an antipsychotic in the United States is loxapine (Daxolin®, Loxitane®). [The demethylation of loxapine has resulted in amoxapine (Asendin®), a compound with antidepressant properties.] A closely related compound called a dibenzodi-

TABLE 1. Currently Available Antipsychotic Drugs[a]

Nonproprietary name	Trade name	Approximate potency[b]	Available as injectable	Chemical structure/representative agent
Phenothiazines				
Aliphatic				
Chlorpromazine	Thorazine®	1:1	Yes	
Triflupromazine	Vesprin®	4:1	Yes	Chlorpromazine
Piperidine				
Thioridazine	Mellaril®	1:1	No	
Mesoridazine	Serentil®	2:1	Yes	
Piperacetazine	Quide®	10:1	No	
				Thioridazine
Piperazine				
Trifluoperazine	Stelazine®	30:1	Yes	
Acetophenazine	Tindal®	5:1	No	
Butaperazine	Repoise®	10:1	No	
Carphenazine	Proketazine®	4:1	No	
Fluphenazine	Permitil®, Prolixin®	50–100:1[c]	Yes[d]	Trifluoperazine
Perphenazine	Trilafon®	10:1	Yes	
Prochlorperazine	Compazine®	7:1	Yes	
Thioxanthenes				
Chlorprothixene	Taractan®	1:1	Yes	
Thiothixene	Navane®	25:1	Yes	Thiothixene
Butyrophenone				
Haloperidol	Haldol®	50:1	Yes	Haloperidol
Dibenzoxazepine				
Loxapine	Daxolin®, Loxitane®	7:1	Yes	Loxapine
Dihydroindolone				
Molindone	Lidone®, Moban®	10:1	No	Molindone

[a]Adapted from Gelenberg.[43]
[b]Milligram equivalence to chlorpromazine.
[c]Oral only. Potency equivalences not established for long-acting injectable forms. Usual dosage for fluphenazine decanoate is 0.5 to 2.5 ml every 3 to 5 weeks.
[d]Available both as short-acting fluphenazine HCl injection and as long-acting enanthate and decanoate esters.

azepine—clozapine—appears to be a nonneuroleptic antipsychotic (see Section III.K). Researchers are currently investigating other members of this group.

The fifth antipsychotic group, the dihydroindolines, are solely represented at present by molindone (Lidone®, Moban®). Rauwolfia alkaloids, such as reserpine and tetrabenazine, are infrequently used as antipsychotics and are primarily of historical interest.

For a tricyclic antipsychotic to be effective, three carbon atoms must lie between the amino nitrogen and the nitrogen of the center ring. The addition of the electronegative substance to the benzene ring (e.g., Cl, SCH_3, CF_3) enhances its efficacy, whereas the piperazine group on the side chain increases its potency. As a rule, **molecules with greater milligram potency produce less sedation and hypotension but more acute extrapyramidal reactions** (see Table 2).

E. General Principles of Use

How does a clinician choose among the various antipsychotic agents? Most importantly, review the patient's medication history. If the patient has previously responded favorably to a given agent, then try that agent again. In fact, if a patient has been taking a drug for maintenance therapy, and an acute exacerbation occurs during a stressful period, then raising the dose of the drug may diminish the symptoms. However, if a patient has responded unfavorably to a given drug, either because of lack of efficacy or unacceptable adverse effects, avoid that agent. On the other hand, if a patient has had no prior experience with antipsychotic drugs, then use the experiences of a family member as a guide. Failing all of these suggestions, the clinician is free to choose among the agents on the basis of his own experience and the spectrum of adverse effects. In general, the high-potency antipsychotic drugs

TABLE 2. Spectrum of Adverse Effects Caused by Antipsychotic Drugs

Low potency	High potency
Fewer extrapyramidal reactions (especially thioridazine)	More frequent extrapyramidal reactions
More sedation, postural hypotension	Less sedation, postural hypotension
Greater effect on the seizure threshold, electrocardiogram (especially thioridazine)	Less effect on the seizure threshold, cardiovascular toxicity
More likely skin pigmentation and photosensitivity	Fewer anticholinergic effects
Occasional cases of cholestatic jaundice	Occasional cases of neuroleptic malignant syndrome
Rare cases of agranulocytosis	

are less sedating, produce less hypotension, less effect on the seizure threshold, fewer anticholinergic effects, less cardiovascular toxicity, less weight gain, and very little effect on the bone marrow and liver. On the negative side, high-potency antipsychotic drugs have a greater incidence of acute extrapyramidal effects. The converse is true of low-potency agents (see Table 2).

F. Pharmacokinetics

The rate and completeness of absorption of drugs determine the rapidity and intensity of onset of their clinical effects. Orally administered antipsychotic drugs are variably absorbed. When given intramuscularly, the drugs produce higher (four to ten times) and more reliable blood levels at a more rapid rate. Antipsychotic agents are highly lipophilic and bind tightly to protein and body membranes. As with other drugs that cross the blood–brain barrier, they also cross the placental membrane to enter the fetal circulation and are transported into mammalian milk.

The half-life of a drug determines the time required to achieve a steady-state concentration in the body (i.e., the point at which tissue concentrations become stable). Steady state is reached after approximately four half-lives. In addition, drugs with longer half-lives may be administered less frequently, and they disappear from the body more gradually when discontinued following chronic treatment. The half-life of an antipsychotic drug in plasma following a single dose is usually 10 to 20 hr. However, the drug's effects typically persist much longer. When these drugs are administered chronically, the brain and body adipose tissues become saturated; these supplies are then released and excreted very slowly. In addition, when an antipsychotic drug has many metabolites (e.g., chlorpromazine), they are detected in the urine for many months after discontinuation of the drug following chronic administration.

As with most psychotropic drugs, lipophilic parent compounds are oxidized to inactive hydrophilic metabolites largely within microsomal enzymes in the liver. These metabolites are excreted primarily in the urine and to a lesser extent in bile. Metabolism and excretion of antipsychotic drugs are greatest in healthy young people and less at either end of the age spectrum.

The blood levels achieved with antipsychotic drugs following a standard dose vary widely among individuals, which may account for some of the differences in clinical effects. Although close correlations of clinical effects with blood levels have not yet been worked out, such a relationship probably exists. A radioreceptor assay that measures the level of dopamine-blocking action in serum appears very promising.[10]

G. Adverse Effects and Toxicity

1. Neurological

a. Extrapyramidal Syndromes

Antipsychotic drugs may cause four types of extrapyramidal syndromes: acute dystonic reactions, akathisia, Parkinson's syndrome, and, after longer-term use, tardive dyskinesia. This section describes each syndrome and its treatment.

i. Acute Dystonic Reactions.

Acute dystonic reactions, including acute dyskinesias (i.e., abnormal involuntary movements of various types) and oculogyric crises, typically occur during the early hours or days following the initiation of antipsychotic drug therapy or after marked dosage increment. Involuntary muscle contractions are common, particularly about the mouth, jaw, face, and neck. The symptoms are episodic and recurrent, lasting from minutes to hours. There may be trismus ("lockjaw"), dystonia or dyskinesias of the tongue, opisthotonus (spasms of the neck that arch the head backward), or eye closure. In oculogyric crises, there is a dystonic reaction of the extraocular muscles, and gaze is fixed in one position.

Acute dystonic reactions are distressing, particularly to the patient, family member, or clinician who is unfamiliar with them. They may be uncomfortable. They are rarely dangerous. However, in rare cases there can be respiratory compromise with the potential for a fatality.

The diagnosis of acute dystonic reaction is usually not difficult if it is clear that a patient has recently begun taking an antipsychotic drug or has had a switch in the type or dosage of medication. At times, however, eliciting this information may be difficult, for example with patients who are taking prochlorperazine suppositories (and say they are not taking any tranquilizer pills), who do not wish to acknowledge use of antipsychotic drugs, or who have sought antipsychotic drugs for illicit use (described recently). Among the many neuropsychiatric syndromes that must be considered in the differential diagnosis of acute dystonic reactions are tetanus, seizures, and conversion reactions.

The highest-potency antipsychotic drugs have the greatest likelihood of producing acute dystonias, the low-potency agents much less, and thioridazine the least. Young people are at greater risk of developing this syndrome than the elderly, and males more frequently than females. When the acute dystonic reactions are frequent or severe in a patient, it may be worthwhile to assay the serum concentration of calcium, since rare cases of hypocalcemia have been detected in this way.

The mechanism underlying acute dystonic reactions is unclear. One hypothesis is that the syndrome reflects an acute increase in dopamine neurotransmission in the basal ganglia, which transiently supervenes the blockade of dopamine receptors brought about by the same drugs. Although dystonic reactions do not occur in naturally occurring Parkinson's disease (paralysis agitans), they are observed in postencephalitic Parkinson's syndrome which shares other features with antipsychotic drug-induced extrapyramidal reactions.

Although the mechanism may be unclear, the treatment of an acute dystonic reaction is straightforward, readily available, and usually dramatically successful. **Parenteral treatment is preferred for the initiation of drug therapy, with intravenous being more rapid than intramuscular.** The intravenous injection of contraactive medication provides both immediate relief and confirmation of the diagnosis. For this purpose, a number of classes of agents have been employed with considerable success. Some clinicians prefer to use a benzodiazepine intravenously, such as diazepam (Valium®), up to 10 mg. This drug is safe and comfortable and does not add additional anticholinergic effects. As with the injection of any other central depressant compound, equipment for support of the airway should be immediately available, should an emergency occur. Injection should be slow (5 mg of diazepam per minute), and care must be taken to avoid accidental intraarterial injection. Other clinicians prefer to administer an antihistamine drug such as **diphenhydramine (Benadryl®)**, 50 mg. An injectable anticholinergic antiparkinson drug such as **benztropine (Cogentin®)**, 1 mg, or **biperiden (Akineton®)**, 2 mg, also may be used. Even injectable caffeine has been used with success.

Following immediate relief of acute dystonic signs, the clinician may wish to place the patient on an oral dose of one of these same drugs. The lowest effective dose should be used (for range, see Table 3). If this successfully prevents any additional reactions, the contraactive medication can usually be tapered and discontinued within several weeks. Would it be wise to co-administer an antiparkinson drug from the beginning of antipsychotic drug therapy in the hope of avoiding an acute dystonic reaction? To date, there is no definitive answer to this question. Some data, however, suggest that one may afford partial protection to some patients through this "prophylactic" approach.[11] Therefore, the physician may want to consider this approach for patients at highest risk (i.e., young males receiving high-potency antipsychotic agents) and for those in whom a reaction is likely to be clinically disruptive. For most other patients, it makes sense to avoid a drug that may be unnecessary, reserving treatment until signs of dystonia appear.

Physicians, nurses, family members, and anyone else who may observe a patient receiving an antipsychotic medicine should be aware of the possible occurrence of a dystonic reaction early in therapy. Treatment should be readily available. For most patients, the risk of dystonic reactions appears to wane with continued antipsychotic drug therapy.

TABLE 3. Antiparkinson Agents[a]

Generic name	Trade name	Type of drug	Usual dose range (mg per day)	Injectable
Amantadine	Symmetrel®	Dopamine agonist	100 to 300	No
Benztropine	Cogentin®	Antihistamine and anticholinergic	1 to 6	Yes
Biperiden	Akineton®	Anticholinergic	2 to 6	Yes
Diphenhydramine	Benadryl®	Antihistamine and anticholinergic	25 to 200	Yes
Ethopropazine	Parsidol®	Antihistamine and anticholinergic	50 to 600	No
Orphenadrine	Disipal®, Norflex®	Antihistamine	50 to 300	Yes
Procyclidine	Kemadrin®	Anticholinergic	6 to 20	No
Trihexyphenidyl	Artane®, etc.	Anticholinergic	1 to 10	No

[a]Adapted from Wojcik.[15]

ii. **Akathisia.** Akathisia is another extrapyramidal reaction associated with both antipsychotic drugs and postencephalitic Parkinson's syndrome. Akathisia is a symptom (i.e., subjective) defined as a **compulsion to be in motion.** Patients describe an inner restlessness, an intense desire to move about simply for the sake of moving. Persons who are virtually paralyzed by the akinesia of postencephalitic Parkinson's disorder have been known to ask other people to move their limbs, just to relieve this intense compulsion. Patients suffering from akathisia are often observed to pace aimlessly, fidget, and be markedly restless. At times, akathisia can cause a worsening of psychosis.[12]

Akathisia can occur early in the course of drug treatment, or it may not appear for several months. It, too, appears to be more prevalent with high-potency drugs. The natural course of akathisia is less clear than that of acute dystonic reaction: at times it appears to wane, yet some patients are troubled by it for a long time. Its mechanism is obscure.

Treatment responses are variable in these patients. Nevertheless, akathisia is an important syndrome to recognize, as it may severely complicate a patient's response to antipsychotic drug therapy; perhaps most important, it makes patients extremely unhappy. Approaches to treatment include attempts to lower the dose of the antipsychotic drug, to switch to a lower-potency agent, or to add a contraactive drug. The same drugs discussed for the treatment of acute dystonic reactions—anticholinergic antiparkinson agents, antihistamines, and benzodiazepines—also may be tried orally in cases of akathisia, although results are less universally successful (see Section III.G.1.a). Whether the dopamine agonist antiparkinson drug amantadine (Symmetrel®) may play a role in the treatment of this disorder is unclear.

iii. Parkinson's Syndrome. Parkinson's is characterized by a triad of
signs: **tremor, rigidity, and akinesia (or bradykinesia).** The tremor (by definition, a regular and rhythmic oscillation of a body part around a point) is in
the neighborhood of 4 to 8 cycles per second and is greater at rest than during activity. A parkinsonian tremor is often observed in the hands, where the
thumb rubbing against the pad of the index finger may produce a characteristic "pill-rolling" appearance. The tremor also can involve the wrists, elbows,
head, palate, or virtually any body part. In neuroleptic-induced Parkinson's
syndrome, tremor is typically bilateral; unilateral tremors should raise questions about the etiology. Although tremor is very common and may be one of
the earlier signs in naturally occurring Parkinson's disease, it is less common
than rigidity and akinesia and may not appear until relatively late in the
drug-related syndrome.

Rigidity is an increase in the normal resting tone of a body part. It is
detectable only by palpation on physical examination. (In other words, a
patient does not **look** rigid; he must **feel** rigid.) In testing for rigidity, the
physician asks the patient to relax completely and allow body parts to be
manipulated without moving them. The examiner then rotates the head on
the neck, moves the major joints in the upper and lower extremities, and
raises each extremity to note the rapidity with which it falls by gravity. An
increased resistance to passive motion and a slow return from a raised position denote the presence of rigidity. When tremor coexists with rigidity, the
rigidity may take on the feel of a "cogwheel." In extreme forms of the condition, rigidity may mimic (or actually become) the waxy flexibility with sustained postures characteristic of catatonia.[13] In antipsychotic drug-induced
Parkinson's syndrome, rigidity tends to be more common than tremor but less
common than the third sign of the triad—akinesia.

Akinesia is a disinclination to move in the absence of paralysis. Literally, akinesia means the absence of motion, whereas bradykinesia, truer to
the clinical reality in most patients, implies a slowness of motion. The bradykinetic patient frequently shows a masklike facies, with diminished expres-
siveness and less frequent eye blinking.

The bradykinetic patient turns his body "en bloc." Instead of turning
first with the eyes, then with the neck, followed in turn by shoulders, hips,
and lower extremities, the Parkinsonian patient turns as if he were one solid
block of wood, without joints. A typical stance includes a flexing of elbows
and wrists together with a stooped posture. The patient's gait is typically
inclined forward, and he may walk with small, rapid steps (marche a petit
pas). In the extreme forms, bradykinesia, as well as rigidity, may shade into
catatonic immobility.[13]

In a less severe manifestation, the slowed movements of the parkinsonian
patient may appear primarily as apathy, boredom, and a "zombielike"
appearance. If other signs of Parkinson's syndrome are not prominent, this

social akinesia may be misdiagnosed as depression.[14] Together with the major triad of Parkinson's syndrome (tremor, rigidity, and bradykinesia), associated signs often include seborrhea and drooling.

Parkinson's syndrome usually occurs within weeks to months after the beginning of antipsychotic drug therapy. Although tolerance develops in many patients, the disorder may persist and require ongoing treatment in others. Women and the elderly are affected more commonly. Again, the high-potency agents appear more likely to promote this disturbance. Probably a late-occurring variant of Parkinson's syndrome is the so-called rabbit syndrome, in which a rapid tremor of the mouth and jaw are reminiscent of the facial expression of a rabbit. The rabbit syndrome appears to respond pharmacologically similarly to other forms of Parkinson's.

Parkinson's syndrome reflects diminished dopaminergic input from the substantia nigra in the midbrain to the head of the caudate nucleus in the basal ganglia (see Fig. 1). In this extrapyramidal network, neuronal systems employing dopamine as a neurotransmitter are in balance with other systems mediated by acetylcholine and GABA. In naturally occurring forms of Parkinson's syndrome, the dopaminergic defect is a result of the destruction of dopamine-containing neurons in the substantia nigra. This destruction may occur as a result of viral infection (e.g., encephalitis), poisoning (e.g., carbon monoxide, manganese), or for unknown reasons (i.e., Parkinson's disease). In the drug-induced variety, a blockade of the dopamine receptors within the caudate nucleus appears to be responsible for the disturbance.

The treatment of Parkinson's syndrome reflects our understanding of the pathophysiology. One approach is to decrease the dose of the antipsychotic drug, presumably thereby decreasing the degree of dopamine blockade at the synaptic receptor. Alternatively, a less potent antipsychotic agent may be employed.

As mentioned earlier, thioridazine has the lowest incidence of parkinsonian reactions. The reason for this differential effect of antipsychotic drugs in causing Parkinson's syndrome may be related to variations in activity within the several dopamine systems. An alternative explanation is that the agents that produce the fewest extrapyramidal reactions, such as thioridazine, have the most potent effect in blocking acetylcholine, thus acting as if they had inherent antiparkinson activity.

Pharmacological contraactive therapy for parkinsonism consists of attempts either to counterbalance the decreased dopamine neurotransmission by blocking acetylcholine transmission [anticholinergic antiparkinson drugs include benztropine and trihexyphenidyl (Artane®)] or by increasing dopamine neurotransmission (e.g., by the use of amantadine). Other dopamine agonist drugs such as L-DOPA and bromocriptine may be useful in other forms of Parkinson's syndrome but are seldom employed for the drug-induced variety.

Table 3 lists available drugs that are useful for the treatment of drug-induced Parkinson's syndrome. The advantages of using one of these agents prophylactically in a patient receiving antipsychotic drug therapy have been debated, but the question remains unresolved. The alternative is to observe the patient for the development of extrapyramidal signs (including an awareness of the more subtle manifestations) and, if and when they appear, to treat them vigorously. Because of additive untoward effects and toxicity, it may be simpler to use antiparkinson drugs only when necessary and to try to discontinue them (gradually) following several months of successful treatment. (Many patients, however, seem to require continued treatment.)

With the exception of amantadine, all of the antiparkinson drugs listed in the table have anticholinergic and/or antihistaminic properties. Among these drugs, trihexyphenidyl has a relatively short half-life, whereas benztropine has a relatively long half-life. Amantadine is a dopamine agonist that has few anticholinergic effects. This feature may make it preferable in patients particularly sensitive to anticholinergic reactions.[15] Amantadine, 100 mg b.i.d to 100 mg t.i.d., may be effective in some cases of drug-induced Parkinson's syndrome, particularly the more severe variety, when anticholinergic antiparkinson drugs have been ineffectual.[16] Amantadine has a relatively long half-life (approximately 24 hr). It is excreted in the urine unchanged and may lead to toxicity (including psychiatric symptoms) in patients with impaired renal function.

Antiparkinson drugs, as well as other chemicals with anticholinergic activity (e.g., belladonna-containing compounds), have been used for "recreational" purposes.[17] It appears that the anticholinergic activity provides a mood-elevating effect for many people, creating a feeling of euphoria or a "high." Some afficionados of the drug culture actually use the drugs to create a toxic delirium, which they perceive as pleasurable. Many schizophrenic patients treated with antiparkinson drugs become more attached to these drugs than to their antipsychotic agents, possibly because of the relief of extrapyramidal symptoms or perhaps because of directly pleasurable effects. Trihexyphenidyl has been reported to be more commonly abused than other antiparkinson agents. If this is true, it could be related to the pharmacology of the drug or simply to its popularity and therefore, availability. Anticholinergic toxicity and its treatment are described in Section III.G.2.

iv. Tardive Dyskinesia. Tardive dyskinesia is characterized by abnormal, involuntary, choreoathetotic movements involving the tongue, lips, jaw, face, extremities, and occasionally the trunk. Not many years after the introduction of antipsychotic agents, patients were described who displayed these movements after a period of drug treatment. However, many questioned the association between these signs and the use of antipsychotic drugs. Instead, they attributed the movements to senile choreas, other brain disorders, schizophrenic stereotypies and mannerisms, or adventitious mouth movements associated with poor dentition and dry mouth. For the most part, clinicians generally ignored the existence of tardive dyskinesia.

By the early 1970s, however, tardive dyskinesia was recognized as more widespread than hitherto appreciated, and a recent review has even suggested that its prevalence has progressively increased over the years since the introduction of antipsychotic medication.[18] Moreover, epidemiologic evidence and clinical opinion now clearly support a drug-related etiology for tardive dyskinesia which has become a serious concern among psychiatrists, other physicians, allied mental health professions—and lawyers.

Tardive dyskinesia typically involves oro–bucco–lingual masticatory movements. These may include lipsmacking, chewing, puckering of the lips, protrusion of the tongue, and puffing of the cheeks. A common early sign is wormlike movements of the tongue. Other movements of the face can be observed, including grimacing, blinking, and frowning.

In the young, movements sometimes begin in the distal extremities and may consist of rapid, purposeless, quick, jerky movements distally—chorea ("dance")—or more sinuous, writhing movements proximally—athetosis. Occasionally, abnormal movements involve the trunk and pelvis. The signs of tardive dyskinesia can range in intensity from minimal to severe. Patients' awareness of the movements similarly varies. Institutionalized chronic schizophrenic patients may deny even very severe movements, whereas a highly functioning patient with a mood disorder could be extremely troubled by the most minimal symptom. The movements may embarrass the patient and interfere with important activities such as eating, talking, and dressing. In rare instances, tardive dyskinesia can impair breathing and swallowing.

It is generally believed that for tardive dyskinesia to occur, a patient must have been exposed, more or less continuously, to an antipsychotic drug for at least 3 to 6 months, although it is probable that a rare, highly sensitive patient may develop this syndrome after an even briefer period. Presumably, increasing exposure to antipsychotic drugs increases the risk of developing tardive dyskinesia, although if a patient has not developed it after some length of time, he is probably less vulnerable. The only risk factor that has appeared consistently in studies of tardive dyskinesia is advanced age, although wide interindividual sensitivity to the development of this syndrome probably exists. There is no convincing evidence that patients taking one type of antipsychotic drug, such as high or low potency, are more or less likely to develop tardive dyskinesia, although there is a hint that patients receiving long-acting preparations may be somewhat more vulnerable. As mentioned previously, it appears that "drug holidays," i.e., regular abrupt discontinuation of antipsychotic drug therapy, do not appear to reduce the risk of tardive dyskinesia. Although it has been suggested that drug holidays may even increase the risk,[18] this is controversial. Prospective studies are only just beginning to link cumulative dosage to the development of tardive dyskinesia. Nevertheless, the assumption that this association exists lies behind the recommendation to maintain patients on the lowest effective dosage over prolonged periods of time.

Estimates of the prevalence of tardive dyskinesia have varied widely—from 1% to over 50% of patients currently taking these drugs.[19] However, when the most minimal cases are removed from consideration, an attempt is made at differential diagnosis, and a careful and reliable screening procedure is used, the prevalence of tardive dyskinesia in a group of patients maintained on antipsychotic drugs for a variable period of time (i.e., a typical outpatient schizophrenic population) is likely to be about 20%.[20] (A comparable group of patients not treated with antipsychotic drugs may have a prevalence rate of 5%.) A more important question concerns the incidence of tardive dyskinesia; preliminary data suggest 3% per year of patient exposure,[20] at least early in the course. (The incidence must "plateau" at some point, perhaps 10 years.)

The movements of tardive dyskinesia may appear during treatment when a patient is taking a constant dose of an antipsychotic, or they may initially appear when the dosage of the drug is lowered or stopped entirely. Conversely, if movements are present, increasing the dose of an antipsychotic drug can make the movements cease. This latter phenomenon has been referred to as "masking" of the movements and gives rise to the concept of "covert dyskinesia," in other words, dyskinesia observed only when an antipsychotic drug has been discontinued.[21] On the other hand, when an antipsychotic drug is discontinued abruptly, a patient may show transient dyskinetic movements which can disappear in a matter of days or weeks. This phenomenon has been known as withdrawal dyskinesia, and it might conceivably indicate that a patient is vulnerable to a persistent dyskinesia if the medication is reinstituted and continued. Tardive dyskinesia itself is believed to be persistent, although evidence suggests that if the movements are detected early and medication is discontinued, many patients will show gradual improvement over time.[22]

The linkage between early development of Parkinson's syndrome and later development of tardive dyskinesia—as well as possible contributing factors to the development of tardive dyskinesia from earlier use of antiparkinson drugs—is unresolved. What is clear is that anticholinergic drugs frequently exacerbate the movements of tardive dyskinesia once they are present and that administration of anticholinergic agents may even "unmask" latent movements. Conversely, discontinuing an anticholinergic drug in a patient with tardive dyskinesia may improve the movements.

The most widely held hypothesis about the mechanism of tardive dyskinesia involves the nigrostriatal dopamine pathway. Chronic blockade of dopamine receptors within the basal ganglia leads first to receptor underactivity, then to overactivity. In other words, the initial receptor blockade from antipsychotic drugs leads to hypoactivity at the receptor neurons. This state is believed to underlie the genesis of Parkinson's syndrome. Prolonged blockade, however, results in a situation analogous to denervation supersensitivity. In fact, chronic neuroleptic administration to animals has been shown to cause an actual multiplication in the number of postsynaptic receptor sites. Thus, long-term administration of antipsychotic drugs leads ultimately to an increase in activity at postsynaptic dopamine receptors. This state of excessive dopaminergic activity is believed to result in the abnormal movements of disorders such as tardive dyskinesia and Huntington's chorea.[23]

Tardive dyskinesia (and Huntington's chorea) are in many ways the opposite of Parkinson's syndrome: the former is a disorder of extraneous movements, the latter a paucity of movements; the former is thought to reflect dopaminergic overactivity (and relative cholinergic underactivity), whereas the latter is caused by too little dopamine neurotransmission (and relatively too much cholinergic). Pharmacological strategies that tend to make one better frequently make the other worse.

Treatment approaches to tardive dyskinesia are based on our understanding (and beliefs) about the nature of antipsychotic drugs and tardive dyskinesia itself. First, of course, comes primary prevention. This means (1) avoiding unnecessary exposure of patients to antipsychotic drugs. In particular, the use of these agents to treat relatively benign conditions or those that could respond equally well or better to other agents (e.g., anxiety, nonpsychotic depression) should be avoided whenever possible. (2) When it is necessary to employ antipsychotic drug therapy, use the lowest dose for the shortest period of time. Of course, most schizophrenic patients will require prolonged therapy with these agents, but the clinician should find the lowest effective maintenance dose. Similarly, in the treatment of patients with other chronic disorders such as mental retardation and organic brain syndrome, the use of drugs should be minimized and constantly reevaluated.

Secondary prevention of a disorder means early detection. For tardive dyskinesia, this entails routine screening and monitoring patients for the presence of abnormal movements. A standard neurological examination can be employed for this purpose, or a clinician may want to use a specific examination procedure and rating scale such as the Abnormal Involuntary Movement Scale designed by the National Institute of Mental Health (see Fig. 2). It is best to perform an examination and note the results prior to the initiation of antipsychotic drug therapy (or before too long into the course) and then to repeat the examination procedure every 6 to 12 months while the patient remains on drug therapy. If early movements are detected, the clinician will want to consider lowering the dose of the antipsychotic drug or discontinuing it altogether. In addition, the patient (or next of kin) should be fully apprised of the clinical dilemma, the options, and the clinician's recommendation for further treatment.

What does one do when the presence of abnormal involuntary move-

INSTRUCTIONS: Complete Examination Procedure (facing page) before making ratings.

MOVEMENT RATINGS: Rate highest severity observed. Rate movements that occur upon activation one *less* than those observed spontaneously.

CODE:
0 = None
1 = Minimal, may be extreme normal
2 = Mild
3 = Moderate
4 = Severe

(Circle one)

FACIAL AND ORAL MOVEMENTS	1. Muscles of facial expression, e.g., movements of forehead, eyebrows, periorbital area, cheeks; include frowning, blinking, smiling, grimacing.	0 1 2 3 4
	2. Lips and perioral area, e.g., puckering, pouting, smacking.	0 1 2 3 4
	3. Jaw, e.g., biting, clenching, chewing, mouth opening, lateral movements.	0 1 2 3 4
	4. Tongue. Rate only increase in movement both in and out of mouth, NOT inability to sustain movement.	0 1 2 3 4
EXTREMITY MOVEMENTS	5. Upper (arms, wrists, hands, fingers). Include choreic movements (i.e., rapid, objectively purposeless, irregular, spontaneous), athetoid movements (i.e., slow, irregular, complex, serpentine). Do NOT include tremor (i.e., repetitive, regular, rhythmic).	0 1 2 3 4
	6. Lower (legs, knees, ankles, toes), e.g., lateral knee movement, foot tapping, heel dropping, foot squirming, inversion and eversion of foot.	0 1 2 3 4
TRUNK MOVEMENTS	7. Neck, shoulders, hips, e.g., rocking, twisting, squirming, pelvic gyrations.	0 1 2 3 4
GLOBAL JUDGMENTS	8. Severity of abnormal movements.	None, normal 0 Minimal 1 Mild 2 Moderate 3 Severe 4
	9. Incapacitation due to abnormal movements.	None, normal 0 Minimal 1 Mild 2 Moderate 3 Severe 4
	10. Patient's awareness of abnormal movements. Rate only patient's report.	No awareness 0 Awareness, no distress 1 Aware, mild distress 2 Aware, moderate distress 3 Aware, severe distress 4
DENTAL STATUS	11. Current problems with teeth and/or dentures.	No 0 Yes 1
	12. Does patient usually wear dentures?	No 0 Yes 1

FIGURE 2. Abnormal involuntary movement scale (AIMS). Asterisk (*) denotes activated movements. From Department of Health, Education, and Welfare, Public Health Service, Alcohol, Drug Abuse, and Mental Health Administration, National Institute of Mental Health.

EXAMINATION PROCEDURE

Either before or after completing the Examination Procedure, observe the patient unobtrusively, at rest (e.g., in waiting room).

The chair to be used in this examination should be a hard, firm one without arms.

1. Ask patient whether there is anything in his/her mouth (i.e., gum, candy, etc.) and if there is, to remove it.

2. Ask patient about the *current* condition of his/her teeth. Ask patient if he/she wears dentures. Do teeth or dentures bother patient *now?*

3. Ask patient whether he/she notices any movements in mouth, face, hands, or feet. If yes, ask to describe and to what extent they *currently* bother patient or interfere with his/her activities.

4. Have patient sit in chair with hands on knees, legs slightly apart, and feet flat on floor. (Look at entire body for movements while in this position.)

5. Ask patient to sit with hands hanging unsupported. If male, between legs; if female and wearing a dress, hanging over knees. (Observe hands and other body areas.)

6. Ask patient to open mouth. (Observe tongue at rest within mouth.) Do this twice.

7. Ask patient to protrude tongue. (Observe abnormalities of tongue movement.) Do this twice.

*8. Ask patient to tap thumb, with each finger, as rapidly as possible for 10 to 15 seconds, separately with right hand, then with left hand. (Observe facial and leg movements.)

10. Ask patient to stand up. (Observe in profile. Observe all body areas again, hips included.)

*11. Ask patient to extend both arms outstretched in front with palms down. (Observe trunk, legs, and mouth.)

*12. Have patient walk a few paces, turn, and walk back to chair. (Observe hands and gait.) Do this twice.

FIGURE 2. (*continued*)

ments is unequivocal? First, consider the diagnosis (see Table 4). Is there any other likely diagnosis? Are the movements characteristic of tardive dyskinesia, or might they be tremors or other movements? Are they chronic mannerisms and stereotypies characteristic of the underlying psychiatric disorder, or have these movements only appeared following chronic drug treatment? Family history should be explored to rule out the presence of hereditary disorders of the central nervous system such as Huntington's chorea or dystonia. The patient's history also should be reexplored to establish a reasonable linkage between drug therapy and the appearance of abnormal movements. Movements that inexorably progress are more likely caused by a degenerative neurological disorder than by tardive dyskinesia. A neurological examination should reveal only abnormal involuntary movements and specifically those characteristic of tardive dyskinesia; other neurologic systems, such as sensory or pyramidal, should not be involved. A physical examination should

TABLE 4. Tardive Dyskinesia: Differential Diagnosis

Disorder	Associated mental disturbances	Family history	Laboratory tests
Dyskinesias on withdrawal from neuroleptic medication	Yes	No	None
Schizophrenic stereotypies and mannerisms	Yes	No	None
Spontaneous oral dyskinesias associated with aging (including Meige syndrome)[a]	Yes	No	None
Oral dyskinesias related to dental conditions or prostheses[b]	No	No	None
Torsion dystonia	No	Yes	None
Idiopathic focal dystonia [oral mandibular dystonia, blephorospasm, spasmodic "habit spasms" (tics)]	No	No	None
Huntington's disease[c]	Yes	Yes	CAT scan
Wilson's disease	Yes	Yes	Serum copper and ceruloplasmin
Magnesium and other heavy metal	Yes	No	Specific for metals
Fahr's syndrome or other disorders with calcification of the basal ganglia	No	Yes	Skull X-rays
Extrapyramidal syndromes following anoxia or encephalitis	Yes	No	None
Rheumatic (Sydenham's) chorea ("Saint Vitus Dance")	No	No	None
Drug intoxications—L-DOPA, amphetamines, anticholinergics, antidepressants, lithium, phenytoin	Yes	No	For specific agents
CNS complications of systematic metabolic disorders (e.g., hepatic or renal failure, hyperthyroidism, hypoparathyroidism, hypoglycemia, vasculitides)	Yes	Possible	For specific disorders
Brain neoplasms (thalamic, basal ganglia)	Yes	No	CAT scan, other brain scans, EEG, etc.

[a]Meige syndrome is a disorder of middle age characterized by progressive oral, lingual, and buccal dystonia together with blephorospasm. The movements are indistinguishable from those of tardive dyskinesia, but patients with Meige syndrome need not have had antedating antipsychotic drug exposure, and Meige syndrome is a progressive disorder.

[b]Be sure to ask patients about the state of their mouth and teeth and whether they have any gum in their mouth when you are examining them for tardive dyskinesia.

[c]The abnormal movements of Huntington's disease are primarily chorea with little dystonia or athetosis. The movements are generalized, producing a "fidgety" appearance in the early stages. Although movements of tardive dyskinesia are more stereotyped and abnormal, the movements of Huntington's disease appear to be normal movements at an increased frequency. Patients with tardive dyskinesia have dyskinesias other than chorea. In general, patients with Huntington's disease have more trouble keeping their tongues out of their mouths, whereas tardive dyskinesia patients may have trouble keeping their tongues in their mouths.

search for the presence of ancillary signs of other extrapyramidal disorders such as the Kayser–Fleischer rings of Wilson's disease. Finally, laboratory testing can rule out other disorders—e.g., copper and ceruloplasmin levels in Wilson's disease, radiological evidence of caudate degeneration in Huntington's disease—if these conditions are suspected. At times, the psychiatrist may wish to seek consultation from a neurological colleague.

If the diagnosis of tardive dyskinesia appears firm, what is the course of treatment? Raising the dose of the antipsychotic drug might succeed in partially (or even completely) suppressing the movements, but the clinician should avoid this strategy, as it might ultimately worsen the disorder. (If the psychosis itself dictates the absolute need to increase the dose of antipsychotic drug, however, this must be done.) The opposite strategy—namely, lowering the antipsychotic drug dose—may produce a temporary worsening of the movements; yet, this is generally the preferred treatment if the psychosis does not deteriorate. From the standpoint of the movement disorder, stopping the antipsychotic agent altogether is preferable. However, making this decision is truly a clinical dilemma and, in most patients with chronic schizophrenia, a most difficult one. Schizophrenic psychosis is usually worse than tardive dyskinesia, and most often the clinician, patient, and family will decide to continue drug therapy, albeit at the lowest effective dose.

Tips for the Diagnosis of Tardive Dyskinesia

Helpful
1. History
   a. Exposure to antipsychotic drug
   b. Nonprogressive disorder
   c. Rule out family history of movement disorders
2. Physical examination
   a. Movements characteristic of tardive dyskinesia
   b. Rule out neurological signs in other systems (e.g., cerebellar, sensory, pyramidal)

Not Helpful
1. What makes movements better (e.g., sleep, relaxation) or worse (e.g., tension, psychological "gain")
2. Whether the patient can voluntarily inhibit movements
3. Whether movements are worsened or "unmasked" by a decrease in the antipsychotic drug dose
4. Laboratory tests—although laboratory tests are not helpful to rule in tardive dyskinesia, they can be helpful in ruling out other disorders.

If the movements continue and are troublesome (and irrespective of whether the patient remains on antipsychotic drug therapy), the clinician will want to alleviate as much of the patient's discomfort as possible. Unfortunately, there is no standard and accepted treatment for tardive dyskinesia. Therapy with a benzodiazepine drug such as diazepam (Valium®) or clonazepam (Clonopin®) may be of assistance to some patients, either by its sedative or muscle-relaxing properties or possibly via its role in increasing GABAergic tone.

Just as Parkinson's syndrome often responds to strategies that increase dopamine neurotransmission, tardive dyskinesia may be alleviated by treatments that diminish dopaminergic tone. Thus, a dopamine-depleting agent such as reserpine or tetrabenezine may be useful. (As mentioned earlier, the use of dopamine blockers such as antipsychotics themselves is generally avoided.) A paradoxical strategy has been to use a dopamine agonist such as L-DOPA in an attempt to desensitize the postsynaptic receptor. One group of investigators has reported success with this treatment, but at the moment, it remains experimental.[24]

Another treatment approach focuses on the cholinergic system. Much as Parkinson's is treated with anticholinergic drugs, so tardive dyskinesia has been approached through the use of cholinomimetics. Deanol was earlier employed for this purpose, but its status as a cholinergic agonist is in question, and its efficacy in tardive dyskinesia is doubtful. Choline chloride has been employed in this fashion, and although results have been encouraging, the many unwanted effects make it clinically troublesome. Phosphatidyl choline, contained in the naturally occurring lipid lecithin, also has been used for this purpose, and our group and others have found it helpful for many patients with tardive dyskinesia.[24] At this time, however, results are preliminary and largely unsubstantiated, and lecithin is far from an indicated therapy. Moreover, "lecithin" sold in so-called health food stores tends to be of doubtful content and purity and may even be contaminated with toxic substances (e.g., heavy metals, pesticides).[25]

Another agent that has been used in tardive dyskinesia with varying degrees of success is baclofen (Lioresal®) which may operate via a GABAergic mechanism. Many other drugs [e.g., propranolol (Inderal®, Inderide®)] also have been administered experimentally in patients with tardive dyskinesia, but unfortunately, no consensus has emerged.

Steps in Diagnosis and Management of Tardive Dyskinesia

Preliminary procedure
1. Base-line neurological examination.
2. Inform the patient and family about the risk of tardive dyskinesia.

Primary prevention
1. Avoid unnecessary exposure to antipsychotics.
2. Use lowest dose of antipsychotic for shortest time.
Secondary Prevention
1. Routine screening for dyskinetic movements [routine neurological examination or rating scale such as Abnormal Involuntary Movement Scale (AIMS)].
   a. Administer at the beginning of treatment.
   b. Administer every 6 to 12 months.
2. Consider lowering dosage or discontinuing antipsychotic drug if early signs develop.
Management
1. First confirm diagnosis by review of symptoms, drug history, and neurological examination.
2. Consider relatively benign drugs first if movements are uncomfortable enough to require treatment.
   a. Benzodiazepines (e.g., diazepam, clonazepam).
   b. ? Baclofen.
   c. ? Propranolol.
3. Refer patient to specialized center.

b. Sedation

It was initially believed that sedation was important for the effectiveness of antipsychotic drugs, but this no longer appears true. Drugs can have a major impact on the primary symptoms of psychosis such as hallucinations and thought disorder without producing somnolence. As mentioned previously, the low-potency antipsychotic drugs such as chlorpromazine, thioridazine, and chlorprothixene tend to be more sedating. If around-the-clock sedation is desired, these drugs can be administered several times daily during the initial days of therapy. If nighttime sedation is indicated, the drugs may be administered once daily at bedtime. Tolerance to sedation tends to develop over a matter of days or several weeks.

c. Seizures

Antipsychotic drugs, particularly the low-potency agents, lower the seizure threshold. For most patients, this is seldom a problem. However, an occasional patient without a history of epilepsy will experience a seizure during treatment with very high doses (or a particularly rapid increase in dose) of a low-potency agent. The problem is more likely to surface in the case of a patient with marginally controlled seizures or in a state of heightened vulnerability such as withdrawal from sedative–hypnotic drugs or alcohol. Each case must be handled individually, but consideration should be given to lowering the dose of the antipsychotic drug, changing to a high-potency agent, and/or adding (or increasing) an anticonvulsant (see Chapter 11).

d. Neuroleptic Malignant Syndrome

The neuroleptic malignant syndrome is a serious disorder consisting of fever, muscular rigidity, and stupor, which develops in association with antipsychotic drug therapy.[26] Other features include autonomic dysfunction (e.g., increased pulse, respirations, and sweating) and occasionally respiratory distress. Laboratory findings commonly indicate leukocytosis and elevated serum CPK. This syndrome typically develops explosively over a 24- to 72-hr period beginning anywhere from hours to months after initial drug exposure. A patient may have received prior treatment with antipsychotic drugs without showing this pattern.

The neuroleptic malignant syndrome has been associated with various antipsychotic drugs but is more prevalent with high-potency agents. Both sexes may be affected at any age, but among reported cases, young adult males predominate. Patients with organic brain disease appear to be at higher risk. Although the incidence of this disorder is unknown, it is probably not as rare as originally believed.

Management consists of discontinuing the antipsychotic drug immediately and instituting supportive measures. In most cases, the syndrome clears within 10 days (longer following long-acting injections); in about 20% of cases, the patient dies. There is no known treatment at this time. The mechanism of this syndrome is believed to involve the basal ganglia and hypothalamus, but the exact pathophysiology remains a mystery.

2. Anticholinergic

a. Peripheral

Antipsychotic drugs block a subtype of cholinergic receptor known as muscarinic. This type of receptor, which responds to interneuronal release of acetylcholine, is located on postganglionic neurons of the parasympathetic branch of the autonomic nervous system (as well as autonomic ganglion cells and certain cortical and subcortical neurons). Thus, the atropinelike action of antipsychotic drugs antagonizes the effects of the parasympathetic nervous system. The most strongly anticholinergic among the antipsychotic drugs is thioridazine, which is almost as potent as the heterocyclic antidepressants. High-potency antipsychotic drugs (e.g., fluphenazine, haloperidol) are comparatively weak in their atropinelike action.

In the skin, anticholinergic drugs can produce warmth, flushing, and dryness; in the eye, dilated pupils, difficulty with visual accommodation, and increased intraocular pressure; in the mouth, dryness; in the lungs, drying of secretions; in the heart, increased rate; in the stomach, decreased acid secretion; in the bowel, diminished motility with potential constipation; in the urinary tract, smooth muscle slowing, which can lead to delayed urination; in the penis, delayed (or retrograde) ejaculation.

In general, the elderly are more sensitive to atropinelike effects than are younger patients. Obviously, certain illnesses are exacerbated by anticholinergic actions of drugs. An abrupt attack of narrow-angle glaucoma is a rare possibility that can occur in a predisposed individual. Fortunately, the more common open-angle glaucoma, particularly when controlled by drugs, is less likely to be made worse by drug administration. Individuals prone to dental problems may suffer from diminished salivation. Patients with respiratory problems could be adversely affected by diminished pulmonary secretions. Similarly, those with cardiac disorders may be compromised by tachycardia as well as by more direct cardiotoxic effects, which are discussed below. Individuals with gastrointestinal disturbances, including those who have recently had abdominal surgery, may be adversely affected by the diminished bowel motility. Similarly, a man with prostatic enlargement could find urination difficult during treatment with an anticholinergic drug.

Some degree of tolerance develops to these effects over weeks and months (and conversely, rebound can occur on drug withdrawal). When peripheral anticholinergic activity of antipsychotic drugs is a problem, the clinician may wish to lower the dose of the drug or switch to a drug with less atropinic activity (i.e., a higher-potency agent). At times, symptomatic treatment may be offered, such as sugarless gum and lozenges for dry mouth, a stool softener or mild laxative for constipation. In occasional patients, the use of a peripherally active parasympathomimetic agent such as bethanechol (Urecholine®) may be indicated.

b. Central

Presumably through their action in blocking central muscarinic cholinergic receptors, antipsychotic drugs can at times produce memory difficulties, confusion, and, in the extreme, delirium.

c. Serious Toxicity

An antipsychotic agent alone, particularly the higher-potency compound, is unlikely to produce serious atropine-type toxicity. However, the more potent antimuscarinic antipsychotic drugs (especially thioridazine) or the combination of an antipsychotic drug with an anticholinergic antiparkinson agent, heterocyclic antidepressant, or other antimuscarinic compound, or a drug overdose can lead to serious toxicity, especially in the elderly and others vulnerable to these conditions. The patient suffering from an atropinelike delirium is typically confused, disoriented, and agitated. Pupils are large (although responsive), mucous membranes are dry, and skin is hot and flushed. Tachycardia and markedly diminished bowel sounds are common.

Intravenously administered physostigmine, 1 to 2 mg in a single, slow injection, can be both diagnostic and therapeutic, as it will reverse both the peripheral and central signs of atropine-type toxicity. (If successful, physostigmine can be repeated IM every few hours until delirium clears.) Physostigmine is a centrally active inhibitor of acetylcholinesterase, and as such it increases the amount of acetylcholine available to cholinergic receptors, thus circumventing the drug's blockade. The infusion of physostigmine should be slow, with careful cardiac monitoring and readily available means to support respiration, should this prove necessary. A physician who wishes to administer physostigmine should be familiar with the pharmacology of this drug and the hazards of cholinergic excess (which can be reversed by the administration of atropine). As a final note, physostigmine should be administered with the greatest caution to a patient who is showing cardiovascular instability as a result of a drug overdose or other medical problems[27] (see Chapter 2).

3. Cardiovascular and Respiratory

a. Hypotension

Orthostatic hypotension during antipsychotic drug administration has been attributed to a combination of hypothalamic actions and peripheral α-adrenergic blockade. Some degree of tolerance may develop. This reaction is more common with the low-potency drugs (e.g., chlorpromazine) and may be more of a problem with the elderly or with patients with preexisting postural hypotension and vascular instability such as those undergoing a sedative–hypnotic withdrawal reaction. It is likely that parenteral administration of an antipsychotic drug may provoke more severe hypotension than oral ingestion of the same drug.

If postural hypotension does develop, it usually can be managed by keeping the patient horizontal. The next step, if necessary, is the administration of intravenous fluids to expand the vascular volume. If these two maneuvers are not effective, then a pure α-adrenergic pressor agent should be administered. Metaraminol (Aramine®) will usually suffice, although norepinephrine (Levophed®) also may be considered. The use of a mixed α- and β-stimulating drug such as epinephrine (adrenalin) could lead to a paradoxical drop in blood pressure, since the α receptors are blocked, and the unopposed β stimulation can promote further hypotension. Similarly, the use of a primarily β-stimulating drug such as isoproteronol (Isuprel®) should be avoided.

b. Cardiac

Antipsychotic drugs have both antiarrhythmic and arrhythmogenic effects on the heart. Antagonism of sympathetic activity in the hypothalamus and a local anesthetic property that stabilizes the cardiac cell membrane (similar to the effects of lidocaine) may cause the antiarrhythmic effect. In addition, antipsychotic drugs have direct quinidinelike effects on the myocardium and cardiac conduction system and affect electrolyte balance. Explanations of the arrhythmogenic action of phenothiazines and other antipsychotic drugs similarly include both central activity and a direct effect on the myocardium. Pathologists have detected microscopic and ultramicroscopic lesions in the cardiac tissue of patients who died suddenly during the course of phenothiazine therapy, suggesting a direct toxic effect.

Whether antipsychotic drugs are protective or toxic to the heart probably depends on the agent, the dose, and the underlying state of a patient's cardiac physiology. Low-potency antipsychotic agents, especially thioridazine, tend to be more cardiotoxic. On the ECG, increased heart rate, prolongation of the QT and PR intervals and T wave, and depression of the ST segment are occasionally observed, most particularly with thioridazine. For most patients, these effects are not clinically troublesome. However, patients with preexisting cardiac disease should be monitored carefully (e.g., clinical examinations, vital signs, ECGs), and low-potency drugs (especially in excessive doses and particularly thioridazine) should be avoided.

Overdoses of antipsychotic drugs (especially thioridazine) can cause cardiac arrhythmias. Because antipsychotic agents have quinidinelike actions, arrhythmias caused by overdoses should not be treated with quinidine or related type 1 antiarrhythmic drugs [procainamide (Pronestyl®) and dysopyramide (Norpace®)]. In the treatment of cardiac arrhythmias that result from overdoses with phenothiazines and related drugs, antiarrhythmics such as lidocaine (Xylocaine®), phenytoin (Dilantin®, etc.), propranolol, and physostigmine (Antilirium®) may have a role. The early use of transvenous pacing also has been recommended.

Combinations of antipsychotic drugs and antidepressants can produce additive cardiotoxic effects. In particular, combinations of thioridazine and heterocyclic antidepressants, especially amitriptyline, are best avoided.

Occasional cases of sudden death reported in patients receiving antipsychotic drugs are difficult to interpret and probably result from various causes. However, episodes of potentially fatal ventricular arrhythmias are a possible factor.

4. Ocular

As already noted, the anticholinergic effects of antipsychotic drugs can affect the eye. Increased mydriasis can make a patient more light sensitive. Interference with visual accommodation may result in complaints of blurred vision. Because of the rare possibility of precipitating an attack of angle-closure glaucoma, prior to treatment with any anticholinergic agent patients should be asked about history of visual symptoms—such as eye pain, blurring, and halos—that could suggest previous narrow-angle episodes. Open-angle glaucoma is less likely to be a problem, but the patient should be managed conjointly with an ophthalmologist.

Prolonged treatment with high doses of low-potency antipsychotic drugs has been associated with the deposition of pigment in the lens, cornea, conjunctiva, and retina, often together with skin pigmentation. Except in extreme cases, these are unlikely to interfere with vision. However, if it is necessary to expose a patient to high doses of a low-potency agent for long periods of time, periodic ophthalmologic examinations would be worthwhile, perhaps annually.

Of greater clinical significance is the pigmentary retinopathy that may accompany thioridazine treatment. This disorder, which can result in visual impairment, is extremely unlikely if doses of thioridazine do not exceed 800 mg per day. Thus, thioridazine is the one antipsychotic agent that should be considered to have an absolute "ceiling dose"—800 mg daily—which must not be exceeded for even brief periods of time. (If a patient does require high doses of an antipsychotic drug, it is best to switch to a different one.)

5. Cutaneous

Virtually any drug is capable of producing an allergic rash in occasional patients, typically between 2 and 10 weeks following initial exposure. This is usually maculopapular, erythematous, and itchy, affecting the face, neck, trunk, and extremities (often the palms and soles of the feet). Allergic reactions vary in distribution and severity, the most extreme being exfoliative dermatitis which can be life-threatening. In most cases, discontinuation of the precipitating agent is followed by prompt remission of symptoms and signs. The itching and rash can be treated symptomatically (with topical steroids). Subsequent antipsychotic therapy should be with a drug from a different chemical group. Occasionally, contact dermatitis occurs in patients hypersensitive to antipsychotic drugs, particularly to liquid preparations.

Patients receiving low-potency antipsychotic medication sometimes become very sensitive to sunlight. The resulting reaction resembles severe sunburn. Management of the acute reaction is the same as for sunburn. Subsequent treatment should include switching to a higher-potency antipsychotic drug or warning the patient to protect himself from sun, whether physically or through the use of a sunscreening preparation [usually one containing *para*-aminobenzoic acid (PABA)].

Occasional patients treated with high doses of low-potency phenothiazines for prolonged periods develop a blue–gray discoloration of the skin, specifically in skin exposed to sunlight. This usually occurs in conjunction with pigmentary changes in the eye. Aside from cosmetic concerns, it is unclear if this reaction has any clinical importance.

As mentioned earlier, seborrheic dermatitis often occurs in conjunction with Parkinson's syndrome.

6. Hormonal, Sexual, and Hypothalamic Reactions

Previously, we discussed how antipsychotic drugs increase prolactin release from the anterior pituitary and consequently cause hyperprolactinemia, probably as a result of dopamine-blocking activity. In females, this occasionally leads to galactorrhea (also, rarely, in males), decreased frequency or flow of menstruation, and in both sexes, a diminished libido. Although so far there is no convincing evidence that chronic antipsychotic drug treatment increases the risk of breast cancer, it is not inconceivable that the growth of prolactin-sensitive tumors may be enhanced by the presence of elevated circulating prolactin concentrations. Therefore, women should be asked about personal and family history of breast cancer, and women receiving long-term antipsychotic therapy should undergo periodic breast examinations. Although there is no evidence that chronic antipsychotic drug treatment can result in increased incidence of pituitary adenomas, it remains at least a theoretical possibility that lactotrophes in the pituitary will be stimulated. Therefore, in the face of chronic hyperprolactinemia, patients should be examined occasionally for possible evidence of pituitary enlargement. Persistent amenorrhea and galactorrhea suggest that the clinician should lower the antipsychotic drug dose. At times, the dopamine agonist bromocriptine (Lergotril®) may be considered, but this should be discussed with an endocrinologist.

Antipsychotic agents appear to lower circulating levels of testosterone, either through a direct or indirect mechanism. Together with the effects of elevated prolactin, decreased testosterone may contribute to the diminished libido observed in some males treated with these chemicals.

Effects on blood sugar, growth hormone, and thyroid hormone also have been reported, although it is doubtful that these are of much clinical import. Chlorpromazine impairs glucose tolerance and insulin release, which may be clinically noteworthy in some prediabetic patients.

Another sexual symptom, already mentioned under anticholinergic effects, is interference with ejaculation. This is most frequently observed in young males treated with thioridazine and is manifested by delayed ejaculation or retrograde ejaculation. In the latter case, the patient reports orgasm without emission, followed by urination that has a "foamy" appearance. Some males also report difficulty maintaining and sustaining erection. In these cases, change to a high-potency drug.

In addition to effects on prolactin and the existence of the neuroleptic malignant syndrome, antipsychotic drugs seem to have many other actions at the level of the hypothalamus. These probably include cardiovascular effects as well as various hormonal and autonomic changes. Temperature regulation is also impaired by phenothiazines and their relatives, particularly the low-potency ones, making patients more vulnerable to hypo- or hyperthermia (depending on the ambient temperature).

Another unwanted effect, probably related to hypothalamic changes, is increased appetite with resultant weight gain. In some patients, this can be most marked and unpleasant. Probably, appetite increase (which may be related to antihistaminic effects) is more common with low-potency drugs. Management may include switching to a higher-potency agent and dietary counseling.

7. Hepatic

The low-potency antipsychotic drugs occasionally produce a syndrome of cholestatic jaundice, probably a combination of a direct toxic effect and an allergic reaction. Typically, within the first month of treatment, the patient develops fever, chills, nausea, malaise, pruritis, and right upper quadrant abdominal pain, followed within a matter of days by jaundice. Liver function tests reveal an obstructive pattern with increased alkaline phosphatase and conjugated (direct) bilirubin. Transaminase enzymes also may be elevated, but they do not reach the levels observed in hepatitis.

The recommended treatment for cholestatic jaundice is discontinuation of the antipsychotic drug, although it is possible that patients will recover despite continued therapy. In almost all cases, recovery occurs over a matter of weeks and is complete and without sequelae. In predisposed patients, cholestatic jaundice may lead to chronic biliary cirrhosis. Subsequent treatment probably should be with a different antipsychotic drug, preferably a high-potency agent.

The presence of preexisting liver disease does not contraindicate the use of antipsychotic drugs. However, when the liver is impaired, metabolism of antipsychotic drugs may be slowed, and other drugs that use similar enzyme pathways could be affected by the addition of another liver-metabolized agent. In addition, the central action of antipsychotic drugs may worsen a case of hepatic encephalopathy.

8. Hematological

Low-potency antipsychotic agents probably are weakly toxic to some elements of the bone marrow, particularly stem cells of the granulocyte series. Almost all patients can compensate for this and show no more than a transient leukopenia. However, a rare patient goes on to develop agranulocytosis.

Perhaps one in 3000 or 4000 patients treated with chlorpromazine (and possibly other low-potency drugs) will develop agranulocytosis. (This occurs rarely, if at all, with high-potency drugs). The onset is typically within the first 2 to 3 months of drug therapy. (It must be remembered, however, that switching to a different agent "restarts the clock.") Many patients treated with antipsychotic drugs show a transient leukopenia, but probably resistant stem cells allow compensation. However, in a patient vulnerable to development of agranulocytosis, the granuloctye count drops precipitously over the course of several days. The white blood cell count may fall below 1000, and practically all of those cells will be lymphocytes.

Routine blood counts will be unlikely to detect the abrupt onset of agranulocytosis unless they are performed two to three times each week for the first several months of treatment. For this reason, they are generally not recommended. Instead, the best approach is to maintain a high clinical index of suspicion. Thus, sore throat, fever, malaise, or other symptoms or signs of infection should prompt **immediate** white blood count with a differential. If the count is low, antipsychotic drugs should be discontinued immediately, and the patient put into reverse isolation to prevent infection. If infection does not supervene, a normal blood count returns within several weeks. If infection does occur, there is a substantial mortality. The mortality rate is considerably elevated if the antipsychotic drug is not discontinued. The experimental antipsychotic drug clozapine was removed from the European market and from experimental use within the United States because of data suggesting that it produced a high incidence of agranulocytosis.

Antipsychotic drugs probably can affect platelet function, although whether this may have therapeutic or toxic significance is unclear. A variety of immunologic and coagulation changes have been described in patients taking chlorpromazine, sometimes in association with hepatomegaly.

About half of a group of patients who had been treated chronically with chlorpromazine had a positive antinuclear antibody test, and more than 75% showed increased serum concentrations of IgM associated with prolongation of partial thromboplastin time. In addition, a number of autoantibodies have been found in patients treated with chlorpromazine, often in association with splenomegaly.[28] Occasional reports have surfaced of the association of antipsychotic drugs with other hematologic syndromes, but no relationship has been clearly established.

9. Pregnancy and Lactation

All antipsychotic drugs can cross the placenta and enter the fetus. Considering all epidemiologic data at present, no consistent evidence has emerged suggesting that any antipsychotic drug is a teratogen. However, the possibility of a low-level association cannot be ruled out. Moreover, antipsychotic drugs may affect the developing nervous system, with possible long-lasting neurochemical and behavioral effects.[29] In addition, newborn babies have shown syndromes of neuroleptic withdrawal from the drugs. For these reasons, if at all possible, a woman should be kept free of antipsychotic drugs during as much of pregnancy as possible.

Similarly, antipsychotic drugs can be detected in human milk at levels roughly similar to those found in blood. Although this means that the nursling would receive relatively small amounts each day, concern about the effects of psychotropic drugs on the developing nervous system, referred to above, must be taken into consideration in weighing treatment decisions (see Chapter 10).

10. Withdrawal Reactions

Tolerance, habituation, and addiction are not believed to occur with antipsychotic drugs. Rarely, these agents have been used recreationally.

As noted earlier, tolerance does develop to some of the unwanted effects of these agents. Partial to complete tolerance may develop to sedation, and some degree of tolerance can occur for hypotension and anticholinergic actions. Conversely, when the drug is stopped, rebound reactions may occur. These can include insomnia, nightmares, and other disturbances of sleep, as well as cholinergic rebound such as increased salivation, abdominal cramps, and diarrhea. To make patients more comfortable, discontinue these drugs gradually (e.g., 5 to 10% of dose per day) rather than abruptly.

Obviously, discontinuation of antipsychotic drugs may be followed by relapse of psychosis. This is generally believed to be a recurrence of the underlying psychiatric disorder. However, it has been suggested that in some patients, psychosis actually is created or exacerbated as a result of supersensitivity created by the drugs.[30] This remains to be established by subsequent studies.

As discussed in the section on tardive dyskinesia, discontinuation of antipsychotic drugs is occasionally followed by transient withdrawal dyskinesias. In other cases, discontinuation of the drug unmasks persistent dyskinesia.

11. Overdose

Fortunately, antipsychotic drugs have a high therapeutic index—the ratio of toxic to therapeutic dose. Ingestion of an antipsychotic drug alone in an overdose attempt seldom results in death. (However, it should always be remembered that another agent may have been ingested along with the antipsychotic drug.)

When an antipsychotic drug is ingested in an overdose, the anticholinergic effects will probably delay gastric emptying; passage of a nasogastric tube with the application of suction should always be attempted, even many hours after the overdose. Instillation of activated charcoal may further diminish absorption. Attempts at inducing emesis may be unsuccessful because of the antiemetic action of these drugs, particularly the low-potency agents. Because antipsychotic drugs have a high lipophilicity coupled with a strong adherence to tissue and proteins, attempts at dialysis are relatively unsuccessful.

Antipsychotic drugs alone seldom produce lethal suppression of vital brainstem centers However, the low-potency agents are capable of inducing serious blood pressure problems which, as noted earlier, should be treated with pure α-stimulating drugs. Low-potency drugs also can occasionally produce serious arrhythmias which, with thioridazine, are most likely to be dangerous. As noted earlier, in the treatment of these arryhthmias, quinidine and other type-1 antiarrhythmic agents (namely, procainamide and dysopyramide) should be avoided because of additive effects (see Section III.G.3).

We previously discussed how physostigmine may have a role in reversing some of the central nervous system effects of atropine toxicity caused by antipsychotic agents. However, physostigmine can worsen some arrhythmias, lower the seizure threshold, and produce respiratory arrest. For this reason, it should be used extremely cautiously, if at all, in conditions of cardiovascular and respiratory instability.[27]

H. Drug Interactions and Combinations

Drugs can interact with each other at two levels—pharmacokinetic and pharmacodynamic. In a pharmacokinetic interaction, one drug interferes with the absorption, distribution, metabolism, or excretion of another drug, effectively raising or lowering blood and tissue levels of the other. In a pharmacodynamic interaction, one drug combines with another to increase or decrease effects at a target organ. There are several reasons why a patient may receive more than one drug at the same time: to enhance a specific therapy, because two or more illnesses must be treated concurrently, or when a second drug must be added to counteract unwanted effects of the first drug.

In general, to minimize potential unwanted interactions, simplify the therapeutic regimen, enhance compliance, and more easily assess specific contributions to a clinical outcome, a physician should prescribe the fewest possible drugs for a patient. However, in a number of clinical situations, a physician will want to coadminister another drug with an antipsychotic agent. We have already mentioned the treatment of extrapyramidal effects with antiparkinson drugs. In such circumstances, several pharmacodynamic interactions are possible. Most antiparkinson drugs (with the partial exception of amantadine) have anticholinergic actions which will add to those of the antipsychotic agent. Many antiparkinson drugs also have antihistaminic effects which can enhance the sedation caused by antipsychotic drugs. In addition, pharmacokinetic interactions also have been reported; it is possible that antiparkinson drugs lower the blood levels of some antipsychotic agents; however, data about this point are inconsistent.[31,32]

Sometimes it may be justified to coadminister a benzodiazepine together with an antipsychotic agent. As mentioned earlier, a drug like diazepam may effectively counteract acute dystonic reactions or akathisia. There appears to be little potential for a pharmacokinetic interaction between these two classes of drugs. However, an important pharmacodynamic interaction is additive sedative effects. Similarly, any sedative–hypnotic drug (including alcohol) has this potential interaction with antipsychotic agents. In the extreme, depression of respiration or blood pressure may occur.

At times (e.g., in the treatment of psychotic depression), a physician may elect to treat a patient with both an antipsychotic drug and a heterocyclic antidepressant. A pharmacokinetic interaction will occur, probably at the level of drug-metabolizing enzymes. This results in higher blood levels of both drugs than if either had been administered alone. In addition, additive sedative, anticholinergic, and cardiovascular effects are likely.

Lithium and an antipsychotic drug are combined in the treatment of many patients with mania. A syndrome of severe neurotoxicity—including neuromuscular signs, cognitive changes, and hyperthermia—was described in four patients receiving treatment with both lithium carbonate and haloperidol.[33] Similarly, EEG abnormalities were reported in several patients who developed encephalopathy during therapy with a combination of lithium and thioridazine.[34] On the other hand, broad clinical experience and a number of published series have testified to the safety of lithium/antipsychotic drug combinations for a vast majority of patients. It is possible, though, that an occasional patient will experience enhanced neurotoxicity from the combination, and any suggestion that this may be occurring should prompt a rapid lowering of dosages or drug discontinuation.[35]

A pharmacokinetic interaction has also been described between lithium and chlorpromazine: mean plasma chlorpromazine levels were significantly lower during combined therapy.[36] Lithium may slow gastric emptying, which would enhance the gut metabolism of chlorpromazine and diminish its absorption, or it may interfere with the absorption of chlorpromazine by diminishing its transport across gut membranes.

Antipsychotic agents also can interact with drugs used for the treatment of nonpsychiatric conditions. Phenothiazines (like heterocyclic antidepressants) can interfere with the antihypertensive actions of guanethidine. Low-potency antipsychotic drugs may potentiate the postural hypotension observed with various antihypertensive drugs. Haloperidol has been reported to cause an organic brain syndrome when combined with methyldopa. By decreasing the metabolism of phenytoin (and perhaps of other anticonvulsant drugs), antipsychotic drugs may elevate anticonvulsant blood levels, potentially producing toxicity. Through their tendency to produce extrapyramidal reactions, antipsychotic drugs can counteract the antiparkinson effects of drugs used to treat naturally occurring Parkinson's syndrome.

Caffeine, contained in many beverages and over-the-counter medicines, also may interact with antipsychotic drugs. At the dynamic level, it can counteract sedative effects, possibly necessitating an increased dose of the antipsychotic drug. At a kinetic level, some caffeine-containing beverages might diminish the absorption of antipsychotic drugs from the stomach, but this is controversial.[37]

The rule of thumb is that when any drug is added to any other drug, the possibility of interactions must be considered. For this reason, as stated at the beginning of the section, the clinician should minimize the use of multiple drugs in the same patient at the same time.

I. Laboratory Tests and Monitoring

In contrast to other drugs, such as lithium, no laboratory tests are essential for patients receiving antipsychotic drugs. Similarly, blood assays of antipsychotic levels have not yet reached the stage of general applicability. However, pretreatment laboratory tests (supplementing a history and physical examination) can be useful to assess a patient's general health status prior to the initiation of antipsychotic drug therapy and for periodic reassessments during treatment. These may include a complete blood count with a differential, a battery of liver function tests, and in men over 30 and women over 40, an electrocardiogram (ECG). (In the initial assessment of a psychotic patient, a differential diagnosis may support assessment of other organ systems or metabolic and endocrine functions. In addition, it would be wise to perform routine screening for syphilis, chest disease, and other illnesses.[38]) During treatment, the clinician should occasionally recheck a patient's health status, although it makes little sense to repeat laboratory tests more frequently than once per year in asymptomatic patients. To recapitulate earlier points: liver disease does not automatically contraindicate the use of antipsychotic drugs; maintaining a high clinical index of suspicion for agranulocytosis and jaundice within the early months of therapy is superior to routine laboratory testing.

As mentioned in the section on tardive dyskinesia, monitoring of patients for early signs of abnormal involuntary movements is wise before and during chronic antipsychotic drug therapy. Prior to treatment and at intervals of 6 to 12 months thereafter, the performance of a basic examination (such as the AIMS) would be worthwhile (see Fig. 2). Because of concerns about breast tumors in patients taking these drugs (see Section III.G.6), women should be periodically examined (and taught to examine themselves, if feasible) for breast lumps.

When patients are taking antipsychotic drugs, various laboratory tests may be artifactually altered. As examples, invalid increases may be reported in serum alkaline phosphatase, serum and urine bilirubin, cerebrospinal fluid protein, serum cholesterol, urine diacetate, serum 17-hydroxy steroids, urine porphyrins, serum transaminases, and urine urobilinogen. In addition, false-positive results may be reported in urinary phenylketonuria and pregnancy testing. Protein-bound iodine (PBI), radioactive iodine, and serum and urine uric acid testing may be inaccurate as well.

J. Clinical Uses of the Antipsychotic Drugs

Based on a medical and psychological evaluation of the patient, the clinician should determine the need for medication and its place within the treatment plan (see Sections I and II in this chapter). The choice of a specific agent depends on the patient's medication history and an understanding of pharmacokinetics, adverse effects, toxicity, and drug interactions. The clinician should discuss his decision to medicate with the patient and/or his family, guardian, etc. (For further discussion of informed consent, competency, etc., see Chapter 12.) Pretreatment laboratory tests might be useful to assess a patient's general health prior to initiating drug therapy (see Section III.I).

1. Acute Treatment

In the early placebo-controlled trials of phenothiazines in the treatment of acute schizophrenic psychosis, about one-fourth of patients who received placebo responded reasonably well. Unfortunately, we are unable to predict in advance those psychotic patients who do not require medication. For each patient, a different amount of medication may be required to contain each exacerbation. Also, a patient may take days or even several weeks to show optimal antipsychotic effect to a given dose of medication. Nevertheless, it is occasionally possible to allow an acutely psychotic person a short drug-free period to improve prior to the institution of the therapy. In an acutely psychotic individual without a long history of psychosis, transferring the patient from a stressful situation to a benign, supportive, and nonconfrontative environment, such as the hospital, may itself be helpful. If the person's behavior is not overtly disruptive, he can be given an opportunity to reconstitute spontaneously over several days. During the diagnostic and psychosocial evaluation procedures, he should be carefully observed. If spontaneous improvement does not occur, if the severity of the psychosis or the nature of the patient's behavior precludes a drug-free interval, or if the patient has a long history of psychotic exacerbations, then vigorous antipsychotic drug therapy should be instituted.

Some physicians employ extremely large doses of high-potency antipsychotic drugs early in treatment. This approach, known as rapid neuroleptization or "digitalizing" treatment, attempts to achieve rapid remission of psychosis and rapid discharge from the hospital. Unfortunately, double-blind studies have been unable to confirm any enhanced efficacy of this form of treatment compared to standard dosage regimens. In other words, treating all psychotic patients with "megadoses" does not control psychosis or allow discharge any more rapidly, and it is associated with an increase in untoward effects. Thus, the clinician should individualize treatment for each patient by gradually increasing the dose of the antipsychotic drug over a period of days to find the most effective level.

However, if a patient is highly excited and/or dangerous, relatively large doses of antipsychotic drugs, administered parenterally, may be a very effective method of containment. High-potency drugs are preferable, since they are less likely to produce hypotension and seizures. For example, 2.5 to 10 mg of haloperidol can be administered intramuscularly every 30 to 60 min until the patient's behavior is controlled. A maximum dose should be 30 mg/half hour and 100 to 120 mg/day. Once behavior is controlled, oral treatment at the lowest effective dose is preferable. (Experimental work has shown intravenously administered haloperidol to be surprisingly safe and impressively effective.) Loxapine (Daxolin®, Loxitane®) and thiothixene (Navane®), among other high-potency drugs, are also available parenterally and may be used for rapid control of psychotic excitement (see Table 1 for dosage comparisons). The use of high doses of parenteral antipsychotic drugs is not without risk, and patients undergoing this regimen should be monitored continuously, including respiration, pulse, and blood pressure measurements.

For most patients, however, who are not out of control, what is the optimal dose for the treatment of an acute psychotic episode? Most patients require at least 400 mg per day of chlorpromazine or its equivalent (see Table 1 for conversion factors). Some will respond to less; many will require much more. Treatment should be individualized, based on a patient's response. If there is a prior history of antipsychotic drug therapy, the dosage found effective at that time might be used initially.

Early in the treatment course, administer antipsychotic drugs in divided doses, perhaps three or four times per day (more frequently during acute titration of severely excited behavior). Once satisfactory levels have been achieved, and the patient has become tolerant to unwanted effects (probably within several weeks), once-daily dosage usually will suffice. If a patient can be maintained out of the hospital, a once-daily dosage, even from the beginning, may enhance compliance. Particularly when a more sedating agent is employed, a bedtime dose may be optimal, as it can improve sleep, and the peak anticholinergic and hypotensive effects will occur while the patient is asleep.

What if a patient does not appear to respond to an antipsychotic drug? First, the clinician must wonder whether the patient is actually receiving the agent. An outpatient may not have filled a prescription or may be taking the drug irregularly if at all. An inpatient might be "cheeking" tablets or capsules. Questions to be asked at this juncture include: Is anyone observing the patient taking the medication, including an inspection of the patient's mouth? Does the patient have any noticeable "side effects" from the drug, such as extrapyramidal reactions? If compliance is a particular problem, consider changing the dosage regimen, administering a liquid preparation, or using a parenteral agent. Always ask patients how they feel about a drug. They might reveal covert effects such as sexual dysfunction or akathisia which may be improved by switching to a different agent; or, one may learn of a patient's wish to remain "crazy."

If compliance is not a problem, yet the patient has not improved, he may require a higher dose of medication. Increase the dosage until improvement occurs or limiting adverse effects develop. Although FDA-approved labeling (contained in the *Physician's Desk Reference* and in the package insert) provides useful guidelines about maximal dosage, the actual upper limit may vary from patient to patient. The one exception to this rule is thioridazine which must not be administered in dosages exceeding 800 mg per day—even for a brief period of time—because of the danger of pigmentary retinopathy with potential loss of vision.

Some patients metabolize antipsychotic drugs very rapidly in the gut and in the first pass through the liver. A physician might suspect that this is the case in a patient who is taking relatively large doses orally, yet experiences neither clinical benefit nor adverse effects. These patients may respond to particularly high oral doses or a parenteral preparation.

Although all antipsychotic drugs are equally effective, some patients appear to do better with one agent than another. Thus, failure to improve with one antipsychotic drug (after the above factors have been considered) is a reason to switch to a different agent. Clinicians should be wary, however, of a tendency to be "too quick on the prescription trigger," switching agents every few days in a vain attempt to "do something." Only after a drug has been given an **adequate trial (in terms of dosage and length of time)** should the clinician switch to a different agent. This means raising doses at least to the FDA-recommended limit (if tolerated) and continuing for at least a month. When it is time to change, it makes most sense to choose a drug in a different chemical class.

One other consideration in the apparently refractory patient is psychosocial factors, which may be "fueling" the psychosis. Antipsychotic drugs raise the threshold at which an individual predisposed to psychosis actually becomes psychotic in response to interpersonal and intrapsychic stresses. A chronic schizophrenic, for example, might remain quite stable and relatively intact (albeit still awkward, isolated, and apathetic) when in a low-stress environment, even with little or no medication. However, given a precipitant (an argument with a "schizophrenogenic mother" or being placed in a "double bind"), he may decompensate into a state of disorganized thinking and be unable to distinguish reality from fantasy.

It takes more medication to "cap" a psychosis in the face of ongoing stresses and threats than in more placid circumstances. In fact, if the pressure is sufficient, psychochemistry alone will not bring the psychosis under control. Hence, the clinician must consider psychological and environmental factors when treating an acutely decompensated patient. If a patient remains at home and is unimproved despite adequate chemotherapy, change the environment; e.g., arrange for hospital admission. If he is in the hospital, inquire about ongoing contacts both inside and outside the hospital. Occasionally, a schizophrenic patient's mother will sit on his lap during visiting hours, another patient may be making sexual advances, or a naive staff member might be getting provocatively close. In such circumstances, decreasing the intensity of the patient's conflict may allow a hitherto ineffective drug to become strikingly efficacious.

And how effective is effective for an antipsychotic drug? The drugs are best at suppressing the most florid symptoms of psychosis such as hallucinations, delusions, excited, assaultive, and belligerent behavior, and disorganized thinking. If the patient has a primary disorder of mood, reconstitution should involve what Bleuler called restitutio ad integrum—in other words, a return to an integrated and normal state of personality and functioning. For a schizophrenic patient, however, recovery from psychosis is likely to involve return to a somewhat strange, awkward, and isolated existence.

2. Transition and Continuation Therapy

When psychotic symptoms have remitted successfully, we pass from the acute phase of active symptom suppression to continuation therapy. Continuation therapy entails the continued administration of medication in the hope of avoiding a relapse. This is analogous to the continuation of antimicrobial therapy past the period of symptom relief and fever defervescence. After the alleviation of an acute psychotic episode, continue therapy for about 6 months.

It is best not to change the type and dosage of antipsychotic medication at the time of an important transition such as discharge from the hospital. If a patient has responded favorably to an antipsychotic drug, continue the same dose of that drug through the return to home, job, and community. Antipsychotic agents presumably provide a buffer for the stresses of the transitional period.

If a person has resumed a normal life without evidence of recurrent psychosis, the physician should gradually lower the dose of the antipsychotic drug. If dosage tapering has proceeded smoothly, within about 6 months consideration may be given to discontinuing the agent entirely. However, when a psychotic illness has shown itself to be chronic, with frequent recurrences (a common pattern among schizophrenic patients), maintenance therapy should be considered.

3. Maintenance Therapy

a. Definition

Maintenance therapy (of any illness and with any mode of treatment) consists of long-term administration of an agent with a goal of preventing or ameliorating future symptoms. By definition, a patient on a maintenance regimen is (more or less) in a state of remission. Treatment is administered not to suppress ongoing symptoms so much as to avoid or attenuate future symptoms. The goal is to make relapse less likely or, if it recurs, less severe. (In treating a chronic schizophrenic person, if overt symptoms of psychosis persist, consider a dosage increase, change of drug, psychosocial intervention, or other factors discussed in Section III. J.1.)

b. Chronic Schizophrenia

If a group of schizophrenic patients in remission is switched from active antipsychotic medication to placebo, roughly 65% to 80% will relapse within about 1 year. How long a patient will go before relapsing is variable and unpredictable. In any given month, roughly 10% of the remaining unrelapsed medication-free patients may be expected to relapse. At the end of 1 to 2 years, a small cohort of schizophrenic patients will not have relapsed despite the lack of antipsychotic drug therapy; they have less need for maintenance treatment. Unfortunately, we are unable to identify these patients in advance. Patients clinically stable on relatively low doses of antipsychotic drugs may be more likely to maintain remission following complete cessation of the agent. Also, patients in relatively low-stress environments are more likely to remain stable without drugs, although the onset of stress can heighten their vulnerability.

Although some have suggested the use of "drug holidays" (i.e., "vacations" from medication) in attempts to assess patients' needs for ongoing medication therapy, this author favors periodically tapering the drug to find the lowest effective dosage for a given patient. For example, a patient who has been maintained on 25 mg per day of a high-potency antipsychotic drug and has been stable clinically for over a year can be tried on a dose of 20 mg per day. If he is maintained adequately at that dose for several months, a further decrease to 15 mg per day may be attempted. In this manner, the lowest effective maintenance dose of an antipsychotic drug can be found for that patient at that time. Patients' need for medication varies over time, and chronic patients should not be allowed to remain at the same dose for many months (and even years) without reassessment of their doses. Just as medication may sometimes be tapered downward, there will be other times during maintenance therapy when symptom exacerbation, possibly linked to stressful periods, may dictate the need to increase dosage. As always, such decisions must be individualized.

Do long-acting antipsychotic preparations afford greater protection against relapse in schizophrenic disorders? At the time of this writing, two long-acting antipsychotic drugs are available by prescription in the United States—the enanthate and the decanoate esters of the phenothiazine fluphenazine. Several similar esters of other high-potency antipsychotic drugs are available in Europe. In addition, penfluridol, an experimental antipsychotic drug chemically related to haloperidol, can be administered only once weekly by mouth. (Unfortunately, concerns about possible toxicity may keep penfluridol from the United States market, but analogous agents are being tested.)

Of the two fluphenazine esters, the decanoate is favored over the enanthate because of its longer duration of action (3 to 6 weeks as opposed to 2 weeks) and fewer unwanted effects. Fluphenazine decanoate is usually administered intramuscularly (but also may be given subcutaneously) in dosages of from 12.5 mg (0.5 cc) through 75 mg (3 cc) every 3 to 4 weeks. Some patients may be adequately maintained on very low doses of fluphenazine decanoate, such as 1.25 mg (0.05 cc) every few weeks.[39] At the higher end of the scale, patients have received more that 125 mg (5 cc) per dose, which necessitates the use of several injection sites. Unfortunately, there is no established conversion factor to equate a dose of oral fluphenazine hydrochloride to a dose of decanoate for a patient treated acutely with the former. Once the decanoate is injected, it cannot be removed for several weeks; therefore, it is safest to start all patients new to this treatment with a low dose, increasing gradually over several weeks.

When determining the dosage of the decanoate, the clinician can administer an initial dose, such as 0.5 to 1 cc, and then supplement the patient as needed with oral fluphenazine or intramuscular fluphenazine hydrochloride. If more medication is necessary, the clinician should administer a "booster" injection of perhaps 0.5 cc decanoate in 3 to 4 days. At the end of 3 to 4 weeks, the clinician can then tally up the total amount of decanoate injected and use this to establish the next dosage. (For example, a patient received 0.5 cc on day 1 and then required another 0.5 cc on day 5 and an additional 0.5 cc on day 12 to become clinically stable. At day 21, he should receive 1.5 cc for the next 3 weeks.) In this manner, a "sliding scale" approach can be used to determine the optimal dose for the patient at that time.

When using the decanoate, the clinician can flexibly adjust not merely the total dosage but also the dosing interval. For many patients, a dose of decanoate will be clinically effective for 6 weeks or longer. If a patient does not show symptoms of relapse toward the end of a dosing interval, the clinician may want to extend this period. Preliminary data suggest that once a patient has been maintained for a year or more on the decanoate, drug effects may last for many months.

The Use of Fluphenazine

1. Initially administer 0.5 cc of fluphenazine decanoate.
2. Supplement with oral or IM fluphenazine as needed.
3. If necessary, give "booster dose" of 0.5 cc on day 3 or 4.
4. Then give 0.5-cc doses every 3 to 7 days to contain symptoms.
5. After 3 to 4 weeks, add total dosage given and administer in a single dose.
6. During chronic treatment, dosage may be lowered slowly, or period between doses extended if symptoms are contained.

Physicians must be sensitive to the medical–legal implications of using long-acting medications. For example, a young schizophrenic man with a long history of medication noncompliance and frequent hospital admissions was readmitted for a 10-day period of observation. After this period had elapsed, the hospital staff felt the patient was not dangerous to himself or others and thus did not meet the state's stringent criteria for involuntary commitment. Because of the patient's poor record of medication compliance, the treating physician administered an injection of fluphenazine decanoate on the day prior to his discharge "so at least we'll be sure he'll get a few weeks more of medicine." Effectively, this approach left the patient without clinical supervision during the period he was most vulnerable to adverse effects from the new drug. In essence, the use of a long-acting phenothiazine was a ploy to prolong involuntary treatment for an additional few weeks without authorization—a highly questionable maneuver, both legally and ethically.

For many years, the bulk of relapses among schizophrenic patients was blamed on medication noncompliance. A patient would come to a clinic showing obvious signs of psychotic decompensation. The clinician would elicit from a family member a history of recent cessation of medication, and the relapse would be attributed to medication noncompliance. However, various unknown factors may lead to relapse, which in turn could prompt a patient to rebel against the medication regimen.

We participated in a large NIMH collaborative study that investigated these different possibilities, randomly assigning patients in double-blind fashion to receive either fluphenazine decanoate or oral hydrochloride. We failed to find significant differences in relapse rates between patients assigned to the oral form of fluphenazine and those receiving the "depot" medication.[40] Similar findings have emerged from other studies with prospective random assignment of patients. In contrast, other investigations have shown that a group of patients initially stabilized on decanoate appear to benefit from continuing this medication.[41]

Thus, it is likely that there is a subgroup of patients who will do better when maintained on a long-acting agent. In the absence of defined scientific criteria, however, clinical judgment must be used to select appropriate patients for each drug regimen. Nevertheless, the scientific data to date strongly suggest that if all schizophrenic patients were changed to the long-acting preparations, thus diminishing the problem of medication noncompliance, a relatively small dent would be made in the public health problem of relapses among schizophrenic patients. And this limitation of the ability of antipsychotic drugs to prevent relapse, even when they are used reliably, accounts in part for the fact that although the total number of beds occupied by schizophrenic patients in hospitals has declined considerably over the past three decades, the rate of admission to large institutions actually has increased.

Clearly, although antipsychotic drugs significantly lower the probability of relapse, they do not provide absolute protection. Thus, clinicians must consider other factors, particularly the psychosocial. Over the long term, addressing these considerations may help to lower the relapse rate among schizophrenics and to improve their ability to function socially.[2] In addition, the clinician must identify the minority of patients who may no longer need maintenance antipsychotic drug therapy. This author recommends periodic tapering to find and follow these patients. Recently, a study has been initiated that contrasts maintenance medication therapy for schizophrenic patients with an alternate approach in which patients are treated vigorously during acute episodes but are allowed to remain medication-free during intervals between active psychosis. Preliminary data suggest that the latter technique may be useful.[42]

c. Other Diagnostic Groups

In no other psychiatric disorder is the indication for maintenance antipsychotic drug therapy as clearly established as it is in the treatment of the schizophrenic syndrome. Nevertheless, clinical experience suggests that patients with other diagnoses occasionally benefit from long-term treatment with antipsychotic drugs. For example, an occasional patient with bipolar affective disorder may benefit from maintenance therapy with an antipsychotic agent, either in addition to or as a substitute for lithium. Similarly, a patient with recurrent episodes of psychotic depression might be assisted. Some patients with uncontrollable behavior caused by mental retardation or an organic brain syndrome will be more manageable on maintenance antipsychotic drug therapy; however, it should be demonstrated that nonpharmacological approaches, such as environmental alteration and behavioral therapy, do not alleviate the problem. Patients with borderline personalities may benefit from antipsychotic drugs, usually in relatively low doses, for long-term assistance with uncontrollable waves of emotions and, at times, destructive impulses. (A proper role for medication in this group of patients has not been established, however.) The butyrophenone haloperidol is often used for chronic symptom suppression in patients with Gilles de la Tourette syndrome.

If antipsychotic drugs are to be used for disorders other than schizophrenia, particularly when they are used over a period of many months and even years, the clinical record should reflect in detail the rationale behind the therapy and the care taken in its administration. In light of the long-term risks of antipsychotic drug treatment, a patient's chart should indicate why alternate treatments were not employed. Finally, the record should also detail the continued need for antipsychotic agents, attempts made to lower the dose or discontinue their use, and steps taken to monitor for unwanted effects and toxicity.

K. New Drugs

Since the introduction of chlorpromazine about 30 years ago, we have seen the development of two other subclasses of phenothiazines and four other distinct groups of antipsychotic drugs. However, with the exception of a spectrum of unwanted effects, there has been little new. Despite advertising ballyhoo, most of the drugs introduced since chlorpromazine have fallen more or less into the me-too category: no better, no worse, no different. This is not to say that the availability of a spectrum of antipsychotic drugs does not facilitate clinical practice; it does. The ability to choose among agents allows physicians to minimize unwanted effects for each patient. Also, a patient may respond better to one drug than to another.

What can we expect in the future? In the past, the drug companies, unwilling to gamble on "long shots," tested the same preclinical compounds for potential antipsychotic action, resulting in rediscovery of the same type of agent despite chemical differences in the molecules themselves. Thus, the pharmacological profile of new drugs displayed a monotonous similarity to the old drugs.

One exception was the dibenzoxazepine drug clozapine, referred to a number of times in this chapter. Clozapine was an effective, low-potency, sedating antipsychotic drug that was distinguished by its lack of extrapyramidal effects. Moreover, clozapine produced little elevation in plasma prolactin. Although other explanations have been given, it is possible that clozapine was a "smart" dopamine blocker, effectively counteracting dopamine receptors in brain centers that run amok in psychosis (mesolimbic and mesocortical pathways?) while having relatively little effect on neurological (nigrostriatal) and hormonal (tuberoinfundibular) tracts. However, clozapine had an unfortunate tendency to produce a high incidence of agranulocytosis as well as hypotension and hyperthermia. Therefore, its manufacturer, Sandoz Ltd., has withdrawn it from worldwide use. An avid search is ongoing among a number of pharmaceutical laboratories to find other clozapinelike compounds but without its toxicity.

Various new chemical compounds are being tested for antipsychotic effects, but most are not much different from the older compounds. Pimozide, a particularly potent dopamine blocker, resembles haloperidol both structurally and clinically. A number of long-acting injectable preparations are being tested, but there seem to be few differences from the fluphenazine enanthate and decanoate esters. Penfluridol, chemically related to haloperidol, may be administered once weekly by mouth. This drug also has problems with toxicity and may not come to market, although a once-weekly preparation would be clinically attractive. However, as with the long-acting injectables, there is no evidence that long-acting oral preparations will reduce the relapse rate among schizophrenics.

A number of chemically and pharmacologically distinct substances have been used experimentally for the treatment of psychosis within recent years. These include the β-adrenergic blocking agent, propranolol, which has been employed alone and in combination with antipsychotic drugs for the treatment of schizophrenia, organic brain disease, and other psychiatric conditions. As of this writing, results with propranolol remain inconclusive although intriguing. The anticonvulsant carbamazepine (Tegretol®), chemically related to the heterocyclic antidepressants, has been effective in treating psychotic conditions associated with mania and depression. A number of other substances also are in various phases of experimentation. The outcome will depend on the quirks of nature, the vicissitudes of public funding for psychiatric research, and the degree to which private industry perceives a potential for profit.

IV. CONCLUSION

Psychiatrists continue to hope that better agents will be developed for the treatment of psychosis. These would include more effective drugs, drugs that could reach that minority of schizophrenic patients who remain refractory to currently available agents, substances with fewer unwanted effects and a lower incidence of toxicity, and a generally broader range of clinical options.

Yet, despite their shortcomings, the current crop of antipsychotic drugs have been strikingly impressive in the relief they have provided for many patients and families. Although imperfect, they have largely been able to quell the onslaught of the more virulent aspects of psychosis. And although they have a broad range of untoward reactions and toxicity associated with their use, they are nonaddicting, have a high therapeutic index, and, considering the extent of their usage, are impressively nontoxic.

REFERENCES

1. May P. R. A., Tuma A. H., Yale C., et al: Schizophrenia—a follow-up study of results of treatment. II. Hospital stay over two to five years. *Arch Gen Psychiatry* 33:431–506, 1976.
2. Hogarty G. E., Goldberg S. C., Schooler N. R., et al: Drugs and social therapy in the aftercare of schizophrenic patients. II. Two-year relapse rates. *Arch Gen Psychiatry* 31:603–608, 1974.
3. Epstein N. B., Vlok L. A.: Research on the results of psychotherapy: A summary of evidence. *Am J Psychiatry* 138:1027–1035, 1981.
4. Gelenberg A. J.: The catatonic syndrome. *Lancet* 1:1339–1341, 1976.
5. *Electroconvulsive Therapy*. Task Force Report #14, American Psychiatric Association, Washington, 1978.
6. Bartlett J., Bridges P., Kelly D.: Contemporary indications for psychosurgery. *Br J Psychiatry* 138:507–511, 1981.
7. Lipton M. A., Mailman R. B., Nemeroff C. B.: Vitamins, megavitamin therapy, and the nervous system, in Wurtman R. J., Wurtman J. J. (eds): *Nutrition and the Brain,* vol 3: *Disorders of Eating and Nutrients in Treatment of Brain Diseases.* New York, Raven Press, 1979, pp 183–264.
8. Gelenberg A. J.: Nutrition and psychiatry, in: Young V., Herman R., Owen G., et al (eds): *The Manual of Clinical Nutrition.* Washington, Nutrition Publications, in press.
9. Borus J. F.: Deinstitutionalization of the chronically mentally ill. *N Engl J Med* 305:339–342, 1981.
10. Cohen B.: Dopamine receptors and antipsychotic drugs. *McLean Hosp J* 6:95–114, 1981.
11. Casey D. E., Clappison V. J., Keepers G. A.: Anticholinergic drugs in neuroleptic-induced extrapyramidal symptoms. Paper read at the American Psychiatric Association meeting, New Orleans, May 11–15, 1981.
12. VanPutten T., Mutalipassi L. R., Malkin M. O.: Phenothiazine-induced decompensation. *Arch Gen Psychiatry* 30:102–106, 1974.
13. Gelenberg A. J., Mandel M. R.: Catatonic reactions to high potency neuroleptic drugs. *Arch Gen Psychiatry* 34:947–950, 1977.
14. Rifkin A., Quitkin F., Klein D. F.: Akinesia: A poorly recognized drug-induced extrapyramidal behavior disorder. *Arch Gen Psychiatry* 32:642–674, 1975.
15. Wojcik J. D.: Antiparkinson drug use. *Mass Gen Hosp Biol Ther Psychiatry Newslett* 2:5–7, 1979.
16. Gelenberg A. J.: Amantadine in the treatment of benztropine-refractory neuroleptic-induced movement disorders. *Curr Ther Res* 23:375–380, 1978.
17. Smith J. M.: Abuse of the antiparkinson drugs: A review of the literature. *J Clin Psychiatry* 41:351–354, 1980.
18. Jeste D. V., Wyatt R. J.: Changing epidemiology of tardive dyskinesia: An overview. *Am J Psychiatry* 138:297–309, 1981.
19. Wojcik J. D., Gelenberg A. J., Labrie R. A., et al: Prevalence of tardive dyskinesia in an outpatient population. *Comp Psychiatry* 21:370–380, 1980.
20. Kane J., Struve F., Woerner M., et al: Results from a prospective study of tardive dyskinesia development: Preliminary findings over a two-year period. Paper read at the NCDEU meeting, Key Biscayne Florida, May 26–28, 1981.

21. Gardos G., Cole J. O., Tarsy D.: Withdrawal syndromes associated with antipsychotic drugs. *Am J Psychiatry* 135:1321–1324, 1978.

22. Quitkin F., Rifkin A., Gochfeld L., et al: Tardive dyskinesia: Are first signs reversible? *Am J Psychiatry* 134:84–87, 1977.

23. Baldessarini R. J., Tarsy D.: Tardive dyskinesia, in Lipton M. A., DiMascio A., Killam K. F. (eds): *Psychopharmacology: A Generation of Progress.* New York, Raven Press, 1978, pp 993–1004.

24. Alpert M., Diamond F., Friedhoff A. J.: Receptor sensitivity modification in treatment of tardive dyskinesia. Paper read at the NCDEU meeting, Key Biscayne Florida, May 26–28, 1981.

25. Gelenberg A. J., Wojcik J. D., Growdon J. H.: Lecithin for the treatment of tardive dyskinesia, in: Barbeau A., Growdon J. H., Wurtman R. J. (eds): *Nutrition and the Brain.* New York, Raven Press, 1979, vol 5, pp 285–303.

26. Caroff S. N.: The neuroleptic malignant syndrome. *J Clin Psychiatry* 41:79–83, 1980.

27. Baldessarini R. J., Gelenberg A. J.: Using physostigmine safely. *Am J Psychiatry* 136:1608–1609, 1979.

28. Zarrabi M. H., Zucker S., Miller F., et al: Immunologic and coagulation disorders in chlorpromazine-treated patients. *Ann Intern Med* 91:194–199, 1979.

29. Gelenberg A. J.: Psychotropic drugs during pregnancy and the perinatal period. *Mass Gen Hosp Biol Ther Psychiatry Newslett* 2:41–42, 1979.

30. Chouinard G., Jones B. D.: Neuroleptic-induced supersensitivity psychosis: Clinical and pharmacologic characteristics. *Am J Psychiatry* 137:16–21, 1980.

31. Rivera-Calimlim L., Castaneda L., Lasagna L.: Effect of management on plasma chlorpromazine in psychiatric patients. *Clin Pharmacol Ther* 14:978–986, 1973.

32. Dysken M. W., Javaid J. I., Chang S. S., et al: Fluphenazine pharmacokinetics and therapeutic response. *Psychopharmacology* 73:205–210, 1981.

33. Cohen W. J., Cohen N. H.: Lithium carbonate, haloperidol, and irreversible brain damage. *JAMA* 230:1283–1287, 1974.

34. Spring G. K.: Neurotoxicity with combined use of lithium and thioridazine. *J Clin Psychiatry* 40:135–138, 1979.

35. Gelenberg A. J.: Is it safe to co-prescribe lithium with a neuroleptic? *Mass Gen Hosp Biol Ther Psychiatry Newslett* 2:13, 1979.

36. Rivera-Calimlim L., Kerzner B., Karch F. E.: Effect of lithium on plasma chlorpromazine level. *Clin Pharmacol Ther* 23:451–455, 1978.

37. Gelenberg A. J.: Coffee, tea, and antipsychotic drugs revisited. *Mass Gen Hosp Biol Ther Psychiatry Newslett* 4:42-43, 1981.

38. Gelenberg A. J.: Psychiatric emergencies: The psychotic patient *Drug Ther,* May 1981 pp 25–36.

39. Kane J., Rifkin A., Quitkin F., et al: A pilot study of "low dose" fluphenazine decanoate in outpatient schizophrenics. *Psychopharmacol Bull* 15:78–79, 1979.

40. Schooler N. R., Levine J., Severe J. B., et al: Prevention of relapse in schizophrenia: An evaluation of fluphenazine decanoate. *Arch Gen Psychiatry* 37:16–24, 1980.

41. Gelenberg A. J.: About long-acting antipsychotic drugs. *Mass Gen Hosp Biol Ther Psychiatry Newslett* 3:17–18, 1980.

42. Carpenter W. T. Jr, Stephens J. H., Raey A. C., et al: Early intervention versus continuous pharmacotherapy of schizophrenia. *Psychopharmacol. Bull.* 18:21–23, 1982.

43. Gelenberg A. J.: Treating the outpatient schizophrenic. *Postgrad Med* 64:48–56, 1978.

44. Lader M.: *Introduction to Psychopharmacology.* Kalamazoo, Upjohn, 1980, p 30.

5

Anxiety

ALAN J. GELENBERG, M.D.

I. INTRODUCTION

A. Anxiety: A Symptom

Anxiety is a universal human experience, a common response to routine daily stress and emotional conflict. There is a spectrum of anxiety—from a normal emotion to a psychopathological symptom of varying severity. When accompanied by other specific symptom constellations, anxiety can form the nucleus of a number of syndromes.

B. Symptoms

1. Psychological

The psychological perception of anxiety varies with the severity of the experience and with the individual's awareness of his own emotional responses. Mild anxiety may be perceived as a vague sense of irritability and uneasiness. More fully experienced, anxiety is a feeling that something terrible is about to happen, such as impending death or doom. In its most severe forms, a sufferer feels terror or panic.

2. Physical

Physical symptoms of anxiety also vary, depending on the intensity of the anxiety as well as the individual's predispositions and awareness of bodily functions. Virtually any body system can be involved. The skin may be

---

ALAN J. GELENBERG, M.D. • Department of Psychiatry, Harvard Medical School and Massachusetts General Hospital, Boston, Massachusetts 02114.

flushed, and a patient may feel hot or cold, possibly associated with sweating. Pupils often are dilated as part of general autonomic arousal, and the patient's eyes may dart around in a terrified scanning. Gastrointestinal symptoms can include dry mouth, a feeling of nausea (and possibly actual vomiting), intestinal cramping, and diarrhea. Cardiorespiratory symptoms and signs can include palpitations (possibly extra beats), tachycardia, a feeling of faintness (and even vasovagal syncope), an experience of shortness of breath, and hyperventilation with light-headedness and paresthesias. Tremulousness, tremor, and restlessness are common, as are headache and urinary frequency.

C. What Anxiety Is Not

Anxiety is not depression, agitation, or excitement, although it may accompany or underlie any or all of these. Depression—marked by a sense of diminished self-esteem not necessarily present in anxiety—often is accompanied by anxiety; the converse, however, need not be true.

Agitation is a sign rather than a symptom. In other words, it is perceived by an outside observer rather than described subjectively by the patient. Agitation, in which a patient is in a state of restless motion (pacing, hand wringing, appearing tormented) may be a sign of anxiety, but patients can be agitated in the throes of depression or psychosis, even when they do not report the symptom of anxiety.

Excitement, a state of greatly increased emotion and activity, is frequently observed in manic and some schizophrenic psychoses. Very often, anxiety generates the state of psychotic excitement. Moreover, excited patients may make others very anxious (indeed, they can be quite intimidating).

II. MODELS

A. Psychoanalytic

Psychoanalysts view anxiety as a manifestation of intrapsychic conflict and describe a continuum of responses. Secondary anxiety signals the ego to mobilize defenses to deal with a stress or conflict. "The anxiety acts as a warning that danger is impending; but the danger is one that the individual is capable of coping with; it is not yet overwhelming or inevitable."[1] Psychoanalysts also have described how anxiety is central to symptom formation and the development of the neuroses (i.e., obsessive–compulsive, phobic, etc.). The symptoms are the end product of the mixture of elements from both an unconscious impulse and the ego defenses directed against it. The symptoms are a compromise formation, the result . . . of vectors of forces showing the summated effects of all the elements.[1]

For example, a ladylike and very proper middle-aged woman little given to displays of emotion—and certainly not anger—becomes manifestly anxious when she is alone with her husband. The clinician learns that the symptoms started after the woman learned of her husband's recent infidelity. She is brimming with a sense of outrage toward her husband, but these feelings are intolerable to her. When they threaten to surface, she becomes overtly anxious.

B. Behavioral

One behavioral explanation of anxiety concerns the pairing of a neutral stimulus with a painful one. For example: turn on a light in a rat's cage, then shock the animal. After several pairings of light with shock, the animal will crouch, shake, urinate, and defecate when the light appears—apparent signs of anxiety. In human terms, a girl may become anxious in the presence of her father because of his heavy-handed style of discipline. When she grows into womanhood, this pattern might generalize from her father to other adult men, in whose presence she will also experience symptoms of anxiety. In this model, anxiety occurs when an individual encounters a sign that "predicts" a painful event. Anxiety also may become a stimulus itself, shaping and conditioning future behavior in adverse ways.

C. Separation Anxiety

Another explanation of anxiety focuses on separation anxiety—a universal experience in infancy. During specific critical periods, when infants are separated from a central and trusted caregiving figure (usually mother), they may initially experience a state of panic, which is vividly communicated to all within range. This reaction has obvious survival value—both for the individual and the species—as it encourages closer attention to the needs of the baby during its long period of dependency. Separation anxiety seems to be an innate rather than a conditioned response. From the outset, the separation itself appears to generate the infant's sense of terror; separation anxiety does not wait for an experience (or series of experiences) in which separation was attended by other adverse consequences (e.g., hunger, physical discomfort). One could imagine that either experiences in early childhood, an innate (biochemical?) predisposition, or a combination of the two could leave some individuals vulnerable to attacks of the same type of panic long after separation anxiety should have been outgrown and no longer serves any useful function. These latter-day panic attacks could be triggered by subliminal cues or unconsciously perceived events, by intrapsychic conflict, or by neurochemical patterns.

D. Biological

The biology of anxiety has been of interest for a long time. Many years ago, James and Lange squared off against Cannon in a debate over whether peripheral autonomic symptoms of anxiety were primary or secondary to the perception of anxiety. The former claimed that it was the racing heart, sweaty palms, and tightness in the stomach that an individual identified as the experience of anxiety; the latter maintained that visceral symptoms **followed** an internal percept.

Recent developments in neurobiology have shed interesting new light on the biology of anxiety. The benzodiazepine drugs (to be discussed shortly) appear to be the most effective, and are beyond a doubt the most popular, antianxiety compounds ever employed in man. How intriguing, then, when it was discovered that the mammalian brain possesses its own receptors specific for benzodiazepine molecules.[2] On the assumption that God (or evolution) did not endow us with benzodiazepine receptors in anticipation of Leo Sternbach's synthesizing Librium® and Valium®, neuroscientists began to search for an endogenous ligand for the benzodiazepine receptor. Although at the time of this writing the search continues, a number of potential candidates have been identified.[3]

Thus, it appears that our brains possess their own anxiolytic molecules (analogues of Valium®) and receptors for these molecules. To generalize from animal studies, it is possible that individuals with chronic high levels of anxiety may suffer from congenital (or acquired) defects in this internal anxiety-regulating system. Two such possibilities would be that (1) these individuals might have too little of the endogenous benzodiazepine and/or (2) they may have some difficulty binding the benzodiazepine to its receptor sites. (To paraphrase an old joke, some folks may have been born 10 mg of Valium® below par.) The administration of exogenous substances such as benzodiazepine drugs or alcohol may alter this internal regulating system. It is also conceivable that nonpharmacological therapies for anxiety, such as meditation and relaxation, may mobilize internal antianxiety substances and enhance their effectiveness.

Other tantalizing biological data include a significantly increased incidence of mitral valve prolapse in individuals with panic attacks,[4] and the fact that the intravenous infusion of lactate is capable of triggering anxiety reactions in predisposed individuals.[5]

III. DIFFERENTIAL DIAGNOSIS

Many patients with anxiety come to their general practitioner or internist complaining of various somatic symptoms. Others who experience anxiety more on a psychological level might request to see a psychiatrist. Whatever the patient's route of entry into the health care system, a physician should carefully evaluate the individual using standard medical procedures: history, physical and mental status examinations, and indicated laboratory tests. A practitioner should always maintain a high index of suspicion about the possibility of a medical etiology and carefully evaluate specific somatic complaints. Psychiatric patients have a high incidence of coexisting medical problems, and therefore, a clinician should not automatically assume that a physical symptom is "merely" a manifestation of the patient's anxiety. Because anxiety accompanies most psychopathological states and many organic problems, the differential diagnosis is extensive.

A. Medical

A list of all possible organic causes of anxiety would constitute much of the index of a textbook of medicine—even without including emotional reactions to physical illness. Many varied types of medical problems result in anxiety symptoms. Endocrine disorders such as hyperthyroidism may produce severe anxiety. Similarly, hypoglycemia, whether caused by an insulinoma or by exogenously administered insulin, can result in anxiety, and so can secreting tumors such as carcinoid and pheochromocytoma. Patients with various neurological abnormalities—including encephalopathies of diverse etiologies, postconcussion syndrome, and seizure disorders—may report anxiety. Others with severe pulmonary disease and hypoxia also complain of anxiety. Excesses of stimulant drugs (including caffeine) and withdrawal from sedative drugs (including alcohol) can be culprits as well.

It would be impossible to memorize all the possible physical causes of anxiety, and it would be a useless exercise to sit before an anxious patient with a checklist. Rather, the clinician should maintain a high index of suspicion and complete a thorough assessment.

When taking a history, inquire about past and present medical illnesses and medications, other treatments, and doctors consulted. Inquire also about the use of over-the-counter drugs as well as "recreational" substances. Hallucinogens, for example, may precipitate a "bad trip" or panic attack. Always ask about alcohol, and do not forget to estimate the amount of caffeine consumption.

Complete a careful review of systems. Although the presence of various symptoms may not have emerged initially when taking a history from an anxious patient, the systems review may reveal a pattern—such as skin and hair changes, heat intolerance, and weight loss (possible hyperthyroidism)— that can suggest further diagnostic evaluation.

The clinician should complete a routine physical examination with specific attention to areas highlighted by the history. Laboratory tests can be ordered on the basis of findings from the history and physical examination and anticipated medication therapy.

B. Psychiatric

Anxiety accompanies most psychiatric disorders. Patients with schizophrenia, other psychoses, affective disorders, borderline states, and personality disturbances may present with severe anxiety. Before prescribing an antianxiety drug, the clinician should complete a thorough evaluation. Psychoses, affective disorders, personality disturbances, and organic brain syndromes (see Section III.A) should be considered in the differential diagnosis of anxiety. Once the clinician determines the diagnosis, the general rule is to treat the primary disorder specifically—antipsychotic drugs for schizophrenia, antidepressants for endogenous depressions, antianxiety drugs for generalized anxiety disorders, etc.

IV. PRIMARY ANXIETY DISORDERS AND THEIR TREATMENT

Current nomenclature divides anxiety disorders into three major subtypes: phobic disorders, anxiety states, and posttraumatic stress disorders. Approximately 2 to 4% of the general population has at some time in their lives experienced one of these conditions.[6]

A. Phobic Disorders

When someone develops a persistent and irrational fear of a situation or object and avoids it at all costs, he has a phobia. The third edition of the American Psychiatric Association's *Diagnostic and Statistical Manual* (DSM-III) describes three types of phobias: agoraphobia (with or without panic attacks), social phobia, and simple phobia.

1. Agoraphobia

Agoraphobia (literally, fear of the marketplace) is characterized by a fear of being cut off from sources of help. At a given time, about 0.5% of the population may suffer from agoraphobia. Among phobic patients seeking treatment, agoraphobia is the most common syndrome. Sufferers are frightened by crowded public places, particularly those from which egress is difficult or impossible. They may fear being alone, often restrict their activities to home or its geographic proximity, and might refuse to go out without a trusted friend or family member. In the most extreme situations, an agoraphobic person will refuse to leave home altogether or to go places without company.

Frequently, panic attacks accompany agoraphobia. In a panic attack, the patient experiences severe anxiety symptoms and an overwhelming sense of terror. The symptoms usually last for minutes (or occasionally hours), although to the sufferer this might feel like ages. Episodes are discrete, often without a discernable precipitant, and occur unpredictably.

Klein has hypothesized that panic attacks are central to the genesis of agoraphobia.[7] In his model, an individual first experiences a panic attack "out of the blue"—perhaps because of vestiges of severe separation anxiety and/or a biochemical predisposition. (Interestingly, an intravenous infusion of sodium lactate may precipitate a panic attack in these patients, and they have a higher than expected prevalence of mitral valve prolapse.)

After an initial panic attack, the patient usually assumes a physical cause and seeks medical attention. Most often none is discovered, and the individual goes back, somewhat perplexed, to his normal life pattern. After a second or third such episode, however, the patient's style of living gradually changes. He avoids circumstances where he feels cut off from immediate help—crowded shopping centers, driving in tunnels, etc. This may progress to a marked constriction of activities and living space and can considerably burden friends and family. At the same time, the individual develops a secondary response—anticipatory anxiety, namely, fear of the panic attacks.

Treatment of agoraphobia and panic attacks has become highly successful in recent years. First and foremost, a large majority of patients with panic attacks are successfully treated with antidepressant drugs. Although most research to date has focused on the tricyclic antidepressant imipramine (Tofranil® and others) and the MAO inhibitor antidepressant phenelzine, clinical experience suggests that almost any antidepressant drug (with one or two exceptions among experimental agents) can effectively alleviate this condition. Preliminary evidence suggests that these drugs block panic attacks by enhancing central nervous system norepinephrine transmission. Dosages of antidepressant drugs vary widely among patients, but many patients respond to amounts far lower than those used to treat depression. Therefore, the clinician should begin treatment with fairly small doses (e.g., 25 to 50 mg per day of imipramine) and increase the dose gradually until panic attacks cease. The therapy should continue for 6 to 12 months at the effective dose; then the clinician may attempt to lower the dose of the drug gradually and discontinue it to assess the necessity of further treatment.

After an antidepressant drug has successfully treated the panic attacks (ideally within a matter of weeks), the clinician should encourage patients to confront the feared situation or object and to overcome their anticipatory anxiety. Various approaches can help: counseling, education, and reassurance from a physician, group therapy with similar patients, trips into "the field" with a therapist. For treatment of agoraphobia to work, in vivo exposure to the phobic stimuli is essential. This approach usually helps to dissipate anticipatory anxiety and allows the patient to resume his usual activities. Adjunctive treatment with a benzodiazepine antianxiety drug [or possibly with a β-adrenergic blocking agent, such as propranolol (Inderal®, Inderide®)] might help diminish anticipatory anxiety if psychosocial and behavioral techniques alone do not suffice. This approach can be combined with insight-oriented psychotherapy. The goal would be both to diminish symptoms and to help the patient understand the nature of internal conflicts (i.e., the source of separation anxiety, etc.). Benzodiazepines tend not to be effective against the panic attacks themselves; however, the new drug alprazolam (Xanax®)— which purportedly possesses antidepressant activity—may be an exception.

2. Social Phobia

Patients with social phobias fear and avoid situations that could lead to public humiliation or embarrassment. For example, a phobic patient might never speak in public, use public lavatories, or perform various functions in the presence of other people.

Psychosocial and behavioral approaches aimed at encouraging a patient to experience and gradually overcome this fear of public performances may help to alleviate the anxiety. Psychotherapeutic techniques can assist a patient to understand the dynamic basis of his concerns. β-Adrenergic blocking drugs such as propranolol can sometimes alleviate social anxiety. Similarly, benzodiazepine drugs might play an adjunctive role.

3. Simple Phobia

Simple phobia is an irrational fear of an object or situation (other than those described in the above two conditions). Examples include fear of animals (zoophobia), closed spaces (claustrophobia), or heights (acrophobia).

Treatment of simple phobia is primarily nonbiological. Although at times psychoanalytic approaches are indicated (Freud's "Little Hans" is a case in point), behavioral treatment is usually more rapid and effective. In some instances, supplementary anxiolytic drugs can be helpful. Many clinicians combine approaches such as insight-oriented therapy (to understand the conflict) and behavioral treatment (to confront the phobic object).

B. Anxiety States

1. Panic Disorder

The description and treatment of panic disorders are the same as those discussed in the section above on agoraphobia.

2. Generalized Anxiety Disorder

This condition is characterized by general persistent anxiety of at least 1 month's duration that does not meet the criteria for the other conditions listed in this section. The clinician must rule out other medical and psychiatric disorders. Treatment varies with the extent and nature of the symptoms, their relation to psychosocial factors, and a patient's resources—psychological, intellectual, and even financial.

A patient who experiences anxiety in intimate relationships may benefit from psychodynamic psychotherapy or psychoanalysis to explore the roots of underlying intrapsychic conflicts. Others, with anxiety that stems from an isolated sexual problem, may benefit from specific sexual therapy. If anxiety is situational and in response to a life stress, then short-term supportive psychotherapy might be indicated. When anxiety is chronic, the clinician could include relaxation training in the therapeutic plan.

Drug therapy for the treatment of anxiety symptoms ideally should be used in the context of an ongoing therapeutic relationship and together with a nonbiological treatment—talking therapy, behavioral techniques, or environmental manipulation. Whenever possible, medication treatment should be relatively brief (i.e., during a time-limited period of specific stress). However, many patients complain of chronic and persistent anxiety and often request "tranquilizers." The clinician then must decide if the potential advantages of an antianxiety drug outweigh possible disadvantages. If drugs are considered in a patient undergoing psychotherapy, transference factors should be explicitly evaluated. In most cases, benzodiazepines are the agents of choice for patients with generalized anxiety disorder (see Section VI).

3. Obsessive–Compulsive Disorder

Obsessions are recurrent, persistent ideas, thoughts, images, or impulses that are experienced as alien and perceived as involuntary intrusions into consciousness. Compulsions are urgent repetitive behaviors; failure to perform the compulsive act often results in anxiety. Common obsessions include thoughts of violence, contamination, and doubt; common compulsions include hand washing and touching of specific places.

Both biological and nonbiological treatments of obsessive–compulsive disorders (to be distinguished from compulsive personality disorders) have been disappointing. Most researchers and clinicians agree, however, that a treatment plan should generally include some form of psychotherapeutic approach.[8]

Pharmacological techniques for the treatment of obsessive–compulsive disorder are still experimental. Some investigators have reported good results with the experimental antidepressant clomipramine, administered intravenously as well as orally. This chlorinated form of imipramine is a particularly potent enhancer of cerebral serotonin neurotransmission, and indeed, there is evidence of irregularities in serotonergic systems within the brain of patients with this condition.[9] For that reason, speculation has arisen about whether the serotonin precursor amino acid tryptophan may help to alleviate this condition. When panic attacks coexist with obsessions and compulsions, MAO inhibitor antidepressants might diminish symptoms.[10,11]

C. Posttraumatic Stress Disorders

The patient with a posttraumatic stress disorder relives a recognizable trauma that would upset most people. He experiences considerable emotional distress (e.g., recurrent dreams, intrusive thoughts) and either withdraws from involvement in current life situations or feels emotionally detached or numbed. Depending on the time course, this syndrome is subcategorized as acute or chronic (delayed).

The typical approach to posttraumatic stress disorder is psychotherapy, usually aimed at encouraging the individual to confront, deal with, and integrate psychological issues raised by the stressful events. At times, the adjunctive use of medication, such as benzodiazepine drugs, can diminish anxiety and relieve insomnia.

V. ANTIANXIETY AGENTS

Anxiety is universal and ubiquitous. Not surprisingly, people continue to search for chemical passports to tranquility—elixirs or pills that will provide rapid relief from the symptoms of anxiety. The benzodiazepine antianxiety agents are currently the most widely used and prescribed drugs in the entire world. Before chlordiazepoxide (Librium®), people took meprobamate (Equanil®, Miltown®, and others), and before that they took barbiturates, chloral hydrate, bromides, and other sedatives—and we probably could trace this pharmacological tree back to roots at the dawn of civilization. Certainly, alcohol is a time-honored (dishonored?) member of this group.

In this chapter, we review benzodiazepine drugs as well as several other classes that occasionally are used to treat anxiety, including antihistamines, barbiturates, propanediols, propranolol, and the antipsychotic drugs.

A. Benzodiazepines

The popularity of this class of antianxiety drugs has generated articles entitled "The Benzodiazepine Bonanza" and "Valiumania." From 1964 through 1973, the number of antianxiety drug prescriptions filled in United States drug stores increased dramatically. Most were for the benzodiazepines chlordiazepoxide and diazepam (Valium®). However, this trend has since reversed, possibly because of adverse publicity among physicians and the lay public. Even with the decline in use, over 60 million prescriptions for benzodiazepines were filled in the United States in 1979.[12] Fifteen percent of respondents to one survey within the United States reported using antianxiety agents in the 1970s—a figure comparable to that reported for other developed countries.[13]

Chlordiazepoxide, the first benzodiazepine antianxiety agent synthesized, was marketed in 1960. Three years afterwards, diazepam was introduced and rapidly became the most widely prescribed drug in the world. The popularity of these agents has spawned a number of chemical siblings.

In the following sections, we discuss the eight benzodiazepine drugs currently labeled for antianxiety use in the United States: chlordiazepoxide (Librium® and others), clorazepate (Azene®, Tranxene®), diazepam (Valium®), lorazepam (Ativan®), oxazepam (Serax®), prazepam (Centrax®, Verstran®), halazepam (Paxipam®), and alprazolam (Xanax®). Two other benzodiazepines, flurazepam (Dalmane®) and temazepam (Restoril®), are indicated for sleep (see Chapter 6). Another, clonazepam (Clonopin®), is labeled for the treatment of epilepsy. The labeled indication for benzodiazepine use (e.g., anxiety vs. insomnia) probably has more to do with corporate marketing decisions and commercial strategies than with the unique pharmacological profiles of the agents.

Benzodiazepines, as noted earlier, are the most widely prescribed antianxiety agents in the world. For that matter, they are the most widely prescribed drugs of any type. Their popularity is deserved. Clinically, they are highly effective for the alleviation of acute anxiety, and they probably retain at least a portion of their efficacy over time. Toxicologically, they are remarkably safe in situations of overdose, and their overall record of safety is unparalleled. Although they are by no means perfect (indeed, much of this chapter is devoted to caveats about their use), benzodiazepine drugs represent a definite step forward in the pharmacological treatment of anxiety.

1. Chemistry

Molecular structures of the eight benzodiazepines currently labeled for anxiolytic use are shown in Fig. 1. There are several subtypes of benzodiazepines with some differences in their pharmacology (see Table 1). Diazepam is a prototype of the 2-keto benzodiazepines, whose other members include desmethyldiazepam (the active agent during administration of clorazepate, prazepam, and halazepam). These drugs are all biotransformed by hepatic oxidative reactions and have long elimination half-lives.

Oxazepam. lorazepam, and the hypnotic temazepam are 3-OH benzodiazepines. They are metabolized by conjugation and have short to intermediate half-lives. The newly released alprazolam is a triazolo benzodiazepine, which also undergoes oxidation in the liver, but whose rate of elimination is considerably more rapid than that of the 2-keto benzodiazepines. Chlordiazepoxide is chemically distinct but pharmacologically similar to the 2-keto drugs. Clonazepam, an anticonvulsant benzodiazepine, is a 7-nitro benzodiazepine, which has a distinct biotransformation.

2. Pharmacological Effects and Mechanism of Action

Benzodiazepines reduce the effects of anxiety on behavior in animals. In a commonly employed behavioral paradigm, the presence of a light in a rat's cage will be followed shortly by a painful electric shock. The animal soon learns the "meaning" of the light and, in its presence, manifests anxiety: shaking, tachycardia, crouching, urinating, and defecating. If he had previously been working on a task (e.g., pressing a bar to obtain food), in the presence of the light (i.e., the anxiety condition) he stops working, remaining immobilized. However, administration of a benzodiazepine would allow the animal to keep on working despite the anxiety-producing stimulus, as if the drug had removed the fear of shock.

Benzodiazepines block nervous system stimulation that originates in the brainstem reticular system and diminish activity in areas associated with emotion such as the septal region, amygdala, hippocampus, and hypothalamus. Benzodiazepines raise the seizure threshold and increase the frequency and activity of brain waves—effects that resemble those of other sedative–hypnotic drugs such as barbiturates.

In one experiment, a single dose of diazepam administered to a group of healthy volunteers impaired both immediate and delayed free recall by interfering with the acquisition of new information. Retention remained unaf-

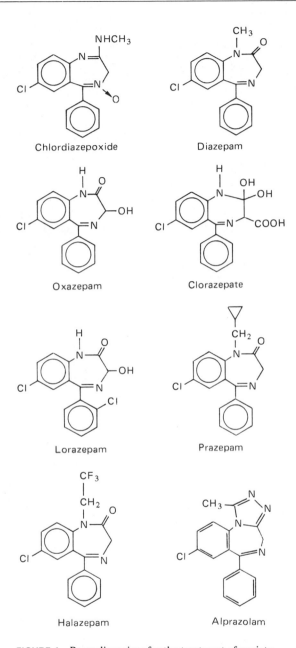

FIGURE 1. Benzodiazepines for the treatment of anxiety.

TABLE 1. Benzodiazepine Antianxiety Drugs[a]

Drug	Approximate dose equivalents (mg)	Available dosage forms	Rapidity of absorption	Active metabolites	Half-life (hr)
Alprazolam (Xanax®)	0.5	0.25-, 0.5-, and 1.0-mg tablets	Intermediate	α-Hydroxyalprazolam, desmethylalprazolam, 4-hydoxyalprazolam	6 to 20
Chlordiazepoxide (Librium® and others)	10	5-, 10-, 25-mg tablets and capsules, 100-mg/2-ml ampule	Intermediate	Desmethylchlordiaz-epoxide, demoxe-pam, desmethyl-diazepam, oxazepam	5 to 30
Clorazepate (Azene®, Tranxene®)	7.5	3.75-, 7.5-, and 15-mg cap-sules (Tranx-ene®) 3.25-, 6.5-, and 13-mg capsules (Azene®)	Fast	Desmethyl-diazepam,[b] oxazepam	30 to 200
Diazepam (Valium®)	5	2-, 5-, 10-mg tablets, 10-mg/2-ml ampules, 50-mg/10-ml vials, 10-mg/2-ml syringe	Fastest	Desmethyldiazepam, oxazepam	20 to 100

Halazepam (Paxipam®)	20	20-, 40-mg tablets	Intermediate	Desmethyl-diazepam, oxazepam	Ca. 14 (parent), 50 to 100 desmethyl-diazepam
Lorazepam (Ativan®)	1	0.5-, 1-, 2-mg tablets, 2- and 4-mg/ml syringes, 2- and 4-mg/ml vials[c]	Intermediate	None	10 to 20
Oxazepam (Serax®)	15	10-, 15-, 30-mg capsules, 15-mg tablets	Slower	None	5 to 15
Prazepam (Centrax®, Verstran®)	10	5-, 10-mg capsules, 10-mg tablets	Slowest	Desmethyl-diazepam,[b] oxazepam	30 to 200

[a] Prepared with the assistance of Jerrold F. Rosenbaum, M.D.
[b] These drugs are pro drugs for desmethyldiazepam; the parent compound is rapidly converted to the active metabolite.
[c] As of this writing, approved by FDA only for preanesthetic use.

fected. After 3 weeks of diazepam administration, partial tolerance developed to the memory impairment, and 1 week following discontinuation of diazepam, memory returned to normal.[14]

The benzodiazepines' mechanism of action has not been completely elucidated. They interact with brain receptors specific to them, and they probably resemble an endogenous ligand to these receptors. Benzodiazepine receptors are located in areas of the brain that might explain some of the pharmacological activity of benzodiazepine drugs.[15] Benzodiazepine receptors in the limbic system (hippocampus and olfactory bulb) may mediate antianxiety effects; receptors in the cortex might explain anticonvulsant activity; and receptors in thalamic nuclei could be involved in sedative effects. The interaction between drug and benzodiazepine receptor allows increased activity of the inhibitory neurotransmitter γ-aminobutyric acid (GABA).

Prolonged administration of benzodiazepine compounds may "turn off" the synthesis of endogenous benzodiazepinelike substances. Various withdrawal effects following drug discontinuation could, in turn, be caused by changes in receptors that follow long-term administration. The time required for recovery from benzodiazepine withdrawal symptoms would then reflect the time it takes to regenerate the endogenous ligand.

The effects of benzodiazepines on other organ systems show a strikingly benign pattern. Although decreased respiration, blood pressure, and cardiac output may be observed, they are unlikely to be of clinical consequence. In fact, clinicians have safely administered these drugs to large numbers of patients with diseases of the heart, blood vessels, and lungs.

Diazepam, especially, produces significant skeletal muscle relaxation, probably by direct action on spinal neurons. Physicians have administered this drug to many patients with skeletal muscle spasm, spasticity, and other muscle disorders, although its efficacy remains to be proved beyond doubt.

3. Kinetics

The rate at which a drug is absorbed from the gastrointestinal tract determines to a large degree the rapidity and intensity of onset of its acute effects.[16] Among benzodiazepine compounds, the rate of absorption varies considerably (see Table 1). Thus, diazepam and clorazepate reach the blood rapidly and produce prompt and intense effects following a single oral dose: peak concentrations of diazepam may be reached within an hour (even more rapidly in children), which could account for occasional reports of euphoria with diazepam. On the other end of the absorption spectrum, prazepam (and, to a lesser degree, oxazepam) is more slowly absorbed, resulting in a less intense and more delayed onset of action after single doses.

For any drug, absorption is most rapid when medication is taken on an empty stomach. Anything that delays gastric emptying—such as food or aluminum-containing antacids—will slow drug absorption, resulting in delayed onset and diminished intensity of acute clinical effects.

After a single dose of a benzodiazepine drug, its action is terminated primarily by drug distribution, which correlates with its lipid solubility. Thus, diazepam—the most lipid-soluble benzodiazepine—is rapidly and extensively distributed to body tissues following a single oral dose. Even though diazepam has a long elimination half-life, following a single dose its duration of action is relatively brief. Moreover, some degree of central nervous system tolerance also appears to diminish the initial action of the drug, even before blood levels have shown much decline. Less extensively distributed drugs, such as lorazepam, have a much longer duration of action after a single dose, even though lorazepam's elimination half-life is much briefer than diazepam's.

Plasma concentrations of benzodiazepine drugs (and their active metabolites) probably correlate to some degree with clinical response, although this relationship is complicated by tolerance that develops within the central nervous system. At present, measurements of benzodiazepine concentrations in blood are not ready for general clinical use, although studies have correlated unwanted effects of these drugs with blood levels and may provide clues to problems of overdose and withdrawal.[17]

Benzodiazepines bind tightly to plasma protein and are highly lipophilic, which means they are difficult to remove from the body by dialysis. They probably recirculate enterohepatically, which could account for an occasional secondary rise in blood levels several hours after the initial rise.

Benzodiazepines are metabolized in the hepatic microsomal enzyme system. Many are biotransformed into desmethyldiazepam—a major active metabolite of diazepam and halazepam, and a metabolite of chlordiazepoxide. In addition, clorazepate and prazepam have little pharmacological activity themselves but serve as precursors for desmethyldiazepam. The conversion of clorazepate to desmethyldiazepam occurs rapidly but depends on an acid medium in the stomach, which is compromised by the presence of antacids or food. The transformation of prazepam to desmethyldiazepam occurs more slowly, accounting for the gradual onset of effects with that drug. The metabolic pathways that transform drugs to desmethyldiazepam are influenced by factors such as age, liver disease, or the coadministration of other drugs that may affect hepatic oxidizing activity.

Three benzodiazepines—oxazepam, lorazepam, and the hypnotic temazepam—have no active metabolites and are simply conjugated with glucuronide in the liver. The elimination half-lives of these compounds is in the short to intermediate range. Their metabolism is less affected by the presence of liver disease, the extremes of age, or drug interactions.

Of what use to a clinician is a drug's half-life? First, the half-life determines the time required to achieve a "steady-state" concentration—which occurs in about four half-lives. (At steady state, the amount of drug excreted equals the amount ingested, i.e., a dynamic equilibrium.) Until a drug reaches steady state, it is accumulating, which means that the optimal dosage cannot yet be determined for a given patient. For example, an elderly woman in a nursing home may gradually become more sedated over the first several weeks on a chlordiazepoxide regimen. The drug is continuing to accumulate in her body until steady state is achieved, which may take longer in an elderly patient. For this reason, the clinician must be aware of this lag and adjust dosage accordingly.

A second significance of the half-life is with regard to the frequency of dosing. Drugs with half-lives greater than 24 hr often may be administered in once-daily doses, whereas drugs with short half-lives should be administered more frequently to achieve constant clinical effects. A third implication concerns the other end of the treatment program—termination. Drugs with long half-lives have a built-in tapering: when they are discontinued, their rates of egress from the body are relatively slow. Even so, all benzodiazepines should be discontinued by tapering rather than by abrupt discontinuation, but this is even more of a concern with short-half-life agents.

4. Adverse Effects

The most common unwanted effects of the benzodiazepines (as for other central nervous system depressants) are drowsiness and ataxia, which correlate with elevated blood concentrations of the drugs (and active metabolites). At even higher levels, gross psychomotor impairment and marked sedation occur. The elderly may be more vulnerable to these reactions because they usually achieve higher blood (and tissue) drug levels for a given dose and also because the aging brain is more sensitive to the effects of sedatives.

An increased tendency to express hostility, particularly in group settings, has been reported with diazepam and chlordiazepoxide but may be less of a problem with oxazepam. Data on this point remain inconclusive,[18] but clinicians may wish to avoid long-acting benzodiazepines in patients who have trouble containing their anger. Occasional patients become depressed during chronic benzodiazepine therapy, but whether this is a causal association remains in doubt.

Aside from the effects noted above, adverse reactions with benzodiazepines tend to be uncommon and are rarely serious. Occasional patients experience increased appetite and weight gain, cutaneous (usually allergic) reactions, nausea, headache, and assorted endocrine changes. Rare reports describe agranulocytosis and cholestatic jaundice, but unusual events in association with drug therapy do not prove an association with the drug. A few investigators have raised the possibility of a relationship between diazepam use and mammary tumors in laboratory animals and in humans; however, a careful review of the data does not support a causal association.[19]

5. Toxicity

Probably the nicest feature about the benzodiazepines is their very high therapeutic index—the ratio of toxic to therapeutic doses. Although frequently ingested in overdose attempts, benzodiazepines alone almost never cause fatalities.[20,21] The combination of a benzodiazepine with alcohol or other sedative–hypnotic agents is more hazardous, although it is unclear whether or not the benzodiazepines actually contribute to the lethality of the combination.[22]

Whenever possible, the use of any drug during pregnancy should be avoided. Some data suggest that benzodiazepines taken during the first trimester may cause an increased incidence of cleft lip/cleft palate. Used late in pregnancy or during nursing, benzodiazepines have been associated with a "floppy infant syndrome." Other observations in infants whose mothers have taken benzodiazepines have included multiple congenital deformities, intrauterine growth retardation, withdrawal symptoms, neonatal depression with poor sucking and hypotonia, hyperbilirubinemia, hypothermia, increased carbon dioxide tension and acidosis, and cardiac arrhythmias (many of which may be coincidental).[23] (See Chapter 10.)

6. Tolerance, Dependence, and Withdrawal Reactions

Tolerance develops to the sedative effects of benzodiazepines, but it is unclear whether tolerance develops to their sleep-maintaining and antianxiety effects. The benzodiazepines probably do retain at least a proportion of their efficacy over many months and possibly longer.

Benzodiazepine drugs have been sought out for "recreational" purposes—i.e., to induce a euphoric state, a "high." Some may have a greater abuse potential than others, conceivably related to their pharmacokinetics (e.g., rapid absorption and onset of action). In general, however, the abuse of these drugs has not been a major problem. On the other hand, clinicians should not prescribe the benzodiazepines to patients with a history of substance abuse, particularly with sedative–hypnotics. Any suggestion that a patient is taking more of the drug than prescribed should be viewed with concern.

Benzodiazepine withdrawal leads to reactions similar to those observed with other sedative–hypnotic compounds (e.g., barbiturates, alcohol). Cross tolerance exists among these various classes, and one agent can treat a withdrawal reaction to another. In fact, benzodiazepines are frequently employed as treatment for alcohol-withdrawal syndromes.

We used to believe that withdrawal reactions to benzodiazepines were relatively rare and occurred only when the drugs were used in dosages considerably in excess of therapeutic recommendations. More recently, however, clinicians have observed that patients taking benzodiazepines for long periods of time—even at standard doses—are vulnerable to withdrawal reactions on abrupt discontinuation (possibly because of a "turning off" of endogenous benzodiazepine substances).[24]

Mild withdrawal symptoms include insomnia, dizziness, headache, anorexia, vertigo, tinnitus, blurred vision, and shakiness. Some of these symptoms indicate a return of preexisting anxiety that had been contained by the benzodiazepine drug. However, if after discontinuing the drug these symptoms increase over several weeks and then begin to wane, a withdrawal reaction is more likely.

Severe signs of benzodiazepine withdrawal include hypotension, hyperthermia, neuromuscular irritability, psychosis, and seizures. Short-acting benzodiazepines, with their relatively rapid egress from the body, might cause a higher incidence of severe withdrawal reactions, including convulsions.

Benzodiazepine Withdrawal Syndrome	
Anxiety	Blurred vision
Agitation	Diarrhea
Tremulousness	Hypotension
Insomnia	Hyperthermia
Dizziness	Neuromuscular irritability
Headaches	Psychosis
Tinnitus	Seizures

Physicians should advise patients who are taking benzodiazepines to consult with them before discontinuing the drug. When it is desirable to stop the treatment, the drug (especially short-acting agents) should be tapered gradually, by 5 to 10% each day. The β-blocker propranolol has been used experimentally in the treatment of benzodiazepine withdrawal reactions, but results have been equivocal.[25,26]

7. Drug Interactions

Benzodiazepines interact with relatively few other drugs, so they can be coadministered safely with various medical and psychiatric medications. Benzodiazepines have relatively little tendency to induce hepatic microsomal enzymes, especially in comparison to barbiturates and other sedative–hypnotics, which means they usually can be administered to patients taking anticoagulants.

A common pharmacodynamic interaction (i.e., additive effects on target organs) is the **enhancement of central nervous system depression when a benzodiazepine is coadministered with another sedative, including alcohol.**

TABLE 2. Benzodiazepine Interactions[27]

Diazepam (Valium®)	↑ Phenytoin (Dilantin® and others) levels
Diazepam	↑ Digoxin (Lanoxin® and others) levels
Disulfiram (Antabuse®)	↑ Chlordiazepoxide (Librium® and others), diazepam levels
Antacids	↓ Clorazepate (Azene®, Tranxene®) absorption; slower chlordiazepoxide, diazepam absorption
Food	Slower diazepam absorption
Cimetidine (Tagamet®)	↑ Levels of long-acting benzodiazepines
Alcohol	?↑ Diazepam levels; potentiates CNS-depressant effects

It is doubtful whether coadministration of alcohol with diazepam can increase blood concentrations of diazepam (a pharmacokinetic interaction). A handful of pharmacokinetic interactions involving benzodiazepines have been reported (see Table 2). In general, benzodiazepines that undergo conjugation as the only metabolic step in biotransformation (i.e., oxazepam, lorazepam, temazepam) have the fewest kinetic interactions. Diazepam increases plasma levels of the anticonvulsant phenytoin and of the cardiac drug digoxin. When disulfiram is coadministered with chlordiazepoxide and diazepam, blood levels of the benzodiazepines can rise. Antacids should not be administered at the same time as clorazepate, since they will diminish the biotransformation of clorazepate to the active compound desmethyldiazepam, thus reducing its potency. Antacids and foods slow the absorption of other benzodiazepines but do not diminish the total amount absorbed. Cimetidine, used for the treatment of acid peptic disease, increases the blood levels of long-acting benzodiazepines (e.g., diazepam, chlordiazepoxide, clorazepate, prazepam) but does not appear to affect the short-acting agents (e.g., lorazepam, oxazepam, temazepam).[27]

8. Nonpsychiatric Uses

Benzodiazepines have a number of uses outside of psychiatry: as anticonvulsants for premedication before surgery and other procedures (such as cardioversion and endoscopy), in treatment of alcoholic withdrawal states, and as muscle relaxants in such diverse conditions as muscle strain, tetanus, spasticity, and stiff-man syndrome.

B. Other Antianxiety Agents

With the availability of the benzodiazepines, most previously employed antianxiety drugs have become obsolete. However, there are times when a physician may seek an alternative; for instance, in a patient liable to substance abuse. In addition, a doctor may "inherit" a patient who is already taking another type of drug, and thus we should all have some familiarity with other antianxiety compounds.

1. Antihistamines

Because of their sedative effects, drugs that block central and peripheral histamine receptors (primarily H_1) are sometimes used to calm anxious patients. Of the antihistamine drugs, clinicians prescribe hydroxyzine (Atarax®, Vistaril®, and others) most often. As shown in Fig. 2, it is chemically unrelated to the antipsychotics, antidepressants, benzodiazepines, or meprobamate.

Data about hydroxyzine metabolism in man are sparse. Apparently the drug is rapidly absorbed, begins to act within 15 to 30 min after a single oral dose, reaches peak plasma levels within 1 hr, and maintains its effect for at least 24 hr. In addition to its sedative and antianxiety effects, hydroxyzine also possesses antiemetic and antihistaminic properties. It may be more sedating than the benzodiazepines, although in some patients it can cause agitation. Although probably not as effective an anxiolytic as the benzodiazepines, hydroxyzine does not cause physical dependence or abuse; therefore, it may be used as an alternative for patients prone to drug dependence. Usual daily doses range from 200 to 400 mg per day in two to four divided doses which can be administered intramuscularly as well as orally.

In addition to the treatment of anxiety, hydroxyzine has been used for motion sickness, as a preanesthetic medication, and to treat allergic dermatoses. It is not as effective as chlordiazepoxide for treating alcohol withdrawal syndromes.

Fatal overdosage is uncommon with hydroxyzine, and withdrawal reactions have not been observed. Occasionally, cases of abnormal involuntary movements have been reported with antihistamines. Hydroxyzine may be teratogenic when administered to a pregnant woman, but this has not been studied definitively. **Whereas benzodiazepines and most other sedative–hypnotic drugs elevate the seizure threshold, antihistamines depress the threshold and thus should be used with caution in patients with seizure disorders.** Both peripheral and central anticholinergic toxicity can occur with antihistamine drugs; the elderly tend to be more sensitive to these actions. On a pharmacodynamic basis, hydroxyzine may show additive toxicity with other drugs that possess CNS-depressing antihistaminic or anticholinergic activity.

2. Barbiturates

The benzodiazepines, which have a much more favorable clinical profile, have largely replaced the formerly popular barbiturates for the treatment of anxiety. Barbiturates are classified according to their duration of action,

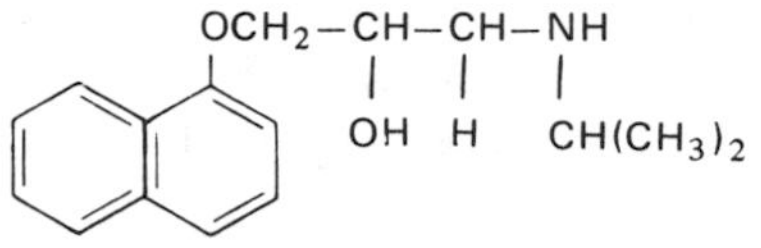

Propranolol

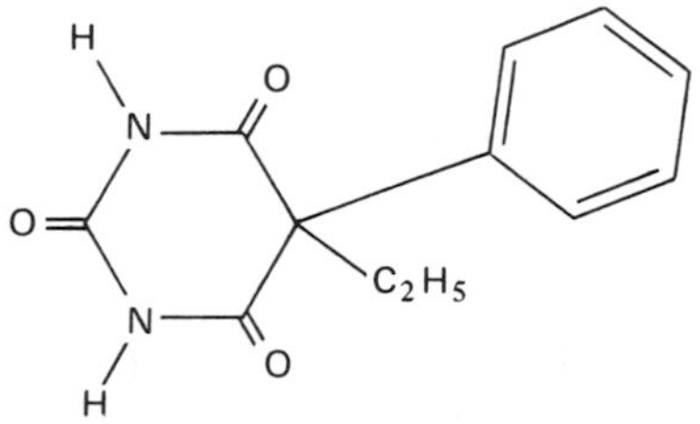

Phenobarbital

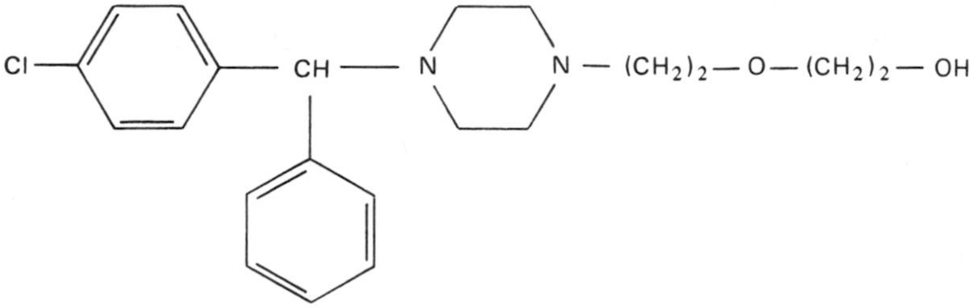

Hydroxyzine

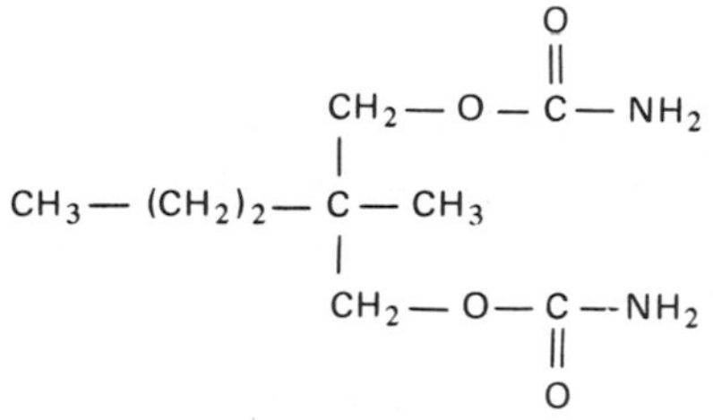

Meprobamate

FIGURE 2. Other drugs used for the treatment of anxiety.

which corresponds with their lipid solubility. The most lipid-soluble and most rapidly acting barbiturate is thiopental which is used primarily as an intravenous anesthetic. The least lipid-soluble, longest acting barbiturate is phenobarbital, usually employed as a daytime sedative, antianxiety agent, or anticonvulsant. Barbiturates that act more rapidly have a faster onset of action, more rapid metabolic degradation, and increased hypnotic potency. Rapidly acting barbiturates are primarily inactivated by metabolism in the hepatic microsomal enzymes of the liver, whereas phenobarbital is eliminated largely unchanged by the kidney.

Barbiturates have a wide variety of effects on the body. They are CNS depressants and, in doses only several times greater than therapeutic, can depress the central respiratory drive. In toxic doses, barbiturates also depress cardiac contractility. Barbiturates interfere with the microsomal drug-metabolizing system in the liver and thus interact with a variety of other drugs.

Barbiturates, most notably phenobarbital, probably have some degree of efficacy in the treatment of anxiety, but they seem to be less effective than the benzodiazepines and produce more sedation. It is likely that tolerance develops to antianxiety effects, which most probably result from their sedative activity. Clinical use of these agents is further complicated by the drugs' tendency to induce dependence, to cause serious withdrawal reactions, and to be dangerous in overdoses.

A barbiturate overdose can be extremely serious. Doses in excess of ten times a standard hypnotic dose are generally dangerous. Death occurs in approximately 0.5 to 12% of cases. Short-acting barbiturates are more toxic than the longer-acting agents: 2 to 3 g of amobarbital (Amytal®), secobarbital (Seconal®), or pentobarbital (Nembutal®) can cause death; in contrast, a lethal dose of the long-acting phenobarbital (Luminal® and others) begins at about 6 to 10 g. Similarly, lethal blood concentrations may be 6 mg/100 ml for phenobarbital and barbital but only 1 mg/100 ml for shorter-acting agents. Obviously, the presence of alcohol or other central nervous system depressants can cause death at lower barbiturate concentrations.

Patients who are moderately intoxicated with barbiturates show central nervous system signs: nystagmus, slurred speech, sedation, and ataxia. More severe levels of intoxication can lead to coma, depressed reflexes, and diminished cardiac contractility. Treatment consists of support of vital functions. Elimination of the drug may be hastened by the use of dialysis or hemoperfusion.

Adverse effects of barbiturates primarily reflect CNS depression. The dose necessary to affect respiration is not much higher than the therapeutic dosage, which gives these drugs a relatively low therapeutic index. Withdrawal reactions are similar to those described for the benzodiazepines but are likely to be much more severe, associated with a high incidence of seizures, and potentially fatal.

Aside from potentiating the sedative and CNS-depressing effects of other similar drugs, barbiturates can interact pharmacokinetically with many other agents, especially oral anticoagulants. **It is best to avoid coadministering barbiturates with anticoagulants,** but if it is unavoidable, the clinician should closely monitor the anticoagulant dosage and prothrombin time.

Barbiturates are contraindicated in patients with acute intermittent porphyria.

3. Propanediols

Meprobamate (Equanil®, Miltown®, and others) and tybamate (no longer available in the United States), two propanediols, are labeled for use as antianxiety agents. Meprobamate was an extremely popular drug in the 1950s, but controlled studies have failed to demonstrate its superiority over the barbiturates for the treatment of anxiety. For a vast majority of anxious patients, there is little reason to prescribe one of these drugs. Moreover, adverse effects, interactions, liability to abuse, and withdrawal syndromes resemble those observed with the barbiturates.

The structure of meprobamate is depicted in Fig. 2. The propanediols, similarly to the barbiturates, are metabolized mainly by hepatic microsomal oxidases and also induce these enzymes. The half-life of meprobamate is about 12 hr, and that of tybamate about half as long.

Pharmacological and clinical effects, toxicity, hazards, tolerance, withdrawal reactions, and interactions of meprobamate and tybamate are all similar to those of the barbiturates.

4. Propranolol

Propranolol (Inderal®, Inderide®) blocks β-noradrenergic receptors in the peripheral sympathetic nervous system and probably centrally as well. Although β blockers have recently been developed that discriminate between β_1 (cardiac) and β_2 (pulmonary) receptors, propranolol blocks both receptors competitively and without discrimination. Propranolol's structure is depicted in Fig. 2. Propranolol is almost completely absorbed following oral administration, but only about one-third of the administered drug reaches the systemic circulation, largely because of extensive first-pass metabolism in the liver. As with most drugs, plasma concentrations after a given dose of the drug vary widely among different people. The acute half-life of propranolol is about 3 hr, but with chronic administration it increases to about 4 hr. The drug is largely bound to plasma protein, which may make total blood concentrations less reliable as an index of clinical response. Propranolol is metabolized to inactive products and then excreted in the urine.

Propranolol has extensive effects on the cardiovascular system. It is used to lower blood pressure, prevent attacks of angina pectoris, and control certain cardiac arrhythmias. By blocking β_2 receptors, which are responsible for dilation in pulmonary bronchi, propranolol increases airway resistance and is thus **contraindicated in patients with asthma.** Propranolol has considerable effects on carbohydrate and fat metabolism and **is best avoided or used with great caution in patients with diabetes.** Unlike some β blockers, it readily penetrates the blood–brain barrier, but researchers are uncertain whether or not the effects of propranolol in the brain result from blockade of β receptors. In fact, although its peripheral mechanism of action appears understood, the way in which propranolol acts to treat certain neurological and psychiatric syndromes is unknown.

Propranolol is probably not as effective an antianxiety agent as the benzodiazepine drugs, although it might more specifically alleviate the sympathetic visceral symptoms of anxiety (e.g., tachycardia). It is possible that propranolol has a central antianxiety effect or, alternatively, that the patient experiences a decrease of anxiety because of a lessening of somatic symptoms (as per the James–Lange theory). Perhaps patients with many somatic symptoms or those prone to substance abuse may do best with this agent, but defining a proper role for propranolol in the treatment of anxiety will require much more research.

Doses of propranolol vary widely, but initially the physician should administer 10 to 20 mg three or four times daily. Its short half-life makes divided doses necessary, but it also means that propranolol can be administered on an as-needed basis. The FDA, however, **has not labeled propranolol for the treatment of anxiety or any other psychiatric condition.** Therefore, a physician will be well advised to discuss risks and benefits thoroughly with the patient, specify alternative treatments, note the innovative nature of this therapy, secure the patient's consent, and document the discussion in the record (see Chapter 12).

The major hazards of treatment with propranolol are those of β blockade. In individuals with cardiac disease, propranolol can lead to heart failure or conduction delays. Patients treated for angina or hypertension sometimes experience potentially hazardous rebound phenomena when propranolol is withdrawn suddenly. As noted earlier, asthma is a contraindication to the use of this drug. Patients taking insulin for the control of diabetes may be more susceptible to hypoglycemia when they take propranolol. Other unwanted effects include nausea, vomiting, diarrhea and constipation, depression, delirium, psychosis, and allergic reactions.

5. Antipsychotic Drugs

At times, clinicians use antipsychotic drugs for the control of anxiety. However, phenothiazines and related compounds are generally less effective for treating anxiety than the benzodiazepines, and the former produce a wider range of more serious adverse reactions, particularly long-term neurological effects (namely, tardive dyskinesia). For these reasons, minimize the use of antipsychotic drugs to treat nonpsychotic anxiety. Occasionally, considerations of abuse, failure to achieve satisfactory response with benzodiazepines, or the presence of overwhelming anxiety (as in the borderline personality) may suggest the use of low doses of an antipsychotic drug (although hydroxyzine and propranolol may be alternatives). In such cases, the physician should administer the lowest effective dose for the shortest period of time, carefully monitor the patient, periodically reevaluate the dose, and use necessary precautions (see Chapter 4).

VI. CLINICAL USE OF ANTIANXIETY AGENTS

A. Introduction

Of all the anxiolytic drugs we have just reviewed, the benzodiazepines are deservedly the most popular: they are both highly effective and have a broad margin of safety. A physician, however, should not use any antianxiety agent as a substitute for listening and talking, developing an ongoing therapeutic relationship, considering environmental, social, and psychological factors, and prescribing nonbiological therapies. At the same time, clinicians should eschew the kind of ideological dogmatism that routinely frowns on the use of substances to alleviate emotional suffering—a state of mind Klerman has dubbed "pharmacological Calvinism."[28]

B. Evaluating the Patient

The physician should prescribe an antianxiety agent only after completing a thorough individual assessment and developing a balanced, custom-designed treatment program for each patient. He must first rule out medical and psychiatric syndromes that may respond to more specific treatments. Next, he should consider a role for various nonbiological approaches, e.g., counseling, psychodynamic psychotherapy, behavioral treatments, relaxation training.

C. Treating Anxiety with the Benzodiazepines

In general, because they are highly effective and comparatively safe, the benzodiazepines are the drugs of choice for the treatment of patients with anxiety accompanying an acute situational disorder or life stress or for patients who chronically experience anxiety, such as those with a generalized anxiety disorder. Benzodiazepines can play an adjunctive role in the treatment of other anxiety disorders such as phobias, obsessive–compulsive disorder, or posttraumatic stress disorder. Although their effectiveness has not been conclusively demonstrated during chronic therapy, benzodiazepines probably maintain some efficacy over the long term. The commonly observed reemergence of anxiety (other than withdrawal symptoms) when benzodiazepine drugs are discontinued following chronic therapy suggests (indirectly) that they do have some continued antianxiety effect.

Ideally, benzodiazepine drugs should be administered for short-term use, typically around a period of stress, and always within the context of an ongoing therapeutic relationship. The physician should see the patient for a follow-up visit within a week or two to assess the patient's overall clinical status and response to the medication.

In the real world, however, many patients take benzodiazepines chronically. Is this ever justified, and if so, what are the risks? To address the latter first, benzodiazepines carry a potential for dependence, abuse, and withdrawal reactions (although all are probably less severe than with other sedatives). Furthermore, the probability of withdrawal reactions (and perhaps the severity) increases with the chronicity of exposure. Also, in occasional patients, long-term use of benzodiazepines may produce chronic sedation and apathy (probably because of excessive levels). To avoid promoting abusive, overly long, and unsupervised use of these substances, physicians should not prescribe large quantities of benzodiazepine drugs (or multiple refills).

Despite our best intentions, however, some patients do take benzodiazepines chronically and function in a relatively stable manner. How does one identify these patients, and how should they be managed? The answer is empirically. If a patient has been taking a benzodiazepine drug for weeks or a few months, the physician should gradually taper the agent. A reemergence of anxiety, however, may prompt a reinstitution of the dose at a level sufficient to suppress symptoms. In some patients, the physician discovers that attempts at tapering the medication are repeatedly followed by a renewed need for the drug. If anxiety symptoms (more than a withdrawal reaction) regularly reemerge when the dose is tapered, and the patient has not shown a tendency to abuse the drug (e.g., to get "high," to increase the dose beyond the physician's prescription), then the most prudent course may be to allow the patient to continue chronically with the medication. Of course, the clinician should attempt to taper the drug periodically, possibly every 6 to 12 months, to find the lowest effective dose that can control symptoms.

Clearly, nonbiological approaches to chronic anxiety are preferable, but in assessing the overall balance between the risks and benefits of the drug and the risks of unchecked anxiety, long-term prescription of a benzodiazepine may be appropriate for some individuals. Perhaps for others, this is merely a "bad habit," but it is equally feasible that some individuals are biologically prone to excessive anxiety—perhaps because of too little endogenous benzodiazepine or difficulty binding this internal anxiolytic substance.

Steps in the Treatment of Anxiety

1. Evaluate the nature of the anxiety.
   a. Rule out medical and specific psychiatric causes.
   b. Define areas of conflict and stress.
   c. Note drugs that may interact with anxiolytics.
2. Evaluate the patient's character structure and intrapsychic issues to help determine psychological risks and benefits of drug taking.
3. Consider nonbiological approaches (e.g., dynamic psychotherapy, ego supportive or crisis intervention therapies, behavioral approaches, hypnosis, or relaxation training).
4. If medication is indicated, discuss plans with the patient.
   a. Outline potential hazards (e.g., problems driving, hangover, additive effects with other drugs).
   b. Propose a short-term trial of drug therapy.
   c. Discuss the need for periodic reevaluation.
   d. Outline the potential harm to the fetus for women of childbearing age.
5. Prescribe short-acting agents in divided doses; long-acting agents may be administered once or twice a day.
6. Give benzodiazepines in low doses initially (in small, nonrefillable prescriptions) and increase until:
   a. Anxiety is adequately contained.
   b. Significant adverse reactions (particularly drowsiness) occur.
   c. Recommended dose limits are reached.
7. Discontinue drugs slowly (i.e., over several weeks—longer after prolonged therapy or with very high doses).
8. Give a sedating antihistamine (i.e., hydroxyzine) or a short trial of an antipsychotic agent to patients who may abuse drugs.
9. Only provide ongoing benzodiazepine therapy for patients who
   a. Have significant anxiety without medication.
   b. Do not respond to other treatment measures.
   c. Do not show signs of abuse.
10. Reevaluate drug use
    a. When symptoms do not respond adequately to treatment.
    b. When the patient requests increasing doses or requires high doses or prolonged administration.
    c. When the period of acute stress passes or after several weeks of acute administration.
    d. Every few months in patients on chronic medication.

Is there a role for benzodiazepine drugs in the treatment of anxiety among patients with so-called borderline personalities? The answer to this question contains more caveats than recommendations. Probably, this diagnostic category represents a heterogeneous group of disorders, possibly containing some individual who will show symptomatic improvement during acute exacerbations of anxiety if treated with standard doses of benzodiazepine drugs. However, for many borderline patients, the dose of a benzodiazepine that would contain the characteristic massive upsurge of anxiety to which they are often prone would be so excessive as to cause unacceptable adverse effects. Moreover, many of these individuals are prone to substance abuse. Additionally, prescription of drugs of this type can vastly complicate therapeutic interactions. Finally, in some individuals, benzodiazepine drugs may disinhibit tendencies to act on socially unacceptable impulses, promoting the expression of hostility or indiscrete sexuality.

Benzodiazepine drugs can also serve as ancillary agents in the treatment of depression and psychosis. Although they probably are not effective for the treatment of most cases of major depression, particularly of the melancholic type (an exception might be the new benzodiazepine alprazolam), benzodiazepines may help to alleviate the anxiety that often accompanies depression and thus serve as useful concurrent therapy for other somatic treatments such as antidepressant drugs. For many patients, an antidepressant alone will suffice, but in the early weeks of treatment (before the antidepressant has become effective) a benzodiazepine may provide welcome symptom relief.

Similarly, in the treatment of patients with psychosis, benzodiazepines may at times be used in addition to antipsychotic agents. Benzodiazepines probably have little inherent antipsychotic efficacy (at least in the usual clinical dose range) and, if administered alone, might precipitate hostile or excited outbursts in an occasional psychotic patient. However, coadministered with an antipsychotic drug, benzodiazepines are sometimes useful for the treatment of certain extrapyramidal syndromes such as acute dystonic reactions and akathisia (see Chapter 4).

D. Indications for Using Other Antianxiety Drugs

Other antianxiety drugs tend to be less effective, more hazardous, or associated with more unwanted effects than the benzodiazepines. For some patients, a β blocker such as propranolol may effectively alleviate some of the somatic manifestations of anxiety. More study will be required, however, before propranolol can be generally recommended or its proper place in therapeutics determined. Clinicians should avoid barbiturates and related sedative–hypnotic compounds (including meprobamate) when treating anxious patients unless there is a specific, compelling reason to employ them.

In patients with a liability of substance abuse, the clinician might want to elect a drug to treat anxiety that does not have potential to produce abuse or dependency. For this purpose, a sedating antihistamine (e.g., hydroxyzine) may be helpful, although it is generally not as effective as the benzodiazepines. In some cases, the physician may want to use low doses of a phenothiazine or other antipsychotic drug; if treatment is likely to be prolonged, however, the physician and patient must consider the possibility of producing long-term neurological effects (namely, tardive dyskinesia) even at relatively low doses.

E. Discussing Treatment with the Patient

Once a decision is made to prescribe antianxiety medication, the physician should discuss the treatment plan and advise the patient about potential hazards such as possible problems driving, morning hangover, dangers of taking alcohol or other sedative–hypnotic drugs concomitantly. In addition, the clinician will want to suggest that prescription of an antianxiety agent is for a limited period of time and that the need for medication will be reevaluated regularly. Also, advise women who may become pregnant about potential hazards to the fetus.

F. Choosing a Specific Benzodiazepine

The choice of a specific benzodiazepine is not crucial, since all are equally effective. However, the clinician should consider pharmacokinetic differences that may help tailor the drug to the patient and situation. For example, the rapidity with which a specific benzodiazepine is absorbed may affect the speed of onset of therapeutic action after a single dose. So if a patient with a social phobia wished to take a single dose of a benzodiazepine shortly before specific engagements, he might prefer diazepam because of its rapid onset of action. Similarly, a choice between benzodiazepines with short versus long durations of action during chronic therapy may be affected by the anticipated schedule of drug treatment. For patients who anticipate being under stress for many weeks, a long-acting benzodiazepine (e.g., diazepam, chlordiazepoxide, clorazepate, prazepam) provides the advantages of once- or twice-a-day dosing as well as consistent tissue levels around the clock. (Once-daily dosages are usually administered at night to avoid excessive sedation associated with peak blood concentrations.)

When the long-acting benzodiazepines are discontinued, their long half-lives provide a built-in gradual tapering. Short-acting drugs, by contrast, are excreted more rapidly, and since the time of appearance and severity of symptoms of a withdrawal reaction may correlate with the rapidity of decline of blood levels, short-acting agents may be associated with earlier onset and more severe withdrawal reactions. Consequently, increased attention should be paid to avoiding abrupt discontinuation of these agents. Of course, any benzodiazepine should be discontinued gradually for the patient's safety and comfort.

When short-acting benzodiazepines are used, steady-state concentrations are achieved more rapidly than with long-acting drugs. In the elderly, in whom half-lives of all drugs tend to be prolonged, steady-state levels of long-acting drugs may not be achieved for a number of weeks. During this time, the dose of the drug must be carefully titrated against anxiety symptoms to avoid excessive sedation. Achieving a steady state in a matter of days with a short-acting agent allows determination of the therapeutic dose more rapidly.

Another point, which has yet to be confirmed, is that the shorter-acting agents (e.g., lorazepam, oxazepam) may have less of a tendency to enhance irritability and hostility in some patients. Better established is the fact that the short-acting drugs have fewer kinetic interactions, as with cimetidine. Finally, because the metabolism of short-acting benzodiazepines is little affected by the presence of liver disease, it may be less complicated to use these agents in patients with hepatic impairment.

Short- vs. Long-Acting Benzodiazepines*

Long-acting	Diazepam
	Chlordiazepoxide
	Clorazepate
	Prazepam
	Flurazepam
Intermediate-acting	Halazepam
	Alprazolam
Short-acting	Lorazepam
	Oxazepam
	Temazepam

*The terms "short" and "long" refer to the drugs' half-lives, which are relevant for chronic administration. With single doses, different rules apply.

Whatever drug is chosen, observe the patient frequently during the early days of treatment to assess his response, monitor unwanted effects, and titrate the dosage until a steady state is reached (i.e., no further accumulation occurs). Dosages will vary widely among patients, based on the fluctuating symptoms of anxiety as well as on individual differences in drug kinetics. If an individual is responding to a transient stress, the drug should be tapered and discontinued soon after the stress has been alleviated.

Chlordiazepoxide, diazepam, and, more recently, lorazepam are available for parenteral use. Chlordiazepoxide and diazepam produce unreliable blood levels when administered intramuscularly; intravenous use, however, leads to rapid and predictable rises in blood drug levels. Therefore, these two drugs are best administered orally or intravenously. Lorazepam has recently been approved for intramuscular administration, although at present the labeling is restricted to preanesthetic use. Blood level increases following intramuscular lorazepam administration are generally smooth and reliable.[29]

Diazepam is adsorbed by plastic intravenous bags and tubing which can result in a loss of potency. Moreover, diazepam can precipitate if mixed for infusion with saline or dextrose. To avoid this problem, increase the diazepam concentration, hasten infusion speed, and/or dissolve diazepam in a lipid emulsion.[30] If accidentally administered intraarterially, diazepam produces severe inflammation with tissue necrosis.[31]

VII. SUMMARY

Anxiety is a common—virtually universal—problem. Most instances of anxiety never come to medical attention. Those that do, however, deserve careful diagnosis and evaluation. Many will improve with support, specific intervention, and/or nonbiological approaches. When nonspecific medication treatment of anxiety is indicated, a benzodiazepine drug will usually be the agent of choice. Used prudently, with appropriate attention to the physician-patient relationship, benzodiazepine drugs can help to alleviate suffering in many distressed patients.

REFERENCES

1. Nemiah J. C.: *Foundations of Psychopathology.* New York, Oxford University Press, 1961, pp. 100, 121.
2. Mohler H., Okada T.: The benzodiazepine receptor in normal and pathological human brain. *Br J Psychiatry* 133:261–268, 1978.
3. Paul S. M., Marangos P. J., Goodwin F. K., et al: Brain-specific benzodiazepine receptors and putative endogenous benzodiazepine-like compounds. *Biol Psychiatry* 15:407–428, 1980.
4. Gorman J. M., Fyer A. F., Gliklich J., et al: Effect of imipramine on prolapsed mitral valves of patients with panic disorder. *Am J Psychiatry* 138:977–978, 1981.
5. Pitts F. M. Jr, McClure J. N.: Lactate metabolism in anxiety neurosis. *N Engl J Med* 277:1329–1336, 1967.

6. American Psychiatric Association: *Diagnostic and Statistical Manual of Mental Disorders,* ed 3 *(DSM-III).* Washington, American Psychiatric Association, 1980.
7. Klein D. F.: Anxiety reconceptualized. *Compr Psychiatry* 21:411–427, 1980.
8. Salzman L., Thaler F.: Obsessive–compulsive disorders: A review of the literature. *Am J Psychiatry* 138:286–296, 1981.
9. Thoren P., Asberg M., Bertilsson L., et al: Clomipramine treatment of obsessive–compulsive disorder: II. Biochemical aspects. *Arch Gen Psychiatry* 37:1289–1294, 1980.
10. Jenike M. A.: Rapid response of severe obsessive–compulsive disorder to tranylcypromine. *Am J Psychiatry* 138:1249–1250, 1981.
11. Isberg R. S.: A comparison of phenelzine and imipramine in an obsessive–compulsive patient. *Am J Psychiatry* 138:1250–1251, 1981.
12. Rosenbaum J. F.: The drug treatment of anxiety. *N Engl J Med* 306:401–404, 1982.
13. Rickels K.: Are benzodiazepines overused and abused? *Br J Clin Pharmacol* 11:71S–83S, 1981.
14. Ghoneim M. M., Mewaldt S. P., Berie J. L., et al: Memory and performance effects of single and three-week administration of diazepam. *Psychopharmacology* 73:147–151, 1981.
15. Snyder S. H.: Benzodiazepine receptors. *Psychiatr Ann* 11:19–23, 1981.
16. Greenblatt D. J., Divoll M., Abernathy D. R., et al: Benzodiazepine kinetics: Implications for therapeutic pharmacogeriatrics. *Drug Metab Rev,* in press.
17. Greenblatt D. J., Shader R. I., Divoll M., et al: Benzodiazepines: A summary of pharmacokinetic properties. *Br J Clin Pharmacol* 11:11S–16S, 1981.
18. Downing R. W., Rickels K.: Hostility conflict and the effect of chlordiazepoxide on change in hostility level. *Compr Psychiatry* 22:362–367, 1981.
19. Jackson M. R., Harris P. A.: Diazepam and tumour promotion. *Lancet* 1:445, 1981.
20. Finkle B. S., McCloskey K. L., Goodman L. S.: Diazepam and drug-associated deaths: A survey in the United States and Canada. *JAMA* 242:429–434, 1971.
21. Greenblatt D. J., Allen M. D., Noel B. J., et al: Acute overdosage with benzodiazepine derivatives. *Clin Pharmacol Ther* 21:497–514, 1977.
22. Divoll M., Greenblatt D. J., Lacasse Y., et al: Benzodiazepine overdosage: Plasma concentrations and clinical outcome. *Psychopharmacology* 73:381—383, 1981.
23. Gelenberg A. J.: Benzodiazepine use during pregnancy. *Mass Gen Hosp Biol Ther Psychiatry Newslett* 3:36, 1980.
24. Gelenberg A. J.: Benzodiazepine withdrawal. *Mass Gen Hosp Biol Ther Psychiatry Newslett* 3:9–10, 1980.
25. Tyrer P., Rutherford D., Huggett T.: Benzodiazepine withdrawal symptoms and propranolol. *Lancet* 1:520–522, 1981.
26. Abernethy D. R., Greenblatt D. J., Shader R. I.: Treatment of diazepam withdrawal syndrome with propranolol. *Ann Intern Med* 94:354–355, 1981.
27. Gelenberg A. J.: Short-acting benzodiazepines and cimetidine (Tagamet): No interaction. *Mass Gen Hosp Biol Ther Psychiatry Newslett* 4:23, 1981.
28. Klerman G. L.: Psychotropic hedonism versus pharmacological Calvinism. *Hastings Cen Rep* 2:1–3, 1972.
29. Shader R. I., Greenblatt D. J.: Clinical implications of benzodiazepine pharmacokinetics. *Am J Psychiatry* 134:652–656, 1977.
30. Winsnes M., Jeppsson R., Sjoberg B.: Diazepam adsorption to infusion sets and plastic syringes. *Acta Anesthesiol Scand* 25:95–96, 1981.
31. Rees M., Dormandy J.: Accidental intra-arterial injection of diazepam. *Br Med J* 281:289–290, 1980.

SELECTED READING

1. Rosenbaum J. F.: Anxiety, in Lazare A. (ed): *Outpatient Psychiatry: Diagnosis and Treatment*. Baltimore, Williams & Wilkins, 1979, pp 252–256. Good overall review of anxiety as a syndrome; includes differential diagnosis.

2. Salzman L., Thaler F. H.: Obsessive–compulsive disorders: A review of the literature. *Am J Psychiatry* 138:286–296, 1981. Overview of recent developments regarding obsessive-compulsive disorder.

3. Baldessarini R. J.: Drugs and the treatment of psychiatric disorders, in Gilman A. G., Goodman L. S., Gilman A. (eds): *Goodman and Gilman's The Pharmacological Basis of Therapeutics,* ed 6. New York, Macmillan, 1980, pp 391–447. Review of preclinical pharmacology of antianxiety agents.

4. Petursson H., Lader M. H.: Benzodiazepine dependence. *Br J Addict* 76:133–145, 1981. Review of important topic.

6

Insomnia

ALAN J. GELENBERG, M.D.

I. INTRODUCTION

Four percent of the United States adult population have used prescription hypnotics, and many others have taken over-the-counter medications to promote sleep.[1] Approximately 17% of patients who visit physicians complain of difficulty sleeping, and doctors prescribe hypnotic drugs for about half of them.

After a period of increasing hypnotic use, between 1971 and 1977 the number of prescriptions written for hypnotics decreased by 39%, and the type of drugs changed. In 1971, barbiturates comprised 47% of hypnotic prescriptions; by 1977, they accounted for only 17%, and the benzodiazepine flurazepam (Dalmane®) had captured 53% of the market. This change in prescribing habits has led to a sharp reduction in the number of suicides from barbiturate overdoses (although, interestingly, the total suicide rate has not declined).

II. SLEEP

A. Normal

Researchers have identified five EEG patterns of sleep. The sleep cycle begins with stage 1, nonrapid-eye-movement sleep (NREM), which is followed successively by stages 2, 3, and 4 of NREM sleep. The deeper NREM stages, 3 and 4, are characterized by increasing quantities of slow (delta) waves and probably play a metabolically restorative function. After the ini-

ALAN J. GELENBERG, M.D. • Department of Psychiatry, Harvard Medical School and Massachusetts General Hospital, Boston, Massachusetts 02114.

tial NREM sleep cycle, the first rapid-eye-movement (REM) period, often associated with dreaming, begins. During REM sleep, muscle tone decreases, the eyes move rapidly, and the EEG shows fast-frequency, low-amplitude waves. Depending on the total duration of sleep, this cycle repeats itself approximately four to six times each night, at intervals of roughly 90 min. During the later cycles, REM periods and stage 2 predominate. The young adult spends approximately 20 to 25% of total sleep time in REM sleep. Total sleep time is greatest in childhood, declines during adolescence, and plateaus until old age, when it again decreases.

B. Insomnia

Insomnia is a symptom. Patients describe difficulty either falling asleep or staying asleep. When they complain of not sleeping restfully, EEG studies frequently show multiple awakenings throughout the night and more time spent in the lighter stages of sleep (1 and 2) than in the deeper stages (3 and 4).

Insomnia has many diverse etiologies: medical, psychiatric, and situational. As in the case of anxiety, the physician should search for specific treatable causes before prescribing a nonspecific therapy such as a hypnotic drug. Various medical and neurological conditions, for example, result in difficulty falling and staying asleep. Conditions that cause pain or discomfort, such as arthritis, can impair sleep; so may many metabolic and endocrine disturbances. Withdrawal from sedative drugs, use of stimulant drugs or caffeine, and "delayed sleep phase," in which people have their biological clock set at the wrong bedtime,[2] also cause insomnia. Although nocturnal myoclonus, which is common and physiological, usually does not disturb the sleeper, it may occasionally lead to insomnia. Drugs such as antidepressants can exaggerate this condition.

Sleep-induced ventilatory impairment, also known as **sleep apnea,** is rare but important to diagnose. In this condition, the **prescription of a sedative compound could prove fatal.** Sleep apnea may result from physical obstruction of the airway or from impairment of the brainstem respiratory centers. The former is more likely to result in complaints of daytime drowsiness, which may prompt a visit to a physician. Both central (i.e., brainstem) and obstructive sleep apnea are likely to affect libido and penile erection. Another common complaint is headaches, especially frontal headaches in the morning. Patients with central sleep apnea frequently complain of disturbed sleep with frequent awakening. Those with obstructive sleep apnea often have a long history of insomnia together with daytime drowsiness. Bed partners and roommates complain of loud snoring in patients with the obstructive variety, and these patients also manifest sudden body movements during the night.

Sleepwalking sometimes occurs in patients with obstructive apnea. The definitive diagnosis of either type of sleep apnea must come from all-night polygraphic monitoring.[3]

Numerous psychiatric conditions are associated with insomnia. Schizophrenics show variable sleep patterns; in some, slow-wave sleep (stages 3 and 4) decreases. Manic patients sleep less than normals, although they usually do not complain of insomnia.

Depression is typically associated with insomnia. Patients with the melancholic (endogenous, endogenomorphic) forms of depression frequently wake up early in the morning, and they also may awaken many times during the night. Depressed patients often spend less time in the more refreshing slow-wave phases of sleep, may have increased periods of REM sleep, and typically have a shorter than normal period before their first REM phase (decreased REM latency). Other depressed patients sleep more or have difficulty falling asleep.

Patients with generalized anxiety disorders or individuals under unusual situational stress often develop insomnia and complain of awakening many times during the night.

III. HYPNOTIC DRUGS

Many patients ask physicians for "sleeping pills." Even if a patient does not make such a concrete request, a physician might still feel obligated to "do something" when a patient complains about sleep difficulties.

Occasionally, the differential diagnosis will reveal specific disorders with clear treatments. More commonly, a nonbiological approach will suffice. When a physician does decide to use a hypnotic drug, he should almost always choose a benzodiazepine because of their record of efficacy and, more importantly, safety. The decision of whether to use a short- versus a long-acting benzodiazepine is discussed shortly.

When may a physician turn to a nonbenzodiazepine hypnotic agent? If a patient has previously taken a different type of drug, has found it effective, and has used it with apparent impunity, the physician may wish to continue prescribing that drug for the patient. Another situation would be a patient liable to substance abuse, in whom a nonaddictive hypnotic [e.g., an antihistamine such as diphenhydramine (Benadryl®)] might be appropriate.

A. Benzodiazepines

The striking popularity of benzodiazepines as hypnotic substances is not without good cause. They are the most effective and safest drugs for the treatment of insomnia. At present, the United States Food and Drug Administration (FDA) designates two benzodiazepine drugs as hypnotics. These include the long-acting benzodiazepine flurazepam and a more recent addition, the short-acting temazepam (Restoril®). Other benzodiazepine drugs, such as nitrazepam and triazolam, are used abroad to facilitate sleep. It is probable that most or all of the benzodiazepine drugs used to treat anxiety also can effectively induce sleep. Corporate marketing decisions often determine whether or not a drug company develops a benzodiazepine as either a hypnotic or an anxiolytic compound. The FDA approves drugs for labeling based almost exclusively on data submitted to them by manufacturers.

Figure 1 depicts the molecular structure of flurazepam and temazepam; Table 1 gives information about their dosages and kinetics. The pharmacology of the benzodiazepines has been discussed in Chapter 5.

Unlike many other hypnotics, benzodiazepines do not cause anesthesia. When the benzodiazepines are administered to an awake subject, the EEG shows decreased alpha and increased low-voltage, fast activity. As with barbiturates, tolerance develops to these EEG alterations. Benzodiazepines decrease sleep latency (the time required to fall asleep), diminish the number of awakenings, and also decrease the length of stages 3 and 4 (slow-wave sleep). However, because the number of slow waves in stage 2 sleep increases, the total number of delta waves (slow waves) during the night does not diminish. Benzodiazepines affect REM sleep in variable ways depending on the individual, his illness, and the type and dosage of the drug. This contrasts with many other hypnotic agents which markedly suppress REM sleep. Most importantly, benzodiazepines used at bedtime usually increase the total amount of time asleep.

Flurazepam is a long-acting drug that resembles diazepam. Its major and active metabolite, N^1-desalkylflurazepam, is formed in the liver and has a half-life of 40 to 250 hr, which indicates that the blood level on the eighth

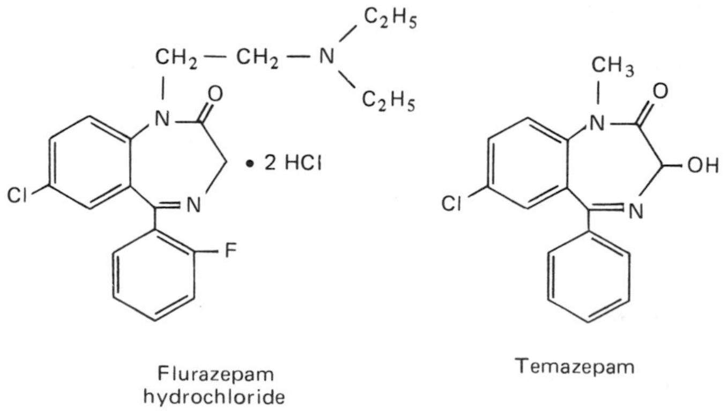

Flurazepam
hydrochloride

Temazepam

FIGURE 1. Benzodiazepines used for the treatment of insomnia.

TABLE 1. Benzodiazepine Hypnotics

Drug	Usual bedtime dose for young adults	Dosage forms	Active metabolites	Half-life (hr)
Flurazepam (Dalmane®)	30 mg	15-, 30-mg capsules	N¹-desalkyl-flurazepam	40 to 250
Temazepam (Restoril®)	30 mg	15-, 30-mg capsules	None	5 to 25 (occasionally longer)

morning after a consecutive week of nightly flurazepam use is likely to be four to six times that found on the first morning. This probably accounts for the observation that sleep on the second or third night of flurazepam therapy is better than on the first. The persistence of the metabolite can also mean that residual sedation and impairment of cognitive and motor skills may persist well after the last dose of the drug. Moreover, potential interactions with other sedatives, including alcohol, may be prolonged. In a study of normal subjects taking flurazepam, tolerance developed to the impairment of cognitive functions but not to the impairment of psychomotor ability.[4] The long-lasting effect of flurazepam may make it preferable for patients with chronic anxiety as well as insomnia. Furthermore, rebound insomnia (i.e., sleep worse than pretreatment levels following drug withdrawal) is less likely with a long-acting agent. However, morning "hangover" (i.e., residual sedation and impaired function) may be a problem for some patients.

Temazepam has a much shorter half-life than flurazepam (approximately 5 to 25 hr, although longer in some subjects and the elderly) and no major active metabolites. It is merely conjugated in the liver as are oxazepam (Serax®) and lorazepam (Ativan®). This results in less of an effect the day after a nighttime dose, although further studies on hangover and impaired performance are necessary.[5] Absorption of temazepam (like that of oxazepam) is comparatively slow, which may be a problem for patients with difficulty **falling** asleep. For this reason, patients should be advised to take it on an empty stomach 1 to 2 hr before sleep is desired. When short-acting benzodiazepines are discontinued after chronic therapy, rebound insomnia might occur; its clinical significance, however, has not been determined.

Tolerance to the hypnotic effects of the benzodiazepines is probably less than with other hypnotics for at least up to 1 month. Problems of adverse effects, toxicity, addictions, and interactions are covered in Chapters 5 and 7.

B. Barbiturates

The barbiturates are discussed in Chapter 5. In general, short- and intermediate-acting barbiturates are used as hypnotics [e.g., amobarbital

(Amytal®), pentobarbital (Nembutal®), secobarbital (Seconal®)], whereas long-acting barbiturates [e.g., phenobarbital (Luminal®)] are used for day-time sedation.

Barbiturates decrease sleep latency, shorten slow-wave sleep, and notice-ably decrease the length of REM periods. With short-acting barbiturates, these effects tend to wear off later in the night. Tolerance develops to the hypnotic effects of barbiturates over a matter of days, and rebound phenom-ena occur following cessation of treatment.

Because of problems of tolerance, abuse, dependence, adverse effects, and the danger of overdose, clinicians should rarely prescribe barbiturates as hypnotics. (See Section III in Chapter 7.)

C. Chloral Derivatives

Chloral hydrate (Noctec® and others) and two closely related com-pounds, chloral betaine (Beta-chlor®) and triclofos sodium (Triclos®), are pharmacologically and clinically similar. All three share the same active metabolite, trichloroethanol, which has a plasma half-life of approximately 4 to 12 hr (see Table 2).

Chloral hydrate decreases sleep latency and the number of awakenings and may slightly decrease slow-wave sleep. It has relatively little effect on REM sleep because some degree of tolerance develops. Therapeutic doses of chloral hydrate have little effect on respiration and blood pressure, but toxic doses may impair both.

Chloral hydrate has an irritating and unpleasant taste. Local irritation of the gastrointestinal tract can cause heartburn, nausea, and vomiting. The relatively short half-life of the chloral derivatives makes hangover less of a problem. Allergic reactions are occasionally observed. Because of its potential to cause direct organ toxicity, chloral hydrate is best avoided in patients with severe hepatic, renal, or cardiac disease. Most adults will require 1 to 2 g of

TABLE 2. Chloral Derivatives

Drug	Usual hypnotic dose	Dosage forms	Half-life (hr)
Chloral hydrate (Noctec® and others)	1 to 2 g	250-, 500-mg capsules; 250-mg/5-cc, 500-mg/5-cc, 800-mg/5-cc syrup	4 to 9½
Chloral betaine (Beta-chlor®)	1740 mg	870-mg tablets	4 to 9½
Triclofos sodium (Triclos®)	1500 mg	750-mg tablets; 1.5-g/15-ml liquid	4 to 9½

chloral hydrate to induce sleep. A 500-mg dose may be no more than a placebo, although an occasional patient might respond at this dosage, which could make it a good starting point. Gastric irritation increases with the dose but may be minimized by administering the drug with milk or an antacid.

Chloral betaine is more palatable and less irritating than chloral hydrate; about 870 mg of the former equals approximately 500 mg of the latter. For triclofos sodium, 1.5 equals about 900 mg of chloral hydrate.

Chloral hydrate affects the hepatic drug-metabolizing system and thus may interfere with a number of other drugs that are metabolized in the liver. Another potential problem arises from the fact that trichloroacetic acid, a metabolite of chloral hydrate, displaces acidic drugs from plasma protein binding sites, resulting in increased plasma concentrations of these drugs. Chloral hydrate also may interact with the diuretic furosemide (Lasix®) to cause a syndrome of sympathetic instability. The combination of chloral hydrate and alcohol is the legendary "Mickey Finn," reputed to have a "knockout punch." Although the potency of this combination is more legend than fact, the two may enhance each other's blood levels, which adds to the sedative potentiation.

The hypnotic dose of chloral hydrate for adults is approximately 1 to 2 g; a toxic dose is approximately 10 g. The range is considerable, however, with death having followed an ingestion of 4 g, and survival after 30 g. Gastric irritation may limit the amount a patient can take at one time, and vomiting diminishes absorption. However, gastric necrosis can produce additional complications. In serious intoxication, support of cardiovascular and respiratory functions is vital. Hemodialysis may enhance excretion.

Tolerance, physical dependence, and addiction are possible with chloral derivatives. A withdrawal syndrome occurs similar to that seen with other sedatives and alcohol (see Section III.C.3 in Chapter 7).

If a patient has previously used a chloral derivative and prefers it, then careful administration is acceptable. In general, however, there is little reason to choose one of these agents.

D. Piperidinedione Derivatives

Two piperidinedione derivatives are available in the United States, glutethimide (Doriden®) and methyprylon (Noludar®). The actions of these two drugs resemble those of barbiturates.

1. Glutethimide

Glutethimide has all of the drawbacks of the barbiturates without any added advantages. What is worse, overdoses with glutethimide are even

more difficult to treat than those with the barbiturates or similar compounds.

The half-lives of glutethimide and its sister compound methyprylon are given in Table 3. The pharmacological profile of glutethimide resembles that of the barbiturates except for its anti-motion sickness effect and anticholinergic activity. Similarly to the barbiturates, glutethimide suppresses REM sleep.

Gastrointestinal absorption of glutethimide varies. It is highly lipophilic and about 50% bound to plasma proteins. Almost all of the drug is metabolized in the liver. The half-life of glutethimide is about 5 to 22 hr. Similar to the barbiturates, glutethimide stimulates the hepatic microsomal enzyme system, which increases the potential for many pharmacokinetic interactions. Glutethimide is contraindicated in patients with acute intermittent porphyria.

One of the reasons glutethimide has maintained some vitality in the marketplace is that, despite its low therapeutic index and high lethality, at therapeutic doses it produces relatively few unwanted effects. Occasionally central nervous system effects occur, including confusion, excitement, hangover, drowsiness and ataxia; anticholinergic effects such as dry mouth, blurred vision, constipation, and difficulty urinating; cutaneous allergic reactions (occasionally serious); gastrointestinal irritation; and rare blood dyscrasias such as thrombocytopenia, aplastic anemia, and leukopenia.

The hypnotic dose of glutethimide is 0.5 to 1 g; as little as 5 g can produce severe intoxication, and 10 g or more may be lethal. In acute glutethimide intoxication, respiratory depression often is less severe than with barbiturate overdoses, but cardiovascular collapse may be worse. Antimuscarinic effects are typically prominent. Neuromuscular irritability can occur with possible seizures. In intoxication, the plasma half-life of glutethimide is prolonged and may exceed 100 hr. Fluctuating levels of consciousness, including lucid intervals, are typical, possibly because of variable absorption and enterohepatic recirculation as well as intermittent release of the drug from lipid stores. The presence of other nervous system depressant compounds obviously will worsen an overdose. Treatment of glutethimide intoxication is aimed at reducing absorption, supporting vital functions, and hastening

TABLE 3. Piperidinedione Derivatives

Drug	Usual hypnotic dose	Dosage forms	Half-life (hr)
Glutethimide (Doriden®)	500 mg	500-mg capsules; 125-, 250-, 500-mg tablets	5 to 22
Methyprylon (Noludar®)	200 to 400 mg	300-mg capsules; 50-, 200-mg tablets	Ca. 4

excretion. The last may be accomplished by hemodialysis, preferably with a lipid solvent such as soybean oil.

Glutethimide can produce tolerance and dependence as well as an abstinence syndrome typical of sedative–hypnotics (see Section III.C.3 in Chapter 7).

2. Methyprylon

Methyprylon (Noludar®) is pharmacologically very similar to its structural relative glutethimide and to the barbiturates. It is a short-acting hypnotic with a plasma half-life of only 4 hr (longer in states of intoxication). Methyprylon suppresses REM sleep, and REM rebound occurs upon its withdrawal.

Methyprylon is almost completely metabolized in the liver, where it stimulates the hepatic microsomal enzyme system. It is contraindicated in patients with acute intermittent porphyria. Adverse effects are essentially the same as those described with glutethimide.

Acute intoxication with methyprylon is clinically similar to that with barbiturates, although it may have less of a tendency to depress respiration. A dose of 15 g or 200 mg per kilogram of body weight can cause serious intoxication and possibly death. In fact, death has been reported after as little as 6 g of methyprylon. However, recovery has followed as much as 27 g. Coma after methyprylon intoxication may last for as long as 5 days. Methyprylon is more readily dialyzed than glutethimide because it is more highly water soluble.

Methyprylon is quite similar to the barbiturates in its liability to produce tolerance, dependence, and withdrawal reactions (see Section III.C.3 in Chapter 7). There would be few reasons ever to select methyprylon as a hypnotic.

E. Methaqualone

Like many other sedatives, methaqualone (Quaalude®, Sopor®) raises the seizure threshold. It also has antispasmodic, local anesthetic, antihistaminic, and antitussive activity. At higher doses, methaqualone can depress myocardial contractility and cause hypotension. Methaqualone probably suppresses REM and stage 4 sleep, at least in higher doses, but this remains to be clarified.

Methaqualone is well absorbed from the gastrointestinal tract and carried mostly bound to protein and plasma. It is virtually completely metabolized in the hepatic microsomal enzyme system and has a half-life of 10 to 30 hr.

Aside from the usual CNS effects observed with practically all hypnotics, methaqualone also has been reported to produce transient and occasionally persisting paresthesias. In some patients, agitation, excitement, and anxiety may be paradoxical responses to this drug, and excessive dreaming, somnambulism, and hangover are often reported. Less common are gastrointestinal irritation, rashes, and, very rarely, blood dyscrasias. Methaqualone potentiates the effects of other central nervous system depressant drugs. Apparently, methaqualone can be administered safely to patients with acute intermittent porphyria.

Intoxication with methaqualone tends to be less severe than that observed with barbiturates. In cases of severe overdose, delirium, increased muscle tone, and seizures may occur. Coma can follow doses in excess of 2.4 g, and death has occurred after 8 g. The presence of alcohol or other CNS depressants can make coma more severe and death more likely. The usual principles of treating sedative–hypnotic overdose apply, although the highly lipophilic nature of methaqualone, together with its strong affinity for serum albumin, make dialysis less than effective.

Methaqualone was widely abused in the 1970s. Afficionados of the drug culture claimed a better "high" from this drug, but it is hard to distinguish pharmacological differences from cultural fads. Tolerance and dependence can occur with methaqualone, and abstinence syndromes, including seizures, may be severe. There is evidence that methaqualone is riding a second wave of popularity in the early 1980s (see Section III.C.3 in Chapter 7). With the possible exception of a patient with acute intermittent porphyria, there would seem to be little indication for selecting this drug. Doses and dosage forms are listed in Table 4.

F. Ethchlorvynol

Ethchlorvynol (Placidyl®) has a rapid onset of hypnotic action (15 to 30 min), and, although its elimination half-life is 10 to 25 hr, rapid distribution terminates its clinical effect within a few hours after an acute dose. (Chronic dosing, however, can lead to prolonged effects.) Ethchlorvynol resembles the barbiturates in its effect on sleep stages, including suppression of REM. Rebound occurs following drug withdrawal.

Adverse effects with ethchlorvynol include confusion, hangover, ataxia, and nausea and vomiting. Other reactions are hypotension, facial numbness, amblyopia, and giddiness. Less common are allergic reactions, blood dyscrasias, and cholestatic jaundice.

Ethchlorvynol seems to interfere with the kinetics of drugs metabolized in the hepatic microsomal system such as anticoagulants. Additive sedative effects can occur with other drugs and alcohol. Delirium has been reported in

TABLE 4. Other Hypnotic Drugs

Drug	Usual hypnotic dose	Dosage forms	Half-life (hr)
Methaqualone (Quaalude®, Sopor®)	150 to 300 mg	75-, 150-, 300-mg tablets	10 to 42
Ethchlorvynol (Placidyl®)	500 to 1000 mg	100-, 500-, 750-mg capsules	10 to 25
Ethinamate (Valmid®)	500 to 1000 mg	500-mg capsules	Brief
Diphenhydramine (Benadryl® and others)	50 mg	25-, 50-mg capsules, 12.5-mg/5-ml elixir, 50-mg/1-ml injection	Unknown
Paraldehyde	10 to 30 ml by mouth	Liquid	Brief

patients taking ethchlorvynol together with tricyclic antidepressants. Ethchlorvynol is contraindicated in patients with acute intermittent porphyria.

Profound coma can follow an acute overdose with ethchlorvynol. Death has been reported after a dose as low as 2.5 g, but the usual lethal range is given as 10 to 25 g. Treatment includes the usual approaches to diminishing absorption, supporting vital functions, and hastening elimination, possibly using a lipid dialysate with hemodialysis.

Physical dependence occurs with regular use of ethchlorvynol, tolerance develops to its sedative effects, and abuse is possible. Withdrawal reactions are similar to those with the barbiturates (see Section III.C.3 in Chapter 7). As with so many other drugs in this section, ethchlorvynol could probably be removed from the market with few adverse consequences. For doses and dosage forms, see Table 4.

G. Ethinamate

Ethinamate (Valmid®) has few differences from the barbiturates. It is a short-acting hypnotic, producing sleep within 30 min and a maximum effect in 45 min (see Table 4). The short duration of action means that hangover is rare. Gastrointestinal irritation occurs in some patients, allergic reactions have been reported, and rare cases of thrombocytopenia have been associated with this drug. Paradoxical excitement may be more common in younger patients.

Acute intoxication resembles that with the barbiturates, and death has occurred after as little as 15 g. Treatment of overdoses is the same as for other sedative–hypnotic compounds. Habituation, dependence, and abstinence reactions are also similar. There is little reason to prescribe this drug. Doses and dosage forms are given in Table 4.

H. Diphenhydramine

Diphenhydramine (Benadryl® and others) is a sedating antihistamine that resembles hydroxyzine (Atarax® and others) (discussed in Chapter 5). A dose of 50 mg can be an effective hypnotic for many adults (see Table 4). Diphenhydramine appears to suppress REM sleep, and REM rebound occurs following its discontinuation. Its duration of action is usually 4 to 6 hr. Anticholinergic effects, including confusion and even delirium, can develop in susceptible individuals, elderly patients, and those taking other drugs with anticholinergic activity. In an occasional patient, paradoxical excitement may occur. Diphenhydramine appears to be a comparatively safe drug, and since it is unlikely to lead to substance abuse, it may be an appropriate hypnotic for an occasional patient with an abuse problem.

I. Paraldehyde

Paraldehyde, a foul-smelling and irritating liquid, remains in therapeutics largely as a historical curiosity. It is a rapidly acting hypnotic and, as such, rarely causes hangover. Sleep typically occurs within 10 to 15 min (for dosages, see Table 4).

Like the barbiturates, paraldehyde raises the seizure threshold. Before the advent of the benzodiazepines, it was commonly employed for the treatment of delirium tremens. In the presence of pain, administration of paraldehyde has been associated with paradoxical excitement. Large doses of paraldehyde can suppress respiration and produce hypotension.

Following oral administration, paraldehyde is rapidly absorbed. Most is metabolized in the liver, but a proportion is excreted unchanged via the lungs (imparting a pungent odor to the patient's breath that permeates a hospital room), and a smaller amount in the urine. In patients with liver disease, less is metabolized and more excreted by the lungs.

Whether administered orally or parenterally, paraldehyde is extremely irritating to the body's tissues. The lethal dose of paraldehyde is probably very high, but death has been reported after as little as 25 g. Tolerance, dependence, and withdrawal syndromes occur and resemble those observed with alcohol. Paraldehyde is unpleasant and difficult to handle, and it affords no benefits over other medications such as the benzodiazepine hypnotics.

J. Bromides

Bromides were introduced into medicine in the mid-19th century for the treatment of epilepsy, and subsequently they were reported to be effective hypnotics and tranquilizers. However, because of their low therapeutic index, they have become compounds of historical interest only.

Both their therapeutic and toxic effects result from the ability of bromides to displace chloride ions in the CNS and elsewhere. Bromide is not metabolized but is excreted by the kidneys. The long half-life of about 12 days is responsible for many cases of gradual accumulation and toxicity. The young, the old, and those with renal failure are most susceptible to bromide toxicity.

Adverse effects with bromides are headache, vertigo, gastrointestinal disturbance, and acneiform rash. Acute intoxication is rare, as the ingestion of large doses causes gastric irritation and vomiting. When bromide use was common, chronic intoxication was familiar, particularly in psychiatric hospitals. Symptoms include rash, confusion, irritability, tremor, anorexia, weight loss, ataxia, stupor, and coma. Treatment consists of administering sodium chloride and water and is augmented by the use of diuretics.

There no longer appears to be a role for bromides as hypnotics or sedatives, and they have been removed from the market of over-the-counter sleep aids.

K. Tryptophan

Tryptophan is an essential amino acid present in various proteins. Tryptophan is a precursor of serotonin (5-hydroxytryptamine, 5-HT), a neurotransmitter believed to play an important role in sleep onset and in the control of slow-wave sleep. Although some studies on laboratory animals have suggested that tryptophan can decrease the latency to the first slow-wave episode and to the first REM sleep, other studies have yielded conflicting results.

Experiments in human volunteers and in patients suffering from insomnia have generally found that tryptophan reduces sleep latency and increases sleep time. The doses have varied considerably, from 250 mg to 15 g, taken at bedtime. Not all investigators, however, have found tryptophan to be an effective hypnotic. Dietary factors also may be relevant: concomitant ingestion of protein together with tryptophan may increase blood levels of other large neutral amino acids which compete with tryptophan for entry into the brain.[6]

Because tryptophan is a natural food substance and not a patentable drug, industry has shown little interest in developing this compound. Consequently, they have not performed the usual pharmacological and toxicologic studies with tryptophan. Generally, clinicians feel that tryptophan causes few unwanted effects other than mild gastric irritation. Unlike many of the other hypnotics, tryptophan does not seem to cause long-term toxicity, acute intoxication, dependence, or withdrawal reactions. One caveat, however, is that substances sold in so-called health food stores are not monitored by the FDA, and many have been found to be variable in composition and contaminated with toxic matter such as pesticides and heavy metals.

L. Over-the-Counter Drugs

Many over-the-counter preparations are available as "sleeping pills" (see Table 5).[7] Most contain one or a combination of the following: scopolamine, an antihistamine, or a salicylate.

Scopolamine, a centrally active anticholinergic agent, depresses the cerebral cortex as well as the reticular formation and hypothalamus. Scopolamine can cause paradoxical excitement and delirium, particularly in the presence of pain. It decreases REM sleep, and when it is discontinued, REM rebound occurs. Common unwanted effects are anticholinergic, such as dry mouth, blurred vision, urinary hesitancy, and constipation. Because of the anticholinergic effects, overdoses, particularly in young children, can be dangerous. Hazards of anticholinergic drugs and treatment of toxicity have been discussed earlier.

Antihistamines have been previously discussed (see Section III.H). The two contained in over-the-counter sleep preparations are methapyrilene and pyrilamine.

Several salicylates are combined with the above agents in many patent medicines. These are salicylamide, aspirin, acetaminophen, and sodium salicylate. Their effectiveness as sleep aids is in doubt, although it is possible that their analgesic activity may promote sleep by alleviating pain in affected patients. Typical problems with salicylates (other than acetaminophen) include gastric irritation and interference with clotting mechanisms. Intoxication with salicylates can produce tinnitus and acid–base disturbances and with acetaminophen may result in hepatic necrosis.

TABLE 5. Some Nonprescription "Sleeping Pills"

Brand name	Contents
Compoz®	Methapyrilene (an antihistamine)
	Pyrilamine (an antihistamine)
Nytol®	Methapyrilene
	Salicylamide (a salicylate)
Sleep-Eze®	Scopolamine hydrobromide
	Methapyrilene
Sominex®	Scopolamine aminoxide
	Methapyrilene
	Salicylamide

There is little evidence that any available over-the-counter sleeping pill is more effective than placebo, although it is possible that in a subset of patients with insomnia, some pharmacological benefit may be derived from these agents. They are not innocuous, however, and some patients may be particularly sensitive to their adverse effects. In addition, when a patient takes an overdose, toxicity (e.g., an anticholinergic syndrome) may occur.

M. Other Psychotropic Drugs for Insomnia

At times, physicians prescribe other types of psychotropic medications for the treatment of insomnia. As noted previously, prescription of a benzodiazepine drug can be rational in the treatment of insomnia, and whether or not the specific drug chosen is labeled for insomnia or anxiety probably makes little difference. Particularly when a long-acting agent is used for treating anxiety, a bedtime dose may alleviate insomnia at the same time.

When insomnia is symptomatic of a psychotic disorder, an antipsychotic drug may promote sleep by containing the underlying problem. Furthermore, a nighttime dose of a sedating antipsychotic agent [e.g., chlorpromazine (Thorazine®), thioridazine (Mellaril®)] can provide additional symptomatic relief. However, antipsychotic agents should not be used solely for the treatment of insomnia in nonpsychotic patients, since their potential toxicity tends to outweigh likely benefits. In addition, tolerance develops over a matter of days (or a few weeks) to their sedative effects.

The same basic principles apply to the use of antidepressant drugs for the induction and maintenance of sleep. When insomnia is a symptom of depression, use an antidepressant. Moreover, sedating antidepressants may help to alleviate sleep even before they normalize mood. In the absence of depression, however, the use of an antidepressant drug specifically as a hypnotic is best avoided, since these agents have a low therapeutic index, and tolerance rapidly develops to their sedative effects.

IV. CLINICAL USE OF HYPNOTICS

Before doctors prescribe medicine for sleep, they should thoroughly evaluate the patient. As discussed in Chapter 5, the physician should obtain a complete history, review of organ systems, and indicated laboratory tests and formulate a thoughtful differential diagnosis. Medical conditions that could interfere with sleep should be ruled out. The clinician should also define psychiatric syndromes (i.e., endogenous depression, anxiety disorders, psychosis) amenable to definitive therapy and, when appropriate, institute specific treatment. In addition, he should decide if transient difficulties, such as a time-limited stress, could be managed effectively by sympathetic listening, problem solving, and information giving.

When a patient complains of persistent difficulty falling asleep, and no other treatable problem is present, the physician will want to determine if the patient's routine living patterns are contributing to the problem. Does the patient "catnap" during the day? Is there excessive stimulation or noise prior to bedtime or during the night? Does the patient drink too much coffee or tea, particularly later in the day?

Clinicians should tell individuals who complain of insomnia to avoid sleeping except during specified nighttime hours. The period preceding sleep should be relatively quiet and calm, perhaps augmented by traditional aids such as warm milk and a hot bath. In a patient without liability to substance abuse and dependence, a "nightcap" may become a helpful ritual. Tell the patient that if he does not fall asleep in approximately 20 min after getting into bed, he should get out of bed and read or watch television. When he feels ready to sleep, he should return to bed. The clinician should reassure the patient, telling him not to worry about lack of sleep and encourage the patient to exercise during the day and to eat a well-balanced diet. At times, formal relaxation training or teaching autohypnosis may help.

If the physician decides to prescribe a hypnotic drug, the patient should understand from the outset that it will be for a relatively brief period of time. There are many trade-offs with hypnotic drugs, such as impaired performance or habituation, and these are often worse than the insomnia itself. Many individuals, however, do take hypnotic drugs nightly for extended periods, and, for the most part, they do not seem adversely affected. Despite evidence that the hypnotics cause chronic distortions in the sleep stages, this effect does not produce evident clinical pathology.

In general, prescribe hypnotics in relatively small quantities and without automatic refills. The drug should be taken as necessary and discontinued once the patient has slept well for several nights. The patient should be warned of possible adverse effects such as hangover and impairment of motor and intellectual performance. If a patient is taking other CNS depressants, a hypnotic should be used with caution, since it potentiates their effects.

Generally, benzodiazepines should be prescribed for short-term or intermittent use. If insomnia persists, requiring continuous long-term (i.e., more than 1 to 2 months) use of a hypnotic, try to identify its cause and develop a treatment program. This may include psychotherapy, mobilization of environmental supports, and the establishment of an ongoing supportive relationship with the physician. It may also involve clearing up a patient's misconceptions about insomnia (i.e., fear of its supposed deleterious effects).

Benzodiazepines are safer and more effective than other sedative–hypnotics (see Chapter 5). The major reason to prescribe a nonbenzodiazepine hypnotic is in patients prone to substance abuse. In these individuals, consider a non-dependency-producing agent such as an antihistamine. There are few patients in whom the use of barbiturates or related sedative–hypnotics is justified.

Steps in the Management of Insomnia

1. Evaluate the nature of the sleep disorder and search for medical conditions and psychiatric disorders with more specific treatments.
2. When practical, provide nonbiological approaches (e.g., psychological support, information-giving, insight-oriented intervention, relaxation training, or self-hypnosis).
3. If sleep disorder is persistent or severe and not caused by another psychiatric disorder, consider the benzodiazepines such as temazepam and flurazepam.
4. Prescribe a sedating antihistamine (e.g., diphenhydramine) for patients with abuse potential.
5. Inform the patient about
   a. Risks and benefits (particularly hangover and impaired motor and intellectual functioning).
   b. The short-term or intermittent nature of treatment for insomnia.
6. Review treatment every few weeks to try to minimize or discontinue medication.

V. SUMMARY

Everyone occasionally suffers from a bad night's sleep. Unfortunately, some complain of disturbed sleep frequently. In many cases, the fear of insomnia is worse than any actual effects from the sleep loss.

Whatever the cause, persistent insomnia merits medical intervention, but medical intervention is not synonymous with medication prescription. The physician should thoroughly evaluate the problem and formulate a diagnosis. If specific treatment is not appropriate, the physician often can offer advice, guidance, and counseling. When a hypnotic drug is necessary, prescribe it for occasional use, limited periods of time, and within the context of an ongoing therapeutic relationship. For most patients, a benzodiazepine is the drug of choice for insomnia, although at times, an antihistamine will be effectively used. Very occasionally, a clinician can prescribe one of the other drugs mentioned in this chapter.

REFERENCES

1. Solomon F., White C. C., Parron D. L., et al: Sleeping pills, insomnia and medical practice. *N Engl J Med* 300:803–808, 1979.

2. Weitzman E. D., Czeisler C. A., Coleman R. M., et al: Delayed sleep phase syndrome. *Arch Gen Psychiatry* 38:737–751, 1981.
3. Derman S., Karacan I.: Sleep-induced respiratory disorders. *Psychiatr Ann* 9:41–62, 1979.
4. Church M. W., Johnson L. C.: Mood and performance of poor sleepers during repeated use of flurazepam. *Psychopharmacology* 61:309–316, 1979.
5. Lydiard R. B.: Temazepam (Restoril)—a new short-acting benzodiazepine hypnotic. *Mass Gen Hosp Newslett Biol Ther Psychiatry* 4:37–38, 1981.
6. Gelenberg A. J.: Use of choline, lecithin and individual amino acids in psychiatric and neurologic disease, in Beers R. J. Jr, Bassett E. G. (eds): *Nutritional Factors: Modulating Effects on the Metabolic Processes.* New York, Raven Press, 1981, pp 239–254.
7. *Handbook of Nonprescription Drugs,* ed 5. Washington, American Pharmaceutical Association, 1977.

SELECTED READING

1. Harvey S. C.: Hypnotics and sedatives, in Gilman A. G., Goodman L. S., Gilman A. (eds): *Goodman and Gilman's The Pharmacological Basis of Therapeutics,* ed 6. New York, MacMillan 1980, pp. 339–375. Review of preclinical pharmacology of sedative–hypnotics.
2. Hartmann E.: *The Sleeping Pill.* New Haven, Yale University Press, 1978. Reviews the entire scope of concerns about medication for the induction of sleep. Suitable for general audiences but also for professionals.
3. Petursson H., Lader M. H.: Benzodiazepine dependence. *Br J Addict* 76:133–145, 1981. Review of important topic.

7

Substance Abuse

STEVEN M. MIRIN, M.D., and
ROGER D. WEISS, M.D.

I. INTRODUCTION AND DEFINITIONS

The self-administration of chemical substances that alter thinking and/or mood has been a widespread practice for centuries. When the use of such substances deviates from societal norms or is deemed harmful to physical and mental health, substance use merges, often imperceptibly, into substance abuse—a term with legal and medical implications.

Traditionally, abuse reflects an underlying emotional disturbance. Many people use psychoactive drugs, including alcohol, to medicate feelings of anxiety or depression. Others, however, find the mood- and mind-altering effects of these drugs innately pleasurable and are "recreational" users. Regardless of initial motivation, however, repetitive use of psychoactive drugs often has adverse consequences. These include the development of psychological and/or physical dependence and, in some, a profound disturbance of psychosocial functionings.

Psychological dependence refers to a profound emotional need for the repetitive use of a particular drug or class of drugs. It has its origin in the ability of some drugs to relieve tension and/or produce euphoria. **Physical dependence** implies a state of altered cellular physiology caused by repetitive drug administration. As a result, abrupt or even gradual withdrawal of the dependence-producing drug may precipitate a characteristic abstinence syndrome.

From a pharmacological perspective, drug dependence also results from the direct reinforcing effects of these agents on the central nervous system.

STEVEN M. MIRIN, M.D., and ROGER D. WEISS, M.D. • Department of Psychiatry, Harvard Medical School, and Drug Dependence Treatment Program, McLean Hospital, Belmont, Massachussets 02178.

The ability of many drugs to relieve tension or produce euphoria may be mediated through their effects on various brain neurotransmitter systems.

Many abused drugs, including the opiates, central nervous system depressants, and stimulants, serve as primary reinforcers in animal models of addiction. For example, monkeys with prior drug experience will work to self-administer their drug of choice. Unfortunately, repetitive use of some agents is accompanied by the development of drug **tolerance,** a state in which increasingly larger doses of the drug must be taken to reproduce its original pharmacological effect. Tolerance may result from an increased rate of drug metabolism (dispositional tolerance) or a change in the sensitivity of target cells to the drug's pharmacological effect (cellular or pharmacodynamic tolerance). In addition, induction of tolerance to one member of a particular drug class (e.g., benzodiazepines) may be accompanied by the development of tolerance to other drugs in the same general class, in this case, depressants. This phenomenon is called **cross tolerance.** The rate of tolerance development depends on the drug used, its dosage, the frequency of administration, and individual physiological variables. It is often, but not always, accompanied by physical dependence.

The development of drug dependence and the experience of withdrawal may cause some individuals to seek medical treatment. The clinical evaluation of such individuals should ideally include a detailed medical and psychiatric history. The clinician should distinguish emotional problems preceding drug abuse from those that result. Since drug dependence and withdrawal often are accompanied by symptoms similar to those seen in patients with other psychiatric disorders (e.g., anxiety, insomnia, depression), a careful developmental and family history, psychological testing, and indicated laboratory tests may be extremely useful. As in other areas of medicine, proper treatment depends on accurate diagnosis. This chapter reviews each major class of commonly abused drugs with respect to basic pharmacology, patterns of abuse, and currently held views about treatment.

II. ABUSE OF OPIATE DRUGS

A. Classification

We can divide the opiates into the following categories based on their derivation:

1. Natural alkaloids of opium derived from the resin of the opium poppy, including opium, morphine, and codeine.
2. Semisynthetic derivatives of morphine, including diacetylmorphine (heroin), hydromorphone (Dilaudid®), and oxycodone (Percodan®).

3. Purely synthetic opiates, which are not derivatives of morphine, including meperidine (Demerol®), methadone (Dolophine®), and propoxyphene (Darvon®).
4. Opiate-containing preparations, such as elixir of terpin hydrate with codeine and paregoric, having abuse liability.

Among the opiates, the semisynthetic derivatives, like heroin and oxycodone, and pure synthetics, like meperidine and methadone, are most commonly abused.

B. Pharmacology

The opiate drugs are readily absorbed from the gastrointestinal tract, nasal mucosa, and lung, but parenteral administration more rapidly elevates blood levels and produces intoxication. For example, following intravenous administration of heroin, the drug is almost immediately hydrolyzed to morphine by the liver, with peak plasma morphine levels attained in approximately 30 min. The drug then rapidly leaves the blood and is concentrated in body tissues. Only small quantities of injected opiates cross the blood–brain barrier, but plasma levels correlate directly with the level of intoxication. Morphine is metabolized primarily by conjugation in the liver. Its half-life (i.e., the amount of time necessary for one-half of a given dose to be cleared from the blood) is approximately 2½ hr and 90% of the total dose administered is excreted in the urine within the first 24 hr. The remainder is excreted through the biliary tract and appears in the feces.

The opiates act by selectively binding to stereospecific neuronal receptor sites which thus far have been identified in the brain (e.g., the hypothalamus) and gut. These opiate receptors probably mediate the action of naturally occurring opioid peptides (i.e., the enkephalins and β-endorphin) as well.

C. Acute Effects

1. Central

Acute administration of heroin, especially intravenously, produces an orgasmlike "rush" lasting 30 to 60 sec. This is usually followed by a brief period of euphoria accompanied by a profound sense of tranquility. This state may last for several hours, depending on the dose administered and the plasma level of morphine attained. It is characterized by drowsiness ("nodding"), lability of mood, mental clouding, apathy, and motor retardation. Respiratory depression (i.e., diminished volume and slower rate) secondary to inhibition of the brainstem respiratory center also occurs. Stimulation of the brainstem chemoreceptor trigger zone for emesis may produce nausea and vomiting. However, with repetitive use, tolerance develops to this effect.

2. Peripheral

In the healthy patient, the cardiovascular effects of opiates like morphine are minimal. In some patients, however, peripheral vasodilation may contribute to orthostatic hypotension. These drugs also decrease secretions in the stomach, biliary tract, and pancreas and inhibit the contractility of smooth muscle. As a result of the latter effect, opiate use may be accompanied by constipation; diminished smooth muscle tone in the ureters and bladder may produce urinary hesitancy. Inhibition of the smooth muscle of the iris results in pupillary constriction, an important sign of opiate intoxication in man.

D. Tolerance and Physical Dependence

Tolerance to some effects of opiate drugs begins to develop after only a week of regular use. Tolerance to other effects develops more slowly. Thus, patients become tolerant rather quickly to the euphoric, analgesic, sedative, respiratory depressant, and emetic effects while continuing to exhibit pupillary constriction and constipation. In most persons receiving therapeutic doses of morphine four times a day for 2 or 3 days, some degree of physical dependence occurs.

E. Acute Intoxication and Overdose

1. Etiology

Among chronic abusers of opiate drugs, overdose is relatively common and may be accidental or reflect suicidal intent. Unintentional overdose stems from two basic preconditions: (1) the user does not know the dose of opiate actually administered; (2) opiate users vary considerably in their level of drug tolerance. Overdose deaths probably are the result of respiratory depression with subsequent anoxia, although anaphylactoid reactions to heroin or its common adulterants may also play a role.

2. Clinical Manifestations

Patients who overdose on illicitly obtained opiate drugs usually are alone, and the untoward effects are immediate. Thus, diagnosis and medical intervention often are too late. When these patients present for treatment, they may be in stupor or coma with constricted pupils and diminished pulse and respiration. Hypothermia and pulmonary edema (usually noncardiogenic) are seen in severe cases.

The clinician must differentiate opiate overdose from other causes of respiratory depression and coma. Although pupillary constriction usually is a reliable sign, it also occurs in severe barbiturate intoxication. Moreover, in the event of circulatory collapse and cyanosis, the pupils become dilated. In narcotic users, look for dermatological evidence of repeated intravenous injections (i.e., needle tracks). Signs of other medical illnesses often associated with chronic opiate use, e.g., hepatitis, infectious endocarditis, and multiple abscesses, also may help to make the diagnosis.

3. Management

a. General Life-Support Measures

The first task in treating acute opiate poisoning is to establish an adequate airway. Aspiration can be prevented either by placing the patient on his side or by using a cuffed endotracheal tube. Gastric lavage should be performed if the clinician suspects recent oral intake of opiates or other drugs. If hypoglycemia complicates the clinical picture, establish a reliable intravenous route and slowly infuse a 50% solution of glucose in water. Pulmonary edema, if present, can be treated with positive-pressure respiration.

b. The Use of Naloxone

Narcotic antagonists can dramatically reverse respiratory depression and other symptoms associated with acute opiate toxicity. The current drug of choice is naloxone (Narcan®), a pure, potent narcotic antagonist with no agonistic (i.e., opiatelike) effects of its own. Naloxone, 0.4 mg (1 ml), administered intravenously, should reverse manifestations of overdose within 2 min. Increase in respiratory rate and volume, rise in systolic blood pressure, and dilation of the pupils indicate a favorable response. If the initial response is unsatisfactory, the same dose may be given twice more at 5-min intervals. Failure to respond after three doses of naloxone suggests either that the diagnosis of opiate poisoning is erroneous or that another problem (e.g., barbiturate poisoning, head injury) may be complicating the clinical picture. Unfortunately, the duration of action of naloxone is much shorter (1 to 4 hr) than that of most opiate drugs. For this reason, patients with severe overdoses should be hospitalized and monitored closely for at least 24 to 48 hr. A significant decrease in respiratory rate or level of consciousness should prompt additional antagonist treatment to prevent relapse into opiate-induced coma.

Most patients who overdose on drugs like heroin or methadone are also physically dependent. Repeated administration of naloxone, which displaces opiates from their receptor sites in the brain and elsewhere, may precipitate an acute abstinence syndrome. Signs and symptoms of opiate withdrawal may appear within minutes and last for several hours. Moreover, they cannot be easily overcome by giving additional opiates. The severity and duration of abstinence symptoms depend on the degree of opiate dependence and the dose and route of administration of naloxone. The use of a small dose (0.4 mg IV) at 5-min intervals may help to avoid this unwelcome complication.

c. Other Considerations

Patients who use opiates tend to abuse other drugs as well, particularly alcohol, barbiturates, antidepressants, and antianxiety drugs. For this reason, the clinician should obtain blood and urine from all patients for toxicological screening. On recovery, the degree of suicidal intent associated with overdose should be assessed; prior to discharge, patients can be referred to an appropriate treatment facility.

F. Opiate Withdrawal

1. Clinical Manifestations

The opiate-dependent patient often comes for treatment when the quality or availability of heroin or other opiates declines on "the street," making it difficult to stave off symptoms of withdrawal. When abstinence symptoms occur, their severity depends on the type of opiate previously used, degree of tolerance, time elapsed since the last dose, and emotional meaning of the symptoms. The symptoms reflect increased excitability in organs previously depressed by chronic opiate use.

In the early stages of withdrawal from heroin (i.e., 6 to 12 hr after the last dose), the patient may yawn and sweat, his nose and eyes may run, and he may experience considerable anxiety. Craving for opiates and drug-seeking behavior intensify. As withdrawal progresses, pupils dilate, and the patient may develop gooseflesh, hot and cold flashes, loss of appetite, muscle cramps, tremor, and insomnia or a restless tossing sleep. Eighteen to 24 hr after the last dose of heroin, nausea, vomiting, and elevations in blood pressure, pulse, respiratory rate, and temperature occur. After 24 to 36 hr, diarrhea and dehydration may develop.

In the case of heroin or morphine, abstinence symptoms generally peak 48 to 72 hr after the last dose. By this time, laboratory values reflect the clinical process. Leukocytosis is common, and ketosis and electrolyte imbalance may develop as a result of dehydration. In untreated cases, clinical symptoms usually disappear with 7 to 10 days, although physiological disturbances may be detected for several months afterward. Withdrawal from methadone is characterized by slower onset (24 to 48 hr after the last dose) and more gradual resolution of symptoms (3 to 7 weeks). Indeed, patients often complain of fatigue, weakness, and insomnia for several months after stopping the drug.

2. Management

a. Detoxification with Methadone

i. Pharmacology. Withdrawal from opiate drugs may be readily treated by using methadone hydrochloride, a synthetic opiate with pharmacological properties qualitatively similar to those of heroin and morphine. Orally, methadone is approximately half as potent as subcutaneous morphine. Its onset of action is approximately 30 to 60 min, and its duration of action ranges from 24 to 36 hr. Methadone is bound to tissue protein and gradually accumulates. Demethylation in the liver is the principal metabolic pathway. Excretion is primarily through the kidneys and gastrointestinal tract.

The acute effects of methadone are similar to those of other opiate drugs: sedation, analgesia, and respiratory depression. During chronic administration, tolerance develops. Brief periods (7 to 14 days) of use in low (i.e., less than 40 mg/day) and decreasing doses does not result in clinically significant physical dependence.

ii. Principles of Use. The use of methadone in the treatment of opiate withdrawal is based on several factors. As a result of the strong cross dependence between methadone and the other opiates, sufficient doses (**10 to 40 mg/day) of methadone will prevent abstinence symptoms** in patients who are physically dependent on other opiate drugs. In addition, methadone is well absorbed from the gastrointestinal tract and is effective orally, thus enabling avoidance of the hazards of intravenous use. Since the drug is more slowly metabolized than heroin or morphine, it has a longer duration of action (24 to 36 hr), allowing for once-per-day administration. Finally, oral administration of therapeutic doses to tolerant individuals does not produce the euphoria that follows intravenous use of shorter-acting opiates such as heroin.

iii. Clinical Application. Detoxification can be complicated by difficulty determining the degree of physical dependence because of uncertainties about the percentage of active drug contained in street samples (usually between 3 and 10%) and the variable reliability of the patients. Given these uncertainties, the clinician can use the following method of detoxification. (1) Observe the patient for objective signs of opiate withdrawal (i.e., a 20% rise over base-line blood pressure and pulse, sweating, and pupillary dilation). When at least two of these four signs are present, give 10 mg of dissolved methadone orally. Signs of withdrawal should abate, at least temporarily, within an hour. If they do not, the patient's symptoms may not be caused by opiate withdrawal. Over the next 24 hr, repeat this process as often as necessary, although the total dose of methadone administered over this period (the stabilization dose) should not usually exceed 40 mg unless the patient has been maintained on methadone at higher doses. (2) Over the next 24 hr, give the stabilization dose in two divided doses. (3) Beginning on the third day, taper the methadone by 5 mg per day, beginning with the morning dose, until the patient is completely withdrawn. Dispense all methadone in liquid form and directly supervise its consumption. During and after detoxification, patients may complain of fatigue, muscle pain, and insomnia. However, prescribing additional methadone merely postpones their inevitable discomfort. Moreover, since these patients frequently abuse central nervous system depressants, the clinician should not prescribe such medications for the treatment of insomnia. Finally, most outpatient programs monitor patient's urines on a daily or twice-weekly random schedule for the presence of illicit drugs. Naturally, care must be taken to ensure that the patient does not substitute "clean" for potentially drug-contaminated urine. In addition, since toxicology laboratories vary considerably in their degree of accuracy and quality control, laboratory participation in an ongoing proficiency testing program is desirable.

The normal course of outpatient detoxification with methadone is from 3 to 21 days. Although inpatient detoxification can be completed in 3 to 7 days, patients generally prefer a more gradual reduction in dosage. Outpatient programs often have difficulty retaining patients through the entire detoxification process. Patients who drop out may voice dissatisfaction with their current dosage of methadone, fear of its long-term effects, and/or generalized distrust of the treatment program. More pertinent, however, is the patients' ambivalence about giving up opiate use and the fact that tolerance develops rapidly to methadone's euphorigenic and analgesic effects. Thus, once the dosage drops to 15 or 20 mg per day, patients may experience a return of abstinence symptoms. Patients should be informed at the outset that they cannot expect a symptom-free withdrawal period.

b. The Use of Clonidine in Opiate Detoxification

In recent years, some investigators have found that clonidine (Catapres®), a nonopiate antihypertensive drug, significantly reduces symptoms of opiate withdrawal. It may act by stimulating α-2-adrenergic receptors in the locus ceruleus of the midbrain and thereby greatly reduce the noradrenergic hyperactivity that usually accompanies opiate withdrawal. Detoxification from methadone requires 2 weeks using initial daily doses of 10 to 17 μg/kg; detoxification from heroin often can be completed in 4 days using lower doses (see Gold et al.[6]). The most common adverse effect of clonidine treatment is hypotension. Patients also may experience a rebound increase in blood pressure when the drug is discontinued. At present, the use of clonidine in the treatment of opiate withdrawal is still experimental.

c. Neonatal Addiction and Withdrawal

The infant born to an opiate-dependent mother presents a special problem. As recently as 25 years ago, the mortality rate among passively addicted neonates with signs and symptoms of opiate withdrawal was almost 90%. At present, the mortality rate is negligible, primarily because of increased awareness of this problem.

Like many other drugs of abuse, opiates cross the placenta. Approximately 75% of infants born to opiate-dependent mothers are physically dependent. Most exhibit symptoms of opiate withdrawal within the first 24 hr of life. In infants born to mothers dependent on methadone, the onset of withdrawal symptoms is delayed but usually occurs within the first 3 days. Some infants, however, may first manifest withdrawal symptoms as late as 10 days after birth.

Although there is marked individual variation, the degree of physical dependence developed by the mother correlates well with the severity of the withdrawal syndrome in her infant. These infants are usually tremulous, with a shrill, piercing cry, increased muscle tone, and hyperactive reflexes. Sneezing, frantic sucking of the fists, sleep problems, and regurgitation after feeding are also common. Other symptoms include yawning, sweating, tearing of the eyes, pallor, and diarrhea. High fever, dehydration, and seizures indicate severe withdrawal.

The diagnosis of opiate withdrawal in the neonate is often complicated by the fact that a mother may withhold her history of narcotic use or leave the hospital before symptoms develop in her offspring. A maternal history of hepatitis, thrombophlebitis, endocarditis, lack of prenatal care, or unexplained neonatal death in the past should raise the clinician's index of suspicion. Other indicators include labor pains that cannot be controlled with the usual doses of analgesics, needle marks along superficial veins, and overt signs of narcotic withdrawal in either mother or infant.

The primary goals in managing neonatal withdrawal are to reduce central nervous system irritability and control diarrhea and dehydration. Although numerous drugs have been used to treat this syndrome, **paregoric,** 0.2 ml PO every 3 to 4 hr, appears to be most helpful. The initial 4-hr dose can be increased in 0.05-ml increments until symptoms are controlled. If symptoms are not alleviated by a dose of 0.75 ml given every 4 hr, the clinician should suspect physical dependence on some other drug class, particularly central nervous system depressants. In such cases, phenobarbital, 5 mg/ kg per day in three divided doses, should be added to the regimen.

After a stabilizing dose has been found and maintained for a week, the total daily dose of paregoric should be tapered by 0.06 ml per day. The importance of concomitant supportive therapy (fluids, proper feeding, etc.) cannot be overemphasized. Indications of therapeutic success include a normal temperature curve, diminished crying and restlessness, increased ability to sleep, weight gain, and vasomotor stability.

Recently, addicted mothers-to-be have been maintained on low doses (40 mg or less) of methadone during pregnancy, tapering the drug a few weeks before delivery. This approach reduces the risk of sepsis from unsterile needle use and makes the mother more available for prenatal care.

G. Treatment of Chronic Opiate Abuse

A wide variety of medical and psychosocial complications accompanies chronic opiate use. These, coupled with poor living conditions and deviant lifestyle, produce significant morbidity and mortality. The death rate among urban addicts is estimated at 1% per year. Drug overdose and violence account for many deaths, but medical complications take their toll as well. We review some of these briefly.

1. Medical Complications

Hepatitis B (serum hepatitis) is a frequent and sometimes lethal complication of chronic intravenous drug use. Up to 65% of urban heroin addicts will develop hepatitis B at some time in their drug-using career. Infected individuals transmit the blood-borne virus by sharing contaminated needles. Recurrent infection and chronic persistent hepatitis also are common. About 60% of current heroin users have chronically elevated serum transaminase levels, possibly related to a high incidence of alcoholism in this population.

Intravenous drug users, even those with no known history of heart disease, also are prone to develop infectious endocarditis, often from *Staphylococcus aureus*. Other medical complications include foreign body emboli, pulmonary fibrosis, pneumonia, lung abscess, and tuberculosis. In patients who inject these drugs subcutaneously or intramuscularly, abscess formation may occur with infection, ulceration, and occasionally gangrene as sequelae. Hyperpigmented scars ("needle tracks") are another common finding. Finally, male opiate users commonly complain of decreased sexual drive, impotence, and delayed ejaculation, whereas females suffer from amenorrhea and infertility. Recent studies have linked these phenomena with opiate-induced suppression of both pituitary gonadotropin and sex hormone (i.e., testosterone) secretion.

2. Treatment Approaches

a. General Considerations

Chronic opiate users who present themselves for treatment are often both physically ill and psychosocially disabled. In addition to the pharmacological effects of these drugs, the addict lifestyle itself may be reinforcing, particularly for individuals with low self-esteem and limited opportunities for success in the mainstream of society. The clinician should view opiate dependence as a chronic relapsing illness. Patients often require a wide range of medical and rehabilitative services. Remedial education, job training and placement, legal assistance, and individual, group, and family counseling should supplement biological intervention.

Successful treatment of chronic opiate use hinges on motivating the patient to seek an alternative life-style—a task that any single treatment modality, whether it be intensive long-term psychotherapy or methadone maintenance, cannot accomplish by itself. Moreover, successful treatment usually incorporates some element of control over patient behavior, whether it be chemical (e.g., methadone maintenance), custodial (e.g., civil commitment), an autocratic peer group (e.g., therapeutic communities), or the self-control provided by regular administration of a narcotic antagonist. Whereas the nature of the controls may differ, all attempt to counteract the patients' impulsivity and covert self-destructiveness. The following sections describe some of these treatment approaches.

b. Methadone Maintenance

i. Background and Theory. As a treatment modality, methadone maintenance evolved out of the clinical observation that some individuals may be unable to abstain totally from opiate drugs. Its theoretical justification derives from the hypothesis that chronic opiate use induces long-lasting, perhaps permanent, physiological changes at the cellular level. As a result, opiate addicts may experience "narcotic hunger" for months or years after withdrawal; the need to satisfy this hunger results in relapse. In this context, medically supervised maintenance on methadone, in doses high enough to satisfy narcotic hunger, becomes a logical alternative to psychological and physical dependence on heroin or other illicitly obtained opiate drugs.

ii. Clinical Application. We have already reviewed the pharmacology of methadone in Section II.F.2.a.i. **Methadone maintenance usually entails administration of 40 to 120 mg PO per day.** After determining that the patient is indeed opiate dependent (i.e., by observing objective signs of withdrawal coupled with a urine specimen positive for the presence of opiates), the clinician should determine a methadone stabilization dose in the manner described in Section II.F.2.a.iii. Thereafter, the daily dose is adjusted to a level at which the patient reports complete blockade of the effects of subsequently administered opiate drugs (e.g., heroin) and random urine samples indicate that the use of opiates other than methadone has ceased.

When it is taken regularly, tolerance develops to methadone's euphorigenic effects, and patients generally function without psychomotor impairment or evidence of intoxication. Some patients, however, continue to complain of sedation, excessive sweating, constipation, ankle edema, and decreased interest in sex. The latter is associated with a drug-induced drop in plasma testosterone, especially at higher doses.

Patients on methadone maintenance generally come to the clinic daily to receive the drug and do not take home any doses until considerable movement toward rehabilitation is noted. Compulsory clinic attendance makes the patient available for participation in individual and/or group counseling which, in some clinics, constitutes a precondition for receiving methadone. Other requirements may include evidence of active job seeking, urine specimens free of illicit drugs, and adherence to clinic rules about antisocial behavior.

iii. Detoxification from Methadone. When patients voluntarily or involuntarily leave methadone maintenance treatment, the clinician can **decrease the dosage by 5 mg per day to a level of 25 mg per day, whereupon withdrawal proceeds more gradually** (e.g., 2.5 mg per day). When detoxification is initiated because the patient is being discharged from treatment, the clinician should consider a more rapid course, but probably in an inpatient setting. Unfortunately, the tapering process is often associated with drop-out from other forms of drug treatment and/or relapse to heroin use.

iv. *l*-α-Acetylmethadol (LAAM). In several programs, this long-acting derivative of methadone has been studied as a replacement for methadone during maintenance treatment. Given at a dose roughly 1.3 times the patient's usual methadone dose, the duration of action of LAAM is approximately 72 hr, thereby eliminating the need for daily clinic visits and the dispensing of "take-home" methadone. Administration of LAAM three times a week helps to minimize the disruptive impact of daily clinic visits on patients' attempts to find or maintain employment. Studies of LAAM treatment indicate that the drug is comparable to methadone in safety and efficacy (i.e., ability to curb illicit opiate use) but that the drop-out rate among LAAM patients is higher. A need by some patients for more frequent clinic contact and the failure of the drug to prevent abstinence symptoms between doses are two reasons frequently cited for LAAM treatment failures.

v. Current Issues in Methadone Treatment. Methadone maintenance boasts the highest retention rate of any opiate treatment modality. It is now the primary treatment modality for approximately 75,000 patients. Fifty to 70% of those who begin on methadone maintenance remain in treatment for at least 1 year. However, some areas of controversy about its use remain. These include the risk that casual opiate users ("chippers") will be inadvertently given methadone, the use, within some programs, of "confrontation" groups that may not be appropriate for all patients, and the fear that methadone programs may overlook the psychological and social problems that contribute to the development of addiction. In addition, since methadone itself produces dependence and euphoria, it is subject to abuse after diversion to the street market. Finally, at least 20% of all patients on methadone continue to abuse other classes of psychoactive drugs, e.g., anxiolytics, hypnotics, and alcohol.

Although methadone maintenance does not constitute a panacea, it does represent an important adjunct to successful treatment. Both illicit opiate use and criminality are decreased, and the rate of employment is increased. In addition, patients on methadone maintenance are more available for other rehabilitative services including job training, supplementary education, and legal, financial, and psychiatric help.

c. The Use of Narcotic Antagonists

i. **Rationale.** The narcotic antagonists are structurally similar to the opiates and occupy the same receptor sites in the central nervous system and elsewhere. In sufficient doses, they completely block the pharmacological effects of subsequently administered opiate drugs through a process of competitive inhibition. If given after opiate dependence has developed, they rapidly displace opiates from their receptor sites and precipitate an acute abstinence syndrome.

The rationale for the use of narcotic antagonists in the treatment of opiate dependence is based on the conditioning model originally proposed by Wikler. He noted the development of socially conditioned abstinence symptoms in former addicts who are exposed to the environment in which they have previously experienced both drug taking and withdrawal. In such individuals, increased craving for opiates frequently occurs and often leads to a relapse of drug-taking behavior. Other external stimuli, such as being in the presence of drugs or observing someone else "get high," may produce conditioned abstinence responses. Internal stimuli include feelings of anxiety, depression, and fear of withdrawal. Wikler theorized that if detoxified addicts were allowed to self-administer opiates but were prevented from experiencing opiate reinforcement (i.e., the heroin effect), extinction of conditioned responding would take place, and the patient might eventually give up trying to "get high." The development of narcotic antagonists has provided the pharmacological tool with which to test this theory.

ii. **Clinical Use.** In both clinical and laboratory settings, patients maintained on narcotic antagonists actually report decreased craving for opiates; their level of opiate consumption also declines. Some, however, continue to manifest conditioned subjective and physiological responses to opiates despite antagonist blockade and tend to be relatively poor candidates for antagonist treatment. Another problem is that some narcotic antagonists such as cyclazocine have agonistic (i.e., opiatelike) effects of their own, resulting in dysphoria which limits their acceptability to patients. Other antagonists, e.g., naloxone and naltrexone, have little or no agonistic effects, but naloxone's short duration of action (1 to 4 hr) makes it impractical for chronic maintenance treatment. In contrast, naltrexone, a relatively pure derivative of naloxone, has a longer duration of action. Fifty milligrams given orally will block the effects of 25 mg of heroin for approximately 24 hr. Adverse effects of naltrexone include drowsiness, lightheadedness, nausea, and occasional feelings of unreality, but these are usually temporary.

Investigators are currently studying buprenorphine hydrochloride, a mixed opiate agonist and antagonist. It is a clinically effective analgesic, 25 to 40 times more potent that morphine; it is also equipotent to naloxone as an antagonist. Experimentally, a subcutaneous dose of 8 mg per day significantly suppressed heroin self-administration in human addicts. Subjects said they preferred buprenorphine to methadone or naltrexone.

Thus far, clinical trials in a number of centers have demonstrated that the long-term acceptability of antagonist treatment is relatively low among addicts. When combined with other modalities, however, antagonists may be a useful adjunct in the treatment of opiate addicts. The development of sustained-release preparations for these agents may enhance their usefulness in certain addict subgroups.

d. Outpatient Drug-Free Treatment

The term "outpatient drug-free treatment" (OPDF) actually encompasses various treatment strategies, all of which do not use methadone or narcotic antagonists. Other psychotropic drugs (e.g., antipsychotics, antidepressants) may be employed as necessary but are usually prescribed temporarily.

Outpatient drug-free treatment often represents the opiate addict's first treatment experience. Many poorly motivated patients choose this type of program, since controls are fewer, and they have to give up little to participate. These programs usually offer individual and/or group counseling. Couple and family work, behavior therapy, and vocational rehabilitation may also be available. Urine screening is used to detect the presence of illicit drug use. Some studies have shown that in highly motivated patients, OPDF treatment is as effective as methadone maintenance in curbing illicit drug use and promoting employment.

e. Therapeutic Communities

Self-help residential treatment programs called "therapeutic communities" or "concept houses" have become one of the primary modalities for the rehabilitation of chronic opiate users, espeically those who fail in other modalities. Ex-addicts generally run these programs. Their special perspective has led to the evolution of a confrontive approach and a refusal to accept psychodynamic, biochemical, or environmental justification for continued drug use. Instead, treatment focuses on interpersonal concerns, particularly responsibility toward the community and the competent handling of aggression and hostility. Residents work their way up through a structured hierarchy within the "community" by demonstrating responsibility and honesty and by remaining drug-free. Those who achieve high status in the system, in turn, serve as role models. Some graduates remain as staff members.

The addict's ambivalence about remaining drug-free coupled with direct and highly critical confrontation by peers results in a drop-out rate of approximately 80% in the first month. More recently, however, courts have begun offering treatment in a therapeutic community as an alternative to jail for addicts convicted of drug-related crimes; this has certainly lowered the overall drop-out rate in these programs. For those who stay, the duration of treatment varies, but the average is about 6 months. "Graduates" from therapeutic communities are as likely to remain opiate free, maintain employment, and stay out of jail as patients in methadone maintenance programs.

III. ABUSE OF CENTRAL NERVOUS SYSTEM DEPRESSANTS

A. Introduction

The central nervous system (CNS) depressants have widely varying chemical structures and include **the barbiturates, the benzodiazepines, and the sedative–hypnotics such as methaqualone, glutethimide, meprobamate, chloral hydrate, paraldehyde, methyprylon, and ethchlorvynol.** The following sections discuss the various abuse syndromes. (See Chapter 5 for a complete discussion of the pharmacology of these agents.)

B. Tolerance and Physical Dependence

With repetitive administration, three types of tolerance develop to the central nervous system depressants. They include (1) **dispositional tolerance,** in which the enzyme systems of the liver become more capable of rapidly metabolizing these drugs; (2) **pharmacodynamic tolerance,** in which the cells of the CNS adjust themselves to the presence of increasing doses of these drugs; and (3) **cross tolerance** to the effects of other central nervous system depressants, including alcohol.

Tolerance to the hypnotic effects of a short-acting barbiturate such as pentobarbital (Nembutal®) begins to develop within a few days, even when it is administered in therapeutic doses. After 2 weeks, the therapeutic effectiveness of a given dose may be reduced by 50%. Moreover, the simultaneous development of cross-tolerance to other CNS depressants makes substitution of a second drug in this general class therapeutically ineffective, since the patient will likely be tolerant to its effects. On the other hand, since some CNS depressants (including barbiturates and alcohol) compete for hepatic metabolism, concurrent use of two or more of these agents will result in clinical effects far greater than either of the drugs alone. Heightened toxicity and accidental overdose are common sequelae of this practice.

C. Classification

1. Barbiturates

The barbiturates are usually classified by their duration of action into ultrashort-, short-to-intermediate-, and long-acting types. The ultrashort-acting barbiturates, including methohexital (Brevital®), and thiopental (Pentothal®), are used primarily as intravenous anesthetics. The short-to-intermediate-acting drugs, including amobarbital (Amytal®), pentobarbital (Nembutal®), and secobarbital (Seconal®), are employed primarily for their sedative and hypnotic properties. The relatively long-acting barbiturates, including phenobarbital (Luminal® and others), may be employed as sedative–hypnotics but are most useful in the control of some seizure disorders. They may also be used to facilitate withdrawal from other sedative–hypnotics.

2. Benzodiazepines

To a large extent, the benzodiazepines have replaced the barbiturates for the pharmacological treatment of anxiety. In addition, the hypnotic effects of these compounds have contributed to their increasing popularity. Taken for brief periods in therapeutic doses, the benzodiazepines are safe and effective; however, chronic use may result in the development of tolerance and physical dependence.

3. Other Sedative–Hypnotics

In addition to the barbiturates and benzodiazepines, a number of other drugs depress CNS functioning and, therefore, have potential utility (and abuse liability) as sedative–hypnotics. Although they vary considerably in their chemical structure and pharmacological properties, the clinical picture in both intoxication and withdrawal is quite similar. Some of the more commonly used (and abused) agents are described below.

Chloral hydrate (Noctec®), the oldest and best-known drug of this group, will induce sleep at doses of 0.5 to 1.0 g PO. Habitual use may produce tolerance and physical dependence. Abrupt withdrawal may result in delirium, seizures, and death. Patients may occasionally display a "break in tolerance," leading to sudden unexpected death by overdose.

Methaqualone (Quaalude®, Sopor®) is a drug that has achieved wide popularity among drug abusers who enjoy the sense of well-being, disinhibition, paresthesias, and ataxia which characterize intoxication ("luding out"). In addition, mathaqualone has been purported to have aphrodisiac properties, a claim that has not been substantiated. Many users find that methaqualone, unlike the barbiturates, does not make them drowsy. The usual hypnotic dose is 150 to 300 mg PO, but some abusers may take up to 2 g per day. Death has been reported after intravenous injection of 8 g, but most deaths occur in abusers who have also been drinking alcohol.

Glutethimide (Doriden®) in an oral dose of 500 mg rapidly induces sleep in most nontolerant individuals. Doses of greater than 2 g per day for a month produce physical dependence. In these individuals, abrupt discontinuation of the drug may result in a general depressant withdrawal syndrome (see Section III.F). When taken in large doses, glutethimide is stored in the body's fatty tissue and is thus difficult to dialyze. In cases of overdose, episodic release from body stores may occur, and so the patient's degree of intoxication may fluctuate widely. Serum concentrations may not correlate well with the level of consciousness. Unlike other CNS depressants, dilated pupils may accompany glutethimide poisoning. Overdose with this drug has been implicated in many suicides.

Methyprylon (Nodular®) in doses of 200 to 400 mg will induce sleep. As is the case with other sedatives, prolonged use of large doses will result in physical dependence. Death has been reported following the ingestion of as little as 6 g, but individuals vary greatly in their degree of tolerance.

Ethchlorvynol (Placidyl®) is a sedative–hypnotic with a rapid onset and short duration of action. Ingestion of 2 to 4 g per day over several months can produce physical dependence. As with methyprylon, the potentially lethal dose varies widely. Ingestion of more than 10 g at once is usually fatal.

Meprobamate (Miltown®, Equanil®), a carbamate derivative, has been widely used as an antianxiety agent and skeletal muscle relaxant. The benzodiazepines have largely supplanted this drug both as a therapeutic compound and as a drug of abuse. The usual therapeutic dose is 400 mg three or four times per day. Chronic administration of slightly higher doses will produce physical dependence with the possibility of seizures on withdrawal. The lethal dose varies between 12 and 40 g. Reports of potential teratogenicity make the ingestion of meprobamate during the first trimester of pregnancy contraindicated (see Chapter 10).

D. Abuse of CNS Depressants

Although less publicized, the prevalence of sedative abuse probably exceeds that of the opiates. In 1976, 128 million prescriptions were written for sedative–hypnotic drugs in the United States. Most physicians would agree that at times these drugs are grossly overprescribed, often without adequate evaluation. Federal legislation has eliminated "open-ended" prescriptions for most of these agents.

Unlike opiate abusers, the vast majority of depressant abusers do not belong to a drug-using subculture and an illicit system of drug distribution. Instead, they are primarily individuals who have received legitimate prescriptions to treat insomnia or anxiety. With prolonged administration, however, tolerance develops to the hypnotic and anxiolytic effects of these drugs, often prompting either an increase in dosage or a switch to another drug in the same general class. At the same time, the cross tolerance that develops between the various CNS depressants limits the effectiveness of this therapeutic maneuver. Eventually, the patient may become physically dependent on one or more of these agents, and subsequent attempts at withdrawal may result in abstinence symptoms.

A second group of sedative abusers are younger, tend to abuse other drugs (e.g., stimulants or heroin), and generally depend on illicit sources of supply. Intravenous drug use is much more common in this group. Generally, they prefer the short-acting barbiturates like pentobarbital, sedatives like methaqualone, and anxiolytics like diazepam (Valium®). They may use these drugs regularly (i.e., daily) or during sprees of intoxication lasting several days. In either situation, they may consume massive doses (e.g., > 300 mg of diazepam per day).

Finally, many stimulant abusers use CNS depressants to "come down" after a prolonged period of amphetamine or cocaine use. Others take pharmaceutical preparations that combine a stimulant such as dextroamphetamine with a short- or intermediate-acting barbiturate, and some develop physical dependence on the CNS depressant component. These individuals are more likely to administer depressants intravenously, increasing their risk of fatal overdose.

E. Acute Intoxication and Overdose

1. Etiology

Not infrequently, depressed patients may make a suicide attempt by overdosing on CNS depressants that they received for the treatment of insomnia and/or anxiety. Occasionally, a patient may become confused after ingesting the therapeutic dose. Ingestion of a second, third, or even fourth dose ("drug automatism") then leads to increased confusion and subsequent overdose.

2. Clinical Manifestations

Mild to moderate intoxication with central nervous system depressants closely resembles alcoholic drunkenness, but patients do not have alcoholic

TABLE 1. Signs and Symptoms of CNS
Depressant Intoxication

Drowsiness	Ataxia
Slurred speech	Hypotonia
Motor incoordination	Hyporeflexia
Confusion/agitation	Memory impairment
Disorientation	Respiratory depression
Nystagmus	Inappropriate affect
Tremor	Rage reactions

breath. The severity of symptoms depends on the drug(s) used, the route of administration, and the presence or absence of other complicating conditions (e.g., head injury). As summarized in Table 1, patients usually present with drowsiness, slurred speech, motor incoordination, impaired memory, confused thinking and disorientation. Physical examination may reveal both horizontal and vertical nystagmus, tremor, and ataxia. In addition, patients may exhibit extreme irritability, agitation, inappropriate affect, and paranoia, sometimes accompanied by rage reactions and destructive behavior. The latter is most common when depressant drugs are combined with alcohol.

Severe overdose with CNS depressants is accompanied by signs of cerebrocortical and medullary depression. Patients may be stuporous or comatose with absent corneal, gag, and deep tendon reflexes. Plantar stimulation may produce no response or an extensor response. They may also have impaired cardiopulmonary function with shallow, irregular breathing, hypoxia, respiratory acidosis, and, in the late stages, paralytic dilation of the pupils. In terminal cases, the patient may develop shock, hypothermia, lung complications (e.g., pulmonary edema, pneumonia), and renal failure.

3. Management

The clinical picture described above, coupled with a suspected or confirmed history of sedative intake, depression, and recent psychiatric or medical treatment, suggests the diagnosis of sedative overdose. Additional history from family or friends also can be quite useful. Chromatographic analysis of blood and urine samples will confirm a drug ingestion.

Adequate treatment of sedative overdose requires a well-trained staff in a hospital setting. Generally, if more than ten times the full hypnotic dose of a drug has been ingested, overdose will be severe, particularly if combined with alcohol intake. When the patient arrives in the emergency room, treatment will be dictated by his state of consciousness. In the awake patient who has ingested a drug in the past several hours, vomiting should be induced or gastric lavage instituted. Samples of the vomitus, blood, and urine should be sent for toxicological analysis. If the patient has ingested a fat-soluble drug such as glutethimide, 60 ml of castor oil may be given via nasogastric tube. If bowel sounds are present, a cathartic (e.g., 15 to 30 g of sodium sulfate) should be instilled into the tube to prevent gastric dilation and regurgitation. If the patient's condition remains stable, he should be continuously observed, with monitoring of respiratory and cardiovascular functioning and the level of consciousness. Following the ingestion of certain fat-soluble drugs including glutethimide, meprobamate, and ethchlorvynol, the patient's level of consciousness may fluctuate widely as the drugs are episodically released from tissue stores. Patients who remain fully conscious and free of cardiopulmonary complications may be released after 24 hr of observation.

Patients who present in a stuporous or comatose state or who are initially awake but then lapse into coma clearly need more intensive treatment. The goal is to support vital functions until the patient is able to metabolize and excrete the drug. Thus, management is directed primarily toward maintaining adequate cardiopulmonary and renal function. If the drug ingestion has occurred within the previous 6 hr, gastric lavage should be attempted, but only after establishing an unobstructed airway by passing a cuffed endotracheal tube. When oxygenation is inadequate, the clinician should ventilate mechanically and administer oxygen. If shock supervenes, transfusions of whole blood, plasma, or plasma expanders should be used to elevate blood pressure and prevent circulatory collapse. The use of vasopressor drugs [e.g., norepinephrine (Levophed®)] has been advocated in some situations.

When renal function is satisfactory, forced diuresis should be attempted; enough saline and dextrose in water (approximately 500 ml/hr) should be administered to produce a urine output of 8 to 10 ml/min. With the longer-acting barbiturates such as phenobarbital, alkalinization of the urine with sodium bicarbonate enhances excretion. Some authors advocate the use of diuretics [e.g., furosemide (Lasix®)] to promote urinary excretion. In cases of profound intoxication, hemodialysis is often effective when more conservative measures fail. For the more lipid-soluble short-acting barbiturates and some of the nonbarbiturate sedative–hypnotics (e.g., glutethimide), the use of a lipid dialysate or hemoperfusion through charcoal or resins (e.g., the lipid-adsorptive AMBERLITE® XAD-4) may promote drug elimination more effectively than traditional dialysis methods.

In general, survival following an overdose of a CNS depressant depends on the maintenance of adequate respiratory, cardiac, and renal function until drug concentrations drop below potentially lethal levels. On recovery, psychiatric consultation should be obtained, and the patient's suicide potential assessed. Patients who purposefully overdose on CNS depressants tend to repeat this action, especially if the underlying problem (e.g., depression) is not effectively managed.

F. Withdrawal from CNS Depressants

Chronic administration of CNS depressants, even in the usual therapeutic doses, may produce tolerance and eventually physical dependence.

Although tolerance develops rapidly to the therapeutic dose, tolerance to a potentially lethal dose develops at a somewhat slower rate. Thus, even chronic users of these substances may become quite intoxicated and even comatose when the dose is raised only slightly.

Physical dependence implies the presence of an abstinence syndrome on withdrawal. In severe cases, withdrawal may carry significant risk of mortality and should be carried out in a hospital setting.

1. Clinical Manifestations

Onset of withdrawal symptoms depends on the duration of action of the particular drug. In the case of the short-acting barbiturates, abstinence symptoms may occur within 12 to 16 hr after the last dose. Withdrawal of a longer-acting drug such as diazepam may not result in abstinence symptoms until 7 to 10 days after the last dose. Severity of symptoms depends on the degree of physical dependence and individual variables which are poorly understood.

Early manifestations of abstinence include agitation, anxiety, anorexia, nausea, and vomiting. As withdrawal progresses, the patient may complain of weakness and develop tachycardia, abdominal cramps, postural hypotension, hyperactive deep tendon reflexes, and a gross resting tremor. Although total sleep time is reduced, the percentage of rapid eye movement (REM) sleep increases, and nightmares become more frequent.

With the exception of the longer-acting barbiturates, withdrawal symptoms characteristically peak 2 to 3 days after the last dose; generalized seizures may occur within this period, either singly or as status epilepticus. About 50% of patients who have seizures develop delirium. The latter is characterized by anxiety, disorientation, frightening dreams, and visual hallucinations. Agitation and hyperthermia can lead to exhaustion followed by cardiovascular collapse. Delirium is not easily reversed, even by giving large doses of the abused drug. If death does not supervene, the patient, after a lengthy period of sleep, usually clears by the eighth day.

2. Management

The treatment of CNS depressant withdrawal is complicated by the fact that sedative abusers are often inaccurate historians. They may wish to obtain as much drug from the clinician as possible and/or may have impaired memory secondary to chronic drug use. For this reason, the **pentobarbital tolerance test** is a useful tool in the management of withdrawal states. The test takes advantage of the fact that cross tolerance exists between the various CNS depressants. As illustrated in Table 2, patients showing signs of depressant withdrawal are given 200 mg of pentobarbital orally. One hour later, the clinician should examine the patient for signs of sedative intoxication such as sedation, nystagmus, ataxia, and slurred speech.

TABLE 2. Detoxification from CNS Depressants Using the Pentobarbital
Tolerance Test

Day 1: 200 mg PO pentobarbital
  If intoxication: 100 to 200 mg PO q.6.h. (nystagmus, ataxia).
  If no intoxication: 100 mg PO q.2.h. until signs of intoxication develop; the total dose
    required to produce intoxication is then given q.6.h. for the next 24 hr.
Day 2: Give pentobarbital in the same dose as was given in the previous 24 hr.
Day 3 and beyond: Subtract 100 mg/day of pentobarbital from total dose given on previous
  day until detoxified. If signs of intoxication develop, eliminate a single dose and resume
  treatment 6 hr later. If signs of withdrawal develop, give 100 to 200 mg pentobarbital PO or
  IM stat.
Phenobarbital substitution: 30 mg phenobarbital for each 100 mg pentobarbital. Advantages:
  more constant plasma level and significant anticonvulsant effects.

If mildly intoxicated by this dose, the patient has probably been taking less than the equivalent of 800 mg of pentobarbital a day.

The clinician can stabilize these patients on a dose of 100 to 200 mg of pentobarbital every 6 hr, depending on the degree of intoxication. If, after an initial test dose (200 mg), no signs of intoxication appear, the patient's tolerance is probably greater than that induced by prolonged, daily use of 800 mg of pentobarbital. Consequently, additional increments of 100 mg of pentobarbital may be administered every 2 hr until signs of intoxication become evident or until a total of 500 mg has been given. The clinician should then calculate the total dose required to produce intoxication and give this dose every 6 hr for the next 48 hr. If the patient becomes grossly intoxicated, the next 6-hr dose may be omitted, and the following day's dose reduced by this amount. Once stabilization has been achieved, the total daily dose of pentobarbital is reduced by 100 mg each day until withdrawal is completed. Patients should be free of tremulousness, insomnia, and orthostatic hypotension. If these signs of abstinence recur during the tapering process, additional 100- to 200-mg doses of pentobarbital may be given. However, it is usually sufficient to stop the dosage reduction for 1 day and then cautiously resume tapering the drug.

One disadvantage of pentobarbital-mediated withdrawal is that patients sometimes require intoxicating doses to prevent the development of seizures and perhaps delirium. Thus, practical reasons exist for substituting a long-acting barbiturate such as **phenobarbital** once stabilization on pentobarbital has been achieved. Use of the longer-acting phenobarbital produces a more constant plasma level than can be obtained with the shorter-acting pentobarbital. Phenobarbital also provides a greater degree of anticonvulsant activity relative to its sedative effects, so that the patient need not be intoxicated to avoid the development of seizures. Finally, since the lethal dose of phenobarbital is several times greater than the intoxicating dose, there is a greater margin of safety. Thirty milligrams of phenobarbital can be substituted for every 100 mg of pentobarbital. The drug can be given in divided doses every 8 hr. Once stabilization on phenobarbital has been achieved, the dose is lowered by 30 mg per day until total withdrawal is achieved. If the patient shows signs of barbiturate toxicity, one or more doses may be omitted. If signs of withdrawal are apparent, an additional 60 to 120 mg of phenobarbital can be given immediately IM, and the total daily dose of phenobarbital increased by 25%. Phenobarbital should not be administered in doses exceeding 500 mg per day.

Treatment with phenobarbital will suppress early symptoms of depressant withdrawal. Once delirium has developed, however, 24 to 72 hr of barbiturate treatment may be required before it clears. Phenytoin (Dilantin®) is of questionable efficacy in preventing withdrawal seizures in these patients. The antipsychotic drugs [e.g., chlorpromazine (Thorazine® and others)], which themselves lower seizure threshold, also should be avoided, although some have advocated their use in the treatment of delirium (see Chapter 11).

Although some patients have been withdrawn from CNS depressants as outpatients, this is risky. Thirty milligrams of phenobarbital are substituted for each hypnotic dose of the substance abused, and the total daily requirement of phenobarbital is given in three divided doses. The total daily dose is then reduced by 30 mg per day over 2 to 3 weeks.

3. Mixed Opiate–Sedative Dependence

In the last decade, simultaneous abuse of more than one class of psychoactive drug has become commonplace. Heroin addicts and patients on methadone maintenance may also abuse sedatives and alcohol. Although there is no cross tolerance between opiates and CNS depressants, sedatives may partially alleviate the symptoms of opiate withdrawal. However, even large doses of methadone or heroin will not prevent sedative withdrawal.

When mixed opiate–sedative dependence is suspected, the clinician should first determine the degree of sedative dependence by using the pentobarbital tolerance test. Once this is done, the most prudent course is to maintain the patient on a dose of methadone sufficient to prevent symptoms of opiate withdrawal while gradually tapering CNS depressants. Some have recommended tapering both classes of drugs simultaneously, but this approach complicates the clinical picture.

G. Treatment of Chronic Sedative Abuse

The majority of patients who abuse sedative–hypnotic drugs are middle-class, middle-aged individuals who have outwardly normal social and occupational adjustments prior to the development of physical and psychological dependence. A smaller group consists of young people with a history of prior drug abuse and relatively poor life adjustment. Both groups have an increased prevalence of psychopathology. It is often difficult to discern, however, whether the psychopathology predates or is a result of the drug abuse. Unfortunately, the treatment available for both groups is inadequate. As yet, no pharmacological measures compare to methadone or the narcotic antagonists. Traditional modalities such as individual or group psychotherapy are of questionable efficacy. Self-help movements similar to Alcoholics Anonymous and the therapeutic communities for opiate addicts have only recently become available.

The paucity of adequate treatment, coupled with the high degree of physical and psychological disability among chronic sedative abusers, makes primary prevention an important priority. The patient's overall psychological state as well as his presenting symptoms should be carefully evaluated before these drugs are prescribed. Careful inquiry into complaints of anxiety and insomnia may uncover emotional problems that may respond to brief counseling or require referral for more intensive psychological treatment. Affective disorder (e.g., major depression) or panic disorder may be treated effectively with antidepressants. Most patients who come to medical attention after the development of sedative dependence require detoxification and then social and psychological rehabilitation to avoid relapse. When the degree of psychosocial impairment limits the effectiveness of psychotherapy, some form of residential treatment may be necessary. In outpatient programs, **randomized urine testing** for the presence of illicit drugs is a useful adjunct to treatment.

IV. ALCOHOL ABUSE

A. Introduction

Of all the drugs mentioned in this chapter, alcohol is the most commonly abused. About 70% of the adult population in this country have consumed alcoholic beverages in the last year. Within this group, it is estimated that the number of problem drinkers approaches 10 million, about half of whom are physically dependent on alcohol.

The criteria for the diagnosis of alcoholism remain controversial. The World Health Organization (WHO) recommends that the term "alcohol-type drug dependence" replace the word "alcoholism." They define the disorder within a cultural context—drinking in a manner that exceeds the social norm for a particular community. Alcohol-induced health problems and disruption of social relationships also qualify an individual for this diagnosis under the WHO criteria. In contrast, the National Council on Alcoholism (NCA) emphasizes biological criteria. Thus, patients who become physically dependent and develop withdrawal symptoms after discontinuing alcohol are, by definition, alcoholic. Individuals who develop alcohol-related diseases such as Laennec's cirrhosis, pancreatitis, or the Wernicke–Korsakoff syndrome) also fulfill criteria for diagnostic level I (i.e., classical alcoholism). Diagnostic levels II and III include less certain indicators of alcohol dependence.

Finally, the American Psychiatric Association (APA) has recently reclassified alcoholism under the broader rubric of "substance use disorders," with pathological drinking subdivided into "alcohol abuse" and "alcohol dependence." "Alcohol abuse" implies a pattern of pathological alcohol use (i.e., binges, blackouts, drinking despite alcohol-induced medical problems, or drinking of nonbeverage alcohol), impairment in social or occupational functioning caused by drinking and a duration of at least 1 month. A diagnosis of alcohol dependence requires either of these first two criteria plus evidence of tolerance or a history of abstinence symptoms following alcohol withdrawal.

B. Risk Factors in Alcoholism

Problem drinking appears to be frequently, although perhaps not causally, related to urban living, low socioeconomic status, and divorce. In addition, certain religious and ethnic groups have a disproportionate share of problem drinkers, e.g., Irish Catholics, American Indians, and Eskimos. Whether this is because of genetic factors, a sense of alienation from the mainstream of society, or social attitudes toward drinking is unclear.

Genetic factors may play a role in the development of alcoholism. The disease appears to run in families. Monozygotic twins, who are genetically identical, have a higher concordance rate for the disorder than dizygotic (nonidentical) twins. Moreover, children of one or more alcoholic parents adopted at birth have a much higher rate of alcoholism over time than the offspring of parents without alcoholism, including those adopted by alcoholics. In the search for possible biological and genetic "markers," an increased ratio of amino-n-butyric acid to leucine has been noted in some alcoholics. However, the significance of this finding is still unclear.

Various attempts have been made to correlate "predisposing" personality variables with subsequent drinking behavior. In this context, alcoholics have often been described as possessing "oral" personality traits including passivity, dependency, pessimism, and self-doubt. However, chronic alcohol use often masks or distorts underlying personality traits, and recent studies have indicated that such personality traits result from, rather than cause, alcoholism.

C. Pharmacology

Alcohol is rapidly absorbed from the gastrointestinal tract, but the rate of absorption is modified by food, the volume of liquid ingested, the concentration of alcohol, and its rate of administration. High concentrations limit intestinal absorption by inducing a reflex pylorospasm. As a result, large quantities of alcohol may remain unabsorbed in the stomach before gradually passing into the small intestine. Thus, following an episode of heavy drinking, an individual may experience fluctuating levels of intoxication.

Once absorbed, alcohol appears to be uniformly distributed throughout most body tissues, including the brain, where an equilibrium with the plasma alcohol concentration is quickly reached. In the liver, alcohol is converted to acetaldehyde through the action of alcohol dehydrogenase. Acetaldehyde, in turn, is converted into acetyl coenzyme A, which is then oxidized through the citric acid cycle or used in other anabolic reactions. In addition to alcohol dehydrogenase, liver microsomal oxidases also play a role in alcohol metabolism. The average rate of liver oxidation is 10 ml/hr with a daily maximum of approximately 450 ml. A small unoxidized portion of ingested alcohol is excreted through the kidneys and lungs.

D. Tolerance and Physical Dependence

The degree of tolerance to the effects of alcohol varies considerably. Certainly, people with identical blood alcohol levels may exhibit markedly different behavior responses. In addition, chronic alcohol ingestion results in the development of both metabolic and pharmacodynamic (tissue) tolerance. Metabolic tolerance implies enhanced activity of those enzymes that oxidize alcohol in the liver, e.g., alcohol dehydrogenase. In most individuals, this type of tolerance quickly reaches an upper limit, and thereafter, is quite uniform. When drinking is steady and does not exceed an individual's metabolic capacity, manifest signs of intoxication may never appear. However, when the rate of consumption rises above this level, blood alcohol concentrations increase rapidly, resulting in intoxication. Within 3 weeks after discontinuing drinking, metabolic tolerance is greatly reduced, even in individuals with a long history of heavy use.

Pharmacodynamic or tissue tolerance implies adaptive changes at the cellular level, particularly in the brain, as a result of prolonged exposure to alcohol. Consequently, higher blood alcohol levels are needed to produce the degree of intoxication previously seen at lower blood levels.

Cross tolerance between alcohol and the other central nervous system depressants results from both pharmacodynamic and metabolic factors. As in the case of other CNS depressants, however, tolerance to the intoxicating effects of alcohol does not imply tolerance to the lethal dose, which is probably not much greater in alcoholics than in nondrinkers.

Chronic ingestion of large amounts of alcohol will result in physical dependence. The time required varies and depends on factors not yet completely defined. In most patients, the presence of physical dependence is confirmed by the development of abstinence symptoms when the drug is withdrawn. Indeed, abstinence symptoms may occur even after a partial drop in the blood alcohol level.

E. Acute Intoxication

1. Simple Type

Although ethyl alcohol affects all organ systems of the body, its most marked and important effect is on the central nervous system (CNS). Alcohol-induced inhibition of the cerebral cortex releases lower brain centers from the inhibitory and integrating control of the cortex. This accounts for the initial stimulatory effect of alcohol on behavior. In the initial stages of intoxication, the user may become outgoing, loquacious, and emotionally labile. Increased confidence and expansiveness often lead to the perception of enhanced verbal and manual performance. Careful testing, however, reveals that efficiency in both areas is impaired. Recent memory, ability to concentrate, and insight also are diminished.

The acute effects of alcohol on the brain are a function of the blood alcohol level, which itself is determined by dose, speed of absorption, rate of metabolism, and the efficiency of alcohol excretion. In addition, CNS effects are more pronounced when the blood alcohol level is rising than when it is falling. In the majority of individuals, a blood alcohol concentration of 50 to 100 mg per deciliter (dl) results in mild intoxication. Concentrations over 100 mg/dl usually impair an individual's ability to operate a motor vehicle. At 200 mg/dl, most users will be grossly intoxicated, exhibiting ataxia and slurred speech. Blood alcohol levels over 400 mg/dl are potentially lethal.

2. Idiosyncratic "Pathological" Intoxication

In some individuals, many of whom are quiet and shy when sober, relatively small doses of alcohol may induce a transitory but profound state of intoxication which develops either during drinking or shortly thereafter. Such patients appear confused, disoriented, and delusional. Consciousness may be impaired, and auditory or visual hallucinations have been reported. Patients also exhibit increased activity, impulsivity, and aggressiveness with accompanying rage reactions and violence. In those with preexisting depression, suicide attempts may occur. Most episodes of pathological intoxication last only 2 to 3 hr, but some may last a day or more. These episodes end with a deep sleep. On awakening, there is usually amnesia for the event.

F. Chronic Intoxication

1. Peripheral and Central Nervous System Effects

Chronic alcohol abuse may lead to substantial nervous system pathology. The most frequent neurological disorder in alcoholics is **polyneuropathy,** which results primarily from an alcohol-induced vitamin deficiency. A direct toxic effect of alcohol also may be a factor. Most patients are asymptomatic, with absent ankle jerks as the only sign. In more severe cases, burning feet, pain, paresthesias, and distal muscle weakness occur. Foot drop and wrist drop are ultimate complications. Prolonged abstinence, adequate nutrition, and vitamin replacement may gradually reverse this syndrome, but in some, the damage is permanent.

Wernicke's disease, the result of an alcohol-induced thiamine (vitamin B₁) deficiency, occurs in some chronic alcoholics. Nystagmus, bilateral sixth cranial nerve palsies, and paralysis of conjugate gaze are frequently seen along with ataxia and various mental disturbances. Most common is a "quiet delirium" characterized by apathy, lassitude, disorientation, and drowsiness. A less common syndrome, **Korsakoff's psychosis** (alcohol amnestic disorder), consists of profound anterograde and retrograde amnesia in an otherwise alert individual. Confabulation also may be present. Wernicke's disease and Korsakoff's psychosis are not separate disease entities; rather, the latter is a variably present component of the former. When both are present, the disease is called the **Wernicke–Korsakoff syndrome.** Postmortem brain examination of these patients often reveals structural lesions in the mammillary bodies.

Prompt diagnosis and treatment of Wernicke's disease is imperative. Immediate administration of **thiamine, 50 mg IV and 50 mg IM, followed by 50 mg IM or PO each day** until the patient is eating well should improve the ocular difficulties within hours to days. Ataxia also may respond during this time period. Delirium, when present, is reversible, but as confusional symptoms recede, the symptoms of Korsakoff's psychosis may become more evident. In such patients, recovery takes longer (i.e., a year or more) and may be incomplete.

Other central nervous system sequelae of chronic alcohol abuse include **cerebellar degeneration,** affecting primarily stance and gait, and **vitamin deficiency amblyopia,** causing blurred vision, central scotomata, and, if untreated, optic nerve atrophy.

2. Effects on Other Organ Systems

Over time, heavy alcohol consumption may damage other organ systems. Liver disease can take the form of alcoholic fatty liver, alcoholic hepatitis, or cirrhosis. Gastrointestinal disorders include gastritis, pancreatitis, gastric and duodenal ulcers, and malabsorption syndrome. Many alcoholics are anemic, in part because of nutritional (e.g., folic acid) deficiencies that often accompany chronic alcohol abuse. Alcoholic cardiomyopathy also is an important cause of morbidity and mortality in chronic heavy drinkers. The reader is referred to standard textbooks of internal medicine for a more complete description of these clinical entities.

3. Fetal Alcohol Syndrome

The offspring of women who abuse alcohol during pregnancy may manifest one or more congenital abnormalities grouped under the term fetal alcohol syndrome (FAS). These may include low birth weight, microcephaly, mental retardation, short palpebral fissures, epicanthic folds, maxillary hypoplasia, abnormal palmar creases, cardiac anomalies (e.g., septal defects), capillary hemangiomas, and a slowed postnatal growth rate. Generally, these infants sleep and feed poorly and are irritable, tremulous, and hyperactive. In one study, the perinatal mortality rate was 17%, and 44% of the surviving children were mentally deficient. Seriously affected infants may never achieve normal growth or intellectual performance, even in an optimal postnatal environment.

The etiology of FAS is unclear, but it may result from a direct toxic effect of alcohol or one of its metabolites on the central nervous system of the fetus. The amount of alcohol exposure required to produce the syndrome is unknown. Some authorities recommend that pregnant women consume no more than two mixed drinks or their equivalent per day; others recommend total abstinence.

G. Alcohol Withdrawal

1. Minor Abstinence Syndrome

a. Clinical Manifestations

In physically dependent users, the initial stages of alcohol withdrawal usually begin several hours after the last drink. Tremulousness ("shakes"), muscle tension, blushing, sweating, and a vague sense of anxiety ("jitters") may be followed by nausea, vomiting, anorexia, and abdominal cramps. The patient appears restless and agitated; signs of generalized central nervous system irritability include hyperreflexia and a tendency to startle easily. As the withdrawal syndrome progresses, the patient develops a marked resting tremor and possibly auditory and visual hallucinations accompanied by paranoid delusions. Although initially he may have some insight, it is lost as the syndrome progresses.

In a minority of alcoholics, seizures ("rum fits") develop. They are typically grand mal and begin within 48 hr after the last drink. Usually seizures are self-limited, but status epilepticus may develop, particularly in patients with preexisting seizure disorder who have discontinued their anticonvulsant medication during the preceding drinking bout. In one-third of cases, seizures are followed by the development of delirium tremens.

b. Management

Minor abstinence symptoms usually resolve within 3 to 4 days, even in untreated patients. However, some degree of insomnia, tremor, and uneasiness may persist for as long as 10 to 14 days. Characteristically, these patients do not come to medical attention unless complications (e.g., seizures) develop. Heavy drinkers soon learn that administration of any central nervous system depressant, including alcohol, will reduce abstinence symptoms. Thus, a drinking bout may be prolonged as the patient attempts to ameliorate abstinence symptoms. If barbiturates or other sedative–hypnotics are used regularly for self-treatment, these patients may develop dependence on those drugs as well.

In patients who seek treatment, the clinician can take advantage of the cross tolerance between alcohol and other CNS depressants by substituting a longer-acting drug for alcohol and then gradually reducing the dose of the drug. Chlordiazepoxide (Librium®) is commonly used for this purpose. Administer 25 to 100 mg PO immediately and repeat the dose in 1 hr. Additional doses of 25 to 100 mg may be given approximately every 4 hr as needed until signs and symptoms of withdrawal are suppressed. The exact dose will depend on the age, size, general health, liver function, and drinking history of the patient. Within the first 24 hr, up to 400 to 600 mg of chlordiazepoxide may be given. Chlordiazepoxide should not be administered intramuscularly because it is poorly absorbed. On the second and third days, the preceding day's dose may be halved. On the fourth day, the drug can be stopped, and the patient observed for signs of withdrawal.

Chlordiazepoxide is metabolized into several active compounds that have slightly longer half-lives than the parent drug. Its onset of action is within 2 hr, with a peak effect in about 4 hr. After a single dose, the half-life of chlordiazepoxide ranges from 6 to 30 hr. The half-life may be longer in the elderly and in patients with liver disease.

The prophylactic use of antiseizure medications in alcohol withdrawal is controversial. Some have recommended that anticonvulsants not be prescribed, even for patients with a past history of withdrawal seizures. Others feel that in patients with a seizure history, combined phenytoin and chlordiazepoxide offer better protection against withdrawal seizures than chlordiazepoxide alone. Following a 1-g intravenous loading dose, 300 mg per day of phenytoin may be given orally throughout the withdrawal period.

2. Major Abstinence Syndrome (Delirium Tremens)

a. Clinical Manifestations

In about 5% of patients who develop withdrawal symptoms, the minor abstinence syndrome described above evolves into a state of confusion, disorientation, agitation, and delirium. This severe form of alcohol withdrawal is called delirium tremens (DTs). Symptoms generally begin **72 to 96 hr after the last drink** and may last for a few hours to a few weeks. Hallucinations (usually visual), tremulousness, disorientation, insomnia, and nightmares are common, as are signs of autonomic nervous system hyperactivity, including fever, sweating, tachycardia, hypertension, and increased respiratory rate. Since other serious medical illnesses (pneumonia, malnutrition, cirrhosis, gastritis, and anemia) often accompany DTs, these should be investigated and promptly treated. Subdural hematomas and meningitis also occur with increased frequency.

The patient with delirium tremens usually has a history of excessive drinking for at least 5 years, along with recent heavy drinking. The severity of the syndrome depends on the degree of prior intoxication, general health, and adequacy of preventive treatment. Once delirium develops, drug treatment and other management efforts may not alter its course. The mortality rate, even in treated cases, is approximately 10%. Death may occur as the result of either hyperthermia or cardiovascular collapse. Autopsy examinations in patients with delirium tremens have failed to elucidate the exact pathophysiology of the problem.

b. Management

Patients with delirium tremens are seriously ill and require intensive inpatient care. The major objectives of treatment are **reduction of CNS irritability, prevention of exhaustion, and correction of potentially fatal fluid and electrolyte imbalances.** Vitamin replacement and treatment of concurrent illnesses also are important considerations. **Diazepam** can reduce CNS irritability: 10 mg IV followed by 5 mg IV every 5 min until the patient is calm but awake. Thereafter, 5 mg may be given IV or PO at 1- to 4-hr intervals until the delirium clears. Careful monitoring of vital signs is necessary to avoid respiratory depression or hypotension.

3. Alcoholic Hallucinosis

Following a prolonged drinking bout, some patients who are physically dependent on alcohol may experience auditory hallucinations. These generally occur within 48 hr after cessation of drinking and take the form of threatening or disturbing voices. Patients may respond by calling the police or arming themselves. Unlike patients with delirium, however, these individuals are oriented to time, place, and person. Alcoholic hallucinations may last from a few hours to a week, although about 10% continue for weeks or months. Some patients will experience a recurrence of hallucinosis following each bout of heavy alcohol use. A few will develop a chronic form of this disorder, which may be mistaken for schizophrenia. **Antipsychotic drugs** such as chlorpromazine or trifluoperazine (Stelazine®) are the treatment of choice. On recovery, there is excellent memory for the psychotic episode.

H. Treatment of Chronic Alcohol Abuse

1. Introduction

The alcoholic individual has developed a life-style in which he is preoccupied with alcohol and has lost control over its consumption. As a result, drinking usually leads to moderate to severe intoxication. As tolerance develops, the alcoholic tends to increase the dose; if he is physically dependent, he drinks to prevent or relieve abstinence symptoms, which perpetuates the disorder. In the later stages, brief periods of abstinence are consistently followed by relapse, with its accompanying physical, emotional, and social costs.

Even a recovered alcoholic still suffers from a chronic, relapsing illness. Periods of stable abstinence may be interrupted by occasional relapse. Thus, abstinence should not be the sole criterion of successful treatment. Moreover, rehabilitation encompasses not only the physical aspects of the illness but psychological and social recovery as well. To achieve these goals, different treatment approaches must be integrated into a comprehensive program.

2. Biological Treatment

a. Disulfiram

The drug disulfiram (Antabuse®) interferes with the metabolic breakdown of acetaldehyde, an intermediate product in alcohol metabolism. As a result, patients on disulfiram who subsequently ingest alcohol often experience rapid buildup of acetaldehyde in the blood, usually accompanied by signs and symptoms of acetaldehyde poisoning. These include sensations of heat in the face and neck, throbbing headache, flushing, and feelings of constriction in the throat. Nausea, vomiting, hypotension, and profound anxiety are common; chest pain, coughing, and labored breathing may also occur. Some cases may be complicated by seizures, respiratory depression, cardiac arrhythmias, myocardial infarction, acute heart failure, and death.

The severity of the "Antabuse reaction" is usually correlated with the dose of disulfiram and the amount of alcohol subsequently ingested. Symptoms peak 30 min to several hours after alcohol ingestion. Patients with preexisting heart disease, cirrhosis, diabetes, or any debilitating medical disorder are particularly at risk for untoward and dangerous complications. These patients in particular should be instructed to avoid even disguised forms of alcohol (e.g., aftershave preparations). When reactions occur, they should be treated supportively by maintenance of blood pressure and correcting hypokalemia when necessary.

Disulfiram is rapidly absorbed from the gastrointestinal tract, but it becomes fully effective only after 12 hr. The drug is oxidized by the liver and excreted in the urine. Excretion is slow, with one-fifth of the administered dose remaining in the body after 1 week. As a result, alcohol ingestion may produce an acetaldehyde reaction up to 2 weeks after disulfiram has been discontinued.

The usual maintenance dose of disulfiram is 250 mg PO per day. Although the drug is largely inert except when combined with alcohol, adverse effects unrelated to alcohol ingestion may include fatigue, gastrointestinal disturbances, acne, tremor, toxic psychosis, restlessness, and a persistent garliclike or metallic taste. A dose of 125 mg per day will suffice in patients who experience such undesirable effects.

Disulfiram is probably most useful in older, well motivated, socially stable patients whose drinking is precipitated by recurrent psychological stress. The drug should be taken each morning, when the level of stress and the temptation to drink is usually lowest. When taking disulfiram, many patients report that situations previously conducive to drinking generate less craving for alcohol than before. On the other hand, patients with poor impulse control, schizophrenia, or depression with suicidal ideation are at considerable risk of drinking when on disulfiram.

Disulfiram, by itself, is not an extremely effective treatment for alcoholism. A recent study indicated that only 23% of patients treated with disulfiram alone remained alcohol-free for 1 year, compared to 12% of a placebo-treated control group. Taking disulfiram is a daily decision which must be supported by other developments in a patient's life. It should be part of a comprehensive treatment program aimed at helping the patient adjust psychologically and socially to an alcohol-free existence.

b. Psychotropic Drugs

Many alcoholic patients drink to medicate an underlying psychiatric disorder, e.g., major depression or schizophrenia. In these individuals, specific pharmacotherapy for the primary disorder may improve the ultimate prognosis. Thus, in alcoholic patients with coexisting depression, a trial of antidepressant medication may be warranted. Such drugs should be prescribed cautiously, however, and only after completing detoxification. Alcohol potentiates the sedative properties of antidepressant drugs, and the antidepressants themselves lower the seizure threshold. The combination of alcohol and antidepressants is commonly found in overdose deaths (see Chapter 2).

Lithium is useful in some alcoholic patients who are also depressed, but nondepressed alcoholics are not particularly helped by this drug (see Chapter 3). Although alcoholics are frequently anxious, the use of anxiolytic drugs (e.g., diazepam) other than in the treatment of withdrawal is problematic, since alcoholics frequently abuse CNS depressants.

3. Behavioral Approaches to Treatment

In the past decade, behavior modification techniques have achieved increasing popularity. The euphorigenic effects of alcohol and the ability of the drug to relieve anxiety and tension are powerful reinforcing effects that promote repeated use. Repeated use, in turn, leads to tolerance and physical dependence, at which point drinking to stave off abstinence symptoms constitutes yet another reinforcer. As in the case of opiate use, chronic, heavy use of alcohol is accompanied by dysphoria and anxiety, which is often forgotten when the patient becomes sober. The latter phenomenon has been called state-dependent learning.

a. Aversion Therapy

In aversion therapy, or counterconditioning, alcohol ingestion is repeatedly followed by an artificially contrived noxious experience, e.g., a mildly painful electric shock. Over time, a powerful association is forged between drinking and the aversive stimulus. In theory, this association persists beyond the immediate treatment experience so that subsequently even the thought of drinking evokes powerful memories of the aversive stimulus. A number of alcohol treatment programs using chemical aversion (i.e., drugs that produce vomiting) have reported success (i.e., 40 to 60% abstinence for at least 1 year) with this method. The high level of motivation required of patients willing to submit to such treatment may account, in part, for the good results. Aversion therapy is probably most useful in the context of other treatments aimed at reinforcing sobriety.

b. Other Behavioral Techniques

Contingency contracting is a system in which the patient and therapist agree on a behavior to be encouraged (abstinence) or eliminated (drinking); a system of rewards or punishments is worked out to expedite these goals. In alcoholics who drink in response to anxiety, **sytematic desensitization** coupled with **relaxation training** may help to teach alternative coping behavior. **Assertiveness training** attempts to teach the patient social skills to handle interpersonal situations that have made him feel angry, frustrated, or manipulated and have led to drinking. Finally, in **blood alcohol level (BAL) discrimination training,** the alcoholic is taught to differentiate between reasonable and excessive blood alcohol concentration. He then attempts to use this skill, often combined with aversive conditioning techniques, to drink in moderation.

Although behavioral techniques are successful in some patients, we need carefully controlled studies to define the indications for such treatments. Certainly most successful treatment programs address not only the issue of drinking but also the intrapsychic and environmental cues that trigger this behavior. As with other modes of treatment, behavioral approaches are most successful when tailored to the individual needs of the patient rather than applied on a wholesale basis.

4. The Psychotherapies

A myriad of psychological therapies have been used to treat chronic alcoholism. These include individual, group, and family therapy. Although the alcoholic is the identified patient, problem drinking is often a symptom of troubled relationships. Sometimes, a couple or family tacitly supports continued heavy drinking. Organizations like **Alanon** and **Alateen** are often helpful (see Section IV.H.5).

An insight-oriented approach may help some patients; however, most researchers feel that psychotherapy alone does not usually constitute adequate treatment for alcoholism. Exploring sources of external stress and unconscious conflict may be useful but is generally insufficient to maintain sobriety when alcohol is available and the desire to drink is high. For this reason, disulfiram, **Alcoholics Anonymous,** and other measures should be combined into a multimodal treatment approach.

5. Alcoholics Anonymous

Perhaps the most successful treatment for chronic alcoholism is Alcoholics Anonymous (AA), a worldwide organization aiming to help its members achieve lasting sobriety. This is essentially a self-help approach in which members share their recovery experiences and support each other in the struggle to avoid relapse. Unlike the help offered by most professionals and social agencies, AA groups are almost continuously available. Experienced group members (sponsors) are assigned to care for new recruits during periods in which the risk of relapse is high. The group meetings themselves provide opportunities for catharsis and mutual support. In this sense, membership gratifies dependency needs while providing an opportunity to give to others, thus enhancing self-esteem. Alanon, a separate organization for spouses, offers support and valuable information about dealing with the alcoholic at home. Alateen provides similar help for the children of alcoholic parents.

6. Adjunctive Services

Halfway houses can be useful for alcoholic patients who are not emotionally prepared to live at home. For some, they are transitional facilities between home and hospital, whereas for others they provide long-term custodial care and supervision. Since job failure frequently accompanies chronic alcoholism, **vocational rehabilitation programs** are also a useful adjunct to treatment. Within industry, in-house alcohol treatment programs emphasize case finding, confrontation of the wayward worker, motivation for treatment (usually through administrative measures), and close monitoring of job performance. Similar programs have also been developed in military organizations.

7. Summary

Concern about the rising cost of health care has naturally prompted questions about the efficacy of various treatments for alcoholism. Some studies have suggested that less intensive treatment, e.g., outpatient group therapy or brief hospitalization for detoxification, does not necessarily result in a poorer outcome compared to other, more intensive treatment regimens. However, as in other addictive disorders, a multimodal treatment approach is clearly the most useful. Reliance on pharmacological intervention alone or on a single psychologically based treatment modality is usually insufficient to disrupt a pattern of repetitive relapse. Finally, although the individual and societal costs of alcoholism are enormous, little attention has been paid to preventive approaches. More research is needed to determine how to teach and promote moderate drinking.

V. ABUSE OF CENTRAL NERVOUS SYSTEM STIMULANTS

A. Amphetamines and Methamphetamine

1. Introduction

A wide variety of drugs stimulate the central nervous system; a number of these have potential for serious abuse. Amphetamine and its related compounds are sympathomimetic agents: their peripheral effects resemble those produced by stimulation of adrenergic (i.e., sympathetic) nerve endings. They also have central stimulatory effects, which contribute to their popularity as drugs of abuse. Dextroamphetamine (Dexedrine®), the *d*-isomer of amphetamine, is three to four times as potent as the *l*-isomer. Other amphetamine derivatives include methamphetamine (Desoxyn®), which is available in injectable form, methylphenidate (Ritalin®), phenmetrazine (Preludin®), and diethylpropion (Tenuate®, Tepanil®). This section focuses on amphetamines as examples of this class of agents.

2. Pharmacology

Both amphetamine and methamphetamine are well absorbed from the gastrointestinal tract and are stored in body tissues, including the CNS. Clinical effects generally appear within 30 min after oral ingestion. The drugs are metabolized primarily in the liver via hydroxylation, demethylation, and oxidation deamination. Following oral administration, more than 50% is excreted unchanged in the urine, particularly when urinary acidity is high.

Structurally, the amphetamine molecule strongly resembles the catecholamine neurotransmitters norepinephrine and dopamine. However, amphetamine is more lipid soluble than either and more readily crosses the blood–brain barrier. The central nervous system stimulation, anorexia, and enhanced psychomotor activity produced by amphetamines probably result from their facilitation of norepinephrine release from nerve terminals. They also may interfere with the metabolic breakdown of norepinephrine, both by inhibiting reuptake of this neurotransmitter by CNS neurons and by inhibiting monoamine oxidase, an important enzyme in norepinephrine metabolism. Some authors feel that amphetamines may directly stimulate adrenergic receptors.

The amphetamines also exert some effects on dopamine-containing neurons by facilitating dopamine release and perhaps interfering with the metabolic breakdown of this neurotransmitter. The paranoid psychosis that sometimes accompanies chronic use of high doses of amphetamines may result from effects of dopaminergic neurons.

3. Acute Effects

In therapeutic doses, amphetamines produce wakefulness, mood elevation, a sense of initiative and confidence, and increased mental alertness and ability to concentrate on simple tasks. Appetite is diminished, probably through a direct effect on the feeding center in the lateral hypothalamus. Systolic and diastolic blood pressure are increased, and heart rate is reflexly slowed. At higher doses, tremulousness, agitation, insomnia, headache, dizziness, confusion, and dysphoria occur. The EEG is desynchronized, and both total sleep time and rapid eye movement (REM) sleep are markedly reduced.

4. Tolerance and Physical Dependence

With repetitive use, tolerance develops to some of the effects of the amphetamines, especially when high doses are administered frequently. The mechanism is unclear, but some have hypothesized replacement of norepinephrine stores with amphetamine metabolites which act as "false transmitters." Tolerance develops rapidly to the mood-elevating and appetite suppressant effects of these drugs. On the other hand, chronic low-dose administration will continue to produce some stimulatory effects.

On sudden drug discontinuation after chronic amphetamine use, abstinence symptoms develop. These include lethargy, fatigue, and depression, along with a rebound increase in rapid eye movement (REM) sleep. These symptoms frequently set the stage for resumption of use and an alternating pattern of intoxication and withdrawal.

5. Patterns of Abuse

Currently, amphetamine and other CNS stimulants such as methylphenidate are widely used in the **treatment of narcolepsy, attention deficit disorder, and exogenous obesity.** Until the late 1960s, these drugs were frequently prescribed for the treatment of fatigue and depression as well. However, as their abuse potential became apparent, their prescription was placed under increased regulatory control which, in turn, created a substantial illicit market. This has led to widespread drug substitution, so that most of what is sold "on the street" as amphetamine often is caffeine or another over-the-counter stimulant.

Many chronic amphetamine users first begin taking the drug in the context of treatment for obesity or depression. Truck drivers, students, and physicians may abuse the drugs to alleviate fatigue. With the development of tolerance, the user tends to raise the dose. Subsequently, attempts at withdrawal may produce abstinence symptoms (see above) and resumption of use.

Some amphetamine abusers use the drug intermittently, ingesting large doses in search of euphoria. Members of this group are often young, tend to abuse other drugs, and are more likely to use stimulants intravenously in the form of methamphetamine ("crystal"). With this pattern of use, the drugs may be injected many times each day in doses as high as 1 g every 3 to 4 hr. Sprees of intoxication may last days or weeks and are usually followed by abrupt withdrawal ("crashing"). They also sometimes concurrently use barbiturates or opiates. After a period of exhaustion and sleep, amphetamine use is resumed.

6. Acute Intoxication

a. Clinical Manifestations

Serious toxic reactions from acute ingestion of amphetamine occur primarily in nontolerant (i.e., infrequent) users who consume relatively large doses (i.e., more than 60 mg/day) over a short period of time. The intoxication syndrome is characterized by restlessness, irritability, tremor, confusion, talkativeness, anxiety, and lability of mood. Peripheral effects include headache, chills, vomiting, dry mouth, and sweating. Blood pressure is variably affected, and heartbeat may be irregular. In more severe cases, auditory and/ or visual hallucinations, seizures, and hyperpyrexia may occur.

Among intravenous methamphetamine users, prolonged episodes of intoxication ("speed runs") are accompanied by anorexia, weight loss, insomnia, and generalized deterioration in psychomotor abilities. Chronic users, while intoxicated, also exhibit repetitive sterotyped behavior (e.g., taking things apart and putting them back together). Prolonged high-dose use may result in hallucinations, parasitosis (i.e., picking at imaginary bugs), lability of mood, and paranoia. These individuals also are prone to episodes of unprovoked violence, especially when amphetamines are combined with barbiturates.

Tolerance to the toxic effects of amphetamine or methamphetamine varies. Some patients can become quite ill at doses of 30 mg, whereas chronic users may tolerate 1 g of dextroamphetamine or more. Even in chronic users, however, large doses of intravenous methamphetamine may be followed by chest pain, temporary paralysis, or simple inability to function. The conscious, but "overamped" individual may experience racing thoughts coupled with euphoric mood and perhaps some degree of catatonia. Although deaths from amphetamine overdose are relatively rare, hyperpyrexia, seizures, and shock are reported in fatal cases. At autopsy, findings include petechial hemorrhages in the brain and congestion of the lungs, brain and other organs.

b. Management

Treatment of acute amphetamine toxicity includes **reducing CNS irritability and autonomic nervous system hyperactivity, controlling psychotic symptoms, and promoting rapid excretion of the drug** and its metabolites. Fevers above 102° F should be treated vigorously. Seizures that occur with acute amphetamine toxicity may take the form of status epilepticus, which should be treated with diazepam, 5 to 10 mg IV, injected at a rate not exceeding 5 mg per minute. This procedure may be repeated every 10 to 15 min as necessary to a total dose of 30 mg. Once the patient is no longer in acute distress, CNS irritability can be further reduced by avoiding excessive stimulation. The excretion of unchanged amphetamine can be enhanced by acidification of the urine. Provided there are no signs of liver or kidney failure, ammonium chloride 500 mg PO may be given every 3 to 4 hr.

Psychotic symptoms that accompany acute amphetamine toxicity are best treated by a dopamine-blocking agent such as chlorpromazine or haloperidol. A test dose of chlorpromazine, 25 mg PO, may be followed by 50 q.i.d. until symptoms disappear, usually within 48 hr. Some patients may require larger doses. If severe agitation or aggressiveness is a problem, intramuscular administration of antipsychotic drugs should be considered. Patients receiving antipsychotics should be monitored for hypotension. In addition, illegally produced amphetamines sometimes are adulterated with anticholinergic substances, which can potentiate anticholinergic effects of antipsychotic agents (see Chapter 4).

7. Amphetamine Withdrawal

Even without treatment, symptoms of acute amphetamine toxicity usually resolve within a week. The withdrawal period is characterized by fatigue, depression, hyperphagia, and rebound increase in REM sleep. As recovery progresses, the clinician should treat the depression, which may be quite severe. The patient's potential for suicide must be evaluated. Treatment with heterocyclic antidepressants* should be considered if the depression fails to remit within a few days. Although the efficacy of these drugs in reversing postamphetamine depression remains in doubt, some patients will experience depression and fatigue for several months and probably deserve a trial of antidepressant medication. In addition, patients with underlying mood disorders appear particularly vulnerable to the depression induced by amphetamine withdrawal (see Chapter 2).

8. Amphetamine-Induced Psychosis

Chronic high-dose amphetamine use may be accompanied by the development of a **toxic psychosis, which resembles paranoid schizophrenia.** In the early stages, patients are euphoric, loquacious, and overconfident in their abilities. As the syndrome progresses, suspiciousness, fear, and increased aggressivity are noted, along with delusions of persecution, ideas of reference, and auditory, visual, and tactile hallucinations. Bruxism, parasitosis, distorted

---

*Since many of the currently used thymoleptic drugs are not tricyclic in structure, we have adopted this term to represent the various cyclic antidepressants. From: Baldessarini R.J.: Overview of recent advances in antidepressant pharmacology. Part II. *McLean Hosp J* 7:1–27, 1982.

time sense, changes in body image, and hyperactivity also are reported. Some patients exhibit compulsive, stereotyped behavior, which may appear purposeful but is characterized by doing and undoing a particular task. Unlike most toxic psychoses, confusion and disorientation are relatively absent.

In most cases of amphetamine psychosis, withdrawal of the drug is followed by slow but complete recovery within days to weeks. In some patients, however, psychotic symptoms may persist for years. Characteristically, there is hypermnesia for the psychotic episode, allowing the patient to describe his condition in great detail.

Some have felt that amphetamine psychosis occurs only in patients who are specifically predisposed to psychosis; however, the syndrome has been produced in normal volunteers given large doses of amphetamine for 5 days. In practice, consistent use of doses over 100 mg per day for weeks or months places the user at greater risk for the development of psychosis. Sudden increases in dosage, even in tolerant individuals, also may precipitate a psychotic episode.

As with acute amphetamine intoxication, withdrawal of the drug and the use of antipsychotics (e.g., haloperidol, chlorpromazine) in doses sufficient to control symptoms is the treatment of choice for amphetamine psychosis. Once the psychosis clears (usually within several days), antipsychotic drugs should be stopped to permit clinical assessment in a drug-free state. If psychotic symptoms recur, antipsychotics can be reinstituted.

B. Cocaine

1. Introduction

Perhaps no other drug has gained as much in popularity over the past decade as cocaine—a local anesthetic and CNS stimulant whose actions resemble those of amphetamine but are of shorter duration and perhaps greater intensity (although research subjects who blindly compared the effects of the two drugs were unable to tell them apart).

Cocaine exerts a direct stimulatory effect on the cerebral cortex, producing excitation, restlessness, euphoria, and feelings of increased strength and mental ability. Its sympathomimetic effects include vasoconstriction, tachycardia, increased blood pressure and temperature, and dilated pupils.

2. Pharmacology

Cocaine is rapidly absorbed when administered intranasally or by smoking of either coca paste or the alkalinized extract ("freebase"). Oral cocaine use is unusual in this country, but Andes mountain Indians have chewed coca leaves (containing the precursor of cocaine) for centuries. The usual street dose of cocaine is difficult to measure, since both purity and the pattern of consumption vary widely. Fifteen to 50 mg is the usual intoxicating dose.

Following intranasal or intravenous (IV) administration, onset of action begins within 2 min. Peak effects occur at 15 to 20 min after intranasal use and 5 to 10 min after IV use. Freebase smoking results in almost immediate intoxication, but the effects last just a few minutes. With oral administration (i.e., chewing coca leaf), the rate of absorption is slower, and the duration of action longer.

In general, the subjective effects of cocaine are related to the plasma levels achieved, but the rate of rise of the plasma level also is important in determining the effects. After a single dose, plasma levels fall rapidly as the drug is metabolized, both in the liver and by cholinesterase enzymes in plasma. The half-life of the drug is approximately 1 hr. The cocaine metabolite benzoylecgonine is excreted in the urine and can be detected by enzyme immunoassay up to 30 hr after the last dose.

3. Tolerance and Physical Dependence

Although cocaine does not produce physical dependence in the classical sense, animal experiments suggest that the drug has powerful reinforcing properties. Given the option, rhesus monkeys with prior cocaine experience will consistently choose intravenous cocaine over food, even after several days of food deprivation. Clinical experience in man suggests that some users develop profound psychological dependence on cocaine and will pursue the drug experience to the exclusion of almost all other activities. In addition, the hypersomnia, hyperphagia, and lassitude ("crash") seen after discontinuation of chronic use constitute a discrete withdrawal syndrome which may precipitate renewed use.

Although some chronic cocaine users may consume very large amounts of the drug, tolerance to the effects of cocaine has not been demonstrated. Indeed, some regular users may develop a "reverse tolerance" or sensitization to the drug's subjective and behavioral effects.

4. Patterns of Abuse

The relatively high cost of illicitly acquired cocaine has contributed to its status as a drug of abuse by the middle and upper classes. The growing market for the drug, especially in urban areas, has also spawned an underground network of dealers who are often heavy users themselves. The drug is usually taken intranasally ("snorted"), although intravenous use is increasingly common. More recently, "freebasing," or smoking the alkaline precursor of cocaine, has come into vogue. Occasionally, cocaine is applied topically to the genitalia to enhance sexual excitement and delay orgasm.

The majority of cocaine users take the drug intermittently (e.g., once per week) and never experience significant physiological or psychosocial problems. Some users, however, develop profound psychological dependence on cocaine and may experience serious emotional, social, and financial difficulties. These individuals may use the drug intensively over periods lasting days to weeks, during which time they sleep very little and remain almost continuously intoxicated.

5. Acute Intoxication

Acute cocaine poisoning is most common among intravenous users, but freebasing and the smoking of coca paste, common in South America, also appear to be particularly hazardous modes of consumption. The symptoms are similar to those of acute amphetamine intoxication and often include intense anxiety, paranoia, and hallucinations. Elevated blood pressure, tachycardia, ventricular irritability, hyperthermia, and respiratory depression are symptomatic of more severe poisoning. Acute heart failure, stroke, and seizures also have been reported. Death from these complications is rare but can occur.

Initial treatment of acute cocaine poisoning should provide **general life support measures,** including establishment of an airway, stabilization of the circulatory system, and reduction of severely elevated body temperature. Manifestations of **sympathetic nervous system hyperactivity** such as hypertension, tachycardia, and tachypnea may be treated with propranolol (Inderal®, Inderide®), 1 mg IV injected slowly every 1 min for up to 8 min. Patients in hypertensive crisis who do not respond to this regimen may be given sodium nitroprusside (Nipride®) or phentolamine (Regitine®). Intravenous diazepam can be used in patients with repeated seizures. Once the patient is stabilized medically, chlorpromazine or haloperidol may be used to treat any psychotic symptoms that remain.

6. Sequelae of Chronic Cocaine Abuse

Infrequent cocaine use, even when sustained over a long period of time, usually does not lead to serious complications. Chronic heavy users, however, may develop perceptual disturbances, including auditory, visual, or tactile hallucinations (e.g., "cocaine bugs" crawling under the skin) as part of a paranoid psychosis similar to that seen in chronic amphetamine users. Heavy intranasal use may lead to chronic inflammation or ulceration of the nasal mucosa, and occasionally to septal perforation. Smoking of freebase cocaine may impair pulmonary diffusing capacity. Patients with underlying affective disorder, e.g., recurrent depression, sometimes remain undiagnosed and untreated when the sequelae of stimulant abuse cloud the clinical picture.

C. Treatment of Chronic Stimulant Abuse

Treatment of patients who abuse amphetamines, cocaine, or other CNS stimulants must be flexible and eclectic. Some patients find Alcoholics Anonymous meetings, with their emphasis on delay of drug-induced gratification, quite helpful. Individual psychotherapy and/or drug-related counseling is often beneficial as well. For those who use stimulants to treat an underlying mood disorder, antidepressants or lithium should be considered. For those unable to function drug-free in an outpatient setting, residential treatment in a drug treatment facility may be advisable.

VI. ABUSE OF HALLUCINOGENIC SUBSTANCES

A. Introduction

The hallucinogens are a group of structurally similar agents that produce perceptual distortion (primarily visual illusions and hallucinations) and enhance awareness of internal and external stimuli. They also induce in the user a sense that mundane events are unusually important, a tendency toward introspection and profound emotional lability. Some have referred to this group of substances as "psychedelic" (i.e., "mind expanding"), but this suggested property may be more illusory than real. The term "psychotomimetic" also has been applied to these drugs because they produce a state that mimics functional psychosis, but the resemblance between hallucinogen intoxication and functional psychosis is superficial.

Popular in the late 1960s, the prevalence of hallucinogen abuse has declined in recent years. The drugs have by no means disappeared, however, and the adverse consequences of their use are still apparent in emergency room settings. Moreover, drugs sold on the street as "hallucinogens" often contain other agents (e.g., amphetamine, phencyclidine), so that patients who present with a "bad trip" presumably from mescaline may, in fact, be suffering from a PCP-induced psychosis.

B. Classification

Pharmacologically, the commonly abused hallucinogenic substances may be divided into two major groups. The **indolealkylamines,** including *d*-lysergic acid diethylamide (LSD), psilocybin, and dimethyltryptamine (DMT), bear a structural resemblance to the neurotransmitter 5-hydroxytryptamine (serotonin). The **phenylethylamines,** including mescaline and the phenyliso-propylamines such as 2,5-dimethoxy-4-methylamphetamine (DOM, "STP"), are structurally related to dopamine, norepinephrine, and the amphetamines.

The commonly abused hallucinogens and their important properties are summarized in Table 3. For purposes of this chapter, discussion focuses primarily on LSD, since it is the best known from a pharmacological and clinical standpoint and is the most commonly abused hallucinogen.

C. *d*-Lysergic Acid Diethylamide

1. Pharmacology

d-Lysergic acid diethylamide is a synthetic hallucinogen derived from an extract of the ergot fungus. It is a potent hallucinogen, with intoxication resulting from doses as low as 50 μg. The drug is colorless, odorless, and tasteless. It is usually ingested as part of a pill or dissolved on a piece of paper. Occasionally, it is administered intravenously. Following oral administration, the drug is well absorbed from the gastrointestinal tract and distributed to body tissues. Only small amounts are detected in the brain, however. Although the mechanism of action is unclear, the drug inhibits the activity of serotonergic neurons in the midbrain dorsal raphe. The plasma half-life of LSD is 2 to 3 hr. It is metabolized into nonhallucinogenic substances, primarily by conjugation in the liver.

2. Tolerance and Physical Dependence

With repeated administration, tolerance develops rapidly (i.e., in 2 to 4 days) to the behavioral effects of LSD. As a result, even chronic users do not take the drug more often than twice a week, and the vast majority take it less frequently. Considerable cross tolerance exists between LSD and other hallucinogens. No physical dependence has been demonstrated in LSD users, and abstinence symptoms are not observed after withdrawal. Only one death has been directly linked to an LSD overdose, although fatal accidents and suicides may occur during periods of intoxication.

3. Acute Intoxication

The effects of LSD begin 20 to 60 min after ingestion, depending on the amount ingested and the degree of tolerance developed. Sympathomimetic effects include tachycardia, increased blood pressure and body temperature, and pupillary dilation. Hyperreflexia, nausea and muscle weakness also are

TABLE 3. Commonly Abused Hallucinogenic Drugs

Drug	Source	Psychedelic dose	Peak symptoms	Duration of action	Prominent somatic effects	Prominent psychological effects
d-Lysergic acid diethylamide	Synthetic (from fungi)	50 μg	2–3 hr	8–12 hr; undulating activity as effect declines	Increased sympathetic nervous system activity: dilated pupils, increased BP, pulse, DTRs, temperature, blood sugar, tremor	Hypervigilance, illusions, emotional lability, loss of body boundaries, time slowing, increased intensity of all sensations
Psilocybin	Mushroom	10 mg	90 min	4–6 hr	Like LSD, but milder	Like LSD, but less intense, more visual, more euphoria; paranoia
Dimethyltryptamine (DMT)	Synthetic	50 mg	5–20 min	30–60 min	Like LSD, but with more intense sympathomimetic symptoms	Like LSD, but usually more intense, in part because of sudden onset. Must be smoked or injected; cannot be taken orally
Mescaline	Peyote cactus	200 mg	2–3 hr	8–12 hr	Nausea, vomiting; otherwise like LSD; perhaps more intense sympathomimetic effects	Like LSD but perhaps more sensory and perceptual changes; euphoria prominent
Dimethoxymethylamphetamine (DOM, "STP")	Synthetic	5 mg	3–5 hr	6–8 hr at doses below 5 mg; 16–24 hr at high doses (10–30 mg)	Minimal effects at low dose; autonomic effects prominent at doses above 5 mg	May resemble amphetamine combined with LSD, but long-lasting; high incidence of flashbacks, psychosis; chlorpromazine may aggravate symptoms

observed. Peak effects occur between 2 and 3 hr after ingestion. Visual illusions, wavelike perceptual changes, macropsia and micropsia, and extreme emotional lability dominate this period. Perceptions in one sensory modality may effect or overflow into another (synesthesias), so that colors are "heard" and sounds "seen." Subjective time is slowed, and a generalized loss of body and ego boundaries is experienced. There is also a tendency toward increased fantasy production, diminished ego function, and feelings of depersonalization. In such a state, the lack of a supportive environment or companion can be detrimental, as the individual struggles to control his anxiety and prevent ego disintegration. As the effects of the drug begin to wane (i.e., 4 to 6 hr after ingestion), the patient experiences intermittent "waves of normalcy." After 8 to 12 hr, the intoxication syndrome is mostly cleared, although aftereffects, including a sense of psychic numbness, may last for days.

D. Adverse Reactions following Use of LSD or Other Hallucinogens

1. Panic Reactions

As summarized in Table 4, the major hazards of hallucinogen use are psychological. The most common adverse reaction is a temporary episode of panic (a "bad trip"). The likelihood of panic is determined by the expectations or "set" of the individual taking the drug, the setting in which the drug is taken, the user's current level of psychological health, and the type and dose of the drug administered. Inexperienced users and those who are constricted, schizoid, anxious, and who fear loss of control have difficulty coping with the disorganizing effects of these drugs. Taking the drug alone or in an unfamiliar or hostile setting also seems to predispose to panic.

TABLE 4. Adverse Reactions to Hallucinogens

Type	Duration	Predisposing factors	Treatment
Acute panic	2–24 hr	Obsessional character, large dose, inexperienced user	Support, reassurance, diazepam if necessary
Toxic delirium	2–24 hr	Large dose, idiosyncratic response	Support, reassurance, antipsychotics, or diazepam if necessary
Drug-precipitated functional psychosis	Indefinite	Vulnerability to schizophrenia or affective disorder	Antipsychotics only after first 48 hr
Flashbacks	Minutes to hours	Recent (< 6 months) use of a hallucinogen; use of marijuana or amphetamines	Reassurance; usually brief and not as intense as original experience

Fortunately, most panic reactions are limited to the duration of action of the particular drug used. Since there are no known methods for rapidly eliminating hallucinogenic substances from the body, the primary goal of treatment is to support the patient through this period, mostly by reassuring him that he is not "losing his mind" and that he will soon return to his normal state. The presence of calm, supportive friends can be very helpful. Such patients should not be left alone. In the majority of users, symptoms subside as the drug is metabolized, usually within 24 hr. When support and reassurance are ineffective and the patient is severely agitated, diazepam, 10 to 30 mg PO can be helpful, but in most cases the use of psychotropic medication is not necessary.

2. Toxic Delirium

Some hallucinogen users experience an acute toxic confusional state characterized by hallucinations, delusions, agitation, disorientation, and paranoia. In this state, assaults and inadvertent suicide attempts may occur (e.g., if the patient believes he can fly or stop a speeding train). No prior history of mental disorder, visual rather than auditory hallucinations, and the presence of some degree of observing ego suggest a diagnosis of toxic drug reaction rather than schizophrenia.

As in the case of any toxic delirium, the primary aim is to support the patient through the period of drug effect. In a majority of users, symptoms will subside gradually as the drug is metabolized. Diazepam may be effective in the treatment of associated anxiety but can also cloud the clinical picture and should be prescribed only when support and reassurance are ineffective. Phenothiazines must be given with caution, especially if atropine-type drugs may have been ingested. Haloperidol might be a better choice in such cases. At times, physical restraint also may be necessary to prevent the patient from harming himself or others. Untreated patients usually become mentally clear within 24 hr (as the drug is metabolized), with no obvious sequelae.

3. Drug-Precipitated Functional Psychosis

Another untoward effect of hallucinogen use is psychosis that fails to clear after the drug is metabolized. This occurs primarily in patients with underlying affective disorder or schizophrenia, some of whom may use these drugs in the hope of achieving psychic reintegration or an anxiety-free state. Such patients often become more disorganized by the drug experience. Treatment may include judicious use of antipsychotic drugs and, when indicated, lithium and/or antidepressants. Following resolution of the acute psychotic episode, attention should be directed toward understanding the precipitants of drug use.

4. Recurrent Drug Experiences (''Flashbacks'')

A fourth adverse consequence of hallucinogen use is the spontaneous recurrence of drug effects a few days to several months after the last drug experience. These "flashbacks," lasting a few seconds to several hours, can be precipitated by internal or external stress unrelated to drug use or by use of marijuana or amphetamines. They are characterized by perceptual distortions, feelings of depersonalization, and emotional lability. Some patients respond to flashbacks with anxiety, depression, and paranoia; others enjoy them. Treatment consists of firm reassurance that the flashback will pass. In some cases, antianxiety agents such as diazepam are helpful.

E. Sequelae of Chronic Hallucinogen Use

In the early 1970s, hallucinogen use was closely tied with the politics and social expectations of the hippie movement. Even then, regular users ("acid heads") were often described as meek, indifferent, and passive–aggressive. It is unclear, however, whether these personality traits were the direct result of drug use or merely characterized a group of people more likely to use the drugs. Today, the vast majority of hallucinogen users are experimenters who take the drug several times out of curiosity or occasionally to intensify a particular experience. Regular users are more apt to exhibit serious psychopathology and abuse other psychoactive drugs as well.

Medical sequelae of chronic hallucinogen use are not well defined. Reports of LSD-induced chromosome damage in humans have aroused concern, but the data are equivocal. In very high doses, LSD does produce an increased number of stillbirths and deformities in pregnant laboratory animals; however, the relevance of these findings to man is unclear. Controlled studies have found no significant increase in the incidence of birth defects among LSD users relative to nonusers. Nevertheless, it is wise to advise pregnant women to avoid the use of this and other drugs, especially during the first trimester.

VII. PHENCYCLIDINE ABUSE

A. Introduction

Phencyclidine (PCP, "angel dust," "hog," "T," "crystal joints," "rocket fuel"), a commonly used animal tranquilizer, has recently achieved considerable popularity among adolescent and young adult drug users. Phencyclidine abuse has become quite widespread in recent years, with approximately one of six young adults between ages 18 and 25 having used the drug knowingly, and more having taken the drug unwittingly in the form of adulterated marijuana or LSD. Street samples of the drug have been shown to contain nearly 30 analogues of PCP, many of which are more potent than PCP itself. Because of its behavioral toxicity, the drug poses a significant health problem, with deaths resulting from drug-induced violence, suicide, and accidents.

B. Pharmacology

Although it is classified as a dissociative anesthetic, PCP has stimulant, depressant, hallucinogenic, or analgesic effects, depending on the dose and route of administration. Phencyclidine is usually administered by dissolving the drug onto marijuana or tobacco and then smoking the mixture. It can also be taken orally, intranasally, or intravenously. The drug is well absorbed via each of these routes, although absorption after oral ingestion may be slow. Phencyclidine is metabolized in the liver and stored in fatty tissues.

Behavioral tolerance to PCP occurs with chronic use, but physical dependence has not been reported. Although the serum half-life is generally about 45 min at low doses, the half-life may be as long as 3 days after an overdose; this is a result of sequestration of PCP in brain and adipose tissue. Phencyclidine may be detected in urine and blood using a gas assay technique. There is some correlation between PCP levels in urine and blood and the degree of intoxication. Blood levels peak 1–4 hr after inhalation, but PCP may be detected in urine for up to a week following high-dose use. Since PCP is a weak base with a pK_a of about 8.5, the drug is increasingly soluble in more acidic aqueous solutions. Thus, acidification of the urine will enhance PCP excretion (see Section VII.D).

C. Acute Intoxication

In low doses (5 mg or less), PCP exerts a depressant effect on the central nervous system, producing a state resembling alcohol intoxication with muscular incoordination, generalized numbness of the extremities, a "blank stare" appearance and mild ptosis of the eyelids. Ocular findings include vertical or horizontal nystagmus, miotic or normal-sized reactive pupils, and absent corneal reflexes. Impaired perception, mild analgesia, and various forms of motor disturbances are also seen. Higher doses (5 to 10 mg) produce nystagmus, slurred speech, ataxia, hyperreflexia, increased muscle tone, and catalepsy. Severe overdose (greater than 20 mg) may result in hypertensive crisis, muscular rigidity, seizure, respiratory depression, coma, and death.

The subjective effects of PCP include changes in body image, feelings of dissociation, perceptual distortions, auditory and visual hallucinations, and feelings of "nothingness". The behavioral state resembles the effects of sensory deprivation. Amnesia for the period of intoxication (usually 4 to 6 hr) is frequent.

Many PCP users experience some mood elevation, but feelings of anxiety are common as well. Indeed, most regular users report unwanted effects, most commonly perceptual disturbances, restlessness, disorientation, and anxiety, during each period of intoxication, whereas desired experiences (e.g., increased sensitivity to external stimuli, dissociation, stimulation, and elevated mood) occur only 60% of the time. This has led clinicians and researchers to wonder why so many people continue to take a drug that they find largely unpleasant. Some clinicians have proposed that the drug has reinforcing properties; some users enjoy the risks of a PCP experience and the fact that phencyclidine, if nothing else, alters consciousness profoundly. For many polydrug abusers (which most PCP users are), the degree of alteration in affective state is far more important than the type of alteration.

Patients acutely intoxicated with phencyclidine generally come to treatment facilities because they have aroused the concern of people around them. These patients are often confused and disoriented and may display bizarre posturing or catatonia. They may seem apprehensive and anxious or euphoric. Slurred speech is common, and the patients often appear to stare blankly into space. Increased bronchial or salivary secretions are common, as are systolic hypertension, horizontal or vertical nystagmus, and ataxia. The symptom picture of bizarre behavior with nystagmus, hypertension, and drooling strongly suggests a diagnosis of PCP intoxication.

Once the diagnosis is made, treatment efforts should be directed toward calming the patient, ensuring the patient's and the staff's safety, and treating any medical complications that arise. The patient should be placed in isolation (i.e., a "quiet room"), which will decrease external stimulation; restraints may be necessary if the patient is combative or self-destructive. Diazepam (10–20 mg PO or 2.5 mg IV) may be useful in decreasing agitation and muscle hypertonicity. Since the patient may also have taken CNS depressants, diazepam should be used cautiously. To increase PCP excretion, the patient may be given cranberry juice (which contains benzoic acid) or oral ascorbic acid (0.5 to 1.5 g). Nasogastric suctioning should be reserved for serious cases in which recent oral ingestion is highly suspected, since PCP use may predispose the patient to laryngospasm. Because of the risk of seizures, ipecac should not be used. Hypertensive crisis may be treated with diazoxide (Hyperstat®, Proglycem®), and status epilepticus, should it occur, is best treated with intravenous diazepam. Most patients improve within several hours after PCP ingestion. However, the patient should be observed until his sensorium has cleared, his vital signs are stable, and he is no longer combative or agitated.

D. Phencyclidine Overdose

Phencyclidine overdose is differentiated from simple intoxication primarily by the level of consciousness of the patient; the patient who has overdosed will be stuporous or comatose. In severe overdose, coma may last from several hours to 10 days. Hypertension is frequently present and may be severe. Respirations may be decreased, and seizures (sometimes leading to status epilepticus) are frequently seen. Horizontal and vertical nystagmus are always present, and muscle tone is increased.

Treatment of PCP overdose usually consists of (1) maintenance of adequate oxygenation, (2) gastric lavage if the drug has been ingested in the previous 4 hr, (3) treatment of hypertensive crisis with diazoxide or hydralazine, and (4) use of intravenous diazepam if necessary for seizures. (5) Acidification of the urine facilitates drug excretion and hastens recovery from psychosis or coma. This may be accomplished by administering ammonium chloride via nasogastric tube in a dose of 2.75 mEq/kg in 60 cc of saline solution every 6 hr, along with intravenous ascorbic acid (2 mg/500 cc IV fluid every 6 hr) until the urine pH drops below 5.5. For comatose patients, ammonium chloride should be given IV, 2.75 mEq/kg, as a 1–2% solution in saline. When the urinary pH has reached 5, furosemide, 20–40 mg IV, should be given to promote further drug excretion. This may be repeated once if necessary. Renal function should be monitored, since high-dose intoxication may decrease urine output.

E. Phencyclidine Psychosis

In some vulnerable individuals, PCP can produce psychotic symptoms that may persist for days or weeks after the last dose. Although this reaction occurs primarily in novice users, it may also occur in chronic users taking moderate to high doses regularly. It is also more likely to occur in patients with a history of prior schizophrenic episodes, even those who are being maintained on antipsychotic drugs.

Generally, the course of PCP psychosis may be divided into three phases, each lasting about 5 days. The initial acute phase of the psychosis, typically the most severe, is often characterized by paranoid delusions, hyperactivity, anorexia, insomnia, agitation or catalepsy, and unpredictable assaultiveness. During this period, patients are extremely sensitive to external stimuli. In the mixed phase of the psychosis, paranoia and restlessness remain, but the patient is usually calmer and intermittently in control of his behavior. In the absence of further drug use, the next 1 or 2 weeks are usually characterized by gradual reintegration and resolution of symptoms. However, in some patients, psychotic symptoms may persist for months. Depression is also a common sequel of PCP psychosis.

The treatment of PCP psychosis is aimed at maintaining the physical safety of the patient and others, decreasing psychotic thinking with the use of antipsychotic drugs, and promoting rapid excretion of the drug through acidification of the urine. If drug ingestion has been relatively recent, gastric lavage may also be helpful. Injury may be prevented by prompt hospitalization and the use of a "quiet room" to reduce external sensory input. Unlike hallucinogen users on "bad trips," patients intoxicated with PCP do not respond well to "talking down." Use of antipsychotics in conjunction with procedures designed to lower tissue levels of the drug (see Section VII.D) may hasten recovery. However, antipsychotic drugs with significant anticholinergic effects (e.g., chlorpromazine) should be avoided, since they may potentiate the anticholinergic effects of phencyclidine. Haloperidol, 5 mg IM given hourly as needed, may be useful, although response to treatment is often slow. Most patients are substantially better after 2 to 3 weeks of treatment—sooner if the drug can be rapidly eliminated from the body.

F. Sequelae of Chronic Phencyclidine Use

Phencyclidine is a readily available, inexpensive drug with very powerful behavioral effects and is, therefore, difficult to give up. Chronic users rarely seek treatment, although they may develop anxiety, social isolation, severe episodes of depression, and occasional violent outbursts. Some patients exhibit schizophrenialike symptoms coupled with aggressive behavior, whereas others develop memory and speech impairment. Most PCP users are also active users of other psychoactive drugs, especially marijuana, alcohol, and hallucinogens. Residential drug treatment programs have had some success in the treatment of chronic users, but for many the prognosis is grim.

VIII. INHALANT ABUSE

A. Introduction

The inhalants comprise a heterogeneous group of volatile organic solvents that have profound toxic effects on the CNS. Some of the commonly inhaled substances and their major active ingredients include: glues and paint thinners (toluene), lighter fluid (naphtha), aerosols (fluorinated hydrocarbons, nitrous oxide), cleaning solutions (trichloroethylene, carbon tetrachloride), and gasoline (benzene).

B. Patterns of Abuse

Inhalants tend to be popular drugs of abuse among boys in their early teens, especially in poor and rural areas, where more expensive drugs of abuse are less available. Although the prevalence of inhalant abuse decreases with age, many users go on to abuse other drugs. Most commonly, the volatile gases are inhaled from a handkerchief or rag that has been soaked with the solvent material. Glue squirted into a paper bag gives off a vapor which can then be inhaled. Aerosol spray cans are a source of volatile hydrocarbons and nitrous oxide.

C. Acute Intoxication

High lipid solubility and rapid passage across the blood–brain barrier account for the rapidly intoxicating effects of the inhalants. Drug effects last up to 45 min, depending on the degree of exposure. The clinical picture resembles that of alcohol intoxication and includes euphoria, giddiness, and lightheadedness. Irritation of the nasal mucosa, conjunctivitis, and unusual breath odor also suggest the diagnosis. Depending on the solvent used, a variety of toxic effects also may occur. These include induction of cardiac arrhythmias, hypoxia, seizures, and death. Tolerance to the effects of inhalants develops rather quickly, but no cross tolerance occurs among the various solvents. Although physical dependence has not been documented, a syndrome resembling delirium tremens has been noted in some chronic users who stop using these agents abruptly. Abdominal pain, paresthesias, and headaches also can occur during drug-free periods. Strong psychological dependence often develops in inhalant abusers and accounts for much of the difficulty in treating these individuals.

D. Sequelae of Chronic Inhalant Use

Although the exact relationship between inhalant abuse and brain damage is unclear, a number of studies have found a greater than expected prevalence of abnormal electroencephalograms, perceptual motor difficulties, and impaired memory in chronic users. Language skills and the ability to process information and think abstractly also may be affected. Peripheral neuropathies and bone marrow depression are the potential consequences of long-term use. Finally, there is some evidence that as a group, inhalant abusers exhibit more self-destructiveness and antisocial behavior than other types of drug abusers.

E. Treatment Approaches

Chronic solvent abusers are notoriously difficult to treat because of the combined effects of low socioeconomic status, family problems, school failure, antisocial behavior, and brain damage. Therapeutic communities emphasizing work programs, remedial education, and other reality-based therapies may offer the best chance of success with these patients. Behavior modification programs might be useful in treating chronic relapsing behavior.

IX. MARIJUANA USE AND ABUSE

A. Introduction

Marijuana, a plant used for recreational and medicinal purposes for centuries, is still widely popular today. The term "marijuana" refers to the dried leaves and flowers of the Indian hemp plant *Cannabis sativa,* which grows freely in warm climates and has psychoactive effects when smoked or ingested.

Recent surveys suggest that between 40 and 45 million people over the age of 12 have tried marijuana at least once, including 60% of those between the ages of 18 and 25.

B. Pharmacology

Although marijuana has both stimulant and sedative properties and will produce hallucinations when taken in high enough doses, pharmacologically it appears to be in a class by itself. The plant is extremely complex, containing over 400 identifiable compounds. The principal psychoactive ingredient, however, appears to be Δ-9-tetrahydrocannabinol (THC), which is found in highest concentration in the small upper leaves and flowering tops of the plant. Hashish, a dried, concentrated resinous exudate of the flowers, is several times more potent.

In this country, marijuana cigarettes ("joints") generally contain 0.5 to 1 g of marijuana leaf with an average THC content of 1 to 2% (i.e., 5 to 20 mg). During smoking, the degree of absorption varies, but the average experienced user will absorb approximately half the total dose into his bloodstream. Drug effects are noticeable almost immediately and reach peak intensity within 30 min. Speed of onset is partly determined by the concentration of THC in the preparation. After an hour, plasma levels begin to decline, and most of the subjective effects disappear by 3 hr after the last dose. Oral administration of marijuana is generally 20 to 30% as effective as smoking in delivering THC to the bloodstream. Onset of action also is slower (30 to 60 min after ingestion), but the subjective effects persist for a longer period of time (3 to 5 hr). Predictably, the rate of absorption is influenced by the food content of the stomach.

Following administration by either route, THC leaves the blood rapidly as a result of both hepatic metabolism and efficient uptake by body tissues. It is stored in fat depots, where it may remain for 2 to 3 weeks. Some also remains bound to plasma protein. The drug is metabolized to 11-hydroxy-THC, which is excreted via the gastrointestinal tract and to a lesser extent by the kidneys. Like the parent compound, THC metabolites also bind tightly to plasma proteins and can be sequestered in fat depots for long periods of time, with subsequent rerelease into the bloodstream. As a result, THC can be measured in plasma for up to 6 days after a single episode of marijuana use; THC metabolites can be detected in urine up to a month after a single dose. Evidence of the slow rate of elimination of THC has fostered speculation that repeated use of marijuana may lead to accumulation of THC or its metabolites in body tissues. The experimental data at this point are unclear.

C. Tolerance

Daily use of marijuana may result in the development of tolerance, especially in those who consume more than five "joints" per day. This finding contrasts with earlier theories that experienced marijuana users exhibited "reverse tolerance," i.e., a greater sensitivity to the drug after repeated use. The latter phenomenon may be more a function of social learning than a drug effect. Mild physical dependence has also been demonstrated in heavy users. Withdrawal symptoms include restlessness, irritability, sleep disturbance, anorexia, sweating, tremor, nausea, vomiting, and diarrhea.

D. Patterns of Use and Abuse

The majority of marijuana users (approximately 60%) may be classified as experimenters who give up the drug shortly after their initial experience. Another 35% use marijuana once or twice per week. The remaining 5% use the drug from several times per week to every day.

Most studies have demonstrated that casual users cannot be differentiated from nonusers on psychological tests or measures of psychomotor performance. On the other hand, heavy users (defined as those who smoke nearly every day) manifest an increased prevalence of all types of psychopathology. The use of other psychoactive substances, including alcohol, also is more frequent. On the other hand, there is no evidence that marijuana use per se leads directly to "harder" drugs. Clinical experience with chronic users suggests that some use the drug to treat predrug psychopathology.

E. Acute Intoxication

1. Subjective Effects

As with other drugs, the clinical effects following a dose of marijuana depend on the strength of the preparation, route of administration, individual variables (e.g., metabolic rate, prior drug experience, and personal expectations), and the setting in which the drug is consumed.

Shortly after inhalation and absorption through the lungs, users experience a sense of well-being or euphoria, accompanied by feelings of friendliness and relaxation. Intoxicated persons also develop an altered time sense or "temporal disintegration," a state in which the past, present, and future become fused. Although awareness of their environment may be heightened, they may have less ability to communicate; their speech is often disconnected and tangential, and some smokers become remote and withdrawn. Thought processes are slowed, short-term memory is often impaired, and users have difficulty concentrating. Some feel that they have achieved special insights; others find mundane events more humorous or more poignant, and there is accompanying emotional lability.

2. Physiological Changes

Two reliable signs of marijuana intoxication are increased heart rate and conjunctival injection. The rise in heart rate is directly related to the dose of THC. Decreases in salivation, intraocular pressure, and skin temperature also are found, and at high doses, orthostatic hypotension can occur. Bronchodilation occurs acutely, but chronic marijuana smoking often results in obstructive pulmonary disease similar to that seen in tobacco smokers. Marijuana only minimally affects the waking surface EEG; the changes are similar to the drowsy state. Sleep EEG recordings show a significant loss of rapid eye movement (REM) sleep and increases in both stage 4 and total sleep time.

3. Cognitive and Psychomotor Effects

Various authors have studied the effect of marijuana on intellectual and psychomotor performance. Generally, naive and casual users given the drug in a laboratory setting demonstrate deterioration in both areas, probably because of memory disruption. Impairment is dose related and depends on the complexity of the task. More experienced users, however, are able to compensate for the acute intoxicating effects of THC. In most users, driving performance is impaired, with frequent misjudgment of speed and longer time required for braking.

F. Adverse Reactions following Marijuana Use

1. Acute Panic

Considering the extent of usage, the incidence of adverse reactions to marijuana use is quite low. The most common are summarized in Table 5. Panic can occur in inexperienced users; the likelihood is related to the dose of THC, the expectations of the user, and the setting in which the drug is taken. The tachycardia, disconnected thoughts, and paranoid ideation that often accompany marijuana use may precipitate panic attacks. A panic state may simulate acute psychosis, but careful examination reveals that the patient is not disoriented or hallucinating, and his ability to test reality is intact; he is aware that his condition is drug-related. In some patients, depression may be more prominent than anxiety.

The treatment of panic centers around firm reassurance in a nonthreatening environment. The patient is told that his symptoms have been caused by a strong dose of marijuana and that he will recover within several hours. Physical restraints, seclusion, or administration of antipsychotic drugs can exacerbate the problem. As drug effects subside, panic wanes, and the individual, although shaken, regains control. The persistence of THC metabolites may cause some patients to feel intermittently intoxicated for several days.

TABLE 5. Adverse Reactions to Marijuana

Type	Predisposing factors	Symptoms	Treatment
Acute panic	Inexperienced users, hysterical or obsessional characters, oral administration	Anxiety, depression, no psychotic symptoms	Reassurance; occasionally anxiolytics; episode usually short-lived
Toxic delirium	Large dose, oral use	Confusion, disorientation, hallucinations, depersonalization, delusions	Most remit in 12–48 hr; antipsychotics if necessary
Flashbacks	Days or weeks after last dose, prior history of hallucinogen use	Like hallucinogenic experience except brief	Reassurance, anxiolytics if necessary
Chronic psychosis	Prolonged heavy use of very potent marijuana or hashish; rare in U.S.	Paranoia, delusions, hallucinations, panic, bizarre behavior, occasionally violence	Antipsychotics
Amotivational syndrome	Prolonged heavy use; existence of syndrome is controversial	Apathy, decreased attention span, poor judgment, poor interpersonal relationships	No known treatment

2. Toxic Delirium

Following large doses of marijuana, taken either orally or by inhalation, users may experience psychic disorganization accompanied by feelings of depersonalization and changes in perception and body image. Some patients are disoriented, with marked memory impairment. Confusion, derealization, paranoia, visual and auditory hallucinations, and dysphoria are also features of this toxic delirium. Individuals usually remain aware that these effects are drug related. Toxic delirium is more likely after cannabis is ingested, perhaps because of the user's inability to titrate adequately the dose of THC. In most cases, the process is self-limited and lasts from a few hours to a few days; it resolves as plasma THC levels decline. Generally, no pharmacological treatment is indicated, but patients should be carefully observed and prevented from doing harm to themselves or others.

3. Recurrent Reactions ("Flashbacks")

Although more characteristic of LSD, recurrent marijuana experiences occurring days or weeks after the last dose have been reported. Such phenomena are more common in individuals who have previously used hallucinogens. Flashbacks are rare in patients who used the drug more than 6 months previously. When these reactions occur long after the last drug use, a psychiatric or neurological disorder should be suspected, particularly if symptoms continue beyond several hours.

G. Sequelae of Chronic Use

1. Cannabis Psychosis

In Western countries psychosis directly attributable to chronic cannabis use is rare. In Middle Eastern and Asian countries, however, chronic use of more potent marijuana or hashish (the concentrated resin) reportedly may result in a cannabis-induced psychosis. Paranoia, persecutory delusions, visual and auditory hallucinations, panic, bizarre behavior, and occasional aggressive outbursts comprise the clinical picture. The role of preexisting psychopathology in these patients is unclear. Patients with this disorder usually respond quickly to treatment with antipsychotic drugs, although relapse is common on resumption of cannabis use.

2. Amotivational Syndrome

A number of authors have described an "amotivational syndrome" which develops gradually in chronic heavy marijuana users. It is characterized by decreased drive and ambition, a shortened attention span, poor judgment, a high degree of distractability, impaired communication skills, and diminished effectiveness in interpersonal situations. A tendency toward introversion and magical thinking also has been observed. The individual frequently feels incapacitated and makes few or no plans beyond the present day. Personal habits deteriorate, and there are a progressive loss of insight and feelings of depersonalization. Aggression is profoundly diminished, and, as a result, these patients appear apathetic and withdrawn rather than antisocial. The contribution of predrug psychopathology in this syndrome remains unclear. Indeed, some authors doubt the existence of the amotivational syndrome, since studies of chronic marijuana smokers in Jamaica, Costa Rica, and Greece found no difference in work output as the extent of use increased.

3. Medical Problems

Chronic users of marijuana report an increased frequency of bronchitis and various upper respiratory infections which improve when drug use is discontinued. Marijuana smoke may impair the ability of alveolar macrophages to inactivate bacteria in the lung. Local irritation and narrowing of the airways also contribute to the problems of these patients.

One study reported pneumoencephalographic evidence of cerebral atrophy in chronic marijuana smokers, but these subjects also were heavy users of other drugs. Subsequent studies using computerized tomography (CT scans) have not revealed any evidence of structural abnormalities in the brains of marijuana users.

Since tachycardia is the most consistent cardiovascular effect of marijuana smoking, the drug may precipitate episodes of angina pectoris in patients with preexisting heart disease. Finally, investigators have variously reported decreased serum testosterone, sperm counts, and sperm motility and an increased prevalance of chromosomal breakage in heavy marijuana users. However, each of these findings has been challenged.

H. Potential Medical Uses of Marijuana

Over the past decade, a number of potential medical uses of marijuana (i.e., THC) have emerged. The drug appears useful in the treatment of the **severe nausea and vomiting** often experienced by patients receiving cancer chemotherapy. Since the drug lowers intraocular pressure, it may also be useful in the treatment of **narrow-angle glaucoma**. Use of marijuana has also been explored in the treatment of asthma, seizures, muscular spasticity, depression, and chronic pain, but with no clear evidence of success.

I. Treatment of Chronic Marijuana Abuse

At present, methods for treating chronic marijuana users are not well developed, primarily because such individuals do not often request treatment. In those who do, however, discontinuing drug use obviously is a prerequisite, since psychotherapy is of little value in chronically intoxicated individuals. An educational approach with emphasis on the unknown aspects of chronic use may be instructive for some but provokes resentment and hostility in others. A more useful approach is to focus attention on the motivation for use, carefully defining those situations in which the drug is taken. Heavy users will often become intoxicated in response to difficult interpersonal situations, particularly those that threaten to arouse hostility or anger. Encouragement in expressing such affects directly but nonviolently is an important part of treatment. The clinician should also explore the possibility of an underlying affective disorder which the patient may be self-medicating. Since chronic cannabis use can be accompanied by increasing social constriction and occupational drift or failure, task-oriented socialization groups coupled with vocational rehabilitation are potentially useful adjuncts to traditional psychotherapeutic approaches.

X. SUBSTANCE ABUSE IN PERSPECTIVE

The epidemic spread of substance abuse is a phenomenon best understood through an eclectic perspective. The behavior of individuals who abuse one or more psychoactive substances is partially the result of developmental, sociocultural, and interpersonal factors. In some patients, genetic and/or biological factors may influence vulnerability as well. Although some have suggested that particular personality traits predispose to the development of drug abuse and dependence, some traits (e.g., passivity, manipulativeness, inability to tolerate frustration) may result from repetitive drug use and the drug-using life-style. Similarly, although the development of insight and the resolution of intrapsychic conflicts are clearly desirable goals, no hard data suggest that insight, by itself, leads to a decline in drug-using behavior.

A number of investigators have focused on the interaction between the effects of abused drugs and individual psychopathology. Thus, substance abusers have been viewed as self-medicating feelings of depression and tension while modifying internal drive states and avoiding the stark unpleasantness of the real world. However, clinical and laboratory studies of substance abusers have consistently found that although all these drugs serve as primary reinforcers in both animals and man, their chronic administration usually results in a host of unpleasant consequences. These may be subtle, like the effects of chronic marijuana use on ambition, or they may be dramatic, like the psychosis that often accompanies long-term PCP use.

Recently, there has been growing interest in the behavioral aspects of substance abuse disorders. Clearly, in some patients phenomena like conditioned abstinence contribute to drug-seeking behavior and relapse. Consequently, patients and their doctors must learn to anticipate the impact of environmental stimuli that may enhance craving and lead to renewed drug use. At the same time, the clinician should attempt to reshape attitudes and behavior through psychotherapy, group pressure, role modeling, and other techniques of social learning. The relative success of self-help organizations like Alcoholics Anonymous is clear testimony to the usefulness of providing concrete guidelines for behavioral change in a supportive setting.

Finally, biological approaches to substance abuse, although appealingly cost effective, also have their pitfalls. In methadone maintenance programs, for example, some opiate addicts become alcoholics, and others spend their time diverting methadone to the street market. The narcotic antagonists, although pharmacologically effective, are not very popular with most opiate users. Disulfiram, an effective deterrent to impulsive drinking, is ineffective by itself in maintaining long-term abstinence.

In summary, substance abuse is an extremely complex and multidetermined behavior, and the treatment of substance abusers presents a bewildering array of theoretical and practical problems. Those who seek to alter such behavior need to recognize this and devise equally complex and multidisciplinary approaches to treatment. As in other areas of medicine, the doctor's adherence to dogma can be hazardous to the patient's health.

SELECTED READING

Opiates

1. Bale R. N., Van Stone W. W., Kuldau J. M., et al: Therapeutic communities vs methadone maintenance. A prospective controlled study of narcotic addiction treatment: Design and one-year follow-up. *Arch Gen Psychiatry* 37:179–193, 1980.
2. Cohen S.: Clonidine (Catapres): Nonopiate detoxification. *Drug Abuse Alcoholism Newslett* 9:1–3, 1980.
3. Cushman P.: The major medical sequelae of opioid addiction. *Drug Alcohol Dep* 5:239–254, 1980.
4. Dole V. P., Nyswander M. E.: Heroin addiction—a metabolic disease. *Arch Intern Med* 120:19–24, 1967.
5. Dole V. P.: Narcotic addiction, physical dependence and relapse. *N Engl J Med* 286:988–992, 1972.
6. Gold M. E., Redmond D. C., Kleber H. D.: Clonidine blocks acute opiate-withdrawal symptoms. *Lancet* 2:599–602, 1978.
7. Gold M. S., Pottash A. L. C., Sweeney D. R., et al: Rapid opiate detoxification: Clinical evidence of antidepressant and antipanic effects of opiates. *Am J Psychiatry* 136:982–986, 1979.

8. Goldstein A.: Heroin addiction: Sequential treatment employing pharmacologic supports. *Arch Gen Psychiatry* 33:353–358, 1976.
9. Goldstein A.: Heroin addiction and the role of methadone in its treatment. *Arch Gen Psychiatry* 26:291–297, 1972.
10. Gritz E. R., Shiffman S. M., Jarvik M. E., et al: Physiological and psychological effects of methadone in man. *Arch Gen Psychiatry* 32:237–242, 1975.
11. Harford R. J.: Comparative validity of random-interval and fixed-interval urinalysis schedules. *Arch Gen Psychiatry* 35:356–359, 1978.
12. Jaffe J. H.: Drug addiction and drug abuse, in Goodman L. S., Gilman A., Gilman A. G. (eds): *Goodman and Gilman's The Pharmacological Basis of Therapeutics*, ed. 6. New York, Macmillan, pp 535–584, 1980.
13. Jaffe J. H., Martin W. R.: Opioid analgesics and antagonists, in Goodman L. S., Gilman A., Gilman A. G., (eds.): *Goodman and Gilman's The Pharmacological Basis of Therapeutics*, ed. 6. New York, Macmillan, pp 494–534, 1980.
14. Jasinski D. R., Pevnick J. S., Griffith J. D.: Human pharmacology and abuse potential of the analgesic buprenorphine: A potential agent for treating narcotic addiction. *Arch Gen Psychiatry* 35:501–514, 1978.
15. Jasinski D. R., Martin W. R., Haertzen C. A.: The human pharmacology and abuse potential of N-allynoroxymorphone (naloxone). *J Pharmacol Exp Ther* 152:420–426, 1967.
16. Kleber H. D., Slobetz F.: Outpatient drug-free treatment, in DuPont R. L., Goldstein A., O'Donnell J. (eds): *Handbook on Drug Abuse*. Washington, National Institute on Drug Abuse, 1979, pp 31–38.
17. Kreek M. J.: Medical safety and side effects of methadone in tolerant individuals. *JAMA* 223:665–668, 1973.
18. Ling W., Blaine J. D.: The use of LAAM in treatment, in DuPont RL, Goldstein A. O'Donnell J. (eds): *Handbook on Drug Abuse*. Washington, National Institute on Drug Abuse, 1979, pp 87–96.
19. Ling W., Klett C. J., Gillis R. D.: A cooperative clinical study of methadyl acetate: I. Three-times a week regimen. *Arch Gen Psychiatry* 35:345–353, 1978.
20. Ling W., Klett C. J., Gillis R. D.: A cooperative clinical study of methadyl acetate: II. Friday-only regimen. *Arch Gen Psychiatry* 37:908–911, 1980.
21. Ling W., Blakis M., Holmes E. D., et al: Restabilization with methadone after methadyl acetate maintenance. *Arch Gen Psychiatry* 37:194–198, 1980.
22. Martin W. R., Jasinski D. R., Haertzen C. A., et al: Methadone—a reevaluation. *Arch Gen Psychiatry* 28: 286–295, 1973.
23. Martin W. R.: Naloxone. *Ann Intern Med* 85:765–768, 1976.
24. Martin W. R., Jasinski D. R., Mansky P. A.: Naltrexone, an antagonist for the treatment of heroin dependence. *Arch Gen Psychiatry* 28:784–791, 1973.
25. Mello N. K., Mendelson J. H.: Buprenorphine suppresses heroin use by heroin addicts. *Science* 207:657–659, 1980.
26. Mello N. K., Mendelson J. H., Kuehnle J. C., et al: Operant analysis of human heroin self-administration and the effects of naltrexone. *J Pharmacol Exp Ther* 216:45–53, 1981.
27. Mendelson J. H., Ellingboe J., Kuehnle J. C., et al: Effects of naltrexone on mood and neuroendocrine function in normal adult males. *Psychoneuroendocrinology* 3: 231–236, 1979.
28. Meyer R. E., Mirin S. M., Altman J. L., et al: A behavioral paradigm for the evaluation of narcotic antagonists. *Arch Gen Psychiatry* 33:371–377, 1976.
29. Meyer R. E., Mirin S. M.: *The Heroin Stimulus: Implications for a Theory of Addiction*. New York, Plenum Press, 1979.

30. Mirin S. M., Meyer R. E., Mendelson J. H., et al: Opiate use and sexual function. *Am J Psychiatry* 137:909–915, 1980.
31. Mirin S. M., Meyer R. E., McNamee H. B.: Psychopathology and mood during heroin use. *Arch Gen Psychiatry* 33:1503–1508, 1976.
32. National Research Council Committee on Clinical Evaluation of Narcotic Antagonists: Clinical evaluation of Naltrexone treatment of opiate-dependent individuals. *Arch Gen Psychiatry* 35:335–340, 1978.
33. O'Brien C. P., Testa T., O'Brien T. J., et al: Conditioned narcotic withdrawal in humans. *Science* 195:1000–1002, 1977.
34. Resnick R. B., Schuyten-Resnick E., Washton A. M.: Treatment of opioid dependence with narcotic antagonists: A review and commentary, in DuPont R. L., Goldstein A., O'Donnell J. (eds): *Handbook on Drug Abuse*. Washington, National Institute on Drug Abuse, 1979, pp 76–104.
35. Sells S. B., Simpson D. D.: The case for drug abuse treatment effectiveness, based on the DARP research program. *Br J Addict* 75:117–131, 1980.
36. Sells S. B.: Treatment effectiveness, in DuPont R. L., Goldstein A., O'Donnell J. (eds): *Handbook on Drug Abuse*. Washington, National Institute on Drug Abuse, 1979, pp 105–120.
37. Senay E. C., Dorus W., Goldberg F., et al: Withdrawal from methadone maintenance: Rate of withdrawal and expectation. *Arch Gen Psychiatry* 34:361–367, 1977.
38. Simpson D. D. , Savage L. J.: Drug abuse treatment readmissions and outcomes: Three-year follow-up of DARP patients. *Arch Gen Psychiatry* 37: 896–901, 1980.
39. Simpson D. D., Savage L. J., Lloyd M. R.: Follow-up evaluation of treatment of drug abuse during 1969 to 1972. *Arch Gen Psychiatry* 36:772–780, 1979.
40. Snyder S. H.: The opiate receptor and morphine-like peptides in the brain. *Am J Psychiatry* 135:645–652, 1978.
41. Snyder S. H.: Opiate receptors in the brain. *N Engl J Med* 296:266–278, 1977.
42. Stimmel B., Adamsons K.: Narcotic dependency in pregnancy: Methadone maintenance compared to use of street drugs. *JAMA* 235:1121–1124, 1976.
43. US Department of Health, Education and Welfare; Public Health Service; Alcohol, Drug Abuse and Mental Health Administration: Clinical management during pregnancy, in *Drug Dependence in Pregnancy: Clinical Management of Mother and Child*. National Institute on Drug Abuse, Services Research Monograph Series, 1979, Chapter 3.
44. US Department of Health, Education and Welfare; Public Health Service; Alcohol, Drug Abuse and Mental Health Administration: Management of labor, delivery and the immediate post-partum period, in *Drug Dependence in Pregnancy: Clinical Management of Mother and Child*. National Institute on Drug Abuse, Services Research Monograph Series, 1979, Chapter 4.
45. Vaillant G. E.: A 20-year follow-up of New York narcotic addicts. *Arch Gen Psychiatry* 29:237–241, 1973.
46. Wikler A.: Dynamics of drug dependence. *Arch Gen Psychiatry* 28:611–616, 1973.
47. Zelson C., Lee S. J., Casalino M.: Neonatal narcotic addiction: Comparative effects of maternal intake of heroin and methadone. *N Engl J Med* 289:1216–1220, 1973.
48. Zinberg N. E.: The crisis in methadone maintenance. *N Engl J Med* 296:1000–1002, 1977.

CNS Depressants

49. Ager S. A.: Luding out. *N Engl J Med* 287:51, 1972.
50. Bakewell W. E. Jr, Wikler A.: Incidence in a university hospital psychiatric ward; Symposium: Non-narcotic addiction. *JAMA* 196:122–125, 1966.

51. Braestrup C., Squires R. F.: Brain specific benzodiazepine receptors. *Br J Psychiatry* 133:249–260, 1978.
52. Cronin R. J., Klingler E. L. Jr, Avashti P. S., et al: The treatment of nonbarbiturate sedative overdosage, in Browne P. G. (ed): *A Treatment Manual for Acute Drug Abuse Emergencies.* Washington, National Institute on Drug Abuse, 1974, pp 58–62.
53. Dorpat T. L.: Drug automatism, barbiturate poisoning and suicide behavior. *Arch Gen Psychiatry* 31:216–220, 1974.
54. Greenblatt D. J., Shader R. I.: Drug therapy: Benzodiazepines (first of two parts). *N Engl J Med* 291:1011–1243, 1974.
55. Haefely W. E.: Central actions of benzodiazepines: General introduction. *Br J Psychiatry* 133:231–238, 1978.
56. Harvey S. C.: Hypnotics and sedatives, in Goodman L. S., Gilman A., Gilman A. G. (eds): *Goodman and Gilman's The Pharmacological Basis of Therapeutics,* ed 6. New York, Macmillan, 1980, pp 339–375.
57. Jaffe J. H.: Drug addiction and drug abuse, in Goodman L. S., Gilman A., Gilman A. G. (eds): *Goodman and Gilman's The Pharmacological Basis of Therapeutics,* ed 6. New York, Macmillan, 1980, pp 535–584.
58. Gelenberg A. J.: Benzodiazepine withdrawal. *Mass Gen Hosp Newslett Biol Ther Psychiatry Newslett* 3:9–12, 1980.
59. Pevnick J. S., Jasinski D. R., Haertzen C. A.: Abrupt withdrawal from therapeutically administered diazepam. *Arch Gen Psychiatry* 35:995–998, 1978.
60. Setter J. G.: Emergency treatment of acute barbiturate intoxication, in Browne P. G. (ed): *A Treatment Manual for Acute Drug Abuse Emergencies.* Washington, National Institute on Drug Abuse, 1974, pp 49–53.
61. Smith D. E., Wesson D. R., Seymour R. B.: The abuse of barbiturates and other sedative–hypnotics, in DuPont R. L., Goldstein A., O'Donnell J. (eds): *Handbook on Drug Abuse.* Washington, National Institute on Drug Abuse, 1979, pp 233–240.
62. Smith D. E., Wesson D. R.: Phenobarbital technique for treatment of barbiturate dependence. *Arch Gen Psychiatry* 24:56–60, 1971.
63. Swartzburg M., Lieb J., Schwartz A. H.: Methaqualone withdrawal. *Arch Gen Psychiatry* 29:46–47, 1973.
64. Victor M., Adams R. D.: Barbiturates, in Isselbacher K. J., Adams R. D., Braunwald E., et al (eds): *Harrison's Principles of Internal Medicine.* New York, McGraw Hill, 1980, pp 982–985.
65. Wesson D. R., Smith D. E.: Managing the barbiturate withdrawal syndrome, in Browne P. G. (ed): *A Treatment Manual for Acute Drug Abuse Emergencies.* Washington, National Institute on Drug Abuse, 1974, pp 54–57.
66. Wikler A.: Diagnosis and treatment of drug dependence of the barbiturate type. *Am J Psychiatry* 125:758–765, 1968.

Alcohol

67. Bean M.: Alcoholics Anonymous: Chapter I: Principles and methods. *Psychiatr Ann* 5:7–21, 1975.
68. Cohen S. (ed): The treatment of alcoholism: Does it work? *Drug Abuse Alcoholism Newslett* 7:1–3, 1978.
69. Edwards G., Orford J., Egert S., et al: Alcoholism: A controlled trial of "treatment" and "advice." *J Stud Alcohol* 38:1004–1031, 1977.
70. Emrick C. E.: A review of psychologically oriented treatment of alcoholism: II. The rela-

tive effectiveness of different treatment approaches and the effectiveness of treatment versus no treatment. *J Stud Alcohol* 36:88–108, 1975.

71. Fuller R. K., Roth H. P.: Disulfiram for the treatment of alcoholism. *Ann Intern Med* 90:901–904, 1979.

72. Goodwin D. W.: Alcoholism and heredity. *Arch Gen Psychiatry* 36:57–61, 1979.

73. Hanson J. W., Jones K. L., Smith D. W.: Fetal alcohol syndrome: Experience with 41 patients. *JAMA* 235:1458–1460, 1976.

74. Kline N. S., Wren J. C., Cooper T. B., et al: Evaluation of lithium therapy in chronic and periodic alcoholism. *Am J Med Sci* 268:15–22, 1974.

75. Kwentus M. D., Major L. F.: Disulfiram in the treatment of alcoholism. *J Stud Alcohol* 40:428–446, 1979.

76. Mendelson J. H., Mello N. K.: Biologic concomitants of alcoholism. *N Engl J Med* 301:912–921, 1979.

77. Mendelson J. H., Mello N. K.: *The Diagnosis and Treatment of Alcoholism.* New York, McGraw Hill, 1979.

78. Merry J., Reynolds C. M., Bailey J., et al: Prophylactic treatment of alcoholism by lithium carbonate: A controlled study. *Lancet* 2:481–482, 1976.

79. Neubuerger O. W., Matarazzo J. D., Schmitz R. E., et al: One year follow-up of total abstinence in chronic alcoholic patients following emetic counterconditioning. *Alcoholism Clin Exp Res* 4:306–312, 1980.

80. Ouelette E. M., Rosett H. L., Rosman N. P., et al: Adverse effects on offspring of maternal alcohol abuse during pregnancy. *N Engl J Med* 297:528–530, 1977.

81. Pattison E. M.: Nonabstinent drinking goals in the treatment of alcoholism: A clinical typology. *Arch Gen Psychiatry* 33:923–930, 1976.

82. Pattison E. M.: Ten years of change in alcoholism treatment and delivery systems. *Am J Psychiatry* 134:261–266, 1977.

83. Pomerleau O., Pertschuk M., Stunnett J.: A critical examination of some current assumptions in the treatment of alcoholism. *J Stud Alcohol* 37:849–867, 1976.

84. Ritchie J. M.: The aliphatic alcohols, in Goodman L. S., Gilman A., Gilman A. G. (eds): *Goodman and Gilman's The Pharmacological Basis of Therapeutics,* ed 6. New York, Macmillan, 1980, pp 376–390.

85. Sampliner R., Iber F. L.: Diphenylhydantoin control of alcohol withdrawal seizures: Results of a controlled study. *JAMA* 230:1430–1432, 1974.

86. Schuckit M. A.: Alcoholism and genetics: Possible biological mediators. *Biol Psychiatry* 15:437–447, 1980.

87. Sollers E. M., Kalant H.: Alcohol intoxication and withdrawal. *N Engl J Med* 294:757–762, 1976.

88. Stinson D. J., Smith W. G., Amidjaya I., et al: Systems of care and treatment outcomes for alcoholic patients. *Arch Gen Psychiatry* 36:535–539, 1979.

89. Thompson W. L., Johnson A. D., Maddrey W. L., et al: Diazepam and paraldehyde for treatment of severe delirium tremens: A controlled trial. *Ann Intern Med* 82:175–180, 1975.

90. Vaillant G. E.: Natural history of male psychological health: VIII. Antecedents of alcoholism and "orality." *Am J Psychiatry* 137:181–186, 1980.

91. Victor M., Adams R. D.: Alcohol, in Isselbacher K. J., Adams R. D., Braunwald E., et al (eds): *Harrison's Principles of Internal Medicine.* New York, McGraw Hill, 1980, pp 969–977.

92. Victor M., Adams R. D.: Deficiency diseases of the nervous system, in Isselbacher K. J., Adams R. D., Braunwald E., et al (eds): *Harrison's Principles of Internal Medicine.* New York, McGraw Hill, 1980, pp 1985–1990.

93. Weissman M. M., Myers J. K.: Clinical depression in alcoholism. *Am J Psychiatry* 137:372–374, 1980.

CNS Stimulants

94. Aigner T. G., Balster R. L.: Choice behavior in rhesus monkeys: Cocaine versus food. *Science* 201:534–535, 1978.
95. Smith D. E., Wesson D. R., Buxton M. E., et al (eds.): *Amphetamine Use, Misuse and Abuse: Proceedings of the National Amphetamine Conference.* Boston, G. K. Hall, 1979.
96. Byck R., Van Dyke C.: What are the effects of cocaine in man? in Petersen R. C., Stillman R. C. (eds): *Cocaine: 1977.* Washington, National Institute on Drug Abuse, Research Monograph #13, 1977, pp 5–16.
97. Catravas J. D., Waters I. W., Walz M. A., et al: Antidotes for cocaine poisoning. *N Engl J Med* 297:1238, 1977.
98. Cohen S.: Coca paste and freebase: New fashions in cocaine use. *Drug Abuse Alcoholism Newslett* 9:1–3, 1980.
99. Ellinwood E. H. Jr: Amphetamine psychosis: Individuals, settings and sequences, in Ellinwood E. H., Cohen S. (eds): *Current Concepts on Amphetamine Abuse.* Washington, National Institute of Mental Health, 1972, pp 143–158.
100. Ellinwood E. H. Jr: Amphetamines/anorectics, in DuPont R. L., Goldstein A., O'Donnell J. (eds): *Handbook on Drug Abuse.* Washington, National Institute on Drug Abuse, 1979, pp 221–231.
101. Ellinwood E. H. Jr: Emergency treatment of acute adverse reactions to CNS stimulants, in Browne P. G. (ed): *A Treatment Manual for Acute Drug Abuse.* Washington, National Institute on Drug Abuse, 1975, pp 63–67.
102. Ellinwood E. H. Jr, Kilbey M. M.: Fundamental mechanisms underlying altered behavior following chronic administration of psychomotor stimulants. *Biol Psychiatry* 15:749–757, 1980.
103. Fischman M. W., Schuster C. R., Resnekov L., et al: Cardiovascular and subjective effects of intravenous cocaine administration in humans. *Arch Gen Psychiatry* 33:983–989, 1976.
104. Goldfrank L., Lewin N., Weisman R. S.: Cocaine. *Hosp Physician* 17:26–44, 1981.
105. Griffith J. D., Cavanaugh J., Held J., et al: Dextroamphetamine: Evaluation of psychotomimetic properties in man. *Arch Gen Psychiatry* 26:97–100, 1972.
106. Grinspoon L., Bakalar J. B.: Cocaine, in DuPont R. L., Goldstein A., O'Donnell J. (eds): *Handbook on Drug Abuse.* Washington, DC, National Institute on Drug Abuse, 1979, pp 241–248.
107. Grinspoon L., Hedblom P.: *The Speed Culture: Amphetamine Use and Abuse in America.* Cambridge, Harvard University Press, 1975.
108. Jaffe J. H.: Drug addiction and drug abuse, in Goodman L. S., Gilman A., Gilman A. G. (eds): *Goodman and Gilman's The Pharmacological Basis of Therapeutics,* ed 6. New York, Macmillan, 1980, pp 535–584.
109. Javaid J. I., Fischman M. W., Schuster C. R., et al: Cocaine plasma concentration: Relation to physiological and subjective effects in humans. *Science* 202:227–228, 1978.
110. Kokkinidis L., Anisman H.: Amphetamine models of paranoid schizophrenia: An overview and elaboration of animal experimentation. *Psychol Bull* 88:551–579, 1980.
111. Kramer J. C., Fischman V. S., Littlefield D. C.: Amphetamine abuse: Pattern and effects of high doses taken intravenously. *JAMA* 201:89–93, 1967.
112. Kramer J. C.: Introduction to amphetamine abuse, in Ellinwood E. H., Cohen S. (eds): *Current Concepts on Amphetamine Abuse.* Washington, National Institute of Mental Health, 1972, pp 177–184.
113. Petersen R. C.: Cocaine: An overview, in Petersen R. C., Stillman R. C. (eds): *Cocaine: 1977.* Washington, National Institute on Drug Abuse, Research Monograph #13, 1977, pp 5–16.

114. Post R. M.: Cocaine psychoses: A continuum model. *Am J Psychiatry* 132:225–231, 1975.
115. Post R. M., Kotin J., Goodwin F. K.: The effects of cocaine on depressed patients. *Am J Psychiatry* 131:511–517, 1974.
116. Rappolt R. T., Gay G. R., Inaba D. S.: Propranolol in the treatment of cardiopressor effects of cocaine. *N Engl J Med* 295:448, 1976.
117. Resnick R. B., Kestenbaum R. S.: Acute systemic effects of cocaine in man: A controlled study by intranasal and intravenous routes. *Science* 195:696–698, 1977.
118. Ritchie J. M., Greene N. M.: Local anesthetics, in Goodman L. S., Gilman A., Gilman A. G., (eds): *Goodman and Gilman's The Pharmacological Basis of Therapeutics*, ed 6. New York, Macmillan, 1980, pp 300–320.
119. Siegel R. K.: Cocaine: Recreational use and intoxication, in Petersen R. C., Stillman R. C. (eds): *Cocaine: 1977*. Washington, National Institute on Drug Abuse, Research Monograph #13, 1977, pp 119–136.
120. Thompson T., Pickens R.: Stimulant self-administration by animals: Some comparisons with opiate self-administration. *Fed Proc* 29:6–12, 1970.
121. Tinklenberg J. R.: The treatment of acute amphetamine psychosis, in Browne P. G. (ed): *A Treatment Manual for Acute Drug Abuse Emergencies*. Washington, National Institute on Drug Abuse, 1975, pp 68–72.
122. Van Dyke C., Jatlow P., Ungerer J., et al: Oral cocaine: Plasma concentrations and central effects. *Science* 200:211–213, 1978.
123. Weiner N.: Norepinephrine, epinephrine and the sympathominetic amines, in Goodman L. S., Gilman A., Gilman A. G. (eds): *Goodman and Gilman's The Pharmacological Basis of Therapeutics* ed 6. New York, Macmillan, 1980, pp 138–175.
124. Weiss R. D., Goldenheim P. S., Mirin S. M., et al: Pulmonary dysfunction in cocaine smokers. *Am J Psychiatry* 138:1110–1112, 1981.
125. Wetli C. V., Wright R. K.: Death caused by recreational cocaine use. *JAMA* 241:2519–2522, 1979.
126. Willis J. H. P.: The national history of anorectic drug abuse, in Garattini S., Samanin R. (eds): *Central Mechanisms of Anorectic Drugs*. New York, Raven Press, 1978, pp 365–373.
127. Woolverton W. L., Kandel D., Schuster C. R.: Tolerance and cross-tolerance to cocaine and *d*-amphetamine. *J Pharmacol Exp Ther* 2:525–535, 1978.

Hallucinogens

128. Blacker K. H., Reese T. J., Stone G. C., et al: Chronic users of LSD: The "acidheads." *Am J Psychiatry* 125:341–351, 1968.
129. Bowers M. B. Jr.: Acute psychosis induced by psychotomimetic drug abuse. I. Clinical findings. *Arch Gen Psychiatry* 27:437–439, 1972.
130. Bowers M. B. Jr.: Acute psychosis induced by psychotomimetic drug abuse. II. Neurochemical findings. *Arch Gen Psychiatry* 27:440–442, 1972.
131. Bowers M. B. Jr., Chipman A., Schwartz A., et al: Dynamics of psychedelic drug abuse: A clinical study. *Arch Gen Psychiatry* 16:560–566, 1967.
132. Brawley P., Duffield J. C.: The pharmacology of hallucinogens. *Pharmacol Rev* 24:31–66, 1972.
133. Cohen S.: Flashbacks. *Drug Abuse Alcoholism Newslett* 6:1–3, 1977.
134. Faillace L. A., Snyder S. H., Weingartner H.: 2,5-Dimethoxy-1-methylamphetamine: Clinical evaluation of a new hallucinogenic drug. *J Nerv Ment Dis* 150:119–126, 1970.

135. Freedman D. X.: The use and abuse of LSD. *Arch Gen Psychiatry* 18:330–347, 1968.
136. Gilmour D. G., Bloom A. D., Lele K. P., et al: Chromosomal aberrations in users of psychoactive drugs. *Arch Gen Psychiatry* 24:268–272, 1971.
137. Glass G. S., Bowers M. B. Jr.: Chronic psychosis associated with long-term psychotomimetic drug abuse. *Arch Gen Psychiatry* 23:97–102, 1970.
138. Grinspoon L., Bakalar J. B.: *Psychedelic Drugs Reconsidered.* New York, Basic Books, 1979.
139. Jacobson C. B., Berlin C. M.: Possible reproductive detriment in LSD users. *JAMA* 222:1367–1373, 1972.
140. Jaffe J. H.: Drug addiction and drug abuse, in Goodman L. S., Gilman A., Gilman A. G. (eds): *Goodman and Gilman's The Pharmacological Basis of Therapeutics,* ed 6. New York, Macmillan, 1980, pp 535–584.
141. McGlothlin W. H., Arnold D. O.: LSD revisited. *Arch Gen Psychiatry* 24:35–49, 1971.
142. McGlothlin W. H., Arnold D. O., Freedman D. X.: Organicity measures following repeated LSD ingestion. *Arch Gen Psychiatry* 21:704–709, 1969.
143. Snyder S. H., Weingartner H., Faillace L. A.: DOET (2,5-dimethoxy-4-ethylamphetamine), a new psychotropic drug: Effects of varying doses in man. *Arch Gen Psychiatry* 24:50–55, 1971.
144. Snyder S. H., Faillace L. A., Weingartner H.: DOM (STP), a new hallucinogenic drug, and DOET: Effects in normal subjects. *Am J Psychiatry* 125:113–120, 1968.
145. Tucker G. J., Quinlan D., Harrow M.: Chronic hallucinogenic drug use and thought disturbance. *Arch Gen Psychiatry* 27:443–447, 1972.

Phencyclidine

146. Domino E. F.: Treatment of phencyclidine intoxication. *Psychopharmacol Bull* 16:83–85, 1980.
147. Fauman M. A., Fauman B. J.: The psychiatric aspects of chronic phencyclidine use: A study of chronic PCP users, in Petersen R. C., Stillman R. C. (eds): *PCP: Phencyclidine Abuse: An Appraisal.* Washington, National Institute on Drug Abuse, Research Monograph #21, DHEW Publ. No. #78-728, 1978, pp 183–200.
148. Gelenberg A. J.: Psychopharmacology update: Phencyclidine. *McLean Hosp J* 2:89–96, 1977.
149. Graeven D. B.: Patterns of phencyclidine use, in Peterson R. C., Stillman R. C. (eds): *PCP: Phencyclidine Abuse: An Appraisal.* Washington, National Institute on Drug Abuse, Research Monograph #21, DHEW Publ. No. #78-728, 1978, pp 176–182.
150. Jaffe J. H.: Drug addiction and drug abuse, in Goodman L. S., Gilman A., Gilman A. G. (eds): *Goodman and Gilman's The Pharmacological Basis of Therapeutics,* ed 6. New York, Macmillan, 1980, pp 535–584.
151. Luisada P. V.: The phencyclidine psychosis: Phenomenology and treatment, in Petersen R. C., Stillman R. C. (eds): *PCP: Phencyclidine Abuse: An Appraisal.* Washington, National Institute on Drug Abuse, Research Monograph #21, DHEW Publ. No. #78-728, 1978, pp 241–253.
152. Peterson R. C., Stillman R. C.: Phencyclidine: An overview, in Peterson R. C., Stillman R. C. (eds): *PCP: Phencyclidine Abuse: An Appraisal.* Washington, National Institute on Drug Abuse, Research Monograph #21, DHEW Publ. No. #78-728, 1978.
153. Smith D. R., Wesson D. R., Buxton M. E., et al: The diagnosis and treatment of the PCP abuse syndrome, in Petersen R. C., Stillman R. C. (eds): *PCP: Phencyclidine Abuse: An Appraisal.* Washington, National Institute on Drug Abuse, Research Monograph #21, DHEW Publ. No. #78-728, 1978.

Inhalants

154. Cohen S.: Inhalants, in DuPont R. L., Goldstein A., O'Donnell J. (eds): *Handbook on Drug Abuse*. Washington, National Institute on Drug Abuse, 1979, pp 213–220.
155. Glaser F. B.: Inhalation psychosis and related states, in Browne P. G. (ed): *A Treatment Manual for Acute Drug Abuse Emergencies*. Washington, National Institute on Drug Abuse, 1975, pp 95–104.
156. Jaffe J. H.: Drug addiction and drug abuse, in Goodman L. S., Gilman A., Gilman A. G. (eds): *Goodman and Gilman's The Pharmacological Basis of Therapeutics,* ed 6. New York, Macmillan, 1980, pp 535–584.
157. Lewis J. D., Moritz D., Mellis L. P.: Long-term toluene abuse. *Am J Psychiatry* 138:368–370, 1981.

Marijuana

158. Bernstein J. G.: Marijuana—new potential, new problems. *Drug Ther* 10:38–48, 1980.
159. Chopra G. S., Smith J. W.: Psychotic reactions following cannabis use in East Indians. *Arch Gen Psychiatry* 30:24–27, 1974.
160. Cohen S.: Cannabis: Impact on motivation. Part I. *Drug Abuse Alcoholism Newslett* 9:1–3, 1980.
161. Cohen S.: Cannabis: Impact on motivation. Part II. *Drug Abuse Alcoholism Newslett* 10:1–3, 1981.
162. Cohen S.: Marijuana: Pulmonary issues. *Drug Abuse Alcoholism Newslett* 9:1–3, 1980.
163. Harding T., Knight F.: Marijuana-modified mania. *Arch Gen Psychiatry* 29:635–637, 1973.
164. Heath R. G.: Marihuana: Effects on deep and surface electroencephalograms of man. *Arch Gen Psychiatry* 26:577–584, 1972.
165. Jaffe J. H.: Drug addiction and drug abuse, in Goodman L. S., Gilman A., Gilman A. G. (eds): *Goodman and Gilman's The Pharmacological Basis of Therapeutics*, ed 6. New York, Macmillan, 1980, pp 535–584.
166. Jones R. T.: Marihuana-induced "high": Influence of expectation, setting and previous drug experience. *Pharmacol Rev* 23:359–369, 1971.
167. Kupfer D. J., Detre T., Koral J., et al: A comment on the "amotivational syndrome" in marijuana smokers. *Am J Psychiatry* 130:1319–1322, 1973.
168. Melges F. T., Tinklenberg J. R., Hollister L. E., et al: Temporal disintegration and depersonalization during marihuana intoxication. *Arch Gen Psychiatry* 23:204–210, 1970.
169. Mendelson J. H., Ellingboe J., Kuehnle J. C., et al: Effects of chronic marijuana use on integrated plasma testosterone and luteinizing hormone levels. *J. Pharmacol Exp Ther* 207:611–617, 1978.
170. Mendelson J. H., Rossi A. M., Meyer R. E. (eds): *The Use of Marihuana: A Psychological and Physiological Inquiry*. New York, Plenum Press, 1974.
171. Meyer R. E.: Psychiatric consequences of marijuana use: The state of the evidence, in Tinklenberg J. R. (ed): *Marijuana and Health Hazards. Methodological Issues in Current Research*. New York, Academic Press, 1975, pp 133–152.
172. Mirin S. M., Shapiro L. M., Meyer R. E., et al: Casual versus heavy use of marijuana: A redefinition of the marijuana problem. *Am J Psychiatry* 127:54–60, 1971.
173. Petersen R. C. (ed): *Marijuana Research Findings: 1980*. Washington, National Institute on Drug Abuse, Research Monograph #31, 1980.

174. Tennant F. S. Jr., Groesbeck C. J.: Psychiatric effects of hashish. *Arch Gen Psychiatry* 27:133–136, 1972.
175. Thacore V. R., Shukla S. R. P.: Cannabis psychosis and paranoid schizophrenia. *Arch Gen Psychiatry* 33:383–386, 1976.
176. Treffert D. A.: Marijuana use in schizophrenia: A clear hazard. *Am J Psychiatry* 135:1213–1220, 1978.
177. Weil A. T.: Adverse reactions to marihuana: Classification and suggested treatment. *N Engl J Med* 282:997–1000, 1970.

8

Geriatric Psychopharmacology

CARL SALZMAN, M.D., STEVEN A. HOFFMAN, M.D., and STEPHEN C. SCHOONOVER, M.D.

I. INTRODUCTION

Older persons, representing more than 10% of the population in the United States, take all forms of medication more frequently than younger individuals. Estimates of psychotropic drug use in the aged ranges from 7 to 92% in institutional settings and up to 30% in medical settings. A greater incidence of polypharmacy accompanies increased utilization of drugs. A recent survey in general hospitals showed that older patients received an average of 5–12 medications per day. These statistics reflect many factors: a longer life-span accompanied by a greater incidence of chronic illnesses; increased medical sophistication; and drug therapy as a substitute for nonbiological interventions.

To care for the geriatric patient, the clinician must not only master the usual skills necessary for effective drug administration but also understand the unique characteristics of older individuals. In this age group, medical disorders commonly mimic or contribute to psychiatric presentations (see Table 1 in Chapter 1). Physical illnesses, medical drugs, and significant organ system alterations increase the number and severity of adverse reactions from psychotropic agents. Age-related physiological changes as well as drug–drug

CARL SALZMAN, M.D., and STEVEN A. HOFFMAN, M.D. • Department of Psychiatry, Harvard Medical School, and Department of Psychopharmacology, Massachusetts Mental Health Center, Boston, Massachusetts 02215.   STEPHEN C. SCHOONOVER, M.D. • Department of Psychiatry, Harvard Medical School and Beth Israel Hospital, Boston, Massachusetts 02215.

TABLE 1. Problems of Drug Taking in the Elderly

Problem	Causes
Forgetting medication	1. Organic, affective, or psychotic disorders may cause the patient to take too much or too little medication.
Poor compliance	1. Drugs are too expensive.
	2. Adverse effects may be prohibitive.
	3. Arthritic patients cannot open bottles (particularly with safety caps).
	4. Elderly cannot get to the pharmacy (particularly in winter months).
Unusual reactions	1. Unknown polypharmacy; patient taking over-the-counter medications or other drugs without doctor's knowledge; more than one doctor is prescribing drugs without knowledge of the other.
	2. Unknown or underestimated use of alcohol, nicotine (smoking), or caffeine.
	3. Undiagnosed illness that will alter absorption, distribution, metabolism, or elimination.
	4. Undiagnosed decline in nutritional status which also may alter drug metabolism.
Confusion over medicine taking	1. Pills which look alike (shape, color, size) may be interchanged; pills taken concurrently but on different schedules (e.g., q.i.d. and t.i.d.) may be confused.
Capricious noncompliance	1. May take either excessive medicines or none at all because of irrational ideas or struggles over control.

interactions may alter psychotropic drug pharmacokinetics; medications often take longer to work, last longer in the body, and produce greater clinical effects per milligram dosage. In addition, older individuals frequently have complicated psychosocial problems that may decrease drug compliance (see Table 1).

II. PHARMACOKINETIC CHANGES

Because of structural and functional changes within the aging body, the clinical effect(s) of psychotropic drugs may be altered. In most individuals, age-related changes result in reduced clinical effect, increased toxicity, and prolonged clinical and toxic effects. Pharmacokinetic studies of psychotropic drugs and drug–drug interactions have focused on age-related changes in (1) drug absorption and distribution; (2) protein binding; (3) metabolism; and (4) excretion.

A. Absorption and Distribution

In the absence of gastrointestinal pathology, the amount of GI absorption is not significantly altered by the aging process. Because of decreased gastric motility, however, the **rate** of gastric absorption sometimes may be lowered. Although this may delay peak blood levels, actual age-related changes in absorption have little clinical or practical relevance.

The use of other drugs, however, commonly alters psychotropic drug absorption in the elderly (see Table 2). Antipsychotic agents may be precipitated in the stomach by coffee or tea. Aluminum-, magnesium-, or calcium-containing antacids, kaolin/pectin preparations (Dormagel®, Parapectolin®, and others), and activated charcoal (Charcodote® powder) can decrease absorption of benzodiazepines and chlorpromazine (Thorazine® and others) and should be given at least 2 hr before or after the psychotropic drug to prevent alterations in the plasma level. Milk of magnesia, which is frequently given to older medical and surgical patients who are taking psychotropic drugs, also may delay psychotropic drug absorption. Similarly, drugs with anticholinergic activity such as atropine (Antrocol® and others), scopolamine (Historal® and others), meperidine (Demerol® and others), antipsychotics, and heterocyclic antidepressants* may decrease gut motility and interfere with absorption. This may result in inadequate blood levels and compromised clinical effects. By delaying gastric emptying and permitting more degradation of the drug in the gut, anticholinergic agents lower chlorpromazine blood levels.

B. Protein Binding

All psychotropic drugs [except lithium (Eskalith®, Lithonate®, and others)] bind extensively to plasma albumin. Since albumin levels decrease with age, older patients may be more susceptible to toxic responses and thus require lower doses of medication. In addition, other drugs given to the elderly may displace psychoactive agents from protein binding sites, resulting in a higher proportion of unbound drug and increased adverse reactions (see Table 2).

---

*Since many of the currently used thymoleptic drugs are not tricyclic in structure, we have adopted this term to represent the various cyclic antidepressants. From: Baldessarini R.J.: Overview of recent advances in antidepressant pharmacology. Part II. *McLean Hosp J* 7:1–27, 1982.

TABLE 2. Pharmacokinetic Effects of Drug Interactions

Psychotropic drug	Interacting agent and effect

Absorption

Antipsychotics	Coffee, tea may cause precipitation in the stomach (although some authorities now doubt this effect).
	Aluminum-, magnesium-, or calcium-containing antacids delay hydrolysis.
	Kaopectate and milk of magnesia decrease absorption.
Benzodiazepines	Aluminum-, magnesium-, or calcium-containing antacids decrease absorption.
All drugs	Anticholinergic agents [e.g., atropine (Antrocol® and others), scopolamine (Historal® and others), meperidine (Demerol® and others)] decrease absorption.

Protein binding

Diazepam (Valium®)	Increases binding of digoxin (Lanoxin® and others).
Heterocyclic antidepressants	TSH (Thytropar®) increases binding.

Excretion

All drugs	Propranolol (Inderal®, Inderide®) increases serum levels from reduced renal blood flow.
Heterocyclic antidepressants	Tetracycline (Surmycin® and others) and spectinomycin (Trobicin®) increase serum levels by reducing clearance.
	Sodium bicarbonate increases serum levels by increasing tubular reabsorption secondary to alkalinization of the urine.
	Ascorbic acid and ammonium chloride decrease serum levels by a decrease in reabsorption secondary to acidification of the urine.
Lithium	Ibuprofen (Motran®), indomethacin (Indocin®) (and perhaps all prostaglandin synthetase inhibitors) increase serum levels by reducing renal clearance.
	Some Na-losing diuretics increase serum levels by increasing reabsorption.
	K^+-sparing diuretics may decrease serum levels by decreasing reabsorption.

Hepatic metabolism

Decreases metabolism of psychotropic drugs (raises blood level)
   Isoniazid (Nydrazid® and others)
   Chloramphenicol (Chloromycetin® and others)
   Methylphenidate (Ritalin®)
   Disulfuram (Antabuse®)
   Antipsychotics (raises heterocyclics)
   Cimetidine (Tagamet®) [affects chlordiazepoxide (Librium®), diazepam, prazepam
      (Centrex®), and clorazepate (Tranxene®)]

(*continued*)

TABLE 2. (*Continued*)

Propranolol (Inderal®, Inderide®)
Norethindrone (Loestrin® and others)
Barbiturates (when toxic doses of heterocyclics are present)

Increases metabolism of psychotropic drugs (lowers blood level)
Alcohol
Barbiturates
Nonbarbiturate sedative–hypnotics [except perhaps flurazepam (Dalmane®)]
Caffeine
Smoking
Carbamazepine (Tegretol®)
Phenytoin (Dilantin® and others)
Chloral hydrate (Noctec® and others)
Antiparkinson agents
Lithium (Eskalith®, Lithonate®, and others) [affects chlorpromazine (Thorazine® and others); also decreases chlorpromazine levels by delaying gastric emptying, inhibiting absorption, and increasing renal excretion)

C. Hepatic Metabolism

The first-pass effect (i.e., degradation of drugs as they initially traverse the liver) removes more than 80% of most psychotropic drugs taken orally and absorbed from the stomach and intestine. This hepatic function depends on liver blood flow which decreases as cardiac output decreases. Thus, the first-pass drug extraction decreases with age and may, therefore, increase the fraction of unmetabolized psychotropic drug that reaches the general circulation and enhance the potential for toxicity. Propranolol (Inderal®, Inderide®) and cimetidine (Tagamet®), which diminish hepatic blood flow, may also contribute to a decreased first-pass effect.

All psychotropic drugs (except lithium) are primarily metabolized in the liver microsomal enzyme system. With age, hepatic enzyme metabolism may be reduced, producing higher blood levels of psychotropic drugs and increased adverse reactions. Medical drugs combined with psychotropic drugs also may inhibit or induce liver microsomal enzymes, further altering psychotropic drug metabolism (see Table 2). In addition, protein–calorie malnutrition and vitamin deficiency (e.g., vitamin A, folic acid, C, and B_{12}) may decrease hepatic microsomal enzyme activity.

D. Excretion

Psychotropic drugs are excreted primarily through the kidney. Reduced renal blood flow, glomerular filtration, and tubular excretory capacity all have been reported in the elderly. Delayed excretion (as well as impaired hepatic metabolism) is reflected in a prolonged elimination half-life ($t_{1/2B}$) of many psychotropic drugs.

The clinical effect of age-related decreased renal function and prolonged half-life may prove hazardous in the case of lipid-soluble psychotropic drugs (e.g., long-acting benzodiazepines, tertiary tricyclic antidepressants, and some antipsychotic drugs) that form active metabolites. Accumulation of these drugs and their metabolites in the increased fatty tissue as well as in plasma may predispose the older patient to substantially increased risk of toxicity. Other coadministered drugs also can affect the excretion of psychotropic agents (see Table 2).

III. ADVERSE REACTIONS

Adverse reactions occur much more frequently in the older patient. In addition to altered pharmacokinetics, the elderly exhibit a generally increased sensitivity to psychoactive medication. The most frequent and troublesome effects involve the central nervous system (sedation, confusion, and extrapyramidal effects) and heart (orthostatic hypertension and alterations of heart rate, rhythm, and contractility) (see Tables 3 and 4). In addition, drug combinations, so prevalent in the elderly, increase the incidence and severity of both central and peripheral adverse reactions (see Table 5).

A. Central Nervous System

1. Sedation

Excessive sedation in the elderly may be caused by many psychiatric medications, including benzodiazepines, the sedating heterocyclic antidepressants [e.g., doxepin (Adapin®, Sinequan®), amitriptyline (Elavil® and others)] and the sedating antipsychotic agents [e.g., chlorpromazine and thioridazine (Mellaril®)]. Oversedation not only can be mistaken for depression but also can decrease the elderly patient's contact with his surroundings, impair his cognitive capacities, and reduce his self-esteem.

Oversedation is also one of the most common and problematic effects resulting from inappropriate drug combinations. In medically ill elderly patients, sedating psychotropic medications are often administered together or with narcotics, analgesics, alcohol, or sedatives. For example, two recent studies showed that one or more narcotics were given to many elderly patients who received a hypnotic drug, a tricyclic antidepressant, diazepam, or an antipsychotic agent. The CNS depression (oversedation) that results from such drug combinations may lead to a lowered mood, a sense of help-

TABLE 3. Adverse Reactions from Psychotropic Drugs That May Be More Common and Severe in the Elderly

Effect	Cause	Clinical examples
Sedation	Most psychotropic drugs either produce or enhance sedation of other medications	Increased daytime sedation and napping; increased confusion and irritability at night
Confusion	Antichlorinergic properties of heterocyclic antidepressants and antipsychotics	Disorientation, visual hallucinations, agitation, assaultiveness, loss of memory
	Lithium Secondary to increased sedation	
Orthostatic hypotension	Results from heterocyclic antidepressants and antipsychotics	Falling when getting out of bed or a chair
Cardiac toxicity	Primarily from heterocyclic antidepressants	Increase in heart rate and in frequency of irregular heart beat rhythms; altered ECG patterns
Extrapyramidal symptoms	Antipsychotics	Akathisia—restlessness which is confused with agitation; akinesia—decreased activity and interest which is confused with depression

TABLE 4. Pharmacological Effects of Psychotropic Drugs That Cause Adverse Reactions in the Elderly

Drug effect	Symptoms
Decreased central nervous system arousal level	Sedation, apathy, withdrawal, depressed mood, disinhibition, confusion
Peripheral anticholinergic blockade	Dry mouth, constipation, atonic bladder, aggravation of narrow-angle glaucoma and prostatic hypertrophy
Central anticholinergic blockade	Confusion, disorientation, agitation, assaultiveness, visual hallucinosis
α-Adrenergic blockade and central pressor blockade	Orthostatic hypotension
Quinidine effect, anticholinergic effect, decreased myocardial contractility	Tachycardia, cardiac arrhythmia, heart block, increased PR interval and widening of QRS complex, decreased inotropic effect, heart failure
Dopaminergic blockade	Extrapyramidal symptoms, (?) tardive dyskinesia

TABLE 5. Unwanted Clinical Effects of Psychotropic–Psychotropic / Medical Drug Combinations

Unwanted effects	Psychotropic drug used	Combination drug
Oversedation: disorientation, confusion, agitation, irritability, hallucinations	Antipsychotics Benzodiazepines Sedative–hypnotics Amitriptyline (Elavil® and others) Doxepin (Sinequan®, Adapin®)	Narcotics Analgesics Alcohol Sedatives
Central anticholinergic: confusion, disorientation, assaultiveness, toxic hallucinosis	Antipsychotics Heterocyclic antidepressants	Narcotics Atropine-containing drugs (often over-the-counter antihistamines)
Stimulation: excitation, hyperpyrexia, convulsions	MAOIs	Heterocyclic antidepressants
Neurotoxic responses		
Confusion, extrapyramidal symptoms, seizures, ataxia, hyperreflexia, abnormal EEGs	Lithium (Eskalith®, Lithonate®, and others)	Antipsychotics
Cerebellar ataxia, polyuria, decreased thyroxine index, decreased libido	Lithium	Phenytoin (Dilantin® and others)
Transient delirium	Heterocyclic antidepressants	Ethylclorvynol (Placidyl®)
Inhibition of response to L-DOPA (Larodopa®, Sinemet®)	Antipsychotics	L-DOPA
Cardiac		
Prolonged conduction	Heterocyclic antidepressants	Quinidine (Quinora® and others) Procainamide (Pronestyl®)
Nodal bradycardia with slow atrial fibrillation	Chlordiazepoxide	Digoxin (Lanoxin® and others) Thiazide diuretics
Inhibition of antihypertensive effects	Heterocyclic antidepressants Antipsychotics (MAOIs, amphetamines?)	Guanethidine (Esimil®, Ismelin®) Debrisoquine, clonidine (Catapres®, Combipres®)
Exacerbation of orthostatic hypotension	Heterocyclic antidepressants	Diuretics
Peripheral anticholinergic		
Dry mouth, urinary stasis, constipation	Antipsychotics Heterocyclic antidepressants	Narcotics Atropine-containing drugs (often over-the-counter) Antihistamines

(continued)

TABLE 5. (*Continued*)

Unwanted effects	Psychotropic drug used	Combination drug
Respiratory depression	Heterocyclic antidepressants Phenothiazines	Meperidine (Demerol® and others)
Lithium-related		
Prolongation of neuromuscular blockade	Lithium	Succinylcholine (Anectine®, Sucostrin®)
Exacerbation of lithium side effects		Pancuronium (Pavulon®)
Increase or decrease in glucose tolerance (?)		Methyldopa (Aldomet® and others) Insulin

lessness, an attitude of "resignation," and withdrawn or disordered behavior. There may be a decline in self-care and social activities, as though the older patient had given up and was quietly awaiting death.

2. Confusion

Confusion in the elderly most often results from three etiologies: CNS depression or oversedation (see above), CNS anticholinergic effects, or toxic effects of lithium therapy. When significant sedation occurs, older individuals often develop difficulties with concentration and recall.

Anticholinergic effects can lead to CNS confusion as well as peripheral toxicity. Central anticholinergic syndromes commonly appear with the use of various antidepressants [e.g., amitriptyline, imipramine (Tofranil® and others), trimipramine (Surmontil®), doxepin, and nortriptyline (Aventyl®, Pamelor®)] and some antipsychotics [e.g., chlorpromazine, thioridazine, chlorprothixene (Taractan®)]. More often, however, confusion results from administration of mutliple drugs with anticholinergic properties. For instance, the combination of an antipsychotic, an antidepressant, and an antiparkinson agent may cause significant toxicity, since the elderly have increased CNS sensitivity to cholinergic blockade. The clinician should remember that even medications with few anticholinergic effects can cause CNS impairment when given alone to sensitive individuals, when given in higher doses, and when administered in combination with other psychiatric or medical drugs.

The elderly patient with organic brain dysfunction is especially susceptible to central anticholinergic toxicity. Antipsychotics and heterocyclics may be prescribed with narcotics (e.g., meperidine), atropine-containing drugs (which are often available as over-the-counter drugs), and antihistamines that can produce either central and/or peripheral effects. In mild forms, it may appear as disorientation, confusion, agitation, and irritability, particularly at night (i.e., the "sundowner's syndrome"). In more severe cases, it may result in a toxic delirium consisting of disorientation, hallucinations, other psychotic symptoms, and even assaultiveness. This condition can be life-threatening because of self-destructiveness, combativeness, or poor self-care. Typically, in general hospital or nursing home settings, such patients attempt to climb out of bed, mistake nurses for family members, have frightening periods of amnesia, or may even hallucinate. A common medical response is to add more sedating drugs, particularly antipsychotics; this, of course, only further aggravates the condition or puts the patient to sleep.

Lithium alone commonly causes confusion and disorientation in the elderly. Confusion secondary to neurotoxicity also may result from the combined use of an antipsychotic drug and lithium. Other symptoms include extrapyramidal features, seizures, ataxia, hyperreflexia, and abnormal EEGs. If lithium and an antipsychotic are used together, we recommend that the patient's status be monitored with EEGs and that the plasma lithium concentrations be kept below 1.0 mEq/liter.

The combination of lithium and phenytoin (Dilantin® and others) also should be used with caution, since patients who overdose with both drugs have developed persisting cerebellar ataxia. In addition, lithium-type toxicity, including polyuria, polydipsia, decreased free thyroxine index, and decreased libido, has been noted despite normal serum levels of both drugs. In one case, substitution of carbamazepine (Tegretol®) for phenytoin resulted in remission of symptoms.

3. Extrapyramidal

Older patients develop frequent and severe extrapyramidal symptoms. This may result from altered pharmacokinetics or decreased dopamine levels in the nigrostriatal pathways of the elderly. The most common effects include akathisia, parkinsonism, akinesia, and the "Pisa syndrome." As in younger patients, akathisia is often misdiagnosed as agitation. Further medication often increases the severity of the symptoms. Akinesia, consisting of decreased speech and energy and mask-like facies, may be mistaken for depression. The "Pisa syndrome" is a form of dystonia in which the trunk is flexed to one side. The clinician can treat these extrapyramidal symptoms with antiparkinson drugs. However, he must weigh the added risk of anticholinergic effects against the possible advantages and disadvantages of switching the class of antipsychotic drug.

Tardive dyskinesia is much more common in the elderly (especially women) and in those with neuropathological disorders. No effective treatment exists, although the condition may remit if medication is stopped shortly after the appearance of symptoms (remission occurs less often in older patients) (see Chapter 4).

Parkinson's disease itself is more common in old age. Antipsychotic drugs may worsen a patient's condition by inhibiting his response to levodopa (i.e., by blocking dopaminergic receptors in the CNS). When the older patient is treated with L-DOPA (Sinemet® and others) and antipsychotics, a change in dosage may be necessary.

4. Other Central Nervous System Symptoms

Sometimes, undesirable CNS effects occur when drug combinations cause excessive stimulation of the noradrenergic system. Heterocyclics or MAOIs, for example, increase the central effect of amphetamines, and MAOIs increase the effect of a large number of agents (see Table 5). In the elderly, this stimulation may increase agitation, excitation, restlessness, and insomnia.

The combination of heterocyclic antidepressants and MAOIs may cause severe reactions with symptoms that include excitation, hyperpyrexia, convulsions, and hypertension; fatalities have occurred. However, in most of these patients one or more of the following three conditions was present:

1. Excessive doses of one or more drugs were used.
2. The heterocyclic was given parenterally.
3. Other psychotropic drugs were also administered.

Generally, the clinician should avoid combining MAOIs and heterocyclics in the elderly unless they do not respond to the usual therapies or have had a previous good response to combination therapy.

Coadministration of ethclorvynol (Placidyl®) and heterocyclic antidepressants may cause a transient delirium and also should be avoided.

B. Cardiac

Unwanted cardiovascular effects from psychotropic drugs and from the combination of psychoactive and medical agents include changes in cardiac conduction, rhythm, and blood pressure. Although less frequent than CNS sedation or anticholinergic effects, cardiovascular changes are particularly hazardous in the elderly, especially if they have preexisting heart disease.

1. Effects on Blood Pressure

Orthostatic hypotension in the elderly probably results from several causes: blockade of central vasomotor centers, negative inotropic effects (decreased cardiac contractility), and peripheral α-adrenergic blockade. This adverse reaction occurs most often with the use of heterocyclic antidepressants (particularly amitriptyline and imipramine) and antipsychotics (particularly chlorpromazine and thioridazine).

In clinical practice, transient hypotension may cause dizziness, falls and fractures, myocardial infarcts, or strokes. In one study, about 40% of geriatric patients reported dizziness and falling. In the elderly, hypotension may occur at night when patients get up to urinate. Therefore, each patient should be checked for orthostatic changes and told to change positions slowly. Sometimes support stockings also can help.

Heterocyclic antidepressants decrease the antihypertensive properties of many drugs, particularly guanethidine (Ismelin®), bethandine, and debrisoquine. Heterocyclics also inhibit the effects of clonidine (Catapres®, Combipres®) but probably not reserpine (Serpasil® and others) or α-methyldopa (Aldomet® and others). Antipsychotic agents, like heterocyclic antidepressants, can also inhibit the effect of antihypertensive agents by blocking their uptake. Low-potency antipsychotics may be more inhibitory than their high-potency counterparts.

2. Effects on Rate, Rhythm, and Contractility

In the elderly patient, there is an increased risk of cardiac effects from antipsychotics and heterocyclic antidepressants. Because of their anticholinergic properties and effects on intracardiac conduction, these agents cause tachycardia. They also may produce an increased incidence of premature ventricular contractions (although at some doses PVCs decrease), heart block, atrial and ventricular arrhythmias, heart failure, or worsening of congestive heart failure (see Chapters 2 and 4 for ECG changes).

Spontaneously occurring atrial and ventricular arrhythmias are commonly seen in the geriatric population. Since heterocyclic antidepressants retard cardiac conduction, their combination with drugs that prolong conduction, such as quinidine (Quinora® and others), procainamide (Pronestyl® and others), or disopyramide (Norpace®), may result in toxic cardiac effects. Digoxin (Lanoxin® and others), when combined with lithium, may cause severe nodal bradycardia with slow atrial fibrillation or sinoatrial block. The combination of thiazide diuretics (which deplete sodium and potassium), lithium, and digoxin is particularly hazardous; sodium depletion leads to lithium retention which, in turn, worsens potassium depletion and increases digoxin toxicity. Permanent ventricular pacemakers are not affected by the tendency of heterocyclic antidepressants to interfere with intraventricular conduction.

C. Other Organ Systems

1. Respiratory depression is a rare effect in all patients; it appears more frequently in the elderly with lung disease who are taking sedative–

hypnotics. Moreover, meperidine-induced respiratory depression is enhanced by both heterocyclic antidepressants and phenothiazines.

2. Ocular and dermatologic effects from long-term antipsychotic drug use usually occur only in older patients after large cumulative doses of medication (most often seen with low-potency phenothiazines).

3. Peripheral anticholinergic effects such as dry mouth may cause oral infections, loss of teeth, and a poor fit for dentures; decreased gastrointestinal and urinary bladder motility appear more often in the elderly.

4. Lithium prolongs the neuromuscular blockade produced by succinylcholine (Anectine® and others) and pancuronium (Pavulon®). Therefore, in lithium-treated patients requiring elective surgery and a muscle-relaxant anesthetic, lithium should be discontinued 48 to 72 hr preoperatively and resumed on return of bowel function. Depressed patients taking lithium who also require ECT should be closely monitored after anesthesia to ensure the return of adequate respiration.

5. The interaction of lithium with insulin and carbohydrate metabolism is complex; controversy exists about whether lithium increases or decreases glucose tolerance. Therefore, glucose control of insulin-dependent diabetics on lithium therapy should be closely monitored.

IV. CLINICAL APPLICATION

A. Principles of Medication Use

To Treat Elderly Patients Safely

1. Know the properties of each drug, including pharmacokinetics, possible adverse reactions, and clinical effects.

2. Take a careful medical history and complete a physical examination to rule out an organic etiology and to document physical symptoms and illnesses that may interfere with psychotropic medication (e.g., bowel obstruction or constipation, kidney disease or urinary tract disease, glaucoma).

3. Be aware of other medications the patient is taking (even over-the-counter preparations).

4. When medication is indicated, do not withhold it because of age.

5. Offer a simple plan for taking medication. For example, show the patient a picture of the pill to be taken, outline an exact dosage schedule, and use family members to help if necessary.

6. Start medication in small amounts and increase slowly while monitoring adverse reactions. Rely on both verbal reports and physical signs.

7. Continue the trial of medication until the patient receives adequate doses or has significant clinical effects or prohibitive adverse reactions (clinicians have a tendency to stop drug trials too early).

8. Avoid polypharmacy by giving only one psychotropic agent whenever possible and by intermittently reviewing all medications.

9. Always provide psychological support.

10. Assume that any older patient taking psychotropic medication who is agitated, confused, restless, forgetful, or depressed may be drug toxic. Consider reducing the dose or discontinuing medication before adding another drug.

B. Clinical Use

1. Agitated Behavior and Psychotic Thinking

In older as well as younger people, antipsychotic medication may be used to treat psychosis. Although a late emergence of schizophrenia is rare, other types of psychoses (i.e., depressive, organic, schizoaffective, and manic) may appear in older patients. Most commonly, however, antipsychotic medication is used in elderly patients to control severe behavioral disturbances such as agitation, wandering, self-mutilation, and assaultiveness.

a. Acute Psychosis or Behavior Problems

No studies show that one antipsychotic medication is more effective than another in controlling acute psychosis or disordered behavior of the elderly. However, adverse reactions differ markedly with different antipsychotic medications. The antipsychotic effects that are frequent and particularly hazardous in older people include sedation, orthostatic hypotension, and extrapyramidal and anticholinergic symptoms. High-potency antipsychotic medications such as haloperidol (Haldol®), thiothixene (Navane®), or piperazine phenothiazine [Trifluoperazine (Stelazine®), perphenazine (Trilafon®), fluphenazine (Prolixin®)] are less likely to produce sedation and hypotension although more likely to produce extrapyramidal symptoms. A low-potency antipsychotic such as thioridazine is strongly sedative and anticholinergic but produces fewer and less severe extrapyramidal reactions in the elderly. The selection of an appropriate antipsychotic medication, therefore, rests on a consideration of unwanted effects. For example, nonsedating antipsychotic drugs are more likely to produce extrapyramidal symptoms; conversely, sedating antipsychotics are less likely to produce extrapyramidal symptoms.

In addition, the clinician can administer other antipsychotics if the older individual has previously responded favorably and safely, and if no new physical conditions preclude their use. Antipsychotics should be started in low oral doses (e.g., 1 to 2 mg of a high-potency drug or 10 to 25 mg of thioridazine) two to three times per day and increased slowly.

b. Treatment of Extrapyramidal Symptoms

Extrapyramidal effects caused by the antipsychotics and occasionally by heterocyclic antidepressants are treated with low doses of antiparkinson agents [e.g., trihexyphenidyl hydrochloride (Artane®, Tremin®), 0.5 mg]. The clinician should increase dosage only after careful assessment of the patient's mental and physical status, since these drugs often combine with antipsychotic agents to produce serious anticholinergic syndromes. In the treatment of dystonias, the antiparkinson medications should be discounted after 3 to 7 days. In the treatment of parkinsonism and akathisia, antiparkinson agents should be stopped after 6 weeks to 3 months. If symptoms reemerge, the clinician should consider changing the antipsychotic medication.

2. Dementia

Chronic brain syndromes may result from many etiologies. Dementias caused by tumors or increased intracranial pressure may be reversible. However, the majority of the elderly with dementia have progressive, diffuse loss of brain cells (Alzheimer's disease accounts for 50 to 75% of cases) and ongoing deterioration of mental capacities and functioning (see Section III.A.2). Less often, older patients may develop dementia from arteriosclerosis. Multiple infarcts often cause a clinical picture in the elderly marked by sudden onset and stepwise progression with a deteriorating mental status and focal neurological signs. About one-third of demented patients have both Alzheimer's dementia and multiple infarcts. Older patients also may present with "pseudodementia." Although not a specific disorder, this term describes a decline in cognitive processes associated with depression. The patient appears somewhat confused and disoriented and has impaired recent memory. In severe cases, there are behavioral disturbances and a deterioration of self care. Adequate antidepressant treatment often brings about a surprising restoration of thinking, memory, and behavior. Factors associated with this condition include:

1. History of affective disorder.
2. Symptoms of major depressive illness accompanying the cognitive disturbance.
3. Poor immediate recall but adequate delayed verbal recall.
4. Intact recognition memory.
5. Few objective deficits on mental status.

6. Improved intellectual functioning when the clinician structures tests, prompts the patient, or allows extra time for answers.

Older patients with well-established organic dementia also may have significant depressive symptoms that compromise thinking and behavior. Administering an antidepressant often improves the patient's depression, memory, orientation, and behavior.

Patients with senile dementia of the Alzheimer's type may have a selective deterioration of acetylcholine neurons. Precursors of acetylcholine such as lecithin and choline have been administered to these patients with equivocal results. Some late-life dementias have been thought to result from decreased central nervous system oxygenation. Clinical and research experience with cerebral vasodilators as well as drugs that increase cerebral blood flow [heparin (Panheprin® and others), papaverine (Cerebid® and others), cyclandelate (Cyclospasmol® and others), and hyperbaric oxygen] have also produced questionable results. The ergot alkaloid combination hydergine has been shown to have slightly positive effects in the mildly demented older patient, but these results have not been striking. Central nervous system stimulants have had no positive therapeutic effect on thinking or memory. Recent research has also focused on new protein complexes, steroids, and metabolic agents such as piracetam, $ACTH_{4-10}$, procaine, and RNA, but the effects of these agents have been either negative or equivocal.

3. Anxiety

The treatment of anxiety in the elderly is similar to that in younger patients. Benzodiazepines are the safest and most effective agents for the short-term management of moderately severe anxiety states that do not respond to nonpharmacological methods. However, the clinician should carefully monitor the drugs, since they often cause sedation, uncoordination, and confusion. Combining benzodiazepines with drugs that have sedative or disinhibiting properties often can produce central nervous system depression, lowered mood, disinhibited behavior, or confusion, disorientation, memory loss, and agitation.

Benzodiazepines in clinical use can be divided into two groups on the basis of their pharmacokinetic properties. In one, the drugs are long-acting, have active metabolites, and tend to accumulate, lasting about twice as long in the elderly as compared with a young or middle-aged adult. These drugs include chlordiazepoxide, diazepam, clorazepate, prazepam, and flurazepam. These drugs may be useful for the older patient who is forgetful or is taking many drugs on different daily schedules and inadvertently omits the benzodiazepine; if a dose is missed, clinical effect will not be compromised. Since these agents tend to accumulate, however, they should be given only once a day or perhaps every other day. Unfortunately, the long-acting benzodiazepines have several disadvantages for the elderly. They take longer to reach steady-state plasma concentrations. Should toxicity occur, elimination of these drugs may take days to weeks, thus subjecting the older patient to prolonged unwanted effects.

The other group of benzodiazepines has a much shorter duration of activity, has no active metabolites, and tends not to accumulate. These agents include oxazepam (Serax®), lorazepam (Ativan®), and alprazolam (Xanax®). They must be administered throughout the day, since their duration of action is measured in hours. Should toxicity occur, however, the drugs will be more rapidly eliminated than the long-acting benzodiazepines. Since the older patient is more sensitive to the benzodiazepines' unwanted effects, and to the problems of polypharmacy, the use of short-acting drugs may be preferred.

When an older patient reacts adversely to benzodiazepines or exhibits persistent, severe, or disorganizing anxiety, the practitioner should avoid other sedative–hypnotic drugs. These medications, particularly the barbiturates, may cause respiratory depression, CNS impairment, and frequent paradoxical responses. Instead, he might consider using low doses of an antipsychotic agent.

4. Insomnia

The elderly patient commonly suffers from insomnia. The clinician should carefully evaluate the patient, since sleep disorders frequently are secondary to various other conditions (e.g., depression, anxiety states, pain, dyspnea, daytime napping, urinary urgency, recent emotional trauma, or caffeine). If medication is appropriate, the practitioner should only administer a hypnotic for a short period. Flurazepam, 15 mg at bedtime, is effective; with longer use, this drug may accumulate and cause sundowning and disinhibition. The shorter-acting benzodiazepines (e.g., oxazepam, 5 to 10 mg, or lorazepam, 0.5 to 1.0 mg) offer other alternatives. Temazepam (Restoril®), 15 mg at bedtime, has strong hypnotic properties and a short half-life. Although there is little experience with this drug in the elderly, it may have significant advantages.

5. Depression

Heterocyclic antidepressants are the drugs of choice for the severely depressed elderly patient. However, older patients are more susceptible to adverse effects than younger individuals. In particular, orthostatic hypotension, cardiac irritability, and anticholinergic toxicity occur more often in the elderly. Since no data suggest clinical superiority of one heterocyclic antidepressant over another, the clinician should choose a heterocyclic on the basis of its adverse reactions. In general, tertiary tricyclic amines such as imipramine and amitriptyline produce more severe untoward effects than their demethylated secondary amine metabolites, desipramine and nortriptyline, respectively. Tertiary amines also last longer and, because of altered hepatic metabolism with age, tend to accumulate more than secondary amines. Desipramine or nortriptyline may be recommended for the depressed elderly patient who has psychomotor retardation or hypersomnia. In those with anxious or agitated depressions, doxepin, which is more sedating, should be used.

Various new heterocyclic antidepressants are rapidly becoming available for clinical use. A number of these drugs, including maprotiline (Ludiomil®) and trazodone (Desyrel®), are thought to have lower anticholinergic toxicity than the secondary tricyclics mentioned above. If so, these drugs may offer significant advantages in the older patient. Controlled clinical comparisons will be necessary to verify these preliminary findings.

Every elderly patient must have a physical examination and a pretreatment ECG prior to the initiation of heterocyclic antidepressant therapy. During the course of treatment, blood pressure, urine output, and ECG should be monitored periodically. Should the patient become toxic or incompletely respond to treatment, plasma levels of the drug should be obtained. Occasional elderly patients will require high doses of medication.

For the severely depressed elderly patient whose life may be jeopardized by the depression (either through inanition or suicidal impulses), ECT should be administrated. Electroconvulsive therapy is also preferred for elderly patients who have responded positively in the past, who have nihilistic or somatic delusions, or who have moderately to severely impaired cardiovascular status.

6. Bipolar Affective Disorder

The manic elderly patient presents a difficult therapeutic challenge. In acute manic states, antipsychotic medication may be necessary to control hyperactivity, which can rapidly lead to exhaustion. Most commonly, high-potency agents such as haloperidol, fluphenazine, or thiothixene are used.

Since lithium may produce serious adverse effects in the elderly, its use in the treatment of mania requires special care. The elderly are sometimes more sensitive to toxicity resulting from the interaction of lithium and an antipsychotic drug. This toxicity is manifested by a confusional state with memory loss, disorientation, fear, and agitation.

Lithium excretion and its elimination half-life tend to be delayed in older patients, leading to increased likelihood of toxicity. For this reason, adverse effects are more common among the elderly than in younger patients.

Symptoms of lithium toxicity may be confused with common symptoms of older patients, such as nausea, vomiting, restlessness, tremor, and confusion.

Lithium, therefore, should be restricted to the treatment of the acute manic episode and for prophylaxis only in patients with well-documented recurrent bipolar illness. Acute mania may be treated with an initial dose of 150 mg of lithium b.i.d.; dosages should be increased by 150-mg increments. Blood levels above 0.8 mEq/liter should **not** be routine. If high levels are necessary, the clinician should carefully monitor the patient's electrolytes, fluid status, and mental status. For prophylaxis, a blood level of 0.4 to 0.8 mEq/liter is often adequate. Cardiac and renal function should be carefully checked, and serum lithium levels, ECGs, thyroid, and kidney function should be reviewed frequently.

V. CONCLUSION

Medicating the elderly presents many difficulties for the clinician. The marked heterogeneity of this population and their special problems (particularly polypharmacy, altered pharmacokinetics, and CNS sensitivity) must be confronted with each patient. Often, serious adverse reactions develop before the clinician can give adequate therapeutic doses of medication. Therefore, the practitioner should carefully monitor each drug and change the regimen if the initial trial fails. Even with skilled pharmacological and nonbiological interventions, older patients may have limited responses. Despite these problems, caretakers who provide comprehensive treatment, including psychosocial, medical, and psychopharmacological approaches often see gratifying results.

SELECTED READING

1. Larny P. P.: *Prescribing for the Elderly*. Littleton, MA, PSG Press, 1980, p 8.
2. Blaschke T. F., Cohen S. N., Tatro D. S., et al: Drug–drug interactions and aging, in Jarvik L. F. (ed): *Clinical Pharmacology and the Aged Patient*. New York, Raven Press, 1981, pp 11–26.
3. Salzman C.: A primer on geriatric psychopharmacology. *Am J Psychiatry* 139: 67–74, 1982.
4. Kalchthaler T., Coccaro E., Lichtige S.: Incidence of polypharmacy in a long-term facility. *J Am Geriatr Soc* 25:308–313, 1977.
5. Salzman C.: Polypharmacy and drug–drug interactions in the elderly, in Nancy K. (ed): *Geriatric Psychopharmacology*. New York, Elsevier/North Holland, 1979, pp 117–126.

9

Pediatric Psychopharmacology

CAROL R. KOPLAN, M.D.

I. INTRODUCTION

The use of psychoactive drugs in children presents a number of problems. First, despite recent attempts at clarifying the diagnostic nomenclature of childhood disorders, emotional disturbances in children do not always present in as discrete and homogeneous a fashion as those commonly observed in adults. Thus, choosing the proper medication for a child may be more difficult. Second, research on the use of psychotropic medications in children is relatively sparse, leaving the clinician with the need to make practical decisions without adequate scientific underpinning. Finally, in children, the emotional, behavioral, and social base on which psychiatric problems are identified and treated is more fluid than in adults. A prescribing physician, therefore, must take into account a child's rapidly changing physical status, developmental stage, relationships within the family, and ongoing environmental stresses in selecting a medication and monitoring response to treatment. Despite all these challenges, however, psychiatric medications can bring marked relief to children with a number of identifiable disorders, including psychoses, severe behavior problems, enuresis, and attention deficit disorder, so that along with psychosocial interventions, medicine can form an important part of a treatment approach for a child psychiatrist (see Table 1).

After a thorough medical and psychiatric evaluation, a practitioner should arrive at a diagnosis and specify target symptoms at which drug treatment will be aimed. In all cases, pharmacological therapy should form part

CAROL R. KOPLAN, M.D. • Department of Psychiatry, Emory University School of Medicine, Atlanta, Georgia 30322.

TABLE 1. Childhood Diagnoses and Their Pharmacotherapy[a]

DSM category	Specific	Symptomatic
Pervasive developmental disorders	None	Antipsychotics
Attention deficit disorders with hyperactivity	Stimulants	Antipsychotics
	?Antidepressants	Antidepressants
Stereotyped movement disorders		
Transient motor tic disorder	None	?Antipsychotics
Chronic motor tic disorder	None	?Antipsychotics
Tourette's disorder	?Antipsychotics	Antipsychotics
Conduct disorders		
Undersocialized, aggressive	None	?Stimulants
		?Antimanics
Eating disorders		
Anorexia nervosa	None	?Antipsychotics
Anxiety disorders		
Overanxious disorder	None	?Anxiolytics
Separation anxiety disorder	?Antidepressants	Antidepressants
Developmental disorders		
Enuresis	None	Antidepressants

[a]Adapted from Gittleman-Klein et al.[11]

of a comprehensive treatment plan which may include individual, group, or family psychotherapy, special education, or an alternative living arrangement such as hospitalization or residential treatment.

Treating an adolescent with medication requires special care. The clinician must handle the therapeutic relationship with skill and sensitivity, explaining in detail the expected course of treatment and adverse effects of the drug. Because adolescents often feel that adults in general are trying to "control" their feelings and behavior, they may be particularly resistant to taking drugs. Therefore, **the most important priority in working with an adolescent is the development of a trusting relationship.**

Drug kinetics are different in children than in adults. For example, a child's liver represents a proportionately larger amount of the total body weight, so children often metabolize agents more quickly. In addition, lower levels of protein binding and percentage of total body adipose tissue result in smaller depots for drug storage, which means quicker onset of action and decreased duration of effect. Therefore, children usually require relatively higher and more frequent doses than adults, but they tend to develop fewer adverse effects. When unwanted reactions do occur, they are generally less severe and respond more readily to a decrease or discontinuation of the medication. Children should be systematically questioned about the development of untoward effects, since they volunteer this information less readily than adults.

As an aid to the practitioner, guidelines for the administration of drugs used in children are presented in Tables 2 through 8.

II. PSYCHOSES AND SEVERE BEHAVIOR DISORDERS

A. Introduction

Functional psychoses in children are often categorized according to their time of onset. Infantile autism develops in children under 3 years of age. These children may benefit from antipsychotic medication, which diminishes their aggressive, self-destructive, or hyperactive symptoms but may not affect the underlying thought disorder. Childhood schizophrenia, which has its onset during latency, is characterized by inappropriate behavior, a thought disorder, and sometimes changes in eating and sleeping habits. Antipsychotic agents are helpful both acutely and in the long term. The treatment of adolescent-onset psychosis with antipsychotic drugs is similar to that of adult schizophrenia and has a better prognosis than the childhood types.

The following symptoms in children also may be helped at times by cautious use of antipsychotic medication:

1. Severe aggressive behavior—toward oneself, others, or property— that cannot be managed by other means. This may be seen in children with attention deficit disorder with hyperactivity, severe conduct disorders, organic brain disease, or mental retardation.
2. Severe debilitating anxiety not responsive to psychotherapy, environmental change, or other drugs.

B. Antipsychotic Drugs

Similarly to adults, children and adolescents with psychotic disorders generally benefit from the administration of antipsychotic drugs. In addition, these drugs have been used to treat children with serious behavior disorders and very severe anxiety. Because experience with phenothiazines—particularly chlorpromazine (Thorazine®) and thioridazine (Mellaril®)—has been more extensive than with most other antipsychotic drugs, they are often preferred (see Table 2).

1. Principles of Use

As in adults, the antipsychotic efficacy of various preparations is generally equivalent. Therefore, the choice of a drug depends on a patient's prior experience and on the spectrum of pharmacological properties (e.g., sedative, neuroleptic effects). For example, the aliphatic phenothiazines are most sedating and therefore may be more useful in psychotic children who manifest severe anxiety and agitation. The piperazines [e.g., fluphenazine (Prolixin®), trifluoperazine (Stelazine®)] are less sedating and may be adminis-

TABLE 2. Major Tranquilizers for Children 6 to 12 Years of Age

Generic name (brand name)	Preparations (mg)	Oral dose—PDR	Comments
Phenothiazines			
Aliphatics			
Chlorpromazine (Thorazine®)	Tablets: 10, 25, 50 Spansules: 30, 75, 150, 200 Syrup: 10 mg/5 ml (1 tsp) Concentrate (for institutional use): 30 mg/ml, 100 mg/ml	¼ mg/lb body wt. q 4–6 hr for outpatients; in severe behavior disorders or psychosis, 50–200 mg/day or more	For an acutely disorganized or agitated child, can give 25 to 50 mg IM; child must be observed for postural hypotension. Acutely disturbed adolescent can be given 25–50 mg IM or 50–100 mg PO or up to 300 mg PO in divided doses while awaiting hospitalization. Watch for hypotension. May be given at bedtime once tissue saturation occurs.
Piperidines			
Thioridazine (Mellaril®)	Tablets: 10, 15, 25, 50, 100, 150, 200 Concentrate: 30 mg/ml, 100 mg/ml	Ages 2–12: 0.5–3.0 mg/kg per day Moderate disorders: 10 mg 2 or 3 times/day Severe disorders: 25 mg 2 or 3 times/day	In children 5–12, may give up to 300 mg/day; over 12, may give up to 800 mg/day.
Piperazines			
Trifluoperazine (Stelazine®)	Tablets: 1, 2, 5, 10 Concentrate (for institutional use): 10 mg/ml	Start with 1 mg once or twice a day; usually, do not exceed 15 mg/day	The piperazines may be chosen for the apathetic withdrawn schizophrenic child or adolescent.
Fluphenazine HCl (Prolixin®) (Permitil®)	Tablets: 1, 2, 5 Elixir: 0.5 mg/ml, 2.5 mg/5 ml (1 tsp)		"Safety and efficacy in children have not been established"
Butyrophenones			
Haloperidol (Haldol®)	Tablets: ½, 1, 2, 5 Concentrate: 2 mg/ml	Over 12; moderate symptomatology: 0.5–2	Researchers have used the following doses in children:

	mg b.i.d. or t.i.d.; severe symptomatology: 3.0–5.0 mg b.i.d. or t.i.d.		(1) severe behavior disorder in outpatient children: 0.5–2.0 mg/day; (2) outpatient schizophrenic children: 10–12 mg/day; (3) for institutional mentally retarded children with behavior disorders: 1.5–15 mg/day; (4) Gilles de la Tourette's syndrome: 2–3 mg/day; (5) autistic children: 0.5–4 mg/day.
Thioxanthenes Thiothixene (Navane®)	Capsules: 1, 2, 5, 10 Concentrate: 5 mg/ml	Not recommended for children under 12	Researchers have found thiothixene effective in (1) autistic 3- to 7-year-olds: 1–6 mg/day to improve mental state; (2) psychotic boys 5–15: 6–30 mg/day to decrease motor activity, more responsive; (3) institutional mentally retarded children: 5–15 mg/day.
Dihydroindolone Molindone (Lidone®) (Moban®)	Capsules: 5, 10, 25 Concentrate: 20 mg/ml		(1) For hypoactive psychotic children. (2) Not recommended by manufacturer for children under age 12. (3) Not recommended for behavior disorder associated with mental retardation. (4) Dosage range: 1–200 mg/day.

tered to hypoactive or withdrawn schizophrenics. Apathetic schizophrenic children may benefit from higher doses in proportion to body weight than adults, and they seem to develop fewer extrapyramidal effects. Several controlled studies suggest that haloperidol (Haldol®) is more effective in treating disruptive behavioral symptoms than either chlorpromazine or thioridazine. Haloperidol seems to increase attention and concentration while not reducing mental alertness.

Children with infantile autism, especially younger children, seem very sensitive to the sedative properties of chlorpromazine and sometimes become more disorganized. Therefore, the less sedative antipsychotics such as thiothixene (Navane®), haloperidol, or trifluoperazine are preferred. Campbell[3] showed that haloperidol (0.5 to 4.0 mg/day) led to a decrease of stereotypies and withdrawal in children $4\frac{1}{2}$ years and older with infantile autism. When these children were treated with drugs plus behavior modification, they learned to imitate speech more rapidly; however, no other behaviors were modified.

The actual amount of drug for acutely disturbed children may approach the recommended minimal dose for adults. Since antipsychotics are long-acting drugs, they often can be administered once a day, increasing compliance. Generally, if children are given a reasonable explanation of why the drug is necessary, they will accept oral medication. Occasionally, however, a child is very agitated. Thioridazine and haloperidol, available in liquid form, should be administered to these disturbed children before the parenteral route is used.

2. Adverse Effects

The child and parents should be questioned intermittently about the presence of unwanted effects, since they often are not reported voluntarily. Most untoward effects in the child are similar to those in the adult (see Chapter 4). The most common include:

1. Anticholinergic effects, particularly nasal congestion, drowsiness, and dry mouth. The child usually becomes tolerant to these effects within the first few weeks, but if they persist, the dose can be lowered or the preparation changed. (The latter measure is usually unnecessary.)
2. Orthostatic hypotension, resulting in a decrease of both systolic and diastolic blood pressure, occurs most commonly with low-potency antipsychotic agents such as the aliphatic phenothiazines. The parents and patient should be cautioned to make postural changes slowly.
3. Photosensitivity reactions occur with most of the phenothiazines but may be less likely with thioridazine. A sunscreen such as *p*-

aminobenzoic acid (PABA) can be used to protect the child from the sun. Allergic skin reactions occur more commonly than photosensitivity.

4. Hyperpyrexia may be caused by antipsychotic drugs. Therefore, if a child develops a fever of undetermined etiology, the dosage should be lowered and the body temperature monitored. If the fever persists, the drug should be discontinued.

5. Leukopenia occasionally occurs in children taking antipsychotic medications. The white blood count usually returns to normal 2 to 4 weeks (although occasionally longer) after discontinuation of the drug. As in the adult, the clinical state of the patient rather than the white blood count should be followed. All infections, particularly those of the oropharynx, should be vigorously worked up. Agranulocytosis rarely occurs in children (see Chapter 4).

6. Abnormal liver function tests have been reported early in treatment in children, but jaundice is rare if it occurs at all (see Chapter 4).

7. Seizures occasionally occur in children taking antipsychotic medication—especially in those with EEG signs of epilepsy or a previous clinical seizure disorder or those receiving aliphatic phenothiazines. In patients at risk, antipsychotic drug doses should be administered in small amounts and increased gradually. If anticonvulsant drugs have been used previously, they should be continued when antipsychotic agents are prescribed.

8. Although studies are contradictory, impaired learning possibly may be related to antipsychotic drug use.

9. Breast enlargement, menstrual irregularities (such as amenorrhea), and lactation have been observed in adolescents.

10. Dose-related frequency, urgency, polyuria, enuresis, urinary incontinence, and erection and ejaculation difficulties have been reported, predominantly with thioridazine. Therefore, in adolescents who are developing sexually, thioridazine is not the drug of choice.

11. Weight gain and appetite increase commonly occur in children taking these drugs.

12. Lens and corneal stippling have been reported in children.

13. Extrapyramidal signs (EPS) are similar to those occurring in the adult and include parkinsonism, akathisias, and dystonias, which are often more severe than in adults. According to a survey by Polizos and Engelhardt,[18] dystonias occurred in 25% of psychotic children given antipsychotic drugs. These extrapyramidal effects are dose dependent and usually occur within the first few days of treatment with the antipsychotic agents. The more severe dystonias are characterized by the sudden onset of muscular rigidity, usually involving the muscles of the neck or upper extremity, and may include torticollis, dysphagia, aphonia, or protrusion of the tongue.

Sometimes the respiratory muscles are involved, although apnea has not been reported. If the patient develops dysphagia or laryngospasm, parenteral medication such as intramuscular or intravenous diphenhydramine (Benadryl®) may be given. However, caution should be exercised, since a slight risk of anaphylaxis exists. Some clinicians prefer IV diazepam (Valium®) for the treatment of laryngospasm and other dystonic reactions. Others administer benztropine (Cogentin®), 1 to 2 mg IM, which can be repeated in ½ hr. For less severe reactions, antiparkinson agents or diphenhydramine may be given by mouth for periods not longer than 3 to 4 months (see Table 3).

14. **Withdrawal emergent symptoms (WES) and tardive dyskinesia.**
When antipsychotic drugs are abruptly discontinued, approximately 50% of children develop WES within 4 weeks. The syndrome most commonly occurs after the administration of antipsychotic drugs associated with a high incidence of EPS. The WES consist of dyskinesias and systemic symptoms (nausea, vomiting, diaphoresis, and hyperactivity) which remit after 8 to 12 weeks. The dyskinesias consist of involuntary movements of the extremities, trunk, and head. Slightly less common symptoms are ataxia, impaired fine coordination, tremor, and hypotonia. A few children have developed solitary oral dyskinesia. Spontaneous remission occurs if the child can remain without medication; most children, however, have to be restarted on the drug because of the severity of their emotional illness. Tardive dyskinesia (TD) is characterized by dyskinesias that last 6 months of more, but, unlike in WES, there are no accompanying systemic symptoms. The signs of TD can be mild or severe and include facial tics and grimaces, choreoathetoid, ballistic, and myoclonic movements of the extremities and trunk, torticollis and retrocollis, abnormal posturing, generalized motor restlessness,

TABLE 3. Antiparkinson Agents for Children 6–12 Years of Age

Generic name (brand name)	Preparations (mg)	Oral dose—PDR	Comments
Diphenhydramine (Benadryl®)	See Table 6		
Trihexyphenidyl HCl (Artane®)	Scored tablets: 2, 5 Elixir: 2 mg/5 ml Sequels: 5	1–2 mg b.i.d.	No specific reference to children by manufacturer
Benztropine mesylate (Cogentin®)	Tablets: 0.5, 1, 2	1 mg b.i.d.; for acute dystonic reactions: 1–2 mg	Because of atropinelike side effects, contraindicated in children less than 3; caution in children over 3

and ataxia. Buccolingual masticatory movements, common in adults, are less common in children.

Sometimes, other movement disorders suppressed by antipsychotic medication reappear when the drug is withdrawn. These include stereotypies, nervous mannerisms, tics, imitative gesturing, psychotic posturing, choreoathetoid movements (i.e., cerebral palsy), or mild choreic movements (i.e., accompanying attention deficit disorder or Sydenham's chorea).

3. Clinical Application

An acute psychosis—characterized by a thought disorder, marked behavioral changes, or disordered sleeping and eating—is an indication for antipsychotic agents. If the family can manage, the child may be kept at home, given medication, and seen frequently as an outpatient. However, depending on the severity of the illness and the family's resources, hospitalization may be necessary.

As stated previously, because most of the experience in children has been with chlorpromazine and thioridazine, these drugs are generally preferred. The clinician should administer the antipsychotic agent in the lowest effective dose and increase as necessary until the patient improves or develops adverse effects (see Table 2). In some children, adverse effects will be so troublesome that the drug will have to be changed to another phenothiazine subgroup or another class (see Chapter 4).

If the child requires chronic treatment, sedation may become a problem. Even when mild, it may affect the child's cognition. Therefore, a drug should be tapered as soon as the causative stress has abated and the child's symptoms are contained. The drug can be reinstituted if there is an exacerbation of symptoms. When antipsychotic drugs are discontinued, they should be tapered over 3 to 6 weeks. Abrupt withdrawal can lead to lethargy, irritability and excitement, and movement disorders.

III. TIC DISORDERS

Tourette's disorder, or Gilles de la Tourette's syndrome, is an uncommon but disabling tic disorder which begins between the ages of 2 and 14. It consists of involuntary movements of the arm and head, which spread to the rest of the body. The patient may make grunting or barking sounds and may develop coprolalia or echolalia. Experts postulate that the disease may reflect a disorder of dopaminergic, noradrenergic, or cholinergic neurotransmitter systems.

In most cases, haloperidol is the treatment of choice and generally alleviates the muscular and vocal tics. The initial dosage in children is 2 to 3 mg/day. Although an average dose in grown patients is 5 mg/day, doses ranging from 40 to 180 mg/day occasionally have been required for control of symptoms. Shapiro[5] recommends that haloperidol be started at a low dose (0.25 mg/day) and that benztropine (0.5 mg) also be given to prevent acute dystonias. If a dystonia still occurs, 1 mg of benztropine can be given immediately, followed by continued treatment of 1 mg/day. The dosage of haloperidol should be increased every 5 days by 0.25 mg until the symptoms are controlled or adverse effects become problematic. Occasionally, a child who has done well in school will begin to do poorly. Slight decreases in the dose of haloperidol usually lead to improved school performance.

Clonidine (Catapres®), an antihypertensive agent with adrenergic agonist (and sometimes antagonist) properties, recently has been successfully used to treat Tourette patients who had not responded to haloperidol. Moreover, agents that enhance the effects of acetylcholine [e.g., physostigmine (Antilirium®) and lecithin] also have been used. Although promising, all treatments other than haloperidol are experimental.

Special education and individual and family psychotherapy may be necessary adjuncts to drug treatment, depending on the duration of symptoms and the degree of disability. Another source of assistance and support is the Tourette Syndrome Association,* founded by patients and their families in 1974. This organization currently (1981) includes more than 8000 members. They can provide the most updated information about tic disorders.

IV. DEPRESSION

A. Introduction

After considerable controversy, child psychiatrists have begun to agree that major depressive disorders do, in fact, occur in both children and adolescents. In part, their disagreement centered around the fact that children, in contrast with adults, do not necessarily exhibit the cardinal features of depression described in DSM-III. Rather, symptoms of depression are significantly modified by the child's level of cognitive and affective development. For example, children with early, profound emotional deprivation may develop an anaclitic depression characterized by apathy, anorexia, and withdrawal. After separation–individuation, the most blatant depressions in children may have symptoms that are similar to, but more muted than, those in adults. A chronic depressive syndrome resulting from repeated separations from important adults may closely resemble a moderately severe adult retarded depression. Frequently, children manifest their depressed feelings

*Tourette Syndrome Association, Inc., 40–08 Corporal Kennedy Street, Bayside, New York 11361.

indirectly: by "acting out," school phobias, running away, changes in school performance, somatization, or regressive symptoms such as withdrawal, insomnia, restlessness, and even enuresis or encopresis. Sometimes the clinician may overlook the child's desperation, reflected by suicidal ideation and intent. Therefore, **evaluation of any depressed child should always include a careful assessment of suicidal potential.**

B. Heterocyclic Antidepressants*

1. Principles of Use

The clinician should evaluate the child's symptoms and situation carefully, including information gathered from parents, teachers, and the child himself. For most depressed and unhappy children, psychotherapy, supportive measures, and environmental manipulation are effective. However, if a child has the symptoms of a major depressive syndrome, a heterocyclic antidepressant should be considered early in treatment. As with adults, those children who have well-defined melancholia respond to pharmacotherapy. (Although the FDA has not approved the use of these agents for depression in children under the age of 12, the final decision rests with the doctor and parents.)

Children may require adult doses. **However, the practitioner should use caution, since young children seldom report adverse effects and may develop serious toxicity at relatively low doses** (e.g., 150 mg). Heterocyclics should be started at low doses (e.g., 25 mg by mouth/day) and increased by 25 mg every few days. Children generally require doses of 3 to 5 mg/kg. A clinical trial must be defined empirically by either alleviation of symptoms or the appearance of worrisome effects. Generally, the time course of response and the management of the clinical trial are the same as in adults. Abrupt withdrawal of heterocyclics should be avoided, since children may develop nausea, vomiting, drowsiness, headaches, and decreased appetite. The practitioner should avoid doses above 5 mg/kg, since children are more vulnerable to cardiovascular toxicity.

The treatment of depressions in adolescents is very similar to that in adults. The clinician should complete a careful diagnostic evaluation, since severe dysphoria in an adolescent may mark the beginning of either a depression or a schizophrenic episode.

2. Adverse Effects

The adverse effects of heterocyclics in children are very similar to those in adults (see Chapter 2). Most frequently reported are anticholinergic

---

*Since many of the currently used thymoleptic drugs are not tricyclic in structure, we have adopted this term to represent the various cyclic antidepressants. From: Baldessarini R. J.: Overview of recent advances in antidepressant pharmacology. Part II. *McLean Hosp J* 7:1–27, 1982.

effects, insomnia, tremulousness, restlessness, hypotension, hypertension (more common in children), and gastrointestinal upset. Other symptoms include weight gain, headaches, anorexia and weight loss, irritability, seizures, mild thrombocytopenia, skin rash, and precipitation of acute schizophrenic episodes. Most of the common effects abate within the first weeks of treatment; if they do not, the dose of medication should be lowered.

Imipramine in doses of 5 mg/kg body weight per day may affect cardiac functioning, but usually not at doses of 1 to 3 mg/kg per day. The Food and Drug Administration (FDA) (1975) approves protocols for imipramine research only if the daily dose does not exceed 90 mg for a 40-lb child, 160 mg for a 70-lb child, and 180 mg for an 80-lb child.

3. Overdose in Children

Overdose is an increasing problem in children. Imipramine poisoning can occur after the intake of 10 mg/kg (e.g., about 150 mg in a 3-year-old). Toxicity is initially inevitable after the ingestion of 20 mg/kg, and an overdose is potentially fatal following a dose of 40 mg/kg. The serious complications occur in children under 2 years old who often develop cardiac complications and require the installation of permanent cardiac pacemakers. Of reported fatalities from imipramine overdoses, all resulted from doses of 250 mg or more. Recovery has been reported after overdoses of up to 1800 mg.

All children poisoned by tricyclics should be admitted to the hospital for continuous cardiac monitoring for at least 24 hr. Tricyclic poisoning is characterized by the **"Three Cs": cardiac arrhythmia, convulsions, and coma.** Additionally, signs of atropine poisoning occur and include flushed and dry skin, dry mouth, mydriasis, hyperthermia, and urinary retention. Physo-

TABLE 4. Physostigmine Salicylate for Children 6 to 12 Years of Age

IV dose—PDR	Comments
For overdosage of imipramine in children: start with 0.5 mg and repeat at 5-min intervals to determine minimum effective dose; do not exceed 2 mg. Because of short duration of action, repeat at 30- to 60-min intervals as necessary. Inject *slowly* to reduce possibility of physostigmine-induced seizures. (Note: Manufacturer does not state minimum age for which physostigmine is safe to use.)	May also be given IM, as is generally done with adults. Ingestion of excessive antiparkinson agents, tricyclics, and major tranquilizers, especially thioridazine; also may lead to central anticholinergic toxicity or acute anticholinergic syndrome responsive to physostigmine. Overdose of physostigmine can lead to cholinergic crisis.

stigmine, an atropine antagonist (see Chapter 2) that penetrates the blood–brain barrier, is an effective antidote when used in the first 12 hr. In children, an intramuscular dose of 0.5 mg physostigmine salicylate should be administered. It may be repeated at 5-min intervals but should not exceed 2 mg. If effective, the dose should be repeated within 30 to 60 min. The injection should be given slowly to avoid physostigmine-induced convulsions, cardiac arrhythmias, respiratory arrest, and cholinergic excess (see Table 4).

C. Monoamine Oxidase Inhibitors

At present, MAOIs should be used only as an experimental treatment, since there have been few clinical trials to determine either efficacy or safety in children.

V. BIPOLAR AFFECTIVE DISORDERS

A. Introduction

Since Anthony and Scott described manic–depressive illness in a prepubescent boy in 1960, there have been additional case reports as well as accounts of successful treatment of selected children with lithium carbonate. Ten criteria have been proposed for the diagnosis of bipolar affective illness in children. Since that time, various investigators have attempted to refine these criteria. In 1979, Davis described "manic–depressive variant syndrome of childhood," characterized by the following: (1) affective storms, (2) family history of affective disorder, (3) hyperactivity, (4) disturbed personal relationships, and (5) absence of psychotic thought disorder. Although not required to make the diagnosis, associated symptoms include sleep disturbance, attention deficit disorder, abnormal EEG, and neurological problems.

Bipolar affective disorders are more common in adolescents than was previously thought. In this age group, manic–depressive illness may not uncommonly be confused with schizophrenia. Also, some patients present atypically with antisocial behaviors and aggressive acting out. When bipolar illness is diagnosed in adolescents, use of lithium should be considered.

B. Lithium

Lithium may play a number of roles in child psychiatry. It has successfully been used to treat "manic–depressive variant syndrome of childhood" (particularly in those with a lithium-responsive parent with manic–depressive illness). Also, lithium has been reported to decrease aggressive behavior and hyperactivity in some autistic children, but it is probably not effective for the treatment of attention deficit disorder. Some children, however, who manifest aggressiveness, explosiveness, and hyperactivity and have not responded to other medications might respond to lithium. Others have reported that lithium has a stabilizing influence on children who have periodic disturbances in mood and behavior. It must be emphasized, however, that although children appear to tolerate lithium well acutely, neither the efficacy nor the long-term safety of lithium has been acceptably demonstrated. Moreover, to date, the FDA has not approved the use of lithium in children under 12 years of age, which means that physicians electing to use this treatment in a selected child should exercise appropriate caution (see Chapter 12). More widespread use of lithium in children should be restricted to carefully designed, institutionally approved protocols.

VI. ENURESIS

A. Introduction

Nocturnal or primary enuresis is the most common type of enuresis and is usually present from infancy. Its etiologies are not completely known. In 2% of cases, it is caused by pyelonephritis or urinary tract malformation. Diabetes mellitus and diabetes insipidus should be ruled out as well. In about 10%, enuresis is symptomatic of an acute emotional disorder or family stress.

Nocturnal or primary enuresis is part of a sleep disorder. The enuretic episode begins in stage 4, not during REM sleep. When the sleep pattern changes to stage 1 or 2, the patient urinates. Some of these patients have a history of EEG disturbances, sleepwalking or nocturia, and a family history of this disorder. Enuresis persists in 10 to 15% of 4- to 5-year-olds. By 7 years of age, 10% are still bedwetters, and by 18 years, only 1 to 3% are estimated to still have enuretic episodes. Obviously, these symptoms often cause considerable distress to a child.

Other types of enuresis include (1) diurnal enuresis—the child who is wet during the day as well as at night; these children are more likely to have an organic or emotional disorder; and (2) secondary enuresis, which follows a completely dry period of several months and is generally a regressive response to stress.

B. Therapeutic Methods

Methods of treating nocturnal enuresis include:

1. Treatment of the underlying organic disease.

2. Supportive treatment, consisting of interviews with the child and parents to discuss the symptom and its impact. The clinician should emphasize that most children will outgrow this disorder and that punishment is useless and, indeed, harmful to the child.
3. Individual or family therapy or both. This may be beneficial when a primary emotional disorder exists.
4. Enuresis alarm (buzzer). A mat attached to a buzzer is placed on the child's bed. It rings and awakens the child when he wets. In time, the child will wake up before wetting and eventually—within 4 or 5 months—will sleep through the night and remain dry. The procedure has a success rate of 75% but is not recommended until the child is about 5½ years old. (This form of treatment is very common in Great Britain.)
5. Medication. The antidepressants amitriptyline and imipramine are effective in the short-term control of bedwetting. Imipramine's effect on nocturnal enuresis remains unclear, but there are several theories. One postulates that these children have immature bladders, characterized by decreased capacity and increased irritability, which leads to poor bladder contractions and enuresis. Imipramine has parasympatholytic (atropinelike) actions which may relax the detrussor muscle and decrease muscle irritability and involuntary contractions. Another theory relates imipramine's effect to the normal sleep pattern. In stages 1 and 2 sleep, there is lower intravesical pressure and fewer spontaneous bladder contractions than in stages 3 and 4, when enuresis occurs. Imipramine increases the time in stage 2 sleep and diminishes the time in stages 3 and 4, when an increase in bladder pressure occurs.

Enuresis should be treated with drugs only when the symptom itself is causing severe emotional distress and other safer methods of treatment have been ineffective. Imipramine should not be used alone but should be viewed as an adjunctive treatment. The long-term effects of these agents in children are not well defined, and they should be used only with extreme caution. The child should be at least school age, since the risks of potential overdose with heterocyclics are serious in younger children. All parents should be reminded to keep medication out of the child's reach. If an overdose occurs, the child should be given rapid medical attention (see Table 2).

Antidepressant drugs are usually well tolerated in children. The most frequent adverse effects are irritability, headache, dizziness, insomnia, or gastrointestinal upset. The dosage range of the tricyclics for the treatment of enuresis is 10 to 100 mg (1 to 2 mg/kg of imipramine) taken entirely at bedtime or in divided doses. Older children require a dose of at least 25 to 50 mg. Both the dosage and schedule should be individually determined (see Table 5). Generally, the drug should be administered until the child is dry

TABLE 5. Antidepressants for Children

Generic name (brand name)	Preparations (mg)	Oral dose—PDR	Comments
Imipramine (Tofranil®)	Tablets: 10, 25, 50	Dose of 2.5 mg/kg should not be exceeded in childhood. ECG changes have been reported in children receiving twice this amount. Enuresis: in children over 6, 25 mg 1 hr before bedtime; if no success in 1 week, increase to 50 mg. In children over 12: 75 mg nightly. Manufacturer does not recommend more than 75 mg/day.	See text for usage in MBD, depression, and school phobia. Manufacturer states that use of drug for conditions other than enuresis is not recommended. When stopping, dose should be tapered.
Amitriptyline (Elavil®)	Tablets: 10, 25, 50		Manufacturer states that drug is not recommended for children under 12.

every night for 3 months. In contrast to the treatment of depression, its onset of action is rapid (suggesting a different mechanism of action).

A high relapse rate follows withdrawal of the heterocyclics. When relapse occurs, the same drug should be reinstituted for at least another 3 months. This often produces lasting symptom control. Although short- and possibly longer-term control of enuresis is effective with heterocyclics, the risks of overdose, as well as the unknown long-term effects of these drugs, should be carefully considered.

Although imipramine has an immediate short-term effect, both the buzzer and placebo still exert a positive effect 4 months after initiation of treatment. They both decrease the frequency of enuretic episodes.

VII. SCHOOL REFUSAL

School refusal, one aspect of **separation anxiety disorder** (DSM-III), is characterized by fear or dread of going to school in the morning and often starts after a vacation or illness. This syndrome may be a depressive equivalent manifesting itself as separation anxiety, but it also may herald the onset of childhood schizophrenia. When it is a manifestation of depression, school refusal is observed much more often in girls than in boys.

School refusal may be an emergency in child psychiatry. The longer the child stays out of school, the more difficult it is to return. The parents should be supported in their attempts to help the child go back to school. For example, they should be permitted to accompany the child and remain at school for short periods if necessary.

Some reports indicate that a comprehensive therapeutic program without drugs is effective in some younger children and in those with short-lived phobia. Adolescents, however, who are more likely to have been symptomatic for a long period, generally respond poorly to the various therapies. Drugs should be administered when other forms of therapy fail to produce results within 1 to 2 weeks. Several medications have been tried, including benzodiazepines, amphetamines, antipsychotics, MAOIs, and heterocyclic antidepressants. Some clinicians, for example, have used benzodiazepines as an adjunct to other therapeutic approaches, but this practice has not been studied extensively enough to document its objective advantages.

More vigorous pharmacotherapy, such as the use of imipramine, may be employed if the child's parents are reliable and cooperative or if the patient is hospitalized. Although other heterocyclics may be effective, imipramine is the only agent whose current use has been well documented. There is also some evidence that imipramine is more effective in adolescents than in younger children. School-phobic patients who respond best to imipramine have accompanying depressive symptoms and may have a family history of severe depressions.

Imipramine, in addition to increasing school return, also improves the child's subjective feeling of well-being. In most children, imipramine should be administered initially in doses of 25 mg/day for 3 days, then 50 mg for 4 days. By the second week, the child should be taking 75 mg/day. Since school children are not in the age group that is most susceptible to adverse effects, this initial dose usually is safe. Thereafter, the dose may be increased by 25 mg every few days. A dose of 75 to 150 mg (approximately 3 to 5 mg/kg) usually is adequate, but the amount should be individualized. Occasionally, higher doses (up to 200 mg) are necessary. Clinical effects usually occur 4 to 6 weeks after instituting treatment. The endpoint is the appearance of a positive clinical effect or prohibitive adverse effects. Children develop adverse effects similar to adults. The dangers of imipramine are described in detail in the preceding enuresis section. The most common symptoms in children include headache, dizziness, insomnia, and gastrointestinal symptoms. Some improvement resulting from pharmacotherapy usually occurs within the first 2 weeks, but full clinical effect may require 2 to 3 months. After complete symptom remission, the heterocyclic should be tapered gradually (to avoid uncomfortable withdrawal symptoms) over the next 3 months.

When a school phobia persists despite outpatient treatment, hospitalization is indicated. Under these circumstances, an antipsychotic agent occasionally is needed to control the child's panic about leaving home. Parents often need support and even medication to cope with this separation.

VIII. ANXIETY DISORDERS

Anxiety may be a symptom of many different emotional disorders. In DSM-III, "anxiety disorders of childhood and adolescence" have been divided into three types: separation anxiety disorder (which includes school refusal discussed above), avoidant disorder of childhood and adolescence, and overanxious disorder. The use of antianxiety agents, however, has not been specifically studied for any of these three categories.

Crisis intervention aimed at facilitating communication with the child/ adolescent and his family can help to relieve anxiety and may be the only therapy necessary. Treatment might consist of both individual and family therapy. When a child's anxiety is disabling enough to interfere with normal activities such as attending school, however, the use of antianxiety agents should be considered. First, though, the child should be evaluated carefully to rule out more serious problems such as depression or psychosis.

In children with less severe anxiety who require medication, antihistamines have been most commonly used to treat acute or reactive anxiety secondary to external stress and chronic anxiety manifested by insomnia or impaired functioning. Since clinicians have limited experience with benzodiazepines in children, and since disinhibition and exacerbation of behavioral disorders may occur, these agents have limited usefulness in younger patients (see Table 6). Some adolescents, however, may benefit from benzodiazepine therapy. In these cases, the clinician should attempt to rule out an impulse disorder, since chlordiazepoxide in particular may lead to disinhibition.

Another use of these drugs is to treat hyperventilation, which is characterized by severe anxiety, rapid breathing, and occasionally fainting. It is common in adolescent girls and may also be seen in latency-aged children. If "suggestion" or breathing into a paper bag does not abort the attack, oral or IV diazepam may be used. Intravenous diazepam should be used cautiously, since it may depress respiration. Supportive therapy and the use of minor tranquilizers are effective in the treatment of conversion reactions as well. The patient should always be carefully evaluated to determine the precipitant of the episode.

A. Antihistamines

Before the introduction of the antipsychotics, the antihistamines diphenhydramine (Benadryl®) and hydroxyzine (Atarax®, Vistaril®) were used to treat psychosis and behavior disorders in children. They are now administered primarily as antianxiety agents and are generally the preferred agent in younger children.

Diphenhydramine also has been used to treat prepubescent children with

TABLE 6. Minor Tranquilizers in Children 6 to 12 Years of Age

Generic name (brand name)	Preparations (mg)	Oral dose—PDR	Comments
Benzodiazepines			
Diazepam (Valium®)	Scored tablets: 2, 5, 10	3–10 mg/day in divided doses; increase as needed	1. Not for use in children under 6 months. 2. Can use 5 or 10 mg to treat acute anxiety or severe hyperventilation. 3. For sleep: 2–10 mg h.s.
Chlordiazepoxide (Librium®)	Capsules: 5, 10, 25 Tablets: 5. 10, 25	10–30 mg/day in divided doses	1. Not recommended for children under 6. 2. May cause excitation. 3. Parenteral dose not recommended for children under 12.
Diphenylmethane derivatives			
Diphenhydramine (Benadryl®)	Elixir: 12.5 mg/5 ml (1 tsp) Capsules: 25, 50	Infants and children up to 20 lb: 0.5–1 tsp 3 or 4 times/day (37.5–50 mg/day) Children over 20 lb: 1–2 tsp 3 or 4 times/day (37.5–100 mg/day) not to exceed 300 mg/day	1. May lose some efficacy in pubescent children. 2. May use IM or IV route for acute extrapyramidal symptoms; however, there is a slight risk of anaphylaxis. 3. May use 25–50 mg h.s. for sleep. 4. Tolerance may develop. 5. In young children, antihistamines may produce excitation.
Hydroxyzine (Atarax®)	Tablets: 10, 25, 50, 100 Syrup: 10 mg/5 ml (1 tsp)	Children under 6: 50 mg/day in divided doses; over 6: 50–100 mg/day in divided doses	Average range of daily dose: 20–100 mg
(Vistaril®)	Capsules: 25, 50, 100 Oral suspension: 25 mg/5 ml (1 tsp)		

impulse problems, especially of neurogenic origin, and young children with tension-relieving repetitive motor activities such as tics, head banging, and body rocking. Documentation of these effects, however, is limited. Other uses include the treatment of transient insomnia and antipsychotic-induced extrapyramidal symptoms.

Diphenhydramine should not be used continuously, since children may become tolerant to its sedative or hypnotic effect. Contraindications include bronchial asthma, narrow-angle glaucoma, and pyloroduodenal and bladder neck obstruction. The drug is better tolerated in children than in adults and usually is effective at doses that do not cause drowsiness.

Hydroxyzine may be a safe and effective alternative to diphenhydramine for the treatment of anxiety in children. Adverse effects include drowsiness and dry mouth.

B. Benzodiazepines

Although clinical reports have suggested that the benzodiazepines are beneficial in children for the treatment of anxiety associated with neurotic conflict and situational disorders, scientific data about the effectiveness of these agents is limited. They also have been useful in the treatment of tics, transient sleep disorders, and persistent night terrors. Diazepam, chlordiazepoxide, or oxazepam (Serax®) should be administered only briefly, intermittently, and as an adjunct to other treatment modalities. If symptoms persist, a more comprehensive treatment approach should be developed.

Oral diazepam in children less than 6 months old has not been studied adequately, nor has the use of chlordiazepoxide or oxazepam in children under 6 years of age. The efficacy and safety of parenteral diazepam and chlordiazepoxide have not been established in children less than 12 years old. In adults (and probably in older children), intramuscular absorption is incomplete and erratic, so this is not the preferred route. Adverse effects from benzodiazepines include nausea, ataxia, constipation, skin sensitivity, drowsiness, and, rarely, syncope. In some children, chlordiazepoxide may cause paradoxical reactions such as acute rage, excitement, and disorganization of thought processes. If this occurs, oxazepam might be preferable. Benzodiazepines are not recommended in hyperactive or psychotic children.

C. Other Sedative–Hypnotics

Barbiturates should not be used for sedation or sleep, since they commonly produce a paradoxical response, resulting in excitation in younger children.

Meprobamate (Equanil®, Miltown®) has been widely used and abused among adults for many years, but no well-controlled studies demonstrate their effectiveness in children. Because of experience with this drug in adults, however, and the existence of less toxic and less addicting antianxiety drugs, meprobamate should not be used in children.

IX. SLEEP DISORDERS

A. Insomnia

Persistent insomnia in latency-age children and adolescents indicates either a situational crisis, such as a death in the family, or a psychological disturbance. Flurazepam (Dalmane®), a very useful and safe hypnotic in the adult, should not be administered to children under 6 years of age and has not been widely used or studied in adolescents. In children with persistent insomnia not responsive to nonbiological measures, antihistamines such as diphenhydramine are beneficial for short-term intermittent use. The usual effective dose of diphenhydramine is 25 to 50 mg orally at bedtime.

Promethazine (Phenergan®) is a phenothiazine that is not used as an antipsychotic agent. Because its main properties are antihistaminic and seda- tive, it is commonly administered for insomnia secondary to anxiety. It can be prescribed for intermittent, short-term use. The drug produces a quiet sleep from which the child can be awakened easily. Autonomic effects include dry mouth, blurred vision, and dizziness. Paradoxical reactions such as hyperexcitability and nightmares have been reported with oral doses of 75 to 125 mg. There have been occasional reports of hypotension and rare cases of leukopenia (see Table 7).

Chloral hydrate (Noctec®) has been commonly used for the treatment of insomnia secondary to anxiety and the initial stages of CNS-stimulant administration. It should not be used if the child has renal or hepatic impair- ment or a history of previous sensitivity to the drug. Adverse effects include gastric irritation and, very rarely, excitement and delirium.

Phenobarbital (Luminal®) is not recommended because it may cause paradoxical excitement.

B. Nightmares

Nightmares ("REM anxiety attacks") are frightening dreams that occur during the middle or latter part of REM sleep. Unlike night terrors, the dreamer does not develop markedly increased heart and respiratory rate. The nightmares can be remembered in detail if the dreamer is aroused. They are usually transient and intermittent, but if they persist, the child should be evaluated for an underlying emotional disturbance.

TABLE7. Hypnotics for Children 6 to 12 Years of Age

Generic name (brand name)	Preparations (mg)	Oral dose—PDR	Comments
Chloral hydrate (Noctec®)	Capsules: 250, 500 Syrup: 500 mg/5 ml (1 tsp)	50 mg/kg h.s.; maximum 1 g for single dose	1. 250–500 mg is usually effective. 2. May precipitate acute intermittent porphyria.
Diphenhydramine (Benadryl®)	See Table 6	25 mg for sedative dose	1. 50 mg is usual hypnotic dose.
Promethazine (Phenergan®)	Tablets: 12.5, 25, 50 Syrup: 6.25 mg/5 ml, 25 mg/5 ml	12.5–25 mg at bedtime will induce a quiet sleep from which patient can be easily aroused	1. Paradoxical excitation has been reported in children receiving 75–125 mg as a single dose. 2. Although it acts as a sedative, it is in the phenothiazine family. 3. May use up to 100 mg h.s.
Phenobarbital (Luminal®)			1. Not recommended in children because of risk of paradoxical excitation.

C. Night Terrors (Sleep Terror Disorder)

Night terrors (pavor nocturnus or sleep terror disorder) may develop because of sexual or aggressive conflict or following a traumatic event. Generally, they are transient, and the parents can be reassured that the child will outgrow them. If they occur frequently and persist over a period of months, however, the child may have an underlying disturbance and should be evaluated.

Night terrors occur during the first third of the night during stages 3 and 4 sleep and are most common in children 3 to 5 years of age. The child awakens with a scream and shows signs of autonomic arousal, including increased pulse and respiratory rate, sweating, and motor activity which may include sleepwalking. If awakened, the child seems disoriented and frightened but in the morning will not remember the event. The EEG will show an awake alpha pattern.

Several uncontrolled reports suggest that imipramine, 10 to 50 mg h.s., or diazepam, 2 to 5 mg h.s., is beneficial for persistent night terrors in some children. Both drugs may be effective because they suppress stage 4 sleep. However, these findings are still experimental and need to be further investigated before these agents can be recommended for general use.

D. Sleepwalking (Sleepwalking Disorder)

Sleepwalking disorder also occurs in the first third of the night during NREM sleep. It begins in children who are between 6 and 12 years old and may last several years. Predisposing factors include seizure disorders, CNS infections, and trauma. During the episode, it is difficult to communicate with or awaken the child. Generally, on awakening, the child does not remember the event. Because benzodiazepines shorten stage 4 sleep, they have been administered to children who endanger themselves by sleepwalking. However, these drugs should be used with caution (see Chapter 4).

E. Narcolepsy

Narcolepsy is irresistible sleep lasting for 15 min or less. The episodes begin in adolescence or young adulthood and can be treated with stimulants. Imipramine has been used for the treatment of the associated symptoms of cataplexy, sleep paralysis, and hypnagogic hallucinations, but it is ineffective for narcolepsy itself. In this situation, because potential benefits do not outweigh the risks, imipramine should not be used.

X. ATTENTION DEFICIT DISORDER WITH HYPERACTIVITY (MINIMAL BRAIN DYSFUNCTION)

A. Introduction

The attention deficit disorder (ADD) with hyperactivity (DSM-III) (or minimal brain dysfunction syndrome) is characterized by hyperactivity, decreased attention span, distractibility, impulsive and aggressive behavior, and restlessness. Some children also manifest low self-esteem, emotional lability, and difficulty in forming stable relationships. It is very important to emphasize that hyperactivity is not a pathognomonic symptom of ADD but, like anxiety, crosses diagnostic categories. The underlying disorder should be diagnosed before the hyperactivity is treated. Similarly, a learning disorder does not necessarily indicate ADD and must be evaluated thoroughly.

Learning-disabled children have been distinguished from ADD children. Mothers of the latter report more difficulties with control and obedience than mothers of learning-disabled children. These children, on the other hand, make more mistakes than ADD children on a test of rapid serial naming. Nevertheless, this is a fine distinction, and many children with ADD have learning disorders. However, those children with just a learning disorder alone do not benefit from CNS stimulants.

Estimates of the prevalence of ADD are varied, but several American authors place it at 5 to 10% of all school children. In other countries such as England, the reported rate is markedly less because of differences in diagnostic criteria.

These children are usually brought for help while in nursery school, kindergarten, or first grade, since their disruptive behavior is not tolerated in a more structured school setting. Some present several years later because of unexplained school failure. The diagnosis should be made only following a psychological, social, and educational evaluation. The Conners Parent–Teacher Questionnaire is now used frequently to help confirm clinical impressions. Once the diagnosis is made with some certainty, a comprehensive treatment plan should be developed that includes the use of medication accompanied by special education, behavior modification, counseling, and/or psychotherapy for both child and parent.

Central nervous system stimulants such as methylphenidate (Ritalin®) and d-amphetamine (Dexedrine®) are the drugs of choice in the treatment of children with ADD. Few disagree that there are many areas of objective improvement in selected children while on drugs. They improve the behavior of 75 to 90% of ADD children over 6 years of age by decreasing hyperactivity, impulsivity, and aggression and by increasing goal-directed behavior and concentration and social interaction. However, they have not been shown to increase learning, nor do they significantly change overall outcome.

Some children first come to clinical attention during adolescence because of poor school performance or delinquent behavior, and clinical evaluation reveals a history of hyperkinesis or ADD. In such cases, a trial of *d*-amphetamine or methylphenidate is indicated. Even though this group of patients often exhibits impulsive and antisocial traits, they usually do not abuse CNS stimulants.

Central nervous system stimulants and other drugs recommended for children with ADD may also be useful in the treatment of children with hyperkinesis associated with organic brain damage or mental retardation. Children with hyperactivity and behavior disorders severe enough to require hospitalization usually respond better to antipsychotics than to CNS stimulants. Haloperidol has proved particularly useful in controlling aggressive hyperactive children, even though it does not improve learning. Chlorpromazine and thioridazine also are recommended for psychotic children with hyperactivity.

B. CNS Stimulants

The CNS stimulants used for attention deficit disorder with hyperactivity include methylphenidate, *d*-amphetamine, and pemoline (Cylert®). Methylphenidate and *d*-amphetamine are preferred because they are more effective (see Table 6). Methylphenidate produces less anorexia than *d*-amphetamine and therefore is the drug of choice for the treatment of ADD with hyperactivity. Because of growth suppression attributed to psychostimulants, periodic drug holidays (i.e., on weekends and during vacations) are recommended. This allows for rebound growth and also an opportunity to see if the child still requires medication.

1. Mechanism of Action

Amphetamines and related stimulants are sympathomimetics that have potent central stimulant effects and less potent cardiovascular effects. Amphetamine acts primarily on the midbrain, the reticular activating system, the hypothalamus, and the limbic structures.

Methylphenidate, which has a similar biochemical structure and pharmacological action, also probably acts in the lower brain. It is less effective than the amphetamines in stimulating mental and motor activity.

The CNS stimulants increase attention span in children with ADD. Research suggests that amphetamines stimulate the reticular activating system, increasing alertness in hyperactive children. This leads to an increase in focused attention and thereby a decreased response to other stimuli.

Researchers have compared the autonomic system activity of ADD children with normal children by measuring heart rate, skin conductance, and skin temperature. No significant differences were found in the base-line levels in the two groups. Since CNS stimulants increase autonomic acitivity level, it is postulated that ADD children may perform better at high autonomic base levels or that their optimal arousal levels may be higher than those of normal children.

2. Types of CNS Stimulants

a. Methylphenidate

i. Principles of Use. **Methylphenidate (Ritalin®) is the drug of choice for the treatment of ADD in children 6 years of age or older.** In several well-designed studies, methylphenidate was superior to placebo in improving the behavior of these children.

ii. Chemistry. Methylphenidate is a piperidine derivative with the following chemical structure:

iii. Adverse Effects. Anorexia is the most troublesome unwanted effect caused by methylphenidate, although it is less severe than with *d*-amphetamine. Taking the drug at mealtime or lowering the dose decreases this effect. The child also may become tolerant to anorexia within the first week or two of treatment. Weight loss occurs at all doses, but particularly at more than 20 mg/day.

Methylphenidate also causes mild, transient insomnia, tachycardia marked by increased heart rate at rest, abdominal pain, increased motor activity, and withdrawn behavior or tearfulness. Occasionally, there have been reports of psychotic behavior. Methylphenidate may lower the seizure threshold in children with a history of seizures. In such cases, either discontinue methylphenidate or add an anticonvulsant.

Methylphenidate may inhibit the metabolism of anticoagulants, anticonvulsants [phenobarbital, phenytoin (Dilantin® and others), and primidone (Mysoline®)], phenylbutazone (Butazolidin®), and heterocyclic antidepressants. Therefore, if any of these drugs are coadministered with methylphenidate, its dose should be decreased.

Habituation to CNS stimulants has not been reported in children. There is no evidence that taking these drugs predisposes to later addiction.

iv. Clinical Application (see Table 8). Methylphenidate is useful in children 6 years of age and older. The starting dose depends on the child's age and size but is usually 0.25 mg/kg daily. To start, the child is generally given 5 mg/day at breakfast or 5 mg b.i.d. at breakfast and lunch. The drug should be administered 30 min before the meal because it is best absorbed at an acid pH (milk, in particular, interferes with its absorption). If the child is below average or of average weight, the medication might be administered after the meal, since it suppresses appetite.

The dose can be increased weekly in 5- to 10-mg increments until the child improves or develops adverse effects. The usual recommended average

TABLE 8. CNS Stimulants for Children 6 to 12 Years of Age

Generic name (brand name)	Preparations (mg)	Oral dose—PDR	Comments
Methylphenidate (Ritalin®)	Scored tablets: 5, 10, 20	6 and over: 5 mg before breakfast and lunch, with gradual increments of 5–10 mg/week. Daily dosage over 60 mg is not recommended. If improvement not noticed in a month drug should be discontinued.	1. Average daily dose range: 10–40 mg (usually 20 mg or less is sufficient). 2. May give entire dose in morning. 3. If persistent anorexia, may give dose at mealtime.
d-Amphetamine (Dexedrine®)	Tablets: 5 Elixir: 5 mg/5 ml (1 tsp) Sustained-release capsules: 5, 10, 15	6 and over: start with 5 mg 1 or 2 times/day; dosage may be raised 5 mg/week until optimum dose is reached; only rarely is a dose over 40 mg necessary.	1. Average daily dose is 5–15 mg. 2. Generally, one dose in morning is sufficient; sometimes noon or 3 p.m. dose is necessary. 3. No controlled studies in 3- to 5-year-old children.
Pemoline (Cylert®)	Tablets: 18.75, 37.5, 75	6 and over: Start with 37.5 mg in morning. Increase by increments of 18.75/week until desired response. The mean effective dose is 56.25–75 mg/day. The maximum recommended dose is 112.5	1. Give dose once a day. 2. Improvement may not be evident until third or fourth week.

daily dose is 20 to 60 mg or 1.0 to 2.0 mg/kg body weight daily. At doses over 20 mg/day, there is an increased incidence of weight loss.

Once the child is stabilized, one morning dose of 20 mg is usually satisfactory. If the child is hyperactive during the afternoon school hours, however, raising the morning dose or giving an additional noon dose is effective. To monitor the effects of the drug, the clinician should obtain information about the child from several different sources, including both parents and teachers. Some physicians discontinue the drug on holidays and weekends and during the summer and then reevaluate the child in the fall when school starts.

The optimum length of treatment has not been determined. The child's continued need for the drug should be evaluated every 6 months by stopping the medication and observing the child's behavior for 1 to 2 weeks. In general, the drug is often stopped when the child is 10 to 12 years old, since hyperkinesis improves with puberty. Although hyperactivity usually decreases, restlessness, poor attention span, and learning disorders often persist. In one study, methylphenidate in doses of 20 to 60 mg/day was useful in adolescents with a history of ADD, particularly those with learning difficulties and EEG abnormalities.

Methylphenidate initially suppresses growth in height and weight. However, a follow-up study of adolescents who took methylphenidate for at least 6 months showed no evidence of retardation of growth or height. The data also suggest that growth rebound, which occurs following termination of the drug, is proportional to growth suppression. Since growth suppression is greater with *d*-amphetamine than with methylphenidate, rebound is greater after discontinuing *d*-amphetamine than after methylphenidate.

A rare effect of methylphenidate treatment is the development of tics in children with a family history of tics. There has been at least one case report of the development of Tourette's disorder following treatment with methylphenidate, 60 mg/day. The syndrome persisted after medication was stopped. Physicians prescribing psychostimulants should inquire about a history of tics in patients and their families. There have also been reports of acute dyskinesias in children and adolescents taking methylphenidate.

b. *d*-Amphetamine

i. Principles of Use. If methylphenidate is ineffective in the treatment of ADD children, *d*-amphetamine should be used. In several controlled studies, *d*-amphetamine was superior to placebo in the treatment of children with hyperactivity and distractability. It is contraindicated in children with hypertension, hyperthyroidism, glaucoma, agitated states, psychosis, and hyperactivity associated wtih psychotic symptoms. It should not be used within 7 days of discontinuation of an MAOI.

ii. Adverse Effects. Trasient adverse effects include insomnia, increased hyperactivity, decreased appetite, epigastric pain, nausea, and vomiting. The anorexia is often more severe than with methylphenidate. Within 1 week, these symptoms decrease. If they continue beyond this time, the dose can be reduced. Approximately 10% of children will become increasingly hyperactive with this drug. *d*-Amphetamine may also change insulin requirements and may decrease the hypotensive effect of guanethidine. Dyskinesias and psychotic episodes occur rarely. Tachycardia, headaches, fine tremors of the extremities, irritability, tension, and crying with little provocation are toxic effects.

iii. Clinical Application: Children 3 to 5 Years Old (see Table 8). Although the manufacturer recommends *d*-amphetamine, no controlled studies demonstrate the effectiveness of this drug in this age group. Therefore, this drug should generally be avoided in these younger children.

iv. Clinical Application: Children 6 Years Old or Older (see Table 8). Depending on the age and size of the child, *d*-amphetamine should be started in doses of 5 mg once or twice per day and increased by 5 mg each week. The dose range is 10 to 40 mg/day, with an average of 20 mg/day. *d*-Amphetamine peaks in the blood in 2 hr and is excreted within 24 to 48 hr. Therefore, divided doses may be necessary and are usually given before breakfast and before lunch. Many children can manage on one dose each day, particularly in those who develop insomnia when the drug is given late in the afternoon. If a child develops tolerance to the drug, a dose somewhat lower than the usual amount can be alternated every 2 days with the effective dose.

Improvement in symptoms usually occurs within a few days after the therapeutic dose is reached. If symptoms do not improve within 2 or 3 weeks, the drug should be discontinued and an alternate medicine chosen. Many therapists give the child a "drug vacation" over long school holidays or during the summer and then reevaluate the child's needs for continued treatment. The drug is usually stopped at puberty.

c. Magnesium Pemoline

Magnesium pemoline is a less commonly used drug that can be administered to children who exhibit a poor response or prohibitive adverse effects with the standard CNS stimulants. It is structurally different from amphetamine and methylphenidate. It has a similar pharmacological action without significant sympathomimetic activity. The onset of action is slower than that of methylphenidate and amphetamine, usually occurring within 3 to 6 weeks. Pemoline has a longer duration of action than these drugs and can be administered in a single morning dose. Caution should be exercised in children with renal failure, since pemoline is excreted primarily by the kidneys.

Pemoline causes anorexia and initial weight loss, which persist for about 3 weeks. Other adverse effects include transient insomnia, headache, stomachache, nausea, skin rash, depression, and hallucinations. Changes in liver function tests occur but revert to normal when the drug is discontinued. Unlike d-amphetamine and methylphenidate, pemoline causes no heart rate or blood pressure changes.

Similar to the case report of Tourette's disorder developing after treatment with methylphenidate, tics were observed in a 10-year-old boy treated with pemoline. The symptoms in this child, however, diminished when pemoline was discontinued. The patient had also been treated with thioridazine, which the authors suggest may have sensitized the patient to the dopaminergic effect of pemoline, thus leading to Tourette's syndrome.

Depending on age and size, a child should be started on 18.75 mg or 37.5 mg/day of pemoline. The dosage should be increased by 18.75 mg/week until improvement or adverse effects occur. The manufacturer states that the mean effective dose is 56.25 to 75 mg/day and does not recommend more than 112.5 mg/day (see Table 8).

C. Other Drugs Used in the Treatment of Attention Deficit Disorder with Hyperactivity

Although the CNS stimulants are the drugs most commonly used, children with attention deficit disorder and hyperactivity do not represent a homogeneous group, and some may improve on other drugs. For children who do not tolerate the CNS stimulants, another drug may be chosen, such as imipramine. It should be remembered, however, that small overdoses of this drug can cause fatalities in children, and recommended doses can cause seizures. Unlike its action in adult depression, the effect of imipramine on the symptoms of ADD is immediate. Also, contrary to adult use, tolerance may develop to the therapeutic effects. The dosage range for children 5 to 12 years old is 25 to 100 mg/day.

Other alternatives include the antipsychotic drugs and minor tranquilizers. Although d-amphetamine and chlorpromazine are equally effective in reducing hyperactivity, d-amphetamine also improves attentiveness. Hydroxyzine may be used but is significantly less effective than d-amphetamine or chlorpromazine. The benzodiazepines are used rarely in children with ADD with hyperactivity. Although some studies show that they are somewhat effective in treating ADD, others suggest they may worsen this condition. No controlled studies demonstrate the efficacy of diphenhydramine in ADD. Barbiturates are contraindicated, since they can exacerbate hyperactivity.

Various authors have investigated the use of caffeine in the treatment of

ADD. Despite early studies suggesting its usefulness, more recent research indicates that it is probably not significantly better than placebo.

Psychotic children with hyperactivity generally should not be given CNS stimulants, since their psychosis may be exacerbated.

D. Diet

A number of anecdotal reports have attributed dramatic improvement in the behavior of large numbers of hyperactive children to the Feingold or Kaiser–Permanente diet. This regimen eliminates foods with artificial coloring and flavoring, natural salicylates, and preservatives such as BHT and BHA. About 20,000 children are now estimated to be on this diet, and Feingold and other advocates claim improvement in about half of hyperactive children who follow his regimen.

Recent controlled studies, however, suggest a much less sanguine outlook for dietary treatment of ADD children. It is possible that a very small number of children may show some transient behavioral or learning impairment, detectable on a limited number of test instruments, following exposure to large quantities of food dyes or additives. These findings suggest that eliminating these substances is beneficial, but for a vast majority of children with this disorder, the Feingold diet provides no benefit that can be scientifically demonstrated. Rather, the large improvement rate reported by Feingold adherents is more likely attributable to the psychosocial impact of a major change, which must affect not only the child but his entire family. (Indeed, the dietary requirements are quite stringent.) This demonstrates the importance of psychosocial factors and the potential benefit from nonbiological therapy in this syndrome.

Similar to the disappointing results in scientific studies of the Feingold regimen, so-called orthomolecular therapies for hyperactive children have yielded no more than a placebo effect. In fact, material sold in "health food" stores is not regulated by the FDA, has variable composition, and has not infrequently been found to be contaminated with pesticides and heavy metals (such as lead). Moreover, the fat-soluble vitamins (A, D, E, and K) are not innocuous, and large doses can be toxic in children (and adults).

XI. CONDUCT DISORDERS

The DSM-III defines four types of "conduct disorders" that reflect the child's or adolescent's degree of aggression and socialization. The essential feature of these disorders is that the patient violates the rights of others and/or societal norms. These patients often come from chaotic or inconsistent homes, frequently have school difficulties, abuse substances, and may exhibit irritability and temper outbursts. Many are labeled "delinquents," whereas others have a history of attention deficit disorder.

Pharmacotherapy for these disorders has not been systematically studied. Many different drugs have been used; generally, the choice has depended on the predominant symptoms, i.e., aggression, irritability, underlying depression. As with most other disorders, drug treatment is used as an adjunct to psychotherapy and appropriate environmental manipulation.

XII. ANOREXIA NERVOSA

Anorexia nervosa is an eating disorder that occurs primarily in female adolescents. It is characterized by a morbid fear of obesity even during periods of weight loss and a conviction about being fat even when cachectic. The adolescent loses 25% of body weight and often has accompanying amenorrhea. Various approaches to treatment include a combination of the following: individual psychotherapy, family therapy, behavioral modification, and hospitalization.

If the patient presents in an acutely malnourished state, she requires hospitalization with close medical management. Once the patient is medically stable, the clinician can institute psychiatric treatment. Psychotropic drugs such as chlorpromazine and the antidepressants (e.g., amitriptyline) have occasionally been used as adjunctive treatment.

XIII. "BORDERLINE" CHILDREN

Although not specifically defined in DSM-III, many psychiatrists recognize another clinical syndrome, the "borderline" child. These children manifest overwhelming anxiety and panic, poorly defend against their impulses, act bizarrely, and may have a distorted sense of self. They are considered different from psychotic children because they have a somewhat higher level of defensive organization, better reality sense and reality testing, and they try to interact socially. Although psychosocial therapies are preferred, various investigators have prescribed imipramine in a dose just less than 5 mg/kg per day to depressed borderline children who were hospitalized. They observed improvement in peer interactions, uncontrollable behavior, and bizarre movements. Further research is necessary to define more specifically the nature of this syndrome in children and to determine effective treatment approaches.

XIV. CONCLUSION

Drug therapies for children should always be part of a comprehensive treatment plan that accounts for presenting symptoms, developmental and dynamic issues, family influences, and environmental factors. Recently, researchers and clinicians have defined more homogeneous diagnostic categories for childhood disorders and specific drug regimens for selected problems. In particular, we now have therapies that offer significant relief for acute psychosis, attention deficit disorders, and hyperactivity, enuresis, and acute anxiety. Moreover, investigators have reported the use of heterocyclic antidepressants in some childhood depressions and lithium in adolescent-onset bipolar illness. With continued research and wider clinical experience, the future promises drug treatments that are safer, more effective, and more widely applicable.

SELECTED READING

General

1. Burrel C.: How to obtain study medication and to file an IND—an open letter. *Psychopharmacol Bull* 9:240–241, 1973.
*2. Campbell M.: Psychopharmacology, in Noshpitz J. P. (ed): *Basic Handbook of Child Psychiatry*. New York, Basic Books, 1979, vol III, pp 376–409.
3. Conners C. K.: Psychopharmacological treatment of children, in DiMascio A., Shader R. (eds): *Clinical Handbook of Psychopharmacology*. New York, Science House, 1970, pp 281–287.
4. Conners C. K.: Rating scale for use in drug studies with children. *Psychopharmacol Bull* 9:24–29, 1973.
5. *Diagnostic and Statistical Manual of Mental Disorders (DSM-III)*, ed 3. Washington, American Psychiatric Association, 1978.
6. DiMascio A., Shader R. I.: Drug administration schedules. *Am J Psychiatry* 126:796–801, 1969.
*7. DiMascio A., Soltys J., Shader R. I.: Psychotropic side effects in children, in DiMascio A., Soltys J. (eds): *Drug Side Effects*. Baltimore, Williams & Wilkins, 1970, pp 253–260.
8. Engelhardt D. M., Polizos P.: Adverse effects of pharmacotherapy in childhood psychosis, in Lipton M. A., DiMascio A., Killam K. F. (eds): *Psychopharmacology: A Generation of Progress*. New York, Raven Press, 1978, p 1463.
9. Fish B.: Children's psychopharmacology unit. *Psychopharmacol Bull* 6:27–28, 1970.
10. Fish B.: Drug use in psychiatric disorders of children. *Am J Psychiatry* 124:31–36, 1968.
11. Gittelman-Klein R., Spitzer R. L., Cantwell D.: Diagnostic classifications and psychopharmacological indications, in Werry J. S. (ed): *Pediatric Psychopharmacology*. New York, Brunner-Mazel, 1978, pp 136–137.

*Recommended reading.

12. Philips I.: Research directions in child psychiatry. *Am J Psychiatry* 137:1436–1439, 1980.
13. Smith W. R.: Determinants influencing the use of psychoactive drugs in the management of psychiatric emergencies in children and adolescents, in Morrison G. C. (eds): *Emergencies in Child Psychiatry*. Springfield, Illinois, Charles C. Thomas, 1975, pp 415–425.
14. Werry J. S.: The use of psychotropic drugs in children. *J Am Acad Child Psychiatry* 16:446–468, 1977.
15. Werry J. S.: *Pediatric Psychopharmacology*. New York, Bruner/Mazel, 1978.
16. Wiener J. M.: *Psychopharmacology in Childhood and Adolescence*. New York, Basic Books, 1977.
17. Wiener J. S.: Organic therapies, in Kaplan H. I., Freedman A. M., Sadock B. J. (eds): *Comprehensive Textbook of Psychiatry,* ed 3. Baltimore, Williams & Wilkins, 1980, vol 3, 2679–2685.

Psychosis and Severe Behavior Disorders

18. Baldessarini R. A., Tarsy D.: Tardive dyskinesia, in Lipton M. A., DiMascio A., Killam K. (eds): *Psychopharmacology*. New York, Raven Press 1978, pp 993–1004.
19. Campbell M.: Psychopharmacology in childhood psychosis. *Int J Ment Health* 4:238, 1975.
20. Campbell M., Anderson L. T., Meier M., et al: A comparison of haloperidol and behavior therapy and their interaction in autistic children. *J Am Acad Child Psychiatry* 17:640–655, 1978.
*21. Campbell M., Cohen I. L., Anderson L. T.: Pharmacotherapy for autistic children: A summary of research. *Can J Psychiatry* 26:265–273, 1981.
22. Casey D. E., Denney D.: Pharmacologic characterization of tardive dyskinesia. *Psychopharmacology* 54:1–8, 1977.
23. Chapman A. H.: *Management of Emotional Problems of Children and Adolescents.* Philadelphia, Lippincott, 1965.
24. Claghorn J.: A double-blind comparison of haloperidol (Haldol) and thioridazine (Mellaril) in outpatient children. *Curr Ther Res* 14:785–789, 1972.
25. Cunningham M. A., Pillar V., Rogers W. J. B.: Haloperidol in the treatment of children with severe behavior disorders. *Br J Psychiatry* 114:845–854, 1968.
26. Duffy B.: Acute phenothiazine intoxication in children. *Med J Aust* 1:676–678, 1971.
27. Engelhardt D. M., Polizos P., Waizer J.: CNS consequences of psychotropic drug withdrawal in autistic children. *Psychopharmacol Bull* 11:6–7, 1975.
28. Engelhardt D. M., Polizos P., Waizer J., et al: A double-blind comparison of fluphenazine and haloperidol in outpatient schizophrenic children. *J Autism Child Schizo* 3:128–137, 1973.
29. Grabowski S.: Haloperidol for the control of severe emotional disorders in children. *Dis Nerv Syst* 34:315–317, 1973.
*30. Gaultieri C. T., Barnhill J., McGimsey J., et al: Tardive dyskinesia and and other movement disorders in children treated with psychotropic drugs. *J Am Acad Child Psychiatry* 19:491–510, 1980.
31. Jorgensen O. S.: Psychopharmacological treatment of psychotic children. *Acta Psychiatr Scand* 59:229–238, 1977.
32. Meyers B., Tune L. E., Coyle J. T.: Clinical response and serum neuroleptic levels in childhood schizophrenia. *Am J Psychiatry* 137:483–484, 1980.

33. Petty L. K., Spar C. S.: Haloperidol-induced tardive dyskinesia in a ten year old girl. *Am J Psychiatry* 137:745–746, 1980.
34. Polizos P., Engelhardt D. M., Hoffman J. P., et al: Neurological consequences of psychotropic drug withdrawal in schizophrenic children. *J Autism Child Schizo* 3:245–253, 1973.
35. Polizos P., Engelhardt D. M.: Dyskinetic phenomena in children treated with psychotropic medications. *Psychopharmacol Bull* 14:65–68, 1978.
36. Serrano A. C., Forbis O. L.: Haloperidol for psychiatric disorders in children. *Dis Nerv Syst* 34:226–234, 1973.
37. Shabry F., Wolk J.: Granulocytopenia in children after phenothiazine therapy. *Am J Psychiatry* 137:374–375, 1980.
38. Shields W. E., Bray P. F.: A danger of haloperidol therapy in children. *J Pediatr* 88:301–303, 1976.
39. Simeon J., Salety B., Salety M., et al: Thiothixene in childhood psychoses. *Adv Biochem Psychopharmacol* 9:519, 1974.
40. Winsberg C. G., Yepes L. E.: Antipsychotics, in Werry J. S. (ed): *Pediatric Psychopharmacology*. New York, Bruner/Mazel, 1978.
41. Yepes L. E., Winsberg C. G.: Vomiting during neuroleptic withdrawal in children. *Am J Psychiatry* 134:574, 1977.

Tic Disorders

42. Abuzzahab F. S., Ehlen K. J.: The clinical picture and management of Gilles de la Tourette's syndrome. *Child Psychiatry Hum Dev* 2:14–25, 1971.
43. Cohen D. J., Dettor J., Young G., et al: Clonidine ameliorates Gilles de la Tourette's syndrome. *Arch Gen Psychiatry* 37:1350–1357, 1980.
44. Dysken M. W., Berecz J. M., Samarza A., et al: Clonidine in Tourette's syndrome. *Lancet* 2:926–927, 1980.
45. Lucas A. R.: Gilles de la Tourette's disease: An overview. *NY State J Med* 70:2197–2200, 1970.
*46. Shapiro, A. K.: Current treatment of Tourette's syndrome, in Shapiro E. S., Brunn R. (eds): *Gilles de la Tourette's Syndrome*. New York, Raven Press, 1978, pp 315–361.
47. Shapiro A. K., Shapiro E. S., Wayne H.: Treatment of Tourette's syndrome with haloperidol: Review of 34 cases. *Arch Gen Psychiatry* 28:92–97, 1973.

Depression

48. Carlson G. A., Cantwell D. P.: Unmasking masked depression in children and adolescents. *Am J Psychiatry* 137:445–449, 1980.
49. Carlson G. A., Cantwell D. P.: A survey of depressive symptoms in a child and adolescent psychiatric population: Interview data. *J Am Acad Child Psychiatry* 18:587–599, 1979.
50. Cytryn L., McKnew D. H.: Proposed classification of childhood depression. *Am J Psychiatry* 129:149–155, 1972.
51. Fish B.: Summary report of the children's psychopharmacology unit of New York University Medical Center. *Psychopharmacol Bull* 9:13–18, 1973.

52. Goel K. M., Shanks R. A.: Amitriptyline and imipramine poisoning in children. *Br Med J* 1:261–263, 1974.
*53. Kashani J. H., Husain A., Shekin W. O., et al: Current perspectives on childhood depression: An overview. *Am J Psychiatry* 138:143–153, 1981.
54. Kashani J. H., Simonds J. F.: The incidence of depression in children. *Am J Psychiatry* 136:1203–1205, 1979.
55. Law W., Petti T. A., Kazdin A. E.: Withdrawal symptoms after gradual cessation of imipramine in children. *Am J Psychiatry* 138:647–650, 1981.
56. Lucas A. R., Lockett J. H., Grimm F.: Amitriptyline in childhood depression. *Dis Nerv Syst* 26:105–110, 1965.
57. Petit J. M., Biggs J. J.: Antidepressant overdose in adolescent patients. *Pediatrics* 59:283–287, 1977.
58. Puig-Antich J., Blau S., Marx N., et al: Prepubertal major depressive disorder: A pilot study. *J Am Acad Child Psychiatry* 17:695–707, 1978.

Bipolar Affective Disorders

59. Anthony J., Scott P.: Manic–depressive psychosis in childhood. *J Child Psychol Psychiatry* 1:53–72, 1960.
60. Campbell M., Fish B., Korein J., et al: Lithium and chlorpromazine: A controlled crossover study in hyperactive severely disturbed young children. *J Autism Child Schizo* 2:234–263, 1972.
61. Campbell M., Scholman P., Rapoport J. L.: The current status of lithium therapy in child and adolescent psychiatry. *J Am Acad Child Psychiatry* 17:717–720, 1978.
62. Delong G. R.: Lithium carbonate treatment of select behavior disorders in children suggesting manic–depressive illness. *J Pediatr* 93:689–694, 1928.
63. Dostal T.: Antiaggressive effects of lithium salts in mentally retarded adolescents, in Annell A. L. (ed): *Depressive States in Childhood and Adolescence.* Stockholm, Almquist and Wiksell, 1972, pp 491–498.
64. Greenhill L. L., Rieden R. O., Winder P. H., et al: Lithium carbonate in the treatment of hyperactive children. *Arch Gen Psychiatry* 28:636–640, 1973.
65. Rifkin A., Quitkin F., Carillo C., et al: Lithium carbonate in emotionally unstable character disorder. *Arch Gen Psychiatry* 27:519–523, 1972.
66. Schow M.: Lithium in psychiatric therapy and prophylaxis, a review with special regard to its use in children, in Annell A. L. (ed): *Depressive States in Childhood and Adolescence.* Stockholm, Almquist and Wiksell, 1972, pp 477–487.
67. Weinberg W. A., Brumback R. A.: Mania in childhood. *Am J Dis Child* 130:380, 1971.
68. White J. H., Shanick G.: Juvenile manic–depressive illness. *Am J Psychiatry* 134:1035–1036, 1977.
*69. Youngerman J., Canino I. A.: Lithium carbonate use in children and adolescents: A survey of the literature. *Arch Gen Psychiatry* 35:216, 1978.

Enuresis

70. Fraser M.: Nocturnal enuresis. *Practitioner* 208:203–211, 1972.
71. Kolvin I., Taunch J., Currah J., et al: Enuresis: A descriptive analysis and a controlled trial. *Dev Med Child Neurol* 14:715–726, 1972.

72. Poussaint A. F., Ditman R. S.: A controlled study of imipramine (Tofranil) in the treatment of childhood enuresis. *J Pediatr* 67:283–299, 1965.
73. Shaffer D., Costello A. J., Hill I. D.: Control of enuresis with imipramine. *Arch Dis Child* 43:665–671, 1968.

School Refusal

74. Eisenberg L.: The pediatric management of school phobia. *J Pediatr* 55:758–766, 1959.
75. Fish B.: Drug use in psychiatric disorders of children. *Am J Psychiatry* 123:31–36, 1968.
*76. Gittleman-Klein R.: Pharmacotherapy and management of pathological separation anxiety. *Int J Ment Health* 4:255, 1975.

Anxiety Disorders

77. DiMascio A., Soltys J., Shader R. I.: Psychotropic side effects in children, in DiMascio A., Soltys J.(eds): *Drug Side Effects.* Baltimore, Williams & Wilkins, 1970, pp 235–260.
78. Kraft I. A., Ardalic C., Duffy J. H., et al: A clinical study of chlordiazepoxide used in psychiatric disorders of children. *Int J Neuropsychiatry* 1:433–437, 1965.
79. Smith W. R.: Determinants influencing the use of psychoactive drugs in the management of psychiatric emergencies in children and adolescents, in Morrison G. C. (ed): *Emergencies in Child Psychiatry.* Springfield, Illinois, Charles C. Thomas, 1975, pp 415–425.
80. Zrull J. P.: Pharmacotherapy, in Sholevar G. P. (ed): *Emotional Disorders in Children and Adolescents.* New York, Spectrum, 1980, pp 65–77.

Sleep Disorders

81. Fisher C., Kahn E., Edwards A., et al: A psychophysiological study of nightmares and night terrors. *Arch Gen Psychiatry* 28:252–259, 1973.
82. Kales A., Kales J.: Sleep disorders. *N Engl J Med* 290:487–499, 1974.
83. Keith P. R.: Night terrors: A review of the psychology, neurophysiology and therapy. *J Child Psychiatry* 14:477–489, 1975.

Attention Deficit Disorder with Hyperactivity

84. Arnold L. E., Huestis R. D., Smeltzer D. J., et al: Levoamphetamine vs. dextroamphetamine in minimal brain dysfunction. *Arch Gen Psychiatry* 33:292, 1976.
85. Arnold L. E., Wender P. H., McCloskey K., et al: Levoamphetamine and dextroamphetamine. Comparative efficacy in the hyperkinetic syndrome. *Arch Gen Psychiatry* 27:816–822, 1972.
86. Bede L., Langford W., Mackay M., et al: Childhood chemotherapy and later drug

abuse and growth curve: A follow-up study of 30 adolescents. *Am J Psychiatry* 132:436–438, 1975.

87. Bremness A. B., Sverd J.: Methylphenidate-induced Tourette syndrome: Case report. *Am J Psychiatry* 136:1334–1335, 1979.

88. Borland B. L., Heckman H. K.: Hyperactive boys and their brothers: A 25 year follow-up study. *Arch Gen Psychiatry* 33:669–675, 1976.

89. Brown D., Winsberg B., Bialer I., et al: Imipramine therapy and seizures. Three children treated for hyperactive behavior disorders. *Am J Psychiatry* 130:210–212, 1972.

90. Comly H. H.: Cerebral stimulants for children with learning disorders. *J Learn Disabil* 4:20–34, 1971.

91. Conners C. K.: Recent drug studies with hyperkinetic children. *J Learn Disabil* 4:476–483, 1971.

92. Conners C. K., Goyette C. H., Southwick D. A., et al: Food additives and hyperkinesis: A controlled double-blind experiment. *Pediatrics* 58:154–166, 1976.

93. Denckla M. B., Bemporad J. R., Mackay M. C.: Tics following methylphenidate administration. *JAMA* 235:1349–1351, 1976.

*94. Dickerson J. W. T.: Diet and hyperactivity. *J Human Nutr* 34:167–174, 1980.

95. Eisenberg L.: Symposium: Behavior modification by drugs. The clinical use of stimulant drugs in children. *Pediatrics* 49:709–715, 1972.

96. Eisenberg L.: Psychopharmacologic experiment in a training school for delinquent boys: Method, problems and findings. *Am J Orthopsychiatry* 33:431–447, 1963.

97. Feingold B. F.: Hyperkinesis and learning disabilities linked to the ingestion of artificial food colors and flavors. *J Learn Disabil* 9:19–27, 1976.

98. Fish B.: The "one child, one drug" myth of stimulants in hyperkinesis. *Arch Gen Psychiatry* 25:193–203, 1971.

99. Garfinkel B., Webster C., Sloman L.: Methylphenidate and caffeine in treatment of children with minimal brain dysfunction. *Am J Psychiatry* 132:723–728, 1975.

100. Greenberg L. M., McMahon S.: Effect of dextroamphetamine, chlorpromazine and hydroxyzine on behavior and performance in hyperactive children. *Am J Psychiatry* 129:44–51, 1972.

101. Harley J. P., Ray R. S., Tomasi L., et al: Hyperkinesis and food additives: Testing the Feingold hypothesis. *Pediatrics* 61:818–828, 1978.

102. Huessey H. R., Cohen A. H.: Hyperkinetic behaviors and learning disabilities followed over seven years. *Pediatrics* 57:4–10, 1976.

103. Huestis R. D., Arnold E., Smeltzer D.: Caffeine versus methylphenidate and *d*-amphetamine in minimal brain dysfunction: A double-blind comparison. *Am J Psychiatry* 132:868–871, 1975.

104. Kershner J., Hawke W.: Megavitamins and learning disorders: A controlled double-blind experiment. *J Nutr* 109:819–826, 1979.

105. Linnoila M., Gualtieri T., Jobson K., et al: Characteristics of the therapeutic response to imipramine in hyperactive children. *Am J Psychiatry* 136:1201–1203, 1979.

106. Lucas A. R., Weiss M.: Methylphenidate hallucinosis. *JAMA* 217:1079–1081, 1971.

107. Mackay M., Beck L., Taylor R.: Methylphenidate for adolescents with minimal brain dysfunction. *NY State J Med* 73:550–554, 1973.

108. McAndrew J. B.: Dexedrine dyskinesia. *Clin Pediatr* 13:69–72, 1974.

109. Mendelson W., Johnson N., Stewart M.: Hyperactive children as teenagers: A follow-up study. *J Nerv Ment Dis* 153:273–279, 1971.

*110. Millichap G. J.: Drugs in management of minimal brain dysfunction. *Ann NY Acad Sci* 205:321–334, 1973.

111. Mitchell E., Matthews K. L.: Gilles de la Tourette's disorder associated with pemoline. *Am J Psychiatry* 137:1618–1619, 1980.

112. Page J. G.: Pemoline (Cylert) in the treatment of childhood hyperkinesis. *J Learn Disabil* 7:498–503, 1974.
113. Rosenfield A. A.: Depression and psychotic regression following prolonged methylphenidate use and withdrawal: Case report. *Am J Psychiatry* 136:226–228, 1979.
114. Safer D. J., Allen R.: Single daily dose methylphenidate in hyperactive children. *Dis Nerv Syst* 6:325–328, 1973.
115. Safer D. J., Allen R., Barre E.: Depression of growth in hyperactive children on stimulant drugs. *N Engl J Med* 287:217–220, 1972.
116. Safer D. J., Allen R., Barre E.: Growth rebound after termination of stimulant drug therapy. *J Pediatr* 86:113–116, 1975.
117. Schlain R. J., Reynard C. L.: Observations on the effects of a central stimulant drug (methylphenidate) in children with hyperactive behavior. *Pediatrics* 55:709–716, 1975.
118. Schleifer M.: Hyperactivity in preschoolers and the effect of methylphenidate. *Am J Orthopsychiatry* 45:38–50, 1975.
119. Schnackenberg R.: Caffeine as a substitute for schedule II stimulants in hyperkinetic children. *Am J Psychiatry* 130:796–798, 1973.
120. Sprague R., Sleator E.: Methylphenidate in hyperactive children: Differences in dose effects on learning and social behavior. *Science* 98:1274–1276, 1977.
121. Stroufe L. A., Steward M. A.: Treating children with stimulant drugs. *N Engl J Med* 289:407–416, 1973.
*122. Swidler H. J., Walson P. D.: Hyperactivity: A current assessment. *J Family Pract* 9:601–608, 1979.
123. Tryphonas H., Trites R.: Food allergy in children with hyperactivity, learning disabilities and/or minimal brain dysfunction. *Ann Allergy* 42:22–37, 1979.
124. Waizer I., Hoffman S., Polizos P., et al: Outpatient treatment of hyperactive school children with imipramine. *Am J Psychiatry* 131:587–591, 1975.
*125. Weiss G., Hechtman L.: The hyperactive child syndrome. *Science* 205:1348–1353, 1979.
126. Weiss G., Kruger E., Danielson U., et al: Effect of long-term treatment of hyperactive children with methylphenidate. *Can Med Assoc J* 112:159–165, 1976.
127. Weiss G., Minde K., Werry J. S., et al: Studies on the hyperactive child. Five year follow-up. *Arch Gen Psychiatry* 24:409–414, 1971.
128. Wender P.: *Minimal Brain Dysfunction in Children.* New York, John Wiley & Sons, 1971.
129. Werry J. S., Aman M. G.: Methylphenidate and haloperidol for children. *Arch Gen Psychiatry* 32:790–795, 1975.
130. Williams J. I., Crum D. M., Tansig F. T., et al: Relative effects of drugs and diet on hyperactive behaviors: An experimental study. *Pediatrics* 61:811–817, 1978.
131. Winsberg B. G.: Effects of imipramine and dextroamphetamine on behavior of neuropsychiatrically impaired children. *Am J Psychiatry* 128:1425–1431.
132. Zahn T. P., Abate F., Little B. C., et al: Minimal brain dysfunction, stimulant drugs and autonomic nervous system activity. *Arch Gen Psychiatry* 32:381–387, 1975.

Conduct Disorders

133. Conners C. K., Kramer R., Rothschild G. H., et al: Treatment of young delinquent boys with diphenylhydantoin and methylphenidate. *Arch Gen Psychiatry* 24:156–160, 1971.

Anorexia Nervosa

134. Crisp A. H.: Clinical and therapeutic aspects of anorexia nervosa—a study of 30 cases. *J Psychosom Res* 9:67–68, 1965.
135. Dully P.: *Anorexia Nervosa*. New York, Grune & Stratton, pp 52–53, 1969.
136. Greenberg L. M., Stephans J. H.: Use of drugs in special syndromes, in Wiener J. M. (ed): *Psychopharmacology in Childhood and Adolescence*. New York, Basic Books, pp 205–208, 1977.

"Borderline" Children

137. Petti T. A., Unis A.: Imipramine treatment of borderline children: Case reports with a controlled study. *Am J Psychiatry* 138:515–518, 1981.

10

The Use of Psychotropic Drugs during Pregnancy and Nursing

CAROL R. KOPLAN, M.D.

I. INTRODUCTION

Treatment of a pregnant or nursing patient presents unusual challenges to the physician, who must consider not only the usual guidelines for administering drugs but also the special problems of pregnancy and the postpartum period. These include:

1. The significant alterations in maternal physiology during pregnancy and delivery.
2. The vulnerability of the developing fetus.
3. The physiological changes in the neonate.
4. The transfer of various agents to the newborn through milk.
5. The possibility of long-term neuroendocrine or behavioral effects on the developing nervous system.

Ethical considerations and logistical problems in designing controlled studies have limited the amount of research on pregnant women. Therefore, the practitioner frequently is presented with a disturbed patient, complex physiological changes, a vulnerable fetus, and little definitive information about the effects of drugs on the baby.

Clearly, the clinician should seek to avoid or delay any pharmacotherapy in a pregnant patient. However, in patients with severe or persistent symp-

CAROL R. KOPLAN, M.D. • Department of Psychiatry, Emory University School of Medicine, Atlanta, Georgia 30322. The author would like to thank Jeffrey P. Koplan for his support.

toms that do not respond to nonbiological measures, drugs may become necessary. This chapter discusses various approaches to medicating the pregnant or nursing patient, noting risks and benefits to both the mother and child.

II. GENERAL THERAPEUTIC APPROACHES: NONBIOLOGICAL

Whenever possible, the clinician should offer nonbiological treatments to a pregnant patient with emotional symptoms. For patients with mild to moderate depressions, anxiety, and sleep disorders, various psychotherapeutic measures often can help. Perhaps most beneficial is the development of a supportive, trusting relationship with a caretaker. In this context, the patient may benefit from reassurance, ego support, exploration of psychological concerns, and environmental manipulation. Nonbiological methods might not provide complete relief but may offer enough support to delay pharmacotherapy until later in pregnancy or after delivery.

In patients with more severe disturbances, such as some major depressive disorders, mania, or psychotic states, the clinician must provide more intensive care. Sometimes, crisis intervention techniques (see Chapter 2) can control or ameliorate symptoms. Frequently, however, even with active therapeutic approaches, hospitalization may be necessary to protect both mother and fetus or newborn and to provide more continuous, extensive treatment. In addition, some pregnant women may require psychotropic medication.

III. GENERAL ISSUES RELATED TO PHARMACOTHERAPY

To evaluate the risks and benefits of administering a psychoactive agent, the clinician should be aware of changes in pharmacokinetics during and after pregnancy and of potential effects of drugs on the developing fetus (i.e., gross and behavioral teratogenesis), the newborn (i.e., direct effects and intoxication and withdrawal), and the nursing infant.

A. Gross Teratogenesis

Teratogens are drugs that can produce major congenital abnormalities. In humans, the greatest risk of gross organ dysgenesis resulting from exogenous chemicals occurs during the first 2 months of pregnancy. Nervous system development in the embryo is most affected from the tenth to the 25th day of gestation, cardiac development between the 20th and 40th day, and limbs from the 24th to 26th day.[1] Although a tragedy on the scale of thalidomide has not been reported with other psychoactive drugs (thalidomide is a sedative), several have been implicated as teratogens. Suggestive associations have been reported between benzodiazepine usage [particularly diazepam (Valium®)] and oral clefts and between lithium and abnormalities of the heart and great vessels. Although the evidence is somewhat less convincing, antihistamine and barbiturate use during the first trimester has been associated with congenital abnormalities. The relationship between phenothiazine administration during pregnancy and resulting congenital malformations remains uncertain. Finally, heterocyclic antidepressant usage is rarely associated with fetal maldevelopment.[2]

B. Behavioral Teratogenesis

Data from animal studies suggest that babies of mothers receiving psychoactive drugs may develop long-term neurochemical and behavioral changes, even in the absence of gross structural abnormalities. Vorhees et al. have referred to drugs that produce these alterations as "behavioral teratogens."[3] Although the extent and type of risk to a human baby remain unclear, the evidence is suggestive enough to extend the clinician's concern beyond the first trimester to the entire pregnancy and nursing period.[3,4] For example, Kellogg et al. reported that the use of diazepam in rats during the final week of pregnancy in dosages of 2.5 mg/kg, 5.0 mg/kg, or 10.0 mg/kg (i.e., higher than in humans) resulted in long-lasting suppression of the behavioral consequences of arousal in the newborn pups.[5] Chronic neurochemical and behavioral alterations in animals have also been documented with antipsychotic drugs and various other psychoactive compounds.[6]

C. Adverse Effects on the Neonate

1. Direct Effects

The newborn babies of mothers taking psychotropic drugs, particularly late in pregnancy, may show direct pharmacological effects. For example, some neonates whose mothers took phenothiazines develop extrapyramidal symptoms, whereas others whose mothers used diazepam have muscle hypotonia ("floppy infant syndrome").

2. Intoxication and Withdrawal Syndromes

Because antipsychotic drugs, heterocyclic antidepressants, and benzodiazepines are lipid soluble and largely protein bound, they are slowly eliminated from the fetus or newborn. Furthermore, the neonate appears more susceptible to central nervous system drugs than adults for several reasons:

1. Liver enzymes are not yet fully developed, resulting in decreased metabolism and elevated drug levels.
2. Plasma protein concentrations are lower in the fetus and newborn, which means increased quantities of free drug are available to act on the brain.
3. The blood–brain barrier is still incomplete.
4. The immature central nervous system appears generally more sensitive to the effects of chemicals.[2]

As a result, many babies develop syndromes of intoxication and withdrawal. Their symptoms depend on the chemical action of the specific drugs involved (see specific sections below).

D. Psychoactive Drugs and Lactation

Generally, drugs that cross the blood–brain barrier also traverse the placental membrane and appear in mammalian milk. Nursing infants, however, typically receive only a small proportion of the drug administered to their mothers. Except for a few instances, e.g., lithium therapy, the amount of medication the neonate receives is not likely to cause direct pharmacological effects.[7-14] Of greater concern, however, is the possibility that even low dosages of medication can lead to subtle, long-term behavioral effects in the baby. Even though such consequences have not been documented in humans, animal studies are suggestive. Therefore, the practitioner should weigh the psychological and biological benefits of nursing for both mother and infant against:

1. Risk to the immature nervous system from medication.
2. Risk to the mother and child from psychiatric symptoms that will result from discontinuing a drug and might interfere with the mother's ability to care for the baby.

IV. EMOTIONAL ILLNESS DURING AND AFTER PREGNANCY

A. Schizophrenic Disorders

Pregnant women are in the age group when schizophrenia often develops or relapses. In the postpartum period, the chance of recurrence of a schizophrenic psychosis is from 13 to 20% following the first or any subsequent pregnancy.[15] This section discusses specific issues related to medicating the pregnant and lactating woman with schizophrenia.

1. Phenothiazines

The risk of organ dysgenesis in babies born to mothers taking phenothiazines during the first trimester remains uncertain. The French National Institute of Health and Medical Research conducted a prospective study in 12 university hospitals in Paris involving 12,764 women. Of these women, 189 gave birth to babies with unequivocal, nonchromosomally based malformations of different types. Of the 315 women who took phenothiazines during the first trimester, 11 gave birth to malformed babies, a significantly greater number than those in the control group (3.5% vs. 1.6%).[16]

The authors of this study divided the phenothiazines into four chemical groups: (1) three-carbon aliphatic side chain, (2) two-carbon aliphatic side chain, (3) piperazine side chain, and (4) piperidine side chain. A significant increase in malformations was found with drugs having a three-carbon aliphatic side chain. The main drug in this group was chlorpromazine (Thorazine® and others); the 57 exposed women produced four malformed offspring. In the two-carbon aliphatic side chain group, the number of malformed babies, although higher than expected, was not significant. In the third [fluphenazine (Prolixin®), perphenazine (Trilafon®), prochlorperazine (Compazine®)], and fourth groups [thioridazine (Mellaril®)], no significant increase occurred. Trifluoperazine (Stelazine®), a drug with a piperazine side chain, was not included because it is not used in France. However, authors cite two prospective studies in which 800 women received trifluoperazine in the first trimester, with no babies developing overt "skeletal abnormalities."[16]

Although the French study reported a significant number of congenital malformations compared to the control group, the larger multicenter study of Slone et al. reviewed 50,282 gravidas and their offspring of which 1309 mothers had taken phenothiazines. Exposure was either sporadic or heavy and regular. They reported similar rates of congenital malformations when the mothers were exposed during the first 4 months compared to those who were unexposed. Other characteristics studied included perinatal mortality, mean birth weight, and intelligence quotient scores measured at 4 years. No differences were found between the exposed and unexposed group.[17]

In addition to the possibility of gross teratogenesis, various authors have studied behavioral effects in animals whose mothers received phenothiazines (prochlorperazine, chlorpromazine) and observed behavioral changes in the animal neonate.[3,18] Investigators also have reported various nonspecific adverse effects on pregnant rats, such as a decrease in the number of viable litters and the length of gestation.[3]

Usage of psychoactive medications in the pregnant woman may occasionally cause acute postpartum syndromes in the newborn. When phenothiazines have been administered during pregnancy, extrapyramidal effects have been observed in the newborn, including parkinsonism (tremor, bradykinesia, and rigidity), choreiform and dystonic movements, increased muscle tone, akathisia, agitation, hypertonicity, tongue protrusion, and uncoordinated sucking and swallowing. The symptoms usually begin within the first day and may last several weeks to 10 months. The mothers may not have extrapyramidal reactions themselves.[19] Some of these babies have been treated with diphenhydramine hydrochloride (Benadryl®), 5 mg/kg per 24 hr.[20] A baby with extrapyramidal symptoms described by Hill et al. was treated successfully with phenobarbital (Luminal® and others).[21]

A second adverse effect of phenothiazines, and also perhaps of antiparkinson agents and antidepressants, which occurs during the postpartum period is "small left colon syndrome" (SLCS), a functional intestinal obstruction in the neonate. The SLCS is characterized by decreased intestinal motility, abdominal distention, vomiting, and failure to pass meconium. The syndrome is usually benign and resolves after the administration of a gastrograffin enema, which is both diagnostic and therapeutic. If SLCS is not recognized, the baby might require surgery or develop an intestinal perforation which could lead to death.[22]

A third, although rare, adverse effect seen in neonates is respiratory depression. It occurs in babies of mothers taking 500 mg/day or more of chlorpromazine. Extrapyramidal reactions, the SLCS, and respiratory depression are relatively uncommon. However, if the mother has continued taking phenothiazines through delivery, the pediatrician should carefully observe the neonate.

Other antipsychotic drugs besides the phenothiazines have been used during pregnancy and the puerperium. Two cases of limb reduction abnormalities have been reported in babies of mothers taking haloperidol (Haldol®). However, in both cases, causal relationships were not definitely established.[23-26] To date, the safe use of thiothixene (Navane®), molindone (Moban®), and loxapine (Loxitane®) has not been established.

As with all psychoactive drugs, antipsychotic agents have been found in breast milk. Although no obvious immediate or longer-term adverse reactions have been observed in the neonate, the possibility of long-lasting behavioral effects must be considered.[27,28]

2. Antiparkinson Agents

The antiparkinson agents are often coadministered with antipsychotic drugs to prevent or treat extrapyramidal reactions. No studies have specifically addressed the safety of these agents in pregnant or lactating women. However, their anticholinergic or atropinelike effects may potentiate the pregnant woman's problems with constipation. As previously described, the small left colon syndrome has also been associated with these medications.[22] Therefore, in pregnancy the antiparkinson agents should be avoided unless absolutely necessary.

B. Depressive and Bipolar Affective Disorders

Women with affective disorders often experience a decrease in symptoms or even remissions during pregnancy. Some women, however, do develop manic and/or depressive symptoms that require treatment, and the postpartum period tends to bring heightened vulnerability to women with mood disorders. The expectant mother may feel overwhelmed by the prospect of new responsibilities, changes in self-image, or issues of closeness and dependency. In each patient, the clinician should carefully evaluate the nature, severity, and timing of the affective episode. Have there been changes in eating, sleeping, or ability for self-care? Is the pregnant woman suicidal? As in all depressive disorders, the physician should rule out organic causes of depression (see Chapter 2). In addition, the clinician should consider the contribution of the usual emotional and physical changes occurring during each phase of pregnancy, such as mood lability, nausea and vomiting leading to weight loss, fatigue associated with increased sleep (i.e., in the first trimester), and poor sleep (i.e., in the third trimester). Within 10 days postpartum, up to two-thirds of women develop "postpartum blues" or feelings of depression of nonpsychotic proportion, which usually remit over time.[29,30] Moreover, many new mothers are tired from the baby's frequent nighttime awakenings and from anxiety about their new responsibility; fatigue alone, however, does not imply a depressive illness.

1. Heterocyclic Antidepressants

Initially, the pregnant patient should be treated by supportive psychotherapeutic measures. However, if the woman does not improve and remains severely distressed and disabled, the clinician should carefully consider administering medication. Heterocyclic antidepressants are the drugs of choice for major depressive syndromes.

Despite sporadic anecdotal reports of limb deformities,[31-35] no definitive association has been shown to exist between the heterocyclics and organ dysgenesis (although any psychoactive drug might affect the developing nervous system).[36,37] However, intoxication and withdrawal syndromes in the neonate have been observed with heterocyclic antidepressants.

Several authors have reported that infants whose mothers took desipramine (Norpramin®, Pertofrane®) and imipramine (Tofranil® and others) developed withdrawal reactions characterized by dyspnea, cyanosis, tachypnea, tachycardia, irritability, and sweating. These symptoms generally improved over a period of a month.[38,39] Similarly, lethargy and urinary retention occurred in a neonate whose mother took nortriptyline (Aventyl®, Pamelor®) near term.[40] In all cases, the neonate made a complete recovery.

As with the other psychoactive drugs, most heterocyclics are excreted in small amounts in breast milk. The long-term effects, however, are unknown.[8-10]

2. Lithium

Women with bipolar illness are at high risk (30 to 40%) of developing mania or depression postpartum. Lithium is indicated for the prevention of affective episodes in bipolar illness and for the treatment of acute mania or hypomania. It also prevents relapse in many patients with various unipolar depressions (see Chapter 3). Lithium, however, has a number of significant risks for mother, fetus, and newborn. Although lithium registries record a selected sample (i.e., they may have more pathological cases reported than normal experiences), cases collected in the United States, Denmark, and Canada showed that 13 of 143 babies exposed to lithium during the first trimester (sometimes in conjunction with other drugs) had cardiac malformations. Of the 11 cardiovascular malformations, ten were significant (i.e., major abnormalities of the heart and great vessels). A much greater than expected ratio of cardiovascular anomalies compared to other significant abnormalities occurred. Many babies had major congenital heart disease, particularly the rare Ebstein's anomaly (i.e., malformed tricuspid valve and patent foramen ovale).[41-44] These observations suggest that lithium is a weak teratogen but has a predilection for the cardiovascular system. It should also be noted that despite medical and surgical intervention, Ebstein's anomaly is associated with a shortened life-span. Therefore, these risks must be balanced against the need for lithium in pregnant patients, especially during the first trimester.

Another point concerns changing kinetics in the mother during pregnancy. During pregnancy, renal clearance is increased (50 to 100%), and if it is necessary to prescribe lithium, higher doses may be required. Renal clearance decreases during delivery, and therefore, the lithium dose must be decreased immediately to avoid toxicity in both mother and baby. The daily lithium dose should be reduced by 50% or more in the last week of gestation and stopped with the onset of labor. Then, the prepregnancy dose may be started immediately after delivery.[45,46] Prior to delivery, anesthesiologists should be informed that the mother is on lithium, since the drug potentiates the effects of anesthetics and muscle relaxants.[47]

Although most babies of mothers taking lithium do not become toxic, an occasional infant born to a mother with normal lithium levels has elevated levels and may exhibit neonatal lithium intoxication. Symptoms include cyanosis, lethargy, hypotonia, jaundice, hypothermia, duskiness, poor sucking, poor respirations, low Apgar scores, absent Moro relfex, and altered thyroid and cardiac function. These babies generally improve within 10 to 13 days. Some women with toxic infants had been on low-salt diets and were taking diuretics, both of which can elevate plasma lithium levels.[46,48–50]

Lithium also affects thyroid function. Several clinicians have reported edema and goiter in babies born to mothers who took lithium during pregnancy. Since these babies may have difficulties at delivery, pregnant women with thyroid abnormalities should have fetal monitoring by ultrasound during pregnancy. Generally, by 2 months, these babies lose the edema and become euthyroid.[7]

Clinically, the practitioner should follow careful guidelines for treating pregnant patients with bipolar disorders:

1. Consider at least temporarily discontinuing lithium maintenance therapy in patients with stable mood.
2. Avoid lithium during the first trimester; consider using an antipsychotic drug (e.g., haloperidol) for the treatment of acute mania.
3. Try to avoid drugs, but use heterocyclic antidepressants for severe major affective disorders.
4. If it becomes necessary to use lithium, administer the lowest dose of lithium that decreases symptoms.
5. Obtain at least weekly serum lithium levels.
6. Avoid fluctuations in serum lithium levels.
7. Use caution when prescribing lithium to women on low-salt diets and/or diuretics.
8. Decrease the lithium dosage by one-half the week prior to delivery.
9. Discontinue lithium when labor begins.
10. Anticipate postpartum mood fluctuations and be prepared to reinstitute treatment as needed.
11. Provide intermittent fetal ultrasound monitoring for mothers who have thyroid abnormalities.

3. Electroconvulsive Therapy

Occasionally, schizophrenia presents with severe catatonia or agitation that does not respond rapidly to antipsychotics. In other cases, a pregnant patient may present with severe depression and serious suicidal risk. In these conditions, electroconvulsive therapy (ECT) may be a life-saving treatment. Sobel reviewed 18 articles in which 49 pregnant women were treated with

ECT. Only one fetal death occurred, which the author felt was not related to ECT. Of 33 pregnant women in eight New York State mental institutions, ECT was chosen as an emergency treatment for patients with severe agitation or catatonic withdrawal who were at risk for malnutrition, dehydration, or violent injury. Two fetal deaths from congenital malformations occurred among these 33 pregnancies: an anencephalic baby of a 42-year-old woman and a baby with congenital cysts of the lung who died of bronchopneumonia. However, the incidence of fetal damage in the treated group (6%) was not significantly different from that in the control group. Although animal studies indicate that ECT given early in pregnancy may be harmful, a review of five patients receiving ECT in the first 6 weeks showed no fetal damage.[51] However, we cannot draw definitive conclusions from such small numbers.

Remick and Maurice recommend the following guidelines for the use of ECT during pregnancy:

1. Complete a thorough physical examination, including a pelvic, before ECT.
2. Include an obstetrician as part of the treatment team to monitor fetus status.
3. Know the nature of high-risk conditions that may induce premature labor, such as multiple pregnancy, hydramnios, antepartum hemorrhage, maternal hypertension, preeclampsia, diabetes, Rh isoimmunization, cardiac disease, renal disease, and intracranial disease (these are relative contraindications to ECT).
4. Perform external fetal monitoring before and after ECT.[51,52]

C. Anxiety States

1. Benzodiazepines

The benzodiazepines, particularly diazepam, might be teratogenic. The use of diazepam during the first trimester of pregnancy has been associated with an increased risk of cleft lip with and without cleft palate.[53-57] According to a large perinatal collaborative study, chlordiazepoxide (Librium®) did not have a significant association with specific congenital anomalies.[58,59] Although the association is not definitely established, benzodiazepines should be avoided during the first trimester whenever possible.

Babies of mothers using benzodiazepines late in pregnancy and during lactation have developed muscle hypotonia, also known as the "floppy infant syndrome."[2] This may be less of a problem, however, with short-acting benzodiazepines. Authors have also described probable withdrawal symptoms in infants of mothers taking chlordiazepoxide and diazepam during the last 2 to 4 months of pregnancy. The babies developed tremulousness, hypertonia, and hyperreflexia, which lasted as long as 8 months postpartum.[7,10,60-62] Other authors have reported intrauterine growth retardation, hyperbilirubinemia, and hypothermia with diazepam.[61-63] Although single case reports prove little, they should heighten the clinician's awareness and concern about potential problems.

During labor, diazepam is sometimes used to treat anxiety. Although in low doses it does not appear harmful, doses above 100 mg can depress neonatal respiration and reflexes and cause severe asphyxia, temporary hypoactivity, hypotonia, and hypothermia.[21]

2. Antihistamines—Diphenylmethane Derivatives

Several studies have looked at the association between diphenhydramine and congenital anomalies. In the Collaborative Perinatal Project, in which 51,977 mother–child pairs were in the cohort, 595 gravidas used diphenhydramine during lunar months 1 through 4. This study suggested a low-level association between diphenhydramine use and abnormalities such as genitourinary malformations, eye and ear defects, inguinal hernia, and clubfoot.[63] In another study, 599 children with oral clefts, reported to the Finnish Registry of Congenital Malformations in 1967 to 1971, were compared to a control group. A significant increase of cleft palate and oral clefts, with additional malformations, in babies of mothers who took diphenhydramine during the first trimester was observed. There were no differences between the study and control group in the second and third trimester.[64] Since the Registry probably contains selected cases (i.e., more pathological cases than normal), these results are suggestive rather than conclusive. The clinician should exercise extreme caution if he feels required to use diphenhydramine during the first trimester.

3. Other Sedative–Hypnotics

During pregnancy, the use of sedative–hypnotics generally should be avoided. Some physicians have administered barbiturates during pregnancy to treat seizures, insomnia, and sedation. However, because of their abuse potential and known adverse effects on the fetus, they should be avoided. However, some patients may require continuous treatment of their seizure disorder.

When taken by the mother in large doses during the first trimester, barbiturates have been associated with significant anomalies, such as growth retardation, facial dysmorphism, oral clefts, and skeletal abnormalities. Since the teratogenic effects are dose related, the clinician should monitor blood levels to attain a low therapeutic dose, thereby theoretically decreasing the risk.[65,66]

Chronic barbiturate use during pregnancy can lead to neonatal withdrawal symptoms, including tremulousness, excess crying, irritability, increased tone, hyperphagia, and hyperacusia. The symptoms develop within 10 days to 2 weeks even when the mother has taken as little as 60 mg of barbiturates during the last weeks of pregnancy.[67] More recently, Hill et al. reported the occurrence of barbiturate withdrawal symptoms within 5 hr postpartum.[68]

D. Insomnia

Difficulty sleeping is a very common problem among pregnant women. This symptom has many causes and warrants careful evaluation. Is the insomnia caused by depression, psychosis, or anxiety, or is it physiological, especially during the third trimester?

Once psychosis and severe depression are excluded, the clinician might ask the patient to keep a record of her sleeping patterns for 1 week. The sleep chart might include the time she went to bed, the time she fell asleep, the number of awakenings, the time of awakening, and the time napping. The total amount of time sleeping per day can then be determined. Generally, the pattern observed in late pregnancy is characterized by a longer sleep latency, frequent awakenings, and shorter sleep time with reduction of deep sleep (stage 4). Limited sleep in the third trimester and early postpartum period is normal. Immediately after delivery, dreaming is suppressed (stage 1–REM) but normalizes by the second week.[69] In most pregnant women, insomnia should be treated by nonpharmacological means.

E. Hyperemesis Gravidarum

Although nausea and vomiting are common during the first 3 or 4 months of pregnancy, hyperemesis gravidarum is more severe and may last longer. It is characterized by weight loss, dehydration, ketonuria, and occasionally fever, irregular pulse, and jaundice. The differential diagnosis includes cholecystitis, hepatitis, peptic ulcer, pyelonephritis, lesions of the GI tract, hyperthyroidism, intracranial neoplasm, and hydatidiform mole. Other rare causes of severe vomiting may also occur.[70]

Initially, the clinician should recommend eating soda crackers or saltless crackers on awakening and then several small meals a day. If this does not relieve the nausea and vomiting, many physicians then prescribe Bendectin® (doxylamine succinate and pyridoxine hydrochloride). The recommended dose is two tablets at bedtime. For more severe cases, one tablet can be added in the morning, or one in the morning and one in the afternoon.[70]

Recently, after a thorough review, the FDA asked the manufacturer of Bendectin® to narrow the indications for its use and has initiated proceedings to require a patient package insert. Concern over Bendectin's safety arose recently because of the publicity surrounding a court case involving birth defects in a baby whose mother took the drug. In September, 1980, the FDA asked the Fertility and Maternal Health Advisory Committee to evaluate both published and unpublished studies. The Committee found no increased risk of birth defects but felt that two studies raised some questions. One suggested the possibility of increased risk of cleft lip and the other of heart defects. Experts felt that these studies were of concern but did not prove an association with these birth defects. Because of the above two studies, caution is advised until Bendectin's safety is further clarified. At this time

> Bendectin is indicated only for nausea and vomiting of pregnancy which are unresponsive to conservative measures such as eating soda crackers or drinking hot or cold liquids, which interfere with normal eating habits or daily activities and are sufficiently distressing to require drug intervention.[71,72]

If the hyperemesis is severe (weight loss, dehydration, and acetonuria), hospitalization is indicated. Sometimes, rest and relative isolation from husband, boyfriend, and/or family for several days or more may be helpful. Correcting the electrolyte disturbance with intravenous fluids can reverse the vomiting and weight loss. In severe cases, when other medical causes have been ruled out, a combination of hospitalization, IV fluid replacement, and an antiemetic drug can lead to fairly rapid reversal of the condition. In the past, severe cases have resulted in death.[72]

F. Ptyalism

Ptyalism is a condition in which the pregnant woman secretes copious amounts of saliva during the first trimester and sometimes beyond. She constantly spits saliva and wets her pillow at night. It is unknown if the cause is psychological and/or physiological.

Anecdotal reports suggest that the antidepressant doxepin (Adapin®, Sinequan®), which decreases secretions, is an effective treatment for ptyalism. However, the use of this drug to treat ptyalism has not been approved by the FDA. Other approaches such as starch restriction, atropine, and phenothiazines have not led to improvement.[73]

G. Substance Abuse

The physician should discuss with a pregnant woman who abuses drugs or alcohol the effects of these substances on the baby. In addition, knowledge of the woman's problem should be shared with the obstetrician, anesthesiologist, and pediatrician (see Chapter 7).

1. Opiates

Drug abuse and addiction are potentially serious problems during pregnancy. The opiates, including heroin and methadone, have numerous effects on the fetus and mother, probably because of both direct drug effect and the mother's lifestyle, which may include smoking, drug ingestion, drinking, and poor nutrition. Whereas some drugs have a teratogenic potential, others produce syndromes of drug intoxication and withdrawal in the baby.[74]

Approaches to treating the pregnant addict include supporting her habit or transferring to methadone and/or detoxification. If the addict remains on heroin, she probably will not obtain proper and regular prenatal care. Therefore, the clincian should usually transfer her from heroin to methadone, but only within a hospital setting where the dose of methadone can be regulated (low doses of 40 mg or less can be used during pregnancy). Mothers on methadone maintenance are more likely to obtain appropriate prenatal care; the risk from infection will be reduced, and the baby may have a shorter hospital stay. However, methadone babies may be more difficult to treat for postpartum withdrawal than heroin babies.[75]

Another problem in managing the pregnant addict is that she may develop many of the usual medical problems such as hepatitis, abscesses, endocarditis, thrombophlebitis, etc. as well as many obstetrical complications such as premature labor, toxemia, breech delivery, abruptio placenta, postpartum hemorrhage, stillbirths, and neonatal mortality.

The pregnant addict's physician should inform both the anesthesiologist and pediatrician as soon as the mother goes into labor. In addition, it is important to have active social service involvement to facilitate appropriate care for mother and baby upon discharge.

During labor, the clinician should determine when the patient had her last dose of heroin or methadone, since many drugs administered for pain have an additive effect. Also, the anesthesiologist should use caution when administering drugs that may be hepatotoxic, since the addict may have decreased liver function from episodes of hepatitis.

About 75% of infants of addicts show signs of withdrawal. More than half develop symptoms within 24 hr and most within 2 weeks. There are conflicting reports regarding the correlation of the severity of withdrawal symptoms with doses of methadone, length of addiction, and time lapse before delivery of dosage. However, it does appear that methadone babies develop more severe symptoms than heroin babies. If a mother is receiving more than 100 mg of methadone, the baby generally will exhibit a withdrawal response.[76-82]

The more prominent symptoms of neonatal opiate withdrawal include

high-pitched cry, irritability, respiratory distress, feeding and sleeping difficulties, increased muscle tone, convulsions, and even death if untreated.[74,75]
Infants of methadone-addicted mothers also exhibit depressed respiratory
responses to carbon dioxide which last for about 2 to 4 weeks. Some authors
have suggested that this disorder may, in part, explain the higher prevalance
of sudden infant death syndrome in babies of addicted mothers.[82]

Treatment of the newborn addict includes sedation and withdrawal. The
drugs most commonly and successfully used include paregoric, phenobarbital,
diazepam, and chlorpromazine. Paregoric appears to be the treatment of
choice. Parenteral treatment with fluids and electrolytes are often required to
treat the associated vomiting and diarrhea.[74]

2. CNS Depressants: Barbiturates, Minor Tranquilizers

As with opiates, babies born to mothers who abuse barbiturates or minor
tranquilizers may develop an abstinence syndrome. The risks of barbiturate
and minor tranquilizer abuse to mother and baby are discussed in Sections
IV.C and IV.D.

3. Stimulants: Caffeine, Amphetamines, Cocaine

Pregnant women who present with symptoms of anxiety should be evaluated for "caffeinism," i.e., coffee ingestion of six cups or more. Caffeine is not
only present in coffee, tea, various soft drinks, and chocolate but also in many
over-the-counter pain and cold combination remedies. Pregnant women who
consume large amounts of caffeine may be subject to spontaneous abortions
and stillbirths.[83] Babies of nursing mothers taking xanthines may become
irritable, have trouble sleeping, and have colic. Therefore, we recommend
that mothers limit their coffee or tea intake to two cups per day.[46]

Amphetamines, which might be used to treat fatigue or narcolepsy and
suppress appetite, should not be prescribed during pregnancy. Although the
data are conflicting, an increased incidence of cardiac defects and cleft palate
may occur with amphetamine use during pregnancy.[46] Another author
reported a possible association between amphetamine use by the mother and
biliary atresia in her baby.[84] Also, the effect of cocaine on the fetus has not
been studied.[84]

4. Marijuana, d-Lysergic Acid Diethylamide, and Phencyclidine

Some studies have suggested an increased incidence of fetal loss, chromosomal damage, and congenital anomalies among marijuana users.[46] Other
reviewers think there is little evidence to suggest that marijuana is a
teratogen.[85]

An association may exist between LSD usage and chromosome damage.

One review reported limb deformities in five of 161 babies of LSD users. Because the mothers had ingested other substances, and because limb reduction abnormalities occur at similar rates in the general population, the role of LSD could not be determined with certainty.[86]

Another study suggested a possible association between phencyclidine (PCP) use by the mother and spasticity and facial dysmorphology in her infant.[87] These drugs and all others without a specific therapeutic purpose should be avoided during pregnancy.

5. Alcohol Use and Abuse

Alcohol ingestion during the first trimester may contribute to fetal anomalies and during the last trimester may effect fetal size. With chronic maternal abuse of alcohol, or possibly "binge" drinking, the baby may develop the fetal alcohol syndrome (FAS). The prevalence of FAS is estimated to be one to two per 1000 live births (although three to five per 1000 live births may show mild symptoms). The FAS includes growth and mental retardation, developmental delay, craniofacial anomalies, incomplete development of the cerbral cortex, microcephaly, heart defects, joint and limb problems, and maxillary hypoplasia.[88]

Newborns of alcoholics may develop acute alcoholic withdrawal syndrome which is similar to neonatal narcotic withdrawal. The baby should be sedated.[88]

Alcoholics have been given metronidazole (Flagyl®) and disulfiram (Antabuse®) to treat relapsing behavior. To prevent fetal damage from exposure to alcohol, the physician may want to use these agents during pregnancy. Neither, however, has been proven safe.[46]

V. CONCLUSION

Whenever possible, pharmacotherapy should be avoided during pregnancy. In particular, the clinician should not administer drugs, such as lithium and the benzodiazepines, that may lead to a higher incidence of organ dysgenesis during the first trimester. Although the evidence is less convincing, antihistamines and barbiturates may cause anomalies following their use during the first trimester. Therefore, the practitioner should minimize both dosage and length of exposure if these drugs are required early in pregnancy. Similarly, the clinician should exercise caution if he must administer the antipsychotics or heterocyclic antidepressants during the first several months of pregnancy; although there is no proof that they are teratogenic, there is also no proof that they are not.

When any psychotropic drugs are prescribed during pregnancy, the possibility of long-term effects on the developing nervous system should also be weighed. When medication is necessary, the practitioner must remember that he has two patients—the mother and fetus or newborn. He also must account for the significant physiological changes that occur during pre- and perinatal periods and weigh the benefits of medication to the mother against possible risks to the developing infant from both the drug and the mother's emotional disturbance.

REFERENCES

1. Nahas C., Goujard J.: Phenothiazines, benzodiazepines, and the fetus, in Scarpelli E. M., Cosmi E. V. (eds): *Reviews in Perinatal Medicine.* New York, Raven Press, 1978, pp 243–280.
*2. Gelenberg A. J.: Psychotropic drugs during pregnancy and the perinatal period. *Mass Gen Hosp Newslett Biol Ther Psychiatry* 2:41–42, 1979.
*3. Vorhees C. V., Brunner R. L., Butcher R. E.: Psychotropic drugs as behavioral teratogens. *Science* 205:1220–1225, 1979.
4. Lewis P. D., Patel A. J., Bendek G., et al: Do drugs acting on the nervous system affect cell proliferation in the developing brain? *Lancet* 1:399–401, 1977.
5. Kellogg C., Yervo D., Ison J., et al: Prenatal exposure to diazepam alters behavioral development in rats. *Science* 207:205–207, 1980.
6. Gelenberg A. J.: Intrauterine drug exposure: A sequel. *Mass Gen Hosp Newslett Biol Ther Psychiatry* 8:32, 1980.
*7. Ananth J.: Side effects in the neonate from psychotropic agents excreted through breast feeding. *Am J Psychiatry* 135:801–805, 1978.
8. Sovner R., Orsulak P.: Excretion of imipramine and desipramine in human breast milk. *Am J Psychiatry* 136:451–452, 1979.
9. Vorherr H.: Drug excretion in breast milk. *Postgrad Med* 56:97–104, 1974.
10. Patrick M. J., Tilstone W. J., Reavey P.: Diazepam and breast feeding. *Lancet* 1:542–543, 1972.
*11. Gelenberg A. J.: Amoxapine, a new antidepressant, appears in human milk. *J Nerv Ment Dis* 167:635–636, 1979.
12. Contamination of the ideal food. *Therapeutics* 1:16–17, 1971.
13. Martin E.: *Hazards of Medication.* Philadelphia, Lippincott, 1971, pp 279–280.
14. Weinstein M., Goldfield M.: Lithium carbonate treatment during pregnancy. *Dis Nerv Syst* 30:828–832, 1969.
*15. Targum S.: Dealing with psychosis during pregnancy. *Ann Pharm* 19:18–21, 1979.
*16. Rumeau-Rouquette C., Goujard J., Huel G.: Possible teratogenic effects of phenothiazines in human beings. *Teratology* 15:57–64, 1977.
*17. Slone D., Siskind V., Heinonen O. P., et al: Antenatal exposure to the phenothiazines in relation to congenital malformations, perinatal mortality, birth weight and intelligence quotient score. *Am J Obstet Gynecol* 128:486–488, 1977.
18. Robertson R., Majka J., Bokelman D.: Effects of prenatal exposure to chlorpromazine on postnatal development and behavior of rats. *Toxicol Appl Pharmacol* 48:A117, 1979.
19. Ananth J.: Side effects on fetus and infant of psychotropic drug use during pregnancy. *Int Pharmacopsychiatry* 11:246–260, 1976.
20. Levy W., Wisnerewski K.: Chlorpromazine causing extrapyramidal dysfunction. *NY State Med J* 74:684–685, 1974.

*Recommended reading.

21. Hill L. M., Desmond M. M., Kay J. L.: Extrapyramidal dysfunction in an infant of a schizophrenic mother. *J Pediatr* 69:589–595, 1966.
22. Falterman C. G., Richardson J. C.: Small left colon syndrome associated with ingestion of psychotropic drugs. *J Pediatr* 97:308–310, 1980.
23. Kopelman A., McCullar F., Haggeness L.: Limb malformations following maternal use of haloperidol. *JAMA* 231:62–64, 1975.
24. Archer J. D.: Another possible teratogen? *JAMA* 231:69, 1975.
25. Hanson J. W., Oakley G. P.: Haloperidol and limb deformity. *JAMA* 231:26, 1975.
26. Ayd F. J. Jr. (ed): Is haloperidol teratogenic? *Int Drug Ther Newslett* 10:8, 1975.
27. Ayd F. J. Jr.: Excretion of psychotropic drugs in human breast milk. *Int Drug Ther Newslett* 8: Nos. 9 and 10, 1973.
28. Yamer A., McKey R., Arias D., et al: Phenothiazine-induced extrapyramidal dysfunction in the neonate. *J Pediatr* 75:479–480, 1969.
29. Yalom I. D., Lunde D. T., Moos R. H., et al: The "postpartum blues" syndrome: Description and related variables. *Arch Gen Psychiatry* 18:16, 1968.
30. Kane F. J.: Postpartum disorders, in Freedman A., Kaplan H. I., Sadock B. J. (eds): *Comprehensive Textbook of Psychiatry II,* Baltimore, Williams & Wilkins, 1975, vol 1, pp 1055–1059.
*31. Howard F. M., Hill J. M.: Drugs in pregnancy. *Obstet Gynecol Surv* 34:643–653, 1979.
32. McBride W. G.: Limb deformities associated with iminodibenzyl hydrochloride. *Med J Aust* 1:192, 1972.
33. Bannister P., Smith C. D., Miller J.: Possible teratogenicity of tricyclic antidepressants. *Lancet* 1:838–839, 1972.
34. Freeman R.: Limb deformities: Possible association with drugs. *Med J Aust* 1:606–607, 1972.
35. Buckfield P.: Major congenital faults in newborn infants: A pilot study in New Zealand. *NZ Med J* 78:195–204, 1973.
36. Australian Drug Evaluation Committee: Tricyclic antidepressants and limb reduction deformities. *Med J Aust* 1:768–769, 1973.
*37. Goldberg H. L., DiMascio A.: Psychotropic drugs in pregnancy, in Lipton M. A., DiMascio A., Killam K. F. (eds): *Psychopharmacology: A Generation of Progress.* New York, Raven Press, 1978, pp 1047–1055.
38. Webster P. A. C.: Withdrawal symptoms in neonates associated with maternal antidepressant therapy. *Lancet* 2:318–319, 1973.
39. Eggermont E., Raveschot J., Deneve V., et al: The adverse influence of imipramine on the adaptation of the newborn to extrauterine life. *Acta Paediatr Belg* 26:197–204, 1972.
40. Hill M., Stern L.: Drugs in pregnancy: Effects on the fetus and newborn. *Drugs* 17:182–197, 1979.
*41. Weinstein M., Goldfield M.: Cardiovascular malformations with lithium use during pregnancy. *Am J Psychiatry* 132:529–531, 1975.
*42. Gelenberg A. J.: Lithium during pregnancy: Risks of cardiovascular malformations. *Mass Gen Hosp Newslett Biol Ther Psychiatry* 4:1, 1981.
43. Nora J. J., Nora H. A., Toems W. A.: Lithium, Ebstein's anomaly and other congenital heart defects. *Lancet* 2:594–595, 1974.
44. Park J. M., Sridaromont S., Ledbetter E. O., et al: Ebstein's anomaly of the tricuspid valve associated with prenatal exposure to lithium carbonate. *Am J Dis Child* 134:703–704, 1980.
45. Targum S. D., Davenport Y. B., Webster M. J.: Postpartum mania in bipolar manic-depressive patients withdrawn from lithium carbonate. *J Nerv Ment Dis* 167:572–574, 1979.

*46. Berkowitz R. L., Constan D. R., Michizuki T.: *Handbook for Prescribing Medications during Pregnancy.* Boston, Little, Brown, 1980.

47. Havdala H. S., Borison R. L., Diamond B. I.: Potential hazards and applications of lithium in anesthesiology. *Anesthesiology* 50:534–537, 1979.

48. Woody J. N., London W. L., Wilbanks G. D.: Lithium toxicity in the newborn. *Pediatrics* 47:94–96, 1971.

49. Wilbanks G. D., Bressler B., Peete H. C. Jr., et al: Toxic effects of lithium carbonate in a mother and newborn infant. *JAMA* 213:856–857, 1970.

50. DiMascio A., Goldberg H.: Psychotropics in pregnancy: Safer than you think. *Curr Prescript* 2:56–58, 1976.

51. Sobel D. E.: Fetal damage due to ECT, insulin coma, chlorpromazine or reserpine. *Arch Gen Psychiatry* 2:606–611, 1960.

52. Remick R., Maurice W.: ECT in pregnancy. *Am J Psychiatry* 135:761–762, 1978.

53. Safra M. J., Oakley G. P.: Association between cleft lip with or without cleft palate and prenatal exposure to diazepam. *Lancet* 2:478–480, 1975.

54. Saxen I.: Associations between oral clefts and drugs taken during pregnancy. *Int J Epidemiol* 4:37–44, 1975.

55. Saxen E., Saxen L.: Association between maternal intake of diazepam and oral clefts. *Lancet* 2:498, 1975.

56. Saxen I.: Epidemiology of cleft lip and palate. *Br J Prev Soc Med* 29:103–110, 1975.

57. Aarskog D.: Association between maternal intake of diazepam and oral clefts. *Lancet* 2:921, 1975.

58. Athinaragan P., Pierog S. H., Nigam S. K., et al: Chlordiazepoxide withdrawal in the neonate. *Am J Obstet Gynecol.* 124:212–213, 1976.

59. Milkovich L., van dan Berg B. J.: Effects of prenatal meprobamate and chlordiazepoxide hydrochloride on human embryonic and fetal development. *N Engl J Med* 291:1268–1271, 1974.

60. Hartz S. C., Heinonen O. P., Shapiro S., et al: Antenatal exposure to meprobamate and chlordiazepoxide in relation to malformations, mental development and childhood mortality. *N Engl J Med* 292:726–728, 1975.

61. Mazzi E.: Possible neonatal diazepam withdrawal: A case report. *Am J Obstet Gynecol* 129:586–587, 1977.

62. Rementeria J. L., Bhatt K.: Withdrawal symptoms in neonates from intrauterine exposure to diazepam. *J Pediatr* 90:123–126, 1977.

63. Heinonen O. P., Slone D., Shapiro S.: *Birth Defects and Drugs in Pregnancy.* Littleton, New York: Publishing Sciences Group, 1977, pp 323–334.

64. Saxen I.: Cleft palate and maternal diphenhydramine intake. *Lancet* 1:407–408, 1974.

65. Siep M.: Growth retardation, dysmorphic facies and minor malformations following massive exposure to phenobarbitone in utero. *Acta Pediatr Scand* 65:617–621, 1976.

66. Smith D. W.: Teratogenicity of anticonvulsive medications. *Am J Dis Child* 131:1337, 1977.

67. Desmond M. M., Schwanecke R. P., Wilson G. S., et al: Maternal barbiturate utilization and neonatal withdrawal symptomatology. *J Pediatr* 80:190–197, 1972.

68. Hill R. M., Verniaud W. M., Morgan N. F., et al: Urinary excretion of phenobarbital in a neonate having withdrawal symptoms. *Am J Dis Child* 131:546–550, 1972.

69. Karacan I., Heine W., Agnew H., et al: Characteristics of sleep patterns during late pregnancy and the postpartum periods. *Am J Obstet Gynecol* 101:579–586, 1968.

*70. Mannor S. M.: Hyperemesis gravidarum, in Iffey L., Kaminetsky H. A. (eds): *Principles and Practice of Obstetrics and Perinatology,* New York, John Wiley & Sons, 1981, vol 2, pp 1155–1164.

71. Indications for Bendectin narrowed. *FDA Drug Bull* 11:1–3, 1981.

72. Williams J. W.: Nausea and vomiting, in Pritchard J. A., MacDonald P. C. (eds): *Obstetrics,* ed 16. New York, Appleton–Century Crofts, 1980, p 342.
73. Mann E. C., Armistead T. N.: Pregnancy and sexual behavior, in Freedman A. M., Kaplan H. I., Sadock B. J. (eds): *Comprehensive Textbook of Psychiatry II,* Baltimore, Williams & Wilkins, 1975, vol 2, p 1437.
74. Perlmutter J.: Heroin addiction and pregnancy. *Obstet Gynecol Surv* 29:439–446, 1974.
75. Reddy A., Harper R., Stern G.: Observations on heroin and methadone withdrawal in the newborn. *Pediatrics* 48:353, 1971.
76. Kandall S., Gartner L. M.: Delayed presentation of neonatal methadone withdrawal. *Pediatr Res* 7:320–392, 1973.
77. Zelson C.: Current concepts, infant of the addicted mother. *N Engl J Med* 228:1393–1395, 1973.
78. Fleming J. W., Rosser P.: The congenitally methadone-addicted infant. *Birth Defects* 15:99–117, 1979.
79. Glass L., Evans H. E.: Narcotic withdrawal in the newborn. *Am Fam Physician* 6:75–78, 1972.
80. Rajegowda B. K., Glass L., Evans H. E., et al: Methadone withdrawal in newborn infants. *J Pediatr* 81:532–534, 1972.
81. Herzlinger R. A., Kandall S. R., Vaughn H. G.: Neonatal seizures associated with narcotic withdrawal. *J Pediatr* 91:638–641, 1977.
82. Olsen G. D., Lees M. H.: Ventilatory response to carbon dioxide of infants following chronic prenatal exposure. *J Pediatr* 96:983-989, 1980.
83. Cohen S.: Caffeine. *Drug Abuse Alcoholism Newslett* 10:1–3, 1981.
84. Levine J. N.: Amphetamine ingestion with biliary atresia. *J Pediatr* 79:130–131, 1971.
*85. Van Blerk G. A., Majerns T. C., Myers R. A.: Teratogenic potential of some psychopharmacologic drugs: A brief review. *Int J Gynecol Obstet* 17:399–402, 1980.
86. Long S. Y.: Does LSD induce chromosomal change and malformations? *Teratology* 6:75–90, 1972.
87. Golden N. L., Sokol R. J., Rubin L.: Angel dust: Possible effects on the fetus. *Pediatrics* 65:18–20, 1980.
*88. Langer A., Caghan E. N.: Drug and alcohol abuse during pregnancy, in Iffy L., Kaminetsky H. A.: *Principles and Practice of Obstetrics and Perinatology,* New York, John Wiley & Sons, 1981, vol 1, pp 543–552.

11

Temporal Lobe Epilepsy

JEFFREY B. WEILBURG, M.D.

I. INTRODUCTION

Complex partial seizures, previously called psychomotor seizures, are brief, episodic changes in mental status and behavior directly associated with the paroxysmal discharge of epileptic foci in the temporal lobes. Long-term, enduring changes in personality and emotionality, referred to as the "**interictal behavior syndrome**" or "temporal lobe syndrome," often appear between seizures in patients who have epileptic foci in the temporal lobe. Temporal lobe epilepsy (TLE) describes the conglomeration of complex partial seizures, the interictal behavior syndrome, and other associated problems.

Temporal lobe epilepsy is the most common focal and adult seizure disorder, making up about 20 to 30% of all forms of epilepsy. Psychiatric problems occur with greater frequency in TLE patients than in those with other types of seizure disorders. Once mental health clinicians recognize the emotional problems associated with TLE, they should provide direct care or collaborate with a medical team. Although our current knowledge and understanding of phenomena associated with TLE and its treatment remain incomplete and somewhat controversial, we discuss various perspectives. This chapter describes the characteristics and treatment, particularly pharmacological, of complex partial seizures and the interictal behavior syndrome.

II. TEMPORAL LOBE EPILEPSY

A. Characteristics of Complex Partial Seizures

1. Aura

An aura lasting several seconds to hours may occur independently but often precedes a complex partial seizure. Malaise and abdominal discomfort

JEFFREY B. WEILBURG, M.D. • Department of Psychiatry, Harvard Medical School and Beth Israel Hospital, Boston, Massachusetts 02215.

are typical sensations. Unpleasant olfactory or gustatory hallucinations that are often difficult to describe may also occur. A dreamy state or feeling of fear and despair or, rarely, elation can also appear. Seizures or auras may begin at any time. Some patients have seizures "triggered" by photic stimulation, strong emotions, colors, and even snatches of song.

2. Complex Partial Seizures

Seizures interrupt normal emotional responses and memory. Penfield described them as periods of "psychoparesis" marked by "absence or automatism." The patient usually cannot recall the events occurring during a seizure. As the seizure begins, the patient's activity usually stops, the level of awareness decreases, and an expressionless stare appears. Oral automatism such as lipsmacking, swallowing, chewing, or grimacing are characteristic of seizures. Stereotyped motor movements include scratching, rubbing, or fumbling with clothes or buttons. The patient may turn his eyes, head, or trunk, but he maintains his posture and does not fall to the ground or become fully unconscious unless a major motor seizure supervenes. Autonomic reactions, which sometimes occur, include sweating, pallor or flushing, pupillary dilation or constriction, tachycardia, and salivation. Urinary incontinence occurs only occasionally, and fecal incontinence is rare.

Rarely, patients manifest a seizure by bouts of excessive water drinking. Other unusual presentations include paresthesias or indescribable, sometimes severe, pains in the limbs or abdomen. The duration of a complex partial seizure generally ranges from several seconds to several minutes. Temporal status epilepticus has been reported but is probably rare.

3. Postictal States

Seizures are always followed by a period of postictal confusion characterized by mild to moderately severe clouding of consciousness. The patient's mental status gradually clears over a period of 2 to 10 min.

4. Pseudoseizures

Pseudoseizures are episodes of abnormal behavior that resemble a seizure and are described by the patients as a "seizure" but are not correlated with EEG evidence of seizure activity (when EEG is monitored during the episode). Pseudoseizures have also been called "conditioned seizures" or "hysterical seizures." Pseudoseizures are not uncommon occurrences in patients who have TLE. They also appear in patients with severe functional psychiatric pathology.

Pseudoseizures are often the dramatic, maladaptive expression of unconscious (or conscious) psychic distress and should be responded to with understanding, support, or behavioral strategies. Of course, a patient may have both actual seizures and pseudoseizures and then will require a mixture of psychological and medical treatment.

Simultaneous monitoring of behavior and EEG with sphenoidal leads (specially placed electrodes that can pick up abnormal activity that surface electrodes may miss) while the patient is given an infusion of medication that may induce a seizure can be used to make the distinction between real and pseudoseizures. This procedure must only be done under carefully controlled conditions by experienced physicians.

B. Interictal Behavior Syndrome

1. Definition

In patients with TLE, long-term stable changes in personality, emotions, and behavior may become evident between seizures (interictally). These changes occur with sufficient frequency to be grouped together as a syndrome, the interictal behavior syndrome (IBS). The nature and severity of these symptoms vary from patient to patient. Some patients are affected only superficially, whereas others suffer impaired mental and emotional functioning that assumes psychotic proportions. The symptoms and behaviors manifested by patients with the IBS may not lead to problems in living and, in some individuals, may be useful qualities not requiring psychiatric treatment. For example, Dostoevski probably had TLE with the IBS, manifested by hypergraphia and intense philosophical interests.

a. Characteristics of the IBS

The deepening of all affects is a central characteristic of the IBS. Even if the patient responds accurately to a real event, his emotions may become inappropriately intense and sustained. He may attribute deep affective significance to random, unimportant details, objects, and intra- or interpersonal events. Patients may thus seem humorless and seriously concerned in an overgeneralized manner. They may tend toward metaphysical speculation, manifest an augmented sense of personal destiny, and become intensely religious (hyperreligiosity).

Patients also can become extremely moralistic and pay excessive attention to rules; they are frequently filled with self-recriminations and guilt. Suspiciousness and paranoia may become part of their style. Temporal lobe epilepsy patients may also become obsessional and circumstantial. Their style of communication is long-winded, repetitive, and overly detailed. Hypergraphia, manifested by the writing of diaries, novels, or detailed notes, is another distinctive feature of the IBS.

Another common feature of the IBS is sexual changes. Clinicians report hyposexuality most frequently, but hypersexuality or alteration in choice of sexual objects also occurs.

b. Dissociative Episodes

Patients with the IBS exhibit dissociative phenomena. The actual incidence is probably low but is higher than in the non-TLE population. These dissociative states occur more frequently in females than in males and often involve expressions of aggression or sexuality.

Dissociative episodes may occur interictally and are probably not directly related to seizure activity. Periods of amnesia (often called "lost time"), voice changes, and alterations in personality, sense of self, and handedness mark these episodes. Multiple personality disorder has been seen in some patients with TLE.

c. Phobias

Phobias may occur in patients with TLE with greater frequency than in other populations. However, their development may be related to the episodes of fear that occur during the ictus or aura; therefore, some clinicians do not feel that these phobias are primary features of the IBS.

2. Aggression and Violence

The relationship between acts of violence or aggression and the ability or propensity of patients with complex partial seizures or the IBS to commit such acts remains controversial. The ongoing debate between Pincus and Delgado highlights some of the factors involved in the controversy. Although it is still subject to dispute, in our view, the following discussion most accurately reflects the currently available data.

Patients with the IBS are often irritable and exhibit a general worsening of temper. Outbursts of anger, hostility, and organized, directed acts of aggression may occur with the patient fully conscious. Such outbursts are usually in response to environmental provocation. Patients typically recall the episodes and often express remorse after the act.

In contrast to the interictal hostility, aggression during the seizures is probably rare. Occasional patients may demonstrate violent behavior, but their behavior is probably less complex and more in response to the internal experience of fear or rage than the anger that occurs during the IBS.

3. Psychoses and the IBS

Many clinicians have reported a "schizophrenialike" or "schizophreniform" psychosis in TLE patients. This psychosis includes visual and auditory hallucinations and a formal thought disorder. Unlike schizophrenics, these patients maintain affective intensity and interpersonal relatedness; they do not progressively deteriorate. The psychosis can become a long-term problem. The symptoms may become severe enough to disable the patient. Symptoms are relieved only partly, if at all, by antipsychotic and anticonvulsant medication. Surgical removal of the temporal lobe for control of seizures refractory to medical management is sometimes followed by a "mellowing" or disappearance of psychotic symptoms, but this effect is not predictable, and the psychosis may even worsen in some patients.

Researchers disagree about the nature, etiology, and prevalence of the "schizophreniform" psychosis but have estimated that 5 to 15% of patients with the IBS develop psychoses as late, severe sequelae of the IBS. Some authors believe that psychoses and left-sided lesions are associated. These symptoms may be refractory to treatment and are infrequently relieved by medication or surgery.

Acute periods of psychosis not specifically related to the IBS also occur and are discussed below.

4. Laterality of the Lesion

The particular features of the IBS manifested by a given patient and the style with which these features are expressed may be directly related to the location of the primary epileptic focus. Those who have foci in the right temporal lobe may demonstrate more emotionality, affective disturbance, and impulsivity. They tend to minimize the unpleasant aspects of their behaviors. In contrast, those who have a focus on the left side may intellectualize their affects and express alterations in ideation such as increased metaphysical speculation and hypergraphia. These patients tend to exaggerate the severity of their behaviors.

C. Acute Psychotic Episodes

Patients with TLE may have periods of acute psychosis dominated by either mania or depression and consistent with organic affective disorders described in DSM-III. Alternatively, they may have disorders of thought and/or perception, consistent with the organic delusional state or organic hallucinosis.

Various factors, either singly or in combination, can induce these episodes.

1. Medication Toxicity

Excessive blood levels of antiepileptic drugs, including phenytoin, carbamazepine, phenobarbital, primidone, and others, can lead to behavioral deterioration and psychosis in some patients. The clinician should be suspicious that the patient is toxic if he becomes silly, disinhibited, confused, agitated, or excited as the dosage of anticonvulsant is increased. Blood levels should be checked, looking for values in the toxic range. The patient should be carefully examined for other signs of toxicity such as severe nystagmus, diplopia, ataxia, or dysarthria. An empirical trial of a lower dosage is indicated if toxicity is suspected.

2. Overcontrol of Seizures

Clinical experience shows that some patients need to have occasional complex partial seizures; they become psychotic if the seizures are completely eliminated by medication. This phenomenon, perhaps associated with the "forced normalization" of the EEG described by Landholt, is poorly understood. The optimum frequency of seizures must be determined on an empirical basis for each patient.

3. Medication Withdrawal

In many patients, acute psychosis marked by agitation and hallucinations can occur after abrupt withdrawal of anticonvulsant medication.

4. Delirium

A delirium may initially present with behavioral disturbances similar to psychotic symptoms. In additon to the common causes of delirium (e.g., drug toxicity, trauma, infection, mass lesion), patients with TLE may manifest repeated or severe postictal delirium secondary to frequent and poorly controlled seizures. Temporal status epilepticus, though rare, may produce a delirium or psychosis.

5. Other

Similarly to other patients, those with TLE may suffer psychotic decompensation secondary to severe environmental stress. Although the point is controversial, some clinicians believe that patients with TLE also have a functional psychiatric illness independent of but occurring concurrently with TLE.

III. DIAGNOSIS OF TEMPORAL LOBE EPILEPSY

A. History

Complex partial seizures may appear at any age; a peak incidence of onset occurs during adolescence. The IBS, if it occurs, does not manifest itself until some time, usually years, after seizures first appear.

The most common lesion found in the temporal lobes of patients who have had surgery is mesial temporal sclerosis. It is widely believed that this lesion may have occurred during febrile convulsions of infancy. There may be a family history of epilepsy, and the genetic "loading" is hypothesized to be a susceptibility to febrile seizures and their sequelae. Hamartomas of the temporal lobe also are frequently found at surgery.

B. Electroencephalogram

The presence of "spikes" over the temporal area confirms the diagnosis of TLE. However, the anatomic position of the temporal lobes makes it difficult to demonstrate abnormalities with surface electrodes alone. **Nasopharyngeal or sphenoidal leads,** which are closer to the temporal lobe, increase the sensitivity of the EEG. Photic stimulation, hyperventilation, and, in carefully supervised cases, methohexital (Brevital®) stimulation during EEG can be used to help reveal otherwise hidden abnormalities. A sleep-deprived EEG, in which the patient is not allowed to sleep the night before the test and has a tracing made during wakefulness and sleep [induced in the EEG lab with chloral hydrate (Noctec® and others), 500 mg by mouth], can also reveal subtle abnormalities. Monitoring the EEG during seizures may help to rule out pseudoseizures. Telemetric EEG monitoring with sphenoidal leads may also help to pick out the presence of a focus. However, TLE is **not** ruled out by multiple negative EEGs if the patient exhibits typical complex partial seizures, auras, and the cluster of changes characteristic of the IBS.

C. Neurological Examination

The neurological examination is often negative, but several abnormalities may appear if specifically tested for. These include:

1. Weakness of involuntary facial expression (contralateral to focus). The patient, for example, may smile symmetrically when instructed "to smile" but may show asymmetry of the mouth when smiling at a funny joke.
2. Anomic aphasia. If there is a left temporal focus, the patient may have difficulty finding words.
3. Deficit in dichotic listening. Simultaneous presentation of a different sound to each ear through a special apparatus may reveal an abnormal pattern of perception, indicating pathology of one of the temporal lobes.
4. A homonymous superior quadrantanopsia may indicate damage to the temporal portion of the optic radiation.

D. Physical Examination and Laboratory Tests

Physical examination and laboratory tests are generally within normal limits if TLE is the only problem. However, any patient who presents with new-onset seizures or with behavioral changes that have an organic basis should have a complete neurological work-up to rule out the presence of lesions that are potentially life-threatening or correctable. The work-up should include CBC, serum electrolytes, glucose, BUN, liver function tests, toxicology screen, and VDRL. Most epilepsy is idiopathic, and no definite lesion is found during a diagnostic work-up. However, the problems listed below may present as seizures or behavioral changes:

1. Intracranial masses including primary neoplasms such as astrocytoma, glioma, or meningioma; metastatic lesions such as breast, lung, melanoma; lymphomas or leukemias; and vascular malformations.
2. Infections such as meningitis or encephalitis; parenchymal, epidural, or subdural abscesses; or granulomas.
3. Toxic, metabolic, or nutritional disturbances.
4. Others, including trauma, subdural or epidural hematoma.

IV. GENERAL THERAPEUTIC MEASURES

Patients with TLE suffer from problems associated with seizures, auras, and the IBS and problems associated with, but not directly caused by, the epilepsy (i.e., speech or motor disorder secondary to brain damage). Each type of problem demands its own special therapeutic strategy. However, considerable overlap and interaction invariably occur. Anticonvulsant medications may suppress seizures and also affect the IBS. Psychotherapeutic intervention may decrease the frequency of pseudoseizures and contribute to seizure control by improving patient compliance. Surgical procedures may lead to better seizure control but worsen a psychosis. Medical intervention may affect seizures and the symptoms of the IBS but may produce serious adverse effects. Thus, although the clinician should "target" interventions towards ictal and interictal problems separately, it is always of primary importance to watch for therapeutic overlap and to treat the patient as a whole person rather than as a set of problems.

Described below are three basic therapeutic modalities used to treat seizures and the IBS. After a brief discussion of psychotherapy and surgery, we describe the anticonvulsants in detail. The application of these data to the treatment of seizures, the IBS, and the psychosis sometimes seen in patients with TLE follows in Section VI.

A. Psychotherapy

Exploratory, analytic psychotherapy has generally not been helpful in treating the problems that arise as part of the IBS. Supportive therapy emphasizing the use of cognitive restructuring to control their difficulties may be more valuable. Groups composed of TLE patients can provide support, information, education, consensual validation, and reality testing and are very helpful. Even if formal psychotherapy is not part of the treatment plan, the patients and their families will feel more comfortable and able to make appropriate use of the clinician if their psychodynamics are considered.

B. Surgery

Surgeons have removed the diseased or electrically active parts of the temporal lobes to treat patients whose seizures cannot be controlled by medication and who are suffering significant disability. However, surgery is **not indicated** for the treatment of the **psychiatric** problems of TLE.

The technique involves block resection of the anterior portion (5.5 to 6.5 cm) of the temporal lobe on the side of the focus or predominant focus. Thus, most of the hippocampus, the parahippocampal gyrus and uncus, and part of the amygdala are removed unilaterally. The results are variable, and the use of surgery remains somewhat controversial.

C. Pharmacotherapy

Psychotropic medication can play a central role in the treatment of TLE. However, patients with TLE frequently have multiple problems, and dispensing medication alone is not enough to ensure proper care. The clinician must also pay attention to the psychodynamic factors that influence the patient's experience of himself and the world and which lead to difficult interactions with his family and caregivers. Ignoring or misunderstanding these factors often leads the patient or medical team to "act out" the confusion, frustration, and distress engendered by the complicated clinical situations that frequently surround the treatment of TLE.

Some patients have significant social and vocational problems which also must be evaluated. Others have mental retardation or neurological handicaps. These additional problems may be treated with medications that have primary CNS effects or that interact with medications used to control TLE. Thus, the clinician must communicate and collaborate closely with the patient's other caregivers. The psychiatrist's understanding of both the psychodynamic factors and medical issues make him able to coordinate a complex treatment program.

The importance of tailoring the drug regimen to the specific needs of each individual cannot be overemphasized. The principles described below are useful guidelines for planning a rational therapeutic strategy. However, because an individual's response to these medications is never fully predictable, the clinician must be flexible and attentive to each individual patient. Awareness of the adverse behavioral effects of medication, the potential for complications with polypharmacy, attention to the overall clinical picture, and sensitivity to the human needs of the patient are critical factors in the drug treatment of TLE.

V. MEDICATIONS

Medication in TLE patients is used to control two types of problems: those directly associated with seizures and those associated with the interictal state. The drugs generally used include carbamazepine (Tegretol®), phenytoin (Dilantin® and others), phenobarbital (Luminal® and others), and primidone (Mysoline®).

A. Carbamazepine

1. Chemistry

Carbamazepine (Tegretol®) is a dibenzazepine derivative structurally related to the heterocyclic antidepressants* [e.g., imipramine (Tofranil® and others)] and to phenytoin. Its structural formula is:

2. Adverse Reactions

a. Neurological

When carbamazepine treatment is started, ataxia, drowsiness, and dizziness often occur and usually disappear after a few weeks. Rarely, confusional

*Since many of the currently used thymoleptic drugs are not tricyclic in structure, we have adopted this term to represent the various cyclic antidepressants. From: Baldessarini R. J.: Overview of recent advances in antidepressant pharmacology. Part II. *McLean Hosp J* 7:1–27, 1982.

states may appear. If the drug is initially administered in low doses, and the dose increased only gradually, these and other commonly occurring unwanted effects can be minimized.

b. Gastrointestinal

Nausea, vomiting, and anorexia are common when treatment is begun but usually resolved within the first few weeks. Hepatocellular and cholestatic jaundice occur rarely but with enough frequency to warrant monitoring SGOT, SGPT, alkaline phosphatase, and bilirubin every 3 months during therapy. If significant changes occur, consultation with a gastroenterologist and close monitoring of liver functioning may allow the drug to be continued.

c. Ocular

Diplopia and blurred vision are common when treatment is started but usually resolve spontaneously over time. Increases in intraocular pressure also may occur, which means that patients with known or suspected glaucoma should be examined by an ophthalmologist before, and periodically during, treatment.

d. Hematological

Bone marrow suppression leading to aplastic anemia, leukopenia, agranulocytosis, or thrombocytopenia is a very rare but life-threatening toxic effect. Deaths secondary to carbamazepine-induced aplastic anemia have been reported. Concern over this problem was probably exaggerated in the past, and the clinician should not withhold the drug on this basis when it is indicated. However, **close hematological monitoring is warranted. Before treatment,** the clinician should obtain a complete blood count, platelet count, reticulocyte count, and serum iron. **Patients who have significant abnormalities of any of these studies or who have a history of blood dyscrasia should not receive carbamazepine. During the initial 3 months of treatment,** obtain a weekly CBC, platelet, and reticulocyte count. **For the next 2 to 3 years,** a CBC, platelet, and reticulocyte count should be drawn every 3 months. If any of the following appear, the drug should be stopped, and hematological consultation obtained.

Hematocrit < 32%
Hemoglobin < 11 g/100 ml
Leukocytes < 4000/mm^3
Platelets < 100,000/m^3
Reticulocytes < 0.3%

Patients should be advised to consult their physician immediately if they develop fever, sore throat, mouth ulcers, easy bruising, petechiae, or purpural hemorrhage. These may be the early symptoms of a hematological problem. The clinician should stop the drug and obtain CBC and platelet counts.

e. Cutaneous

Stomatitis is a not infrequent unwanted effect to which tolerance usually develops. Rashes and other manifestations of drug allergy occur in about 3% of patients. Stevens–Johnson syndrome, lupuslike reactions, exfoliative dermatitis, alterations in skin pigmentation, and photosensitivity also have been reported.

f. Cardiovascular

The cardiac effects of the drug are poorly described but probably are similar to those of the heterocyclic antidepressants. Guidelines for the use of this drug in patients with cardiac disease have not been established.

g. Renal

Renal damage, a rare adverse effect leading to oliguria and hypertension, also has been described.

h. Cross Sensitivity

Cross sensitivity to the allergic effects of the heterocyclics may occur.

i. Pregnancy

Teratogenic effects of carbamazepine have been noted in animals but not in humans. However, until further research is completed, **the drug should be avoided during pregnancy.**

3. Drug Interactions

The major effects on carbamazepine by other medications are mediated through the microsomal enzyme system (see Table 1).

4. Kinetics

Carbamazepine is rapidly absorbed following oral administration. Peak plasma levels are reached within 2 to 6 hr and vary widely in different individuals.

Eighty percent of the drug is bound to plasma proteins. It is metabolized by the liver and may induce its own metabolism. The initial half-life ranges from 25 to 65 hr, whereas the steady-state half-life ranges from 12 to 17 hr.

5. Toxicity

Toxicity is very similar to that of imipramine.

6. Preparation and Dosage/Monitoring

Carbamazepine is available as single scored tablets of 200 mg. Parenteral forms are not available.

Treatment should begin with 200 mg twice a day. Clinicians should increase the dose by 200 mg per week. Adults usually require between 400 and 800 mg per day administered according to a twice- or three-times-a-day schedule.

Blood levels are available and should be kept at 4 to 10 μg/ml. Most patients achieve optimal control of seizures with minimum adverse effects when the level is between 6.5 to 7.5 μg/ml. Some patients will have adequate seizure control with levels of 3.5 and may therefore be maintained at this level. Rarely, a patient may require levels above 8.0 μg/ml for seizure control and may not have too many unacceptable adverse effects.

If seizures continue to occur with unacceptable frequency after the drug has been maintained at a dose sufficient to produce blood levels of 7.5 to 8.0 μg/ml for 3 to 5 days, another drug may be substituted or a second drug added.

B. Phenytoin

1. Chemistry

Phenytoin's (Dilantin®) structure is

The two benzene (aromatic) substituents at the 5 position appear to be essential to the antiepileptic properties of the compound.

2. Adverse Reactions

a. Neurological

The central nervous system effects of phenytoin are generally dose dependent. Therapeutic amounts do not usually produce sedation, but higher doses may lead to CNS depression. Nystagmus, a frequent unwanted effect, appears at blood levels that range between 10 and 20 μg/ml. Ataxia occurs at blood levels around 30 μg/ml and may indicate toxicity.

TABLE 1. Drug Interactions

Phenytoin drug interactions

A. Drugs that increase effects by metabolic inhibition
1. Aminosalicylic acid (Parasal®) and perhaps other salicylates
2. Chloramphenicol (Chloromycetin® and others)
3. Chlordiazepoxide (Librium®)
4. Chlorpheniramine (Dallergy®)
5. Chlorpromazine (Thorazine® and others)
6. Coumarin anticoagulants (also displaces from binding sites)
7. Cycloserine (Seromycin®)
8. Disulfiram (Antabuse®)
9. Estrogens
10. Ethosuximide (Zarontin®)
11. Halothane (Fluothane®)
12. Isoniazid (INH®, Nydrazid®, and others)
13. Methylphenidate (Ritalin®)
14. Oxyphenbutazone (Oxalid®, Tandearil®)
15. Phenylbutazone (Butazolidin® and others)
16. Prochlorperazine (Compazine® and others)
17. Sulfadiazine (Suladyne®)
18. Sulfamethizole (Azotrex® and others)
19. Sulfasoxazole (Gantrisin® and others)

B. Drugs whose effects are decreased
1. Vitamin D (Calciferol® and others) (direct antagonism)
2. Folic acid (Folvite® and others) (decreased absorption)
3. Phenobarbital (Luminal® and others) (enzyme induction)
4. Oral contraceptives (enzyme induction)
5. Corticosteroids (enzyme induction)

C. Drugs that decrease effects of phenytoin
1. Carbamazepine (Tegretol®) (enzyme induction)
2. Doxycycline (Vibramycin® and others) and other tetracyclines (Achromycin® and others) (enzyme induction)
3. Folic acid (Folvite® and others) (inhibit absorption, direct antagonism)
4. Dexamethasone (Decadron® and others) (enzyme induction)

D. Drugs that produce variable effects on phenytoin
1. Alcohol (enzyme induction?)
2. Phenobarbital (balance between enzyme induction and competitive inhibition)
3. Valproic acid (Depakene®) (associated with both lowered and raised serum levels)

E. Drugs that increase the risk of seizures with phenytoin
1. Reserpine (Serpasil® and others)
2. Heterocyclic antidepressants
3. Less often, other threshold-lowering agents

Phenobarbital drug interactions

A. Drugs whose effects are increased
1. MAOIs (decrease metabolism)
2. Phenothiazines
3. Thyroxine (Synthroid® and others) (displaces from binding sites)

B. Drugs whose effects are decreased
1. Chlorpromazine
2. Corticosteroids (enzyme induction)

(continued)

TABLE 1. (Continued)

3. Dicumarol and other oral anticoagulants (enzyme induction and decreased absorption)
4. Digitoxin (enzyme induction)
5. Doxycycline (enzyme induction)
6. Estrogens and oral contraceptives (enzyme induction)
7. Folic acid (Folvite® and others) (decreases bioavailability)
8. Griseofulvin (enzyme induction and decreased absorption)
9. Heterocyclic antidepressants (enzyme induction)
10. Phenylbutazone (enzyme induction)
11. Phenytoin (Dilantin® and others) (enzyme induction)
12. Testosterone (Oreton® and others) (enzyme induction)

C. Drugs that decrease effects
  1. Agents that induce liver enzymes
D. Drugs that increase sedation and CNS depression
  1. Alcohol (central additive effect)
  2. Isoniazid
  3. MAOIs
  4. Methylphenidate
  5. Phenylbutazone
  6. Phenytoin
  7. Valproic acid (displaces from binding sites, and enzyme inhibition)
E. Drugs that combine with phenobarbital to produce liver toxicity
  1. Carbon tetrachloride
  2. Chlorocarbon anesthetics

Primidone drug interactions

A. Drugs that commonly increase toxicity
  1. Disulfuram
  2. Isoniazid
B. Drug whose effects are commonly decreased
  1. Folic acid (decreases bioavailability)
C. Drug that commonly decreases effects
  1. Phenytoin (enzyme induction)
D. Other interactions—similar to phenobarbital (it is a metabolite of primidone)

Carbamazepine drug interactions

A. Drugs whose effects are decreased
  1. Warfarin (Coumadin®, Panwarfin®) (enzyme induction)
  2. Phenytoin (Dilantin®) (enzyme induction)
B. Drug that decreases effects
  1. Phenobarbital (enzyme induction)
C. Drugs that combine with carbamazepine to produce diabetes insipidus-like syndrome
  1. Antipsychotics
  2. Oncologic agents

Toxicity may occasionally be manifest by behavioral deterioration. Hyperactivity, silliness, confusion, drowsiness, and hallucinations may indicate phenytoin toxicity rather than poor control of epilepsy and may be relieved by lowering the dose. Peripheral neuropathy has been reported to occur in 7 to 30% of patients on long-term regimens of phenytoin.

b. Cardiovascular

Rapid intravenous administration of phenytoin may precipitate asystole and cardiovascular collapse. Phenytoin should therefore never be given at a rate greater than 50 mg/min IV push. During IV administration, vital signs should be monitored.

c. Cutaneous

Hirsutism is a frequent and annoying unwanted effect which can usually be kept at tolerable levels by careful dosage management.

Gingival hyperplasia occurs in about 20% of patients on long-term phenytoin therapy and is even more common in adolescents and children. Careful oral hygiene can control this problem.

Morbilliform (measleslike) rashes may sometimes appear and indicate that phenytoin should be stopped. The drug may be cautiously restarted when the rash clears and may be continued if the rash does not recur. Exfoliative, purpuric, or bullous skin rashes indicate a drug allergy; the clinician should stop the drug in these patients and not restart it.

A lupuslike syndrome, accompanied by a positive antinuclear antibody (ANA) and lupus erythematosus (LE) prep, sometimes occurs.

d. Gastrointestinal

Nausea, vomiting, epigastric pain, and anorexia sometimes accompany phenytoin treatment. Administering the drug with meals or milk and in divided doses may minimize the patient's discomfort.

e. Endocrine

Osteomalacia, accompanied by hypocalcemia and elevated alkaline phosphatase, sometimes occurs and may be a result of altered metabolism of vitamin D and calcium. It is relatively resistant to vitamin D therapy. The clinician should check the serum calcium every 6 months.

Phenytoin binds to thyroid-binding globulin, resulting in an artificially lowered protein bound T_4. No treatment is indicated. Hyperglycemia and glycosuria, probably secondary to phenytoin-induced inhibition of insulin secretion, are rare effects of this drug.

f. Hematological

Macrocytic and megaloblastic anemia, secondary to phenytoin's interference with folate and B_{12} metabolism, may appear. The clinician should draw a complete blood count every 6 months to screen for this problem and administer folate and B_{12} if the patient develops an anemia.

g. Pregnancy

The still incomplete data on the human teratogenicity of phenytoin suggest an increased incidence of birth defects in babies born to epileptic mothers on phenytoin. However, maternal seizures themselves may pose a risk to the fetus. Thus, although the clinician should avoid using this drug during pregnancy, the patient, her family, and obstetrician should assess and weigh the risks and benefits in each individual.

3. Drug Interactions

Several drugs can influence phenytoin's metabolism (see Table 1):

1. Barbiturates may increase the rate of metabolism of phenytoin, although this effect is variable and unpredictable.
2. Carbamazepine increases the rate of metabolism of phenytoin.
3. Oral anticoagulants, isoniazid (INH®, Nydrazid®, and others), disulfiram (Antabuse®), phenylbutazone (Butazolidan® and others), and possibly salicylates may inhibit the metabolism of phenytoin, thereby leading to toxicity.

4. Toxicity

The lethal dose of phenytoin in adults is 2 to 5 g. Initial symptoms of nystagmus, ataxia, and dysarthria progress to obtundation. Death is generally a result of respiratory depression.

Supportive measures, such as maintenance of airway, assisted ventilation, and use of vasopressors after the stomach has been emptied, may be adequate. However, some patients may require hemodialysis.

5. Kinetics

Phenytoin can be given orally and intravenously. Intramuscular injection is not recommended, because absorption by this route is erratic, and blood levels are unpredictable.

Phenytoin is well absorbed from the gastrointestinal (GI) tract. Peak blood levels occur 2 to 6 hr following oral administration. The average half-life is about 22 hr, so the drug may be given only once a day.

Phenytoin is extensively bound to plasma proteins, mainly albumin. It is metabolized by the hepatic microsomal enzymes into inactive metabolites which are reabsorbed by the GI tract and excreted in the urine.

Some patients show genetically determined differences in their ability to metabolize phenytoin. Both hyper- and hypometabolizers have been reported. The drug weakly induces the microsomal system and may induce its own metabolism.

6. Preparation and Dosage/Monitoring

The therapeutic range of phenytoin in the serum is 10 to 20 μg/ml. A dose of 5 mg/kg or 300 mg/day in the average adult usually is sufficient to keep blood levels within the therapeutic range. Given the long half-life of the drug at steady state, the maintenance dose may often be given on a once-a-day basis, usually at bedtime.

The rate at which therapeutic blood levels are attained depends on the clinical situation. A stable patient may be given 300 mg PO per day and will attain therapeutic levels in about 5 days (longer if patient is a rapid metabolizer). In emergencies, when seizures need to be controlled rapidly, "Dilantinization" can be rapidly achieved by giving 1000 mg IV push via syringe **at rates never exceeding 50 mg/min** (10 to 15 mg/kg or 25 mg/kg for children) while vital signs are closely monitored. These amounts can produce therapeutic blood levels in 20 min. Various intermediate regimens are also available in many textbooks of neurology.

Phenytoin sodium (Dilantin®) is available as 30- and 100-mg capsules for oral use and as a sterile solution of 50 mg/ml for IV use. Preparations of phenytoin, USP are available in 50-mg tablets and oral suspensions of 30 and 125 mg/5 ml. **Significant differences in bioavailability exist among the preparations of different manufacturers; therefore, the clinician should select one product and continue it.**

C. Phenobarbital

1. Chemistry

Phenobarbital (Luminal® and others) was the first effective anticonvulsant drug and continues to be a potent, widely used antiepileptic. Many anticonvulsants were developed based on the structure of phenobarbital:

2. Adverse Reactions

a. Neurological

Unfortunately, sedation occurs commonly at therapeutic levels and may set the upper dosage limit. In most patients, sedation decreases as tolerance develops. However, tolerance may also develop to the anticonvulsant effects. The drug must then be given in larger doses, but sedation may recur. Nevertheless (and fortunately), most patients experience a decrease in sedation in the few days following the dosage increase without a recurrence of tolerance to the anticonvulsant effects. Patients who remain drowsy may be unable to use this drug. Children sometimes experience paradoxical excitement rather than sedation. Nystagmus and ataxia are frequently seen when the drug reaches toxic blood levels.

b. Hematological

Megaloblastic anemia similar to that seen with phenytoin occurs only rarely. The anemia usually responds well to therapy with folate or B_{12}.

c. Endocrine

Osteomalacia and vitamin D deficiency are seen rarely. Hypoprothrombinemia and hemorrhage have been reported in the newborns of mothers who are using phenobarbital.

3. Drug Interactions

Barbiturates interact with a wide variety of drugs. Most commonly, phenobarbital decreases the effects of selected medications by inducing microsomal enzymes (see Table 1).

4. Toxicity and Withdrawal

Overdosage of phenobarbital can produce profound respiratory depression and death (see Chapter 7).

Withdrawal syndromes may occur, and the seizures that accompany these syndromes may be very refractory to treatment. Large doses of barbiturates may be required to control such withdrawal seizures. Other antiepileptics are generally of little value.

Dependence, addiction, and abuse are all potential dangers with phenobarbital (see Chapter 7).

5. Kinetics

Oral absorption is slow but complete. Peak plasma concentrations appear several hours after oral administration. The plasma half-life is about 90 min in adults.

Phenobarbital is 40 to 60% bound to plasma proteins. Approximately 25% of the drug is excreted unchanged in the urine. The remainder is converted by the hepatic microsomal enzymes into inactive metabolites and excreted in the urine.

6. Preparation and Dosage/Monitoring

Blood levels of 10 to 25 μg/ml are usually required for control of seizures. The drug is available in 15- and 30-mg tablets. Doses of 60 to 120 mg/day are generally sufficient to produce adequate blood levels in most patients. Sedation can be minimized by using a twice- and three-times-a-day dosage schedule. Hospitalized patients or those with refractory seizures may need higher blood levels; sedation or other unwanted effects remain the limiting factors.

D. Primidone

1. Chemistry

Primidone (Mysoline®) is a congener of phenobarbital. Its structure is

2. Adverse Reactions

a. Neurological

Sedation is the major unwanted effect of primidone. It may be severe and is less likely to disappear than the sedation caused by phenobarbital. Sedation may be minimized by beginning with low doses and increasing the dosage only gradually.

Vertigo, ataxia, and an experience of feeling intoxicated may occur during the first few days of therapy but often resolve spontaneously.

Although rare, some patients with TLE may become acutely psychotic soon after primidone is started. If this occurs, the drug should be immediately stopped, and the psychosis treated with antipsychotic agents.

b. Hematological

Megaloblastic anemia secondary to folate and B_{12} deficiency may appear. This usually responds to folate and B_{12} replacement. Patients on primidone should have a complete blood count checked every 6 months.

c. Endocrine

Osteomalacia similar to that seen with phenobarbital may occur.

d. Cutaneous

Allergic skin rash is rare, but if it occurs, the drug should be immediately stopped and not reused.

3. Drug Interactions

Primidone has properties similar to the barbiturates. Therefore, the clinician generally should assume that drug interactions resemble those of phenobarbital (see Table 1).

4. Toxicity

Primidone is very similar to phenobarbital in its ability to produce life-threatening respiratory depression following overdosage. The development of tolerance and withdrawal syndromes and their treatment are also similar to phenobarbital.

5. Kinetics

Primidone can only be given orally. It is rapidly and completely absorbed from the GI tract. Peak plasma levels are observed about 3 hr after ingestion. The plasma half-life of this drug is about 8 hr.

Primidone is converted into two active metabolites: phenobarbital and phenylethylmalonamide (PEMA). Only a small portion of primidone and PEMA is bound to plasma proteins.

6. Preparation and Dosage / Monitoring

Primidone is available as 50- and 250-mg tablets and as an oral suspension of 250 mg/5 ml. The usual daily adult dosage is 300 to 750 mg given in two or three divided doses. The usual starting dose of primidone is 50 to 125 mg per day. Primidone blood levels are available; the therapeutic range is between 10 to 25 μg/ml.

VI. CLINICAL APPLICATIONS

A. Control of Seizures

Anticonvulsants can usually suppress complex partial seizures and auras. They have the following effects: reduction in the frequency and severity of complex partial seizures; control of abdominal pain, paresthesias, excessive water drinking, or other disturbing ictal phenomenon; prevention or control of the grand mal major motor seizures that may sometimes follow a complex partial seizure; and relief from the phobias resulting from the ictal experience of fear.

The drugs generally used singly or in combination to control complex partial seizures include carbamazepine (Tegretol®), phenytoin (Dilantin® and others), phenobarbital (Luminal® and others), and primidone (Mysoline®). Clinicians now view **carbamazepine as the drug of choice for TLE.** If seizure control with carbamazepine is incomplete, the clinician can add either phenobarbital or phenytoin in gradually increasing doses until the therapeutic level is reached, appropriate control is achieved, or toxicity supervenes. On rare occasions, all three drugs are administered to provide adequate control of seizures. Primidone is the third choice, reserved for situations in which the others have failed or cannot be used. Primidone is rarely used in combination with phenobarbital because of similarities between the two.

The suppression of seizures is a general goal in the treatment of epilepsy. However, complete suppression of partial seizures may exacerbate the symptoms of the IBS and in some cases precipitate frank psychosis. Some patients feel better and demonstrate more normal interictal behavior if they have an occasional complex partial seizure. Thus, in practice, the clinician should seek an optimal balance between the control of seizures and the severity of the IBS.

B. Control of Interictal Problems

Anticonvulsants generally do not ameliorate the symptoms of the IBS. Carbamazepine, however, may both control complex partial seizures and alleviate some of the other problems of the IBS. It resembles the heterocyclic antidepressants structurally and may help to improve impulse control and mood.

The effect of carbamazepine on the IBS may be related to its inhibition of an experimental process called kindling. Kindling is a phenomenon in which repeated electrical stimulation, especially delivered to structures of the limbic system, leads to a lowered threshold for convulsive discharge. In the temporal lobe epileptic patient, the focus may act as an indwelling source of repeated stimulation, lowering the threshold of firing in emotional circuits. This may account for the excessive emotional association underlying the IBS. If this mechanism were applicable, suppression of kindling might prevent or ameliorate the IBS. In the future, drugs shown to suppress kindling in experimental animals might be tested for efficacy in controlling the IBS.

Drugs other than carbamazepine that have antikindling properties may be used to ameliorate the symptoms of the IBS. Amitryptiline (Elavil® and others) and imipramine, which have antikindling properties (probably because of their anticholinergic effects), may be useful adjuncts, especially when depression is a problem. Thioridazine (Mellaril®) also has similar effects and may be administered to control paranoia, hallucinations, and disorders of thought.

C. Treatment of Psychosis in the Patient with a Seizure Disorder

The following comments are directed specifically toward the treatment of psychosis in the patient with TLE but may be applied to patients with other forms of seizure disorders.

1. Antipsychotic Drugs

All psychotropic drugs effect the EEG. Antipsychotic drugs usually produce diffuse slowing, which is not pathological. However, abnormal patterns, including spike-and-wave forms, may appear. In the absence of underlying brain disease, these EEG changes rarely, if ever, manifest themselves as clinical seizures.

In patients with a history of epilepsy or organic brain disease or current evidence of organic brain dysfunction, special care is required when prescribing antipsychotic drugs, since they can lower the seizure threshold and be epileptogenic (see Table 2). For such patients, the physician should avoid prescribing antipsychotic drugs with strong epileptogenic properties, i.e., low-potency agents [e.g., chlorpromazine (Thorazine® and others)].

Various other factors influence the seizure threshold, including:

1. Dose: higher doses are more epileptogenic; sudden or large increases in dosage may further lower the seizure threshold. Treatment should be initiated with gradually increasing doses (and terminated in a similar fashion).
2. Stresses: hyperpyrexia, hypoglycemia, and physical exhaustion all independently lower the seizure threshold.

TABLE 2. Relative Epileptogenic Potential[a]

Antipsychotics	
Slight	Thioridazine, mesoridazine (Serentil®), fluphenazine (Prolixin®), molindone (Moban®)
Moderate	Perphenazine (Trilafon®), thiothixene (Navane®), haloperidol (Haldol®)
Marked	Chlorpromazine
Antidepressants	
Slight	Imipramine
Moderate	Amitriptyline
Stimulants	
Slight	Methylphenidate HCL (Ritalin®)
Doubtful	Dextroamphetamine (Dexedrine®)

[a]Adapted from Itil and Soldatos.[25]

2. Lithium

At low therapeutic levels, lithium may have anticonvulsant properties, acting synergistically with drugs such as phenytoin and phenobarbital. Lithium may thus be used to help patients modulate the intense effects of the interictal behavior syndrome. Care is needed, since toxic levels of lithium may significantly lower the seizure threshold, increasing seizure frequency.

3. Antidepressants

Antidepressants occasionally lower the seizure threshold to a clinically significant degree, but they can be used with caution in patients with seizure disorders. When drug interactions are taken into account, many patients who suffer from significant depression as part of the IBS respond to antidepressant medication.

VII. Conclusion

Temporal lobe epilepsy is an illness consisting of discrete, clinically identifiable abnormalities in brain structure and function that can be directly correlated with abnormalities of emotion, personality, and behavior. For researchers, it affords an opportunity to understand further the interaction between brain activity and behavior. For clinicians, it offers challenging opportunity to combine medical, neurological, and psychological models in the treatment of this complex disorder.

In this chapter we have described our current understanding of the clinical features and treatment of TLE. Much work, however, still needs to be completed to refine our knowledge of this important and exciting area.

SELECTED READING

1. Abramowicz A.: Carbamazepine in the management of seizure disorders. *Med Lett* 17:76, 1975.
2. Bear D. M.: Comments on aggressivity in a case of post-traumatic temporal lobe epilepsy. *Behav. Med* 8:32–41, 1981.
3. Bear D. M.: The significance of behavior change in temporal lobe epilepsy, in Blumer D., Levin K. (eds): *Psychiatric Complications in the Epilepsies: Current Research and Treatment. McLean Hosp J* (special issue) June 1977:9–21, 1977.
4. Bear D. M.: Temporal lobe epilepsy—a syndrome of sensory limbic hyperconnection. *Cortex* 15:357–384, 1979.
5. Bear D. M., Fedio P.: Quantitative analysis of inter-ictal behavior in temporal lobe epilepsy. *Arch Neurol* 34:454–464, 1977.
6. Bear D. M., Levin K., North B., et al: Case report in behavioral neurology. *J Clin Psychiatry* 41:89–95, 1981.

7. Bear D. M., Schenk L., Benson H.: Increased autonomic responses to mental and emotional stimuli in temporal lobe epilepsy. *Am J Psychiatry* 138:843–845, 1981.

8. Betts T. A., Kalna P. L., Cooper R., et al: Epileptic fits as a possible side effect of amitriptyline. *Lancet* 1:390–392, 1968.

9. Blumer D.: Temporal lobe epilepsy and its psychiatric significance, in Blumer D., Benson D. F. (eds): *The Psychiatric Aspects of Neurological Disease.* New York, Grune & Stratton, 1975, pp 171–198.

10. Blumer D.: Treatment of patients with seizure disorder referred because of psychiatric complications, in Blumer D., Levin K. (eds): *Psychiatric Complications in the Epilepsies: Current Research and Treatment. McLean Hosp J* (special issue) June 1977:53–73, 1977.

11. Blumer D., Benson D. F.: Personality changes with frontal and temporal lobe lesions, in Benson D. F., Blumer D. (eds): *The Psychiatric Aspects of Neurological Disease.* New York, Grune & Stratton, 1975, pp 151–169.

12. Cereghino J. J., Brock J. T., VanMeter J. C., et al: Carbamazepine for epilepsy. *Neurology* 24:401–410, 1974.

13. Christiansen J., Dam M.: Influence of phenobarbital and diphenylhydantoin on plasma carbamazepine levels in patients with epilepsy. *Acta Neuro Scand* 49:543–546, 1973.

14. Dallas V., Heathfield K.: Iatrogenic epilepsy due to antidepressant drugs. *Br Med J* 4:80–82, 1969.

15. Delgado-Escuela A. V., Mattson R. H., King L., et al: Special report—the nature of aggression during epileptic seizure. *N Engl J Med* 305:711–716, 1981.

16. Denes G., Caviezelo F.: Dichotic listening on crossed aphasia: "Paradoxical" ipsilateral expression. *Arch Neurol* 38:182–185, 1981.

17. Donnelly E. F., Dent J. K., Murphy D. L., et al: Comparison of temporal lobe epileptics and affective disorders on the Halstead–Reitan test battery. *J Clin Psychol* 28:61–65, 1972.

18. Dreyer R.: The long-term administration of anti-epileptic agents, with particular reference to pharmacotoxicological aspects, in Birkmayer W. (ed): *Epileptic Seizures–Behavior–Pain.* Berne, Hans Huber Publishing, 1976, pp 76–87.

19. Falconer M. A.: Reversibility by temporal lobe resection of the behavioral abnormalities of temporal lobe epilepsy. *N Engl J Med* 289:451–455, 1973.

20. Flor-Henry P.: Psychosis and temporal lobe epilepsy: A controlled investigation. *Epilepsia* 10:363–367, 1969.

21. Flor-Henry P.: Schizophrenic-like reactions and affective psychoses associated with temporal lobe epilepsy: Etiologic factors. *Am J Psychiatry* 126:400–404, 1969.

22. Geschwind N., Shader R. I., Bear D. M., et al: Behavioral changes with temporal lobe epilepsy: Assessment and treatment. *J Clin Psychiatry* 41:89–94, 1980.

23. Grant R. H. E.: Carbamazepine in the treatment of severe epilepsy, in Birkmayer W. (ed): *Epileptic Seizures–Behavior–Pain.* Berne, Hans Huber Publishing, 1976, pp 104–111.

24. Itil T. M., Soldatos C.: Epileptogenic side effects of psychotropic drugs. *JAMA* 244:1460–1465, 1980.

25. Jensen I., Larson J. K.: Psychoses in drug-resistant temporal lobe epilepsy. *J Neurol Neurosurg Psychiatry* 42:948–954, 1979.

26. Koella W. P., Levin P., Baltzer V.: The pharmacology of carbamazepine and some other anti-epileptic drugs, in Birkmayer W. (ed): *Epileptic Seizures–Behavior–Pain.* Berne, Hans Huber Publishing, 1976, pp 32–49.

27. Rall T. W., Schleifer L. S.: Drugs effective in the treatment of the epilepsies, in Gilman A. G., Goodman L. S., Gilman A. (eds): *Goodman and Gilman's The Pharmacological Basis of Therapeutics,* ed 6. New York, Macmillian, 1980, pp 448–474.

28. Remick R. A., Wada J. A.: Complex partial and pseudoseizure disorders. *Am J Psychiatry* 136:320–322, 1979.

29. Rett A.: The so-called psychotropic effect of Tegretol in the treatment of convulsions of

cerebral origin in children, in Birkmayer W. (ed): *Epileptic Seizures–Behavior–Pain.* Berne, Hans Huber Publishing, 1976, pp 194–205.

30. Rodin E.: Psychosocial management of patients with seizure disorders, in Blumer D., Levin K. (eds): *Psychiatric Complications in the Epilepsies: Current Research and Treatment. McLean Hosp J* (special issue) June 1977:74–84, 1977.

31. Schenk L., Bear D. M.: Multiple personalities and dissociative responses in temporal lobe epilepsy. *Am J Psychiatry* 138:1311–1316, 1981.

32. Shader R. I., Weinberger D. R., Greenblatt D. J.: Problems with drug interactions in treating brain disorders. *Psychiatr Clin North Am* 1:51–71, 1978.

33. Sherwin I.: Clinical and EEG aspects of temporal lobe epilepsy with behavior disorder: The role of cerebral dominance, in Blumer D., Levin K. (eds): *Psychiatric Complications in the Epilepsies: Current Research and Treatment. McLean Hosp J* (special issue) June 1977:40–50, 1977.

34. Singer H. S., Freeman J. M.: Seizures in adolescents. *Med Clin North Am* 59:1461–1472, 1975.

35. Sironi V. A., Franzini A., Ravaganti L., et al: Inter-ictal acute psychoses in temporal lobe epilepsy during withdrawal of anticonvulsant therapy. *J Neurol Neurosurg Psychiatry* 42:724–728, 1979.

36. Slater E., Beard A. W.: Schizophrenia-like psychoses of epilepsy. *Br J Psychiatry* 109:95–102, 1963.

37. Tollefson G.: Psychiatric implications of anticonvulsant drugs. *J Clin Psychiatry* 41:295–307, 1980.

38. Walker A. E., Blumer D.: Longterm behavioral effects of temporal lobectomy for temporal lobe epilepsy, in Blumer D., Levin K. (eds): *Psychiatric Complications in the Epilepsies: Current Research and Treatment. McLean Hosp J* (special issue) June 1977:85–103, 1977.

39. Waxman S. G., Geschwind N.: The interictal behavior syndrome of temporal lobe epilepsy. *Arch Gen Psychiatry* 32:1580–1584, 1975.

40. Adverse interactions of drugs. *Med Lett* 23:17, 1981.

41. Drugs for epilepsy. *Med Lett* 21:25–28, 1979.

12

Legal Issues in Prescribing Psychoactive Medications

THOMAS F. O'HARE, J.D.

I. INTRODUCTION

The psychiatrist–patient relationship has gradually changed over the past few years. In all areas of practice, psychiatric paternalism has declined. Hospitalization is now sometimes viewed as deprivation of liberty, and psychotropic agents arc increasingly condemned as "unwarranted invasion of privacy" or "involuntary mind control." Such characterizations have bewildered many practitioners. Since psychiatrists have directed their efforts toward liberating the mind from psychotic processes, they have sometimes felt that patient advocates challenge their competency and professionalism and undermine patients' medical needs. Currently, the foremost area of conflict involves the use of psychoactive medications. This chapter describes the legal issues that the clinician must consider when prescribing these drugs.

II. BASIS FOR LITIGATION

A. Tort Action

Two fundamental bases of litigation may arise when a practitioner prescribes psychoactive medications. The first is a tort action based on one or

THOMAS F. O'HARE, J.D. • Department of Legal Services, McLean Hospital, Belmont, Massachusetts 02178.

more causes of action. A tort, literally a "wrong" suffered by an individual, is based on common law traditions. This means that the history of judicial decisions, and not statute or regulation, defines the parameters of action. The goal of such an action is compensation by the tortfeasor (defendant) or the victim (plaintiff) so that the latter is placed in roughly the same position as he was prior to the commission of the act.

A cause of action is a theory of recovery recognized by courts of law and which, if proven, will entitle the plaintiff to recover damages from the defendant. It is a specific basis for tort litigation.

A tort action resulting from the administration of psychoactive medications may allege one (or more) of several possible causes, including negligence, battery, intentional causation of mental distress, or invasion of privacy. All require proof of damages by the defendant to the plaintiff.

To show that the physician was negligent, the plaintiff must prove that:

1. The physician had a duty to the patient created by the doctor–patient relationship.
2. This duty was breached by the physician who failed to meet the required standard of care.
3. The plaintiff was damaged as a direct result of that breach of duty.

For example, a patient taking lithium for his bipolar affective disorder develops signs of toxicity. If the treating physician fails to recognize and interpret these signs, check the serum lithium level, and make the necessary medication adjustments, and if the patient is damaged (loss of income, medical costs, pain, and suffering) as a result of the lithium toxicity, the courts may find the physician negligent.

All other torts require proof of intent on the part of the defendant (doctor) and a concomitant lack of consent on the part of the plaintiff (patient). Battery, a common element in many malpractice suits, is discussed in the section on informed consent (Section III). Most courts would not find a psychiatrist liable for causation of mental distress unless malice was proven (i.e., intent to do harm) or for invasion of privacy, which has more to do with eavesdropping than with medication. Again, the patient's informed consent generally protects the physician from liability.

B. Civil Rights Complaint

The second type of action that may be brought against a clinician prescribing psychoactive medications is a civil rights complaint. Any person who acts "under color of state law" (e.g., as an agent of the state) to deprive an individual of his or her civil rights may have to pay money damages for such violation. An action under color of law relies on the sanctions of statutes or regulations of the state. For example, because only a state law authorizes certain persons (physicians, judges) to commit individuals to a mental health facility, their actions in so doing are clearly under the color of law. The same applies to employees or agents of hospitals or other facilities that are licensed by a state mental health or public health agency and, therefore, subject to regulation by that agency. In contrast, the essentially private relationship between physician and patient would not be subject to such a claim.

Civil rights actions involving psychoactive medications are based on the theory that the involuntary administration of such drugs may constitute an unwarranted invasion of the patient's privacy. Every individual is constitutionally protected from the "nonconsensual invasion of his bodily integrity." Also, at least one court has found that the involuntary use of antipsychotics constitutes an unconstitutional curtailment of the freedom of expression (thought). The involuntary use of medication could also be construed as infringing on the patient's freedom of religion if his sincere religious beliefs prohibit the use of medication.

The medications discussed in this book are controlled substances. As such, their manufacture, distribution, and use are subject to regulation by state and federal law. In this respect, they are no different than other prescription drugs, and violation of relevant statutes may result in criminal penalties.

III. INFORMED CONSENT

Because the relationship between physician and patient involves mutual promises and obligations, the law views it as a contract. The physician promises to evaluate the patient, perform certain tests, and provide treatment for a medical condition. As in all contracts, if both parties do not understand its terms, the agreement may be void or voidable. In the case of medical treatment, the patient must understand the risks and benefits of such treatment and alternatives to the proposed treatment, or his consent may be invalid.

The common law in this country has long held that medical treatment performed without the patient's consent constitutes a battery (unconsented touching). In the past 25 years, this has changed to a requirement for the patient's **informed** consent, thereby expanding the provider's potential liability. Such consent must be knowledgeable, competent, and voluntary.

How much information must the clinician disclose to the patient? Unfortunately, this question has no precise answer. Most hospitals, in conjunction with their liability carriers, have developed printed consent forms to cover the customary procedures performed at their facility. These forms should be written in language that the lay person can understand. They should include a description of the proposed treatment, an analysis of the risks of such treatment, an explanation of alternative treatments, and a place for the patient to give his consent before a witness. This form does not substitute for a full and open discussion between doctor and patient; it aids such discussion and records it.

A properly executed form, however, does not guarantee protection from liability, but it does become an important record should litigation ensue. In some states, it even raises legal presumptions that increase the plaintiff's burden of proof. Although few physicians or facilities employ written consents for administration of psychoactive medications, recent litigation may impel reevaluation of this policy.

The patient's oral consent is just as valid as an executed form, but it is sometimes difficult to prove that such a consent was offered. **At the least, the provider should record that the patient was given information regarding the medication and that he voluntarily consented to its administration.**

Generally, **the clinician must convey enough information so that a "reasonably prudent" patient can make a decision to accept or decline the treatment.** The physician must initiate the process and, at the least, discuss the following:

1. Expected benefits from the medication.
2. Reasonably expected adverse effects.
3. Steps to ameliorate uncomfortable or disturbing adverse reactions.
4. Alternatives to the proposed treatment.

The physician must utilize his professional judgment in deciding when the individual patient has sufficient information but must not take the position that the patient is not entitled to information that might cause him to decline treatment. The courts have unanimously stated that the issue is what the patient would choose given all relevant information and **not** what is medically advisable.

In some situations, it is unnecessary or impossible to obtain informed consent from a patient. **If an emergency occurs** requiring the administration of the drug, the consent of the patient may be immaterial. Clinicians are advised to know what conditions constitute an "emergency" in the state in which they practice. (The United States Supreme Court may address this issue when it decides the Massachusetts case of *Rogers vs. Okin.*) If the medication is intended to restrain the patient's behavior, at the least the criteria for administering involuntary restraint must be met. Such criteria are usually set forth in state administrative regulations or in statutory law.

If the patient is incompetent to give consent, then the clinician should obtain informed consent from a duly authorized surrogate. Minors are incompetent by reason of age; their parents or legal guardians may consent to treatment on their behalf. Individuals who, because of mental illness or retardation, cannot assimilate information in a manner that supports the decision-making process may also be incompetent. For these persons, a surrogate decision maker (guardian, conservator, committee) may be appointed through a judicial proceeding. In some states, other processes, such as review by an independent clinician, may suffice. The clinician should ascertain whether a patient has been declared legally incompetent or whether his status (e.g., as a minor) renders him incompetent to contract in his own name. It is also important to remember that in most states, hospitalization, even if involuntary, does not define incompetency. If a determination of incompetency has been made, the clinician should determine who has specific authority to consent to treatment on behalf of the patient or the procedures required to secure such authority.

The **law of guardianship** is changing rapidly. Courts are requiring greater specificity in the authority sought by the guardian. Thus, "limited" or "tailored" guardianship decrees reserve certain areas of decision-making to the ward when he has demonstrated competency in those areas (e.g., management of limited funds, voting, certain medical treatment decisions). When appointed, the guardian stands in the place of the ward, and the guardian's informed consent to the proposed treatment must be obtained. Since psychiatric treatment is more a process than an event, the guardian's authority should encompass that treatment process for his incompetent ward. Although the court may periodically review the continuing need for guardianship, the guardian should be authorized to make decisions regarding treatment that may span some period of time.

IV. PATIENT'S RIGHT TO WITHHOLD CONSENT

One of the most intensely debated issues in psychiatry today is the patient's right to decline treatment, particularly psychoactive medications. In several lawsuits, the courts have consistently found that psychiatric patients have constitutionally protected privacy rights which may be abridged by involuntary treatment.

> "[It] seems to us to be an intuitively obvious proposition: a person has a constitutionally protected interest in being left free by the state to decide for himself whether to submit to the serious and potentially harmful medical treatment that is represented by the administration of antipsychotic drugs [*Rogers vs. Okin,* #79-1648,9 (1st Cir., Nov. 25, 1980) Slip, p. 2].

This judicial opinion presents several dilemmas for the clinician. First, medication may not only be the treatment of choice, but it may be the only reasonable means of providing help. Second, concomitant with the right to refuse treatment is the hospitalized patient's right to receive appropriate treatment. In most states, even a patient involuntarily committed for "care and treatment" retains a presumption of competency to decide for himself whether or not to take medication. The right of refusal may resurrect concerns about "warehousing" patients without providing any meaningful treatment.

Another problem is that a patient may refuse medication because of psychotic or delusional reasoning; some of these patients, however, are incompetent. This does not mean that the physician can administer the medication over the patient's objection. Rather, a judicial process must authorize a guardian, conservator, or committee to make such decisions on behalf of the patient. The primary issue in such a proceeding is whether or not the patient is capable of understanding the consequence of his decisions and actions and can assimilate information in a manner that supports his decision.

Many patients who refuse medication are indeed competent. These patients may be aware of the adverse reactions (perhaps having previously been on the proposed medication) and understand the consequences of not receiving the medication. Their refusal, although perhaps unwise, may be competent. This determination is a legal, not a medical, one.

As mentioned above, minors are considered incompetent by reason of age, and their parents or legal guardians have inherent authority to consent to or decline treatment on their behalf. Since the specific rights of minors may vary according to the state, the clinician should learn the operative law (e.g., in Massachusetts, a minor of 16 or 17 years of age may be considered an adult for purposes of admission to a mental health facility, termination of care, and, presumably, for purposes of consenting to or refusing treatment therein).

The right to refuse medication is not absolute. The courts recognize that in an emergency the clinician can administer medication without the patient's consent. What constitutes an "emergency," however, varies according to the state. Some states consider clinical conditions (a worsening of the condition) sufficient, whereas others require a present risk of physical harm to self or others. If the patient's situation meets the definition of an emergency in his state, the clinician should fully document this when administering involuntary medications.

V. SPECIFIC AREAS OF LIABILITY

Although almost every intervention may seem to expose the clinician to litigation, in reality, the "high-risk" areas are few. Using psychoactive medications raises specific liability issues. Since "liability" may be freely translated as "damages," it is worthwhile to examine the likelihood of such damages being assessed.

Certainly, the troublesome adverse reactions caused by many of these medications raise the greatest concern. A list of these untoward effects constitutes a large part of the information that the clinician should convey to the patient so that he can sign an informed consent. The fact that most of these adverse reactions are reversible and only moderately uncomfortable tends to modify the amount of damages the court might award for failure to inform adequately.

A major exception to this generalization is **tardive dyskinesia.** Both the clinical and legal literature consider this a dangerous, debilitating, and irreversible adverse reaction. A recent court decision awarded $760,000 to a patient who developed tardive dyskinesia because of administration of a major tranquilizer. The court also found that the drug should not have been prescribed initially, its use should have been monitored, informed consent was not obtained, and its administration was for the convenience of the staff and not for therapeutic reasons. Clearly, the physician and patient together must weigh the costs and benefits of using these drugs.

Although inconclusive, evidence exists that the psychoactive drugs may affect fetal development. Currently, the clinician should prescribe these drugs during **pregnancy** only when the benefit to the mother clearly outweighs any risk to the unborn child. The same risk–benefit assessment should be made when considering the use of these drugs for nursing mothers. Once the clinician decides to use these drugs, the risks should be clearly explained and discussed with the patient, and the patient's (or surrogate's) informed consent documented. Courts usually measure damages by both the degree of injury and its anticipated duration. An infant, for example, who faces a lifetime of disability may be awarded a generous amount. Clearly, both the doctor and the patient must carefully discuss the risks and benefits of prescribing psychoactive medications to pregnant or nursing women.

Consultation by an expert psychopharmacologist regarding such treatment may benefit physician, patient, and family. It will certainly demonstrate that medications were not prescribed for the pregnant patient without concern for possible teratogenic effects.

Increased institutional advocacy enhances the possibility of litigation to enjoin (prohibit) and seek damages for involuntarily medicating in nonemergency situations. Patients' advocates are skilled spokespersons on behalf of civil liberties. Thus far, based on the defense of "good faith," the courts have been reluctant to impose liability on physicians of institutions for providing responsible treatment, even to unconsenting patients. "Good faith" implies that the defendant doctors were seeking to provide treatment where no previous prohibition existed and could not be expected to anticipate constitutional law developments. Because of the publicity surrounding cases such as *Rogers vs. Okin* and *Rennie vs. Klein,* future reliance on such a defense is ill-advised.

A final issue of liability concerns the prescription of medications for diagnoses or at doses outside the Food and Drug Administration's (FDA) recommendations. These are published in the *Physician's Desk Reference* (PDR), which is essentially a compendium of package inserts. The FDA has regulatory jurisdiction over the pharmaceutical industry, not over the practice of medicine or pharmacy, and thus, it is not illegal for physicians to prescribe drugs beyond the FDA's guidelines. However, the more a physician deviates from their guidelines, the greater the potential liability if damage or injury to the patient results from the prescribed medication.

Should the clinician wish to deviate from such guidelines in the treatment of a patient, he should consider certain precautions. He should record the patient's fully informed consent and his own reasoning in recommending the particular medication or dosage. Such reasons should be openly discussed with the patient. It may also be advisable to seek a consultation from a psychopharmacologist regarding the proposed treatment. Finally, the patient's competence to consent to such treatment should be reassessed. An incompetent patient, or one who is subject to an existing guardianship, raises special problems. Whether a guardian may consent to his ward's participation in a research project or in unorthodox treatments without specific judicial approval remains unsettled.

Although FDA regulations do not forbid other uses, they do establish normative standards that may be noted in judicial proceedings. The greater the deviation from such standards, the greater the need for justification in the clinical record.

VI. SUGGESTIONS FOR AVOIDING LITIGATION

The most successful way to avoid litigation is for the doctor and patient to communicate openly. It is not mere coincidence that the increase of lawsuits against physicians came at approximately the same time as the decline in "womb-to-tomb" care by the family physician. As medical practice became increasingly specialized and technological, and decision-making more complex, the lay person's capacity to understand sophisticated techniques and procedures diminished. Many clinicians felt that patients would refuse reasonable treatment out of fear and misunderstanding (see Rosoff[13]).

The widespread use of psychoactive medications generated similar kinds of problems. The unwanted effects of the medications are real, uncomfortable, and sometimes dangerous. Still, these medications made the effective management of persons with a major mental illness more possible and, for the first time, offered a chance for many to return to "normalcy" in the community. The pressure on the patient to agree to the use of medication was often intense.

Legislation and judicial decisions have slowly eroded that "second-class" citizenship of the mentally ill. Patients are generally presumed to possess the same rights and capacities as other persons until an appropriate forum decides otherwise. As a result, they are entitled to information regarding their treatment and to assistance in evaluating the risk–benefit ratio of that treatment.

Physicians who intend to prescribe psychoactive medications should familiarize themselves with the literature, especially with regard to adverse reactions, contraindications, and interactions. They should share this information with their patients and assist them in reaching an informed and reasonable decision. The clinician should also advise the patient if the medication interferes with the mental or physical abilities required to perform hazardous tasks such as operating a motor vehicle. Most often, the patient and his doctor should openly discuss the risks and benefits. Such negotiation might include discussion of alternative medications, a formal reporting system so that the patient can record the effects of drugs as he experiences them, "trial periods" during which the medication is monitored for a specific, limited period of time, or a consultation with an expert psychopharmacologist. Whatever the content of the negotiation, the patient's participation on his own behalf will remove a significant area of legal objection.

Also, the clinician should evaluate the patient's competency to make such decisions and make appropriate recommendations regarding guardianship to family members or others if such competency is in question. Although the legal presumption of competency (or status of incompetency) remains static until changed by court order, clinicians should be sensitive to whether or not an individual's competency fluctuates. The doctor should document both the patient's consent and his competency to give that consent. The patient should know that such consent is freely revocable.

The clinician should always obtain a careful medication history. If the patient is unable to provide reliable information, other sources should be sought (previous physicians, family, friends). The clinician should monitor the patient's response to the medications and record his findings. The patient should also have a reasonable opportunity to describe his reactions to the drugs and to air his complaints.

Although the documentation suggested may appear burdensome, it both records events that may be admissable into evidence and stimulates the writer's memory. Since trials may take place several years after the events in question, such documentation is invaluable.

Relationships characterized by paternalism often generate bitter litigation. Plaintiffs resent the disenfranchisement of their position, and defendants feel hurt and frustrated at being sued by persons for whom they were caring. Relationships in which all parties can feel invested are less likely to generate lawsuits. Most of the institutional suits (right to treatment, right to refuse treatment) and even the more classical malpractice litigation demonstrate this experience.

We are not suggesting that psychiatrists must relinquish their authority;

rather, we are emphasizing that **the patient has the right to participate in treatment decisions to the extent of his capability.** If he cannot meaningfully consider alternatives, the decision must be made in a manner sanctioned by law.

This chapter has dealt with general legal issues surrounding the use of psychoactive medications. Clinicians are strongly urged to learn the law and regulations governing these issues in the locality of their practice and to seek competent legal counsel when issues arise regarding medication usage. Counsel should review any forms used to record a patient's consent to treatment. Above all, clinicians should share information with their patients, monitor the psychopharmacological regimen, and carefully document their experiences.

SELECTED READING

Articles

1. Applebaum P. S., Gutheil T. G.: Drug refusal: A study of psychiatric inpatients. *Am J Psychiatry* 137:340–346, 1980.
2. Applebaum P. S., Gutheil T. G.: Rotting with their rights on: Constitutional theory and clinical reality in drug refusal by psychiatric patients. *Bull Am Acad Psychiatry Law* 7:308–315, 1979.
3. Ford M. D.: The psychiatrist's double bind: The right to refuse medication. *Am J Psychiatry* 137:332–339, 1980.
4. Gutheil T. G., Shapiro R., St. Clair R. L.: Legal guardianship in drug refusal: An illusory solution. *Am J Psychiatry* 137:347–352, 1980.
5. Plotkin R.: Limiting the therapeutic orgy: Mental patients' right to refuse treatment. *Northwestern Univ Law Rev* 72:461–525, 1977.
6. Reiser S. J.: Refusing treatment for mental illness: Historical and ethical dimensions. *Am J Psychiatry* 137:329–331, 1980.
7. Rhoden N. K.: The right to refuse psychotropic drugs. *Harvard Civ Rts Civ Liberties Law Rev* 15:363–413, 1980.
8. Roth L. H., Meisel A., Lidz C. W.: Tests of competency to consent to treatment. *Am J Psychiatry* 134:279–284, 1977.

Books

9. Annas G. J., Glante L. H., Katz B. F.: *Informed Consent to Human Experimentation.* Cambridge, Ballinger Publishing Company, 1977.
10. Halleck S. L.: *Law in the Practice of Psychiatry.* New York, Plenum Press, 1980.
11. Hofling C. K. (ed): *Law and Ethics in the Practice of Psychiatry.* New York, Brunner/Mazel, 1981.
12. Ludlam J. E.: *Informed Consent.* Chicago, American Hospital Association, 1978.
13. Rosoff A. J.: *Informed Consent.* Rockville, Aspen Systems Corporation, 1981.
14. Wexler D. B.: *Mental Health Law.* New York, Plenum Press, 1981.

CASES

1. *A. E. and R. R. vs Mitchell,* (Cen Div Utah, #C-78-466, June 12, 1980).
2. *Clites vs Iowa,* Law No. #46274 (Iowa Dist Ct, Pottawattamie County, August 7, 1980).
3. *Davis vs Hubbard,* #73-205 (ND Ohio, September 16, 1980).
4. *Goedecke vs State Department of Institutions,* 603 p 2nd 123 (Colo, 1979).
5. *In re Boyd,* 403 A 2nd 744 (DC App, 1979).
6. *In re K. K. B.,* 609 p 2nd 747 (Okla, 1980).
7. *In re Richard Roe III,* Mass Adv Sh (1981), 981.
8. *Kaimowitz vs Department of Mental Health,* Civ No. 73-19434-AW (Mich Cir Ct, Wayne County, July 19, 1973).
9. *Mackey vs Procunier,* 477 F 2nd 877 (9th Cir, 1973).
10. *Rennie vs Klein,* 462 F Supp 1131 (DNJ, 1978).
11. *Rogers vs Okin,* 478 F Supp 1342 (D Mass., 1979), aff'd in part, rev'd in part, 634 F 2nd 650 (1st Cir, 1980), cert granted, US, (#80-1417, March 20, 1981).
12. *Roth vs Clarke,* (ED Penn #79-449, January 22, 1980).
13. *Scott vs Plante,* 532 F 2nd 939 (3rd Cir, 1976).

Index

Abnormal Involuntary Movement Scale (AIMS), 135–137, 141, 153
Abstinence syndrome (*see* Substance abuse)
Abuse (*see* Substance abuse)
Acetaldehyde, 246, 252–253
Acetophenazine, 124
Acetylation, 63
Acetylcholine, 5, 38, 79, 121, 131, 308
l-α-Acetylmethadol (LAAM), 232
ACTH, 26
Acute dystonic reaction, 127–128, 129, 302, 307, 319, 322
Acute intermittent porphyria, 334
Adapin® (*see* Doxepin)
Addiction (*see* Substance abuse)
Adenylate cyclase, 21, 80, 90
Adolescents, 313–352
Affective disorder (*see* Bipolar affective disorder; Depression)
Aggression (*see* Violence)
Agoraphobia, 173–174
Agranulocytosis, 40, 149, 319, 383
Akathisia, 129, 299, 302, 307, 319
Akinesia, 130–131 (*see also* Parkinson's syndrome)
Akineton® (*see* Biperiden)
Alanon, 255
Alateen, 255, 256
Alcohol, 235, 236, 238–239, 243, 273, 297, 300
    abuse, 81, 85, 226, 230, 244–256, 386, 387
    central nervous system effects, 247
    definitions of alcoholism, 244–245
    dehydrogenase, 246
    dependence (*see* abuse)

Alcohol (*cont.*)
    intoxication, 247–249
    in pregnancy, 249, 368 (*see also* Fetal alcohol syndrome)
    withdrawal, 249–252
Alcoholic hallucinosis, 251–252
Alcoholics Anonymous, 244, 255–256, 264, 282
Alcoholism (*see* Alcohol, abuse, definitions of alcoholism)
Alprazolam, 35, 37, 71, 174, 177, 178, 179, 180–181, 196, 198, 309 (*see also* Benzodiazepines)
Alzheimer's disease, 307–308 (*see also* Organic brain syndrome)
Amantadine, 129, 131, 132
Amenorrhea, 39, 41, 147, 230, 319
γ-Aminobutyric acid (GABA), 121, 122, 140, 182
Aminophylline, 99
Amitriptyline, 16, 26, 30, 37, 42, 43, 44, 49, 53, 57, 66, 67, 68, 70, 71, 72, 73, 298, 300, 301, 304, 309, 327–328, 344, 394, 395
Amobarbital, 207–208, 236
Amotivational syndrome, 278, 279–280 (*see also* Marijuana)
Amoxapine, 4, 35, 37, 38, 41, 43, 44, 46, 47, 57, 68, 123 (*see also* Antidepressants)
Amphetamine, 26, 74, 256–261, 266, 267, 303
    during pregnancy, 367
    psychosis, 257, 260–61
Amytal® (*see* Amobarbital)
Anaphylactoid reactions, 224

411